Quranic Arabic

Studies in Semitic Languages and Linguistics

VOLUME 106

The titles published in this series are listed at *brill.com/ssl*

Quranic Arabic

From its Hijazi Origins to its Classical Reading Traditions

By

Marijn van Putten

TUTA SUB AEGIDE PALLAS · 1683 ·

BRILL

LEIDEN | BOSTON

Cover illustration: Leiden University Library, Or. 14.545b, verso. This folio belongs to the same ancient manuscript of the Bibliothèque nationale de France, Arabe 331. It was Carbondated at 652–694 AD (89.3%), 747–763 (6.1%) by the *Corpus Coranicum* project. Courtesy Leiden University Libraries.

Library of Congress Cataloging-in-Publication Data

Names: Van Putten, Marijn, author.
Title: Quranic Arabic : from its Hijazi origins to its classical reading traditions / by Marijn van Putten.
Description: Leiden ; Boston : Brill, [2022] |
Series: Studies in Semitic languages and linguistics, 0081-8461 ; volume 106 | Includes bibliographical references and index. |
Identifiers: LCCN 2021058286 (print) | LCCN 2021058287 (ebook) | ISBN 9789004506244 (hardback ; acid-free paper) | ISBN 9789004506251 (ebook)
Subjects: LCSH: Qur'an–Language, style. | Arabic language–Grammar.
Classification: LCC PJ6696 .V36 2022 (print) | LCC PJ6696 (ebook) | DDC 492.7/5–dc23/eng/20211209
LC record available at https://lccn.loc.gov/2021058286
LC ebook record available at https://lccn.loc.gov/2021058287

Typeface for the Latin, Greek, and Cyrillic scripts: "Brill". See and download: brill.com/brill-typeface.

ISSN 0081-8461
ISBN 978-90-04-50624-4 (hardback)
ISBN 978-90-04-50625-1 (e-book)

This book is printed on acid-free paper and produced in a sustainable manner.

Contents

Preface and Acknowledgements XIII
Transcription XV
Abbreviations XVIII
Sigla XX

1 **Introduction** 1
1.1 Previous Scholarship 1
1.2 The Uthmanic Text Type and the Quranic Consonantal Text 8
1.3 Overview 12

2 **What Is the *ʕarabiyyah*?** 15
2.1 Introduction 15
2.2 The Linguistic Variation in the *ʕarabiyyah* 19
2.2.1 *The Third Person Pronominal Suffixes* 20
2.2.2 *The Extra Vowels of Early Classical Arabic* 23
2.2.2.1 i-umlaut 24
2.2.2.2 III-y ʔimālah 25
2.2.2.3 II-w/y ʔimālah 28
2.2.2.4 The Fifth Long Vowel Ō 29
2.2.2.5 The Front Rounded Vowel in Hollow Passives 30
2.2.3 *Najdi Vowel Harmony* 31
2.2.4 *Najdi Syncope* 32
2.2.4.1 Syncope in the Verbs 33
2.2.4.2 Syncope in Nouns 34
2.2.4.3 Pronouns 34
2.2.4.4 Li- + Apocopate for Commands 35
2.2.4.5 Conclusions on the Syncope 35
2.2.5 *Barth-Ginsberg Alternation in the Prefix Vowel* 36
2.2.6 *The Deictic Pronominal System* 38
2.2.7 *Two Subsequent* Hamzahs *within a Single Word* 39
2.3 Where Is Classical Arabic? 39
2.4 Prescriptivism of the Grammarians 44
2.5 Conclusion 45

3 Classical Arabic and the Reading Traditions 47
3.1 Introduction 47
3.2 Reading or Recitation? 52
3.3 Lack of Regular Sound Change 55
3.3.1 *Harmony of the Pronominal Suffixes* 57
3.3.2 *Najdi Syncope* 59
3.3.2.1 Syncope in fa-huwa, wa-hiya Etc. 59
3.3.2.2 Fa/wa-li-yafʕal > fa/wa-l-yafʕal 59
3.3.2.3 CuCuC > CuCC 60
3.3.2.4 CuCuCāt Plurals of CuCCah Nouns 62
3.3.2.5 Faʕi/ul(ah) Nouns 63
3.3.2.6 CaCi/uCa Verbs 64
3.3.2.7 Conclusion 65
3.3.3 *Additional Phonemic Long Vowels* 66
3.3.3.1 Hollow Root Passives 66
3.3.3.2 Hollow Root ʔimālah 67
3.3.3.3 Phonemic Ē on III-y Nouns and Verbs 68
3.3.4 *Lexically Determined* i-*umlaut* ʔimālah 68
3.3.5 *Dual Deictics* 70
3.3.6 *Dialectal Difference in Short Vowels* 71
3.3.6.1 Cu/iCiyy(ah) 71
3.3.6.2 CiCwān Nouns 72
3.3.6.3 Mit- and Dim- 72
3.3.7 *Disagreement in Pluralization* 73
3.3.8 *Cu/iyūC Plurals* 73
3.3.9 *The Readings Do Not Reflect Natural Language* 74
3.4 The Readings Are Not Dialects 76
3.5 Readers Usually Agree on the Hijazi Form 79
3.6 The Readings Are Intentionally Artificial 81
3.6.1 *The Dropping of the* Hamzah *by Warš* 83
3.6.2 *The* ʔimālah *of Word-Final* Āri *Sequences* 83
3.6.3 *Vowel Harmony of* -hum *in Ruways ʕan Yaʕqūb's Reading* 85
3.6.4 *Ḥafṣ' Anthology of Unusual Features* 86
3.6.4.1 Ṣilat al-hāʔ (Q25:69) 86
3.6.4.2 III-y ʔimālah (Q11:41) 86
3.6.4.3 Softening of Second *Hamzah* of Two Subsequent *Hamzahs* (Q41:44) 87
3.6.4.4 Muttum instead of Mittum (Q3:157, 158) 87
3.6.4.5 Unharmonized -hu (Q18:63; Q48:10) 87

3.6.4.6 III-y/w Apocopates/Imperatives Followed by the 3sg.m. Pronoun 87
3.6.4.7 Conclusion 88
3.6.5 *Plural Pronouns of Warš* 88
3.6.6 *Features Dependent on the Structure of the Text* 90
3.6.6.1 ʔabū ʕamr's Phonemic Contrast of Ā and Ā̈ 90
3.6.6.2 The Verse-Penultimate Conditioning of Qutaybah and Nuṣayr ʕan al-Kisāʔī 92
3.7 The Choices of the Canonical Readers 93
3.8 Conclusion 97

4 The Quranic Consonantal Text: Morphology 99
4.1 Introduction 99
4.2 The *ʔalla-* Base Relative Pronoun 101
4.3 The Distal Demonstrative Expansion with *-l(i)-* in *ḏālika, tilka* and *hunālika* 102
4.4 The Plural Demonstratives (hā-)ʔulāʔi/(hā-)ʔulā; ʔulāʔika/ʔulāka 103
4.5 Proximal Deictics with Mandatory *hā-* Prefix 104
4.6 Feminine Proximal Deictic *hāḏih* 105
4.7 Loss of Barth-Ginsberg Alternation 106
4.8 Uninflected *halumma* 107
4.9 Imperatives and Apocopates of II=III Verbs Have the Shape vCCvC Rather Than (v)CvCC 107
4.10 Mā ḥiǧāziyyah 108
4.11 The Morphosyntax of *kāla* 110
4.12 The Presentative *hāʔum* 110
4.13 The Use of *Zawǧ* as 'Wife' 111
4.14 Alternations between G- and C-stems 111
4.15 Morphological Isoglosses Not Recognized by the Grammarians 112
4.15.1 Ta-*prefix in Prefix Conjugation of tD- and tL-stems* 112
4.15.2 N-*prefix in the Suffix Conjugation of N-stems* 113
4.15.3 *The* ʔan yafʕala *Verbal Complement Construction* 113
4.15.4 *Use of the Definite Article* al- 114
4.16 Questionable Morphological Isoglosses 114
4.16.1 *The III-w Passive Participle Is maCCuww Not maCCiyy* 115
4.16.2 *The Passive Participle of II-y Is maCīC Rather Than maCyūC* 115
4.16.3 *Gt-stems of I-w Verbs Is* ītazara *instead of* ittazara 116

4.16.4 *The Hijazi Dual Is Uninflected, Using the Nominative Form* 116
4.17 The Quran Is Morphologically Hijazi 117

5 The Quranic Consonantal Text: Phonology 119
5.1 Introduction 119
5.2 The Loss of the **ʔ* 120
5.3 Development of the Phoneme *ō* 123
5.4 Lack of *Cyī* > *Cī* 123
5.5 Passive of Hollow Verbs 124
5.6 Retention of *ṣirāṭ* 124
5.7 Lack of Syncopation of **u* and **i* 125
5.7.1 *vCCā Rhymes* 127
5.7.2 *vCā Rhymes* 127
5.7.3 *vCC Rhymes* 127
5.7.4 *vC Rhymes* 127
5.7.5 *Discussion* 127
5.7.6 *Alternation between CuCuC and CuCC Nouns* 129
5.8 Development of the Phoneme *Ē* 133
5.9 Hollow Root ʔimālah 135
5.10 Major Assimilation in Gt-stems. 136
5.11 *raʔaya, *naʔaya > rāʔa, nāʔa 138
5.12 Lexical Isoglosses 139
5.13 Phonetic Isoglosses Not Recognized by the Grammarians 142
5.13.1 *Stative II=III Are ẓalla/ẓaltu or ẓiltu* 142
5.13.2 *Pausal Shortening of Final* -ī 142
5.13.3 *Word-Final āy/w > āʔ* 143
5.13.4 *Pharyngealization of the Emphatics* 144
5.14 The Quran Is Phonologically Hijazi 145
5.15 Conclusion 146

6 Classicized Hijazi: Imposition of the *Hamzah* 150
6.1 Introduction 150
6.2 Pseudocorrect *Hamzah* 155
6.3 *Hamzah* among the Quranic Readers 156
6.4 Pseudocorrect Presence of *Hamzah* 157
6.4.1 *Ḍiyāʔ* → *ḍiʔāʔ* 158
6.4.2 *Mūṣadah* → *muʔṣadah* 158
6.4.3 *Ḍiʔzā* 159
6.4.4 *Manōh* → *manāʔah* 159

6.4.5 *ʕādan l-ʔūlā* 160
6.4.6 *Durriyy → du/irrīʔ* 160
6.4.7 *Maʕāyiš* 160
6.4.8 *Mågoġ → Maʔǧūǧ (ʕāṣim)* 164
6.4.9 *Zakariyyā → Zakariyyāʔ* 164
6.4.10 *Sāq, sāqay-hā, sūq → saʔq, saʔqay-hā, suʔq/suʔūq* 165
6.4.11 *Kās → kaʔs* 167
6.4.12 *Yuḍāhūna → yuḍāhiʔūna* 167
6.4.13 *Aṣ-ṣābūna → aṣ-ṣābiʔūna* 167
6.4.14 *Conclusion* 168
6.5 Failure to Insert *Hamzah* 168
6.5.1 *Long Vowels Followed by* Hamzah 171
6.5.1.1 Nabīʔ, nabīʔīn, ʔanbiʔāʔ, nubūʔah 171
6.5.1.2 Barīʔah/bariyyah 173
6.5.1.3 Nasīʔ 173
6.5.1.4 Xaṭīʔah pl. xaṭāyā 'sin' 174
6.5.2 *Post-consonantal* Hamzah 175
6.5.3 *Intervocalic* Hamzah 177
6.5.3.1 Riʔāʔa n-nās → riyāʔa n-nās 177
6.5.3.2 Liʔallā → liyallā 177
6.5.3.3 Kufuʔan, huzuʔan → kufuwan, huzuwan 177
6.5.3.4 Bādiya r-raʔyi → bādiʔa r-raʔyi 177
6.5.4 *Pre-consonantal* Hamzah 178
6.5.5 *Interchange between* III-w/y *and* III-ʔ *Verbs* 179
6.5.6 *Sāla for saʔala* (*Q70:1*) 180
6.5.7 *Šurakā-ya (Q16:27) for al-Bazzī ʕan Ibn Kaṯīr* 181
6.6 Conclusion 181

7 Classicized Hijazi: Final Short Vowels and tanwīn 182
7.1 Lack of Final Short Vowels in the Reading Traditions 192
7.1.1 *Sabaʔ* 192
7.1.2 *As-sayyiʔ* 193
7.1.3 *Maḥyā-y* 193
7.1.4 *Yā-bunay* 194
7.1.5 *Yartaʕ/nartaʕ* 194
7.1.6 *Tatran, tatrā, tatrē* (Q23:44) 195
7.1.7 *Tuḍār* 195
7.1.8 *The 3sg.m. Suffix -h* 196
7.1.9 *The Mysterious Letters* 200
7.2 Was ʔabū ʕamr's Reading an ʔiʕrāb-less Reading? 200

7.2.1 *Al-ʔidġām al-kabīr* 201
7.2.2 *I-umlaut* 203
7.2.3 *Rawm and ʔišmām* 204
7.2.4 *Nunation Blocks Assimilation* 206
7.2.5 *A Non-literalist Reading of ʔabū ʕamr's Traditions* 206
7.2.6 *Ḥamzah's ʔidġām kabīr* 209
7.3 A Phonetic Rule That Requires Absence of Full *ʔiʕrāb* 209
7.4 Conclusion 211

8 From Hijazi Beginnings to Classical Arabic. 215
8.1 The Prophet's Career 216
8.2 The Uthmanic Recension (ca. 30 AH/650 CE) 217
8.3 The Era of the Readers (ca. 40 AH–250 AH) 221
8.4 Crystallization of Classical Arabic (ca. 250–350 AH) 227
8.5 Conclusion 230

Appendix A: Notes on Orthography, Phonology and Morphology of the Quranic Consonantal Text 233
A.1 Introduction 233
A.2 Orthography 233
A.2.1 *The spelling of* ā 234
A.2.2 *Questions of double* yāʔ, wāw *and* ʔalif 235
A.2.3 *ʔalif al-Wiqāyah* 239
A.2.3.1 ʔalif al-wiqāyah for stem final *uʔ 243
A.2.3.2 Treatment of stem-final *ūʔ 243
A.2.3.3 Treatment of word-final *āʔū 244
A.2.3.4 Word-final *aʔū 244
A.2.3.5 Word-final *aʔu(n) 245
A.2.3.6 Word-final *āʔu 245
A.2.3.7 ربا ,الربوا 247
A.2.3.8 Summary 248
A.2.4 *Spelling of* la- *'indeed' as* لا 249
A.2.5 *The prepositions* ʕalā, ḥattā *and* ladā *are often spelled* حتا، علا، لدا 250
A.2.6 *Words starting with /l/ preceded by the definite article.* 251
A.2.7 *Historical* hamzah *spelling with* ای 251
A.2.8 *The spelling of* dāwūd *as* دواد *and* ruʔūs *as* رواس 254
A.2.9 *Plene spelling of short* u 255
A.2.10 *Defective spelling of word-final long vowels before* ʔalif al-waṣl 255

A.3 Phonology 256
A.3.1 *Consonants* 256
A.3.2 *The Loss of the Hamzah* 257
A.3.3 *Vowels* 258
A.3.4 *Loss of final short vowels and* tanwīn 260
A.3.5 *Assimilation across vowels* 261
A.3.6 *Pausal shortening of* -ī 267
A.3.7 *sayyiʔāt *as* سيات *reflecting /sayyāt/* 267
A.3.8 *A case of* n-*assimilation?* 268
A.3.9 *The Genitilic Adjective Ending* 268
A.3.10 *ʔalif al-waṣl* 269
A.3.11 *An isolated case of word-initial* *wu > ʔu 273
A.4 Morphology 273
A.4.1 *Independent Pronouns* 273
A.4.2 *Clitic Pronouns* 274
A.4.3 *Verbal endings* 276
A.4.4 *Demonstrative pronouns* 277
A.4.5 *Relative Pronouns* 280
A.4.6 *The relative possessive demonstrative* 280
A.4.7 *Short compound interrogatives with mā* 281
A.4.8 *Noun Inflection* 282
A.4.9 *III-w and III-y nouns with preceding a vowel.* 283
A.4.10 *III-w/y and III-ʔ nouns* 284
A.4.11 *Nouns in *-āʔ in construct* 286
A.4.12 *Confusion between subjunctive and apocopate* 288
A.4.13 *Partial merger of III-ʔ verbs and III-y/w verbs* 288
A.4.14 *Pausal imperatives/apocopates of III-y/w verbs Iqtadih (Q6:90), yatasannah* 290
A.4.15 *Partial merger of the I-ʔ and I-w verbs in derived stems* 291
A.4.16 */yak/ besides /yakun/* 292
A.4.17 **raʔaya 'to see' and *naʔaya 'to be distant' as* را *and* نا 292

Appendix B: Orthographic Comparison 294
B.1 samāwāt, naḥ(i)sāt, rawḍāt 298
B.2 yī with two yāʔs 298
B.3 ʔalif al-wiqāyah on yaʕfū/yaʕfuwa 299
B.4 Lack of ʔalif al-wiqāyah on words ending in -waw 300
B.5 Spelling of saʕaw and ʕataw 301
B.6 Luʔluʔ 301
B.7 raʔaw 302

B.8 al-malaʔu 303
B.9 nabaʔu(n) 305
B.10 balāʔ 305
B.11 ʔanbāʔ, ʔabnāʔ, duʕāʔ 306
B.12 Fuʕalāʔ plurals 306
B.13 Našāʔu 308
B.14 Ǧazāʔu 308
B.15 Ribā 309
B.16 ʔasāʔū 310
B.17 Dāwūd 311
B.18 Ruʔūs 312
B.19 Bi-smi 313
B.20 Ibn ʔumma/I, ya-bana ʔumma/i 314
B.21 La-ttaxad̲ta 314
B.22 al-munša/iʔāt 315
B.23 Genitive construct nouns in ending in -āʔi 315
B.24 ʔawliyāʔ in construct 317
B.25 ʔadʕiyāʔihim 317
B.26 arjih, nabbiʔnā, nabbiʔ, nabbiʔhum, ʔanbiʔhum 318
B.27 Fa-ǧtabā-hu, ʕuqbā-hā 319
B.28 maḍā 319
B.29 hātayni 319

Bibliography 320
Index of Tribes, Groups and Regions 332
Index of Subjects 333
Index of Modern Authors 335
Index of Medieval Muslim Figures and Authors 337
Index of Quranic verses 340

Preface and Acknowledgements

The monograph you now have before you was written in the context of my post-doctoral Veni project "Before the Grammarians: Arabic in the formative period of Islam" funded by the Dutch Research Council (NWO). It is not at all the work that I expected to write, but it is the one that I believe needed to be written. The original aim of my research was to reconstruct the language of the early Islamic period, as seen through transcriptions of Arabic into non-Arabic script (primarily Graeco-Arabica, Copto-Arabica, Sassano-Arabica, and Judeo-Arabic), and comparing and contrasting these against the Arabic in Arabic script of the early Islamic period as found in the papyri and inscriptions.

While in the past years I have spent considerable time researching this Xeno-Arabic material, as I have dubbed it, it quickly became clear to me that there was one central linguistic source of early Islamic Arabic which had gone almost completely ignored: the Quran. Little to no research had been done into this ancient linguistic source, without an implicit assumption that its reading traditions established at least a century later are an accurate reflection of the language of its composition. This led me to decide to focus my research in this direction, and this book is a culmination of my research of the past years bringing together questions about the nature and origin of Classical Arabic, the part that the Quran played in this, and the manner in which the Quranic reading traditions arose.

There are many people whom I must thank, and without whose help this work would not exist. Let me start with my dear friend Ahmad Al-Jallad. His passion for the topic of Arabic historical linguistics is what drew me into the field, his presence in Leiden is sorely missed. I wish to also thank Hythem Sidky whose engagement with me on the topic of Quranic manuscripts and the *Qirāʔāt* came at just the right time. Without our friendship and long discussions, this book would have been a very different and much weaker book.

There are many other colleagues whom I could thank for helping me think through the topics of this book, but special mention should be made of Benjamin Suchard, Fokelien Kootstra, Phillip Stokes, Imar Koutchoukali, Chams Bernard and May Shaddel. This core group of dear friends and brilliant researchers have supported me throughout this project and commented on the many drafts of my chapter. I also thank my PhD supervisor and mentor, Prof. Maarten Kossmann who continued to support and challenge me even as I transitioned from Berberology to this new field of Arabic linguistics and Quranic studies, and whose critical and meticulous approach to anything scholarly continues to be a great inspiration to me.

Of course, I am also infinitely grateful to my dear Eline, whose love and support for me is invaluable. Her disinterest in my research keeps me sane and helps me remember that there's more to life than research. Last but not least, I thank my mother and brother, and most of all my dear father who passed away unexpectedly during this research project. His unconditional pride of his sons is dearly missed.

Marijn van Putten
Rotterdam

Transcription

Throughout this book, I use a transcription system of Arabic that needs to be quite flexible as it covers a large amount of vowel representations that do not necessarily occur in textbook Classical Arabic as we know it today, for the consonants I have chosen to use a transcription that clearly distinguishes *hamzah* (ʔ) and *ʕayn* (ʕ), and *hamzah* is always written, even when word-initial, whereas the *ʔalif al-waṣl* is written without initial *hamzah* to denote its elidable status. The table below illustrates my transcriptions in comparison to the DMG transcription system and its representation in international phonetic alphabet in the phonetic representation that I believe most likely matches the pronunciation in Quranic Arabic (see van Putten 2019b for more details).

Arabic	Transcription in this book	DMG	International Phonetic Alphabet
ء	ʔ	ʾ or ∅	[ʔ]
ب	b	b	[b]
ت	t	t	[tʰ]
ث	ṯ	ṯ	[θ]
ج	ǧ	ǧ	[ɟ]
ح	ḥ	ḥ	[ħ]
خ	x	ḫ	[χ]
د	d	d	[d]
ذ	ḏ	ḏ	[ð]
ر	r	r	[ɾ], [ɾˤ]
ر	ṛ[1]	r	[ɾˤ]
ز	z	z	[z]
س	s	s	[s]
ش	š	š	[ʃ] or [ɕ]
ص	ṣ	ṣ	[sˤ⁼]
ض	ḍ	ḍ	[ɮˤ]
ط	ṭ	ṭ	[tˤ⁼]
ظ	ẓ	ẓ	[ðˤ]

1 Only distinguished from *r* when this is relevant to the discussion at hand.

(*cont.*)

Arabic	Transcription in this book	DMG	International Phonetic Alphabet
ع	ʕ	ʿ	[ʕ]
غ	ġ	ġ	[ʁ]
ف	f	f	[f]
ق	q	q	[q˭]
ك	k	k	[kʰ]
ل	l	l	[l]
ل	ḷ	l (as in *allāh*)	[lˤ]
م	m	m	[m]
ن	n	n	[n]
ه	h	h	[h]
و	w	w	[w]
ي	y	y	[j]

When transcribing Classical Arabic in running text, I will use pausal forms in pause, context forms in context. When citing titles of books or names of people, I will stick to the customary practice of using pausal forms throughout, except in construct where I will use *ʔiʕrāb*-less forms. The feminine ending in its pausal form is always spelled *-ah* and never, *-a* in line with its pronunciation in careful Classical Arabic speech, as well as Quranic rhyme. Likewise, in running Classical Arabic text, I will transcribe the definite article as assimilating, but in isolated citation of names and titles I will follow the common practice of avoiding assimilation.

When transcribing Classical Arabic, the pronominal suffix *-hu/-hi* is transcribed with vowel length disharmony, *-hū/-hī* after short vowels in line with the normative pronunciation of Classical Arabic.

As for vowels, many more vowel qualities than the standard six (*a, i, u, ā, ī, ū*) occur in our discussion. The table below gives their relative position, in the vowel triangle, as well as the typical technical term for such a pronunciation. Overlong vowels are written, where relevant, by doubling the long vowel: *aḍḍāāllīna*

	Front	Front rounded	Back
Close	i [i], ī [iː]	ü [y], ǖ [yː] *ʔišmām al-ḍamm*	u [u], ū [uː]
Mid-Close	e [e], ē [eː] *ʔimālah*		o [o], ō [oː] *ʔalif al-tafxīm*
Mid-Open	ä [æ], ǟ [æː] *taqlīl, bayna lafẓayn*		
Open	a [a], ā [aː]		

Abbreviations

Verbs Stems

G	*faʕala*, stem I
D	*faʕʕala*, stem II
L	*fāʕala*, stem III
C	*ʔafʕala*, stem IV
tD	*tafaʕʕala*, stem V
tL	*tafāʕala*, stem VI
N	*infaʕala*, stem VII
Gt	*iftaʕala*, stem VIII
Ct	*istafʕala*, stem X

Stem Shapes

I, II, III	First, second and third root consonant
I-ʔ	Roots with *hamzah* as first root consonant
I-w	Roots with *wāw* as first root consonant.
II-*w*/*y*	Roots with *wāw* or *yā* as second root consonant (hollow roots).
III-*w*	Roots with *wāw* as the third root consonant (weak roots).
III-*y*	Roots with *yāʔ* as the third rood consonant (weak roots).

Symbols

C	consonant
R	Any resonant consonant (*r, l, m, n*)
G	Any Maǧhūr consonant (*b, ǧ, d, ḏ, r, z, ḍ, ṭ, ẓ, ʕ, ġ, q, l, m, n, w, y, ʔ* and *ṣ*)
H	Any Mahmūs consonant (*t, ṯ, ḥ, x, s, š, f, k, h*)
v	Short vowel
v̄	Long vowel
U	High long vowels *ū* and *ī*
W	Glide *w* or *y*
√	Root
∅	Zero
*	Before a word indicates a reconstructed form.
>	Becomes (historically)

<	Comes from (historically)
→	Becomes (synchronically; derivationally). In transmission chains: transmits to.
←	Comes from (synchronically; derivationally). In transmission chains: transmits from.
/…/	Phonemic representation
[…]	Phonetic representation

Sigla

Throughout this book I have decided to cite medieval Arabic works through abbreviations rather than an author date citation system. Also, some dictionaries and common encyclopedias are referred to through abbreviations instead. The list below is an overview of the abbreviations that I have used. Note that in the author-date citations that I give here as an equivalence to the sigla used, as well as in the bibliography I make use of the more familiar DMG transcription system to aid ease of reference in the bibliography.

Ṣaḥīḥ al-Buxārī = *Ṣaḥīḥ al-Buxārī*, accessed through http://sunnah.com, citing the title and number of the *kitāb* as cited in Wensick (1927) followed by the name of the *bāb*.
ʔabū Ḥayyān = *al-Baḥr al-Muḥīṭ* (ʾAbū Ḥayyān 2010)
ʔabū ʕubayd (*Faḍāʔil al-Qurʔān*) = *Faḍāʔil al-Qurʔān* (ʾAbū ʿUbayd 1995)
Al-ʔaxfaš (*Maʕānī*) = *Maʕānī al-Qurʔān* (al-ʾAḫfaš al-ʾAwṣat 1990)
Al-Ḏahabī = *Maʕrifat al-Qurrāʔ al-Kabīr ʕalā al-Ṭabaqāt wa-l-ʔaʕṣār* (al-Ḏahabī 1995)
Al-Dānī (*Taysīr*) = *Kitāb al-Taysīr fī al-Qirāʔāt al-Sabʕ* (al-Dānī 1984)
Al-Dānī (*Ǧāmiʕ*) = *Ǧāmiʕ al-Bayān fī al-Qirāʔāt as-Sabʕ al-Mašhūrah* (al-Dānī 2005)
Al-Dānī (*ʕadd ʔāy*) = *al-Bayān fī ʕadd ʔāy al-Qurʔān* (al-Dānī 1994)
Al-Dānī (*Muqniʕ*) = *al-Muqniʕ fī Rasm Maṣāḥif al-ʔamṣār* (al-Dānī 1978)
Al-Fārisī (*Ḥuǧǧah*) = *al-Ḥuǧǧah fī ʕilal al-Qirāʔāt al-Sabʕ* (al-Fārisī 1971)
Al-Farrāʔ (*Maʕānī*) = *Maʕānī al-Qurʔān li-l-Farrāʔ* (al-Farrāʾ 1983)
Al-Farrāʔ (*Luġāt*) = *Kitāb fīh Luġāt al-Qurʔān* (al-Farrāʾ 2014)
Al-Mubarrad (*al-Muqtaḍab*) = *Kitāb al-Muqtaḍab* (al-Mubarrad 1994)
Ibn al-Ǧazarī = *Našr al-Qirāʔāt al-ʕašr* (ibn al-Ǧazarī 2018)
Ibn al-Ǧazarī (*al-Ġāyah*) = *Ġāyat Al-Nihāyah Fī Ṭabaqāt al-Qurrā*ʾ (Ibn al-Ǧazarī 2006)
Ibn Ǧinnī (*Kitāb al-Muġtaṣab*) = *Kitāb al-Muġtaṣab* (ibn Ǧinnī 1903)
Ibn Mihrān (*Ġāyah*) = *al-Ġāyah fī al-Qirāʔāt al-ʕašr* (ibn Mihrān 1990)
Ibn Mihrān (*Mabsūṭ*) = *al-Mabsūṭ fī al-Qirāʔāt al-ʕašr* (ibn Mihrān 1986)
Ibn Muǧāhid = *Kitāb al-Sabʕah fī al-Qirāʔāt* (ibn Muǧāhid 1972)
Sabṭ al-Xayyāṭ (*al-Mubhiǧ*) = *Kitāb al-Mubhiǧ fī al-Qirāʔāt al-Ṯamān wa-Qirāʔat al-ʔAʕmaš wa-Ibn Muḥayṣin wa-ʔixtiyār Xalaf wa-l-Yazīdī* (Sabṭ al-Ḫayyāṭ 1984)
Ibn al-Sarrāǧ (*ʔuṣūl*) = *Kitāb al-ʔuṣūl fī al-Naḥw* (ibn al-Sarrāǧ 2009)
Ibn al-Sarrāǧ (*kitāb al-xaṭṭ*) = *Kitāb al-Xaṭṭ* (ibn al-Sarrāǧ 1971)

Sībawayh = *Kitāb Sībawayh* (Sībawayh 1988)
Sībawayh (*derenbourg*) = *Kitāb Sībawayh* (Sībawayh 1881)
Al-Suyūṭī (*Hamʕ al-Hawāmiʕ*) = *Hamʕ al-Hawāmiʕ fī Šarḥ Ǧamʕ al-Ǧawāmiʕ* (al-Suyūṭī 1998)
Xalīl b. ʔaḥmad (*Kitāb al-ʕayn*) = *Kitāb al-ʕayn* (Ḫalīl b. ʾAḥmad 2003)
Ibn Xālawayh (*Muxtaṣar*) = *Muxtaṣar fī Šawāḏḏ al-Qurʔān min Kitāb al-Badīʕ* (ibn Ḫālawayh 2009)
Ibn Xālawayh (*Ḥuǧǧah*) = *al-Ḥuǧǧah fī al-Qirāʔāt al-Sabʕ* (ibn Ḫālawayh 1979)
Ibn Xālawayh (*Badīʕ*) = *Kitāb al-Badīʕ* (ibn Ḫālawayh 2007)
Ibn Xālawayh (*ʔiʕrāb*) = *ʔiʕrāb al-Qirāʔāt al-Sabʕ wa-ʕilalu-hā* (ibn Ḫālawayh 1992)
Ibn Yaʕīš (*Šarḥ al-Mufaṣṣal*), = *Šarḥ al-Mufaṣṣal li-l-Zamaxšarī* (ibn Yaʿīš 2001)
Al-Zaǧǧāǧ (*Mā Yanṣarif*) = *Mā Yanṣarif wa-Mā Lā Yanṣarif* (al-Zaǧǧāǧ 1971)
Al-Zamaxšarī (*Mufaṣṣal*) = *Kitāb al-Mufaṣṣal fī al-Naḥw* (al-Zamaḫšarī 1879)
Al-Zamaxšarī (*Kaššāf*) = *al-Kaššāf ʕan Ḥaqāʔiq al-Tanzīn wa-ʕuyūn al-ʔaqāwīl* (al-Zamaḫšarī 1966)

Lane *An Arabic-English Lexicon* (Lane 1863)
Lisān *Lisān al-ʕarab* (ibn Manẓūr n.d.)
EI[1] *Encyclopaedia of Islam*, first edition (Houtsma et al. 1913), entries are cited as Author *EI*[1] "Lemma".
EI[2] *Encyclopaedia of Islam*, second edition (Bearman et al. 1960), entries are cited as Author *EI*[2] "Lemma".

Throughout this book, I also refer to several Quranic manuscripts by abbreviated names, such as CPP, BL, D29, T, 330g, 331 etc. If a full reference is not given in that location, I refer the reader to the Appendix B, where a full list of the variants is given.

CHAPTER 1

Introduction

إِنَّآ أَنزَلْنَٰهُ قُرَانًا عَرَبِيًّا لَّعَلَّكُمْ تَعْقِلُونَ

The Quran, Q12:2, in the reading of Ibn Kaṯīr

1.1 Previous Scholarship

The main question the current book aims to answer is: "What is the language of the Quran?" Despite more than a century of in-depth study of the Quran, and a debate on the linguistic nature, I believe the discussion on this question has not progressed significantly, since Vollers (1906). Despite the many deficiencies of Vollers' work, which have already been addressed in detail especially by Nöldeke (1910), and Geyer (1909), I believe that the question it formulated remains essential to furthering our understanding of the linguistic history of Arabic and the context in which the Quran arose: What *is* the language of the Quran and, perhaps more importantly, *how do we know*?

Vollers' radical theory proposed that the Quran was originally composed in the Hijazi common language (*Volksprache*)—a language he considered much more akin to modern Arabic dialects than the literary language (*Schriftsprache*) in which the Quran later came to be recited. He believed it was reworked by Arab grammarians to adhere to the Classical standard of this literary language, the *ʕarabiyyah*. He saw the literature on the Quranic reading traditions (*Qirāʔāt*) and the variants described within them as providing essential traces of the "original" language. From this he concluded that the Quran was reworked in later times by Arab grammarians, making massive changes to the linguistic nature of the text, including pervasive changes to the consonantal skeleton of the text. Especially the supposition of relatively late changes to the consonantal skeleton by grammarians has become difficult to accept. It is now certain that the standardization of the text well preceded the work of the Arab grammarians by over a century (Sinai 2014a; 2014b; van Putten 2019c).

But, while Vollers' theory has several shortcomings that make it not quite convincing today, the fundamental question as to what the language of the

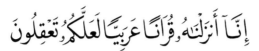

Quran was, is still a valid one, and it has never adequately been answered. Instead, a consensus developed although no evidence seems to have ever been proffered for it. As Rabin (1955, 24) puts it: "Apparently independently, H. Fleisch [(Fleisch 1947, 97–101)], R. Blachère [(Blachère 1947, 156–169)] and C. Rabin [(C. Rabin 1955, 3–4)] arrived in the forties at the conclusion that the language of the Koran, far from being pure Meccan either subsequently revised (Vollers) or slightly adapted to the poetic idiom, was none other than the poetic *koinē*." But the seeds of this later consensus were already laid by Friedrich Schwally in *Geschichte des Korans* part II in 1919. I believe that this is the first explicit endorsement of this view, and with that also one of the more strongly argued iterations of the view. It is worth repeating the whole passage here:

> Generally, any tradition connecting the ʿUthmānic text in any way with dialectal questions must be rejected, since the Koran is not written in a local dialect at all but rather has a language identical to that of the pre-Islamic poems. These, however, cannot possibly have been written in dialectal form, as their authors belonged to quite different tribes, living so far apart that the texts would have to show strong idiomatic differences. Admittedly, when fixing a text in such a defective script as Arabic's, where vowels are generally not indicated and many consonants are expressed by the same sign, some idiosyncrasies of the verbal presentation were simply not recognizable at all. Still, the lexical and grammatical agreement is such that an actual uniform language must be assumed. After all, given what we know about linguo-geographical conditions in other parts of the world, it would be a total contradiction if such a drastic disappearance of dialects were to have occurred in large areas of the Arabian Peninsula. We are, thus, obliged to conclude that the ancient poems, as well as the Koran, were composed in a generally intelligible standard language, the difference of which from the local dialects of cultural centres like Mecca and Medina was naturally less than from that in the more distant areas of the Peninsula.
>
> NÖLDEKE et al. 2013, 260

I have my reservations about the confidence with which it is asserted that the pre-Islamic poems represent a linguistic unity which skips both over the strong classicizing force of the classical Arabic text tradition that without a doubt has affected the language of poetry in many ways.[1] I also believe we should raise

1 For a fascinating and stimulatingly original discussion on this topic see Foreman (forth-

doubts about the true pan-Arabian provenance of the poetry. But this is not our concern here. Rather, this book's topic is to challenge the ease with which the Quran is implicated into being part of this same intertribal pan-peninsular literary language.

Despite the view certainly predating Rabin and his cohorts in the forties, it certainly gained prominence from that point onwards. It is unfortunate that Schwally's passage is never cited, despite being a much clearer formulation of the idea than any of the authors who Rabin cites to have formulated it. It was subsequently wholeheartedly accepted, for example by Zwettler (1978, 160) who says: "most have come to agree that the *ʿarabīya* of the poets and the language of the Qurʾān are essentially identical and that this poetic idiom was not spoken by any group of Arabs as a vernacular tongue." Versteegh (1984, 5) follows as well: "According to the accepted opinion the language of the poems [...] became the language of the *Qurʾān* as well."

Despite the consensus that has developed on this topic, to my knowledge nobody has actually attempted to demonstrate that these two languages are "essentially identical." Instead, this has simply been asserted. Any definition of what the linguistic features of this supposed shared language are is something the field has simply remained silent on. If there is any assertion about its linguistic features at all, scholars have pointed to the Arab grammarians as having codified or standardized it (e.g. Zwettler 1978, 101, 148).

I do not wish to get into the question here whether the language of poetry and the Quran is just the 'Old Arabic' as it was spoken before Islam (e.g. Versteegh 1984) or a specific oral-formulaic register (e.g. Zwettler 1978) and therefore it seems sensible to abstract away from the terms 'Old Arabic' or 'poetic Koiné' and the many other terms that have been used by authors previously, as sometimes the same term may have a different meaning to two different authors. For example, to Rabin (1951, 3) 'Classical Arabic' is the language of pre-Islamic poetry, while Fischer (2002, 1f.) would call that pre-classical. Hence, I will define my own terms here.

First, I will use the term ***ʕarabiyyah*** to mean any form of Arabic that the grammarians deem fit to describe (specifically the earliest grammarians such as Sībawayh and al-Farrāʔ, but later grammarians do not seem to deviate much from them). Both Classical Arabic prose and the language attested in pre-Islamic prose (but less so Quranic prose, as we will see in chapter 3) fall

coming) who presents compelling evidence that one can in fact find systematic phonological differences between different poems, suggesting that the poetry—even after centuries of classicization in their transmission—can still display significant linguistic diversity.

within the range of variation described by the grammarians. By **Classical Arabic**, I refer to the subset of features of the *ʕarabiyyah* that eventually become a strict normative standard, this is the form of Arabic that is described in modern textbooks of Classical Arabic such as Wright (1896) and Fischer (2002). As we will see in chapter 2, this covers only a small subset of many factors of phonological and morphological variation present in the *ʕarabiyyah*. I use the term **Quranic Arabic** to refer to the register in which the Quran was initially composed. I will argue that—contrary to the opinion of other authors—the consonantal skeleton of the standard text is a fairly good guide to its linguistic features.

Of course, viewing the language of the pre-Islamic poetry and Quranic Arabic to be one and the same language is not a new view. The Classical Arabic grammarians themselves do not make a systematic distinction between 'Arabic of Poetry', 'Arabic of Eloquent Arabs' and 'Arabic of the Quran'. All three categories belong to the same eloquent language: the *ʕarabiyyah*. As with all distinctions of language, such distinctions of course remain arbitrary. The differences between Swedish and Norwegian are small enough that there is a high degree of mutual intelligibility—yet for political reasons these languages are considered separate. On the other hand, a Berber speaker from the Souss in Morocco is unlikely to get very far conversing with a Libyan Berber from Zuara, but for pan-Berberist ideological reasons might nevertheless insist that they speak the same language.

As mentioned, while there is near-universal agreement on the idea that the Quranic Arabic and the language of poetry is the same language, the *ʕarabiyyah*, its features and supposed similarities are seldom defined. It is not of much use for a linguist to argue what should or should not be considered the "same language". However, what a linguist can do is evaluate the linguistic features of a distinct corpus. Studying the Quran, for example, we see that it has a highly consistent use of only a *subset* of the linguistic features considered to be *ʕarabiyyah*. As already noticed by the Arab grammarians, for example, the Quran exclusively uses *ḏālika, tilka* and *hunālika* for the distal demonstratives, and never uses *ḏāka, tīka/ḏīka* or *hunāka*. In this the Quran is clearly distinct in its linguistic behaviour from Classical Arabic poetry, and Classical Arabic prose of later times, which use these forms much more freely. While there is no objective way to decide which and how many isoglosses one needs to declare something as not being "essentially identical" to the language of poetry, observing such recurrent and systematic use of only a specific subset of the linguistic variation is meaningful, and therefore important to distinguish, especially if it would otherwise lead to the uncritical acceptance that two corpora—in the case the Quran and pre-Islamic poetry—are essentially identical.

The fact that modern scholars did not sense the need to define this and demonstrate the similarities seems to stem from the fact that they assume that the language of the Quran is more or less identical to the textbook standard of Classical Arabic which is a fairly uniform linguistic system which comes to dominate later Classical literature. This, no doubt, is aided by the fact that the Quranic reading tradition most widely adhered to today, the one of Ḥafṣ ʕan ʕāṣim, has linguistic features that are very close (although by no means identical to) Classical Arabic. However, Ḥafṣ's tradition is just one of the two transmissions of ʕāṣim, and besides him there are yet nine other canonical readings, each with two canonical transmissions; these readings do not just differ in the interpretation of the meaning of certain verses, but, in fact much more frequently and for our purposes more importantly, differ significantly from one another in phonetics, phonology and morphology.

Thus, we find that most modern authors assume that the *ʕarabiyyah* as reflected in the Quran *must* have had the *hamzah*, despite the fact that the grammarians describing the *ʕarabiyyah* clearly allowed for forms that had lost this, without any normative expression of disapproval (see Sībawayh III, 541ff.). For example, Hans Wehr in his review of Fück's *Arabiyya*, commenting on why we cannot trust the orthography of the Quran to learn about the phonology of Quranic Arabic says the following: "Die wesentlichen umgangssprachlichen Merkmale der koranischen Orthographie, das Fehlen der Nunation sowie des Stimmritzenverschlußlautes im Wortinnern und am Silbenende (*bīr, mūmin, nāyim* usw.) rühren wohl aus dieser älteren den Dialekt wiedergebenden Orthographie her und wurden übergenommen, als man vor der Aufgabe stand, die ʿArabīya-Aussprache mit den Mitteln der bereits vorliegenden Orthographie zu fixieren."[2] (Wehr 1952, 184). The implicit assumption here is that the *ʕarabiyyah* must have had the forms *biʔr, muʔmin* and *nāʔim* as in Classical Arabic as it is taught today. Moreover, it is asserted that it was the target pronunciation of Quranic Arabic. Here the overreliance on the widespread reading tradition of Ḥafṣ shows. Had Hans Wehr instead relied on the recitation of the Quran in the Maghreb, he would have indeed heard 'and a well' (Q22:45) not be recited as *wa-biʔrin*, but instead as *wa-bīrin*, and 'A believer' (Q40:28) not as *muʔminun* but as *mūminun*, as this is how the equally valid and canonical recitation of Warš ʕan Nāfiʕ has it, a traditions still popular and broadly

2 The essential colloquial features of the Qurʾānic orthography—absence of nunation and also of the glottal stop within words and at the end of syllables (*bīr, mūmin, nāyim*, etc.)—no doubt the result from this earlier orthography which reproduced the dialects; and they were carried over when the problem arose of setting down the pronunciation of the *ʿarabīya* by means of the orthography available at the time (translation from Zwettler 1978, 123f.).

adhered to by Muslims all over Morocco, Algeria and Tunisia.[3] If, as seems to be implied here, the Quranic recitation of Warš is somehow less reflective of the *ʕarabiyyah* than is the recitation of Ḥafṣ, this should certainly be explained, and not be implicitly assumed.

An equally egregious example of the unintentional but nevertheless highly problematic imposition of modern prescriptive norms of Classical Arabic unto the Arabic of the Quran can be found in Zwettler's (1978, 179, n. 70) discussion of the pronunciation of *nabīʔ* for 'prophet': "the use of *hamz* in *nabīy* was a peculiarly Ḥijāzī pseudo-correction and a feature neither of the *ʿarabiyya* nor of the other dialects."[4] Where Zwettler's certainty comes from that *nabīʔ* does not belong to the *ʕarabiyyah* is unclear to me. Not only is the form *nabīʔ* recognized in lexicographical works like *Lisān al-ʕarab* and by grammarians like Sībawayh (III, 547, 555)—never with the qualification that it is not *ʕarabiyyah*—it is once again a reading that is broadly adhered to even today in Quranic recitation in the tradition of Nāfiʕ.[5] The only reason I can see why one would decide that this is not the *ʕarabiyyah* is due to anachronistic imposition of a much later Classical norm that in no way need be reflective of the *ʕarabiyyah* as it was conceived of at the time of the prophet—even if we would accept that the Quran was composed in that register, for which no compelling positive evidence has been presented.

Nöldeke (1910) criticized Vollers (1906), not altogether fairly, for taking the Gustav Flügel Quran as essentially the standard text, not recognizing the equal validity of reading traditions not reflected in this text edition. This criticism however should be seen as carrying a call to action: if the Quranic reading traditions do not reflect the "true" Quranic Arabic, as opposed to the Arabic of the Flügel Quran, what *do* the Quranic reading traditions represent, and

3 And he is not the only one of the canonical readers that would read these words thus. Likewise, ʔabū Ǧaʕfar and optionally ʔabū ʕamr recited like that. Also, *nāʔimūna* is read with the loss of *hamzah* by the canonical reader Ḥamzah when he pauses on it (as he likely usually would have, as both cases of it stand in verse final position, Q7:97; Q68:19).

4 One may also add that *lā tanbir* neither means—as Rabin, cited by Zwettler, translates—"do not screech" nor as Zwettler suggests "do not raise your voice (i.e. with an expiratory stress)." *nabr* is just an alternative, and seemingly more archaic term for *hamz*. See Xalīl b. ʔaḥmad (*Kitāb al-ʕayn* s.v. نبر) where this meaning is given as its primary meaning (see also, *Lane* 2757a; *Lisān* 4323b). This obviously makes better sense in the context of a (no doubt falsified Hadith) where the prophet tells his follower off for saying *yā-nabīʔa ḷḷāh* 'O prophe' of God!', by answering *lā tanbir bi-smī!* 'don't apply the *hamzah* to my name!'

5 Moreover, whence the certainty comes that *nabīʔ* is the pseudo-correct form and *nabiyy* the proper form is also unclear. As this word clearly comes from Hebrew נביא which, at least historically contains *ʔ* (as evidenced by the final א), it actually stands to reason that it *should* have the *hamzah* in Classical Arabic (see § 6.5.1.1 for further discussion).

which of these (if any) *does* represent the true language? It should be clear from the previous paragraphs that many authors that have opined on the language of the Quran—although occasionally paying lip service to the existence of these readings—have essentially continued to operate on the same simplifying assumption as Vollers, assuming that their print Quran is the standard text and an accurate reflection of Quranic Arabic, and that the other 19 canonical transmissions of the Quran are just inconvenient noise to be ignored.

However, the Quranic reading traditions are not just differences on how to read a certain word or syntagm; the many distinguishing factors between the different reading traditions are in fact linguistic, marking both morphological and phonological distinctions. ʔabū Ǧaʕfar, for example, regularly loses any pre-consonantal *hamzah* (e.g. *rās* 'head'); al-Kisāʔī has a fourth phonemic long vowel (*hadē* 'he lead' but *daʕā* 'he cried out') and Ibn Kaṯīr consistently uses long plural pronouns such as *ʔantumū* 'you (pl.)', *ʕalayhimū* 'upon them'. When scholarship reached the consensus that the language of the Quran is essentially the same as that of the poetry, this should not have been uncritically accepted. One should ask which of these 20 canonical transmissions, if any, is the true language of the Quran. And why should that one be preferred over the other as being representative of the *ʕarabiyyah*? Just because the transmission of Ḥafṣ strikes the modern scholar as most familiar, as it stands closest to the strict classical standard that emerges centuries later—the standard to which also the language of poetry gets mercilessly reshaped (C. Rabin 1955, 21)—it cannot be the reason why we close the book on the investigation into what the language of the Quran is.

As should be clear from the discussion above, despite there now being well over a century of scholarship discussing the language of the Quran in relation to the language of the pre-Islamic period and the language of poetry, the Quran has never been allowed to tell its own linguistic history. Instead, its linguistic history has been co-opted by those telling the linguistic history of the poetry with the automatic assumption that the Quran is part of this same history as well. This is an oversimplification and indefensible from the perspective of historical linguistics. The Quran is a long text with ample linguistic information, not only in its reading traditions, but also in the very structure of the text itself. Scholars have gone to great lengths to disqualify the value of the Quranic orthography to inform us about its language. However, avenues that examine how one can prove that the orthography is meaningful, or indeed rightfully dismissed, have rarely been explored. The orthography of the Quran is quite distinct from the later Classical Arabic orthography, and likewise differs significantly from Arabic orthography that we find in pre-Islamic epigraphy;

this should give us pause: why is this text so different, and why was it so important to preserve?

Moreover, the Quran follows rhyming patterns throughout almost the entire text; only a tiny fraction of the verses does not rhyme with the rest. Rhymed text is an invaluable part of the toolkit of any philologist aiming to reconstruct the language of a certain period, as it helps to break through the otherwise difficult to disentangle question of what parts of an orthography are simply historical spelling and which parts reflect phonetic realty. Vollers (1906, 55ff.) saw the value of Quranic rhyme as a source of linguistic information, but this valuable linguistic resource has been almost completely ignored since then.[6]

1.2 The Uthmanic Text Type and the Quranic Consonantal Text

One of the reasons why the Quran may not have been afforded the ability to tell its own linguistic history originates from a certain amount of skepticism that the text and its orthography, as we have it today, can be confidently projected back to the very period in which the text was composed. Criticism of the transmission history of any tradition of text is a staple of Islamic studies, and certainly in the seventies severe doubts were raised that the Quranic text truly stems from the time that the tradition tells us it comes from.[7] However, times have changed and important advancements have been made especially when it comes to the textual history of the Quran. Early Quranic manuscripts have in recent years become easily accessible as more and more are massively digitized and editions are published. Where previously it may not have been as clear how ancient and well-preserved the Quranic text truly is, and thus what to make exactly of its orthographic idiosyncrasies, it is now clear that the text is considerably ancient. By examining the specific orthographic idiosyncrasies of the Quranic text across a variety of early Quranic manuscripts, Van Putten (2019c) has shown that all early manuscripts come from a single written archetype whose orthographic specificities have been judiciously copied

6 Notable exceptions being Nöldeke et al. (2013, 415) and Rabin (1951, 115f., §bb) who both realized that Quranic rhyme clearly distinguishes *ā* (written with *ʔalif*) and *ē* (written with *yāʔ*) where Classical Arabic pronounces them both as *ā*. But strangely, this view was never picked up and widely accepted. Diem (1979) even goes so far as to explicitly deny that the two spellings of the Classical Arabic *ʔalif maqṣūrah* reflect any pronunciation difference at all—not addressing the evidence from the rhyme to the contrary. See Van Putten (2017a) for a defense of a phonemic distinction of *ē* and *ā* in Quranic Arabic.

7 Most notably through John Wansbrough's work, who argued that the canonical text only came to a close about two centuries after its traditional date around 650 CE (Wansbrough 1977).

over the centuries. All early manuscripts known so far descend from a single text type referred to as the **Uthmanic Text Type (UT)**,[8] which may plausibly be connected with the standardization effort attributed to the third caliph ʕuṯmān b. ʕaffān (reign 23–35 AH/644–656 CE). While the manuscript evidence cannot preclude with absolute certainty an earlier redaction, a time much later than his reign is now a virtual impossibility. We have large portions of the Quran complete in first century manuscripts that all belong to the UT, with carbon dating early enough that much later dating is rather unlikely. In other words, we have evidence and a clear view of the Quranic text in all its linguistic details as it was written down mere decades after the death of the prophet. This should afford it the central and essential role as a primary source for the language of the Quran that it is.

The UT is highly uniform, but there are about 40 variants in the consonantal skeleton of the text in which the original different regional codices differ from one another. These regional variants can be attributed to four regions: Syria, Kufa, Basra and Medina, and these regional variants form a stemma that goes back to a single archetype (Sidky 2021; Dutton 2001; 2004; Cook 2004). These four regional types must be archetypal to the four regions and must be part of the initial distribution of the UT.

A central pillar of the current work is the incorporation of linguistic information of the UT. Whereas the consonantal skeleton of, e.g. the Hebrew bible has long been viewed as an important source of linguistic information of Biblical Hebrew (e.g. Kahle 1947, 95–102; Tov 1992, 47–49; Khan 2013, 13–30 and of course the rich Ktiv/Qere tradition within the Masoretic tradition itself), the same attention has not been accorded to the **Quranic Consonantal Text (QCT)**. As there is no critical edition of the UT, my transcriptions of the QCT will be based to a large extent on the standard text, as we find these in print Qurans today which ultimately descend from the **1924 Cairo Edition (CE)**. Unlike some other earlier print Qurans, such as the 1834 Quran of Gustav Flügel, the orthography of the CE is very conservative, and often is a fairly accurate representation of what we find in 7th century Quranic manuscripts. Due to the impressive uniformity of early manuscripts, and the fairly accurate representation of such documents in the CE, a critical version of the text is of significantly lesser importance than it would be for, say, the Hebrew Bible or forms of the New Testament. Moreover, as the CE is based on traditional medieval works that diligently docu-

8 With the exception, of course, of the spectacular find of the lower text of the Sanaa Palimpsest, which seems to represent another text tradition, plausibly from a tradition deriving from a companion codex (Sadeghi and Bergmann 2010; Sadeghi and Goudarzi 2011; Sinai 2020; Cellard 2021), for a different opinion see Hilali (2017).

mented the orthography and spelling variants of the UT, the QCT of the CE can be thought of in some ways as the result of medieval text criticism, although lacking the diligent critical apparatus that one might wish to have. Despite the impressive conservatism of the CE, the text is not always an accurate reflection of what we typically find in early manuscripts. This is especially the case for the use of *ʔalif*, which is used to write the *ā* significantly more often in the CE than is typical for early manuscripts. But there are also several other orthographic practices innovative in the CE compared to early manuscripts. For example, in early manuscripts the nominative pronoun *ḏū* is consistently spelled ذو, while in early manuscripts it is consistently followed by an *ʔalif*, ذوا. Whenever relevant, I will change the text to better fit what early manuscripts reflect and I will reference the relevant data for such a reconstruction, often discussed in detail in Appendix B.

In my transcriptions of the QCT, I will use the consonantal dotting, even though those were used quite sparingly in early Quranic manuscripts. In fact, it is often suggested that the original redaction of ʕuṯmān's standard text had been completely without consonantal dotting, and was just a bare consonantal skeleton known as the *rasm*. Bursi (2018) has recently pointed out that there is rather little evidence for such a view. The very earliest manuscripts that we have all contain some amount of dotting—although indeed used sparingly.[9] Moreover, he demonstrates that the sparse dotting in early Hijazi manuscripts clearly show similar patterns to the dotting used in the early documentary papyri.

The reason why I provide full dotting for the QCT, first and foremost is because it greatly aids the readability of the text. But I also believe it is justified to assume that we can know the correct dotting for the consonants for two reasons. First of all, whenever dots do appear in the early manuscripts, they overwhelmingly agree with what we find in the CE and in other manuscripts that have dots. This gives us confidence that for the majority of the text, there was a pretty clear idea what the dotting of the consonant was supposed to be, even when early manuscripts were often incomplete in marking it. The second reason is based on the evidence from the reading traditions. Sidky (forthcoming) shows that the canonical reading traditions of the Quran only disagree with each other 284 times on consonantal dotting. This may seem like a large number, but considering the thousands of times that the readers could have

9 In fact, it is rather the later Kufic manuscripts that lose (almost) all dots. One wonders if the traditional view that the UT had a bare undotted *rasm* stems from the examination of the somewhat later Kufic manuscripts, rather than the truly oldest Hijazi manuscripts with significantly more dotting.

plausibly disagreed on the dotting but do not do so, the number is actually strikingly low. This suggests that there indeed was an early consensus on what the consonants of the QCT were, even when the text may frequently have been written ambiguously. This consensus should not be overstated either, of course. Much of the dotting may be filled in by common sense, rather than a shared memory. In most contexts, there simply is no other plausible reading of the sequence دلك than ذلك, that is *ḏālika*. The combination of self-evident readings and consensus on the non-self-evident parts provide a strong basis to transcribe the QCT with these dots.

In my representation of the QCT, I do not distinguish between *ʔalif maqṣūrah bi-ṣūrat al-yāʔ* (e.g. بنى 'he built') and *yāʔ* (e.g. بنى 'sons of (gen./acc.)'), as these are not distinct graphemes in early Quranic manuscripts.[10] In non-final position, both are written with a dotted denticle (e.g. هديه 'he led them', يهديه 'he leads them').

The *hamzah* is never written in early Quranic manuscripts as it lacks any means to express it.[11] If the seat of the *hamzah* is *yāʔ*, it will simply be represented as any other *yāʔ* as we find in the CE, e.g. الذيب 'the wolf' and will not be displayed as a dotless *yāʔ* (الذىب).[12]

The *tāʔ marbūṭah* is never distinguished from the *hāʔ*, as this graphemic distinction does not exist in early Quranic manuscripts, e.g. نعمه الله 'the grace of God'.[13] The earliest *muṣḥaf* that I am aware of that uses the two dots on top

10 Nor are they distinct graphemes, even in much later manuscripts, Quranic or otherwise.

11 We can hardly agree with Zwettler (1978, 179, n. 70) that the *hamzah* is most likely the oldest of the diacritical signs used in the Quranic Arabic manuscripts (citing, but misunderstanding Abbott 1939, 39 f.). To the contrary, the *hamzah* sign does not get expressed with a designated sign in Quranic manuscripts for the first centuries of Islam, even when vowel signs are invented, the *hamzah* is simply expressed with vowel signs which do double duty as markers of the *hamzah*, but in that context are not always unambiguous in whether they denoted *hamzah* or just vowels. Even while at some point Kufic manuscripts start using separate colours for the *hamzah* in the third Islamic century, contemporaneous with this practice there are still many manuscripts that do not distinguish them. The modern *hamzah* sign constitutes the latest layer of Arabic diacritics (Revell 1975, 180).

12 The requirement of a dotless *yāʔ* for the seat of the *hamzah* is a result of typographic constraints, and not a practice that was commonplace in medieval manuscripts. Lack of awareness of Classical Arabic manuscript culture has occasionally led to rather bizarre statements, such as Hopkins (1984, § 20a) affirming that بيس الراى "what a bad opinion!" must lack a *hamzah* because it is written with a dotted *yāʔ*. It is not difficult to find words written with a dotted *yāʔ* where the word carries a *hamzah* in a context where it is *explicit* that the word is to be read with a *hamzah*.

13 As Revell (1975, 180) points out, the dotting of the *tāʔ marbūṭah* constitutes the latest layer of Arabic diacritics, one that was only rarely introduced in Kufic manuscripts. See also Moritz *EI1*, "Arabic Writing".

of *tāʔ marbūṭah* is the Ibn al-Bawwāb Quran from 391AH/1000CE, the earliest dated Nasx Quran written centuries after the ancient Hijazi and Kufic Qurans that we are concerned with.

Whenever there is disagreement between reading traditions on how a certain consonantal skeleton is to be read, the disputed consonant will be left undotted, for example فتىىنوا (Q4:94) which is variously read *fa-tabayyanū* (فتبينوا) or *fa-taṯabbatū* (فتثبتوا).

Finally, while in terms of the spelling of the *ʔalif* for *ā*, I will usually follow the CE, with the important note that the CE frequently spells words *plene* where manuscripts usually write it defectively, when it is relevant to the discussion, I will write the word defectively if it is consistently done so in early manuscripts, or I will use a dagger *ʔalif* to indicate that it is sometimes written with and sometimes without this *ʔalif*. Note here that it means that the dagger *ʔalif* has an explicitly *different* function in my transcription of the QCT compared to how it is used in the Quran today. It does not just note that an *ā* is written defectively, but that the *ʔalif*, which may be of any function, is not always written in the manuscript. An example might be شٰى to denote that *šayʔ* is variously written شاى or شى in the location of the text under discussion in early manuscripts.

1.3 Overview

As it stands now, the Quran has never been allowed to tell its own story as to what its language is; instead, rather convoluted arguments have been developed as to why we cannot and should not use the Quranic orthography as a source of information for its language, all the while (implicitly) assuming that the modern standard Cairo Edition is an accurate reflection of the language of the Quran. But just as we cannot take for granted that the Quran *does* display the language as it was composed, we cannot take for granted that the Quran *does not* display the language as spoken. We *certainly* cannot assume that the language of the Quran must have been linguistically identical to the Classical Arabic or to the *ʕarabiyyah*. The current work aims to close this major lacuna in our understanding of the history of the Arabic language. I believe there are four topics that need to be addressed before we can work towards a final conclusion about the language of the Quran.

In **Chapter** 2, I will explore what the *ʕarabiyyah* is according to those that are said to have standardized it—the Arab grammarians. The *ʕarabiyyah* is all too often equated to Classical Arabic, the fairly uniform standard language described in textbooks and which forms the basis for Modern Standard Arabic. But the early Arab grammarians allow for much more linguistic variation, clearly allowing and even endorsing forms that would not be considered acceptable in Classical Arabic. However, in order to understand the linguistic environment from which the Quran emerged, we must of course be informed by these earlier sources rather than anachronistically project the textbook standard onto this period and expect the Quran to conform to that.

With a clearer picture of the linguistic variation that was accepted in the *ʕarabiyyah* according to the early grammarians, it will be possible to examine the Quranic reading traditions in **Chapter** 3. As has been mentioned, the Quran today is accepted to be recited in ten different reading traditions, of which several still enjoy broad popularity. It will be shown that much of the linguistic variation described by the Arab grammarians is in fact employed in these reading traditions. Showing that the great amount of linguistic variation the grammarians describe are not just odd deviations from an implicit accepted standard language close or identical to Classical Arabic, but that this variation was inherently part of the *ʕarabiyyah* and employed as such. Moreover, the chapter will show that the linguistic variation in the reading traditions cannot be understood as dialects of Arabic. They all have clear artificial linguistic elements which must be understood as conscious decisions to change the language as part of an artificial performance register. However, due to the vastly different approaches found in each of these readings, it will be shown that it is difficult to decide what the true language of the Quran is, as the reading traditions provide twenty mutually exclusive answers.

As the reading traditions seem unable to give a unified answer as to what the language of the Quran is, in **Chapters** 4 **and** 5 I shift focus to the language of the QCT. While some authors have admitted the possibility that the Quran in its original composition may have had some accommodation to a local pronunciation, again and again it is affirmed that grammatically it is essentially the same language as the poetic *koiné*. **Chapter** 4 puts this claim to the test by comparing the isoglosses of the different Arabic dialects collected by the Arab grammarians and comparing them against the linguistic data that can be gleaned from the QCT. **Chapter** 5 subsequently examines the phonological features of Quranic Arabic. While in Chapter 3 it is shown that when doing this with the reading tradition no clear pattern appears at all, all readings haphazardly mix and match features from different dialects, when looking at the QCT a strikingly uniform picture emerges. In its morphological and phonetic features, the language of the QCT is clearly Hijazi Arabic. Occasionally this can be corroborated by pre-Islamic Arabic epigraphic evidence as well. This clear picture that emerges cannot be coincidence, and therefore we must conclude that the QCT is an accurate reflection of the language of the Quran, and that this language is indeed the Hijazi dialect.

Finally, **Chapter** 6 and **Chapter** 7 return to the reading traditions. In previous articles I have shown that Quranic Arabic contained a number of features quite distinct from its later reading traditions. Most notable here is the fact that Quranic Arabic seems to have almost completely lacked the *hamzah* and had lost final short vowels and *tanwīn*. A major source of skepticism of earlier scholars was that, had the language of the Quran been so different from its reading traditions, one would expect to see traces of this in the tradition and moreover one would expect to see pseudo-correct forms. **Chapter** 6 dives deep into the classicization of the *hamzah*, uncovering a variety of unetymological *hamzah*s appearing in the reading traditions as well as many places where a word should have logically had a *hamzah* but inexplicably lacks it. **Chapter** 7 will focus on the many uncertainties and disagreements among the readers on the case inflection—sometimes uncovering words that unexpectedly lack case inflection completely. Moreover, these chapters focus on early reports of the readers, and discussions that followed on some of the controversial readings. These show that at least for some of the readers, for whom we have early reports, it is clear that their choices were not a matter of accurate transmission of how readers believed the prophet would have said it, but rather it was a rational endeavour that required advanced grammatical knowledge. It was the duty of the Quranic reader to rationalize and choose which words should receive which case vowel or *hamzah* and why. This clearly rationalising approach of the readers can be uncovered from the tradition.

CHAPTER 2

What is the *ʕarabiyyah*?

وَكُلٌّ عَرَبِيٌّ

SĪBAWAYH, *al-Kitāb*

∵

2.1 Introduction

In the Western scholarly tradition, it has become customary to consider the language of the Quran to be identical with the language of poetry and the one that established the standard of Classical Arabic, e.g.

> The Qurʾānic language, though virtually identical with the language of pre-Islamic poetry, has a typically religious flavour, manifesting itself in the peculiarities of style and language that must have been absent in other registers.
>
> VERSTEEGH 2014, 65

> [T]he Koran established an unchanging norm for the Arabic language
>
> THACKSTON 1994, xii

> Apparently independently, H. Fleisch, R. Blachère and C. Rabin arrived in the forties at the conclusion that the language of the Koran, far from being pure Meccan either subsequently revised … or slightly adapted to the poetic idiom, was none other than the poetic *koinē*.
>
> C. RABIN 1955, 24

> "At this stage … it seems safe to say that the Qurʾān was revealed and first uttered in a linguistic form that was, if not identical with the language of poetry, close enough to it to be distinguished rather sharply from the spoken dialects …
>
> ZWETTLER 1978, 101

Despite the overabundance of statements of this sort, it remains surprisingly underdefined what the linguistic features of this language are and how we can see what "Classical Arabic" means in these contexts. Even less defined is any concrete evidence that the language of the Quran and poetry are virtually identical despite a near ubiquitous consensus on this point.

Classical Arabic is generally defined by its corpus, rather than through a linguistic definition. The most explicit definition of this corpus that constitutes a single standard form of Classical Arabic was probably formulated by Rabin (1955) "the beginnings of Classical Arabic", who defines Classical Arabic by its traditional corpus, which to him consists of four sources: 1. pre-Islamic and early Islamic poetry, 2. The Quran, 3. The Hadiths and 4. The first century papyri and letters handed down in history works. All but the last of these sources are still considered today to be part of the corpus of the *ʕarabiyyah*. This is closely in line with what the Arab grammarians themselves felt was material necessary to comment upon for the *ʕarabiyyah*. If we look at what the Arab grammarians, and specifically Sībawayh, the earliest of these whose work we have in writing, consider to be part of the corpus worth commenting upon, we find that they agree to a large extent with the definition of Rabin: Poetry, the Quran and Hadiths play a central role in the linguistic evidence proffered by the grammarians, albeit often to highlight unusual practices.

However, we will argue in this chapter that Classical Arabic is not obviously identical to the "poetic *koiné*", nor the basis for all descriptions of the language. Instead, it is rather the outcome of a long negotiation of what "proper Arabic" actually is. The early grammarians only mark the start of this negotiation, and it takes centuries for any clear linguistic standard to develop. While many authors consider Sībawayh the first person to codify and standardize Classical Arabic, he does nothing of the sort.

Central in Sībawayh's work, but also what later grammarians focus on, is what "they" say. This elusive "they" is understood, for example by Carter (2004, 39), to refer to the natural speech of the Bedouin, but this inference does not seem to be based on the actual statements of Sībawayh himself. As Webb (2017, 302 ff.) has shown, whenever Sībawayh explicitly assigns a name to the language of "them", it is generally the "speech of the Arabs" (*kalām al-ʕarab*) that gets mentioned while "bedouin" (*ʔaʕrāb*) are only rarely—and, in such cases often negatively—mentioned. Other contemporary grammarians like al-Farrāʔ (d. 209/824) are much more liberal in assigning tribal association with certain linguistic features found in the *ʕarabiyyah*, but there too, little indication is given that it is specifically the Arabic of the Bedouins that plays a central role. Rather, the main source of the proper use of the *ʕarabiyyah* is by definition a prescriptive one; it is the Arabic of "those whose Arabic can be relied upon" (*man yūṯaqu bi-ʕarabiyyati-hī*) (Carter 2004, 41).

The modern orientalist tradition has mostly been satisfied in following this prescriptive definition of the *ʕarabiyyah*, but follow this up with an (usually implicit) assumption that what the Arab grammarians considered the *ʕarabiyyah* is more-or-less identical to what modern textbooks such as Wright and Fischer call Classical Arabic. The Classical Arabic as we find it in our textbooks is a fairly homogeneous linguistic unit, with little to no morphological, phonetic or syntactic variation. This, however, is not at all what we find in the earliest descriptions of the *ʕarabiyyah*, which are absolutely bristling with linguistic variation. Subsequently the identification of the *ʕarabiyyah* as Classical Arabic with strict norms and little variation all exemplified by the disparate corpora such as the speech of "them", the language of poetry, Quran, and hadiths are all lumped together with assumed linguistic homogeneity without actually demonstrating it.

The assumed linguistic unity of these disparate corpora has frequently led to the imposition of facts of morphology and phonology that cannot self-evidently be deduced from the corpora they discuss. For example, on discussing the development of a standard orthography of "Classical Arabic", Versteegh (2014, 64) says "in the Ḥijāz the *hamzah* was probably absent, but in the variety of the language in which the *Qurʾān* was revealed and the pre-Islamic poems were composed, the *hamzah* was pronounced".[1] While one can indeed make a case for (at least part of) the poetic corpus to have had a *hamzah*, purely on its necessity in the poetic meter, the assumption that this comes part and parcel with the language of the Quran as well, is not demonstrated, nor in fact particularly obvious. Sībawayh, for example, reports in detail on the possibility of dropping the *hamzah*. This is not presented as a non-standard usage, but simply one of the options of Arabic, besides full pronunciation (see Sībawayh, III, 541–556). Considering that Quranic orthography indeed has no way to express the *hamzah*, and our earliest manuscripts make no use of orthographic means to represent it at all, how can we be so sure it was there? Even if we accept that the Quran was composed in the *ʕarabiyyah*, if the *ʕarabiyyah* is the language described and standardized by the grammarians it is still completely possible that the composition was entirely without *hamzah*. As we will see, especially in chapter 3, many of the canonical readings today still lack *hamzah* in many places where the later Classical Arabic would have it.

1 For other quotes of scholars assuming that *hamzah* must have been the norm in the *ʕarabiyyah* see also the previous chapter.

These examples are not just isolated cases, as we will see in this chapter where we will explore the descriptions of the early Arabic grammarians, they allowed for much more variation than the strict norms of Classical Arabic, and no homogeneous standard can be recovered from these works. When one looks closer, we find that the traditional corpora of the *ʕarabiyyah* are noticeably different from one-another, and even within these individual corpora there is significant diversity. Just because they all fall under the aegis of the *ʕarabiyyah*—that is the forms of Arabic the Arab grammarians felt the need to comment upon—does not mean they show no systematic and categorical distinct groups from a linguistic perspective.

With recent advances in the study of pre-Islamic and early Islamic Arabic it has now become clear that the Arabic the grammarians saw fit to comment upon is a highly selective subset of forms of Arabic that were around. Exclusively taking that which the grammarians saw fit to comment upon as "Arabic", ignores a vast amount of linguistic variation that existed in the Pre-Islamic and early Islamic period. As Al-Jallad (2015; 2017a; 2018a) has shown, many other varieties, which are on linguistic grounds evidently Arabic, fall completely outside of the purview of the Arab grammarians. Already in the Pre-Islamic period we find varieties of Arabic that lack the full system of case vowels and nunation, and there is no doubt that such varieties existed in the times the early grammarians were active. Yet, these go completely unmentioned.

Because of this, we now have good reason to doubt the idea that all of Arabic formed a single homogeneous linguistic unit. Moreover, the ambiguities inherent to the Arabic script give a false sense of homogeneity in the "Classical corpora". Little to no skepticism is applied to the vocalizations and interpretations of the originally defective writing of Arabic, even though such disambiguation only appears centuries after the times that these corpora were composed. This is rather surprising as, for example, Rabin (1955, 21) seemed to be well aware of the fact that there was a strong classicizing trend towards even the poetic corpus, which, due to its strict meter, is probably somewhat less susceptible to later classicization than, say, the hadiths or the Quran.

Just because the Arab grammarians considered all of the sources mentioned before to be one and the same *ʕarabiyyah* does not mean that they do not show categorical difference from a modern linguistic perspective. The linguistic unity sought by the grammarians should probably be seen more as a sociolinguistic construct than a claim of similarity on a purely (historical) linguistic grounds. The language, no matter what the corpus, needs to be studied independently, and its linguistic features need to be mapped out. Only when it can be shown that the differences in phonology and morphology can be attributed purely to stylistic differences, does it seem warranted to call these languages "essentially the same language".

As the Quran was evidently one of the most important works of Arabic literature, grammarians have always felt the need to comment on the language of the Quran and its reading traditions. The Quran, and to some extent its reading traditions, therefore naturally feed into the definition of Classical Arabic—that which the grammarians felt the need to comment upon—but this does not necessarily prove that the language of the Quran and the language of the poetry are identical; it only means that the grammarians discussed both within the same grammatical endeavour. Of course, despite possible differences, clearly the linguistic variation was not so large that describing them together was altogether futile, but considering their scope and considerable tolerance towards linguistic variation, it seems very possible that there are appreciable differences present that set these corpora apart.

2.2 The Linguistic Variation in the *ʕarabiyyah*

In the previous section, I argued that the *ʕarabiyyah* (as well as Classical Arabic) is an ill-defined term from a linguistic perspective. It is a language that comes from different sources, all treated by the grammarians as belonging to one single corpus of language. Modern scholars have often accepted the identity of these sources as being all from a single language either called Classical Arabic or "the poetic *koiné*" which I will call here simply the *ʕarabiyyah* (reserving Classical Arabic for the strict standard that emerged later).

This is problematic on a linguistic level. We do not want to take for granted that these languages are identical, we want to be able to test this hypothesis. It is not a given that any two poems are linguistically homogeneous, nor is it clear that the language of any two hadiths is exactly the same. Far from presenting a clear homogeneous linguistic unit, the Arab grammarians record a vast amount of linguistic variation within their grammars. A large amount of this morphological and phonological variation described by the grammarians falls completely outside of the standard Classical Arabic as it is described, for example, by Thackston (1994), Fischer (2002) or Wright (1896).

Many authors, implicitly or explicitly, assume that the Classical Arabic is in fact what the Arab grammarians describe, with some dialectal forms being described parenthetically on the side. For example Classical Arabic seems to be what Rabin has in mind when he speaks of "Literary Arabic", which he considers the "the standardized form [of Classical Arabic], which was used as the international language in the Abbasid empire" (C. Rabin 1955, 3). Even a cursory look at early Abbasid linguistic treaties such as Sībawayh's *al-Kitāb* or al-Farrāʔ's *Luǵāt al-Qurʔān* reveals a vast number of linguistic variants, options and possibilities which are often mutually exclusive. These do not in any way give the impression that there is a single literary standard. They certainly do not suggest that what eventually becomes Classical Arabic is the default and standard form of the language at this time.

The following section will discuss a variety of cases where the grammarians describe morphological or phonological variation that goes beyond the norms of Classical Arabic. Here we will see that, while occasionally some degree of ranking of forms is given, the preferred form is not always what has become the textbook norm, and very often no explicit judgement is given of which form is better.

I will primarily draw on the two earliest grammatical works on the Arabic language available to us, those of Sībawayh (d. 180/796) and al-Farrāʔ (d. 209/824). While Sībawayh often describes an astounding amount of morphological and phonological variation, he is less judicious about explicitly assigning it to certain dialects of Arabic. In his *Luǵāt al-Qurʔān*, al-Farrāʔ is much more cursory in his descriptions, but gives more detailed information as to how certain variation is considered to map onto the different dialects. Occasionally we find that these two early grammarians disagree, which in itself is already interesting: two Arab grammarians sometimes describe linguistic facts that are mutually exclusive, and unresolvable. While such occurrences are rare, we will encounter one such disagreement in the discussion of *ʔimālah* (see §2.2.2.2). In such cases I will also draw on some later grammatical works such as al-Mubarrad (d. 285/898) and al-ʔaxfaš (d. 215/830), to give a sense of where the consensus may have developed after the disagreement in this early period.

2.2.1 *The Third Person Pronominal Suffixes*

Sībawayh devotes two subsequent chapters to the morphological allomorphy that is found in the masculine singular and plural pronominal suffixes. He first devotes a chapter to the length of the final syllable of the pronominal suffixes *-hu* and *-hum* (and *-kum, -tum, ʔantum*) (Sībawayh, IV, 189) and then on the vowel harmony that occurs in these two suffixes (Sībawayh, IV, 195).

According to Sībawayh, the pronominal suffix *-hu/i* is short when it follows a long vowel (*ā, ī, ū*) or a diphthong (*ay, aw*). In all other cases the vowel, in principle, is long. Hence, after any short vowel (*a, i, u*) or consonant the suffix is long *-hū/ī*. This is an interesting deviation from Classical Arabic as it is presented, for example in Fischer (2002, §268.3), who holds that after closed syllables the suffix should be short, i.e. *min-hu* whereas Sībawayh argues for *min-hū*. He says that only "some Arabs" would use the form *min-hu*, but to him the full pronunciation is better (*al-ʔitmāmu ʔaǧwad*). In other words, what is now the normative form in Classical Arabic, seems to have only been a minority form in Sībawayh's view, and moreover a form he explicitly values lower than the other form he describes.

Interesting to our discussion here is that after the discussion of the shortened and lengthened forms, Sībawayh tells us that the Quranic quotes *wa-nazzalnā-hu tanzīlan* (Q17:106), *ʔin taḥmil ʕalay-hi yalhaṯ* (Q7:176), *wa-šaraw-hu bi-ṯamanin baxsin* (Q12:20) and *xuḏū-hu fa-ġullū-hu* (Q69:30) are the "better of the two readings". He does not elaborate on what the other reading would be, but as all of these forms have *-hu* preceded by long vowels and diphthongs, it is obvious that the lengthening of the pronoun is meant in this context (*-hū*, *-hī*). This is the reading of Ibn Kaṯīr, the Meccan reader of the canonical seven (Ibn al-Ǧazarī, § 1212). While Sībawayh values these lengthened forms less than the shortened ones, he explicitly tells us that the lengthening is Arabic (*al-ʔitmāmu ʕarabiyy*). Being 'less good' or 'less common', therefore, does not disqualify a form from being *ʕarabiyy*.

While al-Farrāʔ does not discuss the length of the pronoun *-hu/ū* after a consonant in *Luġāt al-Qurʔān*, he does address this in his *Maʕānī al-Qurʔān* (I, 224f.), where he says that "they" pronounce such forms with short vowels, giving *daʕ-hu yaḏhabu*, *min-hu*, *ʕan-hu* as examples, and announces that "they" hardly ever say [*wa-lā yakādūna yaqūlūna*] *min-hū*, *ʕan-hū*. Al-Farrāʔ here therefore has the opposite opinion of Sībawayh.

Al-ʔaxfaš (*Maʕānī*, 27), direct student of Sībawayh, follows his teacher in preferring *min-hū* while expressing a much more normatively negative opinion of *min-hu* saying it is not good in Arabic [*wa-hāḏā laysa bi-ǧayyidin fī l-ʕarabiyyah*]. Whereas al-Mubarrad (*al-muqtaḍab*, I, 401) explicitly endorses the short form *min-hu*. It therefore does not seem that the competing opinions on what was the proper way of treating such cases was resolved in the generations after Sībawayh.

Sībawayh informs us that speakers have a choice for the plural pronoun -*hum*/-*him*, they can either choose to keep it short, or use lengthened forms -*humū* and the harmonized variant -*himī* pronoun. This lengthening also involves other masculine plural pronominal elements such as *ʔantumū*, *-tumū*, *-kumū* and the independent pronoun *humū*. Al-Farrāʔ (*Luġāt*, 33) agrees with the optionality of this feature, saying, "the Arabs are united in [both options:] not placing a vowel after the *m*, or placing an *u* after it. In their speech it is: *minhum* or *minhumū*; *ʕalaykum* or *ʕalaykumū*; *kuntum* or *kuntumū*. We do not know it as being exclusive to anyone (to have) one of the two linguistic practices (*luġatayn*). All of them say it in both articulations (*al-qawlayn*)."

As for the harmonized form, Sībawayh tells us that 'some of them' use *-himū* instead of *-himī*. Here once again, we find a conflict with Classical Arabic; While Fischer (2002, § 268.4) informs us that lengthened forms like *-humū* and *-himū*, are used in poetry, he makes no mention of the existence of a pronominal *-himī*, and this form seems to have largely fallen out of use in normative Classical Arabic, except when end rhyme in poetry requires it. Moreover, note that the forms presented by Sībawayh and al-Farrāʔ in no way seem to imply that they are to be used in poetry only, or even primarily. This is different, for example with the shortened pronominal suffix *-hu/-hi* after short vowels, which Sībawayh explicitly only allows as a poetic license.

In the second of the two chapters Sībawayh addresses the vowel harmony, which shows that the allomorphs *-hī, -hi, -him* and *-himī* (and *-himū*) are triggered by a preceding *i* or *y*. While the vowel harmony is the general form that Sībawayh presents first, he also informs the reader that the people of the Hijaz say: *bi-**hū*** [بهو] and *laday-**hū*** [لديهو], *ʕalay-**humū*** [عليهمو] and *bi-**humū*** [بهمو], showing that the people of the Hijaz both lacked vocalic length disharmony and vowel harmony. He adds that the Hijazis recite the Quran *fa-xasafnā bi-**hū** wa-bi-dāri-**hū** l-ʔarḍa* (Q28:81), a form that today is uncanonical. There is no obvious expression of derision for these non-harmonizing forms. Al-Farrāʔ (*Luġāt*, 10–11) likewise attributes the lack of vowel harmony to the Qurayš, the people of the Hijaz in general, and the eloquent people from Yemen, whereas the presence of vowel harmony is attributed to the ʔasad and Qays and Tamīm. He adds that Kinānah and Saʕd b. Bakr normally apply vowel harmony to the plural pronoun, but before a two consonant cluster this vowel harmony is removed (e.g. *ʕalayhumu l-qawla*), explicitly mentioning that this is the practice al-Kisāʔī adopts and that it is the most eloquent of linguistic practices. The forms al-Farrāʔ cites for the Hijaz do not have the final long vowels on the plural pronoun forms as Sībawayh mentions, which should probably be understood to mean that at least according to al-Farrāʔ the long forms of the plural pronouns are optional also in Hijazi Arabic, something in line with the optionality of length as a general feature.

We should take the lack of derision as a serious indication that the Hijazi norm is simply considered acceptable. This is clear from the fact that Sībawayh does not avoid derision elsewhere when it comes to pronominal harmony. He considers the *min-him* used by the eastern tribe of Rabīʕah to be a vile linguistic practice [*luġah radīʔah*] and the *ʔaḥlāmi-kim* and *bi-kim* used by one of the branches of Rabīʕah, Bakr b. Wāʔil, to be extremely vile [*radīʔ ǧiddan*]. Clearly the Hijazi forms fell within the purview of what Sībawayh considered eloquent and correct Arabic and he thought of a too liberal use of vowel harmony to be more problematic than its absence.

A final note is given on the shortening of the pronominal suffix vowels before consonant clusters; here Sībawayh seems to allow both *-himu* or *-himi* as the harmonized form.

Sībawayh and al-Farrāʔ do not present a clear single norm and accept a variety of different treatments of the pronominal system. The tables below summarize their descriptions (leaving out the things they consider unacceptable). A ↓ sign marks that a form is explicitly devalued in relation to the basic system, while these are still considered proper and Arabic, while ↑ marks a form that is explicitly considered better., F and S behind the ↓ and ↑ signs mark a difference of opinion between al-Farrāʔ and Sībawayh.

	Base		Lengthened		Classical Arabic		Hijazi
	Base	**i,y_**	**Base**	**i,y_**	**Base**	**i,y_**	**Base**
V̆_	*-hū*	*-hī*	*-hū*	*-hī*	*-hū*	*-hī*	*-hū*
C_	*-hū*		*-hū* ↓F		*-hu* ↓S		*-hū*
V̄_	*-hu*	*-hi*	*-hū*↓	*-hī*↓	*-hu*	*-hi*	*-hū*

Singular pronominal system

	Base		Classical Arabic		Hijazi
	Base	**i,y_**	**Base**	**i,y_**	**Base**
Short	*-hum*	*-him*	*-hum*	*-him*	*-hum*
Long	*-humū*	*-himī*	*-humū*	*-himū*	*-humū*
_CC	*-humu*	*-himi, -humu* ↑F	*-humu*	*-himu*	*-humu*

Plural pronominal system

2.2.2 *The Extra Vowels of Early Classical Arabic*

The medieval Arab grammarians, and with them many modern scholars of the Arabic language, conceive of *ʔimālah* as a shifting from an original *ā* towards the *ī*, ending up generally in between the two, i.e. *ē*. While from a historical linguistic perspective this is true for a part of what the Arab grammarians call *ʔimālah*, it certainly is not true for all of what they collect under this label. Lack of awareness of this has led many a scholar (e.g. Levin 1992) to the incorrect conclusion that in terms of the phonology of the vowel system of Classical Arabic from Sībawayh's lifetime onwards, there was a fairly homogeneous system, namely, one that had three long vowels *ā*, *ī* and *ū* and three short vowels *a*, *i*, *u*. In this interpretation *ʔimālah* would simply be allophonic variation, and belong to the realm of phonetics rather than phonology.

As we will see in this section, this is certainly not the case. Under the rubric of what Sībawayh calls *ʔimālah* there are clear examples of what in modern phonological theory would be thought of as phonemic distinctions; as such Sībawayh describes forms of Arabic that have a phonemic fourth vowel *ē* besides the three base vowels. Some of these distinctions are maintained in the Quranic reading traditions and, moreover, one of these systems corresponds to the fourth long vowel *ē* that can be deduced to exist in the language of the QCT on the basis of orthography and Quranic rhyme (Van Putten (2017a), § 3.3.3 and § 5.8). For a useful translation of Sībawayh's chapters on *ʔimālah* see the translations and analysis of Sara (2007).

Besides this, the early Grammarians also speak of a back vowel in between *ā* and *ū*, that is, *ō* (called *ʔalif al-Tafxīm* by Sībawayh) and even a front rounded vowel *ü* and its long equivalent *ǖ*. None of these variants are presented as incorrect Arabic, and significantly increase the phonological vowel inventory compared to what we might call Classical Arabic.

2.2.2.1 i-umlaut

Sībawayh discusses *ʔimālah* at length, and within this discussion one type of *ʔimālah*, namely the shift of *ā* to *ē* in the vicinity of *i*/*ī*, is most dominant. This shift is blocked whenever there are emphatic or uvular consonants (*ṣ*, *ḍ*, *ṭ*, *ẓ*, *ġ*, *q*, *x*) adjacent to the *ā* or following it, but is not blocked if the umlaut-triggering *i* stands between the blocking consonant and a following *ā* such as in XiCāC stems where X is one of these blocking consonants (Sībawayh 1988, IV, 117–120; 127–136; Sara 2007, 9–16; 56–65; 121–122, 133–134).[2] The consonant *r* holds a special position in this *ʔimālah*. It behaves as an emphatic *ṛ* when followed by *ā* or when it is preceded by *ā* and not followed by *i* or *ī*. As a result, this blocks the *ʔimālah*: *ṛāšid*, *ḥimāṛun* but not of *min ḥimēri-ka*. Interestingly, the sequence *āri* > *ēri* is stronger than blocking emphatic consonants. Thus, one says *qērib* 'boat', *ṭērid* 'expeller'. Likewise nouns with the shape CaCāC and

2 Close parallels of this type of *i*-umlaut *ʔimālah* are well-attested in many modern Arabic dialects, for example in Christian and Jewish Baghdadi (Blanc 1964, 42). For an in-depth discussion on the parallels of Sībawayh's *i*-umlaut *ʔimālah* and what we find attested in the modern dialects see also Levin (1992).

CuCāC, which normally block *ʔimālah* if the genitive follows, undergo *ʔimālah* when the last root consonant is *r*.

This type of *ʔimālah* seems to have been widespread, as Sībawayh only tells us that "the people of the Hijaz apply *ʔimālah* to none of these" (Sara 2007, 12 f.). Al-Farrāʔ (*Luġāt*, 22) does not comment in great detail on this type of *ʔimālah*, mentioning only *al-kāfirūna* is pronounced as such by the people of the Hijaz while some of the people of Najd among the Tamīm and Qays say *al-kēfirūna*. This simple *i*-umlaut does not create a distinction between a phonemic *ā* and *ē*, but should rather be considered a purely allophonic alternation. The table below provides an overview of examples cited by Sībawayh.

Pattern	**Non-emphatic/Uvular environment**	**Emphatic/Uvular environment**
CāCiC	*ʕēbid* 'worshipper'	*ḍāmin* 'guarantor'
CaCāCiC	*masēǧid* 'mosques'	*maʕāliq* 'pluck of animals'
CaCāCīC	*mafētīḥ* 'keys'	*manāfīx* 'bellows'
CiCāC	*kilēb* 'dogs'	No example, but blocked
CiCCāC	*sirbēl* 'shirt'	No example, but blocked

This type of *ʔimālah* is no longer common in Classical Arabic pronunciation today. In fact, it receives no mention at all in many modern grammatical works, such as Fischer (2002), or it is explained as a behaviour of "later times" (Wright 1896, § 6c) despite the earliest grammarian describing it, clearly marking it as part of the *ʕarabiyyah*. It is described in great detail by Sībawayh, and it is not dismissed as 'wrong' or 'less regular'. In fact, Sībawayh does not express any negative judgement of such forms at all. He only tells us that the people of the Hijaz do not do it. We must therefore conclude that using this type of pronunciation was considered acceptable and part of the linguistic variation present in the *ʕarabiyyah* that Sībawayh sought to describe. In fact, about a century later the Basran grammarian al-Mubarrad (d. 285/898) explicitly evaluates the use of *ʔimālah* as better (*Muqtaḍab* III, 42), showing that this is not just a non-standard feature that happened to end up in grammarian descriptions, but rather is part of the variation that can be explicitly endorsed.

2.2.2.2 III-y ʔimālah

The *i*-umlaut *ʔimālah* as discussed above can be plausibly thought of as the allophonic realization of *ā*, as it is predictable when it does and does not occur.

However, there are several other forms of *ʔimālah* that certainly cannot be considered allophonic, but must describe a true phonemic fourth long vowel *ē* that existed beside *ā*, *ī* and *ū*. Sībawayh says that this type of III-*y* *ʔimālah* is uncommon both among the Tamīm and others (Sībawayh, IV, 120; Sara 2007, 20 f.), while al-Farrāʔ (*Luġāt*, 21 f.) says that many of the people of Najd apply it. These statements appear to be contradictory, and their respective descriptions also differ somewhat.

Sībawayh points out that nouns that have a root final consonant *w* do not undergo *ʔimālah*. Hence you get قفا *qafā* 'back', عصا *ʕaṣā* 'stick' القنا *al-qanā* 'the aquiline nose' and القطا *al-qaṭā* 'the sand grouse'. This is different from those with root-final *yāʔ*, which do undergo *ʔimālah* (no examples given, but e.g. الهوى *al-hawē* 'the affection' and الفتى *al-fatē* 'the youth'). Feminine nouns that have the suffix *-ā* (spelled with *yāʔ*) are likewise treated as nouns that have a root final *yāʔ*: معزى *miʕzē* 'nanny goat' and حبلى *ḥublē* 'pregnant'. Derived forms that end in *-ā* (spelled with *yāʔ*) likewise always undergo *ʔimālah*, as derived stems shift their root final consonant from *w* to *y* (as can be seen in the dual, such as *ʔaʕṭayā* 'they (dual) gave' but *ʕaṭawāni* 'two gifts'). Hence, we find *muʕṭē* 'gifted'.

Where nouns (for those who apply this type of *ʔimālah*) have a distinction between root final *wāw* and root final *yāʔ* stems, Sībawayh says this is not the case for verbs. Hence غزا *ġazē* 'he raided', صفا *ṣafē* 'it became clear' and دعا *daʕē* 'he called', just like e.g. رمى *ramē* 'he threw' and بنى *banē* 'he built'.

He explicitly adds that this final weak *ʔimālah* is not blocked by emphatic consonants, thus you have *muʕṭē* 'gifted' and *saqē* 'he watered' (Sībawayh, IV, 132; Sara 2007, 66 f.), clearly indicating that we are not dealing with an allophonic shift from *ā* to *ē* similar to the *i*-umlaut *ʔimālah* discussed in the previous section. Moreover, there are places where the occurrence of *ā* and *ē* cannot be reconstructed from surface forms like **al-fatā* and **al-ʕaṣā*, so we must conclude that for the variety that Sībawayh describes to have this type of *ʔimālah* we are dealing with a phonemic distinction between *ā* and *ē*. Comparative Semitic evidence, most notably the epigraphic old Arabic dialect of the Safaitic inscriptional corpus and Classical Ethiopic show that the long vowel distinction between III-*w* and III-*y* stems is the outcome of two etymologically different sequences (see van Putten 2017a for a discussion). Thus, the contrastive vowels of *al-fatē* and *al-ʕaṣā* come from **al-fatayu* and **al-ʕaṣawu* respectively.

While this etymological distinction is retained in the noun, according to Sībawayh, it is lost in the verb. This is rather surprising, as we would expect that, as with the noun, original **banaya* and **daʕawa* would yield *banē* and *daʕā*, something that is also reflected in Classical Arabic orthography. Sībawayh seems to be quite alone among the early grammarians in maintaining that the verb must lack this distinction. Al-Farrāʔ (*Luġāt*, 21) tells us that "many among the people of the Najd apply *ʔimālah* [lit.: place an *i*-vowel] when they say *qaḍē, ramē* and *sawwē*, and they place an *a* vowel on roots with *wāw* as the third root consonant, for example in *wa-ʔiḏā xalā baʕḍu-hum* (Q2:76) and *mā zakā* (Q24:21), and what is like it." Al-Mubarrad (III, 44) explicitly states that *ʔimālah* is ugly in III-*w* verbs (*qabīḥah*) in ***daʕē*, ***ġazē* and ***ʕadē*, although it might be barely acceptable (*qad yaǧūzu ʕalā buʕd*), while for III-*y* verbs it is considered good (*ḥasanah*) be it a noun, verb, or adjective. Sībawayh's student, al-ʔaxfaš al-ʔawṣat (d. 215/830) endorses both contradictory statements, he says that many of the Arabs (*kaṯīran mina l-ʕarab*; *Maʕānī*, 41) did not apply *ʔimālah* to forms to III-*w* verbs, while many (other) people (*nāsun kaṯīr*; *Maʕānī*, 42) did apply it to verbs with *wāw*.

There is yet another system of final weak *ʔimālah* that Sībawayh discusses as somewhat of an afterthought, but from a modern dialectological perspective highly relevant. As Levin ("Sībawayh's 'Imāla", 87) points out, besides the system where III-*y* and III-*w* verbs are merged towards having *ʔimālah* while nouns remain distinct, there also seem to be dialects where the III-*y*/*w* verb merged towards not having *ʔimālah* and only has *ʔimālah* on the nouns with the feminine ending -*ē*/-*ā*, as examples Sībawayh (IV, 126) cites speakers who say *ramā* 'he threw' but *ḥublē* 'pregnant' *miʕzē* 'goat'. As Levin points out, this corresponds with the *ʔimālah* as we find it in the Mesopotamian Qəltu dialects which have *ḥəble* 'pregnant', *ʔaʕme* 'blind' but *ramā* 'he threw', retaining the ancient vowel contrast.

	Base Sībawayh	**Qəltu-like**	**al-Farrāʔ**	**al-Mubarrad**	**No III-y/w ʔimālah**
III-*y* verb	-*ē*	-*ā*	-*ē*	-*ē*	-*ā*
III-*w* verb	-*ē*	-*ā*	-*ā*	-*ā* ↑, -*ē* ↓	-*ā*
III-*y* noun	-*ē*	-*ē*	?	-*ē*	-*ā*
III-*w* noun	-*ā*	-*ā*	?	-*ā*	-*ā*

While Sībawayh reports final weak *ʔimālah* to be a minority pronunciation, it is in no way judged to be incorrect or less eloquent. Al-Farrāʔ does express a normative preference, but *in favour* of distinguishing *ā* and *ē* saying "the best of that is the case when it is between the strong application of *kasr* and the strong application of *fatḥ*, and following this are most of the Arabs and Quranic readers."[3] This clearly indicates that normatively it is better to pronounce the III-*y* verbs with something that is not identical to a pure *ā* vowel.

This once again shows that we certainly cannot project back the later norms of Classical Arabic to this period. As far as al-Farrāʔ is concerned, the normative pronunciation of Arabic is with four separate phonemic long vowels *ā*, *ī*, *ū* and *ē*.[4]

2.2.2.3 II-w/y ʔimālah

In his chapter on *ʔimālah*, Sībawayh (IV, 120 f.) tells us that "they apply *ʔimālah*" to hollow verbs, whose 1sg. form has an *i* vowel, be they II-*w* or II-*y* (e.g. *xēfa/xiftu* 'to fear', *ǧēʔa/ǧiʔtu* 'to come'). He also adds that this is a linguistic practice for some of the people of the Hijaz. It seems clear that the "they" he refers to more generally in this section are not the people of the Hijaz, as earlier he tells us that "the people of the Hijazi do not apply *ʔimālah* to all of this" (IV, 118). Further dialectal specification of this type of *ʔimālah* is not given, but al-Farrāʔ (*Luġāt*, 17) adds that it is the practice of the common people of the Najd among the Tamīm, ʔasad and Qays.

This, once again, cannot be understood as an allophonic alternation between *ā* and *ē*. One cannot predict from the surface form without *ʔimālah* whether it will have *ā* or *ē*, nor is it conditioned by the presence or absence of emphasis. Instead, it represents two outcomes of etymologically distinct forms of the verb, verbs with a medial triphthong **aWi* yielding *ē* and **aWu* (or **aWa*) yielding *ā* (where *W* is a *w* or *y*). That these verbs once had triphthongs in medial position is quite clear from the Old Arabic dialect reflected in the Safaitic inscriptions, where such verbs often remain uncontracted with a consonantal *y* or *w* (Al-Jallad 2015, 119). For example, we find *byt* 'he spent the night', *ʿwd* 'he returned' and *rwḥ* 'he departed at night'. Safaitic does not make use of *matres lectionis*, and therefore this points to forms like /bayita/, /ʕawada/ and /rawaḥa/ respectively. The original triphthongs of these hollow roots are further confirmed by forms like Gəʕəz *kona* < **kawuna*, and Suchard (2016) shows that a triphthongal origin can also be reconstructed for Proto-Hebrew. This then retains an archaic contrast that is absent in Classical Arabic. The examples with the hollow root *ʔimālah* as discussed here must be a different

3 *Wa-ʔaḥsanu ḏālika ʔamrun bayna l-kasri š-šadīdi wa-l-fatḥi š-šadīdi, wa-ʕalay-hi ʔakṯaru l-ʕarabi wa-l-qurrāʔ.*

4 Considering that his teacher al-Kisāʔī and subsequently also his teacher Ḥamzah both retain a phonemic distinction between *ē* and *ā* in III-*y* and III-*w* verbs respectively in their Quranic readings (see § 3.3.3.3), it is of course not surprising that al-Farrāʔ would consider this the better practice.

outcome from the collapse of these triphthongs, rather than an unmotivated shift from *ā > ē.

Unlike the final weak verbs, where the root consonant determines the outcome of ē versus ā, for hollow roots, it is the second stem vowel that determines the outcome of this collapse. This much is clear from verbs such as *mēta, mittu* whose verbal noun *mawt* leaves little doubt that the root is, in fact, √mwt, and the same can be said for *xēfa, xiftu* whose verbal noun is *xawf* beside forms such as *ṣēra, ṣirtu* with a verb noun *ṣayr*. This is similar to the Hebrew situation where we find *met̠* 'he died' but *mawɛt̠* 'death', which Suchard argues means we must reconstruct **mawita* and **mawt* with a collapse of **awi* in the hollow root to ē. A similar development must be envisioned for forms of Arabic with this type of *ʔimālah*.

Note that this shift does not necessarily take place in varieties that also have an *ā*/*ē* distinction for the III-*w*/*y* verbs. Sībawayh attributes this II-*w*/*y ʔimālah* to the poet Kuṯayyir ʕazzah (Sara 2007, 22 f.), an Umayyad poet whom he quoted in the previous section for not having *ʔimālah* for III-*w*/*y* verbs. The reverse is also true: the dialect on which the Quranic and classical orthography was based clearly only had *ā* for II-*w*/*y* verbs, hence the consistent spelling with *ʔalif* whereas III-*w*/*y* are kept strictly distinct (see § 5.8).

While Sībawayh considers this a rare feature, it is in no way considered bad and is indeed qualified by citing an early Umayyad poet. Al-Farrāʔ (*Luġāt*, 17), like with the previous feature, explicitly endorses having this type of contrast, in very similar wording as in the previous section, saying: "the best of that is the case when it is between the excessive application of *kasr* and the excessive application of *fatḥ*. ʕāṣim applies the *fatḥ* excessively, and Ḥamzah the *kasr* excessively."[5] As al-Farrāʔ only mentions Quranic readers here and does not say that most of the Arabs do it this way, this statement should perhaps be interpreted as only being normative for Quranic recitation, rather than for spoken *ʕarabiyyah*. What is clear, however, is that neither Sībawayh nor al-Farrāʔ considered this practice as incorrect or not belonging to the *ʕarabiyyah*.

2.2.2.4 The Fifth Long Vowel Ō

While Sībawayh spends very few words on the presence of a backed and rounded counterpart to the mid front vowel *ē*, that is, a long *ō*, it is clear from his account that it existed. In a list of sounds that are not basic to the Arabic

5 *Wa-ʔaḥsanu ḏālika ʔamrun bayna l-kasri l-mufriṭi wa-l-fatḥi l-mufriṭi, wa-kāna ʕāṣimun yufriṭu fī l-fatḥi, wa-ḥamzah yufriṭu l-kasri.*

alphabet but acceptable for the recitation of the Quran and poetry, Sībawayh (IV, 432) speaks of an *ʔalif al-tafxīm* typical of the people of the Hijaz in the words *aṣ-ṣalōh* 'the prayer', *az-zakōh* 'the alms' and *al-ḥayōh* 'the life'. While this has been interpreted by Rabin (1951, 107) as a general tendency to pronounce any long *ā* as *ō* in the Hijaz, that is clearly not what Sībawayh is referring to.[6] The three words Sībawayh cites are exactly the words that are spelled with a *wāw* in the orthography of the Quranic Consonantal Text,[7] i.e. الصلوه, الزكوه, and الحيوه. To this we can add several other words such as منوه *manōh* 'Manāt', غدوه *ġadōh* 'morning' and النجوه *an-naǧōh* 'escape'. There are good reasons to think that these were indeed pronounced with an *ō* in Quranic Arabic (see Al-Jallad 2017c; van Putten 2017a), and it can hardly be an accident that it is exactly these words that Sībawayh decided to cite. Al-Farrāʔ (*Luġāt*, 45f.) is aware of such a pronunciation, and states that it is said that the eloquent ones of the people Yemen pronounce it *aṣ-ṣalōh* and *az-zakōh*, but that he has not heard it himself, this may suggest that this pronunciation was already losing popularity by his lifetime.

This *ō* vowel once again does not develop from *ā*, but rather has a clearly distinct etymological origin (nouns ending in **-awat-*) (see Al-Jallad 2017c; van Putten 2017a), and should therefore be considered phonemic amongst speakers that have this *ʔalif al-tafxīm*. This introduces a fifth long vowel, which, moreover, is explicitly considered acceptable by Sībawayh for the recitation of the Quran. It was clearly part of at least some people's speech whose pronunciation Sībawayh respected, and considered this authoritative enough to use it in Quranic recitation.

2.2.2.5 The Front Rounded Vowel in Hollow Passives

The passives of hollow roots are reported by Sībawayh (IV, 342f.) to come in three different forms: He starts with the Classical Arabic *qīla/qiltu*, but then adds that "some arabs" say *xǖfa/xüftu*, *bǖʕa/büʕtu* and *qǖla/qültu*, applying

6 This belief seems to stem from generalized and abridged statements of later grammarians. Al-Mubarrad, for example, copies much of the same wording of Sībawayh considering the sounds that exist in Arabic, but simply mentions the *ʔalif al-tafxīm*, while leaving out the words that serve as an example of the *ʔalif al-tafxīm* as well as the dialectal origin (Al-Mubarrad *muqtaḍab*, I, 330), this is likewise the case for Ibn al-Sarrāǧ (*ʔuṣūl*, III, 487). This lack of precision in later sources should, of course, not be seen as evidence that Sībawayh was wrong and the general statement should be accepted. Ibn al-Sarrāǧ's wording is copied verbatim from Sībawayh's *al-Kitāb*, but has only been abridged. The removal of the reference to the words and tribal identification are simply part of the abridgement process.

7 The edition of al-Kitāb I consulted spells them with *ʔalif*.

lip rounding (*fa-yušimmu*)[8] and "some arabs" say *xūfa/xufta, būʕa/buʕtu* and *qūla/qultu*. While Sībawayh does not specify which dialects use which forms, al-Farrāʔ (*Luġāt*, 14) does: The people of the Hijaz apply the *kasrah*: *qīla/qiltu*; Many of the Qays, ʕuqayl and the common people of ʔasad hint towards the *ḍammah* of the *qāf* (*yušīrūna ʔilā ḍammati l-qāf*) *qǖla/qǖltu* and Faqʕas and Dubayr (branches of ʔasad) say *qūla/qultu*. No specific preference of one form over the other is expressed.[9]

There is no way to derive at *qǖla* or *qūla* from *qīla* historically, and all three reflexes must be seen as different outcomes of the original triphthong **quwila*. Rabin (1951, 159) provides a plausible scenario for these outcomes. He suggests that all the dialects described by the grammarians first underwent a shift of **uWi* > *ǖ*. Subsequently in the Hijaz, this *ǖ* shifted to *ī* retaining the frontness but losing the rounding, whereas Faqʕas and Dubayr shifted it to *ū*, losing the frontness but retaining the rounding. The central dialects of Qays, ʕuqayl and the majority of ʔasad retained the front rounded vowel. But different explanations of the facts may be envisioned as well. The Hijaz and Qays/ʕuqayl/ʔasad forms may have been the outcome of separate collapses of the triphthongs. In Classical Arabic only the *qīla* form has survived, although Fischer (2002, § 246.3) notes that forms like *qūla* may occur in poetry.

2.2.3 *Najdi Vowel Harmony*

One of the phenomena that is attributed to a development in the language of the Tamīm by Sībawayh (IV, 107–109), is the vowel harmony triggered by a sequence of aGi or aGī, where G stands for an intervening guttural consonant, *ʔ, h, ḥ, ʕ, x, ġ*. This affects nouns, adjectives and verbs alike.[10] Forms he cites are:

---

8 *ʔišmām* as lip rounding is clearly explained by Sībawayh (IV, 168–176) in one of the chapters on pause, where it is described as an option for pausing on nouns that end in *-u*.

9 What Sībawayh does say, however, is that the *qīla*/*qiltu* form is the "origin" (*ʔaṣl*). This is a technical term which in Sībawayh's framework means it is the form from which all forms are derived. But this technical term cannot be understood as meaning the "normative" or "Classical Arabic" form. Taking the term *ʔaṣl* as meaning the "normative" form would not result in Classical Arabic. To Sībawayh, for example, unharmonized and long *-hū* and *-humū, naʕima/baʔisa* rather than *niʕma*/*biʔsa* and *wa-li-yaktub* instead of *wa-l-yaktub* are all described as the *ʔaṣl* but do not make it into the Classical Arabic norm. As Sībawayh's approach is not historical, *ʔaṣl* can of course not be understood as "origin" in the historical linguistic sense either.

10 Many modern dialects, as for example Egyptian Arabic, show the exact opposite distribution: if there is no adjacent guttural the adjective is CiCīC, whereas with a guttural adjacent it is CaCīC, e.g. *kibīr* 'big' but *saʕīd* 'happy'. In the modern Arabic dialect of Sanaa, however, we find the exact distribution that is described by Sībawayh (Julien Dufour *personal correspondence*).

- *liʔīm, šihīd, siʕīd, niḥīf, riġīf, bixīl, biʔīs*
- *šihid, liʕib, ḍiḥik, niġil, wixim, miḥik, lihim, wiʕik, xiʔiz, niʕir, fixiḏ*

In the speech of the people of the Hijaz, however, this vowel harmony does not take place. Again, both options are mentioned, but no specific preferences are expressed for either form.

Al-Farrāʔ (*Luġāt*, 5) discusses this same shift for CaGīC nouns, reporting that Hijazis and ʔasad retain the *a* but that Qays, Tamīm, Rabīʕah and those that surround them say *riḥīm, biʕīr, liʔīm, bixīl, riġīf* and *šihīd*. He does not discuss the treatment of CaGiC stems in a systematic way, but comments on several cases where it has clearly taken place. For example, he attributes *niʕim-mā* to Qays and Tamīm, while he attributes *naʕim-mā* to the Hijaz (*Luġāt*, 41). He mentions that some of the Tamīm say *ṭihirta* for *tahirṭa* (*Luġāt*, 125). He also mentions Tamīmī *ar-riḥm* for Hijazi *ar-raḥim* (*Luġāt*, 128) with Najdi syncope (see next section).[11] Once again the grammarians present the two forms as coming from different dialects, but no specific preference is expressed for the *ʕarabiyyah*. In Classical Arabic, however, such harmonized forms have disappeared completely.

2.2.4 *Najdi Syncope*

Both Sībawayh (IV, 113–115) and al-Farrāʔ (*Luġāt*, 29) report a far-reaching syncope of the high vowels *i* and *u* when they are preceded by a light syllable (Cv). Al-Farrāʔ reports this for the people of Najd, while Sībawayh specifies it more and says that it is the linguistic practice of the Bakr b. Wāʔil and many people of the Banū Tamīm. Al-Farrāʔ attributes the full pronunciation to the people of the Hijaz, whereas Sībawayh does not specify what dialect has the full pronunciation.

Al-Farrāʔ mentions three categories to which this development applies: first, to the pronouns *huwa* and *hiya* when preceded by *wa-*, *fa-* and *la-*; second, to nouns of the shapes CaCiC, CaCuC, CuCuC, CiCiC and feminine equivalents; third, it applies to the *li-* placed before the jussive for orders. While not explicitly mentioned by al-Farrāʔ, Sībawayh adds that it also applies in CaCiC, CaCuC, and CuCiC verbs, as well as derived verbs that may have the CaCiC sequence. The development presented by Sībawayh and al-Farrāʔ clearly represents a regular sound law that can be formally represented as follows: **i, *u* > ∅ /Cv.C_. I will discuss the four categories listed by al-Farrāʔ and Sībawayh separately.

11 The editor changed this to *ar-raḥm*, but in a footnote he points out the manuscript said *ar-riḥm*, which is clearly the intended form here.

2.2.4.1 Syncope in the Verbs

Sībawayh (IV, 113) shows that among the dialects that undergo this syncope, it regularly applies in the verb. As examples he cites forms like *karuma* → *karma* 'he is noble', *ʕalima* → *ʕalma* 'he knew', *fuṣida* → *fuṣda* 'he was bled' and *ʕuṣira* → *ʕuṣra* 'it was squeezed'.

He also reports some cases where the CvCu/iC sequence is not followed by a short vowel, and adding an epenthetic vowel to aid word-final CC cluster or CCC cluster that is created. Thus, he lists forms like *lam yalid-hū* → *lam yald-hū* → *lam yalda-hū* 'he begot him' and *inṭaliq* → *inṭalq* → *inṭalqa* 'be free!'. Whether these reports should be understood as exceptional cases, or that the sound law described here is actually independent of the second vowel being in an open syllable, is not entirely clear.

In the following chapter, Sībawayh (IV, 116) points out that CaGiCa verbs that underwent vowel harmony to CiGiCa are also typical of the dialect of the Tamīm (see § 2.2.3 above for a discussion). These too undergo syncope, but only after the vowel harmony. Thus, one gets forms like *šahida* → *šihida* → *šihda* 'he witnessed', *laʕiba* → *liʕiba* → *liʕba* 'he played', *naʕima* → *niʕima* → *niʕma* 'he is glad' and *baʔisa* → *biʔisa* → *biʔsa* 'he is miserable'.

Al-Farrāʔ discusses this development in a less systematic way, but discussions of it can be found throughout *Luġāt al-Qurʔān*. He reports that Rabīʕah and Tamīm drop the *i* in *fuʕila* passives, citing *ʕufya* and *quḍya* 'it is settled' as examples (al-Farrāʔ *Luġāt*, 41). The Hijazi form *ḥasuna* 'he is nice, good' is *ḥasna* among the Tamīm (al-Farrāʔ *Luġāt*, 56). The broader application of this syncope, even affecting words other than CaCuC, CaCiC and CuCiC stems is made clear by the fact that al-Farrāʔ (*Luġāt*, 38) mentions that some of the Tamīm say *yağdu* 'he finds' and *lam ʔağdi/a* 'I didn't find' for *yağidu* and *lam ʔağid*.

These forms discussed by Sībawayh are the result of regular sound laws that allow us to develop a relative chronology of the developments of the vowel harmony followed by the syncope. As with other cases of variation described by the Grammarians, the unsyncopated forms are not presented as 'better' or standard. Rather, both forms are considered part of the *ʕarabiyyah*. In Classical Arabic syncopated forms do not usually occur, the only place where they occur is when the verbs *naʕima* 'he is glad' and *baʔisa* 'he is miserable' are employed as pseudo-verbs of emphatic qualification, such as *niʕma r-rağulu* 'what a wonderful man!' and *biʔsa n-nisāʔu* 'what evil women!' (Fischer 2002, § 259–263). This lexical exception of these two verbs is typical of Classical Arabic but is not described by Sībawayh or al-Farrāʔ for the *ʕarabiyyah*.

2.2.4.2 Syncope in Nouns

While al-Farrāʔ does not refer explicitly to the application of this syncope in the context of verbs, he and Sībawayh both mention its application in nouns. It affects such words as *faxiḏ* → *faxḏ* 'thigh',[12] *kabid* → *kabd* 'liver', *ʕaḍud* → *ʕaḍd* 'upper arm', *raǧul* → *raǧl* 'man'. When the vowel in the first syllable is a high vowel, we see the same development. Thus *qudus* → *quds* 'holiness' (al-Farrāʔ, *Luġāt*, 44) and *huzuʔ* → *huzʔ* 'mockery' (al-Farrāʔ, *Luġāt*, 26), *ʕunuq* → *ʕunq* 'neck' *aṭ-ṭunub* → *aṭ-ṭunb* 'tent rope' and *ʔibil* → *ʔibl* 'camels'. Even CuCuC plural formations are affected, and thus we see *ar-rusul* → *ar-rusl* 'prophets', *ḥumur* → *ḥumr* 'donkeys', *xumur* → *xumr* 'veils', *ʔuzur* → *ʔuzr* 'wraps' and *furuš* → *furš* 'pillows' (Sībawayh, III, 601). Derived nouns that have the expected environment undergo this development according to Sībawayh (although al-Farrāʔ never cites cases of such forms). Thus Sībawayh (IV, 115) cites *muntafixan* > *muntafxan* 'swollen'.

For simple noun stems in Classical Arabic, syncopated forms are still quite frequent but always exist side-by-side with unsyncopated byforms: thus one finds mention in lexicons and grammars of forms like *kabd* besides *kabid*, *ʕunq* beside *ʕunuq* and *ʔibl* besides *ʔibil*, and even for plural forms mention is made of *kutb* besides *kutub* (e.g. Fischer 2002, § 88.2). However, these byforms are presented as fully lexicalized and optional in the language. The regular application of syncope is no longer recognized and forms like *muntafxan* < *muntafixan* do not seem to occur.

2.2.4.3 Pronouns

The pronouns *huwa* and *hiya* do not normally undergo syncope as they stand at the beginning of a word, but when preceded by *wa-*, *fa-* or *la-*, the phonetic environment is created where it would syncopate in the dialects of Najd, thus you get *wa-hwa*, *fa-hya* and *la-hya*. Al-Farrāʔ explicitly connects this practice to the Najdi dialects, whereas Sībawayh (IV, 151) is a bit more circumspect, and says: "the *hāʔ* is quiesced when a *wāw*, or *fāʔ* or *lām* stands before it, and that is your speech: *wa-hwa ḏāhib*, *wa-lahwa xayrun mink*, *fa-hwa qāʔim*. And it is like that for *hiya* […], so they drop the vowel like they drop it in *faxiḏin* → *faxḏin* [etc.]".[13] Those that drop the vowel in *faxiḏ* → *faxḏ* as we saw in section § 2.2.4.2 are the people of Najd.

---

12 One would expect *fixḏ* here for dialects that have the Najdi vowel harmony. It seems that the syncope affected more dialects than those that underwent the vowel harmony.

13 *fa-ʔinna l-hāʔa tasakkana ʔiḏā kāna qablu-hā wāwun ʔaw fāʔun aw lāmun, wa-ḏālika qawlu-ka: wa-hwa ḏāhibun, wa la-hwa xayrun minka, fa-hwa qāʔimun. Wa-kaḏālika hiya,* […], *fa-ʔaskanū ka-mā qālū fī faxiḏin → faxḏun, wa-raḍiya → raḍya, wa-fī ḥaḏirin → ḥāḏrun, wa-saruwa → sarwa.*

In Classical Arabic the normal forms are *huwa* and *hiya*, although Fischer (2002, § 264.3) still makes note of the possibility to syncopate after *wa-* and *fa-* as an option. For the grammarians we discussed here, it is not presented as a free option. Instead, it is clearly presented as the outcome of a regular development that takes place among eastern dialects; and it is not expected to see forms like *wa-hwa* in forms of Classical Arabic that do not also have *kutb* 'books' and *ʕalma* 'he knows'.

2.2.4.4 Li- + Apocopate for Commands

Another connection with the syncope that both Sībawayh (IV, 151f.) and al-Farrāʔ (*Luġāt* 29) provide is the treatment of the *li-* of command (*lām al-ʔamr*). When this form is combined with an apocopate, it represents a command, for example *li-yaʔti* 'let him come!' *li-naʔxuḏ* 'let us take!' (Fischer 2002, § 195). This *li-* of command can be preceded by *wa-* 'and' and *fa-* 'so'. As was the case with *wa-huwa* and *fa-hiya*, the *i* of *li-* now stands in the phonetic environment that would undergo syncope in the Najdi dialects, both grammarians, comparing it with the other forms of syncope discussed so far, say that it is possible to elide this vowel, thus yielding forms like *fa-l-yanẓur* 'so let him see!' and *wa-l-yaḍrib* 'and let him hit!' However, Sībawayh explicitly states that whoever leaves the vowel in *hiya* and *huwa* untouched also leaves the vowel in *li-* untouched. In other words, he explicitly describes the forms *fa-li-yanẓur* and *wa-li-yaḍrib* for those that do not apply syncope.

This is rather different from the situation that we find in Classical Arabic. Where most of the cases described above, the standard prefers the unsyncopated forms, in this case the syncopation is obligatory, whereas forms like *fa-li-yanẓur*, as explicitly endorsed by Sībawayh in non-syncopating dialects, is not considered part of the Classical Arabic language (Fischer 2002, § 195.1).

2.2.4.5 Conclusions on the Syncope

As should be clear from the above discussion, both Sībawayh and al-Farrāʔ make clear and consistent references to the existence of a syncopation rule of the high vowels *i* and *u* in the *ʕarabiyyah* of Najd, this rule can be formulated formally as **i, *u* > ∅ /Cv.C_. The varieties that have this form are by no means considered a 'deviation' from the norm, they are part of the normative construct of the *ʕarabiyyah* that both authors seek to describe.

While in the varieties described by these grammarians the sound law simply applies regularly in those dialects that undergo it, surprisingly in the later Classical Arabic standard, the situation is very mixed. CvCi/uC nominal stems, both as singulars and plurals, make it into this emergent norm in syncopated and unsyncopated forms, although the lack of syncopation seems to be preferred. For verbs, this allowance of syncopation is unheard of except for the verbs *naʕima* and *baʔisa* where the syncopated forms, having undergone vowel harmony as well, *niʕma* and *biʔsa*, and have become specialized as particles of emphatic qualification. For the pronouns both forms are possible, but the unsyncopated form dominates. Finally, for the *li-* of command, only the syncopated form wins out. It should be clear from these many differences that the *ʕarabiyyah* that these early grammarians describe is significantly different from the standard language that eventually becomes dominant.

2.2.5 *Barth-Ginsberg Alternation in the Prefix Vowel*

The Barth-Ginsberg alternation, first identified as a morphological pattern found in Hebrew and Aramaic, states that stative verbs in the prefix-conjugation that have a root vowel *a* will have a prefix vowel *i*, whereas those that have a root vowel *u* or *i* will have a prefix vowel *a*. Thus, yiCCaC versus yaCCiC and yaCCuC. Bloch (1967) convincingly shows that this Barth-Ginsberg alternation was not just a development found in Hebrew and Aramaic, but also a pattern that Sībawayh—and with him many other Arab grammarians—describes for the *ʕarabiyyah*. Since Bloch's revolutionary article, it has become clear that the same alternation is found not only in Classical Arabic, but also in several modern dialects (Najdi Arabic, Ingham (1994, 23f.); and traces in, for example, Maltese, see Van Putten (2020c)) and pre-Islamic Arabic (Al-Jallad and al-Manaser 2015). It is therefore beyond doubt that this alternation should be reconstructed for Proto-Arabic, and subsequently must be part of the shared ancestor of Hebrew, Aramaic and Arabic, that is—at the latest—central Semitic.[14]

Sībawayh (IV, 110–113) considers the use of the Barth-Ginsberg alternation typical for all Arabs except those of the Hijaz. Thus, one says *ʔiʕlamu* 'I know' but *ʔaktubu* 'I write' and *ʔaḍribu* 'I hit'. This high vowel prefix occurs with every person prefix except the *ya-* used for the 3sg.m., and the 3rd person plural/dual forms.[15] Bloch (1967, 24) suggests that this is the result of an Arabic-internal dissimilation of the sequence **yi-* > *ya-*. Further evidence that the inclusion of the *yi-* form is the original situation is found in the fact that certain words where the *yi* shifted to *yī* the dissimilation was avoided, and we simply find

14 Kossmann & Suchard (2018) make a compelling case that the Barth-Ginsberg alternation may even go as far back as the shared ancestor of Berber and Semitic.

15 This is different from the way it behaves in present-day Najdi Arabic which has invariable 1sg. *ʔa-* but variable 3sg.m. *ya-/yi-* (Ingham 1994, 24f.). Hebrew, Aramaic, nor pre-Islamic Arabic (Al-Jallad and al-Manaser 2015) seem to have the exception of the 3sg.m. form as found in the *ʕarabiyyah*.

those original, such as in *yīǧalu* 'he fears' rather than *yawǧalu* and presumably also *yiʔbā* which should likely be understood as a classicized version of a hamzahless form of the verb *yībā* that likewise had the *yī* sequence blocking the dissimilation.

Derived verbs that have a prefix with *-a-* in textbook Classical Arabic, such as N-stem *yanfaʕilu*, Gt-stem *yaftaʕilu*, tD-stem *yatafaʕʕalu*, tL-stem *yatafāʕalu* and Ct-stem *yastafʕilu* are all likewise reported to have the *i*-prefixes for these dialects.

Al-Farrāʔ (*Luġāt*, 6–9) reports many of the same facts, but with more specific attribution: Qurayš and Kinānah always have *a*-vowel in derived stems (N, Gt, tD, tL, Ct), e.g. *nastaʕīnu*; whereas Tamīm, ʔasad and Rabīʕah say *nistaʕīnu*, *ʔistaʕīnu*, *tistaʕīnu* but *yastaʕīnu*. Al-Farrāʔ adds that Quranic reciters read *nistaʕīnu* but also in G(i/a)-stems such as *tirkanū*, *tišāʔūna*, *tixāfūna*, *tīmannā* [for *taʔmanʷnā*], *ʔiʕhad*, *ʔīḏan*, *tiswadd* and *tiṭmaʔinna* and other forms that are like it.

Afterwards, referring to these Barth-Ginsberg forms, al-Farrāʔ says "I followed in this manner, but the recitation follows the first (Hijazi) linguistic practice" (*ʔaǧraytu-hū ʕalā hāḏā l-maǧrā, wa-l-qirāʔatu bi-l-luġati l-ʔūlā*).[16] This confirms that such forms described by Sībawayh and al-Farrāʔ are not just deviations from some unspoken norm, but can even be part of the self-reported speech of said grammarian.

Al-Farrāʔ continues to describe the rules in much the same way as Sībawayh and tells us that for G-stems the prefix is *ʔi-*, *ti-*, *ni-* but *ya-* only in the *faʕila/yafʕalu*. He explicitly adds that it is a mistake to say ***tišrufu* and ***tiḍribu*, a practice widespread in modern dialects.[17] For verbs that are *faʕala/yafʕalu*, and thus are not stative verbs, one does not say ***tiḏhabu* etc. but simply *taḏhab*, because the base verb is not a *faʕila* verb. Al-Farrāʔ adds that al-Kisāʔī heard some of the Dubayr and ʔasad use *i* vowels there.

Neither Sībawayh nor al-Farrāʔ specifically endorse the Hijazi absence of the Barth-Ginsberg alternation as being the proper form of the *ʕarabiyyah*. In Classical Arabic, however, the Hijazi form without the Barth-Ginsberg alternation has become the only acceptable pronunciation (Fischer 2002, §211.2; §241.3).

---

16 Just before this section al-Farrāʔ explicitly cites "the reciters" as using Barth-Ginsberg alternation, so when he speaks of "the recitation", he is either making an explicit statement that those readers are wrong, or he is purely referring to the recitation he learned, which would have probably been from his teacher al-Kisāʔī, who indeed recites without Barth-Ginsberg alternation.

17 This statement should probably be understood as indicating that this practice was already becoming commonplace but was considered normatively unacceptable.

Classical Arabic is often said to have one petrified form with Barth-Ginsberg alternation left, that is, *ʔixālu* 'methinks' (Bloch 1967, 27; Fischer 2002, § 244.3; Huehnergard 2017, 16). Indeed, *Lisān al-ʕarab* (1304c) considers *ʔixālu*, rather than *ʔaxālu* the most eloquent, whereas the latter is analogous. Such a normative preference however does not appear at all with the early grammarians. In fact, neither Sībawayh nor al-Farrāʔ mentions this form at all in their discussion of the alternation.[18]

2.2.6 *The Deictic Pronominal System*

Sībawayh (II, 5, 77 f.; IV, 182, 411) only has a few very short discussions on the deictic pronominal system. Al-Farrāʔ describes the system in more detail (*Luġāt*, 11, 12, 22, 94; *Maʕānī*, I, 109). Principally he identifies a Hijaz versus Najd split, mentioning several forms that explicitly different between the two regions, the differences have been summarized in the table below. Not every form of the paradigm is mentioned explicitly, or assigned to one of the dialect groups explicitly, I have taken the liberty to fill in these forms as seems most likely, and placed them in square brackets.

	Hijaz		**Najd (Tamīm, ʔasad, Qays, Rabīʕah)**	
	Proximal	**Distal**	**Proximal**	**Distal**
sg.	[*hāḏā*], *hāḏihī*	*ḏālika, tilka*	[*hāḏā*], *hāḏī*[19]	*ḏāka, tīka*
du.	[*hāḏāni, hātāni*]	*ḏānika,* [*tānika*]	[*hāḏānni, hātānni*]	*ḏānnika,*[20] [*tānnika*]
pl.	*hāʔulāʔi*	*ʔulāʔika*	(*hā*)*ʔulā*	*ʔulāka*

While the Najdi forms are reported for the *ʕarabiyyah*, it is the Hijazi forms that see the most use in Classical Arabic prose. The Najdi *ḏāka* occurs occasionally in Classical Arabic prose besides *ḏālika*, while *hāḏī, ʔulā*(*ka*) and *ḏāka* are only on occasion used in poetry.

18 Sībawayh does mention the first-person plural form *nixālu*, the fact that he makes no special mention of the 1sg. form suggests it had no special position in his estimation.

19 *Hāḏih* in pause.

20 Al-Farrāʔ's report that *ḏānnika* belongs to the dialects that say *ḏāka* disagrees with al-Mubarrad's report, who says that whoever says *ḏālika* also says *ḏānnika* (III, 275).

2.2.7 *Two Subsequent* Hamzahs *within a Single Word*

Sībawayh (III, 543 ff.) describes the dropping of the *hamzah* in words like *raʔs* > *rās*, *ḏiʔb* > *ḏīb*, *buʔs* > *būs*, *ǧuʔan* > *ǧuwan* and *miʔar* > *miyar*, etc. in great detail, and he does not express any negative (or positive) opinion. It is simply an option when speaking the *ʕarabiyyah*. In the norms as presented in our textbooks today, such forms are not recognized as being part of Classical Arabic at all (Fischer (2002, § 42, § 43), although Wright (1896, § 42) indeed describes the option neutrally).

To Sībawayh (III, 552), however, there is one environment in which the dropping of the *hamzah* is obligatory, namely, when two *hamzahs* follow one another. Thus, one says and *ǧāʔin* (← *ǧāʔīn* ← *ǧāʔiyun* ← *ǧāʔiʔun*) 'going'. While not mentioned explicitly, logically this also affects the verbs *ʔaʔkulu* → *ʔākulu* and *ʔuʔallifu* → *ʔuwallifu* and the plural of *ʔimām*, i.e. *ʔa.immah* (for *ʔaʔimmah*). In Classical Arabic the development of *ʔaʔkulu* → *ʔākulu* is considered regular (Fischer 2002, § 40), whereas other cases are considered to take place only in nouns (Fischer 2002, § 41a) but is said not to occur in the I-ʔ verbs (Fischer 2002, § 41a.1). Sībawayh makes no such distinction between nouns and verbs, and instead presents it as a rule without exception. Al-Farrāʔ does not discuss these cases.

2.3 Where is Classical Arabic?

From the discussion in the previous section (§ 2.2), we have seen that the early grammarians did not establish a single norm as to what the *ʕarabiyyah* is. Instead, they admit a wealth of possibilities, occasionally provided with tribal attribution of certain features, but especially Sībawayh very often simply lists the options without specification. The collection and descriptions of free variation in the *ʕarabiyyah* is a feature typical of the Arab grammarians—it seems to have been part of the very endeavour of being a grammarian. Even if we turn our attention to a grammarian as late as al-Zamaxšarī (d. 538/1144) in his *al-Mufaṣṣal fī al-Naḥw*, we barely see any convergence towards a normative standard in his description. In the chapter on *ʔimālah*, for example, he still describes all the cases of phonemic *ē* found with Sībawayh, even closely following his description (al-Zamaxšarī *mufaṣṣal*, 158–160). Even so, judging from vocalized Classical Arabic manuscripts that predate him, it seems quite clear that what eventually become the prescriptive norms of Classical Arabic had by his time been firmly established.

Rabin (1951, 13) explicitly sees much of the variation discussed above as deviations from the standard: "[The Arab grammarians] never considered the dialects as a form of speech in their own right, but as a collection of curious deviations from the literary language. All their data are measured on Classical Arabic." This, however, reveals more about Rabin's preconceived assumptions about the goals of the grammarians and the homogeneity of Classical Arabic, than it tells us about how the Arab grammarians discussed the possible linguistic variation within the *ʕarabiyyah*. While it is certainly true that the grammarians did not consider the dialects as forms of speech in their own right, it is not true that they are presented as curious deviations from the literary language. All of the variations they described is what they considered to be the literary language. They do not describe them as deviations, but rather as an integral part of the norm.

For example, as we have seen above, both Sībawayh and al-Farrāʔ affirm that eastern dialects tend to drop *i* and *u* in CvCi/u sequences. Never do we find statements of the kind "the people of the Hijaz say *katif*, and the people of Najd say *katf*, and the *ʕarabiyyah* is *katif*." The description of the Hijazi and Najdi forms *is* the *ʕarabiyyah* these grammarians seek to describe. This is often explicit in Sībawayh's writing; when he lists a set of options, he ends such a discussion with a statement that all such options are *ʕarabiyy*. Even when he explicitly calls one better (*ʔaḥsan*, *ʔaǧwad*), he will often end such a discussion with a statement that the dispreferred form is Arabic too. We saw this in Sībawayh's discussion of the long *-hū* and *-hī* after long vowels and diphthongs. While he considers the short forms better, "the full pronunciation is *ʕarabiyy*." At no point is a contrast made between the variation he describes and what the *ʕarabiyyah* is supposed to be.

This necessarily leads us to perhaps an unintuitive conclusion to the modern reader: If one were to read the whole of Sībawayh's *Kitāb*, one would not learn how to speak a single "Classical Arabic". Instead, one would have access to an astounding amount of—often mutually exclusive—variants. In fact, if one takes the statements of Sībawayh seriously, we would find that the forms considered part of the standard language today could simply not exist at all. As an example, in Classical Arabic one would say *taštahī-hi* 'she desires it'. However, in section §2.2.1 we learned that harmonized *-hi* is proper to the dialects of Najd, while in the Hijaz they would say *-hū* (or *-hu*), whereas in section §2.2.5 we learned that *only* the people in the Hijaz have *ta-* as a prefix of Gt-stems while all other regions have *ti-*. Thus, one expects either *taštahī-hū* or *tištahī-hi*; one cannot read the Arab grammarians and learn that the proper Classical Arabic form is *taštahī-hi*, as they at no point explicitly prescribe that.

Still, one might wonder whether the prose of the grammarians themselves would not give away what they considered to be 'the standard'. After all, no matter which modern text edition of Sībawayh's *Kitāb* one consults, these contain all the features of standard Classical Arabic that we know today. But in light of the dominant standard language ideologies present today, and indeed a homogeneous standard having been present for many centuries already, such text editions are of course, quite meaningless. Relentless classicization of orthography and linguistic features is rampant in modern text editing practices, as well as historical copying practices. We do not have an autograph of Sībawayh's book, nor of al-Farrāʔ's works. Copies that have come down to us post-date their lifetimes by centuries, and postdate the establishment of a fairly rigid classical norm by centuries as well. As such, we simply cannot assume that the copies or editions we have today are reliable reflections of the version of the *ʕarabiyyah* they themselves adhered to. Without the strict rules of meter and rhyme, the Classicizing trends which are already strongly present in poetry (C. Rabin 1955, 21), would have been even stronger in prose. I would argue that careful reading of their works can at least lead to a plausible inference that the norms of al-Farrāʔ and Sībawayh may have used in their own prose would have differed from the modern Classical Standard, and also likely differed from one another.

Al-Farrāʔ explicitly endorses the option to make a phonemic distinction between /ā/ and /ē/ in final-weak stems, saying this is most common among the Arabs and the Qurrāʔ (see §2.2.2.2). This distinction was made in Quranic recitation by his teacher al-Kisāʔī, al-Kisāʔī's teacher Ḥamzah, and the teacher of Ḥamzah, al-ʔaʕmaš (see §3.3.3.3). This phonemic distinction appears to have been a venerable Kufan tradition. I see no *a priori* reason to assume that this systematic phonemic distinction was *only* adhered to by these Kufan philologers in Quranic recitation. Al-Farrāʔ's wording does not seem to imply that. Similarly, I see no reason to assume that the lack of harmony of *-hum* when preceding *ʔalif al-waṣl* in, e.g. *ʕalayhumu l-qawl* can transparently be understood as a practice exclusive to Quranic recitation. Al-Farrāʔ explicitly calls this practice 'the most eloquent of linguistic practices' (*ʔafṣaḥ al-luġāt*), and something that 'al-Kisāʔī used to adopt' (see §2.2.1). And indeed, it is also something other Kufans like Ḥamzah and al-ʔaʕmaš adopted, at least in recitation (see §3.3.1).

Neither of these features is explicitly endorsed by Sībawayh, and from what we know of the recitation of the Basran readers, it appears to have rather been typical (at least in Quranic recitation) not to distinguish between /ā/ and /ē/ and say *ʕalayhimi l-qawl* with harmony of both the internal vowel and the connecting vowel (van Putten and Sidky forthcoming). Sībawayh seems to take the 'base' of the harmonized plural pronouns to be *ʕalayhimī*, which could be carefully taken as a possible indication that he would have indeed preferred the *ʕalayhimi l-qawl* form. In light of these differences in description between Sībawayh and al-Farrāʔ, which appear to align with regional practices of Quranic recitation, it seems to me likely that these two grammarians would have differed in these features from one another in neutral prose, while both recognizing each other's options as part of the *ʕarabiyyah*. Whatever the case, it is certainly unwarranted to assume that these two early grammarians would have agreed on a single standard Classical Arabic norm—which they both neglected to describe at all—when speaking and writing prose which just so happens to agree exactly with the modern norms, while it explicitly differed on these points compared to the strongly regional patterns in recitation.[21]

Despite the absence of an explicit normative position from the early grammarians, whenever modern scholarship speaks about the history of Arabic, including the language of the Quran, the assumption that the standard and uniform Classical Arabic was established by the grammarians—and understood by all from the very beginning of the grammarian endeavour to have the limited subset of grammatical features—permeates all argumentation and leads to conclusions that simply do not follow from the data. For example, Rabin adduces that "the dialect of the Quraish must have been more unlike the Classical than the present-day colloquials [...]. Had the Koran been composed in either the dialect of Quraish or in a "vulgar tongue", no amount of revision without altering the consonantal outlines could have made it as similar to Classical as it is." (Rabin 1955, 26). Rabin assumed here that the Arab grammarians had a clearly defined category of *ʕarabiyyah* versus the dialect of Qurayš, but this is not at all what the grammarians present: The dialect of the Qurayš *is* the *ʕarabiyyah*, as are the dialects of Najd. There is no description of Classical Arabic in opposition to the descriptions of the dialects.

Despite the lack of a unified standard, modern Arabists consistently project this homogeneous standard of Classical Arabic back to the period of the early Grammarians or even earlier. For example, Blau & Hopkins (1987, § 25.1) argue that case must be absent in construct in the Judeo-Arabic papyri they study because the 3rd plural masculine is הום- /-hum/, even in genitival position,

21 While the editing process and classicization certainly got rid of many of the more exotic and pre-Classical linguistic features of the *ʕarabiyyah* in the writings of these early grammarians, occasionally traces of it appear to make it into the modern editions of the text. For example, the short form of the apocopate of *kāna* as *yaku, taku* etc. rather than *yakun* and *takun* is generally considered to be a typical feature of Quranic Arabic and poetry, but atypical of the standard Classical Arabic prose that these grammarians are often assumed to implicitly adhere to. Yet, al-Farrāʔ on multiple occasions in his *Maʕānī* in fact uses such short forms in his own prose, and not in order to highlight this feature of Quranic Arabic or the *ʕarabiyyah*, e.g. *fa-ʔin yaku ka-ḏālika fa-yanbaġī ʔan yakūna ḥiṭṭatan manṣūbatan fī l-qirāʔah* "so if it is like that, then it should be recited as *ḥiṭṭatan* in the accusative" (al-Farrāʔ *Maʕānī* I, 38) and *fa-ʔin yaku muwāfiqan li-t-tafsīri fa-huwa ṣawāb* "so if this is in agreement with the explanation, then it is correct" (al-Farrāʔ *Maʕānī* I, 94).

where they say "according to Classical Arabic they should have contained *i*." The papyri they study were written around the same time that Sībawayh and al-Farrāʔ are active as grammarians, and both grammarians find the unharmonized forms of the pronoun completely acceptable. Thus, saying that the form with vowel harmony is the only option Classical Arabic "should" have, is anachronistic. It assumes a linguistic unity of Classical Arabic that is not shown to have existed and certainly is not presented as such by the early Arab grammarians.

Hopkins (2020, 72*) claims that "in Classical Arabic (CA), the final vowel -*ā* is sometimes written with *alif* and sometimes written with *yāʔ*. According to early grammarians, Quranic *tajwīd* and traditional pronunciation of CA, the two spellings are in sound identical". But early grammarians in fact describe them as having different sounds (see § 2.2.2.2), and even much later grammarians like al-Zamaxšarī express no normative opinion that Hopkins ascribes to the early grammarians.[22]

Another example is found in Blau (1967, § 4.1) who interprets سُلنا "we were asked" as a shift of *i* > *u*, apparently taking the hollow root passive *silnā* as the Classical Arabic form, although, according to the early grammarians, for hollow roots both *CüCnā* and *CuCnā* are admitted besides *silnā* (see § 2.2.2.5).

Blau (1967, § 8.3) likewise seems convinced that the *li-* of command always has to syncopate when *fa-* precedes, when he says "the copyist (or the author), … *perhaps* wrongly pronounced *fali* [instead of *fa-l-*, MvP]." However, *fa-li-yaktub* rather than the now standard *fa-l-yaktub* was by no means considered wrong by the early grammarians (see § 2.2.4.4 and also § 3.3.2.2).

However, it is not just those working on Middle Arabic that anachronistically project back later linguistic norms to the early Islamic period. Also, historical linguistic work on modern dialects often takes the Classical Arabic standard as the norm, subsequently misinterpreting archaisms in the dialects as innovations. An example of this is Blanc (1964, 44) who describes the retention of III-*y* *ʔimālah* in Christian and Jewish Baghdadi—like *ʔaʕmi* 'blind' < *ʔaʕmē*, *k*(*a*)*sāli* < *kasālē* 'lazy', *bali* 'yes' < *balē* and *ḥəbli* 'pregnant' < *ḥublē*—as shifts from Old Arabic **ā* to *i*, rather than clear evidence that these dialects developed from varieties of Arabic that have a distinct phonemic *ē* in this position rather than *ā*.

In order to understand the linguistic history of Arabic, the position of the *ʕarabiyyah* within it and how we should understand the position of Middle

22 Incidentally, also the claim that the sounds are merged in *taǧwīd* is incorrect. Four of the ten canonical readers keep them perfectly distinct, see § 3.3.3.3.

Arabic and the modern dialects in relation to it, it is important not to essentialize the *ʕarabiyyah* according to the rigid standard placed upon it today, but rather with the diversity which the Arab grammarians described it.

2.4 Prescriptivism of the Grammarians

The lack of explicit prescriptivism in the early grammatical tradition concerning a large amount of phonological, morphological and syntactic variation should not be understood as evidence that the data presented by the grammarians is an uncurated representation of the dialects of Arabic. In fact, if we compare what the grammarians describe to contemporary Arabic texts written in scripts other than Arabic, we find one very striking difference: The Arabic of this period, not filtered through the grammarian lens, lacks the full *ʔiʕrāb* and *tanwīn* system which so quintessentially marks Classical Arabic and the *ʕarabiyyah*. Some examples of such documents are the following:

(1) The Damascus Psalm fragment, written in Greek letters, datable to right around the active period of the earliest grammarians (end of the 8th, early 9th century), seems to reflect a variety of Arabic that has mostly lost case, occasionally reflecting a genitive in construct before pronominal suffixes and using a marker *-ā* for adverbials. See Al-Jallad (2020b) for a discussion.

(2) The Arabic as reflected in Greek transcriptions of the 7th century has lost all word-final short vowels and *tanwīn*, but retains evidence that *ʔabū* 'father of' was still inflected for case (Al-Jallad 2017d). The pre-Islamic Graeco-Arabic material from the southern levant (around the 6th century) reflects a similar situation (Al-Jallad 2017a).

(3) The Judeo-Arabic papyri written in the early phonetic Judeo-Arabic spelling, a purely phonetic orthography that does not calque Arabic orthography, likely dated around the 8th or 9th century, show no sign of case inflection save for the inflection of the 'five nouns', which are found in the correct genitive forms in address lines (מין אכיה *min ʔaxī-h* 'from his brother'; [לא]בי עמרין *[li-ʔa]bī ʕimrēn*[23] 'to ʔabū ʕimrān'; לאבי עלי *li-ʔabī ʕalī* 'to ʔabū ʕalī'; לאבי יעקוב *li-ʔabi yaʕqūb* 'to ʔabū Yaʕqūb') (Blau and Hopkins 1987).

(4) The pre-Islamic Arabic written in the Safaitic script lacks *tanwīn* and seems to have only retained the accusative *-a* for both definite and indefinite nouns, while word-final *-u* and *-i* had been lost (Al-Jallad and al-

23 Note the *i*-umlaut *ʔimālah* of a CiCCāC noun, as discussed above in section § 2.2.2.1.

Manaser 2015; Al-Jallad 2015, 69 f.). The pre-Islamic Arabic written in Hismaic script may have had all the case vowels, but likewise lacked *tanwīn* (Al-Jallad 2020a).

Indeed, regardless of the period from which an Arabic manual of grammar comes, one would hardly ever know that there was Arabic spoken at all without *ʔiʕrāb* and *tanwīn*,[24] if one would rely on just these grammars. In this sense the Arab grammarians are highly, but only implicitly, prescriptive; there was an essential part of Arabic variation and innovation present in what modern linguists would call "Arabic" that completely escapes any acknowledgement by the grammarians. Clearly to them any form of Arabic that did not have the full system of *ʔiʕrāb* and *tanwīn* was not considered proper "Arabic". This is also clear from the word used to denote these Arabic-defining final case vowels: *ʔiʕrāb*, as a causative verbal noun of the root √ʕrb, it is literally "the thing that makes something Arabic".

2.5 Conclusion

In this chapter we have examined several linguistic features described by the early Arab grammarians Sībawayh and al-Farrāʔ. From this discussion it is clear that these grammarians did not fix a prescribed homogeneous linguistic norm. Instead, we find that they described a large variety of different linguistic options, which are very often presented as equally valid without any normative opinion being expressed, far from establishing a rigid linguistic standard to which all speakers were expected to adhere. It, therefore, can hardly be said that "from its earliest times to the present, [Classical] Arabic has remained superficially almost unchanged" (Fischer 2002, 1). Instead, the Classical language as we know it today has become much less diverse than what the early Kufan and Basran grammarians allowed.

Whenever the grammarians do express a normative preference towards certain forms, they often take pains to point out that the other options are valid too, and when such a preference is expressed, this does not mean that the preferred option is the one that ends up in Classical Arabic. This we see for example in the case of having a fourth long vowel *ē* as the reflex of ancient triphthongs written with the *ʔalif maqṣūrah*, which al-Farrāʔ explicitly endorses, whereas in textbook Classical Arabic this phonemic distinction does not exist (§ 2.2.2.2).

24 Rare admissions are found in the early fourth Islamic century (see Versteegh 1995, 167, n. 11; Larcher 2018).

Moreover, the features described by the grammarians often seem to represent clear, regular phonological developments in the varieties they describe, giving an impression that we are dealing with natural language that has undergone regular sound changes (especially Najdi vowel harmony and syncope, see § 2.2.3, § 2.2.4). However, in Classical Arabic as we know it today, the outcomes of these sound laws that still seemed regular at the time of the early grammarians have now lexicalized and grammaticalized in mixed forms. This is something we see for example with the syncopation of the *li-* before apocopates of command (§ 2.2.4.4), the use of the Barth-Ginsberg variant only for the fossilized form *ʔixālu* 'methinks' (§ 2.2.5), and the lexically determined vowel harmony and syncope in *niʕma* and *biʔsa* (§ 2.2.4.1).

While there are clear prescriptive parameters within which the *ʕarabiyyah* operates, it is clear that what they consider to be the *ʕarabiyyah* was much broader than what becomes the Classical standard. It takes centuries before any kind of homogeneous standard comes forward from the grammarian enterprise. Suggesting that such a homogeneous grammatical standard was already recognized in the late 8th/early 9th century or even the pre-Islamic period is anachronistic. Moreover, as we will see in the next chapter, the linguistic variation described by the grammarians was not of mere theoretical interest but was actually liberally employed in the Quranic reading traditions.

The abundance of different options does not help us to achieve a clear answer as to *what* the language of the Quran is. Even if we accept the assertion of the Arab grammarians that the Quran it was revealed in the *ʕarabiyyah*, that definition is clearly too broad to be meaningful, and we are left with the question: "which *ʕarabiyyah*?" In the following chapters I will further explore this question.

CHAPTER 3

Classical Arabic and the reading traditions

The Quran, Q17:23, in four different readings

∵

3.1 Introduction

It is often stated that the Quran was composed in Classical Arabic, and that, moreover, the Quran served as a basis for Classical Arabic. These statements, taken at face value, seem to neatly wrap up our history of Arabic from the Islamic period onwards. The Quran introduced Classical Arabic as the main cultural language, and from that point forward all Islamic writing proceeded to imitate the linguistic standard set by the Quran. However, these claims have never been demonstrated, and I hope to show here that this definition is unsatisfactory. Already in the previous chapter we saw that the *ʕarabiyyah* in the definition of the early grammarians is very broad, allowing for many different answers to what the language of the Quran really was. It is only in later times that what is considered Classical Arabic becomes strongly restricted. In this chapter, I will show that what was accepted as proper Arabic to recite the Quran in far exceeded the strict norms of the literary language that came to be accepted.

When we ask ourselves what the language of the Quran is, we should in turn ask ourselves "which Quran?" All too often, authors (often implicitly) assume that the Quranic text, in its full and ubiquitous form as we know it from the Cairo Edition of 1924, is the language in which it was pronounced by the prophet Muhammad. This text only represents the transmission of ʔabū ʕumar Ḥafṣ b. Sulayman b. al-Muġīrah al-ʔasadī al-Bazzāz al-Kūfī (d. 180 AH/796 CE), colloquially known as Ḥafṣ, one of the transmitters of ʔabū Bakr ʕāṣim b. ʔabī al-Naǧūd al-ʔasadī (d. 127 AH/745 CE),[1] colloquially known as ʕāṣim. Ḥafṣ' trans-

1 N.B. Not ʿĀṣim al-Ǧaḥdarī as the new translation of Nöldeke et. al. (2013) *History of the Quran* claims, which sadly has conflated these figures with identical death dates and *isms*, while they

mission is by far the most dominant reading today, and linguistically his reading is rather close—but not identical—to Classical Arabic as it is described in our modern textbooks and, by extension, also very close to Modern Standard Arabic.[2] This closeness may very well have given rise to the notion that the language of the Quran is more-or-less identical to the later norms of the literary language. But Ḥafṣ' reading is not the only reading of the Quran available, nor is it considered in any way more normative than other ones. Even today, there are millions of Muslims in Morocco and Algeria (and their diaspora in Europe) who recite the Quran according to the reading of ʔabū Saʕīd ʕuṯmān b. Saʕīd al-Maṣrī (d. 197 AH/812 CE) commonly known by his agnomen Warš, who was a transmitter of ʔabū Ruwaym Nāfiʕ b. ʕabd al-Raḥmān b. ʔabī Nuʕaym (d. 169 AH/785 CE). Warš's reading not only differs from Ḥafṣ in specific word choices, but also shows clear phonological and morphological differences with that of Ḥafṣ. To illustrate this, let us look at Q3:13 in both Ḥafṣ's and Warš's reading.[3] I have marked every word that is pronounced differently between the two in bold, and provide an IPA transcription of both readings.

Hāfṣ	**IPA**
qad kāna **lakum ʔāyatun** fī fiʔatayni t-taqatā fiʔatun tuqātilu fī sabīli llāhi **wa-ʔuxrā** kāfira- tun **yarawna-hum** miṯlay-him raʔya l-ʕayn^{i} #	[qɑdə̆ ka:na **lakum ʔa:jatuŋ:** fi: fiʔatajni t:aqɑta: fiʔatuḓ̃: tu.qa:tilu fi: sabi:li l:a:hi wa**ʔuχrˤɑ:** ka:firatuj̃ jarawnahum miθlajhim rˤɑʔja lʕajn]
wa-ḷḷahu **yuʔayyidu** bi-naṣri-hī man **yašāʔ^{u}** #	[walˤ:ɑ:hu **juʔaj:idu** binasˤrihi: maj̃ **jaʃa::ʔ**]
ʔinna fī ḏālika la-**ʕibratan** li-ʔulī **l-ʔabṣār^{i}** ##	[ʔin:a fi: ða:lika laʕ**ibə̆rˤɑtal liʔuli lʔabə̆sˤɑ:rˤ**]

were separate in the original German. Replace ʿĀṣim al-Jaḥdarī with ʿĀṣim b. Abī al-Naǧūd on pp. 414, n. 168; 457, n. 578; 469, n. 641; 470; 474, n. 23; 480; 483; 483, n, 88; 486; 491, n. 141; 492; 492, n. 147; 493; 494; pg. 500; 501; 507, n. 15 (twice); 520 (thrice); 521; 522, n. 94; 523 (four times); 524 (twice); 527; 530; 532 (five times); 533 (twice); 538; 539; 576; 594; 604. Replace Abū Bakr al-Ṣiddīq (sic!) *ʿan* ʿĀṣim al-Jaḥdarī by ʾAbū Bakr Šuʿbah *ʿan* ʿĀṣim b. Abī al-Naǧūd on p. 501 n. 201.

2 It seems to me that this correlation is unlikely to be a coincidence. Ḥafṣ was the dominant transmission in the late Ottoman empire, and this is the time in which Modern Standard Arabic also started to be standardized. The historical development of the standard form of Classical Arabic, when it became standardized, and whether it was Ḥafṣ's transmission that influenced the formation of the standard or whether he rose to prominence because of his closeness to this standard is something that has not yet been adequately studied, and is outside the scope of this monograph.

3 Reconstructed on the basis of the description of al-Dānī's *Taysīr*, and matched with the pho-

(*cont.*)

Warš	IPA
qad kāna **lakumū ʔāyatun** fī fiʔatayni t-taqatā fiʔatun tuqātilu fī sabīli llāhi **wa-ʔuxrā̈** kāfira-tun **tarawna-hum** miṯlay-him raʔya l-ʕayn^{i} #	[qɑdə̆ kaːna **lakumuː:: ʔaː::jatuŋ:** fiː fiʔatajni tːaqɑtaː fiʔatuð̰̃ː tuqaːtilu fiː sabiːli lːaːhi wa**ʔuχræː** kaːfiratuð̰̃**ː tarawnahum** miθlajhim rˤɑʔja lʕajn]
wa-ḷḷahu **yuwayyidu** bi-naṣri-hī man **yašāʔ^{u}** #	[walˤːɑːhu **juwajːidu** binasˤrihiː maj̃ **jaʃaː::ʔ**]
ʔinna fī ḏālika la-**ʕibratan** li-ʔulī **l-abṣā̈r^{i}** ##	[ʔinːa fiː ðaːlika la**ʕibə̆ratal liʔuli labə̆sˤæː::r**]

In terms of the specific wording, the two readings are nearly identical. The only difference is that Ḥafṣ reads *yarawna-hum miṯlay-him raʔya l-ʕayn* "they see them as being twice their (number) by their own vision" whereas Warš reads *tarawna-hum* "you see them as …".

The morphological and phonetic differences of Warš compared to Ḥafṣ, however, are much more numerous.

- Warš lengthens the plural pronouns *-kum, -hum, ʔantum, hum, -tum* with an extra *ū* whenever it is directly followed by a word that starts with a *ʔ* (*lakumū*).
- Warš replaces the *ʔ* with a glide whenever it is the first root consonant and not word-initial (*yuwayyidu*).
- Warš and Ḥafṣ (and all other readers) agree that a long vowel *ā, ī, ū* should be pronounced overlong whenever a *ʔ* follows. But Warš also pronounces the vowel overlong whenever the *ʔ* precedes these long vowels (*ʔāyatun*).
- The overlong vowel in Warš' recitation is pronounced significantly longer than that of Ḥafṣ (e.g. *yašāʔ*).
- Warš, as a rule, has a distinction between two vowels that are merged to *ā* for Ḥafṣ. Whenever this vowel is written with a *yāʔ*—pointing to its etymological origin—it is pronounced as *ā̈* (*ʔuxrā̈*).
- The sequence *ra* is pronounced emphatically by Ḥafṣ and the other canonical readers, with the exception of Warš who reads it without emphasis if *i* stands in the previous syllable and no emphatic consonants intervene.

---

netics through the recitations of Muḥammad Ṣiddīq el-Minšāwī (Ḥafṣ) and al-ʕuyūn al-Kūšī (Warš), https://www.nquran.com/ar/index.php?group=ayacompare&sora=3&aya=13.

- The sequence *āri* is raised to *ǟri* if the *-i* is the genitive case vowel (*l-abṣǟri*) by Warš.
- For Warš, if a word that starts with a glottal stop is preceded by a word that ends in a consonant, or the definite article, the glottal stop is dropped. Preceding long vowels are still shortened before the definite article, as if it were a two-consonant cluster (*l-abṣǟri*).
- A final effect in Warš's reading not found if one pauses on *yašāʔ* (an optional pause) but present if one does not is the dropping of the second *ʔ* whenever two of those meet with one short vowel in between across word boundaries. Thus *yašāʔu ʔinna* would be pronounced *yašāʔu inna* [jaʃaːːːʔu.inːa].

This overview gives a taste of some of the pervasive linguistic effects of the different readings. They can have variations in their phonological vowel systems, their phonetic realization, morphology and indeed specific wording. While differences in the specific wording are significantly less common than those concerning the linguistic details, these still concern thousands of words. As for the linguistic details, the vast majority of the verses are affected in some way by changes in sound and form of the Quranic readings.

Today, ten readings are accepted as canonical (Nasser 2013a; Nöldeke et al. 2013, 529 ff.). The first seven of these were canonized by the end of the 3rd or beginning of the 4th century AH when Ibn Muǧāhid (d. 324 AH/936 CE) wrote his *Kitāb al-Sabʕah fī al-Qirāʾāt*. This is the earliest extant book on the readings and probably the first to make a real effort to restrain the number of readings that existed in this period.[4] However, for these seven readers, Ibn Muǧāhid reports no less than 49 immediate transmitters. Today, only two transmission paths for each of the canonical readers are considered canonical (thus making it 14 transmissions in total; not all these paths are immediate transmitters). This "two-*Rāwī* Canon" seems to have been first introduced by ʔabū al-Ṭayyib b. Ġalbūn (d. 389 AH/998 CE), but really took off when ʔabū ʕamr al-Dānī (d. 444 AH/1052–1053 CE) wrote his *Al-Taysīr fī al-Qirāʔāt al-Sabʕ*, and Al-Šāṭibī (d. 590 AH/1194 AH) summarized it into a didactic poem popularly known as *al-Šāṭibiyyah*. These two works are still dominant in the teaching of the seven readings today (Nasser 2013a).

The seven readers are associated with five important districts, one each for Medina, Mecca, Damascus and Basra and three for Kufa. The seven readers and their transmitters are as follows (after Watt and Bell 1991, 49):

4 There were almost certainly several works on the readings before ibn Muǧāhid, such as ʔabū ʕubayd's and al-Ṭabarī's, but these appear to have been lost (Nasser 2013b, 36 ff.).

District	Reader	Transmitters	
Medina	Nāfiʕ (d. 169/785)	Warš (d. 197/812)	Qālūn (d. 220/835)
Mecca	Ibn Kaṯīr (d. 120/738)	al-Bazzī (d. 250/864)	Qunbul (d. 291/904)
Damascus	Ibn ʕāmir (d. 118/736)	Hišām (d. 245/859)	Ibn Ḏakwān (d. 242/856)
Basra	ʔabū ʕamr (d. 154/770)	al-Dūrī (d. 246/860)	al-Sūsī (d. 261/874)
Kufa	ʕāṣim (d. 127/745)	Ḥafṣ (d. 180/796)	Šuʕbah (d. 193/809)
Kufa	Ḥamzah (d. 156/773)	Xalaf (d. 229/844)	Xallād (d. 220/835)
Kufa	al-Kisāʔī (d. 189/804)	al-Dūrī (d. 246/860)	al-Layṯ (d. 240/854)

Some of these transmitters differ more from each other than others. The differences between Ḥafṣ and Šuʕbah, for example, are so numerous that they disagree with one another more often than two separate readers like Ḥamzah and al-Kisāʔī. While all other transmitters have differences as well, these transmitters agree with each other much more often, at least when it comes to the choice of specific words.

While Ibn Muǧāhid tends to be seen as the 'canonizer' of the seven readers, his canonization only cemented the seven as taking up a central position in the canon, but did not necessarily prevent other readings from being added to the canon. Shortly after him, many works were written that added more and more readers to these initial seven. While many of these other readings have not reached general acceptance in the Muslim community, three more readers have eventually been accepted into the canon. The definitive canonization of the three after the seven is attributed to Ibn al-Ǧazarī (d. 751 AH/1350 CE) who adds the Basran Yaʕqūb al-Ḥaḍramī, Medinan ʔabū Ǧaʕfar and the Kufan Xalaf (the same Xalaf that is a transmitter of Ḥamzah) as extra eponymous readers, once again with two transmitters each, in his phenomenal work *Našr al-Qirāʔāt al-ʕašr*.

District	Reader	Transmitters	
Medina	ʔabū Ǧaʕfar (d. 130/747)	Ibn Wardān (d. 160/776)	Ibn Ǧammāz (d. 170/786)
Basra	Yaʕqūb (d. 205/820)	Ruways (d. 238/852)	Rawḥ (d. 234/849)
Kufa	Xalaf (d. 229/844)	ʔisḥāq (d. 286/899)	ʔidrīs (d. 292/905)

In the *Našr* Ibn al-Ǧazarī also records in detail a second path of the transmission of Warš, namely that of al-ʔaṣbahānī, which has significant differences with the one recorded already by al-Dānī, the path of al-ʔazraq.

When we see statements that claim that "the Koran established an unchanging norm for the Arabic language" (Thackston 1994, xii) or "the Koran [...] was none other than the poetic *koinē*" (Rabin 1955, 24), this is not very informative. When we actually want to examine what this alleged unchanging norm looked like, we are confronted not with a single answer, but instead with more than twenty different ones. All of these readings differ in significant linguistic ways from what is now considered the standard and, moreover, contain linguistic features that not infrequently fall outside of the purview of the kind of linguistic variation that is described by the Arab grammarians.

In this chapter I will examine what the Quranic readings are, and what they are not. First, I will show that the readings cannot be considered dialects of Arabic or simply Classical Arabic with some dialectal specificities added onto them. Moreover, I will show that there is a high amount of purposeful artificiality to the linguistic practices present in the readings showing what must be considered a concerted effort to make the readings unusual, exotic and eloquent. As a result, I conclude that in terms of what the readings can tell us about the language of the Quran, they fail to give a consistent and uniform answer. As such, the readings cannot serve as the sole source to inform us about the language of the Quran.

3.2 Reading or Recitation?

The term *qirāʔah*, the Arabic name used for a reading tradition, is ambiguous, as it can mean both "recitation" or "reading". The first meaning might imply the readings (as I translate *qirāʔāt* here) are a purely oral transmission of the Quran. Muslims today often envision the readings in such a way, seeing the canonical readings as unbroken and mass-transmitted (*mutawātir*) of the Quranic text from the prophet until today.[5] In the early 20th century, Gotthelf Bergsträßer (Nöldeke et al. 2013, 472 ff.) already saw that this strict way of envisioning the readings as purely oral "recitations" is untenable, which led him to conclude that the Quranic consonantal text was in many cases primary to the readings

5 The view that the transmission of the Quran is *tawātur* seems to develop some significant time after the canonization of the readers. For an in-depth discussion on the emergence of view of *tawātur* of the readings see Nasser (2013b).

that exist. I follow him in this conclusion, but it is worth examining in detail some of the arguments in favour of seeing the readings being dependent on the written form of the text.

First of all, each and every canonical reading basically agrees with the Uthmanic *rasm*, something that is even deemed necessary for a reading to be considered valid (at least as early as al-Ṭabarī (d. 310/923), see Nasser 2013b, 45). Companion readings such as those reported for ʔubayy and Ibn Masʕūd are considered invalid recitations in part because they do not agree with the *rasm*. If even well-respected companions of the prophet had readings that allowed for more oral variation than the Uthmanic readings, it is highly unlikely that so many different oral traditions just so happened to agree with the *rasm*. For example, Ḥamzah ultimately traces his reading back to the famous companion Ibn Masʕūd (al-Dānī *Taysīr*, 9). Ibn Masʕūd's reading does not agree with the *rasm* while Ḥamzah's reading does. The most likely explanation for this discrepancy is that Ḥamzah purposely changed his reading in order for it to agree with the *rasm*, rather than Ibn Masʕūd having used two readings, one not agreeing with the *rasm*, and another one that just so happened to agree with the (not yet extant) *rasm*.[6]

Occasionally it is possible to envision those variant readings indeed have origins in a pre-existent oral tradition where the *rasm*, by accident, accommodated both readings. For example, in Q33:68 ʕāṣim is the only one to read *wa-ʔalʕan-hum laʕnan kabīran* "and curse them with great cursing", rather than *wa-ʔalʕan-hum laʕnan kaṯīran* "and curse them with many a curse." (Ibn al-Ǧazarī, § 3952). The difference between these two readings comes down to a difference in dotting in the word كىرا which could either be read *kaṯīran* or *kabīran*, but these two readings are semantically and phonetically so close, that it does not seem unlikely that such variants could have existed in the oral transmission of the Quranic text before canonization, and by sheer accident happened to agree with the *rasm* when it was instated. However, there are other

6 See also the highly interesting work of Shahpasand & Vahidnia (2018) who show that Ḥamzah and al-Kisāʔī overwhelmingly choose for reading verbs as masculine when the *rasm* allows both a masculine or feminine reading, which they convincingly argue is based on the fact that Ibn Masʕūd's told his students to do so, saying: *ʔiḏā xtalaftum fī qirāʔati yāʔin wa-tāʔin, fa-qraʔū ʕalā yāʔin, wa-ḏakkirū l-qurʔān, fa-ʔinnahū muḏakkar* "when you disagree on the reading of a *yāʔ* or a *tāʔ* [of a prefix-conjugation verb] then read it with a *yāʔ*, and make the Quran masculine, for it is masculine." In a highly engaging paper presented at the Reading the Rasm II symposium (3–5 December 2019, Berlin), Shahpasand further showed that especially Ḥamzah consistently chooses readings that agree with Ibn Masʕūd's reading as much as the *rasm* could allow, even occasionally reading the consonantal skeleton in rather unintuitive ways in order to accommodate such readings.

variants where the phonetics are rather different, and it is by coincidence that in the ambiguous script of Arabic they happen to be written the same. It is unlikely that these kinds of variants do not have their basis in the Uthmanic *rasm*. Some salient examples of this point are the following: فىىىوا *fa-taṯabbatū* 'proceed with caution!' (al-Kisāʔī; Ḥamzah; Xalaf), *fa-tabayyanū* 'be clear!' (the others) (Q4:94; Q49:6, Ibn al-Ǧazarī, § 2951); ىعص الحو *yaquṣṣu l-ḥaqq* 'he tells the truth' (Nafīʕ, ʔabū Ǧaʕfar Ibn Kaṯīr, ʕāṣim), *yaqḍi l-ḥaqq* 'he decides the truth' (the others) (Q6:57; Ibn al-Ǧazarī, § 3029);[7] ىلوا *tatlū* 'recites, recounts' (al-Kisāʔī; Ḥamzah; Xalaf) *tablū* 'tests' (the others) (Q10:30; ibn al-Ǧazarī, § 3354). In such cases, the most likely explanation as to why the readers disagree is not that they were transmitting an oral transmission, but rather that the readers were confronted with an ambiguous *rasm* and interpreted it in two ways that both made semantic sense.[8]

A final point that shows that the readers are to a significant extent dependent on the written form of the text, can be gathered from the fact that the canonical readers all agree with the *rasm* of their respective regions. The tradition has it that when Uthman standardized and distributed the text, he had (at least) four copies of the text made, and distributed these to Medina, Basra, Kufa and Syria (most likely Homs, not Damascus[9]). This traditional account is corroborated by Quranic manuscripts, as it is clear that all Quranic manuscripts of the Uthmanic Text Type descend from a single archetype (van Putten 2019c) and we can indeed identify which of these four regional traditions a Quranic manuscript belongs to by comparing the differences in the *rasm* they have (Sidky 2021).

There are about 60 locations in the Quran, where these regional codices have a slightly different consonantal skeleton. The way that these variants are distributed form a perfect, uncontaminated, stemma (Cook 2004). When such regional difference in consonantal skeleton appears, it is consistently followed closely by the readers of these different regions.[10] For example, the Syrian

7 For a discussion of this variant see Sadeghi (2013).

8 For a similar case where a direct interpretation of the *rasm* by one of the canonical readers can be observed is the reading of Hišām ʕan ibn ʕāmir who reads *ʔibrāhām* and *ʔibrāhīm* wherever the Archetypal QCT has ابرهم and ابرهيم respectively (van Putten 2020b).

9 Sidky (2021).

10 There are a small number of exceptions to this general rule. Ḥafṣ ʕan ʕāṣim deviates from the Kufan Codex in Q36:35 reading *ʕamilat-hu*, instead of *ʕamilat* (Ibn al-Ǧazarī, § 4006) and Q43:71 *taštahī-hi* instead of *taštahī* (Ibn al-Ǧazarī, § 4169). ʔabū Ǧaʕfar in one case deviates from the Medinan *rasm* favouring the Syrian variant Q10:22 *yanšuru-kum* over *yusayyiru-kum* (Ibn al-Ǧazarī, § 3251). ʔabū ʕamr reads Q40:26 *wa-ʔin* instead of *ʔaw ʔin* (Ibn al-Ǧazarī, § 4101).

codex exclusively has Q7:141 احىكم whereas the other codices have احىٮكم. This is reflected in the readings where the Syrian reader Ibn ʕāmir reads *ʔanǧā-kum*, whereas all other readers read *ʔanǧaynā-kum* (Ibn al-Ǧazarī § 3137). Likewise, the Medinan and Syrian codices have Q5:54 ٮرٮدد where the Basran and Kufan codices have ٮرٮد; the Syrian Ibn ʕāmir, and the two Medinans Nāfiʕ and ʔabū Ǧaʕfar read this word as *yartadid* where the other readers read *yartadda* (Ibn al-Ǧazarī § 2989).

The agreement of the readings with the *rasm* cannot be explained by an intentional accommodation of the *rasm* to already existing local oral traditions. Had this been the case, we would be unable to explain how the Syrian *muṣḥaf* shares all variants with the Medinan codex and not a single one with the Basran and Kufan codex, etc. So, whatever oral tradition existed was evidently subjected to a requirement to agree with the *rasm* rather than the *rasm* being updated to match the regional *qirāʔāt*. It is for these reasons that we must think of the Quranic reading traditions as being just that, primarily *readings* of the *rasm*.

3.3 Lack of Regular Sound Change

Many differences among the readings come down to different interpretations of the meaning of the text, reading words differently which here and there can have significant impact on the meaning of a verse and the theology that flows from it. However, most of the differences do not come down to textual/interpretational differences, but rather involve linguistic differences. For example, while most readers read *ʕalay-him* 'upon them', Ḥamzah and Yaʕqūb read *ʕalay-hum* and Ibn Kaṯīr, ʔabū Ǧaʕfar and optionally Qālūn read it *ʕalay-himū*. These differences do not affect the meaning in any way, yet they are linguistically salient. These kinds of purely linguistic differences are what gives these readings their distinct flavour, and are the features that helps one most easily distinguish the different readings from one another.

As we saw already in the previous chapter, the Arab grammatical tradition records a vast amount of linguistic variation within the *ʕarabiyyah*. This variation is often presented through clear and regular rules by these grammarians. Such reports seem to reflect actual sound changes that have taken place in the dialects of the *ʕarabiyyah*, and the agreement of the descriptions between the different early grammarians seems to lend considerable confidence to at least the general dialect geography they sketch. The most comprehensive account of the grammarian reports of the linguistic variation of the *ʕarabiyyah* is still the monumental work by Rabin (1951), which will serve to some extent as a basis for the following examination. However, because it is almost 70 years old now, there is some room for this work to be updated. Most importantly, an edition of one of the earliest accounts of the Arabic dialects has recently been published. At the time of Rabin's writing, this work was known to have existed, but no manuscript was known to have been preserved. This work is al-Farrāʔ's (d. 207/822) *Kitāb fīh Luġāt al-Qurʔān*. As a student of al-Kisāʔī—the Quranic reader, grammarian and famous rival of Sībawayh[11]—al-Farrāʔ constitutes the earliest example of the Kufan school of grammar of which there are extant works available. It is now clear that an enormous amount of the dialectal data recorded by later grammarians is highly dependent on al-Farrāʔ's work. This is often confirmed explicitly by later grammarians who cite either al-Farrāʔ or al-Kisāʔī (often on al-Farrāʔ's authority) for many of the data they adduce.

In the following sections, we will examine some of the linguistic features reported for the *ʕarabiyyah*, and we will focus primarily on the accounts of al-Farrāʔ and Sībawayh. While later grammarians may occasionally adduce features of the Arabic dialects not mentioned by either of these authors, the amount of such data that is relevant to the Quran seems rather more limited. Moreover, as we are interested in the Arabic of the time the Quran was composed, it seems worthwhile to stick to the secondary sources that are as close to this period as possible.

Rabin's (1951, 7) claim that "the grammarians of the Basrian school evinced little real interest in the dialects" and that "Sībawayh mentions mainly usages as were permissible in Arabic as he conceived it." gives perhaps too little credit to the monumental importance of Sībawayh's work on Arabic. It is true that *al-Kitāb* has far fewer attributions of features of Arabic to different tribes than *Luġāt al-Qurʔān*, but this seems to a large extent dependent on genre. The express goal of al-Farrāʔ's work was to record and classify all the different linguistic practices as they occur in the Quran, whereas Sībawayh's is much more concerned with a description and explanation of the grammatical workings. Much of the variation described by al-Farrāʔ is likewise described by Sībawayh, but often lacking the explicit tribal attribution.

The profound influence that al-Farrāʔ's work had on later grammarians and lexicographers in forming the classificatory framework in which variation of Arabic is understood may have led to the impression that that was the focus of the Kufans *par excellence*. As we will see, Sībawayh's work often does comment

11 He famously bested Sībawayh in a debate known as *al-Masʔalah al-Zunbūriyyah*, which is said to have led to Sībawayh's untimely demise (Carter 2004, 13f.).

on dialectal uses, and when he does it more often than not coincides with the description of al-Farrāʔ, although the latter is generally more detailed.

As more or less contemporaneous grammarians of two different schools,[12] finding the observations of the one grammarian corroborated by the other should help alleviate some of the unease a modern linguist might feel about the reliability of such accounts. While the Arab grammarians were certainly not interested in everyday speech, which must have already have developed significantly towards a form closer to the modern dialects as we know them today (see § 2.4), whatever these rival grammarians are describing and agreeing upon must have represented some linguistic reality.

Nevertheless, the following sections will not depend on the assumption that the Arab grammarians are necessarily reporting reliable data of the dialects: these sections will examine certain linguistic processes in their own right, regardless of what tribe they are attributed to. When phonetic sound changes take place in a natural language, these operate without exception. Thus, for example, English underwent a development where word-initial /kn-/ lost the /k/, and therefore all modern English words that are still written, through historical orthography with this cluster, all pronounce it simply with /n-/, e.g. *knight, knee, knot, knead.* Dutch, having not undergone this development retains and pronounces the *k* in all of these places, as in *knecht, knie, knot* and *kneden.* It would be highly unexpected to find that some English words preserved the /kn-/ pronunciation, or that only some Dutch words lost the /k-/. Regularity of sound change, also called "sound laws" is one of the fundamental principles of historical linguistics, and when such regularity fails to apply, and there is no obvious explanation for this, this is a strong indication that we are dealing with a significantly mixed literary register (Hock 1991, 34–51).

In the following sections, we will examine a number of sound changes that are described by the Arab grammarians as clear and regular sound laws that apply in some of the dialects. As we will see, in the Quranic reading traditions these fail to apply in a consistent way. Regardless of whether the attribution of such developments to different tribes by the grammarians is accurate, the failure of these developments to apply regularly is enough to show that the Quranic reading traditions do not make up consistent linguistic systems.

3.3.1 *Harmony of the Pronominal Suffixes*

According to al-Farrāʔ (*Luġāt*, 10 f.), Qurayš and the people of the Hijaz had unharmonized *ʕalay-hum*, *ʕalay-humā*, *ʕalay-hunna* and *ʕalay-hu/ū*. The peo-

12 Al-Farrāʔ was born in 144/761 (Blachère EI² *al-Farrāʾ*), whereas Sībawayh was presumably born around 135/752 (Carter 2004, 10).

ple of Najd (i.e. ʔasad, Qays and Tamīm) harmonized *-hum*, *-humā*, *-hunna* and *-hu/ū* after *i*, *ī* or *ay*, e.g. *ʕalay-him*, *ʕalay-himā*, *ʕalay-hinna*, *ʕalay-hi*. Sībawayh (IV, 195–198) likewise attributes the unharmonized forms to the Hijaz, and does not specify where the harmonized forms are used.

The majority of the readers read in the Najdi manner in terms of vowel harmony. This is the case for ʕāṣim, ibn ʕāmir, ʔabū ʕamr, and even for the Hijazis ibn Kaṯīr, ʔabū Ǧaʕfar, and Nāfiʕ. Clearly, the Quranic preferences do not correspond to the dialectal geography of the readers. There are two reciters who on occasion use the Hijazi form of the plural pronoun. For Ḥamzah this is lexically determined, he only recites *ʔilay-hum, laday-hum* and *ʕalay-hum* without vowel harmony. Other cases of *-ay-* + 3pl.m. suffix undergo vowel harmony, e.g. *ǧannatay-him* (Q34:16) and other pronouns do too, e.g. *ʕalay-himā* (e.g. Q2:229).

As for Yaʕqūb, he blocks vowel harmony of all the plural and dual pronouns (*-hum, humā, hunna* but not the singular pronoun *-hū/u*) when *ī* or *ay* precedes, but not when *-i* precedes. While both of our early grammarians describe vowel harmony, neither of them seems to be aware of varieties that make a distinction in harmonization between *ī* and *ay* as against *i* (Ibn al-Ǧazarī § 1120). This kind of lexically or phonetically conditioned harmony is not described by the Arab grammarians and seems to be an innovation specific to the Quranic reading register (van Putten and Sidky forthcoming).

While neither grammarian assigns a dialectal identification to length disharmony and long plural pronouns, it is worth mentioning for completeness' sake the treatment of this among the readers as well. Ibn Kaṯīr lacks vowel-length disharmony of the singular pronoun, and always has long pronouns, e.g. *fīhī* (Q2:1) and *xuḏūhū fa-ʕtulū-hū* (Q44:47), all other readers do have this vowel length disharmony (Ibn al-Ǧazarī § 1212). All readers (except Ibn Kaṯīr) also agree with al-Farrāʔ's preference to pronounce the pronoun as short after a consonant such as *minhu*, rather than Sībawayh's preference of *minhū* (see § 2.2.1).

Both Ibn Kaṯīr and ʔabū Ǧaʕfar always use the long forms of the plural pronouns, *humū, ʕalayhimū, ʔantumū*, etc., whereas Qālūn ʕan Nāfiʕ has the option to read with long or short pronouns (Ibn al-Ǧazarī § 1122). Warš ʕan Nāfiʕ also makes use of the long pronouns but the conditioning will be discussed in more detail later in this chapter (§ 3.6.5). Thus, long pronouns seem to have been a typical feature of Hijazi recitation, but this does not align with the dialect geography as described by the Arab grammarians, who do not associate long pronouns with the Hijaz at all, and instead suggest it may be used in any dialect freely (§ 2.2.1).

3.3.2 *Najdi Syncope*

One of the well-known features of the Najdi dialects compared to the dialects of the Hijaz, is their conditioned dropping of short high vowels (e.g. Rabin 1951, 97f.). In section §2.2.4 we have discussed the treatment of this syncope as it is described by the Grammarians. From this description it becomes clear that both Sībawayh and al-Farrāʔ describe a regular linguistic development that spans a variety of different environments. While several readers have the syncope in some cases, they fail to apply regularly in all phonetically comparable environments. Even when it concerns a single class (such as nouns of the shape CuCuC syncopating to CuCC), not a single reader treats these in a similar manner.

The following sections will look at six different environments in which this syncope is expected to take place when we follow the descriptions of the Arab grammarians. These will be discussed as separate categories as their treatment is different between the reading traditions.

3.3.2.1 Syncope in fa-huwa, wa-hiya Etc.

According to al-Farrāʔ and Sībawayh (see §2.2.4.3), the third person singular pronouns *huwa* and *hiya* undergo syncopation of the *u*/*i* whenever *wa-*, *fa-* or *la-* would precede among the people of Najd, yielding *wa-hwa, fa-hwa, la-hwa, wa-hya, fa-hya, la-hya,* whereas language the people of the Hijaz did not undergo this development, retaining *fa-huwa, fa-hiya* etc. (al-Farrāʔ *Luġāt*, 29).

Al-Farrāʔ adds that the Quranic reciters can use either the syncopated or the full form. This is in line with what we find. Qālūn ʕan Nāfiʕ, ʔabū ʕamr, al-Kisāʔī and ʔabū Ǧaʕfar apply this syncope to the pronouns, while the rest opts for the Hijazi form (Ibn al-Ǧazarī, §2641).[13] Note that in terms of geographical distribution, no pattern appears, the Medinese readers, a single Basran and a single Kufan follow the Najdi pattern, while the others follow the Hijazi one.

3.3.2.2 Fa/wa-li-yafʕal > fa/wa-l-yafʕal

Sibawayh (IV, 151f.) and al-Farrāʔ (*Luġāt*, 29) mention that the *li-* of command may either syncopate or be maintained when *wa-* or *fa-* precedes, thus the Najdi manner is *wa/fa-l-yafʕal* while the Hijazi manner is *wa/fa-li-yafʕal* (see also §2.2.4.4). Sībawayh explicitly mentions that those who say *wa/fa-l-yafʕal* also reduce the vowel in *wa-hwa*, and *wa-hya* reduced it.

13 Al-Kisāʔī also reads *ṯumma hwa* (Q28:61) and ʔabū Ǧaʕfar *yumilla hwa* (Q2:282).

This view had clearly shifted by the time of Ibn Muǧāhid (454), who discusses the reading *wa-li-yaḍribna* (Q24:31) 'let them (f.) draw' attributed to a non-canonical transmitter of ʔabū ʕamr, ʕabbās b. Faḍl. Ibn Muǧāhid comments that this reading is as if it had the meaning of "in order to" (understanding it as *wa-li-* + subjunctive rather than *wa-l(i)-* + apocopate), which semantically does not make sense in this context. Thus, Ibn Muǧāhid concludes "I don't know what this is" (*wa-lā ʔadrī mā hāḏā*). From this it is clear that that to Ibn Muǧāhid the *li-* in such a context needs to be syncopated for it to designate the *li-* of command, and indeed all canonical readings have undergone this syncope, even those that do not syncopate *wa-huwa* and *wa-hiya*. The relation as drawn by the grammarians is therefore not applied regularly in the canonical readings.

The unsyncopated form, however, is still well-attested in non-canonical readings, both as they are reported in the literary tradition (see, for example Ibn Xālawayh *muxtaṣar*, 12, 17 f., 18), as well as how they occur in early vocalized Quranic manuscripts. In BnF Arabe 330f, 34r (Q4:102), for example, we find clear evidence for *fa-li-taqum, wa-li-yaʔxuḏū, fa-li-yakūnū, wa-li-taʔti, fa-li-yuṣallū* and *wa-li-yaʔxuḏū*. It is therefore clear that we are not so much dealing with a fixed literary standard that preferred this syncopation, but instead this consensus developing in the time between the early Islamic period and the time that Ibn Muǧāhid canonizes the seven readings.

3.3.2.3 CuCuC > CuCC

The people of the Hijaz pronounced singular and plural nouns of the shape CuCuC, along with other stems with this shape, with both vowels, whereas the Tamīm dropped the second vowel in all of these cases. The readers usually agree on the archaic Hijazi pattern, but occasionally a lexical item has the Tamīm form.

While al-Farrāʔ does not comment on every single CuCuC noun present in the Quran, he mentions a fair number of them explicitly as being a Hijazi practice. Of the nouns mentioned by al-Farrāʔ (*Luġāt*) that show disagreement among the readers we have *huzuʔan, kufuʔan* (pg. 26) *qudus* (pg. 44), *qurubah* (pg. 72) *ǧuruf* (pg. 72), *ʔukul* (pg. 86), *nukur* (pg. 87). If we examine how the different readers treat these nouns, we find that not a single reader consistently opts for the Hijazi (H) or Tamimi (T) form, although ʔabū Ǧaʕfar comes fairly close to a regular treatment of the form as Hijazi (Ibn al-Ǧazarī, § 2669–2694):

	IK	N	AJ	IA	AA	Y	K	Ḥ	X	Š	Ḥṣ[14]
al-qud(u)s	T	H	H	H	H	H	H	H	H	H	H
ǧur(u)f	H	H	H	?[15]	H	H	H	T	T	T	H
ʔuk(u)l	T	T	H	H	–	H	H	H	H	H	H
nuk(u)r	T	H	H	H	H	H	H	H	H	H	H
nuk(u)ran	T	H	H	?[16]	T	H	T	T	T	H	T
ʕur(u)ban	H	H	H	H	H	H	H	T	T	T	H
huz(u)ʔan	H	H	H	H	H	H	H	T	T	H	H+
kuf(u)ʔan	H	H	H	H	H	T	H	T	T	H	H+
al-yus(u)r	T	T	H	T	T	T	T	T	T	T	T
yus(u)ran	T	T	H?	T	T	T	T	T	T	T	T
yus(u)rā	T	T	H	T	T	T	T	T	T	T	T
al-ruʕ(u)b/ruʕ(u)ban	T	T	H	H	T	H	H	T	T	T	T
al-ʕus(u)r	T	T	H	T	T	T	T	T	T	T	T
ʕus(u)rah	T	T	H	T	T	T	T	T	T	T	T
ʕus(u)rā	T	T	H	T	T	T	T	T	T	T	T
al-suḥ(u)t	H	T	H	T	H	H	H	T	T	T	T
(al-)ʔuḏ(u)n	H	T	H	H	H	H	H	H	H	H	H
qur(u)bah	H	T?	H	H	H	H	H	H	H	H	H
ʕuq(u)ban	H	H	H	H	H	H	H	T	T	T	T
ruḥ(u)man	T	T	H	H	T	H	T	T	T	T	T
xuš(u)b	H	H	H	H	T	H	T	H	H	H	H
fa-suḥ(u)qan	T	T	H?	T	T	T	H?	T	T	T	T
ṯul(u)ṯay	H	H	H	T?	H	H	H	H	H	H	H
ǧuz(u)ʔun, ǧuz(u)ʔan	T	T	T	T	T	T	T	T	T	H	T
šuġ(u)l	T	T	H	H	T	H	H	H	H	H	H
ʕuḏ(u)ran	H	H	H	H	H	T?	H	H	H	H	H
nuḏ(u)ran	H	H	H	H	T	H	T	T	T	H	T
ʕum(u)ri-hī	H	H	H	H	T?[17]	H	H	H	H	H	H
ǧub(u)lan	H				T	H	H	H	H		
Total Tamim/Hijazi	15/14	15/13	1/27	10/16	16/12	10/19	11/18	18/11	18/11	13/15	14/14

14 IK = Ibn Kaṯīr; N = Nāfiʕ, AJ = ʔabū Ǧaʕfar, IA = Ibn ʕāmir, AA = ʔabū ʕamr, Y = Yaʕqūb, K = al-Kisāʔī, Ḥ = Ḥamzah, X = Xalaf, Š = Šuʕbah ʕan ʕāṣim, Ḥṣ = Ḥafṣ ʕan ʕāṣim.

15 Ibn Ḏakwān has *ǧurfin*, for Hišam both the Tamimi and Hijazi form are transmitted.

16 Ibn Ḏakwān has *nukuran*, Hišām has *nukran*.

17 While Ibn al-Ǧazarī and al-Dānī (*taysīr*) do not report disagreement on the noun *ʕumur*,

Besides these words there are three more words that have undergone a syncope in ʔabū ʕamr's reading when heavy syllable suffixes (*-hā*, *-nā*, *-hum*, *-kum*) follow: *ʔukul* 'food', *rusul* 'messengers' and *subul* 'paths', yielding forms such as *ruslu-hum*, *subla-nā*, and *ʔukla-hā* (Ibn al-Ǧazarī, §2676, 2678, 2683). For the nouns of the shape CuCuC in his reading, the syncope conditioned by heavy syllable suffixes is almost regular. Only *nuzulu-hum* is normally not included in this syncope (although there are non-canonical transmissions that include it, see Ibn Muǧāhid, 623).

From the words disagreed upon no clear pattern emerges. Most readers apply the Tamīmī syncope with some frequency (with the exception of ʔabū Ǧaʕfar), with some of the eastern readers being less prolific than some Hijazi readers in applying it and vice versa. However, many of the remaining words—quite a few of which are explicitly mentioned by al-Farrāʔ as undergoing this development in Tamīmī—unanimously have the Hijazi form among all the readers, e.g. *kutub* 'books' (pg. 31),[18] *nusuk* 'sacrifice' (pg. 33), *nuzul* 'hospitality' (pg. 53), *sudus* '⅙' (pg. 54), *ṯuluṯ* '⅓' (pg. 54), *qubul* 'front' (pg. 77), *dubur* 'back' (pg. 77), *ʕunuq* 'neck' (pg. 80), *ǧuruz* 'barren' (pg. 85), *ʕumur* 'life' (pg. 99). Besides this there are words in the Quran that have the right word shape to undergo syncope but are not explicitly mentioned by al-Farrāʔ, these too are consistently unsyncopated, e.g. *zubur* 'psalms', *rubuʕ* '¼', *ṯumun* '⅛', *ǧunub* 'a distance', *ḥurum* 'in consecrated state', *nuṣub* 'idol', *ẓufur* 'nail', *xumus* '⅕', *furuṭ* 'something excessive', *ḥuqub* 'long period of time', *ṣuḥuf* 'leaves', *xumur* 'veils', *ḥulum* 'dream; (+ *balaġa* 'attain puberty')', *xuluq* 'disposition, nature', *suquf* 'roofs', *ḥubuk* 'celestial paths, orbits', *dusur* 'nails', and *suʕur* 'insanity'. Every single reading therefore overwhelmingly adheres to the Hijazi forms, but the reasons why readers occasionally switch to the Tamimi form are unclear and unpredictable and cannot be obviously understood as an intrusion of the local dialect of the readers into their otherwise overall Hijazi reading.

3.3.2.4 CuCuCāt Plurals of CuCCah Nouns

Syncope also happens in the plural formation of short vowels of CuCCah nouns. According to al-Farrāʔ (*Luġāt*, 16), the people of the Hijaz and the ʔasad form their plurals of *ẓulmah*, *ḥuǧrah*, *ġurfah* and *xuṭwah* with the infixation of *u* before the last root consonant, before adding the regular feminine plural *-āt*,

---

Ibn Muǧāhid (534) transmits a single case of Tamīmī syncope of this noun in Q35:11 through two non-canonical transmitters of ʔabū ʕamr.

18 Vocalized Quranic manuscripts show that syncopated plurals may have been more common, e.g. *ar-rusla* (Q38:14) is found in Wolfen. Cod. Guelf. 12.11 Aug. 2°, 5v, l. 4.; Arabe 334d, 58r, l. 6; Arabe 347b, 81v, l. 2.

i.e. *ẓulumāt, ḥuǧurāt, ġurufāt, xuṭuwāt* (also *ḥurumāt, qurubāt*). The Tamīm and some of the Qays are said to have not had this infixed vowel, i.e. *ẓulmāt, ḥuǧrāt, ġurfāt, xuṭwāt*.

In the Hijazi/ʔasad Arabic reported by al-Farrāʔ the infixed vowel is always *u*, but historically this probably derived from an infixed **a* (see Suchard and Groen 2021). Traces of forms with the original *a*-infix are attested in the reading of the Medinan ʔabū Ǧaʕfar who reads *al-ḥuǧarāt* (Q49:4) rather than *al-ḥuǧurāt* as it is read by the other readers (Ibn al-Ǧazarī, §4247). Al-Farrāʔ (*Luġāt*, 132) explicitly mentions ʔabū Ǧaʕfar's reading as an option besides *ḥuǧurāt* and *ḥuǧrāt* (*Luġāt*, 16). Despite ʔabū Ǧaʕfar's archaic retention of the unharmonized plural CuCaCāt in this case, all the other plurals of this type just follow the reported Hijazi/ʔasad form.

Al-xuṭuwāt (Q2:168 etc.) is read in the Tamimi/Qaysi manner *al-xuṭwāt* by the Nāfiʕ, al-Bazzī ʕan Ibn Kaṯīr, ʔabū ʕamr and Šuʕbah ʕan ʕāṣim, Ḥamzah and Xalaf. The other readers have the Hijazi/Asadi form (Ibn al-Ǧazarī, §2673). In all other cases the readers are in agreement in following the Hijazi/ʔasad form. Here once again we see that the syncope is not applied regularly.

3.3.2.5 Faʕi/ul(ah) Nouns

Al-Farrāʔ (*Luġāt*, 29) explicitly states that the people of Najd, who syncopated *huwa* and *hiya* after *wa-*, *fa-* and *la-*, also syncopate *harim* > *harm raǧul* > *raǧl*. Later, al-Farrāʔ (*Luġāt*, 39) reports that the Tamīm and Bakr b. Wāʔil syncopate the vowel of original *faʕil* and *faʕilah* nouns, while the Hijaz and ʔasad retain the original vowel. Thus, one gets *kalmah* instead of *kalimah* in the east. He also reports that 'others' say *kilmah*, with vowel harmony of the first vowel to the syncopated following vowel.

Most words of the shape CaCiC are unanimously read in the Hijazi way without syncope. Thus *ʕaqib, malik, kalim, laʕib, xaḍir, nakid* (when not read as *nakad*), *ṣaʕiq, fariḥ, ʕarim* and *ʕaṣir*. There are two exceptions, where some of the readers stick to the Tamimi form. The first of these is *raǧili-ka* (Q17:64) which is read as *raǧli-ka* by everyone but Ḥafṣ (Ibn al-Ǧazarī, §3471). Considering the striking consensus (with the exception of Ḥafṣ), one may wonder whether we are not simply dealing with different lexical items, where most readers understood this word as a verbal noun *raǧl* 'going by foot', and Ḥafṣ understood it as an adjective. The other case is *bi-wariqi-kum* (Q18:19), explicitly discussed by al-Farrāʔ (*Luġāt*, 85), which is read as *bi-warqi-kum* by ʔabū ʕamr, Šuʕbah ʕan ʕāṣim, Ḥamzah, Rawḥ ʕan Yaʕqūb and Xalaf (Ibn al-Ǧazarī, §3492).

The Eastern syncopated form is not attested in the canonical readings for the feminine nouns of the shape of CaCiCah. There is complete consensus on the full vocalization of *kalimah* 'word',[19] *naẓirah* 'postponement', *naxirah* 'decayed' (when not read as *nāxirah*, Ibn al-Ǧazarī, § 4508), *waǧilah* 'afraid'. This syncope only occurs once in the plural form, namely *naḥisāt* 'unlucky', which is read by Ibn Kaṯīr, Nāfiʕ, ʔabū ʕamr and Yaʕqūb as *naḥsāt* (Ibn al-Ǧazarī, § 4120).

As with *faʕil(ah)*, nouns with the original shape *faʕul(ah)* are also recorded with syncope of the second stem vowel for the eastern dialects. These contain much fewer lexical items, and there is consensus on the Hijazi form among the canonical readers. The lexical items present in the Quran are *ṣaduqah* and *maṯulah* (Tamīm: *ṣudqah, muṯlah*, al-Farrāʔ *Luġāt*, 54), *ʕaḍud* (in the Hijaz also *ʕaḍid*, Tamīm: *ʕaḍd*, Rabīʕah *ʕuḍd*, al-Farrāʔ *Luġāt*, 85). The fourth of these nouns is *raǧul*. While al-Farrāʔ (*Luġāt*, 36) explicitly assigns the form *raǧul* to the Hijaz, the Tamīmī form is not mentioned specifically, and he simply mentions alternative singular formations such as *rāǧil* and *raǧil*. Sībawayh (IV, 113) explicitly assigns the expected form *raǧl* to Bakr b. Wāʔil and many people of the Banū Tamīm.

3.3.2.6 CaCi/uCa Verbs

As we have seen so far, some reading traditions irregularly undergo the Najdi syncope of nouns in only some lexical items. The grammarians also report the syncope of *i* and *u* in open syllables for verbs of the shape CaCiCa and CaCuCa. Sībawayh explicitly cites *ʕalima* > *ʕalma, ʕilma* and *šahida* > *šihda.*

Among the canonical readers, there is consensus on the Hijazi forms of these verbs, except for two lexical items, namely, *niʕma* 'how good an X' and *biʔsa* 'how bad an X', both of which are transparently from the verbs **naʕima* and **baʔisa* respectively.[20] For these there is complete consensus on the Tamīm forms. A trace of the original Hijazi form of the verb can be found in the reading of نعما which is read as *naʕim-mā* by Ibn ʕāmir, al-Kisāʔī, Ḥamzah and Xalaf (Ibn al-Ǧazarī, § 2806). Indeed, al-Farrāʔ (*Luġāt*, 41) reports that *naʕim-mā* is the practice of the people of the Hijaz. The other readers are either *niʕim-mā*, *niʕ(ĭ)m-mā* or *niʕmmā* (all ultimately < **naʕima mā*). Al-Farrāʔ attributes *niʕim-mā* to Qays and Tamīm, whereas Sībawayh (IV, 439 f.) says "some of them say in recitation" *niʕim-mā*. He argues that the form *niʕim-mā* belongs to the dialect of those who say *niʕima* rather than *niʕma*, and reports that ʔabū al-Xaṭṭāb reports

19 *Kilmah* occurs on BnF Arabe 342a, 6r, l. 3 as a secondary reading, suggesting syncopated forms of these kind may have been more widespread, but nevertheless this reading is quite rare also in the manuscript evidence.

20 Traces of the verbal origins can still be gleaned from the fact that these verbs can agree in gender with their subject (although this is optional) in Classical Arabic, e.g. *niʕma/niʕmati l-marʔatu* 'what a perfect woman!' (Fischer 2002, § 259.1).

this as the dialect of Huḏayl who also say *liʕibun* rather than *laʕibun*. Here is a clear admission that to Sībawayh readings that used both these forms were linguistically mixed.

In all other positions, the canonical readers all read *niʕma* and *biʔsa* in their Tamīmī forms. This distribution is surprising, but seems to reflect a trend that continues in Classical Arabic where words of 'emphatic qualification' (all transparently originally stative verbs) generally have both unsyncopated and syncopated forms.[21] Fischer (2002, § 259–263), in his discussion of these verbs, for example cites *ḥasuna, ḥusna, ḥasna* 'how beautiful, magnificent', *ʕaẓuma, ʕuẓma, ʕaẓma* 'how powerful, mighty', *saruʕa, sarʕa, surʕa* 'how swift!'[22] What the exact motivations are for preferring (or at least allowing) the Tamīmī forms in these constructions, whereas otherwise it is strictly avoided in the Quranic readings and the later Classical Arabic norm is difficult to reconstruct. But it seems likely that the grammarians felt they had a license to use these forms, because they were no longer felt to be verbs.

Sībawayh (IV, 115) goes further in his description, showing that *any* sequence of CaCiC is said to have been syncopated. Thus, he also reports that *muntafixan* would become *muntafxan* for example, and the imperative *inṭaliq* would become *inṭalq(a)*. This is absent in the reading traditions, which consistently opt for the unsyncopated forms typical of the Hijaz.

3.3.2.7 Conclusion

While the syncopation of *i, u* when such words follow a short syllable seems to be a regular process in the Najdi Arabic, the application of the rule is highly erratic in all of the canonical readers. This is not at all something that we would expect if the reading traditions were the outcome of natural language change. Likewise, we do not find that the region where different readers were active is a particularly good predictor of whether they will undergo syncope. The table summarizes the treatment of the six syncope categories discussed among the readers, where N stands for Najdi, H for Hijazi. For some of these the distribution is not absolute. In such N is given followed by the number of words that are

21 Nöldeke, however, astutely points out that especially in early prose it is difficult to know whether people would have pronounced these as the syncopated *biʔsa* and *niʕma* rather than *baʔisa* and *naʕima*. In poetry the norm seems to be the syncopated for, but Nöldeke cites a verse of Ṭarafah where metrically it is certainly trisyllabic (Nöldeke 1910, 217).

22 Besides these, there are some verbs that cannot show such syncopated forms such as *sāʔa* 'how evil' and *ṭāla* 'how often', or are the result of syncope of geminated roots, a syncope that is attested in all forms of Arabic, e.g. *ʕazza, hadda* 'how mighty', *ǧalla* 'how great!' *šadda* 'how much', *qalla* 'how rare'.

read in the Najdi manner. When H/N is given it means that there is disagreement among the two canonical transmitters.

		IK	N	AJ	IA	AA	Y	K	Ḥ	X	Š	Ḥṣ
1.	*wa-huwa* → *wa-hwa*	H	H/N	N	H	N	H	N	H	H	H	H
2.	*wa-li-yafʕal* → *wa-l-yafʕal*	Consensus on the Najdi form										
3.	CuCuC → CuCC	N15	N15	N1	N10	N16	N10	N11	N18	N18	N13	N14
4.	CuCuCāt → CuCCāt	H/N1	N1	H	H	N1	H	H	N1	N1	N1	H
5a.	CaCiC → CaCC	H	H	H	H	N1	H/N	H	N1	N1	N1	H
5b.	CaCiCah → CaCCah	Consensus on the Hijazi form										
5c.	CaCuC(ah) → CaCC(ah)	Consensus on the Hijazi form										
6.	CaCi/uCa → CaCCa	Consensus on the Najdi form in: *baʔisa* → *biʔsa* and *naʕima* → *niʕma* Otherwise: Consensus on the Hijazi form										

3.3.3 *Additional Phonemic Long Vowels*

Several of the Quranic readings have more than three phonemic long vowels (*ā*, *ī*, *ū*). The categories of additional vowels described by the grammarians have already been discussed in section § 2.2.2 and here we will examine how these forms are distributed across the readers.

3.3.3.1 Hollow Root Passives

As we saw in section § 2.2.2.5, the Arab grammarians report three different vocalic options for the passives of hollow roots, which according to al-Farrāʔ can be attributed to the following tribes:

1. People of the Hijaz (Qurayš and those that neighbor them): *xīfa/xifnā*, *bīʕa/biʕnā*, *qīla/qilnā*.
2. Qays, ʕuqayl, and majority of ʔasad: *xǖfa/xüfnā*, *bǖʕa/büʕnā*, *qǖla/qülnā*
3. Banū Faqʕas and Banū Dubayr branches of ʔasad: *xūfa/xufnā*, *būʕa/buʕnā*, *qūla/qulnā*.

Ibn al-Ǧazarī (§ 2629) reports that al-Kisāʔī,[23] Hišām ʕan ibn ʕāmir, Ruways ʕan Yaʕqūb all read in the manner of Qays, ʕuqayl and ʔasad for all the verbs *qǖla*, *ġǖḍa*, *ǧǖʔa*, *ḥǖla*, *sǖqa*, *sǖʔa*, *sǖʔat*.[24] These are all the hollow root passives

23 Al-Farrāʔ (*Luġāt*, 14) also explicitly mentions that al-Kisāʔī reads it as such and that many of the readers followed him in it.

24 Rabin (Chaim Rabin 1951, 159) puzzlingly states that "the Kufan Kisā'ī, however, read in each case *ü* […]. Apparently the Classical language adopted the forms with *ü*, but with the Hijazi spelling." It is difficult to understand what Rabin means by this, but the underlying assumption seems to be that "Classical Arabic"—the Arabic as considered normatively

present in the Quran. More mixed is the treatment of this class by other readers. Ibn Ḏakwān ʕan ibn ʕāmir reads only the verbs *ḥūla, sūqa, sūʔa, sūʔat* while the other verbs that are expected to undergo this development are read with the Hijazi *ī* vowel. Likewise, Nāfiʕ and ʔabū Ǧaʕfar only read *sūʔa, sūʔat* and read the rest with *ī*. All other canonical readers consistently follow the Hijazi practice.

3.3.3.2 Hollow Root ʔimālah

Hollow root *ʔimālah* as found in hollow verbs that have an *i* vowel with consonant initial suffix forms (e.g. *ṭēba/ṭibtu*), as discussed in section § 2.2.2.3, is attributed to Tamīm, ʔasad and Qays by al-Farrāʔ (*Luġāt*, 17) and to some people of the Hijaz according to Sībawayh (IV, 120). Among the canonical readers, only Ḥamzah has this type of *ʔimālah* quite regularly. He applies it to *zēda* 'to increase', *šēʔa* 'to want', *ǧēʔa* 'to come', *xēba* 'to fail', *rēna* 'to seize', *xēfa* 'to fear', *zēġa* 'to wander', *ṭēba* 'to be good', *ḏēqa* 'to taste' and *ḥēqa* 'to surround', and any other form of these verbs where the long vowel is retained, such as *zēdahum* and *ǧēʔū* (Ibn al-Ǧazarī, § 2063). While he is fairly consistent in this regard, Ḥamzah fails to apply this *ʔimālah* to *māta* 'he died',[25] *kālū-hum* 'they measured them' (Q83:3; *kiltum* Q17:35), *zālat* '(did not) cease' (Q21:15; *ziltum* Q40:34). He also makes an exception for *zāġat* (Q33:10; Q38:63) although other forms of this verb do undergo *ʔimālah*.[26]

So even within Ḥamzah's reading, which is the closest to the regular application of this type of *ʔimālah*, this sound change has irregular lexical exceptions. The other readers are less regular in its application. Ibn Ḏakwān and Xalaf only applied *ʔimālah* for forms of the verb *šēʔa* 'he wanted' and *ǧēʔa* 'he came', and Ibn Ḏakwān adds to this *zēda* 'he increased'. All transmissions agree that he applied it to *fa-zēda-hum* (Q2:10), but the others are a cause for disagreement among his transmitters. There is also disagreement as to whether Ibn Ḏakwān reads *xēba* 'to fail' (Ibn al-Ǧazarī, § 2064–2065). For the other transmitter of Ibn

acceptable by the Arab grammarians—could only have one of these forms, rather than all three. It is difficult to reconstruct what caused Rabin to conclude that "the Classical language" had *ū* and only *ū*. It seems to stem from the fact that al-Kisāʔī read it as such, apparently assuming that this Quranic reader and grammarian could not have recited in any other language but the "Classical language". But if this is what Rabin meant, I do not understand what he would make of the majority of readers that read with *ī* instead.

25 Ḥamzah consistently has an *i* vowel in the short stem, which means it would require *ʔimālah* according to the grammarians, ibn al-Ǧazarī (§ 2881).

26 Ibn al-Ǧazarī adds that ibn Mihrān transmits in the transmission of Xallād that *zēġat* does undergo *ʔimālah*.

ʕāmir, Hišām, there is disagreement whether the words *šēʔa, ǧēʔa, zēda* and *xēba* are to be read with *ʔimālah* (Ibn al-Ǧazarī, § 2066). Finally, al-Kisāʔī, Xalaf and Šuʕbah read *rēna* (Ibn al-Ǧazarī, § 2067). From this overview it should be clear that not a single one of the readers consistently follows a regular dialectal distribution for this development.

3.3.3.3 Phonemic Ē on III-y Nouns and Verbs

As discussed in section § 2.2.2.2, some forms of Arabic made a distinction between the *ʔalif maqṣūrah* written with *ʔalif* and with *yāʔ*. Those written with *yāʔ*, being mostly III-*y* roots, derived forms and the feminine ending such as in *ḥublē* 'pregnant' have a phonemic vowel *-ē*. According to al-Farrāʔ (*Luġāt*, 21) the people of the Najd had *ramē* 'to throw', *qaḍē* 'to conclude, decree' etc. whereas the people of the Hijaz had *ramā, qaḍā* etc. for III-*y* verbs, while both have *-ā* for III-*w* verbs. Al-Kisāʔī and Ḥamzah are well-known for having this phonemic distinction (Ibn al-Ǧazarī § 1968). Warš ʕan Nāfiʕ (along the most popular transmissions in the path of al-ʔazraq) likewise retains this distinction but has a lower realization *ǟ* (Ibn al-Ǧazarī § 2023).[27] These three can therefore be seen as having a fairly regular reflex of this development.

Other readers apply *ʔimālah* only sporadically: Ḥafṣ ʕan ʕāṣim reads it only once in *maǧrē-hā* (Q11:41, Ibn al-Ǧazarī, § 1992). Šuʕbah ʕan ʕāṣim reads it for *reʔē* 'he saw' (Ibn al-Ǧazarī, § 2004),[28] *ramē* 'he threw' (Ibn al-Ǧazarī, § 1996) whenever they occur, and *ʔaʕmē* 'blind' in its two attestations in Q17:72, and not in any of its 12 other attestations (Ibn al-Ǧazarī, § 1998). ʔabū ʕamr has a special, and rather artificial treatment which will be discussed in more detail in § 3.6.6.1 below. This highly lexically specified application of the III-*y ʔimālah* is unlikely to be the result of natural language change.

3.3.4 *Lexically Determined* i-*umlaut* ʔimālah

The Arab grammarians recognize multiple types of *ʔimālah*, two of these we have discussed already and must essentially be thought of as representing a phonemic distinction between *ē* and *ā*. However, the type of the *ʔimālah* that takes up the largest amount of Sībawayh's discussion is best thought of as a form of *i*-umlaut where any *ā* that is adjacent to an *i* or *ī* is raised to *ē*, unless it is directly adjacent to one of the emphatic (*ṣ, ḍ, ṭ, ẓ*) or uvular consonants (*q, ġ, x*) or if any of these consonants occur later in the word. This conditioning is well-

27 Ibn Muǧāhid (145) reports *ǟ* for both Warš and Qālūn. Ibn al-Ǧazarī reports the reading of Qālūn from a different transmitter.

28 N.B. also with *ʔimālah* of the first syllable.

known and quite similar to several modern Arabic dialects.[29] While this type of *ʔimālah* is frequently attributed by modern scholars to the tribes of Najd, or more specifically Tamīm, Sībawayh's comprehensive description does not explicitly attributed it to any eastern tribe, only mentioning that that the people of the Hijaz never apply *ʔimālah* in such cases. Al-Farrāʔ is much less systematic in his description of this phenomenon, but more explicit in which tribes do apply it. He reports the people of the Hijaz back the vowel (*yufaxximūna*) of الكافرون whereas the people of Najd among the Tamīm and Qays say *al-kēfirūna* (*yušīrūna ʔilā l-kāfi bi-l-kasr*).

While the *ʔimālah* of this type is clearly non-phonemic in Sībawayh's description, and mostly the result of a regular predictable historical process in the modern dialects that have it as well, oddly enough its occurrences in the Quranic reading traditions are highly lexically determined. The transmitters of Ibn ʕāmir most frequently apply this type of *i*-umlaut *ʔimālah*, but even for this reader it is entirely lexically determined and most of the nouns that would qualify following Sībawayh's description do not undergo it. Ibn al-Ǧazarī (§ 2068–2083) discusses these cases, and they have been summarized below.

Both Hišām and Ibn Ḏakwān (according to some transmission paths) apply the *i*-umlaut to one case of an unemphatic *CaCāCiC* plural, namely, *mašēribu* 'drinks' (Q36:73). However other words that qualify just as well for this shift, are not read in such a way, for example *al-ǧawāriḥi* 'the predators' (Q5:4), *al-ḥanāǧira* 'the throats' (Q33:10), *manāzila* 'positions' (Q36:39), and even *manāfiʕu* 'benefits' which is the word that directly precedes *mašēribu* in Q36:73.

Hišām (according to some transmission paths) also applies *i*-umlaut to one CāCiCah noun, namely, *ʔēniyatin* 'boiling' (Q88:5) while other nouns of the same shape, such as *ʔātiyah* 'coming' (Q15:85; Q20:15; Q22:7; Q40:59) do not undergo it.

The noun *ʕēbidun* and *ʕēbidūna* undergo *i*-umlaut in Hišām's transmission (again according to some transmission paths) in Q109, 3, 4, 5 but not in any of its other attestations. So, without *i*-umlaut are *ʕābidūna* (Q2:138; Q23:47), *al-ʕābidūna* (Q9:112), *ʕābidīna* (Q21:53, 73, 106), *li-l-ʕābidīna* (Q21:84); *al-ʕābidīna* (Q43:81) and *ʕābidātin* (Q66:5). As such, the *i*-umlaut of this word is not just lexically determined, but determined by position in the Quranic text.[30] This is especially striking because another word that would have qualified in this

29 See Levin (1992) for a compelling discussion and compare the conditioning to Christian Baghdadi, for example Abu-Haidar (1991, 29 f.).

30 Phonemic distinctions determined by the position in the text are a phenomenon also found in the reading tradition of the Hebrew Bible (Suchard 2018, 200).

Surah, namely, *al-kāfirūna* (Q109:1) does not undergo the *ʔimālah*. One therefore cannot argue that Hišām is transmitting this single Sūrah in a different dialect that did undergo the *ʔimālah*.

Similar irregularity can be seen for Ibn ʕāmir's other transmitter Ibn Ḏakwān, who has an *i*-umlaut on some, but not all, nouns with the shape CiCCāC. He read *al-miḥrēb*, and *ʕimrēn*, *al-ʔikrēm* and *ʔikrēhi-hinna* in its one attestation (Q24:33) (the latter three all in only some transmission paths) but other nouns are not affected, e.g. *zilzālan* (Q33:11), *al-ʔislām* (Q61:7), *ʔiḥsānan* (Q46:15). Finally, Ibn Ḏakwān (in some transmission paths) reads *ʔimālah* in the words *al-ḥawēriyyīna and li-š-šēribīna.*

Ḥamzah has an even more limited application, only using it in the phrase *ʔana ʔētī-ka bi-hī* (Q27:39, 40) but for example not ***ʔētī-kum* (Q28:29). Besides this he has *i*-umlaut in *ḍiʕēfan* (Q4:9).

A final example is the *i*-umlaut in the pronunciation of (*al-*)*kēfirīna* 'the disbelievers' by ʔabū ʕamr and al-Dūrī ʕan al-Kisāʔī (NB not with the nominative (*al-*)*kāfirūna*, which would qualify in Sībawayh's definition). Warš also has his distinctive in-between ʔimālah (*ā̈*) for this word only.

Sībawayh's system clearly represents a linguistic reality, and its linguistic reality is confirmed by the fact that it describes the system as found in many modern dialects quite accurately. This *i*-umlaut is attested among several different canonical readers. But nowhere does it form the regular, phonetically conditioned system in the way that Sībawayh describes it. This is unexpected if we take the Quranic readings as a reflection of a natural language.

3.3.5 *Dual Deictics*

Al-Farrāʔ (*Luġāt*, 94) reports a clear split of the deictic system between the Hijaz and Najd when it comes to the dual deictics. Qays and Tamīm have *hāḏānni* (proximal masculine), *hātaynni* (proximal feminine) and *ḏānnika* (distal masculine). These same tribes also have *allaḏānni, allaḏaynni* for the dual relative pronoun. The dialect of the Hijaz and ʔasad have a *-āni/-ayni* in all these cases.

The Meccan Ibn Kaṯīr has the Qays and Tamīm form for both the proximal and the distal: *hāḏānni* (Q20:63; Q22:19) *hātaynni* (Q28:27), *fa-ḏānnika* (Q28:32) as well as the dual relative pronoun *allaḏānni, allaḏaynni* (Q4:16; Q41:29). The Basrans ʔabū ʕamr and Yaʕqūb follow Ibn Kaṯīr in using the eastern form only for the distal demonstrative *fa-ḏānnika* (Ibn al-Ǧazarī § 2915). The other canonical readers, however, adhere to Hijazi and ʔasad forms of the deictics and relative pronoun.

3.3.6 *Dialectal Difference in Short Vowels*

3.3.6.1 Cu/iCiyy(ah)

The Fuʕūl(ah) nouns for III-*y* can either retain the initial *u* as per the Hijazi practice, or they can have a harmonized *i*, as per the practice of ʔasad and those who surround them (al-Farrāʔ *Luġāt*, 68).[31] Once again we find that there is significant disagreement among the readers whether to follow the Hijazi or ʔasadī practice, although for *ʕiṣiyy* all readers agree on the ʔasadī form (Ibn al-Ǧazarī, § 3143, § 3549). Probably related to this development is the pronunciation of *ḏurriyyah* as *ḏirriyyah* 'offspring' (al-Farrāʔ *Luġāt*, 39). In this case al-Farrāʔ is less specific and says the people of the Hijaz say *ḏurriyyah* and 'other Arabs' say *ḏirriyyah*. But it seems safe to consider this part of the same development. There is consensus on the Hijazi pronunciation of this word.

The noun Q24:35 دري 'shining', read variously as *durriyyun, dirrīʔun, durrīʔun* (Ibn al-Ǧazarī § 3731) is plausibly explained as a *nisbah* derivation of *durr* 'pearls'. This yields more or less the same phonetic environment as the CuCiyy nouns discussed so far, and thus undergoes the same development. The word-final *ʔ* present among some of the readers is likely pseudocorrect (see § 6.4.6). The Table below illustrates the forms and shows that not a single one of the readers shows a regular pattern, though the Hijazi pronunciation is most common, H = Hijazi, A = Asad, +ʔ = the word has a stem-final ʔ.

	IK	N	AJ	IA	AA	Y	K	Ḥ	X	Š	Ḥṣ
ǧuṯiyyan	H	H	H	H	H	H	A	A	H	H	A
ṣuliyyan	H	H	H	H	H	H	A	A	H	H	A
ʕutiyyan	H	H	H	H	H	H	A	A	H	H	A
bukiyyan	H	H	H	H	H	H	A	A	H	H	H
ḥuliyyi-him(ū)	H	H	H	H	H	–[32]	A	A	H	H	H
ʕiṣiyyv-hum(ū)	A	A	A	A	A	A	A	A	A	A	A
ḏurriyyah	H	H	H	H	H	H	H	H	H	H	H
durriyyun	H	H	H	H	A+ʔ	H+ʔ	A+ʔ	H+ʔ	H	H+ʔ	H

31 Presumably the vowel harmony of CuCyah nouns towards CiCyah is related to this phenomenon. This is reported by al-Farrāʔ (*Luġāt*, 64, 74). He attributed the *xifyah* pronunciation to Quḍāʕah whereas *miryah* is attributed more broadly to the Hijaz, while *muryah* is considered the ʔasad and Tamīm form. There is consensus among the readers on reading *xufyah* and *miryah*.

32 Yaʕqūb reads *ḥalyi-him* instead.

3.3.6.2 CiCwān Nouns

Al-Farrāʔ (*Luġāt*, 47, 62, 77) on multiple occasions reports that nouns that historically probably had the shape *CiCwān undergo harmony of the high vowel **i* to *u* under influence of the following *w* among the Qays and Tamīm, while the vowel remains *i* in the Hijaz. The four words explicitly discussed by al-Farrāʔ that show this dialectal distribution in the Quran are *riḍwān* 'approval', *ʔixwān* 'brothers', *qinwān* 'cluster of dates' and *ṣinwān* 'trees growing from a single root'.

For *ʔixwān*, *qinwān* and *ṣinwān* there is complete consensus on the Hijazi form among the Quranic readers. For *riḍwān* most readers read *riḍwān* in all contexts, but Šuʕbah ʕan ʕāṣim always reads *ruḍwān* with the exception of Q5:16, where he reads it as *riḍwān* (Ibn al-Ǧazarī, § 2832).

Besides this, we must likely also include *ʕudwān*, *ʕidwān* 'enmity' in this discussion, which is recorded by the Arabic lexicographical tradition with both forms (*Lisān*, 2846b). There is consensus among the Quranic readings on the Qays/Tamīm form *ʕudwān*.

3.3.6.3 Mit- and Dim-

Al-Farrāʔ (*Luġāt*, 49) tells us that the hollow verbs *māta* 'to die' and *dāma* 'to last' have a vowel *u* in the short stem *mutta* and *dumta* among the people of the Hijaz, while the Tamīm have *mitta* and *dimta*. From a comparative perspective, it is clear that for *māta* at least, the form with an **i* vowel is original, having developed from an earlier **mawita* (Suchard 2016; van Putten 2017a). This is less clear for *dāma*, but seems likely as well. The readers display a highly mixed treatment of these forms for *māta* where Ḥafṣ even uses both forms in specific locations in the Quran (Ibn al-Ǧazarī, § 2881). There is, however, full consensus on the Hijazi form for the *dāma*.[33]

	IK	N	AJ	IA	AA	Y	K	Ḥ	X	Š	Ḥṣ
mittum Q3:157, 158	H	T	H	H	H	H	T	T	T	H	H
mittum Q23:35	H	T	H	H	H	H	T	T	T	H	T
mittu Q19:23; Q19:66	H	T	H	H	H	H	T	T	T	H	T
mitta Q21:34	H	T	H	H	H	H	T	T	T	H	T
mitnā Q23:82; Q37:16, 53; Q50:3; Q56:47	H	T	H	H	H	H	T	T	T	H	T
dumta Q3:75	H	H	H	H	H	H	H	H	H	H	H

33 Yaḥyā b. Waṯṯāb is attributed as reading Q3:75 *dimta*, Q5:96 *dimtum* (Ibn Xālawayh *muxtaṣar*, 21, 35).

(*cont.*)

	IK	N	AJ	IA	AA	Y	K	Ḥ	X	Š	Ḥs
dumtum Q5:96	H	H	H	H	H	H	H	H	H	H	H
dumtu Q5:117, Q19:31	H	H	H	H	H	H	H	H	H	H	H

3.3.7 *Disagreement in Pluralization*

The plural of *ʔasīr* 'prisoner' among the people of the Hijaz is *ʔusārā*. The people of the Najd most commonly use *ʔasrā* (Al-Farrāʔ *Luġāt*, 29). Al-Farrāʔ goes on to say that the plural *ʔasrā* "is the best of the two options in Arabic, because it has a similar pattern as *ǧarīḥ* pl. *ǧarḥā* and *ṣarīʕ* pl. *ṣarʕā*." This plural occurs three times in the Quran, and there is significant disagreement on which form is to be used, most readers in fact use both the Hijazi and the Najdi forms (Ibn al-Ǧazarī, § 2708, 3192).

	IK	N	AJ	IA	AA	Y	Ḥ	X	K	Š	Ḥs
Q2:85	H	H	H	H	H	H	N	H	H	H	H
Q8:67	N	N	H	N	N	N	N	N	N	N	N
Q8:70	N	N	H	N	H	N	N	N	N	N	N

3.3.8 *Cu/iyūC Plurals*

There are some cases where we likewise find unexpected and mixed treatments even when the early grammarians whom we examine here do not explicitly attribute these forms to specific dialects. This is the case, for example, for the plurals of several CayC nouns like *bayt* 'house', *ġayb* 'a hidden thing', *ʕayn* 'eye, well', *ǧayb* 'bosom' and *šayx* 'elder' which show disagreement of the first vowel of the plural stem. Sībawayh (III, 589) describes these explicitly as having a CuCūC plural pattern and mentions no other options. He does mention that for diminutive we find *šiyayx, siyayd* and *biyayt* as options besides *šuyayx, suyayd* and *buyayt*, although he explicitly considers the form with *u* better (Sībawayh III, 481). Al-Farrāʔ (*Luġāt*, 56) discuss three different options for the plurals: *buyūt, biyūt* and *büyūt*. He considers the last of these three to be the best and most common.

While Ibn Muǧāhid (178 f.) reports *ġuyūb*, but *biyūt, ʕiyūn, ǧiyūb* and *šiyūx* for al-Kisāʔī, one of the manuscripts used in the edition has an extra anonymous attribution that reports the front rounded vowel *ü* for al-Kisāʔī (probably only those reported with *i*, but the wording is ambiguous).[34] For Ḥamzah, he reports that he pronounces *i* for all of these words, but that Xalaf and (the now non-canonical transmitter) ʔabū Hišām ← Sulaym ← Ḥamzah read *ǧüyūbihinna*. *Ǧüyūbihinna* is also reported for Yaḥyā b. ʔādam ← Šuʕbah ← ʕāṣim. Al-Dānī (*Ǧāmiʕ*, 416 f.) brings many more transmissions with *büyūt*-type plurals, for all three Kufans. The forms with the front rounded vowel have been lost in the canonical transmissions as they are adhered to today (and reported on by al-Dānī *taysīr* and Ibn al-Ǧazarī), but it is clear that this was once quite popular in the Kufan tradition, which helps us understand al-Farrāʔ's approving tone of this pronunciation.

The shift of **uy* > *iy* is otherwise very irregular, something we would not expect if it had been the outcome of a regular sound shift. Warš ʕan Nāfiʕ, ʔabū ʕamr and Ḥafṣ ʕan ʕāṣim, ʔabū Ǧaʕfar and Yaʕqūb all regularly have CuyūC, whereas Ḥamzah (in the now-canonical transmission) regularly has CiyūC. The remaining readers all have a single exception to their general pattern, though which word constitutes the exception differs per reader (Ibn al-Ǧazarī, § 2755). Such behaviour is hard to explain as the outcome of the development of natural language and should rather be seen from the perspective of different readers consciously incorporating different dialectal forms into their readings, while not doing so in other places.

	IK	N		AJ	AA	Y	IA		Ḥ	X	K	A	
		W	Q				H	ID̠				Š	Ḥṣ
بيوت	*biyūt*	*buyūt*	*biyūt*	*buyūt*	*buyūt*	*buyūt*	*biyūt*	*biyūt*	*biyūt*	*biyūt*	*biyūt*	*biyūt*	*buyūt*
غيوب	*ġuyūb*	*ġuyūb*	*ġuyūb*	*ġuyūb*	*ġuyūb*	*ġuyūb*	*ġuyūb*	*ġuyūb*	*ġiyūb*	*ġuyūb*	*ġuyūb*	*ġiyūb*	*ġuyūb*
عيون	*ʕiyūn*	*ʕuyūn*	*ʕuyūn*	*ʕuyūn*	*ʕuyūn*	*ʕuyūn*	*ʕuyūn*	*ʕiyūn*	*ʕiyūn*	*ʕuyūn*	*ʕiyūn*	*ʕiyūn*	*ʕuyūn*
جيوبهن	*ǧiyūb*	*ǧuyūb*	*ǧuyūb*	*ǧuyūb*	*ǧuyūb*	*ǧuyūb*	*ǧuyūb*	*ǧiyūb*	*ǧiyūb*	*ǧuyūb*	*ǧiyūb*	*ǧuyūb*	*ǧuyūb*
شيوخا	*šiyūx*	*šuyūx*	*Šuyūx*	*šuyūx*	*šuyūx*	*šuyūx*	*šuyūx*	*šiyūx*	*šiyūx*	*šuyūx*	*šiyūx*	*šiyūx*	*šuyūx*

3.3.9 *The Readings Do Not Reflect Natural Language*

As should be clear from the discussion of the previous sections, all of the linguistic developments discussed above fail to apply consistently in the Quranic

34 *Wa-ruwiya ʕani l-kisāʔiyyi ʔannahū kāna yaqraʔu hāḏihi l-ḥurūfa bi-ʔišmāmi l-ḥarfi l-ʔawwali ḍ-ḍammi muxtalisan miṯli qūla, wa ġūḍa wa-mā ʔašbaha ḏālik.* I am indebted to Nasser (2020, 225) for making me realize that these variants were reported by Ibn Muǧāhid.

reading traditions. This is rather surprising from the perspective of the descriptions of the grammarians, who clearly present these processes as regular rules, often stating explicitly things like 'those who say *wa-l-yafʕal* also say *wa-hwa*'. The readings fail to reflect any regular relation of the sort presented by the grammarians. The lack of regular sound change clearly implies that the readings do not reflect any form of natural language.

Seemingly irregular outcomes of sound changes may be the result of borrowing between closely related languages (Hock 1991, 47 ff.). While in principle, one could try to explain what we find in the readings in this manner, the sheer amount of dialect borrowing that would have to be assumed and the lack of clear patterns among the readers would be difficult to square with the data as presented by the grammarians. Alternatively, one might imagine we are looking at several sound changes in progress. As Labov (1994, Part D, pp. 419–543) shows, sound change can surface as irregular distributions of the sound change in ways that are not entirely predictable while the sound change is still in progress. One might imagine that some of the sound changes discussed above may be understood as part of this kind of distribution, fossilized in time as the reading traditions were transmitted with the utmost precision. However, the great amount of sound changes that would have to be considered to have been caught 'mid shift' by the Quranic reading traditions would be highly unusual, especially considering the fact that the Arab grammarians, active around the same period as the readers of these reading traditions give no indication whatsoever that these shifts were changes in progress, and rather point to regularly conditioned sound changes that can be clearly formulated, and by all intents and purposes seem complete in the different dialects they are attributed to.

Therefore, the chaotic situation that we see among the canonical readers must, in part, be the result of conscious incorporation of different linguistic forms into a single reading. The exact motivation for the haphazard incorporation of such features is not readily recoverable. It seems clear that some amount of regional influence plays a role in this regard. For example, it is unlikely to be a coincidence that three of the four Kufan readers all have regular phonemic *ē* on III-*y* stems (§ 3.3.3.3), which strikes one as likely to be the result of the Teacher-Student relationships that Ḥamzah, al-Kisāʔī and Xalaf have with one another. As ʕāṣim falls outside that cluster, only sharing a teacher several generations higher up, his deviation from the Kufan norm can be understood.[35]

35 For teacher student-relationships I have relied here on the description of al-Dānī (*taysīr*, 9–10). Other sources report slightly different details as to how Ḥamzah relates to al-Sulamī, reporting that he learned from ʔabū ʔisḥāq, who studied directly under al-Sulamī, whereas, Yaḥyā b. Waṯṯāb did not learn from al-Sulamī (Ibn al-Ǧazarī § 751–752).

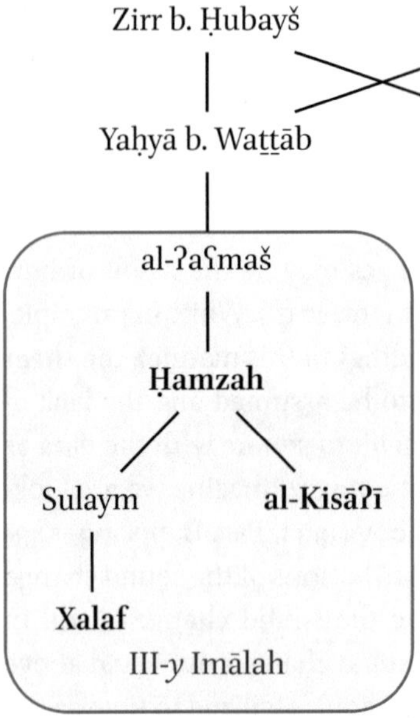

FIGURE 1 III-*y* *ʔimālah* among Kufan Reciters

While teacher student relations can explain some amount of the variation, many of the disagreements are not easily explained in this manner. If we turn, for example, to the syncopation of CuCuC nouns (§ 3.3.2.3), we are confronted with a striking lack of agreement between the two Medinan readers ʔabū Ǧaʕfar and Nāfiʕ, while the latter is a direct student of the former. Likewise, the disagreements between nouns of this type between Ḥamzah, Xalaf and al-Kisāʔī are not easily explained in this manner. There is no straightforward explanation why Ḥamzah and Xalaf chose to read جرف (Q9:109) as *ǧurfin* while al-Kisāʔī chose *ǧurufin*, while with the word نكرا (e.g. Q18:74) it is al-Kisāʔī and Ḥamzah that agree on the syncopated form *nukran*, whereas Xalaf opts for *nukuran*.

3.4 The Readings Are Not Dialects

It should be clear from the discussion in section § 3.3 that there is a significant amount of linguistic variation present in the Quranic reading traditions. These linguistic differences between the readings are often explained today as being the result of regional pronunciations or dialects of Arabic. This is a view commonly espoused by Muslim scholars and laypeople alike, as it is believed that the prophet Muhammad taught his followers in their native dialect, sometimes claiming that the angel Gabriel revealed it to the prophet as such (As-Said

1975, 53; al-Azami 2003, 62 f., 154 f.). This is not a view that seems to have been endorsed in the early *qirāʔāt* works, but that of course need not mean that this is incorrect.

The report is easily dismissed in its most literal interpretation, though. It is readily apparent that Hijazi readers do not employ Hijazi pronominal forms, for example. Likewise, a client of ʔasad (such as ʕāṣim) does not exclusively use ʔasadī forms. Of course, it need not be the case that a reader would be employing his own local dialect, but we find that none of the readers stick to regional forms with any consistency at all. For example, the widespread syncopation and vowel harmony associated with the eastern tribes only shows up erratically in the reading traditions with no obvious patterns discernable.

Especially in the general principles of the readings—widespread features that apply regularly to words whenever they occur—we do find some regional trends. Van Putten & Sidky (forthcoming), for example, show that the use of long plural pronouns of the type *ʔantumū*, *humū*, *ʕalay-himū* etc. is typical for the Hijazi readers, not just the canonical ʔabū Ǧaʕfar, Nāfiʕ (both Medina) and Ibn Kaṯīr (Mecca), but also the non-canonical Meccan Ibn Muḥayṣin. Yet, the Arab grammarians are explicit in pointing out that this is not a regional dialectal feature, but an option for any speaker of Arabic of whatever tribe.

One could, of course, call into question the accuracy of the reports of the grammarians. Perhaps, for some reason, the reports about the dialectal features simply did not map onto reality in any way. It is difficult to envision a motivation for the grammarians to fabricate a vast and intricate system of dialectological data that was agreed upon by the otherwise rivalrous grammatical schools of Basra and Kufa. Moreover, the data they present often seems to show a clear and regular application of sound laws, which makes these developments look like natural linguistic data even though the concept of regular sound laws was not part of the framework of the grammarians, which makes such data look even more natural.

Had this data been fabricated, we would expect it to serve (and be employed for) theological or ideological purposes. It would, for example, have been quite advantageous for al-Farrāʔ to claim that all the features that the readers have (or at least what his teacher al-Kisāʔī or the other Kufan readers read), were a perfect reflection of the dialect of the Qurayš and therefore the most eloquent and authentic form of recitation, but this is not what he reports. Very often al-Farrāʔ explicitly mentions the reading of the Kufan readers even when they are at odds with the dialectal forms of the Hijazis or Qurayš. An example of this is the presence of the vowel *ṻ* in hollow root passives (§ 3.3.3.1), which al-Farrāʔ explicitly attributes to his teacher, al-Kisāʔī, while also explicitly calling it a non-Hijazi form.

Further evidence for a lack of correlation of readers to any one dialect may be found among lexical isoglosses. Al-Farrāʔ (*Luġāt*) discusses many differences between the dialects in the vocalism of specific lexical items. In most cases these seem to be different stem formations, in line with a certain freedom of stem formation seen across the Semitic languages (Fox 2013, 102ff.). With such cases we once again find significant disagreement among the readers, where each of the readers incorporates forms from a variety of different dialects. I will discuss these variants in the list below. Each lexical item will be listed with the tribe or region its associated with, followed by the page number where this is mentioned in al-Farrāʔ's work. After that the reading that has the fewest readers in agreement is mentioned. The unmentioned remainder then has the remaining form.

1. *nabṭušu* (Hijaz), *nabṭišu* (ʔasad), p. 24. ʔabū Ǧaʕfar: *nabṭušu* (Ibn al-Ǧazarī §3162).
2. *maysurah* (Hijaz), *maysarah* (Tamīm, Qays, and people of the Najd), p. 41. Nāfiʕ: *maysurah* (Ibn al-Ǧazarī, §2811).
3. *buxul* (Hijaz), *buxl* (Tamīm), *baxal* (ʔasad), *baxl* (Tamīm, Bakr b. Wāʔil), p. 54f. Ḥamzah, al-Kisāʔī and Xalaf: *baxal*. Rest: *buxl* (Ibn al-Ǧazarī, §2930).
4. *ḥiṣād* (Hijaz), *ḥaṣād* (Najd and Tamīm), p. 63. ʕāṣim, ʔabū ʕamr, Yaʕqūb, Ibn ʕāmir: *ḥaṣād* (Ibn al-Ǧazarī, §3076).
5. *rubamā* 'perhaps' (Hijaz), *rubbamā* (ʔasad, Tamīm), *rabbamā* (Taym al-Rabāb from Tamīm), p. 78. ʕāṣim, Nāfiʕ, ʔabū Ǧaʕfar: *rubamā*. Rest: *rubbamā* (Ibn al-Ǧazarī, §3390).
6. *ka-ʔayyin* (Hijaz), *kāʔin* (Tamīm), p. 101. Ibn Kaṯīr, ʔabū Ǧaʕfar: *kāʔin* (Ibn al-Ǧazarī, §2875).
7. *fawāq* (Hijaz), *fuwāq* (ʔasad, Tamīm, Qays), p. 123. Ḥamzah, al-Kisāʔī, Xalaf: *fuwāq* (Ibn al-Ǧazarī, §4057).
8. *salm* (Hijaz, Tamīm, ʔasad), *silm* (Qays), p. 131. Šuʕbah ʕan ʕāṣim (Q2:208; Q8:61; Q47:35), Ḥamzah, Xalaf (Q47:35): *as-silmi* (Ibn al-Ǧazarī, §2761).
9. *wuǧd* (Hijaz), *waǧd* (Tamīm), p. 141. Rawḥ ʕan Yaʕqūb: *wiǧdi-kum* (Ibn al-Ǧazarī, §4409), the rest has the Hijaz form.
10. *naṣūḥ* (Hijaz), *nuṣūḥ* (some of Qays), p. 141. Šuʕbah ʕan ʕāṣim: *nuṣūḥan* (Ibn al-Ǧazarī, §4417).
11. *tafāwut* (Hijaz), *tafawwut* (some Arabs), p. 142. Ḥamzah, al-Kisāʔī: *tafawwut* (Ibn al-Ǧazarī, §4420).
12. *ruǧz* (Hijaz), *riǧz* (Tamīm and the common people of the Arabs), p. 147. Ḥafṣ ʕan ʕāṣim, ʔabū Ǧaʕfar and Yaʕqūb have *ar-ruǧza* (Q74:5) (Ibn al-Ǧazarī, §4472).
13. *watr* (Hijaz), *witr* (Qays, Tamīm, ʔasad), p. 157. Ḥamzah, al-Kisāʔī, Xalaf: *wa-l-witri* (Q89:3) (Ibn al-Ǧazarī, §4547).

14. *ḍuʕf* (Hijaz), *ḍaʕf* (Tamīm), p. 71. ʕāṣim: *ḍaʕf* (disagreement on Ḥafṣ' authority both *ḍuʕf* and *ḍaʕf*); Ḥamzah and Xalaf have *ḍaʕfan* in Q8:66 but *ḍuʕf(an)* in Q30:54; ʔabū Ǧaʕfar has *ḍuʕafāʔ* in Q8:66, *ḍuʕf* in Q30:54 (Ibn al-Ǧazarī, § 3898). The rest has the Hijaz form in all positions.
15. *ʔuffin, ʔuffi* (Hijaz), *ʔuffa* (People of Yemen and Qays), *ʔuffu* (Some Arabs), *ʔuffan* (ʔasad), p. 80. Ḥafṣ ʕan ʕāṣim, Nāfiʕ, ʔabū Ǧaʕfar: *ʔuffin*. Ibn Kaṯīr, Ibn ʕāmir, Yaʕqūb *ʔuffa*; The rest: *ʔuffi* (Ibn al-Ǧazarī, § 3457).
16. *mansak* (Hijaz), *mansik* (most from Najd), p. 99. Ḥamzah, al-Kisāʔī, Xalaf: *mansikan* (Ibn al-Ǧazarī, § 3657).
17. *hayhāta* (Hijaz), *ʔayhāti(n)*, *hayhāti(n)* (Tamīm, ʔasad), *ʔayhātan* (some Tamīm), *ʔayhāta, ʔayhātun, ʔayhātu, ʔayhāna* (some Arabs), p. 102. ʔabū Ǧaʕfar: *hayhāti*. The rest has the Hijaz form (Ibn al-Ǧazarī, § 3689).
18. *wuddan* (Hijaz), *waddan* (ʔasad), p. 145. Nāfiʕ, ʔabū Ǧaʕfar: *wuddan*, the rest has *waddan* (Ibn al-Ǧazarī, § 4452).

As with the sound laws discussed in the previous section, it is clear that the reading traditions are highly mixed, showing features of different dialects. There is not a single 'base' from which readers have then occasionally imported regional dialectisms. In fact, one frequently finds the opposite trend. For example, in the case of reading *ka-ʔayyin* versus *kāʔin*, we find that only the Hijazi readers have the Najdi forms, while all the non-Hijazi readers have the Hijazi forms. Likewise, the readers whose pronominal systems contain the most Hijazi forms are Ḥamzah (Kufa) and Yaʕqūb (Basra), whereas all the Hijazi readers have perfectly Najdi forms.

Assuming that there was a single 'standard' *ʕarabiyyah*—which for some reason does not get explicitly described by the grammarians—we would have to conclude that readers are moving away from an accepted standard by incorporating features that were explicitly not local to them. Considering the complete silence of the grammarians of this single standard, this strikes me as an assumption we cannot make based on the evidence at hand. Rather, the data seems to suggest that through a process of imperfect transmission and explicit choices, the readers assembled their own reading of the Quran, with no regard as to whether this amalgamation of linguistic features had ever occurred in a single dialect of the *ʕarabiyyah*.

3.5 Readers Usually Agree on the Hijazi Form

So far, we have discussed many phonological, morphological and lexical isoglosses that are reported as differences among the Arabic dialects by the Arab grammarians. We see that very often readers have no real consensus on what dialectal form to use, and that even within a single reading, an alternation between different dialectal forms occurs. These disagreements are frequent and clearly show that the Quranic readings cannot be thought of as "dialects" of Arabic. Nevertheless, there are still many examples where al-Farrāʔ mentions differences in specific words and grammar, where all the readers are in agreement amongst one another.

One might imagine that the points where the readers agree with one another is what could be considered the "Classical Arabic" base. However, whenever such consensus exists, almost invariably, the readers agree on the form attributed to the Hijaz. These cases clearly far outnumber the cases where there is disagreement among the canonical readers. By and large the basis of all the Quranic readings therefore seems to be Hijazi Arabic. This is already clear from some of the classes discussed above. While CuCuCāt forms do show a couple cases where the Najdi syncopated CuCCāt form is employed, the majority of the cases show agreement among the readers on the Hijazi form. The same is true for CuCuC, CaCiC(ah) nouns, CiCwān nouns etc.

In cases of complete agreement among the readers, the consensus almost always falls upon the Hijazi form. For example, the grammarians inform us that the initial vowel of the prefix conjugation of verbs is *i* when the second vowel is *a* (i.e. *ʔifhamu* 'I understand') among the Tamīm, whereas the Hijazis have the innovative *a* vowel there (i.e. *ʔafhamu*) (see § 2.2.5). There is consensus among the canonical readers to read all of these forms in the Hijazi manner.

Also, when it comes to lexical isoglosses, the vast majority of the cases mentioned by al-Farrāʔ there is consensus on the Hijazi form. Below follows a list of some of the words where two local variants are mentioned by al-Farrāʔ, but where the canonical readers consistently opt for the Hijazi form. The page number is the page where the form occurs in al-Farrāʔ's *Luġāt*.

- *zuǧāǧāh* (Hijaz), *zaǧāǧah*, *ziǧāǧah* (Tamīm Qays), p. 107.
- *tuxsirū* (Hijaz), *taxsirū* (ʔasad), p. 136.
- *šararah*, *šarar* (Hijaz, ʔasad), *šarārah*, *šarār* (Tamīm, Qays), p. 151.
- *ṣulb* (Hijaz), *ṣalab* (ʔasad, Tamīm), p. 155.
- *musayṭir* (Hijaz, ʔasad), *musayṭar* (Tamīm), p. 156.
- *kidta* (Hijaz), *kudta* (Common people of Qays), p. 81.
- *baʕudat* (Hijaz), *baʕidat* (Some of Qays), p. 71.
- *ǧuhd* (Hijaz), *ǧahd* (Tamīm), p. 72.
- *ġilẓah* (Hijaz, ʔasad), *ġulẓah* (Tamīm), p. 72.
- *miryah* (Hijaz), *muryah* (ʔasad, Tamīm), p. 74.
- *qaṭirān* (Hijaz, ʔasad), *qiṭrān* (Some of Tamīm and Qays), p. 77.
- *surur* (Hijaz), *surar* (Tamīm, Kalb), p. 78.

- *šaǧar* (Qurayš and its neighbours of the people of the Hijaz), *šiǧar* (the common people among the Arabs), p. 79.
- *sukārā* (Hijaz, ʔasad), *sakārā* (Tamīm), p. 55.
- *kusālā* (Hijaz), *kasālā* (Tamīm, ʔasad), p. 59.
- *yurāʔā* (Hijaz), *yuraʔʔā* (the common people of Qays, Tamīm and ʔasad), p. 37
- *al-hady* (Hijaz, ʔasad), *hadiyy* (The Tamīm and lowest of the Qays), p. 34.
- *al-qiṯṯāʔ* (Hijaz), *al-quṯṯāʔ* (Tamīm and some of the ʔasad), p. 25.
- *maxāḍ* (Hijaz, ʔasad), *mixāḍ* (Tamīm, Qays), p. 89.
- *laʕalla* (Hijaz), *laʕalli* (Some of ʔasad), p. 103.
- *niṣf* (Hijaz), *nuṣf* (ʔasad, Tamīm), p. 42.
- *ḥūb* (Hijaz), *ḥawb* (Tamīm), p. 54.
- *ʔaṯar* (Hijaz), *ʔiṯr* (Najd), p. 58.
- *min ʔaǧl* (Hijaz), *min ʔiǧl* (Tamīm), p. 62.
- *zaʕm* (Hijaz), *zuʕm* (ʔasad), *ziʕm* (some of Qays), p. 63.
- The contextual form of the first-person pronoun: *ʔana* (Hijaz), *ʔanā* (Arabs, Qays, Rabīʕah), p. 64.
- *iṯnatā ʕašrah* (Hijaz, ʔasad), *iṯnatā ʕaširah* (Rabīʕah b. Bizār, Tamīm), p. 24.

Cases where all readers agree on the non-Hijazi forms are rare. So far, I have only identified two cases:

- *ǧubullah* (Hijazi), al-Farrāʔ reports the reading of ʕāṣim and al-ʔaʕmaš is *ǧibillah*, p. 110. It is also the reading of the other readers.
- *baxalat* (Hijaz), *baxilat* (Arabs), p. 53. Consensus on *baxila*.

3.6 The Readings Are Intentionally Artificial

As we have seen above, none of the readings make up any single consistent linguistic system, nor do they show a clear signal of any one dialect of Arabic. Instead, they are an mix of different dialectal forms, distributed in a way from which no obvious pattern can be deduced. The linguistic character of the reading traditions appears to be the result of an artificial amalgamation of different features. In the following sections we will develop this further. We will argue that the irregular patterns we see are not just the result of—perhaps faulty—transmission, but that this configuration of exotic features was to some extent the express purpose of the readers. The lack of regular patterns in the application of sound laws as we saw in § 3.3 could be understood as the result of unintentional mixing. One may imagine that native varieties interfering with incomplete and conflicting reports on how to recite certain words in the context of a nascent grammatical theory could lead to such mixing, although the reasons and patterns cannot meaningfully be deduced from the reading traditions as they have come down to us.

However, this cannot account for all linguistic variation among the reading traditions. In several cases we find that certain general rules that are operative in the readings are highly dependent on Arabic grammatical theory. And it is difficult to imagine how users of the language could have employed these rules before the development of this theoretical framework. In other cases, we find examples of complex conditioning that is dependent not on grammatical theory but on the very structure of the text, keeping in mind strictly where the verse divisions are, for example. Finally, there are many cases of lexical specification of certain sound laws. In several cases, readers will follow a regular phonological rule, only to be broken a single time in a single word. In several cases this involves words that occur in their regular form elsewhere in the text.

Such features do not point to a genuine (and perhaps failed) attempt to transmit the Quran verbatim, as, for example Versteegh (1984, 10), following Beck (1945; 1946) claims the situation was in the first half of the 8th century CE. Rather, such features should be seen as a deliberate attempt at showcasing a reader's knowledge of the text and grammar, including complex structures not otherwise attested within the description of Arabic.

Many of the general principles that take place in the Quranic readings are only made possible because Arabic grammatical theory allows readers to formulate complex grammatically conditioned changes. But this does not mean that the Quranic readings fall within the purview of the descriptions of the Arab grammarians. While much, if not all, of the linguistic variation that we find in the Hadith and poetry fall within the possible variations described by the grammarians, the reading traditions very often have features and linguistic rules that transcend the boundaries of linguistic variation that the Arab grammarians describe.[36] Moreover, the readings often go beyond what we might expect to occur in natural language. In the following sections I will describe some of the artificial features as they are present in the Quranic reading traditions.

36 While this statement strikes me as true in principle, I warn the reader not to essentialize it too much. The Quranic readings have a complex and specialized oral and written tradition that keeps track of highly specific phonological and morphological rules that govern these readings. The Hadith and poetic corpus do not enjoy the same specialized tradition when it comes to communicating specific linguistic facts. It may very well be the case that these corpora also had linguistic features that go beyond what the grammarians describe; the incessant move towards classicizing these corpora as already pointed out by Rabin (1955, 21) to norms stricter than what the Arab grammarians allow, and more towards the

3.6.1 *The Dropping of the* Hamzah *by Warš*

Warš, one of the two canonical transmitters of Nāfiʕ, is well known for his frequent dropping of the *hamzah* with compensatory lengthening such as *yaʔkulu* > *yākulu*, *yastaʔxirūna* > *yastāxirūna* or with the replacement with a glide when the *hamzah* occurs intervocalically *yuʔaxxiru-hum* > *yuwaxxiru-hum*. Regular dropping of the *hamzah* is by no means unique to Warš. ʔabū Ǧaʕfar regularly and ʔabū ʕamr optionally drop any pre-consonantal *hamzah* (Ibn al-Ǧazarī, §1466; §1472–1474). However, the dropping of the *hamzah* of Warš' tradition is not universal. It exclusively applies to the *hamzah* when it is the first root consonant, thus he reads *yākulu* but *ar-raʔsu*; *mūmin* and *muwaḏḏinun* but *luʔluʔan* (Al-Dānī *taysīr*, 34; Ibn al-Ǧazarī, II, 1230f., 1240f.). The difference between first, second and third root consonants is a morphological one, and a concept that was known to medieval grammarians, but not something that we would expect to be a factor in natural language change. In historical linguistics, we consider language change as taking place on the phonological surface form, and being purely phonetically conditioned (Hock 1991, 34–51); this is not the case for Warš' dropping of the *hamzah*, as it is dependent on grammatical theory. This way of recitation therefore cannot have been introduced before the development of Arabic grammatical theory, and therefore cannot be projected back to manners of recitation among the first generations after the standardization of the Quran.

3.6.2 *The* ʔimālah *of Word-Final* Āri *Sequences*

A similar case of sound change dependent on grammatical theory is found with the raising of *ā* to *ē* (ʔabū ʕamr; al-Dūrī ʕan al-Kisāʔī; Ibn Ḏakwān ʕan Ibn ʕāmir) or *ǟ* (Warš ʕan Nāfiʕ) next to *ri*. This rule, which clearly represents a kind of *i*-umlaut, occurs for several different readers, but their principles all have one thing in common: *āri* only raises if the *r* is the third root consonant, or formulated differently: if *-i* is the vowel that marks the genitive case (al-Dānī *Taysīr*, 51; Ibn al-Ǧazarī, §2046–2062).

On the surface, this type of *ʔimālah* looks very similar to the *ʔimālah* involving *āri* as described by Sībawayh (see §2.2.2.1 and Sībawayh, IV 136ff., Sara 2007, 82ff.). While to Sībawayh the sequence *āri* is stronger than other sequences of *āCi*, and therefore can undergo *ʔimālah* for example if the preceding consonant is uvular or emphatic, it is clear from his description that those that have *ʔimālah* of the sequence *āri* also have it, for example, in *kātib* > *kētib*.

standard form of Classical Arabic make it very difficult to judge to what extent the material can be trusted. These corpora deserve an in-depth and careful study of their features too.

However, the readers that have this type of *ʔimālah* exclusively apply it with *āri*, and not with other sequences.

Even if one does not accept that *āri ʔimālah* applies only in dialects that have other forms of *ʔimālah* too (Sībawayh is not very explicit about this), the behaviour in the readings is still markedly different from what Sībawayh describes. While the genitive case vowel can indeed cause *ʔimālah* e.g. *min ʕawāri-hī* → *min ʕawēri-hī* 'from his blindness' and, *mina d-duʕāri* → *mina d-duʕēri* 'from dizziness', it is by no means the case that *only* the genitive *i* can be the cause of this *ʔimālah*, thus Sībawayh cites forms like *qārib* → *qērib* 'boat' and *ṭārid* → *ṭērid* 'expeller'.

For none of the Quranic readings however, such word-internal *āri ʔimālah*s take place. Thus we see *nārin* → *nērin* 'fire' (Q7:12; Q22:19; Q38:76; Q55:15, 35); *an-nahāri* → *an-nahēri* 'the day' (Q2:164) but not active participles like *laysa bi-xāriǧin* → ***laysa bi-xēriǧin* 'not coming out' (Q6:122), *al-wāriṯ* → ***al-wēriṯ* 'the heir' (Q2:233), or verbs like *yuḥāribūna* → ***yuḥēribūna* (Q5:33),[37] *ʔuwāriya* → ***ʔuwēriya* 'I hide' (Q5:31), or plurals like *mašāriqa al-ʔarḍi wa-maġāriba-hā* 'the eastern regions of the land and the western ones' (Q7:137). These are all forms that would undergo this development if we would follow Sībawayh's description. While one can envision that in such productive morphological patterns, the forms without *ʔimālah* might be analogically levelled to forms that are otherwise expected to undergo *ʔimālah*,[38] such an explanation cannot be invoked with all nouns that fail to undergo the *āri ʔimālah*. For example, *al-ḥawāriyyīna* (Q5:111) *al-ḥawāriyyūna* (Q5:112; Q61:14), *li-l-ḥawāriyyīna* (Q61:14) 'the disciples' is a unique noun formation due to its status as an Ethiopic loanword (< Gəʕəz *ḥäwari* 'traveler'). It seems that the *āri-ʔimālah* found among the readers is an artificial rule that requires a clearly developed grammatical theory. Those who apply need to distinguish when a certain sequence is a final root consonant, something that would not be possible without the formal linguistic model of the consonantal root.

The extent of grammatical thinking that is involved in the application of this rule becomes clear when we examine nouns with the exact same phonetic

37 Note however that prefix conjugation forms of *sāraʕa* 'to hasten' undergo *ʔimālah* in the reading of al-Dūrī ʕan al-Kisāʔī *yusēriʕūna* (Q3:114, 176; Q5:41, 52, 62; Q21:90; Q23:61), *nusēriʕu* (Q23:56) (Ibn al-Ǧazarī, §1980).

38 A development in the opposite direction is found in Maltese, for example, where all active participles undergo *ʔimālah*, even if they historically contain consonants that would have blocked it, e.g. *ħieles* 'being free' << *xāliṣ* on the pattern of *liebes* 'being dressed' < *lābis*, while lexicalized words of this pattern do have blocked *ʔimālah*: *ħakem* 'governor' < *ḥākim*.

shape with *āri* word-finally, but where the *-i* is not the genitive case vowel. A word like *al-ǧawāri* 'the ships' (Q42:32; Q55:24; Q81:16) is *not* included in this shift because it comes from the root √ǧry with a shortened final vowel, likewise it is not applied to *fa-lā tumāri* 'do not argue' (Q18:22) because the root is √mry. In other words, these readings make a distinction in the application of *ʔimālah* depending on whether the final *-i* is *ǧarr/xafḍ* (the inflectional *-i*) or *kasr* (the non-inflectional *-i*), and is thus morphologically rather than phonetically conditioned. This conditioning therefore does not look like a natural sound change, and moreover, falls outside the purview of what the Arab grammarians describe.

The other transmitter of al-Kisāʔī, ʔabū al-Ḥāriṯ has an even more specific conditioning for *āri-ʔimālah*. He only applies *ʔimālah* in these cases if the last root consonant is an *r* followed by the genitive *i*, but only if the root under consideration is a geminate root, so *al-ʔabrāri* → *al-ʔabrēri* but not *al-ʔaxbāri* → ***al-ʔaxbēri* (al-Dānī *Taysīr*, 51; Ibn al-Ǧazarī, III, 1676). Such specific conditioning of *ʔimālah* falls completely outside of the types of *ʔimālah* described by the Arab grammarians.

3.6.3 *Vowel Harmony of* -hum *in Ruways ʕan Yaʕqūb's Reading*

Another illustrative example where we see the reading traditions in dialogue with the grammatical tradition, leading to an artificial treatment of the pronominal suffixes is the one found in Ruways' transmission of Yaʕqūb. Yaʕqūb's basic rules shared between his two transmitters, Rawḥ and Ruways, already fall well outside of the kind of variation that Sībawayh and other grammarians describe. To the grammarians it is clear that *i*, *ī* and *ay* preceding either the singular or plural pronouns may trigger vowel harmony (yielding *-hi*, *-hī*, *-him*, *-himā*, etc.) or may be avoided, as is the Hijazi practice. Yaʕqūb, however, has a different kind of conditioning. For the 3rd person singular ending, the conditioning is harmonized as with all other readers if it follows *i*, *ī*, and *ay* (Ibn al-Ǧazarī, § 1210–1212). But for the plural, the conditioning is different and only *i* triggers vowel harmony.[39] Thus, one gets: *bi-hī*/*bi-him*, *fī-hi*/*fī-hum* and *ʕalay-hi*/*ʕalay-hum* (Ibn al-Ǧazarī, § 1120). This pattern is not described by the Arab grammarians, and is specific to this Quranic reading tradition.[40] It is difficult

39 Yaʕqūb's direct teacher, Sallām ʔabū al-Munḏir (d. 171/788) conditions the harmony of the singular in the same way as the plural, where only *i* but not *ay* and *ī* trigger vowel harmony (van Putten and Sidky forthcoming).

40 In fact, it is also attested in several other non-canonical Basran reading traditions, see van Putten & Sidky (forthcoming).

to envision such conditioning as a natural development. It rather seems to be a concerted effort of the reader to have an exotic and complex harmony rule.

Ruways takes this exotic conditioning even further. Because the apocopate of final weak verbs is envisioned in grammatical theory as shortened forms of the long imperfect stems, that is, *yaʔti* is considered a shortened form of *yaʔtī*, Ruways treats these forms as having a long vowel, and thus final weak apocopates block vowel harmony of *-hum*, while other cases of final *-i* do not, thus Ruways reads: *bi-him*, *bi-ḏanbi-him* but *lam yaʔti-hum* (Ibn al-Ǧazarī, § 1121). Making a morphological distinction between word-final *-i* that is part of an apocopate and that which is not. The vowel harmony is clearly dependent on Arabic grammatical theory and a model of the 'apocopate', and must be seen as artificial.

3.6.4 *Ḥafṣ' Anthology of Unusual Features*

Nowhere is the artifice of the Quranic reading traditions so apparent as in the readings of Ḥafṣ ʕan ʕāṣim. Ḥafṣ' general principles, grammar and morphology to a large extent agree with Classical Arabic. While this classical and standardized look is striking, it is even more striking that more than any other reader, Ḥafṣ' reading has a very specific and clearly calculated incorporation of single lexical items that break his general rules by incorporating a feature typical of other Quranic readings. Such features are used in determined places, usually only once and occasionally twice in the whole of the Quran. This clearly conscious, and we may even say playful, use of language was already observed in a footnote of an article by Laher (forthcoming), but it is worthwhile here to expand on this observation and give it a full description.

3.6.4.1 Ṣilat al-hāʔ (Q25:69)

A unique feature of the reading of Ibn Kaṯīr is that he has long vowels in the third person singular masculine pronoun *-hū*/*-hī* which are not shortened after a heavy syllable as we find it among the other readers. While Ḥafṣ follows the general practice of shortening of the *-hū*/*-hī* after a heavy syllable, he has a single exception, namely in Q25:69 he reads فيه 'in it' not as *fī-hi* as he does in the 129 other occurrences of this word, but as *fī-hī* (Ibn al-Ǧazarī, § 1212).

3.6.4.2 III-y ʔimālah (Q11:41)

Unlike the other Kufans, Ḥamzah, Xalaf and al-Kisāʔī, ʕāṣim does not regularly have *ʔimālah* for III-*y* verbs and nouns. Ḥafṣ, however, makes a single exception to this, namely in the word *maǧrē-hā* 'its course' in Sūrat Hūd (Q11:41) (Ibn al-Ǧazarī, § 1992).

3.6.4.3 Softening of Second *Hamzah* of Two Subsequent *Hamzahs* (Q41:44)

It is typical of the Kufans and Ibn ʕāmir to not weaken the *hamzah* when two vowelled *hamzah*s follow each other; This is different from the other readers which lose the second *hamzah*, and instead create a hiatus (*tashīl al-hamzah*). Hence, Ḥamzah, al-Kisāʔī, Xalaf, ʕāṣim and Ibn ʕāmir all read Q2:6 *ʔa-ʔanḏartahum* 'do you warn them?', where the other readers read *ʔa-anḏartahum, ʔā-anḏartahum* or even *ʔānḏartahum* (Warš) (Ibn al-Ǧazarī §1384–1387). However, Ḥafṣ, unlike the other Kufans, makes a single exception: he reads Q41:44 as *ʔa-aʕǧamiyyun* with hiatus (Ibn al-Ǧazarī §1394).

3.6.4.4 Muttum instead of Mittum (Q3:157, 158)

There is disagreement among the readers on how the verb *māta* 'to die' should be treated in the short stem of the suffix conjugation. Ibn Kaṯīr, ʔabū ʕamr, Ibn ʕāmir and Šuʕbah ʕan ʕāṣim all read it with a *ḍammah*, that is *muttum, muttu, mutnā* whenever they occur; On the other hand, Ḥamzah, al-Kisāʔī, and Nāfiʕ read it as *mittum, mittu* and *mitnā* whenever they occur. Ḥafṣ generally follows the *i*-norm, but in the two attestations in Sūrat ʔāl ʕimrān (Q3:157, 158), he chooses to use the *u*-norm instead *muttum* instead (Ibn al-Ǧazarī, §2881).

3.6.4.5 Unharmonized -hu (Q18:63; Q48:10)

All canonical readers are in agreement that after *i, ī* and *ay* the third person masculine pronoun should undergo vowel harmony and be reflected as *-hi* (or *-hī* for Ibn Kaṯīr). While Ḥafṣ usually just applies vowel harmony as expected, he has two exceptions, one after *ī* and one after *ay*: *mā ʔansā-nī-hu* 'he did not make me forget it' (Q18:63) and *ʕalay-hu* 'upon it' (Q48:10) (Ibn al-Ǧazarī, §1212).[41]

3.6.4.6 III-y/w Apocopates/Imperatives Followed by the 3sg.m. Pronoun

As we will see in §7.1.8, there is disagreement between the readers on how to treat the vocalization of the 3sg.m. clitic pronoun when it follows an apocopate or imperative of a III-*y/w* verb. Ḥafṣ as a general rule follows the Classical Arabic rule, which simply uses the long pronouns *-hī* after *-i* and *-hū* after *-a*, e.g. *yuʔaddi-hī* 'he returns it' (Q3:75), *lam yara-hū* 'he did not see it' (Q90:7). Other readers either have shortened pronouns *-hu/-hi*, or have a fully unvocalized pronominal form *-h*. Ḥafṣ however has occasional exceptions to this

41 A few other readers have a similar lack of harmony in a few cases. Ḥamzah reads *li-ʔahli-hu mkuṯū* (Q20:10; Q28:29) and in the transmission of al-ʔaṣbahānī for Warš ʕan Nāfiʕ we find *bi-hu nẓur* (Q6:46) (Ibn al-Ǧazarī, §1232).

general rule, instead following the practices of other readers. So, he reads *fa-ʔalqi-h* 'so deliver it!' (Q27:28), *ʔarǧi-h* 'postpone him' (Q7:111; Q26:36) without a final vowel (typical of ʔabū Ǧaʕfar, ʔabū ʕamr, Šuʕbah ʕan ʕāṣim), *yarḍa-hu* 'he likes it' (Q39:7) with a short vowel (typical of Qālūn ʕan Nāfiʕ and Yaʕqūb). Moreover, he uniquely reads *yattaq-hi* 'he fears him' (Q24:52) with dropping of the apocopate vowel, and a following pronoun still harmonized as if the preceding vowel was present. None of the canonical reading traditions show that behaviour, and it is irregular in his reading as well (Ibn al-Ǧazarī, § 1217).

3.6.4.7 Conclusion

These features listed above are isolated in the transmission of Ḥafṣ, and they are moreover unique among the transmitters of ʕāṣim. Neither Šuʕbah nor the extensively described non-canonical transmitter al-Mufaḍḍal have such a wide collection of 'one-off' exceptions to their general rules. It therefore seems that these isolated readings by Ḥafṣ are innovations introduced by him, and should probably be considered conscious 'homages' to other readings that were around in his lifetime, showing off not only his knowledge of grammar but also the knowledge of linguistic variation present in the Quranic reading traditions.

3.6.5 *Plural Pronouns of Warš*

Sībawayh (IV, 191) and al-Farrāʔ (*Luġāt*, 33), and with them many other grammarians (see van Putten and Sidky forthcoming) are in agreement that the plural masculine pronouns such as *hum*, *ʾantum*, *-tum*, *-hum*, *-kum* may optionally be followed by a long vowel *-ū*.[42] Both grammarians present this as this basically being a free option, and in poetry we indeed find both forms used within the same text, as the meter requires it. Some of the canonical readers regularly have these lengthened forms. This appears to have been typical for the reading traditions of the Hijaz. Both ʔabū Ǧaʕfar and Ibn Kaṯīr use it regularly (see Ibn al-Ǧazarī, § 1122). For Nāfiʕ, Ibn Muǧāhid (108 f.) reports that Qālūn (and along with him, now non-canonical transmitters such as ʔismāʕīl b. Ǧaʕfar, Ibn Ǧammāz and al-Musayyabī) all optionally pronounced it either in the short or long form. ʔaḥmad b. Qālūn ← Qālūn said "Nāfiʕ used to find no fault in

42 An outstanding question is how these long pronominal forms should be understood in light of comparative Semitic evidence. While most Semitic languages have the short forms of these pronouns, Ancient South Arabian generally attests long forms (but occasionally short forms are attested), as does Gəʕəz and Akkadian. The situation reported for Classical Arabic, which seems to have both forms, is not detailed enough to recover how these forms relate to one another.

adding the vowel to the *mīm*." From which Ibn Muǧāhid concludes that Nāfiʕ's original reading was without the vowel, and he reports that he himself reads in this way.

Warš, however, uses both the long and short forms of the pronominal suffixes, and these are phonetically conditioned: Whenever a *ʔ* immediately follows, Warš uses the long forms (Ibn al-Ǧazarī, § 1123; Ibn Muǧāhid 108 f.). While this conditioning is purely phonetic it is not altogether easy to recover what exactly would have caused this. Even if we assume that the Proto-Arabic form was **-humu* etc. there is nothing about a *ʔ* in the following word that would cause it to be lengthened, nor is its absence an obvious reason for syncopation. It seems rather that Warš made the explicit choice to incorporate both options condoned by Nāfiʕ and constructed this condition in order to be able to accommodate both options in a single recitation, where, when reciting in the transmission of Qālūn, one chooses either for the long or the short forms of the pronouns.

A distinct euphonic motivation of this choice by Warš must certainly be considered.[43] Warš' recitation is well-known for its excessive use of overlong vowels. Overlong vowels (*madd*) in Tajwīd are applied by all readers to long vowels that precede *hamzah* and *shaddah* (*samāāʔu, aḍ-ḍāāllīna*) (Ibn al-Ǧazarī § 1234–1238). Warš, together with Ḥamzah, is said to have had the longest overlong vowels (al-Dānī *Taysīr*, 30). Unlike all other readers, Warš also lengthens long vowels if they are *preceded* by *hamzah*, thus yielding *ʔāādamu* (versus the rest *ʔādamu*) (al-Dānī *Taysīr*, 31), and even to diphthongs followed by *hamzah*, e.g. *šayyyyʔun* and *sawwwwʔata* (al-Dānī *taysīr*, 72). Moreover, unlike some other readers (Ibn Kaṯīr, Qālūn (with disagreement) and as-Sūsī do not do this), Warš would also lengthen long vowels if the *hamzah* is the beginning of the next word, thus *māā ʔunzila*. All of these features give the recitation of Warš a very distinct stretched out sound compared to all other readers. Due to Warš' application of overlong vowels if the next word starts with a *hamzah*, Warš' specific conditioning of the long pronouns to only appear before *hamzah* gives him yet another opportunity to apply his signature *madd*.

Therefore, Warš seems to have adapted available linguistic options but has reconfigured them in a way that seems to have been unique to Quranic recitation. While descriptions of the reading traditions use the same terminology and categories as the grammarians, the phonological and morphological phenomena that are found go far beyond what we find in the descriptions of the grammarians. Therefore, if we are to accept that the Quranic readings really

43 I thank Hythem Sidky for suggesting this to me.

did form subsystems of the *ʕarabiyyah*, it was either not considered eloquent enough to be considered *ʕarabiyyah* by the grammarians, or the grammarians were woefully incomplete. Considering both the high regard for these readings and the breadth of knowledge displayed by the earlier grammarians, neither scenario should be considered particularly plausible.

This is an important point: while the descriptions of the reading traditions use the same terminology and categories as the grammarians, and are able to describe the variation found in the readings within this framework, at no point do the descriptions of the reading traditions invoke the mention of dialects that may have had the same system as these readings. Similarly, grammarians never describe such patterns of pronominal use as found in, for example, the reading of Warš as acceptable (or unacceptable) for the *ʕarabiyyah*. This system stands on its own, separate from the grammatical theory of Arabic, going beyond what is considered the "regular" *ʕarabiyyah* that the grammarians would comment upon.

3.6.6 *Features Dependent on the Structure of the Text*

Besides the features discussed above that mix and match phonological and morphological features in clearly artificial ways from a historical linguistic point of view, there are several cases where the reading traditions specifically rely on the structure of the text, which seems to be designed to show off the in-depth knowledge of this text.

3.6.6.1 ʔabu ʕamr's Phonemic Contrast of Ā and Ā̈

ʔabū ʕamr's *ʔimālah* of III-*y* verbs and nouns is another clear example of the Quranic readings not being interpretable as the outcome of natural language change, as it is dependent on which position in the verse a word occurs. While ʔabū ʕamr usually merges the *ʔalif maqṣūrah*s of III-*y* versus III-*w* stems and etymological **ā* (whereas other readers such as al-Kisāʔī, Ḥamzah and Warš ʕan Nāfiʕ always keep them distinct), he keeps them distinct exclusively in verse-final position—which by extension accommodates the rhyme of several Sūrahs that rhyme in Quranic Arabic /-ē/, for example, prominently Q20, Q53, and Q91. Whenever a III-*y* verb or noun occurs at the end of a verse, it is pronounced with *ā̈* (Ibn al-Ǧazarī, § 1986).[44]

It is not uncommon for specific sound changes to take place only in pausal position. This is even fairly common among the modern Arabic dialects. For

44 There are also transmitters of al-ʔazraq ← Warš ← Nāfiʕ that only uses *ā̈* in verse final position, and not elsewhere (Ibn al-Ǧazarī, § 2017, § 2022–2023).

example, we find palatalization of *$^{*}t$* in Shammari (van Putten 2017b), glottalization in Sanaani (Watson and Heselwood 2016) and vowel lengthening in Levantine dialects (Fischer and Jastrow 1980, 179) all taking place specifically in pause. However, in the case of ʔabū ʕamr's reading we are not dealing with a sound change that takes place in this position, but rather the absence of merger in this position, while the two sounds merge in other positions.[45]

A lack of a merger of a phonemic contrast in pause, while the merger is found in all other positions is rare cross-linguistically. The only other parallel that comes to mind, where however it has become a part of morphology, rather than a phonemic contrast that is retained, is found in another reading tradition of a holy text, namely that of Biblical Hebrew. There, stressed short vowels in pause get lengthened to long vowels. This lengthening precedes certain later stress shifts that took place, and therefore historical vowels that are lost elsewhere show up as long vowels in pause (Suchard 2019, 115 ff.). However, in Hebrew such pause-conditioned variants have mostly morphologized and do not generally revive phonemic contrasts lost everywhere else.[46] Suchard (2019, 115) expresses doubt that this kind of contrast could have been obtained in natural speech where such contrasts would have quickly been leveled by analogy. I agree with this assessment, and by extension it is particularly difficult to imagine that ʔabū ʕamr's results from natural language use, as he retains a phonemic contrast only in rhyme position, and nowhere else.

Even if the reciter chooses to not pause at the end of the verse, the contrast needs to be maintained, and pausing on non-verse final recommended pauses of III-*y* nouns or verbs does not cause them to be read with *ā̆*. The phonemic distinction introduced by ʔabū ʕamr, then, is specifically conditioned by the structure of the text, making a distinction between verse-final pauses and other types of pauses. This should probably be understood as a conscious awareness of ʔabū ʕamr (or perhaps his main transmitter al-Yazīdī) to harmonize the clear end rhyme in /ē/ of some of the Sūrahs (van Putten 2017a, 57 f.), while otherwise maintaining a preference for merging the two sounds into a single *ā*—perhaps

---

45 There are in fact a few other positions where ʔabū ʕamr retains the contrast. Namely in the case of feminine nouns with the shape Ca/i/uCCā̆, and whenever the consonant preceding it is *r*, in which case it is pronounced as *ē* (see Ibn al-Ǧazarī, § 1986, § 2032). These too can hardly be considered regular outcomes of sound change, and present situations beyond what the grammarians discuss.

46 The occasional distinction between *CaCC- and *CiCC- nouns that have merged in non-pausal independent position being the only clear example of an ancient phonemic contrast occasionally resurfacing, e.g. *kɛsɛp̄* 'silver' in pause *kåsɛp̄* (< **kasp-*), but *ṣɛdɛq* 'righteousness' in pause *ṣɛdɛq* (< **ṣidq-*). But these too often gets levelled out, thus *rɛḡɛl* 'leg', is *råḡɛl* in pause, despite coming from **rigl-* not ***ragl-*.

anticipating the trend that has led to the now standard form of Classical Arabic which does not have a distinction between these vowels.

3.6.6.2 The Verse-Penultimate Conditioning of Qutaybah and Nuṣayr ʕan al-Kisāʔī

Two transmitters of al-Kisāʔī that do not make it into the two-*rāwī* canon but are nevertheless described in quite some detail in more extensive works like al-Dānī's *Ǧāmiʕ al-Bayān* and Ibn Mihrān's *al-Ġāyah* and *al-Mabsūṭ* are Qutaybah and Nuṣayr (Ibn Mihrān *Ġāyah*, 141 f.; *al-Mabsūṭ*, 89). Both of these transmitters, unlike the canonical transmitters of al-Kisāʔī, make use of the long forms of the plural pronouns. There are some minor differences, especially in the precision of the description, between al-Dānī's *Ǧāmiʕ* and Ibn Mihrān's works. I will limit myself to the description of al-Dānī (*Ǧāmiʕ*, 160 ff.).

For Nuṣayr, the plural pronoun is eligible for the use of long pronouns:

A. If it is unharmonized, i.e. *-hum* does not follow *-i-*, *-ī-* or *-ay-*. Non harmonizing pronouns like *-kum* are therefore not affected by this condition.
B. If the word it is attached to consists of five letters or fewer as written in the *Muṣḥaf* (but he did not count *wa-* and *ʔa-* as part of the word for this count). The independent pronouns *ʾantum* and *hum* are of course not affected by this condition.

If these two conditions apply, then Nuṣayr uses the long pronouns:

1. If a word beginning with an *m* directly follows (e.g. *wa-min-**humū** man yaqūl*, Q9:49 but not *wuǧūhu-hum muswaddah*, Q39:60 because وجوههم is six letters).
2. If a word beginning with a *hamzah* directly follows (e.g. *wa-ʾiḏā qūla la-**humū** ʾanfiqū*, Q36:47 but not *wa-ʾa-ʾanḏarta-hum ʾam lam*, Q2:6 because وانذرتهم is 6 or 7 letters).
3. It is directly followed by the last word of the Aya (e.g. *wa-bi-l-ʾāxirati **humū** yūqinūn#*, Q2:4 but not *razaqnā-hum yunfiqūn#*, Q2:3 because رزقنهم is six letters)

For the last of these three conditions an intervening one letter word such as *wa-*, *bi-* or *fa-* is not considered an intervening word, thus one reads *fa-kubkibū fīhā **humū** wa-l-ġāwūn#* (Q26:94).

While Qutaybah's treatment is similar, it is less complex. Condition A applies, but B does not. And only conditions 2 and 3 apply, but 1 does not. Moreover, no short words may intervene in the last word of the verse and the pronoun (e.g. *mimmā razaqnā-**humū** yunfiqūn#*, Q2:3 but *fa-kubkibū fīhā **hum** wa-l-ġāwūn#*, Q26:94).

These two practices of transmission require and showcase intimate knowledge of the text, and a condition which would be impossible to achieve in any form of natural language. So, for example, verses 5 and 6 of Q107 are read: *(a)lladīna* ***hum*** *ʕan ṣalāti-****him*** *sāhūn(a)* # *(a)lladīna* ***humū*** *yurāʕūn(a)* #. And for example Q40:16 *yawma hum bārizūn(a)* is not read with a long pronoun because *bārizūn(a)* is only the end of the verse in the Damascene verse count and not in the Kufan verse count (Spitaler 1935, 56).

3.7 The Choices of the Canonical Readers

With the large amount of variation found in the readings, many variations of which are difficult to understand as the result of natural language change, one comes to wonder what the reasons for this mixed status would be. It might be tempting to see, for example, Ḥafṣ' reading of unharmonized *-hu* in *ʔansānī-hu* and *ʕalay-hu ḷḷāh* (§ 3.6.4.5) as coming from a report that said "Ḥafṣ would recite words such as *ʔansānī-hu* and *ʕalay-hu ḷḷāh* with *-hu* instead of *-hi*", and in an overzealous attempt to apply the rule as accurately as possible, the transmitter would have applied it to *only* the words mentioned, rather than generalize it to its full implication as was intended by our hypothetical report.[47]

However, in most cases I am disinclined towards an interpretation of faulty or incomplete transmission to be the reason for the irregularities that we find to have taken place between the period of the canonical readers and when the readings were first described in detail, as it seems that the transmission from the canonical readers up until Ibn Muǧāhid is quite accurate. This can be confirmed independently for several of the readers. While before Ibn Muǧāhid we have no extant complete transmissions of the canonical readings, we do have early reports of these readings in works not primarily concerned with the reading traditions.

Al-Farrāʔ (d. 209 AH), a direct student of al-Kisāʔī (d. 189 AH), and thus also a younger contemporary of Šuʕbah (d. 194 AH) and a generation removed from Ḥamzah (d. 156 AH) often reports on the readings of these three reciters (in the case of Šuʕbah invariably just referred to as the reading of ʕāṣim (d. 127 AH)) in his *Maʕānī al-Qurʔān* and *Luġāt al-Qurʔān*. His reports in these works are

47 Rabin (1951, 99, §f) seems to have understood a report in the generalized sense rather than the specific, as he claims that Ḥafṣ read without vowel harmony fairly consistently. Something not claimed in the classical literature, to my knowledge. While I have been unable to consult the edition of *hamʕ al-hawāmiʕ fī šarḥ jamʕ al-jawāmiʕ* that he references, the only attestation of Ḥafṣ in this book indeed discusses his lack of harmony but certainly not as a general rule, but simply the two known places only as discussed in § 3.6.4.5. (al-Suyūṭī *hamʕ al-hawāmiʕ*, I, 196).

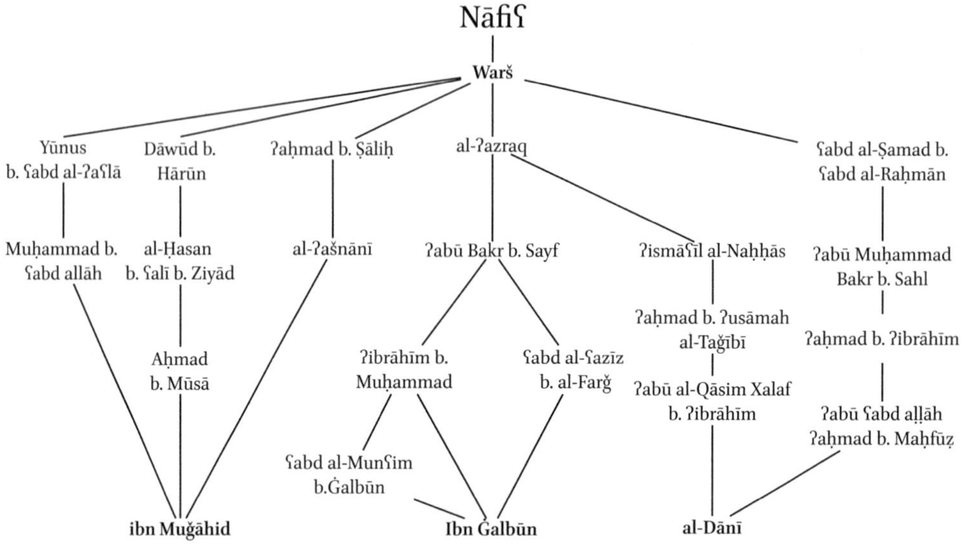

FIGURE 2 *ʔisnād*s of Warš from different medieval authors

almost always in line with what Ibn Muǧāhid reports, while none of his *ʔisnāds* to these readers go through al-Farrāʔ. This lends significant credibility to the accuracy of the transmission. Likewise, Ibn Muǧāhid and later authors like al-Dānī, Ibn Ġalbūn or Ibn al-Ǧazarī frequently have independent paths to the transmitters without this resulting in massive disagreement among these works.[48]

In some cases, we can pinpoint an innovation with accuracy, such as Warš' lengthening of the plural pronouns exclusively before words with a *hamzah* (§ 3.6.5). Examining the ʔisnāds of Ibn Muǧāhid (89, 91), Ibn Ġalbūn (*al-tad̲kirah*, 18 f.) and al-Dānī (*al-taysīr*, 11) we see that the three authors have fairly independent transmissions back to Warš, and all invariably report this same conditioning. This leaves little doubt that indeed Warš was the innovator of this system, and not someone further down his transmission path.

In other cases, it is not always possible to be certain whether a transmitter innovated or not. For example, Ḥafṣ reads the word *raʔūf* with a long vowel whenever it occurs, whereas Šuʕbah reads *raʔuf*. Both transmitters trace their reading back to ʕāṣim, so how do we decide which reading ʕāṣim *actually* read? We might rely on outside factors, such as the fact that all other Kufans also read

48 The overall soundness of transmission of the readings is affirmed, although not exactly demonstrated, by Nasser (2013b, 136) as well.

raʔuf to consider Ḥafṣ' reading to be the innovative one, while Šuʕbah's is the original as it is more typically Kufan. But it is fairly easy to turn that argument on its head: one could argue that Šuʕbah's reading was influenced by the other Kufans around him, whereas Ḥafṣ retained the original reading.[49]

Modern Muslim orthodoxy tries to reconcile cases where the transmitters disagree by asserting that the eponymous reader must have taught both options (As-Said 1975, 91–93). While this is often just used as a convenient excuse for resolving the issue of conflicting readings, there is of course no reason to think that an eponymous reader did not, indeed read certain words in different ways on different occasions or changed their mind during their career as teacher. Whatever is the case, specific variants can only seldomly be rationalized as the result of faulty transmission.

When we turn to the eponymous readers themselves, we quickly lose the ability to gain insight into the development of different options. In some cases, eponymous readers stand in a teacher-student relationship such as ʔabū Jaʕfar → Nāfiʕ; Ibn Kaṯīr → ʔabū ʕamr; and Ḥamzah → al-Kisāʔī; Ḥamzah → Sulaym b. ʕīsā → Xalaf. These relationships help us understand similarities between the readers; all these teacher-student relations show up as obvious similarities of specific word choices when we compare their readings (see Sidky forthcoming; Melchert 2008). However, it is difficult to recover any reason for the differences they have in their linguistic systems. Why, for example, do al-Kisāʔī and Xalaf simply apply vowel harmony to *ʕalay-him*, *ʔilay-him* and *laday-him*, unlike Ḥamzah? Why did their teacher choose to not apply harmony in only those three words?

All of these readers had more teachers than just the canonical readers, and some of the variation and irregularity is probably to be attributed to this fact. Presented with multiple teachers, each teaching different options, a reader was tasked with deciding themselves which form they considered to be the most correct and most eloquent. Such choices would probably not always have been made through purely linguistic reasoning, but the exact methods through which this happened are mostly unrecoverable.

One might envision, for example, the case of Ḥamzah's unique *i*-umlaut *ʔimālah* of *ḍiʕēfan*, that one of the teachers of Ḥamzah transmitted to him a report that the prophet used to recite "*wa-l-yaxša llaḏīna law takrahū min xalfi-him ḏurīyyatan ḍiʕēfan xēfū ʕalayhum fa-l-yattaqù ḷḷāha wa-l-yaqūlū qawlan*

49 This may, in fact, be made plausible by the fact that Ibn Muǧāhid brings a transmission of al-Kisāʔī ← Šuʕbah that he did in fact read *raʔūf* and not *raʔuf*, despite al-Kisāʔī reading *raʔuf* himself (Ibn Muǧāhid, 171).

sadīdan (Q4:9)" which could have been an accurate transmission of *i*-umlaut or perhaps the result of the transmitter speaking with affected recitation due to his own dialect having *i*-umlaut. Not wanting to misrepresent this alleged prophetic reading, Ḥamzah would have piously inserted the *i*-umlaut of *ḍiʕē-fan* into his own recitation, without further thinking or analysing the broader implication of *i*-umlaut being present in this word out of conservatism. While such a hypothetical scenario is not necessarily unrealistic, it does not seem possible to recover why a reciter chose the forms he chose, and what other options he had access to.

One interesting and rare case where the tradition gives us a direct piece of insight into the selection procedure of readings is found with Nāfiʕ. His method of constructing his reading is reported by Ibn Muǧāhid (61f.), who says that Nāfiʕ said: "I looked to what two among them [his teachers] agreed upon, and I adopted it [in reading], and if any was alone [in reading a certain word], I removed it, until I had constructed this reading made up of these aspects."[50] Such a method as laid out by Nāfiʕ makes sense of the mixed linguistic nature of this reading, even if the teachers that he drew his data from all had fully regular and natural readings—which they likely did not, as they themselves may have had similar methods of constructing their reading.

From the very earliest transmissions of the reading traditions, we find that they already contain a collection of different dialectal features. Some of these features can be considered clear and conscious innovations, but many of them are likely the result of a similar 'construction' of different features as the parameters of the eloquent *ʕarabiyyah* were being negotiated by different readers. The mixed character did not come about through faulty transmission in between the time that the readers were active and when the readings were canonized. This mixed form seems quite reliably attributable to the eponymous readers that they are said to represent. As can be seen from Nāfiʕ's reported method of constructing his reading, the primary concern of the canonical readers was not to transmit a consistent linguistic system, but rather to construct a reading containing eloquent features by whatever standard they considered it to be eloquent. A standard which, more often than not, was probably not a linguistically motivated one.

50 *Fa-naẓartu ʔilā mā ǧtamaʕa ʕalayhi ṯnāni minhum fa-ʔaxaḏtuhū, wa-mā šaḏḏa fīhi wāḥidun taraktuhū, ḥattā ʔallaftu hāḏihi l-qirāʔata fī hāḏihi l-ḥurūf.*

3.8 Conclusion

In this chapter we have examined the language of the Quranic reading traditions. While it is often accepted as a truism that the language of the Quran is Classical Arabic, actually examining this statement reveals subtleties that cannot be glossed over if we want to examine what the language of the Quran really is. Looking at the language of the reading traditions it is clear that the answer is not so simple. The tradition presents us with 20 different answers to what the language of the Quran really is.

Second, looking closer, we find that none of these readings represent anything like natural language, or in fact any kind of language described by the Arab grammarians. Regular sound changes that are described in great detail by the Arab grammarians fail to apply with any consistency in the Quranic reading traditions. As such, none of the readings can be considered 'dialects of Arabic', nor in fact any form of natural language.

While the reasons for these irregularities are not always recoverable, it is clear that the artificial nature of the readings is not just the result of incomplete or faulty transmission of the 'true' language of the Quran. The readings in many cases embrace artificial features for a certain artistic effect, which suggests a conscious attempt of the readers to beautify their recitation with unusual and exotic features.

Nöldeke (1910, 2) already remarked on this well over a century ago, he feels that one can still recover the true language below this, saying that "among these reading traditions there are certain things that were more or less alien to living language. The oriental has the tendency to artificially ornament the solemn recitation of their holy texts; [...] But the real language shines through everywhere."[51] I believe that Nöldeke's confidence that the real language shines through everywhere is not borne out by the evidence. Due to these artificial features, it is not altogether obvious that we can recover the "language of the Quran" through reflection on the Quranic reading traditions. None of them form a consistent system (as also noted by Nöldeke et al. 2013, 543), and it is unclear which layers of artifice and irregularity one should remove to get to the "true" language of the Quran, and which ones to keep. The early grammarians like Sībawayh and al-Farrāʔ, active around the same period as the early transmitters of the readers, likewise fail to give a unified answer to what this "real

51 Unter diesen Lesarten ist sicher manches, was der lebenden Sprache mehr oder weniger fremd war. Der Orientale neigt dazu, den feierlichen Vortrag heiliger Texte künstlich zu gestalten; das taten auch die Juden und die Syrer. Aber die wirkliche Sprache blickt doch überall durch.

language" would have been exactly (see chapter 2). So, the gaps that the removal of the "artificial ornaments" would yield—provided we could confidently identify all of them—cannot simply be filled with a unified answer coming from the data of the grammarians.

Moreover, even if it would be somehow possible to filter out from the material of the grammarians which parts of their description represents Nöldeke's "real language", we would still have to accept that the grammarians' conception of this "real language"—living more than 150 years after the rise of Islam—would be an accurate representation of what the "real language" was felt to be at the time of composition. I do not believe that this is convincingly demonstrated by anyone.

What is clear, however, is that contrary to the common conception that the *ʕarabiyyah* is based on eastern dialects, whenever the readers agree on a feature, they primarily converge upon forms that are said to be Hijazi by the Arab grammarians. If anything is to be gained from the readings to inform us about what language the Quran represents, the answer would seem to be that at its core there seems to be traces of a Hijazi dialect, and that this is what shines through if we were to remove Nöldeke's "artificial ornaments".

It seems that the reading traditions cannot give us a more accurate understanding of what the language of the Quran would be, as they are clearly not trying to accurately represent its original language. The only aspect of the Quran that can certainly be projected back to the very beginning of the Islamic period with little to no change is the Quranic Consonantal Text. This therefore functions as the only direct source of the language of the Quran. The QCT as a source of linguistic information will be examined in the next chapter.

CHAPTER 4

The Quranic Consonantal Text: Morphology

أَمَّا أَهْلُ ٱلْحِجَازِ فَيَقُولُونَ ﴿ذَٰلِكَ﴾ بِاللَّامِ وَبِهِ جَاءَ ٱلْكِتَابُ فِي كُلِّ ٱلْقُرْآنِ

AL-FARRĀʔ, *Kitāb fīh Luġāt al-Qurʔān*

∴

4.1 Introduction

In the previous section we have shown that when looking to answer the question what the language of the Quran is, the reading traditions fail to give a consistent answer. They are linguistically diverse, none of them look like natural language, and they must be considered to be a concerted effort to beautify the recitation of the Quran through the use of exotic linguistic features from a variety of different dialects, augmented with completely innovative forms that do not seem to have been part of anyone's natural speech. These reading traditions take shape with the eponymous readers, and it is difficult to see further back than these readers through internal reflection.

However, there is a source of the Quran that carries linguistic information that does go back to the very first decades of Islam: the written text itself. In recent years it has become clear that virtually every early Quranic manuscript that we have access to today goes back to a single archetypal copy (Cook 2004; Sinai 2014a; 2014b; van Putten 2019c). The dating of these manuscripts is so early that a date much later than the date attributed to it by the Islamic tradition (that is, during the reign of ʕuṯmān b. ʕaffān, 644–656 CE) is quite difficult to envision. This primary source, while written in a highly defective script still carries a lot of linguistic information that we can likewise date back to this early period: the spelling is not random, but forms a clear system. This orthography must be seen as an important source of linguistic data, and its frequent deviations from the later standard Classical Arabic orthography can give us important insights into the nature of the language and how it differs from Classical Arabic. Moreover, as the Quran is a rhymed text, we receive a unique insight into some phonological features of the language which are not easily recoverable from other texts from this period, such as the early Islamic papyri.

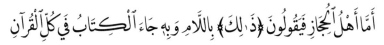

In a series of papers, I have already explored what the QCT can tell us about the phonology and nominal morphology of Quranic Arabic (van Putten forthcoming; 2017a; 2017b; 2018; 2019b; van Putten and Stokes 2018). What has not yet been explored, however, is the historical linguistic affiliation of Quranic Arabic. What morphological and phonological isoglosses does Quranic Arabic have? And how does it relate to pre-Islamic Arabic varieties as found in the epigraphic record and dialects as reported by the Arab grammarians?

Throughout modern Arabist literature, we find many statements that suggest that the Quran was written in a kind of mixed dialect, drawing freely from different dialects—much in the way as the Arabic poetry. The idea that the Quran was written in a mixed dialect seems to ultimately originate from the medieval Islamic tradition, but received its modern articulation in Chaim Rabin's monumental work on the Ancient West Arabian dialects where he stated with some confidence that the Quran was composed in the 'poetic koine' (Rabin 1951, 3 f.).[1] Rabin admits that the form of the poetic koiné used in the Hijaz may have had a local pronunciation, primarily, having lost the glottal stop as reflected in the orthography (Rabin 1951, 4 f.). However he tells us that "in morphology, on the other hand, an almost complete conformity with the 'Arabiyya' could be achieved" (Rabin 1951, 4). The claim then, is that morphologically we should be able to see that the text of the Quran adheres to the 'Classical Arabic' speech norms as opposed to the local dialect of the Hijaz.

This chapter will examine the morphological features of Quranic Arabic as reflected in the QCT, while the next chapter will tackle its phonological features. These features will be compared against the reports of the Arab grammarians as well as the linguistic data found in epigraphic pre-Islamic Arabic. From this discussion it will become clear that whenever the QCT allows us to identify linguistic features it almost universally agrees with what the Arab grammarians attributed to the dialect of the Hijaz, and as such Quranic Arabic should be understood as a reflex of a Hijazi Arabic vernacular and not "Classical Arabic". Moreover, frequently we will see that a large amount of the relevant isoglosses visible in the epigraphic record clearly point away from a northern origin, and on occasion give clear evidence that the isoglosses present in the QCT are an innovation typical for Hijazi Arabic.

In Al-Jallad's (2020b) revolutionary work on the Damascus Psalm fragment, he already listed several morphological features which appear to form unique Hijazi innovations in comparison to forms of Old Arabic found in Northern

1 Rabin (1955, 24) credits Fleisch (1947, 97–101), and Blachère (1947, 159–169) for coming to this conclusion independently from him that the Quran was composed in the poetic *koiné*. Neither author is much more informative as to what this elusive poetic *koiné* entails.

varieties such as Safaitic, Hismaic and Nabataean Arabic. These isoglosses occur in Quranic Arabic as well, and as such, the language of the Damascus Psalm fragment and the Quranic Arabic are closely related to each other. Some of the isoglosses that can be identified as Hijazi innovations from the epigraphic record are also identified as typically Hijazi isoglosses by the Arab grammarians, and there are yet other isoglosses identified by the Arab grammarians for which not as much evidence has been found in the epigraphic record yet. In the following section we will look at morphological isoglosses present in Quranic Arabic as can be gleaned from the QCT which can either be compared to the epigraphic record, or those reported by Sībawayh and al-Farrāʔ (or both). Whenever relevant, I will also cite the discussion of isoglosses that are discussed by Rabin (1951).

4.2 The *ʔalla*- Base Relative Pronoun

Quranic Arabic forms its relative pronoun on a base *ʔalla*- followed by deictic elements *ʔalla-ḏī, ʔalla-tī, ʔalla-ḏīn* etc. This form is innovative in relation to the ancient Semitic relative pronoun *ḏū*, a relative pronoun which continued to exist in Quranic Arabic with a more restricted possessive meaning 'possessor of …', e.g. ذوا فضل /ḏū faḍl/ 'possessor of favour'. This innovation is also acknowledged by Rabin (1951, 154).

The *ḏ*-base relative pronoun is the one that should likely be reconstructed for Proto-Semitic and is cognate to the Aramaic relative pronoun, e.g. Nabataean Aramaic די/זי (Cantineau 1978, 61), Biblical Aramaic דִּי (Rosenthal 1961, 21 f.) and Gəʕəz *zä*. It is the relative pronoun found in the Northern epigraphic varieties of Old Arabic: Safaitic (m. *ḏ*, f.sg. *ḏʾt, ḏt, ḏ* (?) pl. *ḏw*, see Al-Jallad 2015, 85–88), and the one that seems to be attested in the Nabataean Arabic of the Namārah inscription: דו אשר אלתג /ḏū ʔasara al-tāǧ/ 'who bound the crown', (Rabin 1951, 205; Cantineau 1978, 49), cf. also the theonym דושרא /ḏū śarā/ 'the one of the Sharā mountain' (Cantineau 1978, 80).

The earliest attestation of the *ʔalla*-base relative pronoun seems to be JSLih 384, an Old Arabic inscription in the Northern Hijaz, in the Dadanitic script, which has the feminine relative pronoun spelled *ʾlt*, presumably to be read /ʔallatī/. See Müller (1982) and Macdonald (2000, 49) who identify the use of the *ʔalla*-base in this inscription as an Arabic isogloss, and see Al-Jallad (2015, 13, n. 17; 2018b, 8 f.; 2020b, 60) who identifies it as a specifically Old Hijazi isogloss within Arabic.

While the *ʔalla*-base is quite clearly an innovation and seems to have its origins in the Hijaz, by the time the grammarians start discussing the linguistic variation of Arabic, it seems to have become extremely dominant. Neither Sībawayh nor al-Farrāʔ consider any other relative pronouns.[2] A few later grammarians attribute archaic forms of the relative pronoun to Yemeni dialects who used *ḏī* (Rabin 1951, 39) and the Ṭayyiʔ who used *ḏū* (Rabin 1951, 204 f.).

4.3 The Distal Demonstrative Expansion with *-l(i)-* in *ḏālika, tilka* and *hunālika*

A typical feature of Quranic Arabic is the exclusive use of the distal demonstratives that have an additional element *-l(i)-* between the demonstrative element and the addressee agreement suffix *-ka/-kum* etc. Thus, in the QCT we find ذلك and تلك and never forms like ذاك *ḏāka* and تيك *tīka* or تاك *tāka*. The latter forms are reported for Classical Arabic (Wright 1896, § 342; Fischer 2002, § 275a), and especially *ḏāka* occasionally occurs in poetry and Classical Arabic prose (often co-occurring besides *ḏālika*).

The difference between these two pronouns is widely identified as a Hijazi isogloss already in the time of al-Farrāʔ (*Luġāt*, 11), who recognizes the exclusive use of the *ḏālika* form as typical for the Quran and attributes it to the Hijaz, while the people of Najd among the Qays, ʔasad, Tamīm and Rabīʕah use *ḏāka*. As far as can be gleaned from the fragmentary pre-Islamic data, it seems that the archaic forms without the *-l(i)-* insertion were original to the northern Old Arabic varieties, and that *-l(i)-* extension is a Hijazi innovation (Al-Jallad 2020b, 61 f.). *tk* as a feminine distal demonstrative appears to be attested in a single Safaitic inscription (Al-Jallad 2015, 84).

While Rabin (1951, 154) recognizes the identification of the *-l(i)-* extension as Hijazi, he remains skeptical of this identification because some Western Arabs have sayings and poems attributed to them that use *ḏāka* as well. He is also suspicious of the claim because Arab grammarians that claim this to be a Hijazi feature tend to cite the Quran as evidence for this, as it exclusively has *-li-* extension. This seems to me to be the wrong conclusion based on the facts available.

First, as *ḏālika* is the innovative form and *ḏāka* the original, the fact that an archaic form is used by Western Arabs—assuming this attribution is valid—is hardly an argument why *ḏālika* is not a Hijazi feature. At most it is an argument

2 Al-Farrāʔ (*Luġāt*, 12) does talk about relative pronouns however, and attributes an inflecting form of the plural to Huḏayl: nom. *allaḏūna* obl. *allaḏīna*.

that *ḏāka* is not an exclusively eastern feature. Just because *ḏāka* occurs in the Hijaz as well, does not exclude the possibility that *ḏālika* is indeed a uniquely Hijazi innovation.

His second point seems to presuppose the conclusion that the Quran is composed in the poetic koine and therefore *cannot* be evidence of dialectal data, but this has not been demonstrated by him, nor by anyone else. The very fact that Al-Farrāʔ (*Luġāt*, 11) feels the need to *explicitly* state that *ḏālika* is the form that occurs in the Quran in fact highlights that this is a fact considered remarkable and distinctive of Quranic Arabic, and something that he did not consider to follow automatically from the statement that this is the Hijazi form.

In Classical Arabic prose and poetry alike *ḏāka* and *ḏālika* co-occur, and its absence in the Quran is in fact striking, and a clear deviation from the Classical Arabic norms. The very fact that al-Farrāʔ, nor any other grammarian, feels the need to attribute all features present in Quranic readings to the Hijaz (as we saw in chapter 3), seems to confirm that the observation on the Hijazi character of *ḏālika* is quite independent from the observation that it is the only form that occurs in the Quran.

To *ḏālika* and *tilka*, we may also add that the distal locative demonstrative receives the -*l*(*i*)- expansion to form هنالك rather than *hunāka* as a Hijazi feature (al-Farrāʔ *Luġāt*, 47). The Tamimi *hunāka* becomes the dominant form in literary Arabic production but is absent in the QCT.

4.4 The Plural Demonstratives (hā-)ʔulāʔi/(hā-)ʔulā; ʔulāʔika/ʔulāka

Another isogloss that is attributed to the Hijaz is the shape of the plural distal demonstrative. Here al-Farrāʔ (*Luġāt*, 12) reports *ʔulāʔika* for Qurayš and the people of the Hijaz, while *ʔulāka* is reported for Qays, Tamīm, Rabīʕah and ʔasad, *ʔullāka* for some of the Banū Saʕd and Tamīm, and *ʔulālika* for "some of them".[3] The QCT is unambiguous in this regard as it only attests the spelling اولىك and never اولاك, and therefore it is only compatible with the Hijazi form.[4]

The proximal plural demonstrative likewise is reported by al-Farrāʔ (*Luġāt*, 22) to have a difference between Qurayš and those that surround them who have *hāʔulāʔi* as opposed to Tamīm, Qays, Bakr and the common people of

3 From the context it is unclear whether Al-Farrāʔ intends "some of the Banū Saʕd and Tamīm" or "some of the Arabs". Considering that the -*l*(*i*)- infix is a Hijaz feature in the singular forms, it seems probable that the latter is intended, and that it is a feature found, probably, among some Hijazis, but this is not made explicit.

4 For this isogloss see also Rabin (1951, 153, §g).

ʔasad who say *ʔulā* (spelled أُلَى in the edition) or *hā-ʔulā* (spelled هَاؤُلَى in the edition) with an *ʔalif maqṣūrah* (as opposed to an *ʔalif mamdūdah*). He adds that 'some Arabs' drop the first *ʔalif* of the word and say *hawlāʔi* and cites a piece of poetry that adduces this.[5]

The QCT does not allow us to infer with certainty the shape of the proximal deictic (although it definitely has the initial *hā-*), as both *ʔalif* and *yāʔ* can represent the *ʔalif maqṣūrah* whereas *ʔalif* can also represent *ʔalif mamdūdah*. Thus, the QCT هولا is consistent both with *hāʔulāʔi* and *hāʔulā*.

However, al-Farrāʔ explicitly writes the *ʔalif maqṣūrah* with a *yāʔ*, which means he likely intended the Najdi pronunciation to have been *(hā)ʔulē*, since the Kufans, including his teacher al-Kisāʔī, would regularly read *ʔalif maqṣūrah bi-sūrat al-yāʔ* with *ʔimālah* (see § 3.6.4.2).[6] Since the QCT distinguishes between /ē/ (spelled with *yāʔ*) and /ā/ (spelled with *ʔalif*) the QCT would only be consistent with *hāʔulāʔi* and not with *hāʔulē*.

4.5 Proximal Deictics with Mandatory *hā-* Prefix

In the QCT all proximal deictics, be they masculine هذا, feminine هذه, plural هولا or locative ههنا are prefixed by *hā-*. This is remarkably different from what is reported from Classical Arabic where forms without *hā-* are broadly reported, e.g. masculine *ḏā*, feminine *ḏih*, *ḏī*, *tī* plural *ʔulā* locative *hunā*. In Classical Arabic prose especially the form *hunā*—absent in the QCT—becomes standard, while others are rare.

Al-Farrāʔ (*Luġāt*, 22) reports the addition of the *hā-* prefix as optional for the plural among eastern tribes, but mandatory in the Hijaz. Forms without *hā-* are not explicitly mentioned for singular masculine *ḏā* or feminine *ḏī*/*ḏih* by al-Farrāʔ, although later grammarians like al-Zamaxšarī (*al-Mufaṣṣal*, 55) do report them. Even the locative deictic consistently has the *hā-* prefix in Quranic Arabic ههنا 'here' (Q3:154; Q5:24; Q26:146; Q69:35).

In the pre-Islamic record, we find that the Northern varieties consistently lack the addition of the *hā-* so its mandatory addition appears to be a typical

5 It is interesting to note that "dropping of the *ʔalif*" for al-Farrāʔ seems to mean that *āʔu* automatically becomes *aw*, while one might expect it to become *aʔu* instead. With this single occurrence it is difficult to decide what to make of this observation.

6 Modern mesopotamian dialects that retain a reflex of word-final *ē* as *-i* (*ḥəbli*) occasionally seem to treat *ʔalif mamdūdah* the same way, hence *šəti* 'winter'. This seems to point to a merger of word final **-ay-* and word final **-āy-* towards *ē* before the shift of **-āy-* to *-āʔ-* took place, cf. Safaitic *śty* /śetāy/ 'winter'. See on this topic also Levin (1992, especially 86 f.).

innovation of Quranic Arabic. For example, Safaitic only attests *ḏ*, presumably /ḏā/ (Al-Jallad 2015, 80), and the same is true for the late Nabataean Arabic inscription at Harran (568 CE), which clearly attests دا المرطول /ḏā al-marṭūl/ 'this Martyrion' (Fiema et al. 2015, 414), a feminine deictic תי without the initial *hā-* is likewise attested in the Nabataean Arabic of the Namārah inscription, e.g. תי נפש (328 CE) (Fiema et al. 2015, 405). Thus, while the epigraphic data does not allow an identification of this isogloss of typical for the Hijaz, it is clear that North of the Hijaz the addition of the *hā-* was not mandatory, as no attestations of it have been found so far.

4.6 Feminine Proximal Deictic *hāḏih*

According to Sībawayh (IV, 182) the Tamīm dialect has the feminine proximal deictic *hāḏī* form in context which becomes *hāḏih* form in pause. This is also what Rabin (1951, 152, §f) claims is the "strict Classical Arabic" form.[7] The Hijazi dialect would have borrowed this pausal form from Classical Arabic. No argument is given why it would not be the other way around or how he envisions a spoken dialect like Hijazi would go about borrowing such a basic category as a demonstrative from a poetic register. The existence of *tī/tā* demonstratives in *ḥadīṯ*s[8] and poems does not disprove that the *hāḏih* form was the common form in the Hijaz—only that some archaic forms were also in use, if we would accept that poetry and *ḥadīṯ*s are representative of Hijazi Arabic. The feminine proximal deictic throughout the QCT is هذه, which is in line with the report for Hijazi Arabic, which is said to use *hāḏih(ī)* both in pause and context.

In the northern Old Arabic dialects evidence is found for both *tī* and *ḏī* but not (*hā-*)*ḏihī*. For example, the ancient Namārah inscription (dated 328 CE) written in Nabataean Arabic starts with תי נפש 'this is the funerary monument of …'. Safaitic seems to attest a feminine demonstrative that has an initial *ḏ*, presumably /ḏī/, rather than *t* a feminine deictic also reported by the Arab grammarians (Al-Jallad 2015, 81). The forms with final *h*—the only form found in the Quran—is currently unattested in pre-Islamic Arabic.

7 I do not understand what the category of "strict Classical Arabic" is based on. It would imply that Sībawayh's own prose is not a representation of 'strict Classical Arabic', as he exclusively uses *hāḏihī* in context.

8 In fact, the prophetic narration that Rabin cites does not have the proximal deictic, but rather the distal deictic: *kayfa tī-kum* 'how is that one (spoken to a plurality of addressees)?' As prophetic narrations are not necessarily verbatim narrations, the use if *tī-kum* probably says more about the dialect of ʕāʔišah (who narrates this tradition), or the common link of this Hadith (which seems to be Ibn Šihāb al-Zuhrī) than it does about the prophet's speech.

4.7 Loss of Barth-Ginsberg Alternation

As discussed in § 2.2.5, Sībawayh and al-Farrāʔ agree that one of the features absent in Hijazi Arabic that is present in all other dialects is the use of *i*-prefixes in the prefix conjugation of stative *faʕila* verbs, thus they say *ʔanā ʔiʕlamu ḏāka* 'I know that' rather than the Hijazi *ʔana ʔaʕlamu ḏālika*.[9]

The Barth-Ginsberg alternation must certainly be reconstructed for Proto-Arabic (see § 2.2.5). Thus, the disappearance of it is a specific innovation typical of Hijazi Arabic. Indeed, there is evidence for this being a Hijazi innovation from the epigraphic record as well: Two Graeco-Arabic inscriptions from North Arabia attest verbs that unambiguously have *i*-prefixes with a stem vowel *a*: ιραυ /yirʕaw/ 'they pastured' (Al-Jallad and al-Manaser 2015) and εσρατ /yisrat/ 'he served in the army' (Al-Jallad et al. 2020). There is epigraphic evidence in the Northern Hijaz of the innovative generalization if the *a*-prefixes, namely in a Greek inscription which contains the name Ιαλης (UJadhGr 2) (Nehmé 2018, 286 f.), identified by Ahmad Al-Jallad (personal correspondence) as representing the Arabic verbal name /yaʕlē/, rather than the expected /yiʕlē/, had Barth-Ginsberg been operative. Thus, the epigraphic record seems to confirm that the lack of Barth-Ginsberg alternation is a Hijazi isogloss, in line with the reports of the grammarians.

In the QCT it is generally difficult to find unambiguous evidence for or against the Barth-Ginsberg alternation of the prefix, because of the short vowels being unwritten. However, there are two types of verbs, identified by Sībawayh and al-Farrāʔ alike, where this dialectal difference shows up in the consonantal skeleton of the text. As they both point out, stative verbs with I-*w* and I-*ʔ* stems, in the case of the application of Barth-Ginsberg, will end up with a *yāʔ*, thus one gets *tīǧalu* 'you fear' and *tiʔbā* 'you refuse' (Sībawayh, IV, 111). In this place, the QCT provides us with evidence that Quranic Arabic follows the Hijazi innovation of not having Barth-Ginsberg alternation, as we find لا توجل /lā tawǧal/ 'do not fear!' (Q15:53) rather than **لا تيجل, explicitly mentioned by al-Farrāʔ (*Luġāt*, 8) to be the expected form in the non-Hijazi dialects. For the I-*ʔ* stems, we find more evidence in the QCT that the Barth-Ginsberg alternation did not operate: ان تامنه /ʔin tāman-h/ 'if you entrust him' (Q3:75, twice), لا تامنا /lā tāman-nā/ 'you do not entrust us' (Q12:11), تالمون /tālamūn/ 'you are

9 For this feature, see also Rabin (1951, 158, §p, q), who suggests that this feature is borrowed from North-West Semitic, rather than a shared retention. This seems to be the result of imposition of the late Classical Arabic norms which lacks this alternation, taking this standard as a stand-in for Proto-Arabic. There is no obvious reason to assume that the Classical Arabic situation is original in this case.

suffering' (Q4:104, twice), فلا تاس /fa-lā tās/ 'so do not grieve' (Q5:26, 68), لكيلا تاسوا /likay-lā tāsaw/ 'in order that you do not grieve' (Q57:23), وتابى /wa-tābē/ 'but [their hearts] refuse' (Q9:8). اسى /āsē/ 'I grieve' (Q7:93), ان اذن /an āḏan/ 'that I give permission' (Q7:123; Q20:71; Q26:49), امنكم /ʔāmanu-kum/ 'I entrust you' (Q12:64); لا ياب /lā yāb/ 'he should not refuse' (Q2:282, twice); فلا يامن /fa-lā yāman/ 'he does not feel secure' (Q7:99); ويابى /wa-yābē/ 'and he refuses' (Q9:32) حتى ياذن /ḥattē yāḏan/ 'until he permits' (Q12:80); لم ياذن /lam yāḏan/ 'he did not allow' (Q42:21); ان ياذن /an yāḏan/ 'that he permits' (Q53:26) ان يامنوكم ويامنوا قومهم /an yāmanū wa-yāmanū qawmahum/ 'that they entrust you and they entrust their people' (Q4:91); يالمونك /yālamūna/ 'you are suffering' (Q4:104).

These examples thus confirm that Quranic Arabic follows the innovative Hijazi practice of lacking the Barth-Ginsberg alternation.

4.8 Uninflected *halumma*

Rabin (1951, 162 f., §z)—following al-Farrāʔ (*Luġāt*, 63) and Sībawayh (III, 529)—points out that in the Hijaz *halumma* 'come on!' was uninflected, while the Tamīm conjugated it as an imperative verb, sg.m. *halumma*, sg.f. *halummī*, du. *halummā*, pl.m *halummū* pl.f. *halmumna*, (al-Farrāʔ reports the unexpected feminine plural forms *halummanna, halumunna*). In the QCT, هلم is uninflected in the two places it occurs (Q6:150; Q33:18), which in both cases has a plural addressee. The QCT therefore agrees with the Hijaz in this regard. The Hijazi form here is probably archaic, as it seems likely that this is a presentative particle *hal*[10] followed by *-umma*, the same particle as the vocative suffix that one finds in *aḷḷāh-umma* 'O God!' The innovation of the Tamīm would have then been to interpret this as an imperative verb.[11]

4.9 Imperatives and Apocopates of II=III Verbs Have the Shape vCCvC Rather Than (v)CvCC

Imperative and apocopates of geminate verbs have a metathesized form in non-Hijazi dialects (*urudd(a/u)*), whereas in the Hijaz they are un-metathesized (*urdud*) (Rabin 1951, 161 f., §y). This according to Rabin (1951, 4) is one of "the few Hijazi forms [...] that appear sporadically [in the Quran]". It should be

10 Compare for example Ugaritic *hl* 'see; here is/are; now (then)' (Huehnergard 2012, 146).

11 I thank Ahmad al-Jallad for suggesting this analysis to me.

clear by now that many more Hijazi features than just the treatment of geminate verbs appear in the Quran. The claim that this form is sporadic among the readers is not in keeping with the attestations in the Quran. The unmetathesized Hijazi form is the norm. The apocopate occurs without metathesis 43 times, and the imperative 8 times. The metathesized forms never occur for the imperative, and for the apocopate there are only three, or four cases. The first is يشاق 'opposes' (Q59:4), while the unmetathesized form of the same verb is attested as يشاقق 'opposes' (Q4:115). The second and third are تضار 'suffers' (Q2:233) and يضار 'suffers' (Q2:282), which do not occur in unmetathesized forms elsewhere. The last case is a bit more involved. In the Kufan and Basran codices يرتد 'turns back' (Q5:54) occurs besides يرتدد 'turns back' (Q2:217) (Al-Dānī *muqniʕ*, 107), but in the Syrian and Medinan codices Q5:54 is spelled يرتدد.[12]

Rabin suggests that the Hijaz used the unmetathesized forms exclusively, while the Tamīm used the metathesized forms. This is indeed how Sībawayh (III, 529–532) reports it. However, al-Farrāʔ (*Luġāt*, 36) seems to accept the possibility of metathesized forms in Hijazi dialects as he says that Hijaz and ʔasad place the vowel *a* after metathesized final root consonants such as in *tuḍārra* while Tamīm and Qays have *tuḍārri*. The isogloss therefore seems to be that Hijazi was able to use both metathesized and unmetathesized forms whereas Tamīm used the metathesized forms exclusively. The QCT overwhelmingly has forms that are not metathesized, clearly showing this Hijazi isogloss. The metathesis found in Hijazi would appear to be a reflex of a type of assimilation across syllable boundaries that occasionally occurs in the QCT, also in other positions (see Appendix A.3.5 for a discussion).

4.10 Mā ḥiǧāziyyah

The vast majority of the nominal negation using *mā* is constructed with the predicate marked with *bi-*, e.g. وما هم بمومنين 'they are not believers' (Q2:8). Only on rare occasions is the *bi-* left out, and in those cases a disagreement is said to occur between the people of the Hijaz and Najd. This much is also admitted by al-Farrāʔ (*Luġāt*, 28): "the people of the Hijaz say *mā zaydun bi-qāʔim* 'Zayd is not standing', and hardly ever do they drop the *bi-* from their speech,

12 It is surprising that Rabin (1951, 162) reports to not have found variants for Q5:54, as *yartadid* is the reading of the canonical Syrian and Medinan readers, Ibn ʕāmir, Nāfiʕ and ʔabū Ǧaʕfar—in accordance with their regional rasm (Ibn al-Ǧazarī, § 2989).

and this is how it is in the Quran except in His speech: *mā hāḏā bašarā* and *mā hunna ʔummahāti-him*, they apply the accusative when they leave out the *bi-*. Tamīm, Qays and ʔasad (also) say it with the *bi-*, but when they remove the *bi-*, they apply the nominative."[13] This use of the accusative is usually known as *Mā Ḥiǧāziyyah*, whereas using the nominative is called the *Mā Tamīmiyyah*, this feature is well-known among the grammarians (see also Sībawayh, I, 57). At the time of writing, Rabin (1951, 174 ff., §p-t) seemed to lack sources that explicitly comment on the frequency of this construction, and as he points out it seems to have been quite rare. We now know that this was also recognized by Al-Farrāʔ as well. Indeed, in the QCT, only one unambiguous case of the *mā Ḥijāziyyah* can be discerned, namely the famous ما هذا بشرا "this is not a man" (Q12:31). The one other commonly cited example ما هن امهتهم "they are not their mothers" (Q58:2), universally read in the Hijazi manner by the canonical readers *mā hunna ʔummahāti-him(ū)* (not *ʔummahātu-hum(ū)*[14]) is ambiguous in the QCT, and could reflect both the *mā ḥiǧāziyyah* and the *mā tamīmiyyah*. Rabin tentatively supplies another option ما منكم من احد عنه حجزين "not one of you can shield against it" (Q69:47). This one does show the Hijazi form in the QCT, but does not get commented upon by the Arab grammarians, perhaps because they took *ḥāǧizīna* as a *ḥāl*.

As pointed out by al-Farrāʔ and Rabin, all other cases of nominal negation with *mā* mark the predicate with *bi-*. The anomalous nature of ما هذا بشرا (Q12:31) was the reason for Ahmad al-Jallad (2020b, 68 f.) to suggest that it is a grammatical anomaly included as a conscious choice in the direct speech, perhaps to give a colloquial effect to the quotation in the Quran. He likewise observes that another grammatical anomaly, the famous ان هذان لسحران "These two are wizards!" (Q20:63), likewise occurs in direct speech. It should be noted that, unless there is another plausible interpretation of ما هن امهتكم, the use of the nominal negation with *mā* without *bi-* seems exceedingly rare, but not unique to direct speech. With the caveat that this is admitted to be a marginal feature in the Hijaz as well as that it is extremely marginal in the Quran, the grammarian data does seem to assign a Hijazi origin to the isogloss that find in the QCT.

---

13 *ʔahlu l-ḥiǧāzi yaqūlūna: mā zaydun bi-qāʔimin, fa-lā yakādūna yulqūna l-bāʔa min kalāmi-him, bi-ḏālika ǧāʔa l-qurʔānu ʔillā qawlahū "mā hāḏā bašaran", "mā hunna ʔummahāti-him" wa-yanṣibūna ʔiḏā ʔalqawi l-bāʔ. tamīmun wa-qaysun wa-ʔasadan yaqūlūna bil-bāʔi, fa-ʔiḏā ṭaraḥū l-bāʔa rafaʕū.*

14 Although the non-canonical transmitter of ʕāṣim, al-Mufaḍḍal, is said to have read this with the nominative (Ibn Muǧāhid, 628; Ibn Xālawayh, 154).

4.11 The Morphosyntax of *kāla*

Al-Farrāʔ (*Maʕānī*, II, 245f.) tells us that there is disagreement on the how the verb *kālū* "to allot s.th. to s.o." should be treated. He says that the people of the Hijaz and those that neighbour Qays treat the recipient of the allotment as a direct object, giving examples such as *qad kiltu-ka ṭaʕāman kaṯīran* 'I have allotted to you a lot of food', and *kilta-nī* 'you have allotted to me', the more regular syntax appears to be with the preposition *li-*, i.e. *kilta lī* and *kiltu laka*. As al-Farrāʔ points out himself, the QCT follows the Hijazi practice in this regard كالوهم 'they allotted to them' (Q83:3).

4.12 The Presentative *hāʔum*

Al-Farrāʔ (*Luġāt*, 143f.) reports a difference between the presentative particle *hāʔa* 'voilà' and how it is inflected among the people of the Hijaz in contrast to the people of Najd (Qays, Tamīm, ʔasad). The Najdi tribes treat this presentative particle morphologically as an imperative verb, whereas the Hijazi dialect seems to base its endings on the 2sg. pronominal endings where the *k* has been swapped out with *ʔ* for unclear reasons. Al-Farrāʔ also reports that it has reached him that some Arabs indeed have *kāf* in place of the *hamzah* giving as example *hā-ka* and *hā-ki*.

	Hijaz	Najd
m.sg.	*hāʔa*	*haʔ* or *hāʔa*
f.sg.	*hāʔi*	*hāʔī* sometimes *hāʔi*
dual	*hāʔumā*	*hāʔā*
m.pl.	*hāʔum*	*hāʔū*
f.pl.	*hāʔunna*	*haʔna*

While this presentative particle is not attested particularly often in the QCT, the one time it does show up, it clearly takes on the Hijazi morphological form هاوم (Q69:19).

4.13 The Use of *Zawǧ* as 'Wife'

One of the reported differences between Hijaz as opposed to Tamīm and many of Qays and the people of Najd, according to al-Farrāʔ (*Luġāt*, 32–33) is that *zawǧ* is a unisex word meaning both 'husband' and 'wife' depending on the context in Hijazi whereas in the east *zawǧ* is 'husband' and *zawǧah* is 'wife'. The QCT clearly aligns with the Hijazi distribution, e.g. يادم اسكن انت وزوجك الجنه 'O Adam, dwell, you and your wife, in Paradise' (Q2:35).

4.14 Alternations between G- and C-stems

On multiple occasions al-Farrāʔ (*Luġāt*) reports that some dialects have a C-stem where other dialects have a G-stem, with the same meaning. These are in essence lexical isoglosses, based on what kind of morphology they follow, and they allow us to compare them against what we see in the QCT. We find that whatever is reported to be the Hijazi form is the form that we find in the QCT. Verbs reported to have a C-stem in the Hijaz, and a G-stem elsewhere, are the following:

- *ʔawḥā* 'to inspire' (Hijaz), *waḥā* (ʔasad), p. 146. QCT: Hijazi اوحى (Q99:5).
- *ʔawfā* 'to fulfill' (Hijaz), *wafā* 'id.' (Najd), p. 49. QCT: Hijazi اوفى (Q3:76) 'he fulfills'.

Cases where the Hijaz rather has the G-stem whereas other tribes have a C-stem are more numerous, examples of these are the following:

- *fatana* 'to tempt' (Hijaz), *ʔaftana* 'id.' (Tamīm, Rabīʕah, ʔasad, Qays), p. 57. QCT: Hijazi فتنا (Q29:3).
- *ḥaruma* 'to be forbidden', *ḥarām* pl. *ḥurum* 'forbidden' (Hijazi), *ʔaḥrama* 'to be forbidden', *muḥrim* 'forbidden' (ʔasad, Tamīm, Qays), p. 60 f. QCT: Hijazi الحرام (Q2:144).
- *ʕaṣafa* 'to blow violently' (Hijaz) *ʔaʕṣafa* (ʔasad), p. 73. QCT: Hijazi G-stem active participle عاصف (Q10:22; Q14:18); عاصفه (Q21:81); عصفت (Q77:2), rather than the C-stem *muʕṣif*.
- *maraǧa* 'to release' (Hijaz), *ʔamraǧa* (Najd), p. 108. QCT: Hijazi مرج (Q25:53; Q55:19).

In one case the QCT seems to have both the G- and the C-stem with the same meaning attested.

- *nakira* 'to not know' (Hijaz), *ʔankara* (ʔasad, Tamīm), p. 75. The QCT uses the G-stem once نكرهم 'he did not know them' (Q11:70), the C-stem usually means 'to reject, deny' e.g. ينكرونها 'they deny it' (Q16:83), but the active participle at least once seems to have the G-stem meaning in Q12:58 وهم له منكرون 'they did not know/recognize him'.

These lexical isoglosses of verbal stem formation in the QCT therefore seem to follow the patterns as they are reported for the Hijazi dialect.

4.15 Morphological Isoglosses Not Recognized by the Grammarians

In Quranic Arabic, there are several morphological developments which based on comparative evidence with modern dialects and Old Arabic must certainly be seen as innovations typical of Quranic Arabic, yet are not recognized or discussed as isoglosses by the Arab grammarians. In these cases, whatever we find in Quranic Arabic is identical to the *ʕarabiyyah*—that which the grammarians describe as valid and eloquent Arabic. While these do not help us better classify Quranic Arabic within the context of the dialects as described by the grammarians, they occasionally do allow us to set it apart from modern dialects and attested forms of Old Arabic in the epigraphic record.

4.15.1 Ta-*prefix in Prefix Conjugation of tD- and tL-stems*

In Gəʕəz, the tD- and tL-stems the suffix conjugation has the shape *tä-* for the formation prefix whereas the prefix conjugation has the shape *t-*, i.e. *täqäṭṭälä*, *yətqäṭṭäl*. Classical Arabic has *ta-* in both forms, while most modern dialects have *t-* in both stems. It was already noted by Diem (1982) that these *t-* forms cannot be explained as the outcome of regular sound change from *ta-*, and therefore both the *ta-* and *t-* forms must have been around in Proto-Arabic. He subsequently suggests that Proto-Arabic probably had the distribution as it is attested in Gəʕəz. Since Diem's article, dialectological data has become available that shows there are dialects that generalize the *ta-* like Classical Arabic, and more importantly, that there are some rare dialects that indeed retain the alternation as it is present in Gəʕəz. See for example: Douz Arabic *tⁱḥaššam*/*yitḥaššam* 'to be ashamed', *tᵃʕāṛak*/*yitʕāṛak* 'to fight' (Ritt-Benmimoun 2014, 349–350; 355–357),[15] Gulf Arabic *taġayyir/yitġayyar* 'to change', *tiwāfag/yitwāfag* 'to help each other' (Holes 2010, 404f.) and finally in Saudi Arabic we find Ghāmid *takallam/yitkallam* 'to speak', Qauz *tikallam/yitkallam* 'to speak', Hofuf *taḥarrak/titḥarrak* (3sg.f.) 'to move' (Prochazka 1988, 40–50). From this evidence we must conclude that this alternation of the *ta-* and *t-* prefix can securely be reconstructed for Proto-Arabic. The fact that this aligns with what we find in Gəʕəz, make it clear that this allomorphy can even be reconstructed for Proto-West Semitic.

15 The ultrashort vowels ⁱ and ᵃ are the regular outcome of **a* in open syllables.

While the evidence is sparse, the data available suggest that Quranic Arabic underwent the same generalization as Classical Arabic. For the suffix conjugation it is clear it always has the *ta-* prefix, because it does not have a prothetic *ʔalif* to break up the CC cluster, e.g. تقطع 'to be severed' (Q6:94) rather than **اتقطع that one would expect for **/itqaṭṭaʕ/. Evidence that the prefix was *ta-* in the prefix conjugation is sparser, but it can be deduced from يتاخر '(that) he stay behind' (Q74:37), which could only represent /yatāxxar/ or if the *hamzah* is retained in this context /yataʔaxxar/. Had the prefix been *t-* we would have expected **يتخر for /yataxxar/ from **yatʔaxxara*.

Thus, we can conclude that Quranic Arabic has innovated by generalizing the *ta-* prefix to both suffix and prefix conjugations. This generalization seems to have become the prestigious form early on, as any mention of a situation with *ta-/t-* alternation or a generalized *t-* so abundant among the modern dialects seems to be entirely absent in the descriptions of the Arab grammarians. It is thus a clear morphological innovation of Quranic Arabic compared to Proto-Arabic, but it is not explicitly attributed to the Hijaz.

4.15.2 N-*prefix in the Suffix Conjugation of N-stems*

Much like the tD- and tL-stems, the N-stem appears to have had a vocalized allomorph *na-* in the suffix conjugation and an unvocalized allomorph *-n-* in the prefix conjugation in Proto-Arabic. Evidence for this distribution is found in Safaitic where the lack of assimilation of the *n* in the suffix conjugation such as in *nġḍb* /naġḍaba/ 'he was angered' clearly suggests a vocalised prefix. The form *yqtl* /yiqqatel/ 'to be killed' on the other hand appears to represent an assimilated *n*-prefix (Al-Jallad 2015, 134 ff.). The fact that this Old Arabic reflex finds a parallel outside of Arabic in, e.g. Hebrew Pf. *nip̄ʕal* Impf. *yippaʕel* < **na-pʕala, *yi-n-paʕilu* (Suchard 2019, 49 f.) suggests that Safaitic retains the Proto-Arabic situation. Quranic Arabic, like Classical Arabic and, to my knowledge, all modern dialects has generalized the unvocalized allomorph *-n-* to both stems, yielding forms such as pf. انقلب 'he turned' (Q22:11) impf. ينقلب 'he turns' (Q2:143). While the Arab grammarians do not comment on the vocalized prefix form at all, from the epigraphic record and comparative Semitic data it is clear that the Quranic Arabic form is innovative.

4.15.3 *The* ʔan yafʕala *Verbal Complement Construction*

Al-Jallad (2020b, 61) identifies the *ʔan yafʕala* verbal complement construction as yet another isogloss of Hijazi Arabic, in contrast to epigraphic Old Arabic. Both the language of the Quran, and the Old Hijazi of the Damascus psalm fragment form verbal complements with the particle *ʔan* followed by the subjunctive verb, where in Old Arabic of the Levant and North Arabia an infinitive construction would be used (Al-Jallad 2015, 112f.). This seems to be a Hijazi innovation, as its earliest attestation occurs in a fragmentary Dadanitic inscription from al-ʕulā in the Northern Hijaz (Al-Jallad 2020b, 61). However, this is an innovation that Quranic Arabic shares with Classical Arabic, and is thus not identified as a Hijazi isogloss by the grammarians.

4.15.4 *Use of the Definite Article* al-

An interesting isogloss that is not exclusive to the Hijaz, but nevertheless forms a clear linguistic isogloss in the Old Arabic linguistic record is the shape of the definite article. In the Old Arabic present in the corpus of Safaitic inscriptions the definite article is usually represented by a *h*- (presumably /haC-/), not infrequently *ʾ*- and only rarely by *hn*- or *ʾl*- (Al-Jallad 2015, 11, n. 10), and the Old Arabic of the Hismaic corpus seems to lack a definite article altogether (Al-Jallad 2018b, 12). In Nabataean Arabic, on the other hand, it is always written אל, suggesting an unassimilated /al-/ in all contexts. This same lack of assimilation is also found in the Arabic of the Damascus psalm fragment (Al-Jallad 2020b, 24). For Quranic Arabic, the evidence is difficult to interpret, the QCT would suggest an unassimilated article, but this might be a purely orthographic convention—as it is in Classical Arabic—adopted from the Nabataean writing system. Van Putten (2019b, 14f.) gives some not particularly binding arguments why an assimilated article before apical consonants, as in Classical Arabic, might be preferable over an unassimilated situation as found in the Damascus psalm fragment. Whatever the interpretation of the QCT in this case, that it uses the *al*- article, as opposed to the *haC*- article, the Yemeni *an*-/*am*- articles or a completely absent definite article certainly distinguishes it from the Old Arabic present in the northern varieties of Safaitic and Hismaic, and puts it closer to Nabataean Arabic in this regard. The early Arab grammarians, however, do not recognize this as a Hijazi isogloss at all, and rather see the *al*- article with assimilation as the only acceptable form of the *ʕarabiyyah*.

4.16 Questionable Morphological Isoglosses

There are a few morphological isoglosses of the Hijaz discussed by Rabin (1951) which can be deduced from the QCT where it does not agree with the reported Hijazi form. However, in these three cases, we will see that it is to be doubted whether the isogloss is to be attributed to the whole Hijaz, or to the Hijaz at all, as early sources of the grammarians give conflicting reports.

4.16.1 *The III-w Passive Participle Is maCCuww Not maCCiyy*

Al-Farrāʔ (*Maʕānī*, II, 169 f.) claims it is a linguistic practice of the people of the Hijaz to retain the consonant **w* in passive participles of III-*w* stems, e.g. *marḍuwwan* rather than *marḍiyyan* "pleasing". This disagrees with the QCT مرضيا (Q19:55). Rabin (1951, 161, § x) seems skeptical of this isogloss and calls it a "curious statement". His skepticism seems warranted, because elsewhere al-Farrāʔ (*Luġāt*, 92) is explicit in saying that it is only "some of the people of the Hijaz" that do this. Therefore, it does not appear to have been a general innovation found in all of the Hijaz.

This neutralization appears to be part of a more widespread neutralization of III-*w* and III-*y* in derived nominal stems. In the QCT we also see عصيهم /ʕu/iṣiyyu-hum/ (Q20:66, Q26:44) as the CuCūC plural of عصا 'rod'. Interestingly, the CuCūC verbal nouns seems to mostly keep III-*w* and III-*y* roots distinct. Thus, we see علوا /ʕuluwwā/ (Q17:4, 43; Q27:14; Q28:83) as the verbal noun of علا 'to be high, elevated', and عتوا /ʕutuwwā/ (Q25:21), عتو /ʕutuww/ (Q67:21) as the verbal noun of عتا 'to be insolent', whereas we find لرقيك /li-ru/iqiyyi-ka/ (Q17:93) as the verbal noun of رقى 'to ascend' and مضيا /mu/iḍiyyā/ (Q36:67) as the verbal noun of مضى 'to go away'. The Quran however exploits verbal nouns that have undergone this neutralization for the purpose of rhyme in Sūrat Maryam (Q19): عتيا /ʕu/itiyyā/ (Q19:8, 69) as an alternative verbal noun of عتا besides عتوا mentioned above, and جثيا /ǧu/iṯiyyā/ (Q19:68, 72) as the verbal noun of جثا 'to kneel'.

4.16.2 *The Passive Participle of II-y Is maCīC Rather Than maCyūC*

A doubtful isogloss is the Tamīmī practice of using *madyūn* instead of the Hijazi *madīn* for passive participles of II-*y* roots (Rabin 1951, 160, §u). As Rabin points out, it is likely that the Tamīmī form is an innovative analogical formation of the passive participle, rather than the Proto-Arabic reflex, in which case Hijazi would simply have the Proto-Arabic form. The QCT indeed has the alleged Hijazi form, but contrary to Rabin's claim, this does not occur only once in مهيلا 'poured down' (Q73:14), but also مدينون (Q37:53), مدينين (Q56:86) 'indebted; judged', مكيدون 'tricked' (Q52:42).

Sībawayh (IV, 248) does report that 'some Arabs' say *mabyūʕ* 'bought' rather than *mabīʕ*, but he does not explicitly identify it as a non-Hijazi or Tamīmī form, nor does he identify *mabīʕ* as the Hijazi form.[16] The much later grammarian Ibn

16 Some of these "Tamīmī" forms have made it into the Classical Arabic language. Fischer (2002, § 247.2) mentions *mabyūʕ* 'sold', which occurs besides *mabīʕ*. Wehr (1979, s.v.) also mentions *madyūn* besides *madīn* for 'indebted'. In Classical Arabic the alleged Hijazi form is dominant.

Ǧinnī (d. 392/1002) in his *Kitāb al-Muġtaṣab* (p. 3) does identify the *mabyūʕ* type as Tamīmī, but considering how late a source Ibn Ǧinnī is, we should be skeptical of this attribution.

4.16.3 *Gt-stems of I-w verbs Is* **ītazara** *instead of* **ittazara**

According to some grammarians Hijazi Arabic had *ītazara* rather than *ittazara* for I-*w* verbs in the Gt-stem (Rabin 1951, 158f., §r). If correct, this would be an example where the QCT does not follow the Hijazi formation, cf. فاتقوا 'so fear!' (Q2:24) and اتسق 'to become full' (Q84:18). The identification seems doubtful however, as early sources give conflicting accounts. For example, al-Farrāʔ (*Luġāt*, 20) explicitly attributes the form *ittaqū* with an initial long consonant to the people of the Hijaz, while he attributes *taqū* to Tamīm and ʔasad. He makes no mention of a form *ītaqū*.

4.16.4 *The Hijazi Dual Is Uninflected, Using the Nominative Form*

Rabin (1951, 156, § m) suggests that, at least in the dialect of Mecca, the dual did not inflect for case and the nominative was used in all positions. If this is correct, then Quranic Arabic disagrees with the Meccan dialect in this regard, as the dual is fully functional. However, this dialectal explanation seems to exist exclusively as a pious explanation of the problematic reading *ʔinna hāḏāni lasāḥirāni* (Q20:63) (Ibn al-Ǧazarī, § 3590–3591), where from a Classical Arabic grammatical perspective ʔabū ʕamr's *hāḏayni* would be expected. There is, of course, no *a priori* reason to assume that the demonstrative inflected for case in Quranic Arabic; other demonstratives do not inflect for case either. It might not be that the dual in general did not inflect in Hijazi, but that it was specifically the dual demonstratives that did not. Such an interpretation seems to be implicitly suggested (and attributed to the southern Hijazi tribe Banū al-Ḥāriṯ b. Kaʕb) by al-Farrāʔ (*Luġāt*, 94) who only mentions the non-inflecting nature of *hāḏāni*. هذن (Q20:63, Q22:19) is the only form of the masculine dual attested in the QCT, whereas the feminine is only attested as هتين (Q28:27), there is therefore no way to confirm that the Quranic Arabic had an inflecting dual. However, the QCT also allows for a different interpretation. While the particle *ʔinna* requires the accusative, the particle *ʔin* with the same function requires the nominative. The QCT ان هذن لسحرن simply accommodates such a reading, and is indeed the canonical reading reported for Ḥafṣ ʕan ʕāṣim and Ibn Kaṯīr.

Other case of *ʔin* in the function of *ʔinna* are found among several canonical readers, e.g. Q86:4 *ʔin kullu nafsin lamā ʕalayhā ḥāfiẓun* "Every soul has a guardian over it" (majority reading), as opposed to *ʔin kullu nafsin* ***lammā*** *ʕalayhā ḥāfiẓ* "there is no soul but has a guardian over it." (ʕāṣim, Ibn ʕāmir,

Ḥamzah, ʔabū Ǧaʕfar). Similar constructions with disagreement on *lamā* versus *lammā* are found in Q36:32 and Q43:35 (Ibn al-Ǧazarī, § 3312–3313).

Whatever the explanation, the use of *ʔin* in this function, an uninflected dual deictic or even a mere mistake in the QCT—as suggested by a transmission brought by al-Farrāʔ (*Luġāt* 94 f.) in which ʕāʔišah supposedly proclaimed this[17]—this can hardly be used as evidence of an isogloss of a completely uninflecting dual in Hijazi Arabic. Note that the use of this dual is specifically used in direct speech, which Al-Jallad (2020b, 68 f.) suggests may have been a context which uses explicitly colloquial features for rhetorical effect, see section § 4.10 for more details.

4.17 The Quran Is Morphologically Hijazi

As mentioned in section § 4.1 it was Rabin's claim that, while Quranic Arabic was phonologically perhaps somewhat adapted to the local Hijazi dialect, it morphologically adhered almost completely to the poetic koiné. The problem is that Rabin—nor to my knowledge any other author—ever defines what exactly the features morphological or otherwise of this poetic koiné are.

As we have elaborated upon in chapter 2 the very category of a 'poetic koiné' as opposed to 'dialects' is not a dichotomy the Arabic grammarians operated within. In fact, whenever we find Sībawayh discussing a variety of different morphological or phonological options he frequently qualifies this with a *wa-kullun ʕarabiyy*—All is Arabic, even when these options are explicitly attributed to tribes. I think we should take these statements of the grammarians seriously. If we do not impose a dichotomy between an undefined and undescribed poetic koiné versus the dialects, and look at which dialectal features that can actually be recognized in the QCT, a rather clear picture emerges: all the morphological features attributed to the Hijaz that can be gleaned from the QCT indeed confirm that it is a Hijazi text.

It is worth appreciating just how different the view from the QCT is in comparison to what we find in the reading traditions. As I showed in chapter 3, the reading traditions are very mixed, sound laws do not operate regularly and each reading incorporates Hijazi and non-Hijazi features in a haphazard manner and in different configurations from other readers. From the readings, no real

17 Along with two examples of seemingly mistaken case in the sound masculine plural, in both cases related to the *ʔin*(*na*) and *lākin*(*na*) particles, namely *lākini r-rāsixūna* […] ***wa-l-muqīmīna*** (Q4:162) and *ʔinna lladīna ʔāmanū wa-lladīna hādū* ***wa-ṣ-ṣabiʔūna*** (Q5:69), cf. the doublet of this phrase the expected case in Q22:17.

signal from any dialect can be recovered. Therefore, it is all the more striking that the QCT gives such a regular picture. This is unlikely to be a coincidence.

Whenever we are dealing with innovative features of Hijazi Arabic, where the pre-Islamic epigraphic record can give us insight into this feature, we find that likewise the northern varieties of Safaitic and Nabataean Arabic do not appear to have undergone these innovations. This lends some credibility to the comments of the grammarians that these innovations should indeed be sought in the Hijaz. The table below summarizes the isoglosses discussed so far. Some of these cases are retentions while others are innovations, but all in all the picture is clear. Thus, let me recast Rabin's quote mentioned at the top of this section, in terms of what the linguistic evidence actually brings us: As for the Quran, in morphology we find an almost complete conformity with *Hijazi Arabic* has been achieved; the few *Najdi* forms, such as the biliteral jussive and imperative of verbs med. gem. only appear sporadically.

The table below summarizes the morphological isoglosses of Quranic Arabic that have a clear tribal attribution among the Arab grammarians. As should be clear, all of them invariably agree with Quranic Arabic being a Hijazi text. The column next to it examines the presence or absence of these isoglosses in epigraphic Old Arabic such as Nabataean Arabic, Safaitic and Hismaic. Whenever the epigraphic record allows us to discern this, we find that in these northern varieties said isoglosses are absent, which lends credence to the grammarian data that suggests these are Hijazi innovations.

	Grammarians	**Old Arabic**
ʔalla- base relative pronoun	All non-Ṭayyiʔ tribes	North: Absent, Hijaz: Present
Distal demonstratives with *-l(i)-*	Hijaz	Absent
pl.dist *ʔulāʔika* (not *ʔulāka*)	Hijaz	?
m.sg.prox *ḏā* > *hā-ḏā*	Hijaz	Absent
f.sg.prox (*hā*)*-tī*/*ḏī* > *hāḏih*	Hijaz	Absent
Loss of Barth-Ginsberg alternation	Hijaz	Absent
Uninflected halumma	Hijaz	?
Uncontracted II=III imperative/apocopate	Hijaz	?
Mā Ḥiǧāziyyah	Hijaz	?
Presentative *hāʔa* with pronominal endings	Hijaz	?
Zawǧ as Wife	Hijaz	?
Lexical isoglosses of G- and C-stems	Hijaz	?

CHAPTER 5

The Quranic Consonantal Text: Phonology

فَاكْتُبُوهُ بِلِسَانِ قُرَيْشٍ فَإِنَّمَا نَزَلَ بِلِسَانِهِمْ

ʕUṮMĀN B. ʕAFFĀN

5.1 Introduction

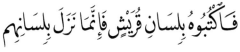

It has long been recognized that the orthography of the QCT, in principle reflects the phonology of Hijazi Arabic. Most notably the way that the *hamzah* is (not) spelled, seems to reflect the purported loss of this sound in the Hijazi dialect. While some authors see this tendency of the orthography as a purely orthographic convention, envisioning that the *actual* language of the Quran was pronounced with the non-Hijazi pronunciation with *hamzah* (e.g. Zwettler 1978, 124; Versteegh 2014, 64) others do not express a clear opinion to what extent the Hijazi orthography can reveal anything about the language of the Quran itself (e.g. Diem 1976; 1979). However, Rabin (1951, 3f.) (also Nöldeke 1904, 11; and Blau 1977, 15f.) is quite confident that the orthography in fact reveals something about the way the Quran was actually pronounced, saying "the pronunciation of the literary language was of course largely accommodated to their native dialect, to which the Koran spelling is therefore a fairly reliable guide." On other occasions, Rabin likewise expresses that the orthography is to be taken seriously for the phonetics of Quranic Arabic. I agree with this view, and I believe that the correctness of this assumption is confirmed to a large extent by the Quranic rhyme (see van Putten 2018). Indeed, whenever the rhyme allows us to examine the presence of the *hamzah*, for example, we must conclude that it was in fact not there whenever the orthography suggests its absence. Thus شان (Q55:29) breaks the strict |-ān| rhyme of Sūrat al-Raḥmān if read as *šaʔn*, whereas this problem is resolved if read as /šān/, the same is clear for شيا (Q19:9) which breaks the rhyme when read as *šayʔā* but is perfectly consistent with the |-i/ayyā| rhyme if read as /šayyā/ or /šiyyā/. The QCT thus clearly reveals a *hamzah*-less pronunciation. To understand the linguistic nature of the language of the Quran, we must let the text tell us, rather than impose a set of mutually contradictory norms presented by the canonical reading traditions.

This chapter will look at some of the phonetic isoglosses that can be deduced from the QCT, in order to connect them with the phonetic features discussed by the grammarians. Some of the features discussed here are isoglosses that Rabin considered part of morphology. While these indeed have an effect on the morphology, they are the outcome of regular sound laws, and therefore I choose to discuss them here. Here too, we will compare the isoglosses to those found in Northern Old Arabic like Safaitic and Nabataean Arabic, showing that several important innovative features are indeed unattested in northern varieties, while they are attested in the QCT.

There are several phonetic isoglosses of the QCT that do not get explicitly referred to as Hijazi features according to the grammarians. Most of the time grammarians do discuss such features, as one of the goals of the grammatical works was to account for the language of the Quran. Even when there is a lack of attribution from the grammarians of certain features to the Hijaz, Rabin (1951) frequently attributes these features to the Hijaz by virtue of them being present in the Quran. This is circular, and rather surprising as Rabin often expresses skepticism of any attribution to Hijazi Arabic when medieval grammarians cite the Quran as evidence for it (as he does, for example in the *ḏālika* rather than *ḏāka* isogloss, see §4.3 above). We will only count features as confirmed to be part of Hijazi Arabic whenever it is explicitly done so by the Arab grammarians, or epigraphic evidence suggests that the innovation is at least absent in Northern Old Arabic. It should be noted, however, that the grammarians report linguistic data from a not insignificant time after the composition of the Quran. As a result, it is possible that when data reported by the grammarians does not align with the QCT being Hijazi, this could still rather be the result of a difference in time, rather than a true disagreement. Often it is not possible to prove this with any certainty, but at times papyri and early Islamic epigraphy may yield some insights.

5.2 The Loss of the *ʔ

As Rabin (1951, 130, §l,m,n) says: “the most celebrated feature of the Hijaz dialect is the disappearance of the *hamza*, or glottal stop.” Indeed, this is a feature universally attributed to the Hijaz by the Arab grammarians, and it is widely recognized to be the foundation for the Islamic Arabic orthography (Diem 1976). Van Putten (2018) argues that, not only does a *ʔ*-less dialect form the basis of the orthography of the QCT, but the Quranic rhyme confirms that the orthography is, in fact, an accurate representation of the Quranic Arabic phonology and therefore had lost ʔ in almost every position. The table below summarizes the evidence of the loss of *hamzah* that can be derived from the Quranic rhyme. First listing the QCT spelling, and the readings, and finally the reconstructed reading that is consistent with the rhyme context it occurs in.

	QCT	Reading traditions	Reconstructed reading	Rhyme
Q55:29	شان	*šaʔnin, šānin*	/šān/	|-āN|
Q69:9	بالخاطيه	*bi-l-xāṭiʔati, bi-l-xāṭiyah*	/bi-l-xāṭiyah/	|-āCiyah|
Q96:16	خاطيه	*xāṭiʔatin, xāṭiyatin*	/xāṭiyah/	|-āCiyah|
Q19:9, 42, 60, 67	شيا	*šayʔan*	/šayyā/ (or /šiyyā/)	|a/iyyā|
Q19:30, 41, 49, 51, 53, 54, 56	نبيا	*nabīʔan, nabiyyan*	/nabiyyā/	|a/iyyā|
Q19:74	وريا	*wa-riʔyan, wa-riyyan*	/wa-riyyā/	|a/iyyā|

One exception to this general loss seems to have been the word-final *ʔalif mamdūdah* (i.e. *-āʔ*) which appears to have retained some phonetic trace of the *ʔ, either as stress + hiatus, or indeed a true glottal stop realization (see Van Putten 2018: 103–105). Rabin (1951, 141, §ee) alludes to the possibility that this may be a place where the Hijaz retained the *hamzah* whereas eastern dialects lost it. Later lexicographical works shows some lexical items with Hijazi *-āʔ* corresponding to eastern *-ā/-ē* but among the early grammarians I have only found evidence for this correspondence in the plural deictic which is said to be *hāʔulāʔi* in the Hijaz while it is (*hā*)-*ʔulā/ē* in the eastern dialects (see §4.4).

Despite an almost universal attribution of *hamzah*-loss to the Hijaz by later grammarians, neither Sībawayh nor al-Farrāʔ are very explicit in attributing this loss to the Hijaz. Sībawayh gives a detailed account in the manner that the *hamzah* may be lost in Arabic (Sībawayh IV, 541ff.), but at no point does he attribute this dropping specifically to the Hijaz. The developments he discusses are clearly similar to those suggested by Van Putten (2018) and Diem (1980) to have taken place in the (orthography of) the QCT. However, to Sībawayh this form of dropping of the *hamzah* was acceptable within what he considered *ʕarabiyyah*, and the highly conservative application of the *hamzah* so closely associated with Classical Arabic today, does not seem to have been the stereotypical feature of proper Arabic in his time. Al-Farrāʔ does not explicitly attribute the complete loss of *hamzah* to the Hijaz either, but when we examine the cases where he does attribute the loss of *hamzah* to certain tribes, it is invariably to the people of the Hijaz or Qurayš. If we were to generalize these isolated statements (something that is not necessarily warranted, nor explicitly unwarranted from the structure of the text), we indeed end up with all the developments typically associated with the Hijazi *hamzah*-loss, and a situation that closely matches the QCT. The list below is a comparison of what is reported in terms of *hamzah*-loss in al-Farrāʔ's *Luġāt al-Qurʔān*.

- *mustahziʔūna* > *mustahzūna* (Qurayš and the common people of Ġaṭafān and Kinānah, p. 15); QCT مستهزون (Q2:14)
- *sayyiʔah* > *sayyah, sayyiyah* (People of the Hijaz, p. 30); QCT سييه (Q2:81). The collapse of the *yyiy* sequence to *yy* seems to take place in the plural السيات (*passim*)
- *ʔanbiʔū-nī* > *ʔanbū-nī* (Qurayš, p. 22); QCT انبونى (Q2:31).
- *isʔal* > *sal* (People of the Hijaz, p. 34); QCT سل (Q2:211 and *passim*).
- *ridʔan* > *ridan* (People of the Hijaz, p. 113); QCT ردا (Q28:34).
- *riʔyan* > *riyyan* (People of the Hijaz, p. 90); QCT ريا (Q19:74).[1]
- *al-minsaʔah* > *al-minsāh* (People of the Hijaz, p. 119, cf. *Maʕānī al-Qurʔān*, II, 256); QCT منسته (Q34:14).
- *at-tanāʔuš* > *at-tanāwuš* (People of the Hijaz, p. 119, cf. *Maʕānī al-Qurʔān*, II, 365); QCT التنوش (Q34:52).

To this we may add the following Isolated statements in his *Maʕānī al-Qurʔān*:

- *yaklaʔu-kum* > *yaklawu-kum, yaklā-kum* (Qurayš, vol. II, p. 204); QCT يكلوكم (Q21:42).

Al-Farrāʔ's statements therefore seem to confirm the conclusion that the Hijazi dialect lacked *hamzah*.

The loss of *hamzah* is a Hijazi feature to the Arab grammarians, and this seems to be corroborated by the epigraphic record. The northern varieties of Nabataean, Safaitic (as well as Hismaic) perfectly retain the *hamzah* in all positions (e.g. Al-Jallad 2015, 45, 53; van Putten 2018, 96). This is especially relevant in the case of Nabataean Arabic. As the Nabataean script is the one ancestral to the modern Arabic script, the difference in orthographic practice between Nabataean Arabic and the QCT is striking. We find that Nabataean Arabic consistently employs the *ʔalif* to denote the *hamzah*, even in places where in the QCT it would go unwritten or would be written with a glide. The fact that the QCT's orthography differs appreciably in this regard and abandons manners of writing the *hamzah* in favour of *hamzah*-less spellings is a strong indication of an orthographic innovation to accommodate the vernacular.

---

1 Al-Farrāʔ that al-ʔaʕmaš and ʕāṣim read with hamzah, but that without hamzah is more well-formed for recitation (*ʔahyaʔu fī l-qirāʔah*), a nice example of an explicit endorsement of a hamza-less form. This opinion of al-Farrāʔ is no doubt inspired by the fact that *riyyan* is better in line with the rhyme of this Sūrah than the reading *riʔyan*.

5.3 Development of the Phoneme *ō*

Quranic Arabic has several cases where a *mater lectionis wāw* is used where all canonical reading traditions read it with *ā*, these are: الصلوه 'the prayer', الزكوه 'alms', الحيوه 'the life', منوه 'Manāt (pre-Islamic goddess)', النجوه 'the salvation', مشكوه 'lamp niche' and الغدوه 'morning'. Modern scholars have generally taken these as purely orthographic idiosyncrasies of these words—often suggested to be inspired by Aramaic—and assumed they simply had a vowel *ā* as in Classical Arabic, but as the Arabic roots clearly have a distinct etymological origin (containing a **w* in the root) and predictable phonetically conditioned behaviour, it seems more likely that these words in fact had a long vowel /ō/ in the final syllable, that is /aṣ-ṣalōh/, /az-zakōh/, /al-ḥayōh/, /manōh/, /an-nağōh/, /miškōh/ and /al-ġadōh/ (Al-Jallad 2017c; van Putten 2017a).

There are good QCT-internal and comparative reasons to see this as an innovation of Quranic Arabic, for example Safaitic still retains an original triphthong here *ngwt* /nagawat/ 'salvation' (Al-Jallad & Jaworska 2019, 102), also the Arab grammarians clearly saw this pronunciation for specifically these words as typical for the Hijaz, as opposed to the pronunciation with /ā/ found elsewhere. Sībawayh (IV, 432), for example, calls it "the *ʔalif al-tafxīm*, by which is meant the linguistic practice of the people of the Hijaz in their speech of *aṣ-ṣalōh*, *az-zakōh* and *al-ḥayōh*." This statement has often been taken to mean that all cases of /ā/ where pronounced backed/rounded by the people of the Hijaz, or word-final stressed /ā/ was (e.g. Rabin 1951, 105f.; Testen 2005, 219), but this is not in keeping with the evidence. The feminine plural *-āt* is never spelled with *wāw* nor are nouns of the shape CaCāC, CiCāC, CuCāC etc. The fact that Sībawayh specifically cites the words that are spelled with a *wāw* in the QCT, and not any other words suggests that it is words specifically of this type, i.e. original *CaCawat- nouns that undergo this shift.

5.4 Lack of *Cyī* > *Cī*

Al-Farrāʔ (*Luġāt*, 21) reports that the Qurayš and commonly among the Arabs *yastaḥyī* is pronounced with the expected *yī* sequence, but Tamīm and Bakr b. Wāʔil read it *yastaḥī*. While the modern Cairo Edition text agrees with the Tamīmī form, this is an idiosyncrasy of the print edition. The QCT as it is reflected in early Quranic manuscripts consistently agrees with the common form also found among the Qurayš, e.g. يستحيي (Q2:26) يحيي (Q2:258) (for a further discussion, see Appendix A.2.2).

5.5 Passive of Hollow Verbs

The passive perfect of hollow verbs had three forms. In the Hijaz *qīla*, with the Qays and part of ʔasad dialect with a front rounded vowel *qǖla* and *qūla* among the Tamīm, Faqʕas and Dabr (§ 2.2.2.5; Rabin 1951, 159, §t; al-Farrāʔ *Luġāt*, 14).[2] These are different dialectal outcomes of what in Proto-Arabic was probably still a triphthong **quwila*.[3] The QCT aligns with the Hijazi form, e.g. قيل (Q2:11 and *passim*).

5.6 Retention of *ṣirāṭ*

Al-Farrāʔ (*Luġāt* 9 f.) tells us that the word *ṣirāṭ* 'road' is the form used by the Qurayš, while other pronunciations exist:
- *sirāṭ*, a reading attributed to Ibn ʕabbās
- Qays is supposed to have pronounced it with the initial sound in between *s* and *ṣ*.[4]
- *zirāṭ*, a reading he attributed to Ḥamzah[5] and the tribes of ʕuḏrah, Kalb and Banū Qayn.

Al-Farrāʔ points out the QCT explicitly agrees with the Qurashi form: "as for الصراط, there are four linguistic practices: the perfect practice is the first practice of the Qurayš, which is what the book (the Quran) brings (written) with a *ṣād*." Indeed 'path' is always spelled صرط, الصرط in the QCT.

The grammarians seem to have considered the form *sirāṭ* the original and the Qurayš form the result of emphasis spread, but from an etymological perspective this is to be doubted.[6] This word being a loan from the Latin *strata* (presumably through Greek and Aramaic), it seems that the *ṣ* was used as a

2 Sībawayh (IV, 342 f.) discusses these forms but does not attribute the forms to specific tribes.
3 Other triphthongs such as *awi*, *awu*, *awa* appear to have not yet collapsed in Proto-Arabic as Safaitic generally retains them (Al-Jallad 2015, 119 f.).
4 This might be seen as further corroboration that Al-Jallad (2014a) is right to see Sībawayh's description of the *ṣād* as an affricate, and that this description should be seen as endorsing a pronunciation that is an emphatic sibilant *ṣād*, as it is pronounced in modern dialects today.
5 In modern recitation, Ḥamzah's reading is said to be pronounced in between *ṣād* and *zāy*, which in practice means it is pronounced as an emphatic *z*, i.e. [zˤ] (Ibn Muǧāhid 105–107; Ibn al-Ǧazarī § 119).
6 See for example *Lisān* (1993b) which says *ṣirāṭ* is a dialectal form (*luġah*) and that *sirāṭ* is the origin (*ʔaṣl*). This seems to be mirrored in other lexicographical works, as *Lane* (1348c) mirrors the same perspective from several sources.

means to represent the cluster *st*. This strategy is found elsewhere in Arabic, for example in *qaṣr* < Lat. *castrum*.[7] The Qurayš form should therefore probably be considered a retention, rather than an innovation.

5.7 Lack of Syncopation of **u* and **i*

Hijazi was known for its conservative syllable structure compared to Najdi. As discussed in § 2.2.4, whenever two short syllables follow, and the second contains a high vowel *u* or *i*, it would syncopate, while Hijazi retains such forms. Basic noun formations affected by this are the following:

Hijaz	Najd
CuCuC	CuCC
CiCiC	CiCC
CaCuC	CaCC
CaCiC	CaCC
CuCiC	CuCC
CaCiCah	CaCCah
CaCuCah	CaCCah

Due to the QCT not recording short vowels, it is difficult to be entirely sure what the status of the syllable structure is in Quranic Arabic, however words of this type occasionally stand in rhyming position, which lets us make some deductions about the application of this syncopation.

However, as we can only examine these forms in rhyme, another complication is added to this examination, as Sībawayh (IV, 173 ff.) reports that "some Arabs" would insert vowels to break up final CC-clusters in pause. In CaCC nouns the nominative and genitive are inserted giving *hāḏā bakur#* (for *bakrun*) and *wa-min bakir#* (for *bakrin*). Sībawayh does not explicitly state what

7 This borrowing strategy should either be understood as the *ṣ* still being an affricate at the time these words were borrowed and [ᵗsˤ] being considered the closest equivalent to [st]. But alternatively it may be the case that these words entered Hijazi Arabic through a dialect where the reflex of Proto-Arabic **ṣ* was [st] or [ṣṭ], much like some of the modern dialects of the Saʕdah region in Yemen today (Behnstedt 1987, 7).

happens to the accusative, except that the *a* is not inserted. For the indefinite one of course gets *bakrā#* (for *bakran*), but for *al-bakra* it is unclear, perhaps it is optionally to be read as *al-bakir#* or *al-bakur#* (see Sībawayh, IV, 174, l. 3). For CiCC and CuCC nouns it is clear that the vowel simply harmonizes with the preceding vowel, and the case vowel has no effect: *hāḏā ʕidil#* (< *ʕidlun*) or *fisil#* (< *fislun*), *fī l-busur#* (for *busrin*), *raʔaytu l-ʕikim#* (for *al-ʕikma*), *raʔaytu l-ǧuḥur#* (*al-ǧuḥra*). While Sībawayh does not explicitly attribute these forms to a certain dialect, he does mention that those who insert vowels in those cases are those who weaken *al-busuru* to *al-busru* in context; these are the Najdi dialects, and it therefore seems clear that this is an eastern practice, not part of Hijazi Arabic. Therefore, comparing the Hijazi to Najdi forms in pause we would expect the following reflexes.

	Hijaz		**Najd**	
	Context	**Pause**	**Context**	**Pause**
CaCC	*bakrun*	*bakr#*	*bakrun*	*bakur#*
CiCC	*ʕidlun*	*ʕidl#*	*ʕidlun*	*ʕidil#*
CuCC	*ǧuḥrun*	*ǧuḥr#*	*ǧuḥrun*	*ǧuḥur#*
CaCiCan	*kaḏiban*	*kaḏibā#*	*kaḏban*	*kaḏbā#*
CaCuCan	*rağulan*	*rağulā#*	*rağlan*	*rağlā#*
CuCuC	*busurun*	*busur#*	*busrun*	*busur#*
CuCuCan	*busuran*	*busurā#*	*busran*	*busrā#*
CiCiC	*ʔibilun*	*ʔibil#*	*ʔiblun*	*ʔibil#*
CiCiCan	*ʔibilan*	*ʔibilā#*	*ʔiblan*	*ʔiblā#*

It is not clear how CaCiCun and CaCuCun nouns would behave in the Najdi dialects as Sībawayh does not explicitly discuss them, but it seems likely that the etymological vowel would simply return in such environments in pause.

Now if we turn to the Quranic rhyme, we can make some predictions on which forms can rhyme with which, depending on whether the Quran had Najdi or Hijazi style syllabification. If Quranic Arabic had Najdi style syllabification, one would expect original CvCiCā, CvCuCā to rhyme freely with CvCCā, while in Hijazi syllabification these would be expected to remain distinct.

Moreover, due to the probable lack of epenthesis in CC-clusters in pause in Hijazi, it seems likely that if the Quran had Hijazi syllabification that non-indefinite accusative CvCiC, and CvCuC nouns should not rhyme freely with CvCC nouns. Indeed, on examining the different rhymes in the QCT, we find a distribution that is consistent with Hijazi syllabification.

5.7.1 *vCCā Rhymes*

There are many examples of indefinite accusative rhymes where the preceding sequence is consistently a long consonant or a consonant cluster. These, as a rule, do not rhyme with words where one expects a vowel in between the two consonants in Hijazi. There are a few exceptions to this among the Quranic reading traditions, most of which can be explained, and these will be discussed below. Sequences with a consonant cluster indefinite accusative rhyme are: Q18:65–83; Q19:76–98; Q20:97–115; Q37:1–3; Q51:1–4; Q65; Q77:1–6; Q79:1–5; Q80:25–31; Q100:1–5.

5.7.2 *vCā Rhymes*

vCCā rhymes are clearly distinct from rhymes that do not have a consonant cluster before the indefinite accusative ending and thus rhyme in vCā. Examples of this type of rhyme are: Q18:1–64 and Q72.

5.7.3 *vCC Rhymes*

Rhymes in a consonantal cluster vCC are relatively rare, but common enough that their lack of rhyming with vC rhymes seems consistent. Examples are Q77:32–33, Q86:11–14, Q89:1–5; Q97; Q103.

5.7.4 *vC Rhymes*

vC rhymes are relatively rare, only showing up in Q51:7–9 and the whole of Q54. The rhyming patterns in Q54 are especially telling. Word-final geminates are treated as a single consonant, and thus *al-qamar* (Q54:1) may rhyme with *mustamirr* (Q54:2).

5.7.5 *Discussion*

The general pattern of these rhymes is clear: as a rule *u* and *i* were not syncopated, following the Hijazi Arabic practice. This is clear for nouns that end in aCiC or aCuC, which can be seen in the table below. Counterexamples to this pattern do not exist. While aCi/uC rhymes not followed by the indefinite accusative would likely have this shape in Najdi as well due to the epenthesis discussed above, we would expect such cases to rhyme freely with aCC nouns, which they do not.

Unsyncopated word	Preceding rhyme	Following rhyme
كذبا /kaḏibā/ (Q18:5)	ولدا /waladā/	اسفا /ʔasafā/
كذبا /kaḏibā/ (Q18:15)	شططا /šaṭaṭā/	مرفقا /mirfaqā/ or /marfiqā/[8]
رجلا /rağulā/ (Q18:37)	منقلبا /munqalabā/	احدا /ʔaḥadā/
مقتدرا /muqtadirā/ (Q18:45)	عقبا /ʕuqubā/[9]	املا /ʔamalā/
عذدا /ʕaḏudā/ (18:51)	بدلا /badalā/	موبقا /mawbiqā/
كذبا /kaḏibā/ (Q72:5)	شططا /šaṭaṭā/	رهقا /rahaqā/
منتشر /muntašir/ (Q54:7)	نكر /nukur/[10]	عسر /ʕasir/
فانتصر /fa-ntaṣir/ (Q54:10)	وازدجر /wa-zdağir/	منهمر /munhamir/
مدكر /muddakir/ (Q54:15)	كفر /kufir/	نذر /nuḏur/
مدكر /muddakir/ (Q54:17)	نذر /nuḏur/	نذر /nuḏur/
منقعر /munqaʕir/ (Q54:20)	مستمر /mustamir(r)/	نذر /nuḏur/
مدكر /muddakir/ (Q54:22)	نذر /nuḏur/	بالنذر /bi-n-nuḏur/
الاشر /al-ašir/ (Q54:26)	اشر /ašir/	واصطبر /wa-ṣṭabir/
المحتظر /al-muḥtaẓir/ (Q54:31)	نذر /nuḏur/	مدكر /muddakir/
مدكر /muddakir/ (Q54:40)	نذر /nuḏur/	نذر /nuḏur/
مقتدر /muqtadir/ (Q54:42)	نذر /nuḏur/	الزبر /az-zubur/
منتصر /muntaṣir/ (Q54:44)	الزبر /az-zubur/	الدبر /ad-dubur/
مدكر /muddakir/ (Q54:51)	بالبصر /bi-l-baṣar/	الزبر /az-zubur/
مقتدر /muqtadir/ (Q54:55)	نهر /nahar/	

For some of the readers *waladā* seems to rhyme with CvCCā stems in some contexts and CaCaCā in others. ولدا occurs seven times in rhyme position, three times in an expected CaCaCā rhyme, and four times in a CvCCā rhyme. However, when look at the other reading traditions, we find that in the CvCCā rhyme, Ḥamzah and al-Kisāʔī read this word as *wuldā* in the places where the rhyme seems to conflict (Ibn al-Ğazarī, § 3570). The table below tabulates the words in their context.

8 Ibn al-Ğazarī (§ 3489).

9 Also read as *ʕuqbā*, see discussion below.

10 Also read as *nukr*, see discussion below.

	Preceding rhyme	Following rhyme
ولدا /waladā/ (Q18:4)	ابدا /abadā/	كذبا /kaḏibā/
ولدا /waladā/ (Q18:39)	احدا /aḥadā/	طلبا /ṭalabā/
ولدا /waladā/ (Q72:3)	احدا /aḥadā/	كذبا /kaḏibā/
ولدا /wuldā/ (Q19:77)	مردا /maraddā/	عهدا /ʕahdā/
ولدا /wuldā/ (Q19:88)	عهدا /ʕahdā/	ادا /iddā/
ولدا /wuldā/ (Q19:91)	هدا /haddā/	ولدا /wuldā/
ولدا /wuldā/ (Q19:92)	ولدا /wuldā/	عبدا /ʕabdā/

There are two cases in Q18, where the rhyme word seems to conflict, where we find a word universally read as CvCCā in both cases flanked by CaCaCā, these are تسعا /tisʕā/ (Q18:25; preceding rhyme /rašadā/ and following rhyme /aḥadā/) and زرعا /zarʕā/ (Q18:32; preceding rhyme /murtafaqā/, following rhyme /naharā/). Both of these words end in ʕ, and one wonders whether there was a vocalic epenthesis under the influence of this guttural to yield /tisaʕā/ and /zaraʕā/. In the case of Q18:32 another solution, however, may simply be that the verse does not end there. According to the Meccan and old Medinan verse count زرعا is not the end of the verse (Spitaler 1935, 42).

5.7.6 *Alternation between CuCuC and CuCC Nouns*

Remaining exceptions are primarily found with nouns of the shape CuCuC or CuCC, where in several cases the rhyme suggests that Quranic Arabic had the shape CuCuC, but CuCCā for the indefinite accusative, i.e. following a syncopation and epenthesis model that is more similar to what is reported for Najd. However, not all nouns with the CuCuC shape seem to behave this way, which makes it difficult to evaluate the evidence.

Several CuCuC nouns, from their rhyme context should clearly be understood as non-syncopating in all contexts. For some of these words, several of the readers adhere to CuCC readings, but it seems evident from the rhyme that this is not the correct reading.

	Preceding rhyme	Following rhyme
جرزا /ǧuruzā/ (Q18:8)	عملا /ʕamalā/	عجبا /ʕajabā/
فرطا /furuṭā/ (Q18:28)	ملتحدا /multaḥadā/	مرتفقا /murtafaqā/
حقبا /ḥuqubā/ (Q18:60)	موعدا /mawʕidā/	سربا /sarabā/
شهبا /šuhubā/ (Q72:8)	احدا /ʔaḥadā/	رصدا /raṣadā/
قبلا /qubulā/ (Q18:55) /qibalā/ Nāfiʕ, Ibn Kaṯīr, ʔabū ʕamr, Ibn ʕāmir, Yaʕqūb (Ibn al-Ǧazarī § 3514)	جدلا /ǧadalā/	هزوا /huzuwā/
هزوا /huzuwā/ Ḥafṣ (Q18:56) /huzʔā/ Ḥamzah, Xalaf /huzwā/ Ḥamzah on pause /huzuʔā/ Rest (Ibn al-Ǧazarī § 2667, 2670).	قبلا /qubulā/, /qibalā/	ابدا /abadā/
هزوا /huzuwā/, /huzʔā/, /huzwā/, /huzuʔā/ (Q18:106)	وزنا /waznā/	نزلا /nuzulā/
رعبا /ruʕbā/ (Q18:18) /ruʕubā/ Ibn ʕāmir, al-Kisāʔī, ʔabū Ǧaʕfar, Yaʕqūb (Ibn al-Ǧazarī, § 2677)	مرشدا /muršidā/	احدا /ʔaḥadā/
عقبا /ʕuqubā/ (Q18:44) /ʕuqbā/ ʕāṣim, Ḥamzah, Xalaf (Ibn al-Ǧazarī, § 2684)	منتصرا /muntaṣirā/	مقتدرا /muqtadirā/
ودسر /wa-dusur/ (Q54:13)	قدر /qudir/	كفر /kufir/
وسعر /wa-suʕur/ (Q54:24)[11]	بالنذر /bi-n-nuḏur/	اشر /ašir/
الزبر /az-zubur/ (Q54:43)[12]	مقتدر /muqtadir/	منتصر /muntaṣir/
والدبر /wa-d-dubur/ (Q54:45)	منتصر /muntaṣir/	وامر /wa-ʔamarr/

In two cases, however, rhyme seems to suggest a pronunciation with CuCuC in every form but the indefinite accusative, where the indefinite accusative is CuCCā with syncope in the indefinite accusative. In the case of *nuḏur* 'warnings' the *nuḏur*/*nuḏrā* alternation is agreed upon by all readers, but for *nukur* 'denial' the *nukur/nukrā* alternation is disagreed upon by the readers, although the majority also has *nukur/nukrā* as the rhyme suggests.

11 See also Q54:47.

12 See also Q54:52.

	Preceding rhyme	Following rhyme
النذر /an-nuḏur/ (Q54:5)[13]	مزدجر /muzdağar/	نكر /nukur/, /nukr/
ونذر /nuḏur/ (Q54:16)[14]	مدكر /muddakir/	مدكر /mudakkir/
نذر /nuḏrā/ (Q77:6)	ذكرا /ḏikrā/	لوقع /lawāqiʕ/
نكر /nukur/ (Q54:6) /nukr/ Ibn Kaṯīr (Ibn al-Ğazarī, § 2688)	النذر /an-nuḏūr/	منتشر /muntašir/
نكرا /nukrā/ (Q18:74) /nukurā/ Nāfiʕ, Ibn Ḏakwān ʕan Ibn ʕāmir, Šuʕbah ʕan ʕāṣim, ʔabū Ğaʕfar, Yaʕqūb (Ibn al-Ğazarī, § 2685)	عسرا /ʕusrā/ (Q18:73) /ʕusurā/ ʔabū Ğaʕfar (Ibn al-Ğazarī, § 2674)	صبرا /ṣabrā/
نكرا /nukrā/, /nukurā/ (Q18:87)	حسنا /ḥusnā/	يسرا /yusrā/, /yusurā/
نكرا /nukurā/, /nukrā/ (Q65:8)	يسرا /yusrā/, /yusurā/	خسرا /xusrā/

Finally, the nouns *nuz*(*u*)*l* 'lodging' and *yus*(*u*)*r* 'ease' occur in environments where the reading /nuzlā/ and /yusrā/ seems to work best for the rhyme, and others where /nuzulā/ and /yusurā/ work better.

	Preceding rhyme	Following rhyme
نزلا /nuzulā/ (Q18:102)	سمعا /samʕā/	صنعا /ṣunʕā/ (Q18:104)[15]
نزلا /nuzulā/ (Q18:107)	هزوا /huzuwā/, /huzʔā/, /huzwā/, /huzuʔā/	حولا /ḥiwalā/
يسرا /yusrā/ (Q18:88) /yusurā/ ʔabū Ğaʕfar (Ibn al-Ğazarī, § 2674)	نكرا /nukurā/, /nukrā/	سببا /sababā/
يسرا /yusrā/, /yusurā/ (Q51:3)	وقرا /wiqrā/	امرا /amrā/
يسرا /yusrā/, /yusurā/ (Q65:4)	قدرا /qadrā/	اجرا /ağrā/
يسرا /yusrā/, /yusurā/ (Q65:7)	اخرى /uxrē/	نكرا /nukurā/, /nukrā/

This conflicting evidence does not allow for a simple resolution, and from a broader Semitic perspective, it is not easy to solve this either. In other Semitic

13 See also Q54:41.

14 See also Q54:21, 23, 30, 37, 39.

15 Q18:103 ends in اعمالا /ʔaʕmālā/, which breaks the rhyme. This verse break does not exist for the Meccan, or either of the Medinan verse counts (Spitaler 1935, 43).

languages, nouns with the shape CuCuC are excessively rare (Fox 2013, 203ff.). Fox (2013, 205) suggests this may have been the shape of the infinitive construct in Hebrew, e.g. *qəṭol* < **qutul-*, while **qtul-* has also been suggested (Suchard 2019, 246). Besides this, only the isolated nouns *bəḵor* 'first-born' (cf. Syr. *bŭḵur*, *buḵrā*) and *ḥălom* 'dream' (cf. CAr. *ḥulum*, *ḥulm*) seem to point to such a noun shape.

Arabic CuCuC nouns often have byforms with the shape CuCC (generally attributed to eastern dialects by the grammarians), but frequently correspond to formations in other Semitic languages that unambiguously point to CuCC. For example, fractions like such as *rubuʕ*, *rubʕ* 'fourth' and *xumus*, *xums* 'fifth' correspond to Hebrew *roḇaʕ* 'fourth' and *ḥomɛš* 'fifth'; the Hebrew forms unambiguously point to **rubʕ-* and **xums¹-*. A similar conflict is found with CAr. *ʔuḏun*, *ʔuḏn* 'ear', Hb. *ʔozɛn* < **ʔuḏn*. For this reason, many authors (e.g. Rabin 1951, 97f.; Fox 2013, 150) have suggested that these forms are the result of dialects with vocalic epenthesis of *CuCC > CuCuC and in other cases syncope *CuCuC > CuCC. However, this cannot entirely account for the variation that we see.

In the Arabic as described by the early grammarians, CuCuC and CuCC nouns are contrastive. CuCuC nouns are frequently used for plural nouns whose singular has a CvCv̄C shape, e.g. *kitāb* pl. *kutub* 'book' and *rasūl* pl. *rusul* 'messenger' (Ratcliffe 1998, 105) whereas the plural of elatives and adjectives of colour and bodily defects have a plural pattern CuCC, for example *ʔakbar* pl. *kubr* 'greater' and *ʔaḥmar* pl. *ḥumr* 'red'. Minimal pairs such as *ḥumur* (sg. *ḥimār*) 'donkeys' versus *ḥumr* (m.sg. *ʔaḥmar*) 'red (pl.)' suggest that we are dealing with a genuine contrast.[16]

The possibility of the existence of CuCuC nouns besides CuCC nouns, even within a single dialect would allow to explain why specifically nouns of this shape seem to yield conflicting results in terms of the syllable structure reflect in the rhyme. Therefore it seems that Fox (2013, 150) is correct to say that not all CuCuC ~ CuCC alternation can be explained as the result of epenthesis and syncope, and that, for reasons that are not entirely clear anymore, some forms of Arabic, including Quranic Arabic, had the freedom to use CuCuC and CuCC shapes side by side.

---

16 One might cast doubt on this contrast as it appears in a literary language, and could be envisioned to be an invention of the grammarians to form a contrast between the two. While in quite a few dialects the two patterns do merge (either towards CuCuC or towards CuCC), at least in Cairene Arabic the contrast appears to be maintained, e.g. *kitāb* pl. *kutub* but *ʔaṭraš* pl. *ṭurš* 'deaf'.

5.8 Development of the Phoneme *ē*

Rabin (1951, 160, § v) points out that a distinction between *ʔalif maqṣūrah* when the root is III-*y* and III-*w* both in verbs and in nouns is clearly present in the rhyme and spelling of the QCT (see also Nöldeke et al. 2013, 415; van Putten 2017a). Thus, we find هدى /hadē/[17] 'he guided' (Q2:143) versus دعا /daʕā/ 'he called' (Q3:38), and الهدى /al-hudē/ 'guidance' (Q3:73) versus سنا /sanā/ 'flash' (Q24:43). While Rabin takes the form *hadē* etc. as analogical innovations from **hadā*, it is now clear from Pre-Islamic Arabic and comparative evidence that the vowels *ē* and *ā* have distinct etymological origins, where *ē* develops from *ayV, whereas *ā* either descends from original **ā* or from **awV* (van Putten 2017a).

Al-Farrāʔ (*Luġāt*, 21 f.) explicitly states that the people of the Hijaz merge the III-*y* and III-*w* verbs towards *ā*, whereas the people of Najd have *ē* for III-*y* verbs and *ā* for III-*w* verbs. He adds that it is best to pronounce the vowel in between "extreme *i*" (*al-kasr al-šadīd*) and "extreme *a*" (*al-fatḥ al-šadīd*) and that the majority of Arabs and readers follow that practice. This comment is surprising on several levels. First, al-Farrāʔ seems to explicitly endorse making a distinction between the two long vowels, different from what becomes the standard in Classical Arabic which merges the two towards *ā*, and second that it is certainly not the majority of readers or Arabs who make this distinction today. This latter comment should probably be understood from the Kufan context from which al-Farrāʔ writes. The Kufan readers Ḥamzah, al-Kisāʔī and Xalaf all read the III-*y* with /ē/. Warš ʕan Nāfiʕ also makes this distinction consistently, pronouncing the III-*y* with /ǟ/. The rest of the readers of the 10 all regularly merge the sounds (with the exception of ʔabū ʕamr at the end of a verse, see § 3.6.6.1). The comment that the 'majority of the Arabs' apparently had a phonemic distinction between /ǟ/ (if in between extreme *i* and extreme *a* does not just point to /ē/)

17 Rabin takes this final *ē* to have been phonetically a diphthong [ay]. The spelling in the QCT does not allow us to distinguish the monophthongal value [ē] from [ay], but I take the monophthongal pronunciation in the readings of Ḥamzah and al-Kisāʔī to be significant here. I am not convinced by Owens' (2006, 199) argument for seeing *ʔimālah* as a rising diphthong [iə] or [ia]. This analysis is primarily based on the idea that *ʔimālah* is spelled with a *kasrah* in front of the *ʔalif* by Sībawayh and that other authors such as Ibn Muǧāhid even describe *ʔimālah*, for example in a word like *ṭēba* as having "*kasr al-ṭāʔ*". This analysis (although by no means certain) might work in front of *ʔimālized ā*s that are written *ʔalif*, but breaks down in words like *hadē* spelled هدى, by Owens' logic these words should be pronounced ***hadī*. Indeed, such cases of *ʔimālah* are explicitly described in the same terms, e.g. Al-Farrāʔ (*lughāt*, 21): *wa-kaṯīrun min ʔahli naǧdin yaksirūna, fa-yaqūlūna* , قضِى, رمِى, وسوِّى, *wa-yaftaḥūna ḏawāt al-wāw* [...].

and /ā/ does highlight that whatever 'Arabic' was at the time of al-Farrāʔ, was clearly distinct from textbook Classical Arabic.

If al-Farrāʔ is correct in attributing the *ē*/*ā* contrast of this feature to the Najd, then this would mean we have a phonetic feature of Quranic Arabic that is proper to Najdi Arabic rather than to the Hijaz. If this feature was ever part of Hijazi Arabic, it seems that at the time that Sībawayh and al-Farrāʔ were active, this distinction had clearly fallen out of use in the Hijaz, some 150 years after the codification of the Quranic text. There are perhaps a few remaining memories of the feature in the Hijaz to be discovered in Sībawayh's *Kitāb*. Rabin points to the passage in Sībawayh (IV, 256) where he tells us that "some Arabs say *ṣawaray*, *qahalay* and *ḍafaway*, so they make it (the *ʔalif maqṣūrah*) a *yāʔ*, and they are like those they agree with those who say *ʔafʕay*, and these are people from Qays and the people of the Hijaz". This appears to be a reference to Sībawayh (III, 414) where he says that "some Arabs say *ʔafʕay*, with the hiding of the *ʔalif* in pause; and if it is pronounced in context, it is not done. And from them there are some that say *ʔafʕay* in pause and in context, so they make a *yāʔ* follow it." All of these statements exclusively pertain to the feminine ending *-ē*, it is difficult to decide how we should understand this with stem-internal forms such as *al-hudē* and *banē*.

More salient evidence that a shift of the treatment of *ē* towards *ā* was under way in the early Islamic period can be found in early transcriptions and developing orthography in papyri and inscriptions of this period. Graeco-Arabic transcriptions of the first century show that *ē* was still distinct among the conquerors of Egypt in the first Islamic century, e.g. μαυλε /mawlē/ 'client', ιαειε /yaḥyē/ 'Yaḥyā (personal name)', ιαλε /yaʕlē/ 'Yaʕlā (personal name)' (Al-Jallad 2017d, 431). By the time that the Damascus Psalm Fragment was written, which may be as early as the 8th century, the contrast that was present in the first Islamic century has disappeared (Al-Jallad 2020b, 47 f.).

In Arabic papyri and inscriptions, we find evidence for such a shift as well. One of the typical features of Quranic orthography is that the *ē* is written with *yāʔ* in all contexts. While Classical Arabic orthography continues to distinguish III-*y* and III-*w* in word-final position, e.g. هدى *hadā* and دعا *daʕā*, the contrast is neutralized before pronominal suffixes, e.g. هداه *hadā-hu* and دعاه *daʕā-hu*. In Quranic orthography however, such suffixed forms are not written with an *ʔalif* but are written with a *yāʔ* just like in final position, i.e. هديه, clearly suggesting the vowel was not yet homophonous to the *ʔalif*.

Finding spellings of either type in the early Islamic period is difficult, but the Muʕāwiyah dam inscriptions from 58 AH has the Quranic style of spelling: بنيه 'he built it', instead of **بناه (Miles 1948). By the time the formulation benediction *ʔabqā-ka/hu ḷḷāh* 'may God preserve you/him' becomes popular in papyri the eighth century, the Classical spelling is the only one attested, e.g. اسماه الله (CPR XXI 5, l. 3; 182 AH).[18] If we assume the inscriptions and papyri to be direct continuations of the language of the Quran, this data could be interpreted as showing a diachronic development of Quranic/Hijazi Arabic from a situation that distinguishes *ē* and *ā* to one that has merged the two sounds. The eastern dialects would then appear to have held off this merger for a longer time, and thus make it into the descriptions of the grammarians.[19] The fact that the Arab grammarians consider this *ē* purely a by-form of the *ʔalif*—even though it is a separate phoneme—also suggests that the base language the grammarians are arguing from is a dialect that has merged these forms.

From a pre-islamic epigraphic perspective we can see some interesting developments that, however, do not help much towards solving this conundrum. In Safaitic the historical triphthongs are still actual triphthongs, i.e. **aya* and **awa* (Al-Jallad 2015, 47), e.g. *ʿlw* [ʕalawa] 'to ascend'. However III-*w* often merges towards III-*y*, e.g. *ngw* [nagawa], *ngy* [nagaya] 'to escape' (Al-Jallad and Jaworska 2019). In Hismaic, the **awa* seems to have collapsed towards *ā*, while the **aya* was still distinct, i.e. *dʿ* [daʕā] 'he called' but *bny* [banay(a)] 'he built' (Al-Jallad 2020a). For Nabataean Arabic, the sounds appear to have collapsed to *ā*, as final **ayV* sequences are spelled with *aleph*: אלעזא /al-ʕozzā/ 'al-ʿUzzā' (Cantineau 1978, 128) and דושרא /ḏū šarrā/ 'Dousares' (Cantineau 1978, 80). The QCT in having the ē/ā contrast is thus archaic (and more archaic than Nabataean Arabic) and not innovative in this regard.

5.9 Hollow Root ʔimālah

Where Quranic Arabic appears to have retained a distinction between word-final triphthongs with III-*w* and III-*y*, the triphthong in hollow roots has quite clearly collapsed to *ā*. These are still distinct triphthongs in the Old Arabic reflected in most Safaitic inscriptions (Al-Jallad 2015, 47), and al-Farrāʔ (*Luġāt*, 17) indeed confirms what the QCT suggests (see § 2.2.2.3): The people of the Hijaz pronounced with a pure *ā* regardless of whether the second root consonant was *w* or *y*. But the common people of the Najd, among the Tamīm, ʔasad and Qays would apply *ʔimālah* to the II-*y* roots such as *šēʔa, ǧēʔa, xēfa, ṭēba, kēda* and *zēġa*.

18 This papyrus has been accessed through the Arabic Papyrology Database (https://www.apd.gwi.uni-muenchen.de/apd/project.jsp)

19 Although even there not unscathed, the descriptions of Sībawayh and al-Farrāʔ are irreconcilable, which suggests even there a merger may have been under way (§ 3.3.3.3).

Rabin (1951, 111–113) sees this quote (which he gets indirectly from Ibn Yaʕīš) as a contradiction with what Sībawayh says. As Sībawayh (IV, 120) says that it is a linguistic practice among some of the people of the Hijaz (*wa-hiya luġatun li-baʕḍi ʔahli l-ḥiǧāz*). Thus, he suggests that Ibn Yaʕīš mistakenly reversed the attribution of this type of *ʔimālah* to the Najdi tribes. Now that we no longer need to rely on the indirect quote of Ibn Yaʕīš (*Šarḥ al-Mufaṣṣal*, V, 188), but have access to the quote of al-Farrāʔ directly, it is now confirmed that Ibn Yaʕīš was quoting al-Farrāʔ correctly, despite the apparent contradiction with Sībawayh.

However, one wonders whether this should be understood as a contradiction between the two authors, rather than a lack of specificity of Sībawayh. Sībawayh (IV, 120 f.) attributes the collapse of the medial triphthong to *ē* to be "a linguistic practice among some of the people of the Hijaz; but the general populace does not apply *ʔimālah*." He makes no mention of whether this is practiced outside of the Hijaz. This interpretation would seem to resolve the apparent contradiction between the report of al-Farrāʔ and Sībawayh. The fact that it is explicitly mentioned to be a marginal feature in the Hijaz means that we should not find it particularly surprising that the feature is absent in the QCT.

5.10 Major Assimilation in Gt-stems.

Another case where a feature that we find in the Quran does not get attributed to the Hijaz is the occasional assimilation of coronal consonants across vowel boundaries. Al-Farrāʔ (*Luġāt*, 27) reports that many of Qays and Tamīm say *muhaddūna* or *muhuddūna* for *muhtadūna* whereas the people of the Hijaz avoid such assimilations.

There are three places in the Quran where the QCT could be understood as having undergone such an assimilation. First is Q10:35 يهدى which is variously read as, *yahaddī, yahăddī, yahiddī, yahddī, yihiddī* and *yahdī* (Ibn al-Ǧazarī, § 3256), second Q36:49 يخصمون which is variously read as *yaxaṣṣimūna, yaxăṣṣimūna, yaxiṣṣimūna, yaxṣṣimūna* and *yaxṣimūna* (Ibn al-Ǧazarī, § 4010) and finally Q4:154 تعدوا variously read as *taʕddū, taʕaddū, taʕăddū* and the rest *taʕdū*. These three verbs also occur unassimilated elsewhere in the Quran (e.g. Q10:108; Q3:44; Q2:231). Whether we are really dealing with assimilated forms of this type, however, depends on the trust one places in the majority of the readers to properly reflect the language of the QCT, and how much trust one places in the linguistic facts as presented by al-Farrāʔ.

On discussing the form Q10:35 يهدى, al-Farrāʔ (*Luġāt*, 72) tell us that among the people of the Hijaz *hadā* 'to lead' may have the same meaning as *ihtadā* 'to be rightly guided' and that the readers used to recite this verse as *ʔam-man yahdī ʔillā ʔan yuhdā* using that meaning thus: "or he who is rightly guided only if he is guided (himself)" rather than the straightforward understanding of this reading with *yahdī* "or he who guides only if he is guided (himself)." If we accept al-Farrāʔ's report that *hadā* may have the meaning of *ihtadā* in the dialect of the Hijaz, then we are not clearly dealing with the QCT reflecting a non-Hijazi form, as this verse may have been read as *yahdī*, lacking the non-Hijazi assimilation. However, there is some reason to doubt this account. Al-Farrāʔ's teacher al-Kisāʔī and his teacher Ḥamzah are the only canonical readers that read *yahdī*. Al-Farrāʔ's comment may be a fabrication to simultaneously defend the semantics of the majority reading and the pronunciation of his fellow Kufans. We do find examples where G- and Gt-stems of the same root have (more or less) the same meaning, this tends to happen when the Gt-stem has a medial transitive, not passive meaning, and therefore has a meaning close to the transitive G-stem, e.g. *šarā-hu* 'he bought it' and *ištarā-hu* 'he bought it (for himself)'. In the case of *hadā* in the meaning of *ihtadā*, however, we are not dealing with a medial transitive meaning of the Gt-stem but a passive meaning of the G-stem. I know of no example where the G-stem can have a passive meaning where the Gt-stem does too.

Q36:49 يخصمون yields less obvious semantic problems. Both *xaṣama* and *ixtaṣama* may have more or less the same meaning "to quarrel", although the former also has a transitive meaning "to quarrel with someone". Al-Farrāʔ (*Luġāt*, 120) comments on the different outcomes of the assimilation of the *ixtaṣama* reading, but makes no special comment on the semantic of Ḥamzah's reading *yaxṣimūna*. He gives a more in-depth discussion of the meaning of this reading in his *Maʕānī al-Qurʔān* (Al-Farrāʔ *Maʕānī*, II, 379).

Q4:154 تعدوا likewise yields few semantic problems. Both *ʕadā* and *iʕtadā* can have the meaning "to transgress". Al-Farrāʔ does not discuss this variant, presumably because in this case the G-stem interpretation is the majority reading (and the reading of the Kufans he was most intimately familiar with).

If we take these forms as assimilated, then they are the only cases of Gt forms in the QCT with an assimilation that al-Farrāʔ attributes to Tamim and Qays. In all other cases the QCT explicitly agrees with the Hijazi form. However, throughout the Quran, not infrequently, we find examples of assimilation of especially coronal consonants or identical consonants across vowels. This is especially commonly attested with tD- and tL-stems, such as *fa-taṭahharū* → فاطهروا *fa-ṭṭahharū* (Q5:6). It also occurs in cases where two consonants assimilating are identical, examples in the QCT are: اتحجونى *ʔa-tuḥāǧǧūn-nī* 'do you argue with me?' (Q6:80),[20] تامرونى *taʔmurūn-nī, tāmurūn-nī, taʔmurūn-niya, tāmurūn-niya*

20 Also read as *ʔa-tuḥāǧǧū-nī* (Ibn al-Ǧazarī, § 3037).

'you ordered me' (Q39:64),[21] تامنا *taʔmanʷ-nā, tāmanʷ-nā, tāman-nā* 'you trust us' (Q12:11)[22] and مكنى *makkan-nī* 'has established me' (Q18:95),[23] فنعما, نعما *niʕim-mā, niʕĭm-mā, naʕim-mā, niʕm-mā* 'how good' (Q2:271; Q4:58).[24] To this we may also add the rare contraction of geminated apocopates that we discussed in § 4.9 above.

It seems then that this kind of assimilation across vowels was somewhat productive in Quranic Arabic. Such forms do not usually get attributed to specific dialects of Arabic at all, and seem to be quite particular to Quranic Arabic.

5.11 *raʔaya, *naʔaya > rāʔa, nāʔa

Another feature suggested by Rabin (1951, 142 f., § ii) to be a Hijazi development is the apparent metathesis of original II-*ʔ* III-*y* verbs to II-*y* III-*ʔ*, thus original **raʔaya* 'to see' and **naʔaya* 'to move away' shift to *rāʔa* and *nāʔa* rather than *raʔē* and *naʔē*. These verbs are registered in the Arabic lexicographical tradition (*Lane* 1197b; *Lisān* 4590c), and it is quite clear that their spelling in the QCT as را (e.g. Q6:76, 77, 78) and نا (Q17:83; Q41:51) should be understood as reflecting such forms (as also recognized by Rabin). While none of the canonical readers read *raʔā/ē* as *rāʔa*—despite the *rasm*—Ibn Ḏakwān ʕan Ibn ʕāmir and ʔabū Ǧaʕfar both read *naʔā/ē* as *nāʔa* (Ibn al-Ǧazarī, § 3478).

The suggestions that this form is Hijazi is confirmed by al-Farrāʔ (*Luġāt*, 80 f.) who comments on these words. He claims that both *naʔā* and *raʔā* are the Qurashi form and he adds that this is how one recites the Quran (he is seemingly unaware of Ibn ʕāmir and ʔabū Ǧaʕfar's reading). He follows this up by a list of mostly Hijazi tribes that do have *nāʔa* and *rāʔa* however: for Hawāzin among its branch of the Saʕd b. Bakr, the Banū Kinānah, Huḏayl and many of the Medinans (specifically the ʔanṣār). He adds that in the *faʕaltu* form this metathesis does not take place and they say *raʔaytu* and *naʔaytu*. This is indeed in line with what we see in the QCT where suffixed forms of *rāʔa* 'to see' are usually spelled رايت and occasionally ريت in early Quranic manuscripts, pointing to /rāyt/ or /raʔayt/. All the tribes and people mentioned

21 Also read as *taʔmurū-niya, tāmurū-niya* (Ibn al-Ǧazarī, 4091). Ibn ʕāmir reads *taʔmurūna-nī*, following the Syrian *rasm* تامرونني (Sidky 2021).

22 Almost universally read with labialization of the first *n*, but ʔabū Ǧaʕfar reads *tāman-nā* (Ibn al-Ǧazarī, § 3326).

23 Also read as *makkana-nī* by Ibn Kaṯīr (Ibn al-Ǧazarī, § 1208). This is also reported as a *rasm* variant for the Meccan *rasm* (Sidky 2021).

24 Ibn al-Ǧazarī, § 2806.

are situated in or around the Hijaz, and thus this feature is clearly Hijazi, although strikingly explicitly denied to be Qurashi.

5.12 Lexical Isoglosses

Besides some of the generalizable phonological details as discussed on the sections above, al-Farrāʔ in his *Luġāt al-Qurʔān* lists many isoglosses of specific lexical items, which represent certain differences in vocalization or metathesis. These cannot always be confidently be seen as the result of a regular sound law, and some certainly reflect the outcome of some irregular shift. Nevertheless, such forms can be compared against the QCT, to see to what extent they support a dialectal identification. Whenever the QCT allows us to distinguish such lexical isoglosses, it invariably points towards the Hijazi form.

This is significant, as this is not at all what we find among the reading traditions when the QCT is ambiguous. Even in such cases the readings quite often agree with the form attributed to the Hijaz, but far from always. In other words, the Quranic readers did not feel forced to stick to what was believed to be the Hijazi/Qurashi forms (see § 3.4). But when the *rasm* leaves no other choice, the readers fall in line, and as a result end up having the Hijazi form. This is strong evidence of the Hijazi character of the QCT. The following list gives examples of forms cited by al-Farrāʔ (*Luġāt*). After each option the tribal attribution is given in brackets, followed by the page number where the isogloss is discussed. Finally, the QCT form is listed. While it is not possible to define more specific sound laws for these isoglosses, I have categorized them into several general types.

Metatheses
- *ṣāʕiqah* pl. *ṣawāʕiq* 'thunderclap' (Qurayš and those eloquent Arabs around them), *ṣāqiʕah* pl. *ṣawāʕiq* (Tamīm, Rabīʕah), p. 16. QCT: Qurayš الصعقه (Q2:55 etc.) pl. الصوعق (Q2:19; Q13:13).
- *ʕamīq* 'deep' (Hijaz), *maʕīq* (Tamīm), p. 99. QCT: Hijazi عميق (Q22:27).
- *ʕaṯā* 'to act wickedly' (Hijaz), *ʕāṯa* (Tamīm, Qays and ʔasad), p. 25. QCT: Hijazi تعثوا (Q2:60).
- *ḥāša* 'to shun, forbid' (Hijaz), *ḥāšā* or *ḥašā* (others), p. 83. QCT: Hijazi حش (Q12:31).[25]

25 It is worth noting here that ʔabū ʕamr ignores the *rasm* and reads *ḥāšā* (Ibn al-Ǧazarī § 3335).

Alternations with semi-vowels or long vowels

- *qinwān* 'cluster of dates' (Hijaz), *qunwān* (Qays), *qinyān* (Kalb), *qunyān* (Tamīm, Ḍabbah), p. 62. QCT: Hijaz or Qays: قنوان (Q6:99).
- *quṣwā* (Hijaz),[26] *quṣyā* (widespread practice [*al-luġah al-fāšiyah*]), p. 71. QCT: Hijazi القصوى (Q8:42). The merging of III-*w* and III-*y* roots towards III-*y* in this formation is well-attested elsewhere, e.g. QCT العليا (Q9:40) and الدنيا (*passim*).
- *ʔaḏān* 'announcement' (common speech among the people of the Hijaz, and Najd), *ʔaḏīn* (Some of the Qays), p. 72. QCT: non-Qays اذن (Q9:3).

Hamzahs

- *tawkīd* 'affirmation' (Hijaz), *taʔkīd* (other Arabs), p. 79. QCT: Hijazi توكيدها 'its confirmation' (Q16:91). This form is likely the result of the reanalysis of the I-*ʔ* verb as a I-*w* verb, due to its use in the D-stem leading to a partial merger. See § 6.4.2 for a discussion.
- *waṣīd* 'entrance' (Hijaz), *ʔaṣīd* (Najd), p. 86. QCT: Hijazi بالوصيد (Q18:18).
- *ḏaʔama* 'to blame' (Hijaz), *ḏāma* (√ḏym) (ʕuḏrah, Qayn, many of Quḍāʕah), p. 64.[27] QCT passive participle مذوما (Q7:18) 'disgraced' is not consistent with II-*y* where *maḏīm* is expected (see also § 4.16.2).

Irregular consonantal correspondences

- *ladun* 'near, close' (Hijaz), *ladu* (Tamim), p. 49. QCT: Hijazi لدن (Q27:6).
- *quṭr* pl. *ʔaqṭār* 'region' (Hijaz), *qutr* pl. *ʔaqtār* (Qays), p. 117f. QCT: Hijazi اقطارها (Q33:14).
- *ǧadaṯ* pl. *ʔaǧdāṯ* 'great' (Hijaz), *ǧadaf* (Tamīm), p. 98. QCT: Hijazi الاجداث (Q36:51).
- *ʔaǧāʔa* 'to bring' (Hijaz) *ʔašāʔa* (Tamīm),[28] p. 89. QCT: Hijazi فاجاها 'So he brought her' (Q19:23).

---

26 In fact, also the masculine elative retains a trace of the root final consonant **w*, as it is spelled اقصا /ʔaqṣā/ with the regular outcome of Proto-Arabic **ʔaqṣawu*, rather than **اقصى /ʔaqṣē/ (van Putten 2017a, 60). This is not commented on by the Arab grammarians, as they do not distinguish between the two etymologically distinct *ʔalif maqṣūrah*s.

27 One might wonder how to understand this statement of al-Farrāʔ in light of the fact that *hamzah* has been lost in the Quran. But II-*ʔ* verbs remain distinct from II-*w*/*y* verbs morphologically, even though it is likely the *aʔa* sequence had shifted to *ā*, e.g. *saʔalta* > /sālta/ but, e.g. *kunta* > /kunt/.

28 One wonders whether this description of the Tamīmī form is intended to designate the voiced post-alveolar fricative pronunciation of the *ǧīm* as is common in many Levantine Arabic dialects today. But there is no way to be certain.

- *qāb* 'a distance' (Hijaz), *qīd* (Najd), *qidā* (some of Ġaṭafān), p. 134. QCT: Hijazi قاب (Q53:9).
- *xasafa* 'to darken' (Hijaz), *kašafa* (Tamīm, Qays, ʔasad), p. 149. QCT: Hijazi خسف (Q75:8).
- *kušiṭat* (Qurayš); *qušiṭat* (Qays, Tamīm, ʔasad) p. 153. The QCT: Qurayš كشطت (Q81:11).

As this list illustrates, the QCT invariably has the Hijazi or Qurashi form. In Al-Farrāʔ's list I have identified one case where the QCT gives a mixed answer and both reported dialectal forms are attested. One must keep in mind in this case that al-Farrāʔ's wording is seldomly explicitly exclusive. Just because a certain form occurs in the Hijaz, while another form occurs elsewhere need not mean that one or the other did not have both. The example I have found is the following:

- *ʔamalla* 'to dictate' (Hijaz, ʔasad), *ʔamlā* (Tamīm, Qays), p. 41. As al-Farrāʔ points out, the QCT has both: تملى 'they are dictated' (Q25:5), وليملل 'so let him dictate' (Q2:282).[29]

There is one more example where the QCT seems to have both forms reported. Hijazis treat *ṭaġā* 'to overflow' as a III-*w* verb, while some of the Tamīm treat it as a III-*y* verb (al-Farrāʔ *Luġāt*, 143). The QCT has both forms, but seemingly with a semantic distinction. طغى /ṭaġē/ 'he transgressed' (Q20:24, 43; Q53:17; Q79:17, 37) and طغا /ṭaġā/ 'it overflowed' (Q69:11). Van Putten (2017a, 60f.) argues that the meaning 'to overflow' is the original inherited word, whereas 'to transgress' is borrowed from Aramaic, with its treatment as a III-*y* verbs borrowed along with it. While these two verbs are often taken to be the same verb (e.g. Diem 1979, 239), and thus the spelling with *ʔalif* as evidence that the two *ʔalif maqṣūrah*s denote the same sound, it seems that this may not have been the case for al-Farrāʔ. Al-Farrāʔ usually cites dialectal variants at their first appearance in the Quran in his *Luġāt al-Qurʔān*, but the discussion of *ṭaġā/ṭaġawtu* versus *ṭaġē/ṭaġaytu* does not appear at the first mention of the verb *ṭaġē* spelled طغى at Q20:24, but instead at the first and only mention of its spelling as طغا (Q69:11) where it means 'to overflow'. This may perhaps be taken as an indication that al-Farrāʔ indeed considered these two verbs to be different, and mentions here that they may merge in Tamīmī.

For these lexical isoglosses, it should be clear that whenever the QCT allows us to identify the dialectal form of the text it consistently sides with Hijazi Arabic. The only exception I have found attests both the Hijazi and the non-Hijazi dialectal form.

---

29 Interestingly, al-Farrāʔ also cites واملى لهم /wa-ʔumlī la-hum/ (Q68:45), now generally understood with the other meaning of the verb *ʔamlā* as 'And I will give them reprieve'.

5.13 Phonetic Isoglosses Not Recognized by the Grammarians

There are several phonetic isoglosses in Quranic Arabic that from a comparative perspective clearly set Quranic Arabic apart from Proto-Arabic in its ancestral stage, but whose features either are not recognized at al by the grammarians, or do not receive an explicit dialectal identification.

5.13.1 *Stative II=III Are ẓalla/ẓaltu or ẓiltu*

While Classical Arabic generally breaks up geminated stative verbs like *ẓalla/ẓaliltu* in the suffixed forms, the QCT treats these verbs differently from *ẓanna/ẓanantu*, and has a biliteral form ظلت (Q20:97), فظلتم (Q56:65). Rabin (1951, 163, §aa) suggests that this might be a specifically Ḥijazi innovation but this does not seem to be corroborated by the two early grammarians we examine here. Sibawayh (IV, 421) discusses such forms but just discusses it in 'their speech' as opposed to *ẓaliltu* forms which he says is 'your speech'. Al-Farrāʔ (*Luġāt*, 93) does not seem to consider the *ẓaliltu* form at all (though see al-Farrāʔ *Maʕānī*, II, 190). He says *ẓalta* is the speech of the Arabs, and some of the Tamīm say *ẓilta*. The presence of this feature of the QCT does not seem to have been considered specifically Hijazi.

5.13.2 *Pausal Shortening of Final* -ī

Rabin (1951, 119, § ii) notices that the 1sg suffixes *-nī* and *-ī* often appear shortened in the QCT. In fact, this overwhelmingly occurs in pause (see van Putten and Stokes 2018, 156–158), but appears to have been optionally available outside of pause as well. Moreover, it does not just affect these suffixes but every single case of word-final *-ī* in the QCT. This feature is suggested by Rabin, and likewise by Blau (1977, 15) and Nöldeke (1910, 4) to be a colloquialism of the Meccan dialect. All authors appear to be under the assumption that this feature is not part of the *ʕarabiyyah*, but this is not backed up by the comments of the grammarians—nor are such forms explicitly attributed to the Hijaz by them.

Sībawayh (IV, 183) reports that indefinite III-*y* nouns of the type *qāḍin* and *ġāzin* are normally pronounced *qāḍ*, *ġāz* in pause, although "some Arabs whose Arabic is to be trusted" say *rāmī*, *ġāzī*. But some among the Arabs (no dialect given) are said to shorten the forms in pause, even for the definite form, thus *al-qāḍ* in pause for *al-qāḍī*. No specific example is given, but this is exactly the

The fact that al-Farrāʔ cites it here, suggests he understood this verse to mean 'And I will dictate for them.'

type of distribution that we find in the Quran, thus الزانى 'the adulterer' (Q24:2) in context, but بالواد 'the wadi' (Q89:9) in pause.

For the verb, Sībawayh (IV, 184f.) considers this an anomalous practice (*šāḏḏ*), but does say it occurs, thus you get forms like *lā ʔadr* for 'I do not know', and he specifically says it is more fit (*ʔaǧdar*) to do this with nouns (citing the Quran), but points out that it occurs for verbs at the ends of phrases in the Quran (*fawāṣil*) citing *wa-l-layl ʔiḏā yasr#* 'by the night when it passes' (Q89:4) and *mā kunnā nabġ#* 'what we have been seeking' (Q18:64).[30]

For the 1sg. suffixes Sībawayh (IV, 185f.) considers the shortening to be the more regular and more common practice in pause, citing forms such as *hāḏā ġulām-ø#* 'this is my slave boy', *wa-qad ʔasqā-n#* 'he has given me to drink'. For these pausal shortenings of *-ī*, Sībawayh cites no regional preferences and cites a variety of Quranic verses and lines of poetry.

Al-Farrāʔ (*Maʕānī*, I, 90) discusses the phenomenon of shortening final *-nī* and *-ī* to *-ni* and *-i* respectively, and says that both the retention of length and the shortening is correct. He does not connect it with pausal pronunciation, presumably because in the Quran it occurs not infrequently outside of pause as well. He adds that it is common to shorten these forms, but does not consider it specific to the Hijaz or to any eastern tribe, but as a general phenomenon.

So, while this isogloss is certainly part of Quranic Arabic, there does not seem to be compelling external evidence to connect this feature with the Hijaz. Its identification as Hijazi is therefore purely based on its appearance in the QCT, this is, of course circular when investigating the linguistic character of the Quran.

5.13.3 *Word-Final āy/w > āʔ*

In word-final position, the sequence **āy* (and probably also **āw*) has shifted to *āʔ* in Quranic Arabic. Rhyme suggests that this was one of the few places where Quranic Arabic retained a reflex of the *hamzah* (van Putten 2018, 103ff.). Comparative evidence with Safaitic shows that this variety of Northern Old Arabic retained **āy* in this positio, e.g. *s¹my* /samāy/ 'sky' and *ʾʿrḍy* /ʔaʕreṣāy/ 'valleys'.[31]

It has been suggested by Rabin (1951, 141, §ee) that one of the dialectal isoglosses between Hijazi Arabic and Najdi Arabic is that Hijazi Arabic has *-āʔ*

30 Note that apparently to Sībawayh *fāṣilah* does not just mean 'end a verse in the Quran', but even 'end of a phrase in the Quran', as *mā kunnā nabġ(i)* is not a verse ending in any regional verse count (Spitaler 1935, 43; al-Dānī 1994, 189).

31 Some dialects in Yemen, like Safaitic, but unlike Quranic Arabic never underwent this development, and still have *-āy* in, e.g. *samāy* (Behnstedt 1987, 59ff.). This is not likely to be an otherwise unmotivated shift from **ʔ > y*, as Behnstedt assumed.

(i.e. *ʔalif mamdūdah*) as an outcome of **āy*, whereas Najdi Arabic has *-ā/ē* (i.e. *ʔalif maqṣūrah*). This isogloss works well for the plural demonstrative which in Hijazi is *hāʔulāʔ(i)*, and Tamīm, Qays, Bakr have *(hā-)ʔulā/ē* instead (see § 4.4). But, the evidence of the early grammarians does not give very strong evidence that Hijazi *-āʔ* versus Najdi *-ā/ē* to words other than the demonstrative, however. Al-Farrāʔ (*Luġāt*, 18 ff.) reports that the Qurayš and those that surround them, and the people of Najd lengthen nouns of the type *bināʔan*, whereas some Arabs shortened it (i.e. *binan*). He adds that some of Qays say *ʔinšāyan* and *bināyan*, retaining (at least in this context) the original **y* consonant. He adds that he does not approve of shortening forms like *bināʔan* and *māʔan* to *binan* and *man* "because it mixes up the lengthened (i.e. nouns that end in *-āʔ*) and the shortened (i.e. nouns that ends in *-ā/an*)."

He also discusses انيه *ʔinā-hu, ʔinē-hu* 'the extent of it' (Q33:53), mentioning that it is a widespread Qurašī practice, while (other) people of the Hijaz, Najd and Huḏayl say *ʔiny* whereas some Arabs says *ʔanāʔ* instead. Here the *ʔalif maqṣūrah* form is specifically connected with the Qurayš, but the lengthened form not with any specific tribe (al-Farrāʔ *Luġāt*, 117).

For بسيمهم 'by their mark' al-Farrāʔ (*Luġāt*, 41) reports for *bi-sīmā-hum* for the Quraysh while 'another practice' is *bi-sīmāʔi-him* and that Ṯaqīf and some of al-ʔasd (= al-ʔazd?) say *bi-sīmyāʔi-him*.

There can be no doubt that the language of the QCT retained a distinction between the *ʔalif mamdūdah* and *ʔalif maqṣūrah*, yet the evidence in favour of a geographical split remains sparse, and conflicting.

5.13.4 *Pharyngealization of the Emphatics*

In the pre-Islamic Graeco-Arabica of the southern Levant, presumably reflective of the local dialect of Nabataean Arabic, the emphatic consonants *ḍ* and *ẓ* are represented with σ and τ respectively. These transcriptions certainly point to unvoiced realizations, which suggests that they may have still been ejectives (which cannot be voiced). Moreover, the lack of any effect of the emphatic consonants on the surrounding vowels, seems to further corroborate that they are ejectives rather than pharyngealized consonants (Al-Jallad 2017a, 128).

While it is not possible to tell from the QCT whether these emphatic consonants were voiced or not, it is clear from the spreading effect that the emphatic consonants have on surrounding consonants that they were pharyngealized, as ejectives are typically non-spreading (van Putten 2019b). This is a specific development of Quranic Arabic as opposed to the northern dialects, and gets described for Arabic more generally by the Arab grammarians. No specific mention seems to be made of ejective realizations, which may have largely fallen out of use by the time the Arab grammarians were active.

5.14 The Quran Is Phonologically Hijazi

As with the morphological features of Quranic Arabic, the phonetic features likewise give a clear picture: Whenever the QCT allows us to examine the phonetic features of the language of the Quran, it quite consistently points in the direction of the Hijaz. Only occasionally the data of the Arab grammarians does not agree with the attested data, most notably with the treatment of the word-final /ē/. In this case, a plausible case can be made that Quranic Arabic is archaic in this regard and the descriptions of the grammarians might simply be an inaccurate reflection of early first century AH Arabic because by the late second century Hijazi Arabic had lost this phoneme. The table below once again lists the features found in the Quran and to which tribe they have been attributed by the grammarians. Likewise, it is shown which innovations can be shown to have not taken place in Northern Old Arabic. Once again, we find that the QCT overwhelmingly points to the Hijaz in terms of its phonetic features, and that many of those features are absent in Northern Old Arabic varieties.

	Grammarians	**Northern Old Arabic**
Loss of the glottal stop	Hijaz	Absent
The Phoneme *ō*	Hijaz	?
Lack of Cyī > Cī	Hijaz	?
Passive hollow roots CīCa	Hijaz	Absent
Retention of ṣirāt	Hijaz	?
No syncope of CvCu/iC > CvCC	Hijaz	?
III-y -*ē* distinct from III-w -*ā*	Najd	Absent
Major Assimilation of Gt-stems	Hijaz, perhaps two words Najdi	Absent
Absence of Hollow root *ʔimālah*	Hijaz	?
**Caʔaya > Cāʔa*	Hijaz (but not Qurayš)	Absent
Lexically specific isoglosses	Hijaz	?
**āy > āʔ*	General *ʕarabiyyah*	Absent
Pharyngealization of emphatics	General *ʕarabiyyah*	Absent

5.15 Conclusion

In this and the previous chapter we have examined the morphological and phonological isoglosses of the language of the Quran, not as it is presented by the—often conflicting—reading traditions, but as it is reflected by the only part of the text that certainly existed in the very beginning of the Islamic period, the Quranic Consonantal Text.

Very different from the view we get if we would take any one of the reading traditions, a very consistent picture emerges: All its features align with what the early Arab grammarians identify as Hijazi Arabic. I believe that this evidence should be taken seriously. There is no positive evidence at all that the Quran was composed in an intertribal poetic koiné whose features remain undefined by those that have advocated such a position. Instead, it seems best to consider the Quran to be composed in the native dialect of the audience it was originally addressed to, that is, the local dialect of Mecca and likely also Medina. This should be seen as strong, and independent, evidence for the location in which the Quran took its form, namely: the Hijaz.[32]

Taking the language of the Quran to be identical with the Hijazi vernacular is something that will strike many readers as familiar. After all, this has been the position of many classical Muslim authors on the one hand, and Karl Vollers (1906) on the other. It is worth exploring here how the current view should be seen in light of these views.

First, Vollers work should be seen in the context in which it was written. He advocated that the Quran was originally composed in the Hijazi vernacular, which he considered to be considerably closer to the features many modern dialects have today; he argued for a complete absence of the case system for example. To his mind, grammarians later 'upgraded' the text to be in line with Classical Arabic. This perspective now may strike us as flagrantly ahistorical—

32 Linguistically, Durie's (2018, 16 f.) suggestion for the location of the Quran's dialect being in the Southern Levant is untenable. While Durie mostly correctly identifies several features of Quranic Arabic as also occurring either in Nabataean Arabic or in Safaitic, he brings no evidence that those take place in the Southern Levant to the exclusion of the Hijaz. The argument at best can therefore only serve as opening the possibility that the Quran is from either the Southern levant or the Hijaz. However, a more detailed analysis shows that the Southern Levantine option is less attractive, as Durie mixes freely linguistic features of distinct dialects of Arabic, and ignores clear isoglosses present in Quranic Arabic completely absent in the Southern Levant. Therefore, contrary to his claim, the linguistic evidence rather speaks in favour of the traditional narrative of the origin of the Quran, and speaks against more exotic suggestions that place the origins of the Quran in Petra or elsewhere in the Nabataean realm.

it is clear that the text of the Quran was standardized long before the first grammarians became active, any reworking that requires a wholesale reworking of the *rasm*—which his work does—must be discarded.

However, Vollers' confusion about these facts in the beginning of the 20th century can hardly be considered entirely his fault. At the time, access to early Quranic manuscripts was almost non-existent, and in fact even access to a print Quran that attempted to reproduce the Uthmanic *rasm* was not available. He therefore worked with the Flügel Quran of 1834, and indeed if one examines this text carefully and compares it against the reports of the Arabic grammarians and *qirāʔāt* works one gets a strong impression that the text has been reworked towards a classical standard. The Flügel Quran has fully classicized spelling in keeping with the presumably Ottoman exemplar that was used for producing this print edition. Thus, all cases of *ā* are spelled *plene*, the *ʔalif maqṣūrah* of III-*y* verbs before pronominal clitics is spelled with *ʔalif*, not *yāʔ*, and even post-consonantal *hamzah* is spelled with an *ʔalif*, such as in *yasʔalūna-ka* as يَسْأَلُونَكَ, rather than the QCT's يسلونك. Indeed, the Quranic text *had* been reworked, but much later than Vollers himself imagined.

Further examples of Classicization in the Flügel Quran can be found in its representation of the reading tradition as well. While the Flügel Quran largely follows the reading of Ḥafṣ ʕan ʕāṣim many of the typical non-classical features of that reading had been edited out by Flügel. Thus Hafṣ' typical *kufuwan* and *huzuwan* instead of *kufuʔan* and *huzuʔan* have been systematically 'classicized' by Flügel as كُفُؤًا and هُزُؤًا. Vollers (1906, 85) thus found that the Hijazi readings *kufuwan* and *huzuwan* had been edited out of the text. Many other typical features of Ḥafṣ' reading have been edited out of the text, thus *ʔansānī-hu* and *ʕalay-hu ḷḷāh*—both likewise Hijazi readings—have been classicized to *ʔansānī-hi* and *ʕalay-hi llāh* respectively. The Quranic text therefore *was* reworked, but not by the Arab grammarians but by a German orientalist.

Regardless of these issues in Vollers' work, the massive amount of disagreement between the Quranic readings on all kinds of forms, between the readers *should* have made his contemporaries aware that they did not know what the true language of the Quran was, and it is to his credit that he tried to answer this question. Moreover, reworking by the early Arabic readers can be uncovered through careful examination of the reading traditions, this will be discussed in more detail in the next two chapters.

Besides Vollers, also the medieval Muslim philologists seem to have considered the language of the Quran to be Hijazi. These statements—and especially those of al-Farrāʔ, as presented in a translation by Kahle (1947, 79 f.)—that proclaim that the language of the Quran is the Qurashi dialect require more careful examination. Western scholars have usually taken the claims of the Quran as being Qurashi to be pious fabrications, as these scholars take it for granted that the language of the Quran was the 'poetic koiné' and not the dialect of the Qurayš. Thus, Rabin (1955, 26) says "had the Koran been composed in either the dialect of Quraish or in a "vulgar tongue", no amount of revision without altering the consonant outlines could have made it as similar to Classical [Arabic] as it is."[33]

Zwettler (1978, 112) commenting on al-Farrāʔ's explanation why the Qurashi dialect is the most correct says that "al-Farrā' has evoked here a fairly superficial picture of the classical *ʿarabīya* (though, of course, not of the actual dialect of Qurayš)". Zwettler is commenting here on a tradition brought by al-Farrāʔ translated by Kahle of ʕumar b. al-Xaṭṭāb writing to ibn Masʕūd (admonishing him to never say *ʕattā ḥīna* instead of *ḥattā ḥina* again): "The Koran came down in the language of the Ḳuraish and it came not down in the language of the Hudhail. So, do you teach men to recite it in the language of the Ḳuraish and not in the language of Hudhail." Here the central view that the Quranic language is Qurashi is already found at the earliest possible date that we can expect to encounter it, with the second earliest grammarian whose works have come down to us.

Such commentaries have often been seen as a "dogma which equated the literary language with the Quraish dialect" (Rabin 1951, 21), but those familiar with the work of al-Farrāʔ should immediately see a problem with asserting the existence of such a dogma with this author. While al-Farrāʔ may have been in the business of extolling the qualities of the Qurayš dialect, from his work it should be obvious that this by no means meant that the Quran could only be read in the dialect of Qurayš, or that he equated the literary language he or his teachers used for recitation to the dialect of Qurayš. Al-Farrāʔ frequently discusses and approves of forms that are explicitly non-Qurashi even for recitation of the Quran (as we saw in chapter 3). He even transmits readings that by his standards are clearly non-Hijazi. One explicit example is that al-Farrāʔ (*Luġāt*) reports that *wariq* is the Hijazi form, whereas *warq* is the Tamimi form and that al-ʔaʕmaš and ʕāṣim read the Tamimi form *bi-warqi-kum* (Q18:19) and not the Hijazi form *bi-wariqi-kum*.[34] This is presented as self-evident fact which required no explanation or apology.

The statement that the Quran was sent down in the dialect of Qurayš therefore should not be taken as a pious fabrication, nor should it be seen as a reflection of a dogma that equates the dialect of Qurayš to the 'poetic koiné'/classical

33 NB since Classical Arabic remains completely undefined, this statement is untestable.

34 Indeed, Šuʕbah ʕan ʕāṣim, of whom al-Farrāʔ is a transmitter reads it thus (Ibn Muǧāhid, 389).

arabic. It is clear that the language of *recitation* could be much broader than the language of revelation, and that this was not considered an issue. The language of the Quran as reflected in the QCT is evidently Hijazi and the fact that the readings do not reflect the dialect of the Qurayš does not disqualify this, the classical authors themselves did not consider it to be disqualifying either.

CHAPTER 6

Classicized Hijazi: imposition of the *hamzah*

لَا تَنبِرْ بِاسْمِي

MUḤAMMAD

6.1 Introduction

In 2020, Ahmad Al-Jallad put forward the bold hypothesis that Classical Arabic as we know it today is not a single linguistic system but rather the outcome of a complex interaction between Old Hijazi, i.e. the language of the Quran and early Islamic Arabic on the one hand and the poetic register of the Qaṣīdahs of the Maʕaddites on the other (Al-Jallad 2020b, 69 ff.). This suggestion is very much in line with what we have argued for so far in the previous chapters and previous studies (van Putten 2017a; 2017c; 2018; 2019b; van Putten and Stokes 2018).

While Quran today is read with a certain amount of linguistic variation, these reading traditions, despite their variation still agree on several central features such as the retention of the *ʔ (in most environments), and a full case inflection with final short vowels and *tanwīn* both of which appear to have been absent in the original form of Quranic Arabic as reflected by the QCT. To get from the language of the QCT to the language(s) used in recitation, this language has to have been 'classicized' over time. This claim will, of course, bring to mind the work of Karl Vollers (1906), who famously claimed that the Quran was composed in the Hijazi vernacular and only later reworked by the Arab grammarians towards Classical Arabic. His hypothesis was criticized by many, and few authors have taken his book particularly seriously but even fewer have seriously answered his arguments in a coherent way.

Vollers (1906, § 39–43) considered the original Hijazi vernacular—and by extension the language of the Quran—to have lacked all forms of case inflection. This is not in keeping with the primary source material. First of all, the QCT very likely reached closure during the reign of ʕuṯmān, around 650 CE (Sidky

2021; Sinai 2014a; 2014b; van Putten 2019c). This is clearly before the development of grammatical theory, and reworking of the text by Arab grammarians towards a literary standard which gets established by the Arab grammarians over a century later is chronologically no longer defensible. Much of his argumentation requires us to assume that the consonantal text was changed in the decades after 650 CE. With this new material evidence, this part of his argumentation has lost most of its explanatory power. Likewise, evidence adduced from canonical and non-canonical readings alike only tells us something about the linguistic variation that was considered acceptable as part of the *ʕarabiyyah*, and nothing about the language of the Quran itself as it is reflected in the QCT. The only argument that relies on the rhyme of the Quran is his argument for the absence of the indefinite accusative (§ 42). He suggests that the indefinite accusative ending was invisible to rhyme, but this is clearly not the case and the presence of this vowel is in fact essential for the choice between certain otherwise identical formulae (e.g. ان الله عليم حكيم versus ان الله كان عليما حكيما, see van Putten and Stokes 2018, 145 f.). Any expression of case that is explicitly present in the QCT is certainly part of the language that the QCT was written down in, and likely (and sometimes demonstrably so) present in the language of the original composition as evidenced by the rhyme.

However, those arguing against Vollers have frequently taken the argument to the opposite extreme: any sign of any case at all must mean that Quranic Arabic had full case inflection exactly how the Arab grammarians present it, with full case/mood inflection and *tanwīn*. But this conclusion is not borne out by the evidence either. Between a stage of full case inflection, which must certainly be reconstructed for Proto-Arabic (Al-Jallad and Putten 2017), and no case at all, there must be a whole spectrum of case systems that were in the process of losing it. Already in the pre-Islamic period there were clearly varieties that had lost their case inflection to various degrees.

While the loss of case and mood has often been seen as a catastrophic event that very rapidly, or instantly changed the language from its Old Arabic stages to its Neo-Arabic stage (e.g. Ferguson 1959; Blau 1977; Versteegh 1984), discoveries of the past decades in Arabic dialectology and especially of recent years in Old Arabic epigraphy have made it clear that such a simplified scenario cannot account for the variation that we see. Safaitic, for example, seems to have only marked the accusative case, while not marking *tanwīn* at all, centuries before the rise of Islam (Al-Jallad 2015, 69). Also, the case system of Nabataean Arabic, lacks *tanwīn* in the earliest period but still seems to have a tripartite case inflection. Only later this case distinction seems to be lost, exchanged with an invariable ⟨-w⟩ ("wawation")—a trace of the original nominative (Al-Jallad forthcoming; Diem 1973). Likewise, the case system present in the Damascus psalm fragment is almost completely on its way out, despite being written around the same time as the activities of the early Arab grammarians (Al-Jallad 2020b). However, if we would follow the indications of the Arab grammarians, we would never know such varieties existed at all, as these clearly fell outside of their normative framework of proper Arabic.

It is now clear that certain forms of pre-Islamic Arabic with clearly archaic features—often more archaic than what we find in Classical Arabic—existed which, nevertheless had a different and frequently more reduced *ʔiʕrāb/tanwīn* system than Classical Arabic. It is therefore not a given that this system, whose linguistic reality is proven by the rhyme and meter in pre-Islamic poetry, could be imposed onto the language of the Quran, even if it is present in all the Quranic reading traditions.

Van Putten & Stokes (2018) argued that the Quran did not completely lack the Proto-Arabic case system as Vollers suggests, but rather had a transitional system where final short vowels and nunation had been lost (where *an* had become *ā*). Case expressed by long vowels was generally retained, as well as case vowels for nouns in construct. In other words, we have argued and adduced evidence that case was only retained in places where the QCT actually reflects it. Examples usually invoked to prove that the case system must have operated, tend to not counter such a system particularly well. In countering Vollers' suggestion, for example Fück (1950, 2) cites the following examples which he considered ambiguous had case been lost. All of the examples would be unambiguous in the case system that Van Putten & Stokes reconstruct. The examples of Fück are given below along with the likely form they may have taken in Quranic Arabic as I would reconstruct it:

انما يخشى الله من عباده العلموا /innamā yaxšē ḷḷāh min ʕibādi-h al-ʕulamō[1]/ (Q35:28)

'Only the knowledgeable among his servants fear God'

واذا حضر القسمه اولوا القوربى /wa-iḏā ḥaḍar al-qismah ulū l-qurbē/ (Q4:8)

'And when relatives, at the time of division, are present'

1 The interpretation of the final *wāw-ʔalif* sequence in what in Classical Arabic is pronounced *al-ʕulamāʔu* remains somewhat difficult to determine. It seems fairly clear that it does not represent *āwu* or *āw*. *ō* seems like a reasonable option. See Appendix A.2.3.6 for a discussion.

ان الله برى من المشركين ورسوله /anna ḷḷāh bariyy min al-mušrikīna wa-rasū-lu-h/ (Q9:3)

'That God is free from the idolaters, as is his messenger'

واذ ابتلى ابرهم ربه /wa-iḏ ibtalē ibrāhām rabbu-h/ (Q2:124)

'And when his lord tried Abraham'

The first two of these are in fact distinguished by the *rasm*, and certainly did not present any problem to the understanding. The other two would not be ambiguous if, as we have argued, case vowels had been retained in construct. One should note, however, that even if such phrases would be fully ambiguous, pragmatically such phrases hardly ever pose true ambiguity—it is unlikely that anyone would think that it is God who fears the servant in Q35:28, for example. The very fact that Classical Arabic writing manages to communicate the intended meanings with a writing system that generally does not express case, should make it clear that such ambiguities can be resolved to a large extent through pragmatic considerations.

Moreover, many extra-linguistic hints such as intonation and pause, which are likely to have played a role in the original composition of the Quran, are systematically erased almost completely in Quranic recitation. These too would have helped with the resolution of ambiguities, even with a strongly reduced case system. It is therefore difficult to accept unusual word order to hold much weight as an argument for a full case system, and evidence for its presence or absence needs to be found elsewhere.

Starting from the linguistic situation where *ʔ and final short vowels and nunation were lost completely, one would naturally expect that at times the Quran had been imperfectly classicized towards a variety that did have these features. It has, on multiple occasions, been claimed that the Quran cannot have been classicized for the exact reason that there are no such traces of imperfect classicization, as exemplified, for example by Blau saying that "the total lack of Neoarabic and pseudo-correct features in the Koran establishes a linguistic situation in which the differences between the literary and spoken language could not have been too far-reaching" (Blau 1977, 15). I agree with Blau that the Arabic of the Quran was probably close to the vernacular of the Hijaz, and that little to no reworking has been undertaken on the consonantal text. However, this implies that the language of the Quran did not have *hamzah*, and indeed that it had a reduced case/*tanwīn* system. Blau seems to admit the possibility that Quranic Arabic had a somewhat reduced system that had lost (at least) word final *-i* (pg. 15f.), but does not commit to a strong opinion on what this system may have looked like.

However, we frequently find evidence in the Quranic reading traditions that these texts *have* been grammatically reworked by its reciters. Pseudo-correct features that clearly point to conscious and artificial tampering with the language of recitation frequently appears in them. In fact, Vollers found many examples of this in his *magnum opus*, although many of his critics seem to have missed these points, and have rather chosen to attack his admittedly much weaker argumentation in favour of his 'caseless Quran'.

As I see it, there are three main systematic features that differentiate Quranic Arabic as it can be reconstructed from the QCT, and how it appears in the Quranic reading traditions. The first, and the most widely admitted difference is that Quranic Arabic seems to have lost the *hamzah* entirely, something that is obvious from the orthography and can be clearly demonstrated from Quranic rhyme (van Putten 2018). In this chapter we will show that the pattern of both the pseudocorrect presence and absence of *hamzah* frequently occurs in the Quranic readings, clearly showing that later philologists have inserted the *hamzah* into the recitation of the Quran and were not always successful in doing so with regard to the placement that would be expected from its etymology.

The second feature, is the quintessentially Classical Arabic feature, namely the system of *ʔiʕrāb* and *tanwīn*, which the language of the QCT appears to have largely lost (van Putten and Stokes 2018). In chapter 7, I will show that to the Quranic reciters, placement of *ʔiʕrāb* and *tanwīn* was a highly theoretical undertaking, not one that unambiguously stemmed from its prototypical recitation and composition. Within this theoretical framework, there are also occasional cases where the reciters fail to fully apply the final short vowels in a manner that would be expected, yielding forms without final short vowels, where we would have expected them.

The third feature, is the retention of a phonemic distinction between the two *ʔalif maqṣūrah*s, the one written with *ʔalif* reflecting /ā/ and the one written with *yāʔ* reflecting /ē/, a distinction clearly reflected in the Quranic rhyme (van Putten 2017a). This feature is different from the previous two. While all readings have, to a greater or lesser extent, retained a good number of cases of etymological *hamzah*, and all of them in principle reflect the Classical Arabic system with *ʔiʕrāb* and *tanwīn*, this last feature is a topic of disagreement among the canonical readers. While normative Classical Arabic eventually opts for a merger of these two sounds, the Quranic reading traditions give ample evidence for an original distinction between the two sounds. This is found regularly in the readings of Ḥamzah, al-Kisāʔī, Xalaf and Warš ʕan Nāfiʕ. It is self-evident that not both retention and loss can be true simultaneously for the original composition of the Quran, and rhyme clearly favours the readings that retain this distinction. I will therefore not discuss this feature in more detail in these chapters.

6.2 Pseudocorrect *Hamzah*

In § 5.2 and Van Putten (2018) we have argued that the language of the QCT lacked a *hamzah* altogether and that the reading traditions eventually classicized Quranic Arabic. Van Putten (2018, 98–101) showed already that the reading traditions treat the *hamzah* rather inconsistently. In phonetically identical environments sometimes the *hamzah* is lost while other times it is not, occasionally based on grammatical principles, other times seemingly by rhyme. The fact that the Quranic readings fail to undergo regular sound changes clearly suggests that the readings are not natural language, but rather a mixed literary register (see § 3.3).

Evidence for a transition from a Hijazi *hamzah*-less pronunciation of the Quran, as confirmed by the rhyme and orthography, towards a more classical system can be seen by the presence of pseudocorrection of the *hamzah* in the Quranic reading traditions. Indeed, we would expect to see the application of *hamzah* where it should have never appeared etymologically, and likewise failure to insert the *hamzah* where we would etymologically expect it. Cases of both types of pseudocrrection can indeed be found in the reading traditions (as well as in Classical Arabic). This is a strong indication that Quranic Arabic originally lacked the *hamzah* and that it was only later artificially inserted, as it became fashionable for proper Arabic to have a *hamzah*.

There appears to be a historical memory of this transition taking place in the beginning of the second Islamic century, at least for Medina, as Ibn Muǧāhid (60) reports that Qālūn said: *kāna ʔahlu l-madīnati lā yahmizūna ḥattā hamaza bnu ǧundabin, fa-hamazū mustahziʔūna, wa-stahziʔ* "The people from Madīnah used to not apply the *hamzah* until [Muslim] Ibn Ǧundab (d. 130 AH/747 AH) applied the *hamzah*. From then on they applied the *hamzah* to *mustahziʔūna* and *istahziʔ*"[2]

2 See also al-Ḏahabī (I, 59); Ibn al-Ǧazarī (*al-Ġāyah*, II, 260).

6.3 *Hamzah* among the Quranic Readers

Before we discuss the cases of pseudocorrect *hamzah* it is worth discussing the generalizable treatment of the *hamzah* in the different canonical reading traditions, as this way we are better able to appreciate the instances when readers deviate not just from the imagined classical Arabic norm, but also from their own norms.

The majority of the Quranic readers regularly retain the *hamzah* in most environments. Readers such as ʕāṣim, Ibn Ḏakwān ʕan ibn ʕāmir, Qālūn ʕan Nāfiʕ, Ibn Kaṯīr, al-Kisāʔī, Xalaf and Yaʕqūb by and large retain the hamzah in all positions. That is: in pre-consonantal position, post-consonantal position and in intervocalic positions. The only position where all readers agree that etymological *hamzah* is to be dropped is in sequences of two *hamzah*s, where the first one is followed by a vowel and the second by a consonant, within a single word, e.g. *ʔaʔmuru-hū* → *ʔāmuru-hū* 'I order him' (Q12:32).

The remaining readers adhere to several general principles of the dropping of the *hamzah*. In the following discussion we will only discuss cases of pseudocorrect *hamzah* that cannot be explained by the general rules of the readings.

ʔabū Ǧaʕfar drops each pre-consonantal *hamzah*, with compensatory lengthening, e.g. *muʔminūna* → *mūminūna*, *šiʔta* → *šīta*, *yaʔkulu* → *yākulu*. He likewise does the same for word-final vowel + *ʔ* sequences: *iqraʔ* → *iqrā*, *nabbiʔ* → *nabbī* (Ibn al-Ǧazarī, § 1466). Besides this he also regularly shifts the sequences *iʔūna*, *iʔīna* and *iʔū* to *ūna* and *ī*(*na*) respectively, e.g. *mustahzūna* (Q2:14; Q15:95), *ʔa-tunabbūna* (Q10:18), *muttakūna* (Q36:56), *fa-mālūna* (Q37:66; Q56:53), *al-munšūna* (Q56:72), *al-xāṭūna* (Q69:37), *al-xāṭīna* (Q12:29, 91, 97), *al-mustahzīna* (Q15:95), *muttakīna* (Q18:31), *yuṭfū* (Q9:32). He has a single exception to this: *xāsiʔīna* (Q2:65; Q7:166) (Ibn al-Ǧazarī, § 1496). He would also drop the *hamzah* whenever it stood in the sequence *uʔa*, where *ʔ* was the first root consonant, e.g. *yuʔaddihī* → *yuwaddihī*, *yuʔāxiḏu* → *yuwāxiḏu* (Ibn al-Ǧazarī, § 1485).

ʔabū ʕamr has the option to drop prescononsantal hamzah, or to conservatively keep it (Ibn al-Ǧazarī, § 1472–1474). However, even with the option to drop the *hamzah*, ʔabū ʕamr would not drop it if *hamzah* was root-final, and in the apocopate or imperative. This is not just in word-final position such as *našaʔ* and *tasuʔ*, but also on morpheme boundaries such as *ʔanbiʔ-hum* and *ʔarǧiʔ-hu*, where the *hamzah* is pre-consonantal within the same word (Ibn al-Ǧazarī, § 1475).

Warš ʕan Nāfiʕ has two main treatments. In the transmission path of al-ʔazraq the rule is that Warš drops pre-consonantal and intervocalic *hamzah*, but only if it is the first root consonant. Hence: *muʔminun* → *mūminun* and *yaʔxiḏu* → *yāxiḏu*, and *yuʔaxxiru* → *yuwaxxiru* but not *biʔsa, ǧiʔta*, or *yašaʔ* (Ibn al-Ǧazarī, §1471).

The other path of transmission of Warš, that of al-ʔaṣbahānī, has a principle that is closer to that of ʔabū Ǧaʕfar. He drops any preconsonantal *hamzah*, regardless of the position in the root. He, however, has a list of exceptions to this general rule, causing him to retain significantly more *hamzahs* than ʔabū Ǧaʕfar. These exceptions are: *baʔs, baʔsāʔ, (al)-luʔluʔ, riʔyan, kaʔs, ar-raʔs, ǧiʔta* (and other forms of the verb such as *ǧiʔnā-hum*), *nabbiʔ* (and other apocopates derive from that root), *qaraʔta* (and other suffixed forms of the verb); *hayyiʔ/yuhayyiʔ* and *tuʔwī/tuʔwī-hi* (Ibn al-Ǧazarī, §1469). Like Warš in the path of al-ʔazraq, he also drops any word-internal intervocalic *hamzah* when it is the first root consonant (Ibn al-Ǧazarī, §1485).

Both transmissions of Warš are in agreement that post-consonantal *hamzah* is dropped if there is a word boundary between the word-final consonant and the next word, or if the word preceding the *hamzah* is the definite article. Thus, *qad ʔaflaḥa* → *qadaflaḥa* and *al-ʔarḍu* → *alarḍu* (Ibn al-Ǧazarī, §1541).

Ḥamzah and Hišām ʕan ibn ʕāmir both have conservative *hamzah* treatment, but make a special exception in pause. Hišām drops all word final *hamzahs* in pause (after dropping the final short vowels), whereas Ḥamzah drops *all hamzahs* in pause. That is, words like *yaʔkulu, yasʔalu, al-luʔluʔi, as-samāʔu* and *al-ʔarḍu* would be pronounces *yākul, yasal, as-samā,*[3] *al-lūlū* and *alarḍ* in pause (Ibn al-Ǧazarī, §1541).

6.4 Pseudocorrect Presence of *Hamzah*

In several cases throughout the Quran, we find examples where readers have a *hamzah* where clearly none was ever present etymologically. Such pseudocorrections fall into three types. First, some words can be shown to behave irregularly within the system of the *ʕarabiyyah* in the appearance of the *hamzah*. Second, some words are loanwords from Hebrew or Aramaic where the *hamzah* is absent, but has been inserted into the Arabic form. Finally, there are several inherited Semitic words which on comparative Semitic grounds can be shown to have never had a *hamzah* in their stem but have acquired them in the readings.

3 Optionally with an overlong vowel triggered by the following, now dropped *hamzah*, or without the length.

6.4.1 *Ḍiyāʔ → ḍiʔāʔ*

Qunbul ʕan Ibn Kaṯīr pronounces the verbal noun of *ḍāʔa* (√ḍwʔ) not as *ḍiyāʔ*, as one would expect for a *fiʕāl* pattern of such a root, but as *ḍiʔāʔ* (Ibn al-Ǧazarī §1534). This is clearly pseudocorrect: the root consonant *w* (which appears in the also Quranic *ḍawʔ*) is simply expected to shift to *y* after *i* (for example II-*w* roots with CiCāC plural like, *diyār* 'dwellings', or verbal nouns like *qiyāmah* 'resurrection').[4]

Ibn Muǧāhid (323), who was a direct student of Qunbul, was clearly bothered by this reading. He reports that Ibn Kaṯīr read it as such and that that is how he learned it from Qunbul. However, he brings transmissions of not just al-Bazzī, one of the transmitters he also reports in his discussion of his *ʔisnāds* of Ibn Kaṯīr but also Ibn Fulayḥ, that they rejected the reading and that Ibn Kaṯīr only read with one *hamzah*. He discusses this word again at Q28:71, where Ibn Muǧāhid (495) says: "Only Ibn Kāṯīr read *bi-ḍiʔāʔin* with two *hamzahs*. And I learned it thus from Qunbul, but he was wrong (*ġalaṭa*)."[5]

6.4.2 *Mūṣadah → muʔṣadah*

The C-stem passive participle written as موصده 'closed' (Q90:20; Q104:8) is read by the majority of the readers as *mūṣadah*. However, Ḥafṣ ʕan ʕāṣim, ʔabū ʕamr and Ḥamzah read it as *muʔṣadah* (Ibn al-Ǧazarī, §1484). This variant is a clear pseudocorrection. The verb *ʔawṣada* 'to close' (√wṣd) is also recorded as *ʔāṣada* (√ʔṣd) in classical lexicons, but within the QCT the verb clearly has √wṣd as its root, as is confirmed by *waṣīd* 'threshold, doorstep' derived from the same root and also attested in the Quran الوصيد (Q18:18). As the root is √wṣd in Quranic Arabic, *mūṣadah* is the expected form and *muʔṣadah* the pseudocorrection resulting from the ambiguity of the *hamzah*-less Quranic Arabic, where C-stem participles (and imperfect) of I-*ʔ* regularly merge with I-*w* roots.

This pseudocorrection did not go unnoticed by classical authors either. Al-Zamaxšarī (d. 538 AH/1144 CE) in his *al-Kaššāf* (IV, 257) brings a report (without *ʔisnād*) on the authority of Šuʕbah—who read *mūṣadah*—saying: "our Imam [i.e. ʕāṣim] would apply the *hamzah* to موصده; and I wanted to plug my ears whenever I would hear it." This story may be apocryphal, designed to explain the difference between Ḥafṣ and Šuʕbah in their transmission of ʕāṣim. Nevertheless, it highlights that clearly this reading was disturbing enough to the grammarian and theologian al-Zamaxšarī, that it was worth relating it.

4 Vollers (1906, 95) sees the *hamzah* as the transitional stage between an original **ḍiwāʔ* and the form *ḍiyāʔ*. There is no reason to assume nor is there evidence that such a transitional stage took place.

5 This line is missing in the first edition of this text, but the third edition has this line added.

The confusion between I-*ʔ* and I-*w* roots is well-known for the D-, L- and C-stems in Middle Arabic (Blau 1967, §72.1), and is the result of subsequent analogies after the loss of the *hamzah*, which is common to Quranic Arabic and Middle Arabic alike. This results in a merger of the two root types in the prefix conjugation and participial derivations. This leads to the frequent appearance of pairs of I-*ʔ* and I-*w* verbs with identical meaning. We find a similar case of such a development for توكيدها 'their affirmation' (Q16:91), which looks like the verbal noun of *wakkada* 'to affirm', but Classical Arabic lexicons also record *taʔkīd* and *ʔakkada* with the same meaning. When cognates in other Semitic languages are lacking, it is often difficult to recover whether the I-*ʔ* form was originally a pseudocorrection, or that the I-*w* is simply a generalized form from an original I-*ʔ* verb in a dialect that has lost the *hamzah*.

6.4.3 *Ḍiʔzā*

Another case of pseudocorrection in Ibn Kaṯīr's reading is the word ضيزى 'most unfair' (Q53:22) as he reads it as *ḍiʔzā* rather than *ḍīzā*/*ḍīzē* (Ibn al-Ǧazarī, §1484). While this word seems to be basically only known to the Arabic lexicographers and grammarians from its Quranic context, its morphology is transparent: it must be a feminine elative, as there are no other feminine adjectives that end in *ʔalif maqṣūrah*. It being an elative, one would expect the pattern to be CuCCā, had the noun indeed been derived from a root √ḍʔz, then we would expect *ḍuʔzā*, not *ḍiʔzā*, which rather is a pseudocorrect insertion of *hamzah* on the vocalic pattern of a √ḍyz root, cf. CAr. *ʔaṭyab* f. *ṭībā* 'better', CAr. *ʔarʔaz* f. *ruʔzā* 'more roaring'.[6]

6.4.4 *Manōh* → *manāʔah*

The majority of the readers read the name of the pre-Islamic goddess Manāt as *manāh*. But Ibn Kaṯīr reads this as *manāʔah*. The goddess Manāt is a personification of Fate, whose name is deribed from the root √mnw alternating with √mny. This root is well-attested in Pre-Islamic Arabic, the deity Manāt is spelled *mnwt* in Nabataean, and the fates are also an often invoked in Safaitic as *mny* /manāy/ (Al-Jallad and Jaworska 2019). The insertion of the *hamzah* by Ibn Kaṯīr cannot be seen as anything but a pseudocorrect reading.

6 Arabic lexicographers appear to have been aware of the weakness of this reading, as, for example *Lisān* (2540c) lists *ḍuʔzā* first, then *ḍūzā* (the expected form if one would drop the *hamzah*) and only then *ḍiʔzā* and *ḍīzā* respectively.

6.4.5 *ʕādan l-ʔūlā*

Q53:50 contains a unique sequence in the Quran, the only place where a word ending in *tanwīn* is followed by the definite article, which is followed by a word that starts with a *hamzah*. This sequence yields a cluster of three consonants /ʕāda**n l-ʔ**ūlā/, which is resolved differently by different readers (Ibn al-Ǧazarī, § 1547–1557s). Normally, in the case of a clash of nunation with the definite article, an epenthetic *i* is inserted, and that is the reading of the majority of the canonical readers: [ʕādani l-ʔūlā]. Warš ʕan Nāfiʕ and ʔabū ʕamr, however, resolve this cluster differently in this specific case. The *tanwīn* is assimilated to the *lām* and the subsequence /llʔ/ is resolved by eliding the glottal stop of the word, yielding [ʕādal-l-ūlā].

Qālūn ʕan Nāfiʕ however, applies yet another development and reads the [ʕādal-l-uʔlā]. Qālūn must have interpreted the feminine elative as being phonemically /ʔuʔlā/, after the application of the regular development ʔvʔC > ʔv̄C, as seen for example in **ʔaʔkulu* > *ʔākulu* 'I eat', **ʔuʔtiya* > *ʔūtiya* 'it was given'. With the loss of the initial *hamzah*, the second *hamzah* gets a chance to reappear, a phenomenon we mostly see in imperatives such as *ʔīti* /(i)ʔti/ but *wa-ʔti* /wa-ʔti/. The problem here, however, is that the interpretation of *ʔūlā* as /ʔuʔlā/, is clearly pseudocorrect due to the inherent ambiguity of the surface form. The root of this form is √ʔwl, and thus the underlying form is not **/ʔuʔlā/ but /ʔuwlā/.

6.4.6 *Durriyy* → *du/irrīʔ*

كوكب درى "a brilliant star" (Q24:35) is read by the majority of the readers as *kawkabun durriyy*, where the latter word is clearly to be understood as a denominal adjective of *durr* 'pearls' followed by the *nisbah*-ending. However, ʔabū ʕamr and al-Kisāʔī read this word as *dirrīʔ* and Šuʕbah ʕan ʕāṣim and Ḥamzah as *durrīʔ* (Ibn al-Ǧazarī, § 3731).

Ibn Xālawayh (*ḥujjah*, 262) explains that the reading *dirrīʔ* should be understood as an intensive adjective (like *sikkīt* 'intensely silent') of the root *drʔ* 'to avert; rush out (said of a torrent)', hence 'rushing out intensely' likening the rushing out to the intensity of the light. This explanation is probably a *post hoc* rationalization of a reading with a pseudocorrect *hamzah*. Ibn Xālawayh suggests that *durrīʔ* has the same meaning as *dirrīʔ*, but *fuʕʕīl* nouns like this otherwise do not exist in Arabic, so such an explanation is not particularly convincing.

6.4.7 *Maʕāyiš*

An interesting point where what is considered correct and what is transmitted comes into conflict is in the plural of *maʕīšah* 'livelihood', which in the reading traditions today is *maʕāyiš* (Q7:10, Q15:20). The use of a *yāʔ* in this case is surprising, other nouns with a similar structure consistently have a *hamzah* in this position, e.g. *madīnah* pl. *madāʔin* 'town'; *ḥadīqah* pl. *ḥadāʔiq* 'garden'; *xalīfah* pl. *xalāʔif* 'successor'; *qabīlah* pl. *qabāʔil* 'tribe', etc.

The shift of *āyi, āwi* to *āʔi* is essentially a regular development, and we find it not just in the broken plural pattern here, but also active participles of hollow roots, e.g. *qāʔim* 'standing', and this development may also be the origin of word final *āʔ* such as in *samāʔ* 'sky'.[7]

The only place in Classical Arabic where both **y* and **w* are retained after *ā* and before *i* is in the verbal system, the L-stems retain the root consonant in the imperfective, even though the regular development would require a shift to *āʔi*. This, however, can be easily explained as the result of analogy. The perfective form regularly retains the root consonants, and this is simply expanded to the imperfect, where it would have regularly been lost. This development can be seen as a three-stage development as follows:

1. Proto-Arabic	**2. **āyi*, **āwi* > *āʔi***	**3. Analogical levelling**
qāwama/yuqāwimu	*qāwama/yuqāʔimu*	*qāwama/yuqāʔimu* >> *yuqāwimu*
ʕāyaša/yuʕāyišu	*ʕāyaša/yuʕāʔišu*	*ʕāyaša/yuʕāʔišu* >> *yuʕāyišu*

For the plural *maʕāyiš* no analogical basis to which the **y* could be restored can be found. As such, *maʕāyiš* is a deviation from what we would expect a form of Arabic that underwent the **āyi*, **āwi* > *āʔi* shift to produce. It turns out that in the reading traditions, the form *maʕāʔiš* is in fact known.[8] Ibn Muǧāhid, who does not usually spend time discussing *šāḏḏ* readings in his *Sabʕah fī al-Qirāʔāt* discusses this form and is curt about it:

7 See Brockelmann (1908, 138 f.) for a discussion on this development, which has striking similarities with a development as found in Aramaic (see also van Putten 2020a, 61). Note however that this development cannot be reconstructed for Proto-Arabic, as varieties of Old Arabic still retain the glide in such places, e.g. Safaitic *s¹my* /samāy/ 'sky', *ḫyṯ* /xāyeṯ/ 'travelling', *gyʿ* /gāyeʕ/ 'starving'. Moreover, the shift does not seem to have taken in several dialects of Yemen, where we find forms such as *samāy* 'sky', *ʔalḥāy* 'jaws' (pl. of *liḥi*) and *ʕamyāy* 'blind' (cf. CAr. *samāʔ*, *ʔalḥāʔ* and *ʕamyāʔ*) (Behnstedt 1987, 59–61).

8 Vollers (1906, 95) takes the plural *maʕāʔiš* as a pseudocorrection. Fück (1950, 39 f.), rather prescriptively, considers the reading *maʕāʔiš* a mistake and evidence that there was a lack of a developed grammatical school in Medina.

> The word معيش: All of them read *maʕāyiš* without the *hamzah*. But Xāriǧah, on the authority of Nāfiʕ transmits *maʕāʔiš* with an overlong vowel and a *hamzah*. And ʔabū Bakr [ibn Muǧāhid] said: this is a mistake.[9]

Sadly, Ibn Muǧāhid does not elaborate on why he considers it a mistake. An answer is found in Sībawayh's *al-Kitāb* however, who is in agreement with Ibn Muǧāhid that this word should not have a *hamzah*. He argues that, because this word is derived from a root where the *yāʔ* is part of the root √ʕyš, this *yāʔ* should be retained (Sībawayh, IV, 354–357). Sībawayh is right to observe that this makes the word objectively different from the other words cited so far, where the *ī* of the singular formation is part of the pattern CaCīCah, rather than part of the root, e.g. *madīnah* has √mdn[10] and *ṭarīqah* has √ṭrq.

In this argument, Sībawayh is undoubtedly thinking of words such as the imperfective L-stem verbs such as *yuʕāyišu* where the root consonant is retained as well. However, we must conclude that this is a *post hoc* argumentation. First of all, we cannot assume that speakers of Arabic were themselves grammarians like Sībawayh, and therefore a sound law that would *only* apply to CaCīCah nouns, when the *ī* happened to not be the result of a root consonant, is not something that is likely to have occurred in natural language, as it requires a highly abstract model of formal grammatical thinking. Second, the argument that because the *yāʔ* is part of the root it could not undergo the **āyi > āʔi* shift clearly breaks down in other derivational forms. The active participle of 'to live', after all is *ʕāʔiš*, not *ʕāyiš*, nor is 'bird' *ṭāyir*, but rather *ṭāʔir*. Sībawayh's opinion, which Ibn Muǧāhid upholds as the status quo, therefore cannot be seen as anything other than rationalization for his choice to prefer *maʕāyiš* over *maʕāʔiš* when he was confronted with the choice between the two.

While later scholars of the *qirāʔāt*, such as Al-Dānī (*ǧāmiʕ*, 511), simply fell in line with Ibn Muǧāhid's opinion, not all scholars found themselves in agreement with his judgment. ʔabū Ḥayyān al-Andalusī (d. 754AH) in his *al-Baḥr al-Muḥīṭ* (V, 15) brings forth a rather spirited argument in favour of *maʕāʔiš* as a correct and acceptable reading.[11]

---

9 *qawluhū "*معيش*", kulluhum qaraʔa "maʕāyiša" bi-ġayri hamz. Wa-rawā Xāriǧatu ʕan Nāfiʕin "maʕāʔišah" mamdūdatan mahmūzah. Wa-Qāla ʔabū Bakrin: wa-huwa ġalaṭ.* (Ibn Muǧāhid, 278).

10 Note that it is synchronically correct to consider this noun to be from a root √mdn in Arabic, as can also be seen from the other plural *mudun*, but ultimately in Aramaic, from which the word stems, *mḏīnṯā* 'province, city' is a noun of place of the root √dyn 'to judge' (Jeffery 2007, 260).

11 I thank Hythem Sidky for pointing me to this reference.

The general public reads *maʕāyiš* with the *yāʔ*, this is an analogy (*qiyās*), because the *yāʔ* in the singular is part of the root, and not an extra letter to the pattern so that it receives a *hamzah*. When it is an extra letter of the pattern, they add the *hamzah*, for example *saḥāʔif* of *ṣaḥīfah*. Al-ʔaʕraǧ and Zayd b. ʕalī and al-ʔaʕmaš and Xāriǧah, on the authority of Nāfiʕ and Ibn ʕāmir in their (respective) transmission read *maʕāʔiš* with a *hamz*. This is not analogy (*qiyās*), because they reported it, and they were trustworthy, so it is necessary to accept it (as a valid reading). This *hamzah* is irregular in the same way as it is irregular in *manāʔir*, the plural of *manārah*—it is originally *manwarah*—and [it is irregular in the same way as it is irregular] in *maṣāʔib*, the plural of *maṣībah*—it is originally *maṣwibah*. *Manāwir* and *maṣāwib* are analogies as they would say *maṣāwib* on the basis of the root, in the same way that they say the plural of *maqāmah* as *maqāwim*; [the plural of] *maʕūnah* as *maʕāwin*.

Al-Zaǧǧāǧ said "all of the Basran grammarians decided that adding a *hamzah* is a mistake, but I know nothing of this perspective; [I know] only that [adding hamzah makes] it similar to *ṣaḥīfah*, *ṣaḥāʔif* and it is not proper to rely on this reading [i.e. *maʕāʔiš*]."

Al-Māzinī said: "The origin of the dispute of this reading is on the authority of Nāfiʕ, but he did not know what the *ʕarabiyyah* was, and the speech of the Arabs [i.e. correct Arabic] is to correct it [i.e. towards *maʕāyiš*] in such cases."

But we are not worshippers of the opinions of the grammarians of Basra! (*lasnā mutaʕabiddīna bi-ʔaqwāli nuḥāti l-baṣrah*).

Al-Farrāʔ said: "sometimes the Arabs added a *hamzah* to this and what is like it, supposing that it is a *faʕīlah*, and they liken *mafʕilah* to *faʕīlah*".[12] So, this is an account from al-Farrāʔ on the authority of the Arabs that they would sometimes add a *hamzah* to this and what is like it.

He brought an account of the reading of trustworthy people: Ibn ʕāmir, he is a pure Arab, and he received the Quran from ʕuṯmān before corruption [of the Arabic language] manifested itself. As for al-ʔaʕraǧ, he was among the greats of the readers of the followers [of the companions of the prophets]. Zayd b. ʕalī, with regard to eloquence and knowledge and cases one seldomly encounters, in that [more than] anyone. As for Al-ʔaʕmaš, he was, with regard to precision, perfection, memory and trustworthiness of high status. As for Nāfiʕ, he was taught by 70 of the followers [of the

---

12 ʔabū Ḥayyān is citing al-Farrāʔ (*Maʕānī*, I, 373) whose wording is slightly different in the edition we have.

companions of the prophet] and with regard to eloquence, precision and trustworthiness he was of high status, as he was not ignorant. Therefore, it is necessary that we accept what they relate to us, and [we should] not pay heed to the disagreement of the grammarians of Basra in this example.

As for the words of al-Mazānī "The origin of the dispute of this reading is on the authority of Nāfiʕ", this is incorrect, because it is (also) reported on the authority of ibn ʕāmir and on the authority of al-ʔaʕraǧ, Zayd b. ʕalī and al-ʔaʕmaš; As for the words "Nāfiʕ did not know what the *ʕarabiyyah* is", this is the evidence for the rebuttal: If we suppose that he did not know what the *ʕarabiyyah* was; is it this skill [i.e. knowing what the *ʕarabiyyah* is] which gives him access to speaking the language of the Arabs? He does not have to [know what the *ʕarabiyyah* is] to do that [speaking the *ʕarabiyyah*]! For he is eloquent of speaking the *ʕarabiyyah*, as he is a transmitter of the reading on the authority of the eloquent Arabs. And many among those grammarians think badly of the readers, but it is not correct of them [to do] that.

This account clearly shows that, despite the objections of the Basran grammarians, such forms were known and at least allowed by some, and may have indeed been the regular outcome in the dialects that gave rise to the CaCāʔiC style plurals.

6.4.8 *Måḡoḡ → Maʔǧūǧ*

ʕāṣim is the only reader who reads the names of Gog and Magog as *yaʔǧūǧ and maʔǧūǧ*, whereas the other readers read *yāǧūǧ* and *māǧūǧ* (Ibn al-Ǧazarī, §1484). As these names are clearly borrowed from the Hebrew גוג ומגוג *goḡ u-måḡoḡ*, which do not have a *hamzah* in either word, ʕāṣim's reading is an innovation from its original source.

6.4.9 *Zakariyyā → Zakariyyāʔ*

Most readers are in agreement that the Biblical name Zachariah in Arabic is supposed to end in a *hamzah*, i.e. *zakariyyāʔ*, this despite the fact that the Quranic rhyme in Q19:3 clearly suggests the name was pronounced /zakariyyā/ in Quranic Arabic. Only Ḥafṣ ʕan ʕāṣim, al-Kisāʔī, Ḥamzah and Xalaf lack this *hamzah* (Ibn al-Ǧazarī, §2840). Considering that the Hebrew name is זכריה *Zəḵaryå*, (or Greek Ζαχαρίας) without a final glottal stop, we must conclude that the majority of the readers are pronouncing the name with a pseudocorrect *hamzah*.[13]

13 Larcher (2021, 49, n. 40) suggests that the "Classical Arabic" form of this name has the

6.4.10 *Sāq, sāqay-hā, sūq → saʔq, saʔqay-hā, suʔq/suʔūq*

Another case of pseudocorrection is found in the plural and dual of *sāq* 'thigh, shank' in the canonical reading traditions. While in Classical Arabic this word is pronounced *sāq* pl. *sūq*, Ibn al-Ǧazarī (§ 3810) reports that Qunbul ʕan Ibn Kaṯīr read بالسوق (Q38:33) and سوقه (Q48:29) with a *hamzah* (= *bi-s-suʔq* or alternatively *bi-s-suʔūq*), but his transmitter al-Bazzī read it without a *hamzah*. He also reports the presence of the *hamzah* for the dual ساقيها (Q27:44), i.e. *saʔqay-hā* 'her two shins'.

Ibn Muǧāhid (483) explicitly points out that the singular *sāqin* (Q68:42, and by extension presumably its other attestation in Q75:29) was not pronounced with a *hamzah*. Eventually the form without the *hamzah* wins out in the classical norm, and it is clear that even by Ibn Muǧāhid's time this was the norm, but it is also clear that the form with *hamzah* was a serious contender at least in the tradition that sprouted from Ibn Kaṯīr. For the plural, the forms *suʔq* and *suʔūq* have become canonical in Qunbul's transmission, rather than the expected form *sūq*.

Unease with these forms used by Ibn Kaṯīr can also be gleaned in the discussion of ʔabū Ḥayyān (VIII, 244 and also IX, 155), who quotes ʔabū ʕaliyy[14] as saying that forms like *saʔq*, *saʔqay-hā* and *suʔq* are weak, and that it is based on a 'well-known linguistic practice' (*luġah mašhūrah*) to apply the *hamzah* to a unvowelled *wāw* when a *ḍammah* precedes, citing a piece of poetry from ʔabū Ḥibbah al-Numayrī: *ʔaḥabbu **l-muʔqidīna** ʔilayya **muʔsā*** 'Moses is the most beloved of kindlers[15] to me'. This explanation fails to account for the presence of the *hamzah* in the dual *saʔqay-hā*, and presumably for that reason ʔabū Ḥayyān disagrees. He says that the form is acceptable because there is a *hamzah* in the root, clearly showing that as late as his lifetime there still had not

---

hamzah. This is a typical example of the imposition of modern norms onto the opinions of the Arab grammarians. Both Sībawayh (III, 394) and al-Farrāʔ (*Luġāt*, 47; *Maʕānī*, I, 208) explicitly state that this name may be pronounced *Zakariyyā* or *Zakariyyāʔu* with no normative preference for one over the other. Incidentally, as there is no reason to consider *Zakariyyāʔu* as more original, it is of course incorrect to take its appearance in Q19:3 in rhyme as evidence that word-final *āʔ* had lost its *hamzah*, in Quranic Arabic. It simply never had it, unlike the examples I adduce of *āʔ* that does seem to rhyme with words that end in a final consonant, and are words that derive from ancient **āy* sequences that shifted to *āʔ* (van Putten 2018, 103–105).

14 Presumably ʔabū ʕaliyy al-Fārisī (d. 377 AH) a student of Ibn Muǧāhid (Ibn al-Ǧazarī *al-ġāyah*, I, 189). While ʔabū ʕaliyy discusses these variants in detail in his *Ḥuǧǧah* (IV, 109–111), nowhere does he call the hamzated forms weak.

15 In one of the two places that this line is cited, this form is vocalized *al-muʔqidayni*, but I would not know who these two kindlers would be.

developed a complete consensus as to whether the root of *sāq* should be understood to be √sʔq or √swq.

The Arab grammarians were unable to resolve the question as to whether the root was supposed to contain a *hamzah* or not. But from a comparative linguistic perspective it is clear that the *hamzah* in the word is pseudocorrect. Other Semitic languages show no sign of the **ʔ* in this word. Aramaic has *šāq*, but the sequence **aʔC* should yield *ēC* in Aramaic. This is clear from the verbal system, e.g. *yēmar* 'he says' < **yaʔmuru* and also from other words of the shape CaʔC, e.g. *rēš* 'head' (cf. Ar. *raʔs*, Hebr. *roš* spelled etymologically as ראש), *kēḇ* 'grief' (cf. Ar. *kaʔb* 'id.' and Hebr. *kʔeḇ* 'id.').[16] Hebrew has *šoq*, spelled שק; this points to the absence of the **ʔ* as Hebrew usually retains the spelling of the **ʔ* spelled with *ʾålɛp̄* in the consonantal text, but *šoq* is not spelled **שאק. Finally, in Ugaritic, which retains the Proto-Semitic **ʔ* with a variety of signs, lacks it completely in this word ⟨šq⟩ (not the expected **⟨šˀiq⟩). This evidence leads us to an unambiguous reconstruction of this word for Proto-West Semitic as **sāḳ*, without a glottal stop. The form *sāq* is therefore etymological and forms with a *hamzah* are pseudocorrect.[17]

On the discussion of *sāq*, Ibn Xālawayh (*ʔiʕrāb*, II, 152f.) explicitly calls out 'Arabs' for placing the *hamzah* in places where it is incorrect.

> Others said: *sāq* is like *bāb*, because the root is s-w-q, and the *wāw* is changed to an *ʔalif*, so it is incorrect to give it a *hamzah*. This is what is among the things in which the Arabs make mistakes, so they do apply the *hamzah* on what does not have a *hamzah*, and similarly with what has a *hamzah* they do not give it the *hamzah*, so *kaʔs* and *raʔs* and *sāq* their stem shape (*waznuhā*) is the same (i.e. as *CāC*), so they make them similar to one-another, yes, he has seen that Arabs say: *ḥallaʔtu s-sawīqa*, but originally it is *ḥallaytu*, and likewise, with *ḥallaʔtu l-ʔinsāna ʕani l-māʔi wa-l-ʔibili*. However, the plural of *sāq*, through replacement (*qalb*) (of the *hamzah*) is *ʔaswuq* without *hamzah* and if you wish (can be) *ʔasʔuq* with *hamzah*.[18]

16 An interesting exception appears to be Aramaic *ʕānā* 'sheep', which has lost the *ʔ* already in Official Aramaic times, spelled קן where Hebrew *ṣōn* צאן, Arabic *ḍaʔn* and Akkadian *ṣēn* point to a reconstruction **ṣaʔn*. This is probably the result of a dissimilation of the two guttural consonants occurring in a row.

17 As already recognized by Vollers (1906, 94). Vollers also noticed that such pseudocorrect forms entered the classical language through other channels than Quranic recitation, this is clear from the variable *bāz/baʔz* 'falcon', which, considering that it comes from Persian *bāz*, must certainly be considered a pseudocorrection as well.

18 This is the result of a fairly regular rule in the *ʕarabiyyah* that sequences of **wu* or **wū*

6.4.11 *Kās → kaʔs*

As already noticed by Blau (1970, 56), much like the case of *saʔq* discussed above, comparative Semitic evidence shows that *kaʔs* 'cup' must have a pseudocorrect *hamzah* in Arabic. The reflexes in Hebrew כוס *kos* (spelled without *ʾålɛp̄*) and Aramaic *kās* as well as Ugaritic ⟨ks⟩ leave no doubt that the reconstruction of this noun in Proto-West Semitic is **kāᵗs* and the *hamzah* in the Quranic reading traditions must be pseudocorrect. What is different from the case of *saʔq*, however, is that this word is read with *hamzah* universally by all the canonical readers. Moreover, this pronunciation has become the *de facto* standard in Classical Arabic, although the form *kās* is known to exist among the lexicographers (*Lane* 2639c; *Lisān* 3802c).

6.4.12 *Yuḍāhūna → yuḍāhiʔūna*

ʕāṣim is unique in reading يضهون 'they imitate' (Q9:30) as a III-*ʔ* root *yuḍāhiʔūna*. All other readers treat the verb as a III-*w/y* verb, reading *yuḍāhūna* (Ibn al-Ǧazarī, § 1532). This verb is attested in an Old Arabic inscription in Safaitic script as *ḍhw* 'to copy' (Al-Jallad and Jaworska 2019). As Safaitic regularly retains the *hamzah* (Al-Jallad 2015, 45, 53), ʕāṣim's reading is evidently pseudocorrect here, and the majority reading is the original.

6.4.13 *Aṣ-ṣābūna → aṣ-ṣābiʔūna*

There is disagreement among the readers on how to read الصبين/الصبون 'the Sabians' (Q2:62, Q5:69, Q22:17), which is variously read as *aṣ-ṣābū/īna* (Nāfiʕ[19]) an *aṣ-ṣābiʔū/īna* (the others) (Ibn al-Ǧazarī § 1496). That is, either as an active participle from a root √*ṣbw/y* or from a root √*ṣbʔ*.

Neither the root √*ṣbw/y* nor √*ṣbʔ* is attested in Arabic in a meaning that would elucidate the meaning of the word Sabians as an Arabic word; hence it is usually taken to be a loanword. If Wellhausen (1897, 237) is correct to identify this word as a plural active participle derived from the Mandaic verb *ṣḇā* 'to baptize' then we must conclude that the *hamzah* is a pseudocorrection. As the Mandaic form is a final weak verb, we would expect the plural active participle to simply be *aṣ-ṣābūna*.[20]

---

become *ʔu*, therefore the plural *ʔaswuq* is expected to shift to *ʔasʔuq*. Note that this explanation is unable to make sense of the reading of the dual with *hamzah*, or in fact the other plural *suʔq/suʔūq*.

19 ʔabū Ǧaʕfar also reads *as-ṣābū/īna*, but this is part of his regular pattern of dropping the *hamzah* (see section § 5.2).

20 The Mandaic form is likely ultimately from a root **ṣbġ* which yields Ar. *ṣabaġa* 'to dye, baptize' and Aramaic *ṣḇaʕ* with the typical loss of the gutturals of Mandaic.

6.4.14 *Conclusion*

While the cases where *hamzah* is applied to a word which etymologically never had it is relatively rare, it is common enough to show that there was a real attempt to classicize the readings towards an ideal that included *hamzah*, by people to whom it was not necessarily obvious which words were supposed to have a *hamzah* or not. This is certainly consistent with what we would expect to find, considering that rhyme evidence shows that the Quran was originally composed in the Hijazi dialect without a *hamzah*.

It is remarkable that a good number of these pseudocorrections are found with Ibn Kaṯīr, the Meccan reciter. Ibn Kaṯīr, despite being a Hijazi, has a remarkably conservative use of *hamzah* in his recitation. Considering how the Hijazi vernacular appears to have mostly lost the *hamzah*, it is by no means surprising that it is exactly this reader that is most prone to pseudocorrection. It should be noted, however, that pseudocorrections are also found with other readers. All readers read *kaʔs*, and the Kufans have several forms with pseudocorrect presence of *hamzah* as well.

6.5 Failure to Insert *hamzah*

While the amount of pseudocorrect insertions of *hamzah* in places where the word historically lacked the *hamzah* is a fairly rare occurrence among the readers, failure to insert the *hamzah* is more common. The tradition also explicitly acknowledges this: the dropping of *hamzah* is part of the *ʕarabiyyah* (Sībawayh, III, 541ff.) and therefore grammarians did not see it as a problem to, in general, retain *hamzah*, but in cases that one was uncertain whether the root had a *hamzah*, to opt for the *hamzah*less form instead. However, the pseudocorrect application of *hamzah* was considered something to be avoided. This can be seen, for example in ʔabū ʕamr's statement concerning his reading of *minsaʔata-hū* as *minsāta-hū* (Ibn al-Ǧazarī, §3962). On this topic al-Farrāʔ (*Maʕānī* II, 356f.) reports:

> ʔabū Jaʕfar al-Ruʔāsī (d. 187 AH) declared to me (al-Farrāʔ, d. 208 AH) that he asked ʔabū ʕamr (d. 154 AH) about it [i.e. the pronunciation of منسته], and (ʔabū ʕamr) said: "*minsāta-hū* is without *hamzah*", and he also said: "Because I do not know it, I remove its *hamzah*."

A slightly more expanded version of this account is related by ʔabū Ḥayyān (VIII, 531):

> ʔabū ʕamr said: "I do not apply *hamza* to it, because I do not know its derivation; If it was among those (roots) that are not *hamzat*ed, I have been (sufficiently) cautious (*iḥtaṭtu*), and if it was *hamzat*ed, then it would be permissible for me to take away the *hamzah* in what contains a *hamzah*."

This account clearly shows that the leaving out the *hamzah* in places where it is etymologically present was not considered a mistake, while adding it where it should have been was. Moreover, it shows that adding the *hamzah* was a rational and theoretical endeavour by the readers, and in case of uncertainty they could decide to leave it out.

The reading of Ibn Ḏakwān of this word is *minsaʔta-hū* (sic!). This is evidently ungrammatical as it suggests a miCCaCt stem formation, something that does not occur in any form of Arabic. It rather seems like an attempt at inserting the *hamzah* into a word that he originally learned to recite as *minsāta-hū*. If one disregards any forms of grammar, there is no way to decide whether a base for *minsāta-hū* is to be pronounced *minsaʔta-hū* or *minsaʔata-hū*.

Al-Dānī (*Ǧāmiʕ*, 680) points out that Ibn Ḏakwān's reading was considered extremely weak by the Arab grammarians in general, because the feminine ending should always be preceded by *-a-* or an *ʔalif*. But, he says, there is a line of poetry, transmitted by al-ʔaxfaš (the same person who transmits this reading for Ibn Ḏakwān), which serves as evidence that the form *minsaʔt-* exists:

× × ⏑ – | × × ⏑ – | × × ⏑ – ||	× × ⏑ – | × × ⏑ – | × × ⏑ – ||
ṣarīʕu xamrin qāma min wakaʔti-hī	*ka-qawmati š-šayxi ʔilā minsaʔti-hī*
'A drunk stood up from his reclination,	like the standing up of an old man on his stick.'

The problem with this poetic evidence is that *minsaʔti-hī* is metrically identical to *minsāti-hī*, and therefore this poem can hardly be used as evidence for it. This is assuming that this line of poetry is not an outright fabrication, which seems more likely in this case. This anonymous line of poetry is only ever cited to explain Ibn Ḏakwān's reading, and al-ʔaxfaš seems to be the originator of the line.

The contemplative and theoretical nature of the reading with or without *hamzah* is also displayed in a colourful exchange between al-Kisāʔī and Ḥamzah on the discussion of al-Kisāʔī reading *ḏiʔb*, as *ḏīb* (Xalaf, Warš and regularly by his principles ʔabū Ǧaʕfar follow him in this exceptional reading, see Ibn al-Ǧazarī §1472). This is related in several Ṭabaqāt works, such as the one of al-Ḏahabī (153f.):

> [...] Muḥammad b. ʕalī b. Sulaymān al-Marwazī said: I asked Xalaf b. Hišām: why is al-Kisāʔī called al-Kisāʔī? And he said: al-Kisāʔī entered Kufa and came to the as-Sabīʕī mosque where Ḥamzah was teaching recitation, and al-Kisāʔī came forward and he was wrapped in a black robe. When Ḥamzah was done praying he said: who goes first? And it was said: "al-Kisāʔī", and they meant the guy in the (black) robe, and they turned their gaze to him and said: if you are a weaver,[21] you will recite Sūrat Yūsuf and if you are a salt vendor (or sailor (?), *mallāḥ*), you will recite Sūrat Ṭāhā. So, he heard them and started to recite Sūrat Yūsuf, and when he arrived at the pericope of the wolf, he recited it without *hamzah* (i.e. *aḏ-ḏīb*). So, Ḥamzah said: "*ad-ḏiʔb* is with *hamzah*." So, al-Kisāʔī replied: "So should I apply the *hamzah* like that in *al-ḥuʔt* (for *al-ḥūt* 'the whale') as well?"—this is about (the verses) *fa-ʔakala-hu ḏ-ḏiʔb* (Q12:17) and *fa-ltaqama-hu l-ḥūt* (Q37:142). Ḥamzah looked to Xallād the cross-eyed, and they argued as a group, but nobody was able to (answer him). Then they said (to al-Kisāʔī): "liberate us, please!" Then (al-Kisāʔī) said: "Learn from what this weaver has to say! When you compare a man to a wolf, you say *qad istaḏaʔaba r-rağul* 'the man was fierce like a wolf', and if you would say *istaḏāba* without *hamzah*, then it is as if you attribute to him emaciation (*huzāl*) [because *ḏāb* means 'vice, fault, defect']. But when you liken him to a whale, you say: *istaḥāta r-rağul*"—which means he eats a lot, because a whale eats a lot—and then he recited:
>
> *ʔayyuhā ḏ-ḏību wa-bnu-hū wa-ʔabū-hū*
> *ʔanta ʕindī min ʔaḏʔubin ḍāriyātī*
>
> 'O wolf, and his son, and his father!
> You are to me among the voracious wolves!'
>
> And he is known as al-Kisāʔī ever since that day.

This account once again shows that, while eliding the *hamzah* is considered acceptable—after all that is how the star of the story recites it—it is *not* allowed to pseudocorrectly apply the *hamzah* to words that do not have it in their root.[22]

---

21 Clearly meant as an insult, weavers were despised in medieval Islamic society, a position they share with the *textor* of Roman times (EI² s.v. *ḥāʾik*).

22 Another humorous story about al-Kisāʔī's reading of *ḏiʔb* as *ḏīb* exploits the polysemy of the verb *hamaza* which means both 'to apply the hamzah' and 'to prod'. Someone asked al-Kisāʔī: *lima lā tahmizu ḏ-ḏīb?* "why do you not hamzate/prod the wolf?". To this al-Kisāʔī answers: *ʔaxāfu ʔan yaʔkula-nī!* "I am afraid that it would eat me!" (al-Ḏahabī, 300) where al-Kisāʔī is playfully riffing on the verse in which his reading *aḏ-ḏīb* occurs: *wa-ʔaxāfu ʔan yaʔkulahu ḏ-ḏīb* "I fear that a wolf will eat him" (Q12:13).

It is worth mentioning here a not quite as colourful, but related account on the authority of Nāfiʕ related by al-ʔaṣmaʕī → ʔabū Saʕīd al-Ḥāriṯī → Ibn Muǧāhid: "I asked Nāfiʕ about الذيب and البير, and he said: 'If the Arabs provide a *hamzah* to them, then provide them with a *hamzah*'" (Ibn Muǧāhid, 346). This quote is related in the context of disagreement among the transmitters of Nāfiʕ on these words. While most transmitters are in agreement that he read these words with *hamzah*, Warš and the non-canonical transmitter Ibn Ǧammāz read them as *al-bīr* and *aḏ-ḏīb*, a practice that Ibn Muǧāhid considered mistaken (*wa-hāḏā wahm*). What this quote illustrates is the rather practical nature of reading with or without *hamzah*. Nāfiʕ gives a rather non-committal answer to the question, telling the readers to follow what they believe what "the Arabs" do.[23]

Once we look closer among the canonical readers, we find numerous examples where there is uncertainty on whether a word is supposed to carry a *hamzah* or not, several readers opt for *hamzah*-less forms where according to their general principles of recitation we would expect them to have been retained. In the following section, we will examine the many cases of incomplete application of the *hamzah* as they occur among the readings.

All of this uncertainty about where the *hamzah* should go is difficult to understand, if we assume that the language of the Quran was indeed pronounced and transmitted with a *hamzah* from the very start. On the other hand, such discussions make perfect sense if the Quranic language was—as is admitted for Hijazi Arabic—without the *hamzah*, and as a new linguistic ideal of the classical poem gained prominence, reciters started adapting features, including the use of the *hamzah*, into their recitation.

6.5.1 *Long Vowels Followed by* Hamzah

6.5.1.1 Nabīʔ, nabīʔīn, ʔanbiʔāʔ, nubūʔah

The majority of the Quranic reciters do not pronounce the *hamzah* in the word نبي, النبي 'prophet' or its plurals النبين, انبيا nor النبوه 'prophecy'. The Medinan reciter Nāfiʕ, however is an exception to this, as he consistently recites these words as *nabīʔ, an-nabīʔīn, ʔanbiʔāʔ* and *an-nubūʔah* (Ibn al-Ǧazarī, §1531).

23 Ibn Muǧāhid seems to have understood this quote as meaning that one is indeed to pronounce these words as *biʔr* and *ḏiʔb*, which reveals a significantly developed view of what 'Classical Arabic' is in the late third/early fourth century AH. To him what 'Arabs' say is clearly the form with *hamzah*. But one wonders if Nāfiʕ truly meant it in such a manner. To Sībawayh, for example, *bīr* and *ḏīb* are acceptable and certainly also something that 'the Arabs' say (Sībawayh, III, 541ff.).

This has frequently been construed as pseudocorrect application of the *hamzah* (e.g. Vollers 1906, 95; Rabin 1951, 131–133; Fischer 2002, 26), where Zwettler (1978, 179 f., n. 71) even claims that it was never part of the *ʕarabiyyah*. From an etymological perspective it is not clear that this is correct. This word is ultimately a loanword from Aramaic or perhaps Hebrew, and while in later forms of both Aramaic and Hebrew the **ʔ* is lost, Biblical Hebrew and Aramaic still retain the *ʾålɛp̄* spelling, suggesting its original presence and pronunciation in these respective corpora, cf. Biblical Aramaic Ktiv נביאה */nabīʔā/; Qre *nḇiyy-å* pl. Ktiv נביאיא **nabīʔ-ayyā* Qre *nḇiyyayyå* (Ezra 5:1); Hebrew נביא *nåḇi* < **nabīʔ* pl. נביאים *nḇiʾim* < **nabīʔīm*. Cf. also Hebrew נבואה *nḇuʔå* 'prophecy' and Biblical Aramaic Ktiv בנבואת חגי /*bi-nabūʔat/ Qre *bi-nḇuʔaṯ* 'the prophecy of (Haggai)' (Ezra 6:14). As the Aramaic loanwords in the Quran consistently show exceptionally archaic phonology (see van Putten 2020a, 69 ff.), it is not *a priori* obvious that the presence of the *hamzah* in these words was never part of the Classical language.

The belief that this must be a pseudocorrection seems to be based on the fact that Sībawayh (III, 555) expresses a clear normative bias against pronouncing the word as *nabīʔ* (and *idem* for *barīʔah* for *bariyyah* see the discussion below), saying that this is the manner of pronunciation of the people of the Hijaz who pronounce the *hamzah*, calling it rare and abhorrent (*qalīl radīʔ*). But while this is the case, he clearly considers the base of this word and *barīʔah* to contain a *hamzah*, as he discusses it as part of the shift of *īʔ, ūʔ, ayʔ → iyy, uww, ayy* including words which in Classical Arabic are usually realized with the *hamzah*, e.g. *xaṭīʔah → xaṭiyyah* 'sin', and *maqrūʔ → maqruww* 'readable'. For the formation of diminutives Sībawayh (III, 547) explicitly allows both *nubayy* and *nubayyiʔ*, but the diminutives of *barīʔah/bariyyah* and *nubūʔah/nubuwwah* he only endorses the forms with *hamzah*, i.e. *burayyiʔah* and *nubayyiʔah*. So, while he has a normative opinion for the dropping of *hamzah*, he clearly considers the *ʔaṣl* of the word to have had the *hamzah*. We cannot conclude from this that *nabīʔ* or *barīʔah* are pseudocorrect, but only that the now normative form without *hamzah* had gained enough ground in Basra in Sībawayh's time that it was considered normative despite being exceptional among the people that usually preserve the *hamzah*. But Nāfiʕ is Medinan and a contemporary of Sībawayh's teacher al-Xalīl b. ʔaḥmad, so clearly it was still part of the *ʕarabiyyah* at that time despite Sībawayh's misgivings.

Despite the archaic nature of Nāfiʕ's reading, it is quite clear that this was not the reading that belonged to the language of the QCT. The broken plural pattern the QCT uses (ʔaCCiCāʔ) is almost exclusively applied to final weak and geminate roots only a few sound roots have this pattern, e.g. *ġaniyy → ʔaġniyāʔ* 'rich' and *šadīd → ʔašiddāʔ* 'strong', *qarīb → ʔaqribāʔ* 'relative' (van Putten

2020a, 64). Had the Quranic Arabic form indeed been *nabīʔ*, we would have rather expected a plural *nubaʔāʔ*.[24] This plural pattern therefore suggests that in Quranic Arabic, as would be expected in Hijazi Arabic the final *hamzah* had been lost and the word was indeed pronounced as the majority of the readers read it.

Nāfiʕ's reading in this case is therefore an archaism, and one that was not considered proper by everyone. A commonly cited prophetic Hadith has someone address the prophet by *yā nabīʔa ḷḷāh*, which is promptly denounced by the prophet. This tradition is explicitly invoked as one of the reasons why a reciter might read *nabiyy* instead of *nabīʔ* by Ibn Xālawayh (*Ḥuǧǧah*, 80f.): "the first reason is that applying the *hamzah* is heavy on their speech, and the evidence for this is his speech (PBUH): I am not the prophe' of God (*lastu nabīʔa ḷḷāh*); it is as if he disliked applying the *hamzah* because he was of Qurayš who do not apply the *hamzah*".

6.5.1.2 Barīʔah/bariyyah

Another loanword from Arabic or Hebrew is البريه 'creature' (Q98:6,7), which like *nabīʔ*, is read as *al-barīʔah* by Nāfiʕ, but in this case Ibn Ḏakwān ʕan Ibn ʕāmir joins him in this reading, other reciters read *al-bariyyah* (Ibn al-Ǧazarī, §1536).

Here too we are likely dealing not with a pseudocorrection, but an accurate transmission of the ancient pronunciation of an original in Hebrew בריאה *bri'å* and/or Aramaic (Jeffery 2007, 76), which is a derivation from the verb ברא 'to create' (Hebrew *bårå*), which likewise was borrowed into Arabic as *baraʔa*.

6.5.1.3 Nasīʔ

النسى (Q9:37) 'the postponement' is read by Warš ʕan Nāfiʕ (in the path of al-ʔazraq) and ʔabū Ǧaʕfar as *an-nasiyy* while the other readers read it as *an-nasīʔ* (Ibn al-Ǧazarī §1525). In the context, it seems quite clear that we should derive this word from the root *nasaʔa* 'to postpone; to drive', and not from *nasā* 'to forget', where *an-nasiyy* would end up meaning 'the forgotten one; that which is to be forgotten'. Note that *minsaʔah*, also a word derived from this root, likewise yielded uncertainty among the readers as to whether or not it should have the *hamzah* (see §6.5 above).

---

24 This plural is in fact attested in a poem by al-ʕabbās b. Mirdās (d. ca. 18–35 AH) starting with *yā xātama n-nubaʔāʔi ʔinnaka mursalun* "O seal of the prophets, you are sent" (al-Ǧabbūrī 1968, 95), another piece of evidence that the form *nabīʔ* pl. *nubaʔāʔ* indeed existed in the *ʕarabiyyah*, also outside of Quranic recitation.

Ibn Muǧāhid (314) reports several other readings. In non-canonical transmission paths of Ibn Kaṯīr we find *an-nasʔ* (ʕuqayl ← Šibl ← Ibn Kaṯīr)—a reading that seems to disagree with the *rasm*—and *an-nasiyy* (ʕubayd ← Šibl ← Ibn Kaṯīr). He also reports *an-nasy* on Ibn Kaṯīr's authority, but without *ʔisnād*.

6.5.1.4 Xaṭīʔah pl. xaṭāyā 'sin'

A clear example of failure to apply *hamzah* in the QCT which has subsequently made it into the Classical Arabic language is the plural formation of *xaṭīʔah* 'sin', its plural, *xaṭāyā*, not only lacks the expected *hamzah* altogether, it could never have even had this *hamzah*, as the plural formation it employs is one typical of final-weak roots. Fischer (2002, § 99b) cites as examples *hadiyyah* pl. *hadāyā* 'gift', *hirāwah* pl. *harāwā* 'club' and *zāwiyah* pl. *zawāyā* 'corner, angle'.

There are some other contexts in which the CaCāCā plural appears, but none of them apply to *xaṭīʔah*.[25] There are a few isolated lexical items that take this plural of sound roots, for example *yatīm* pl. *yatāmā*. Note, however, that if *xaṭīʔah* would belong to this group of nouns we would have expected ***xaṭāʔā* rather than the inexplicable *xaṭāyā*.

As such we would expect the original singular of this noun in Quranic Arabic to have been the *hamzah*less form *xaṭiyyah*, following the same derivation as *hadiyyah*. The reading *xaṭiyyah* was subsequently classicized to *xaṭīʔah* by all readers, while failing to classicize the plural formation along with it.[26] The issue of this specific broken plural pattern associated with this singular was not lost on the Arab grammarians, and *Lisān al-ʕarab* has a lengthy discussion on what was evidently perceived as a problematic plural. The regular plural of CaCīCah nouns is CaCāʔiC (cf. *ḥadīqah* pl. *ḥadāʔiq*; *madīnah* pl. *madāʔin*), and as such the expected plural is *al-xaṭāʔiʔu*,[27] due to the regular elision of the second *hamzah* when two hamzahs follow in a row, this should have become *al-xaṭāʔī*, in the same way that the active participle of 'to come' turns from *al-ǧāʔiʔu* into *al-ǧāʔī*, and it would therefore be expected to have merged with the *faʕālin* type plurals. Sībawayh (III, 552 f.) starts his discussion of this plural

25 For example, it is a regular plural (besides CaCāCin) for nouns that end in the feminine endings *-ā* and *-āʔ*, e.g. *fatwā* 'legal opinion', pl. *fatāwin*, *fatāwā* and *ʕaḏrāʔ* 'virgin' pl. *ʕaḏārin*, *ʕaḏārā* (Fischer 2002, § 99a).

26 The expected for *xaṭiyyah* is attested in Classical Arabic lexicons (*Lane* 761c; *Lisān* 1193b).

27 Al-Zamaxšarī (*mufaṣṣal*, 167) cites ʔabū Zayd as having heard someone use this original plural in *aḷḷāhumma ġfir lī xaṭāʔiʔī* "O God, forgive me my sins."

with: "it is as if [the *hamzah*] was turned into a *yāʔ* and the end of *xaṭāyā* (i.e. the *yāʔ* of *xaṭāʔī*) was replaced with an *ʔalif*". He then commences to explain how one could get from a singular *xaṭīʔah* to the plural *xaṭāyā* without having to assume a singular base *xaṭiyyah*. He likens the replacement of the final *yāʔ* of the hypothetical **xaṭāʔī* (from earlier *xaṭāʔiʔ*) with *ʔalif* to this happening in the final weak plural *maṭāyā* (plural of *maṭiyyah* 'mount'), it is striking here that Sībawayh has to draw an analogy with a CaCiyyah noun, to be able to explain the presence of this plural pattern, while the discussion seems explicitly aimed to avoid this. This brings him to an intermediary form **xaṭāʔā*. The *hamzah* of **xaṭāʔā* is subsequently replaced with a *yāʔ* because it stands between two *ʔalifs*. While *hamzah* as a root consonant can stand between two *ʔalifs* such as in *kisāʔāni, kisāʔā, hanāʔā*, this is not the case for **xaṭāʔā* because its *hamzah* is not a root consonant, but part of the plural pattern (CaCāʔiC), therefore it is weakened to a *yāʔ* instead, yielding *xaṭāyā*. The change from *ī* → *ā* is, of course, *ad hoc*, as is the rule for replacing the *hamzah* with a *yāʔ* to go from *xaṭāʔā* to *xaṭāyā*, which as far as I can tell is not applied to any other word in the lexicon.

The complexity of discussion ultimately comes down to the fact that Sībawayh, and grammarians after him (see the discussions in *Lisān*, 1193, for example) refuse to use a surface form like *xaṭiyyah*—a form explicitly considered to be allowed—for the derivation of the plural. This constraint that the grammarians imposed upon themselves does not lead to a convincing explanation, and that does not seem to have been the point. The grammarians were simply trying to find an explanation of how one could *hypothetically* come from the idealized source form *xaṭīʔah* to *xaṭāyā* without having to assume the loss of *hamzah* as the basis. The self-evident explanation for the plural *xaṭāyā* is that it was formed upon the form *xaṭiyyah*, not *xaṭīʔah*, thus betraying an original *hamzah*less form, despite its absence in the canonical readings.

6.5.2 *Post-consonantal* Hamzah

Above, we discussed a class of words with the lack of the expected *hamzah* when it occurs after a long vowel. But this is not the only position where we find that readers irregularly lose the *hamzah*. We also find it in post-consonantal position.

The very name of the Quran itself is one of these cases where the presence of the *hamzah* is disagreed upon. The word is spelled both defectively قرن and plene قران in early manuscripts, and it is usually read as *qurʔān*, however Ibn Kaṯīr reads it as *qurān* (Ibn al-Ǧazari, §1571). There can be no doubt that the root of *qurʔān* 'recital' is *qaraʔa* 'to recite', and thus in *qurān* the expected *hamzah* is missing. Attempts of Arab philologers to see Ibn Kaṯīr's *qurān* as a derivation from *qarana* 'to bring together' are obviously not very satisfying (Jeffery 2007, 233).

Nāfiʕ treats two CiCC verbal nouns derived from III-ʔ roots as CiC stems, ردا *ridan* (versus the other readers *ridʔan*) 'as help' (Q28:34; Ibn al-Ǧazarī, §1559) and مل *milu* 'fullness' (Q3:91; Ibn al-Ǧazarī, §1560, only in the path of al-ʔaṣbahānī from Warš, and with disagreement among his transmitters). Thus here, like our previous word, post-consonantal *hamzah* was incompletely reinserted in this reading.

The QCT of the Quran makes it clear that there was no *hamzah* in the imperative *saʔala* 'to ask', as it is consistently spelled سل. Had this word had a medial *hamzah*, we would have expected a prothetic *ʔalif* in the imperative **اسل for *isʔal*. As such, to agree with the *rasm*, readers have to read *sal* if nothing is prefixed to the word. However, whenever *wa-* or *fa-* precede the imperative, readers generally include the *hamza*, as now the *rasm* allows the correct syllable structure, hence: *wa-sʔal al-qaryah* 'ask the village' (Q12:82) and *fa-sʔalū ʔahla ḏ-ḏikr* 'ask the people of remembrance' (Q16:43). Ibn Kaṯīr, al-Kisāʔī and Xalaf, however, always read the *hamzah*less form regardless of context (Ibn al-Ǧazari, §1562). Either reading is, of course, irregular as the imperfect forms of this verb have the same phonetic context but are invariably read as *yasʔalu* etc.

There are several words that are expected to have a post-consonantal *hamzah* on comparative grounds, but where all readers are in agreement to not read the *hamzah*. The most obvious of these is the word ملك *malak* 'angel'. This word is generally taken to be a loanword from Gəʕəz *mälʔäk* pl. *mälaʔəkt* 'id.', mostly because it shares the same plural formation as the Arabic مليكة *malāʔikah*, which is a plural formation that is rare, and mostly restricted to loanwords (van Putten 2020a, 66). The Gəʕəz form itself is, of course ultimately derived from the Hebrew מלאך *malʾåḵ* 'id.' or Aramaic *malʾaḵā* 'id.'

The Arabic plural itself clearly points to a missing postconsonantal *hamzah*; there are no other CaCaC nouns that have such a quadriradical plural formation (or more common formations like CaCāʔiC). The lexicographical tradition does in fact record the expected form *malʔak* (*Lisān* 4269b), but the canonical readers are in agreement that the form is *malak*, despite this being an irregular outcome within the phonologies of these reading traditions.

The imperfect of the verb *raʔā* forms a surprising exception to the retention of postconsonantal *hamzah*, as it is not *yarʔā* but *yarā/yarē* among all the canonical readers. The irregular behaviour of this verb seems to have already been a feature of the *ʕarabiyyah* by the time of Sībawayh (III, 546), as he explicitly mentions the exceptional nature of this word: "all Arabs agree on the dropping of it (the *hamzah* in forms like *ʔarā, tarā, yarā, narā*) because of its frequent use", but he adds: "ʔabū al-Xaṭṭāb told me that he has heard one say *qad ʔarʔā-hum* bringing the verb in its original form *raʔaytu*, among the trustworthy Arabs." Al-Farrāʔ (*Luġāt*, 165) also says that all Arabs agree on dropping the *hamzah* with the exception of the Banū ʔasad and Taym al-Rabāb.[28]

6.5.3 *Intervocalic* Hamzah

6.5.3.1 Riʔāʔa n-nās → riyāʔa n-nās

ريا الناس 'to be seen by men' (Q2:264; Q4:38; Q8:47) is read by most readers as *riʔāʔa n-nās*, the regular outcome of a *fiʕāl* stem of the root √rʔy, but ʔabū Ǧaʕfar has irregularly shifted the medial *hamzah* to *yāʔ*, yielding *riyāʔa n-nās* (Ibn al-Ǧazarī § 1490).[29]

6.5.3.2 Liʔallā → liyallā

Warš ʕan Nāfiʕ in the path of al-ʔazraq reads ليلا as *liyallā* 'so that not' (Q2:150; Q4:165; Q57:29), while the rest of the Quranic readers read *li-ʔallā* (Ibn al-Ǧazarī, § 1495). This is irregular behaviour in the reading of Warš, which otherwise retains the *hamzah* in such environments.

6.5.3.3 Kufuʔan, huzuʔan → kufuwan, huzuwan

While Ḥafṣ is generally very conservative in the retention of the *hamzah*, he is unique in dropping the *hamzah* in كفوا 'an equal' and هزوا 'contempt', reading them as *kufuwan* and *huzuwan* respectively, while the other readers read these words either as *kufuʔan/huzuʔan* (the majority reading) or *kufʔan/huzʔan* (Ḥamzah) (Ibn al-Ǧazarī § 2668).

6.5.3.4 Bādiya r-raʔyi → bādiʔa r-raʔyi

An interesting point of disagreement among the readers on the placement of the *hamzah* occurs in the phrase بادى الراى (Q11:27). The majority of the readers reads بادى الراى as *bādiya r-raʔyi*, only ʔabū ʕamr reads it with *hamzah*,

---

28 A few early manuscripts appear to give evidence that in earlier times such readings were more widespread. The vocalization of Arabe 334a's يروا (Q36:31), places a *fatḥah* sign on the *rāʔ* which likely denotes the presence of a *hamzah*, thus suggesting *yarʔaw*, and the spelling يراى in DAM 01.29-1 leaves little doubt the scribe intended *yarʔā/yarʔē*, as this manuscript frequently employs the *ʔalif* to denote the presence of *hamzah* (van Putten 2019a, 370, n. 210).

29 This should not be considered part of the dissimilation of two consecutive *hamzah*s as in **ʔaʔimmah* > *ʔayimmah* 'Imāms' and **ǧāʔiʔun* > *ǧāʔin* 'coming' as suggested by Fischer (2002, § 41a). The dissimilation, at least as described by Sībawayh (III, 552) is always progressive, not regressive, and only occurs if a short vowel intervenes.

i.e. *bādiʔa r-raʔyi* (Ibn al-Ǧazarī, § 1535). However, it is not entirely clear that we are dealing with a pseudocorrection or irregular absence of *hamzah*.

Ibn Xālawayh (*Ḥuǧǧah*, 186) takes ʔabū ʕamr's reading as primary, saying that whoever reads it as *bādiya* is deriving it from the verb *badaʔa/yabdaʔu* 'to begin' and is dropping the *hamzah* thus understanding the phrase as "beginning in opinion". If this interpretation is correct, we are indeed dealing with the absence of the expected *hamzah* which is irregular among each of the readers that reads it thus.

However, al-Farrāʔ (*Maʕānī*, II, 11) clearly has a different opinion and views *bādiya* and *bādiʔa* as two separate lexical items. He tells us: "you should not apply the *hamzah* to *bādiya*, because the meaning *yabdū* 'it is obvious' seems more obvious to us [i.e. "obvious in opinion"]; if you were to apply the *hamzah* to it, then you would intend the meaning *ʔawwal al-raʔy* "first/beginning in opinion."" If al-Farrāʔ is correct to see the two readings as intending two different meanings, this obviously still stems from an ambiguity of the text which only became ambiguous when readers started to add the *hamzah* to the recitation of the Quran.

6.5.4 *Pre-consonantal* Hamzah

Among the canonical readers, the dropping of *hamzah* in pre-consonantal position is by far the most common, because it is a regular practice in a restricted form with Warš, and mostly unrestricted for ʔabū Ǧaʕfar and ʔabū ʕamr (optional for the latter). For the other readers, however, such dropping of the *hamzah* is not regular, but despite that, it is occasionally attested in isolated words among the other canonical readers.

At the start of this section (§ 6.5) we already mentioned that al-Kisāʔī read *aḏ-ḏīb* 'the wolf' without *hamzah*. Xalaf joins him in this reading. Warš likewise drops the *hamzah* in this word, but adds to it also *bīr* 'well', and *bīsa, bīsamā* 'how bad!' (Ibn al-Ǧazarī § 1471–1472). Also, the reduplicated noun *luʔluʔ*, Šuʕbah ʕan ʕāṣim goes against his general principles reads *lūluʔ* in all its attestations (Ibn al-Ǧazarī § 1482). Qālūn ʕan Nāfiʕ and Ibn Ḏakwān ʕan Ibn ʕāmir read ريا (Q19:74) as *riyyan* rather than *riʔyan* (Ibn al-Ǧazarī § 1483). Finally, Qālūn ʕan Nāfiʕ, with disagreement among his transmitters, reads *al-mūtafikah* (Q53:53) and *al-mūtafikāt* (Q9:70; Q69:9) 'that which is overthrown', rather than *muʔtafikah/muʔtafikāt* (Ibn al-Ǧazarī § 1482).

التين 'the fig' (Q95:1) is an example where all readers are in agreement that the word is to be read as *at-tīn*, without *hamzah*, whereas from an etymological perspective, it seems that this word should have had a *hamzah*. Hebrew תאנה[30]

30 The pronunciation *tʔenå* of the Tiberian reading tradition is likely also pseudocorrect, as the glottal stop is expected to have been lost here.

and Syriac ܬܐܬܐ *tettā* both point to a reconstruction **tiʔn-(at-)*, which would be expected to just yield *tiʔn* in varieties that retained **ʔ*.

The suppletive imperative *hātū* 'give!' lacks a *hamzah* among all readers where it would be expected to exist. The verb is transparently historically derived from an imperative of the C-stem of √ʔty, i.e. *ʔātā* 'to give', and it still inflects as an imperative of this type in Classical Arabic *hāti* (m.sg.); *hātī* (f.sg.); *hātiyā* (du.); *hātū* (m.pl.); *hātīna* (f.pl.). In the Quran only the masculine plural *hātū* is attested (Q2:111; Q21:24; Q27:64; Q28:75).

The initial *h* is an ancient retention of the Central Semitic C-stem, which had an **h-* as can be seen, for example in the Hebrew C-stem that has the shape *hip̄ʕel*. So, where the causative in Classical Arabic is expected to be *ʔāti* < **ʔaʔti*, the form *hāti* developed from a form with retained **h-*, i.e. **haʔti*.[31] While Classical Arabic undergoes a dissimilatory process of **ʔvʔ* > *ʔv̄* that can explain the lack of the glottal stop in the regular imperative *ʔāti*, this same sound law cannot be used to explain the absence of the glottal stop in *hāti*, which has irregularly lost the *hamzah* in Classical Arabic as well as all reading traditions. This form probably developed because the form *hāt(i)* was not transparently analysable to the speakers anymore as coming from the root √ʔty, and thus the *hamzah* could not be reinstated.

6.5.5 *Interchange between* III-w/y *and* III-ʔ *Verbs*

In most, if not all, modern Arabic dialects, III-*w/y* and III-*ʔ* merge completely. This merger is already well on its way in the language of the QCT. In the imperfect, the verbs appear to have been indistinguishable from final weak verbs, and in the imperative and jussive, etymological III-*ʔ* verbs behave as III-*y* verbs three of the seven times they occur (see Appendix A.4.13). The result of this partial merger has also led to disagreement between the readers as to whether a verb form should be treated as a III-*ʔ* or a III-*y* verb.

Most conspicuous of the verbs that show this disagreement is the verb *ʔarǧaʔa/ʔarǧā* 'to postpone' forms of which occur throughout the Quran, with clear disagreement between the readers (Ibn al-Ǧazarī, §1229; §1533).

---

31 For an account of the development of the C-stem from **s¹* to **h* and ultimately to *ʔ* in Arabic, see Al-Jallad (*yusapʕil*). Al-Jallad argues that **s¹* regularly becomes *h* on word-boundaries in Proto-Central Semitic. For Arabic, **h* becomes *ʔ* in pre-stress position, thus explaining the shift of **him* 'if' and **hinna* 'verily' to *ʔin* and *ʔinna*. He moreover argues that **hafʕala* > *ʔafʕala* is the result of the same sound shift, drawing upon stress marking in the Damascus Psalm fragment to argue that the stress of C-stems was **ʔafʕála* in Proto-Arabic, something that would be corroborated by Hebrew which likewise carries the stress in this position. If this is correct, it would seem that the imperative form of the verb of **haʔti* carried the stress on the penultimate, i.e. **háʔti*, which would explain the retention of the **h* in this position.

	IK IA H	AA Y	IA ID	N AJ Q IW	N AJ K X W IJ	Ḥ A Ḥṣ	A Š
ارجه (Q7:111; Q26:36)	*ʔarǧiʔ-hū*	*ʔarǧiʔ-hu*	*ʔarǧiʔ-hi*	*ʔarǧi-hi*	*ʔarǧi-hī*	*ʔarǧi-h*	
مرجون (Q9:106)	*murǧaʔūna*			*murǧawna*			*murǧaʔūna*
ترجى (Q33:51)	*turǧiʔu*			*turǧī*			*turǧiʔu*

Leaving the unusual treatment of the pronominal suffix of ارجه aside for now (for a discussion on that see § 7.1.8), there is a mostly regular split: The Damascene, Meccan and Basran readers treat the verb as a III-*ʔ* root, whereas the Medinans and Kufans treat it as a III-*y* root, with the exception of Šuʕbah ʕan ʕāsim who has a mixed paradigm where the imperative is III-*y* and the other forms III-*ʔ*. As I have found no cognates of this verb in other Semitic languages, it is difficult to be sure whether the form with the *hamzah* is the original form, or a pseudocorrection.

Another verb that shows disagreement between the readers are derivations from *waṭiʔa* 'to tread, step on'. ʔabū Ǧaʕfar in accordance with a general rule of his reads يواطوا (Q9:37) as *yuwāṭū* rather than *yuwāṭiʔū* as the rest. However, the forms of the G-stem يطون (Q9:120), تطوها (Q33:27), تطوهم (Q48:25) he reads as *yaṭawna, taṭaw-ha* and *taṭaw-humū* respectively, where the other readers read *yaṭaʔūna, taṭaʔū-hā* and *taṭaʔū-hum(ū)*. These forms are not the regular outcome of his general *hamzah* loss rules. Other verbs of this type simply retain the *hamzah*, e.g. يقرون (Q10:94; Q17:71) as *yaqraʔūna*. He also reads موطيا 'step' (Q9:120) as *mawṭiyan* rather than *mawṭiʔan*. ʔabū Ǧaʕfar is inconsistent on the treatment of this sequence, cf. سيا *sayyiʔan* (Q9:102) but خاسيا *xāsiyā* (Q67:4).

However, he treats وطا 'impression' (Q73:6) as a III-*ʔ* stem, reading *waṭʔan*. This is rather surprising as *wiṭāʔan* is also consistent with the *rasm* and would have matched the treatment of this root as both III-*y* and III-*ʔ*, and this is in fact how ʔabū ʕamr and Ibn ʕāmir read (Ibn al-Ǧazarī, § 4467).

6.5.6 *Sāla for saʔala (Q70:1)*

Nāfiʕ, ʔabū Ǧaʕfar and Ibn ʕāmir read سال in Q70:1 (and *only* there) as *sāla*, with the expected *hamzah* not reinstated, which they do have elsewhere in their reading. Thus, for both of them سالك is read as *saʔala-ka* in Q2:186, for example (Ibn al-Ǧazarī, § 4441).

6.5.7 *Šurakā-ya (Q16:27) for al-Bazzī ʕan Ibn Kaṯīr*

Most readers are in agreement that شركاى (Q16:27) should be read with *hamzah*, *šurakāʔ-iya* 'my partners', but al-Bazzī ʕan Ibn Kaṯīr (with disagreement among his transmitters) reads it as *šurakā-ya*, treating this plural as a *ʔalif maqṣūrah* rather than an *ʔalif mamdūdah* (according to Ibn Muǧāhid, 371, and al-Dānī *al-taysīr*, 137, but not according to Ibn al-Ǧazarī, § 3417). This is not the regular behaviour of al-Bazzī with this noun. In fact, even the other cases of the phrase شركاى 'my partners' (Q18:52; Q28:62, 74; Q41:47) are read by al-Bazzī as *šurakāʔ-iya*.

6.6 Conclusion

In the above sections we have examined the position of the *hamzah* among the canonical readers. As is clear from this discussion we can find ample examples both of the application of *hamzah* where it is evidently pseudocorrect and places where the reading traditions lack *hamzah* where their regular rules would not predict it. These findings show that Blau's assertion that there is no trace of pseudocorrection in the Quran is incorrect. Besides a good number of pseudocorrect *hamzah*s, we also find many examples where the readers fail to insert the *hamzah* where we would expect it. This combined with reports of introduction of *hamzah* in the second century (at least in Medina) suggests that application of the *hamzah* into the text was part of the goals of the Quranic readers. These readers would not always have the means to do this correctly, sometimes overzealously applied it to words that certainly never had it, and in other cases refrained due to uncertainty.

Of course, this does not show that the language was composed without *hamzah*, that evidence can only be retrieved from Quranic rhyme and orthography. What it does show is that the Quranic reading traditions cannot be taken as a reliable guide for the language of the Quran in this regard. The readers were actively trying to apply *hamzah* in what they considered to be the correct way (mistaken or not), and there is no indication that these attempts had anything to do with what the situation was in the original composition. As such, the presence and pervasive use of *hamzah* in the Quranic reading traditions cannot inform us as to what the treatment of the *hamzah* in the original language of the Quran was.

CHAPTER 7

Classicized Hijazi: final short vowels and tanwīn

أَعْرِبُوا۟ ٱلْقُرْآنَ فَإِنَّهُ عَرَبِيٌّ

IBN MASʕŪD

One of the quintessential features of Classical Arabic, but one that is strikingly elusive in both the epigraphic pre-Islamic record and the orthography of early Islamic Arabic is the presence of *ʔiʕrāb* and *tanwīn*. Much has been said about the question whether this system was part of the spoken language, or purely part of a poetic oral tradition. Some authors argued that this case system must have been part of the general spoken register (e.g. Blau 1977) while others felt that it must have been purely part of the poetic performance (e.g. Zwettler 1978). These arguments have now for a large part been superseded by material evidence not available at the time. The view that everyone who spoke Arabic in the pre-Islamic period must have had the full inflectional system of *ʔiʕrāb* and *tanwīn* can be discarded with certainty, as we now have thousands of inscriptions and papyri that prove the contrary (Al-Jallad and al-Manaser 2015; Al-Jallad 2015; 2017a; 2018a). This should change our perspective of what we should expect the inflectional system of the Quran to look like: if multiple varieties of Old Arabic from Syria and Jordan lacked the full inflectional system of Classical Arabic, how can we be certain that this is not also the case for the language of the Quran?

Blau appears to have not found such argumentation compelling because he considered Arabic in Syria and Jordan to be peripheral and, explicitly discussing the case system of Nabataean and what the implications may be for the language situation of the Hijaz, he concludes that "nothing must be inferred from border dialects for central dialects" (Blau 1977, 9). While certainly we must agree that one cannot conclude that just because the Proto-Arabic case system seems to have started to deteriorate in Nabataean Arabic, this must have necessarily been true for Hijazi Arabic as well, I see no reason to dismiss this possibility either, just because these varieties are "peripheral". In fact, it has long been recognized in dialectology that it is rather the peripheral dialects,

 | DOI:10.1163/9789004506251_008

where certain innovative waves may not reach are often the ones that tend to be most archaic (Owens 2006, 29). However, even taking Nabataean Arabic (and by extension Safaitic) as a "border dialects" and Hijazi Arabic as a "central dialect" rather belies an adherence to an unfounded assumption that it is indeed Nabataean Arabic that is peripheral and Hijazi Arabic that is central. As more and more pre-Islamic epigraphy, Arabic and otherwise, has become available it seems to become ever more clear that it is in fact Arabic spoken in Arabia that was the peripheral form of pre-Islamic Arabic, rather than central as the historiographical and genealogical myth making of the early Islamic empire may make us believe (Al-Jallad 2018b, 34).

Rather than relying on notions of periphery and centrality, we must rather turn our gaze to the data at hand. The fact that Old Arabic from Syria and Jordan lacked the full inflectional system known to Proto-Arabic—whether these varieties were peripheral or not—at least prove that such varieties did exist before Islam, and that the case system did not only begin its collapse at the start of (or even due to) the Islamic conquests as suggested, for example by Blau (1977, 16) and Versteegh (1984, 91). When referring to what the language of the Quran is, indeed nothing must be inferred from border dialects but they must not be inferred from central dialects either. The evidence of the Quran must speak for itself.

When addressing the question of the case system of the Quran however, certainly nothing must be inferred from statements by the Arabic grammarians, who seemingly admit no other option but speaking with full inflection. This is for two reasons. First, the grammarians are not contemporary with the Quran and therefore can hardly be considered direct witnesses of the language of the Quran. Second, the grammarians' treatment of the case system is highly ideological. They famously ignore the existence of non-inflectional forms of Arabic completely even in times where there can be little doubt this system had been lost completely in any vernacular spoken at the time, e.g. in the time of al-Zamaxšarī (d. 538/1143). One is hard pressed to find any admission that such forms of Arabic exist at all in his work, despite its disappearance in most, if not all, vernaculars.[1]

I will not discuss here whether the full inflectional system of Classical Arabic was part of the spoken register of some people, or a purely poetic register. For our current discussion, I do not think that this question is relevant. The ques-

1 The earliest admissions by grammarians that people do not quite seem to speak the way they prescribe the language seems to first start to appear in the fourth century AH, by al-Zaǧǧāǧī (d. 337/948) and Ibn Ǧinnī (d. 392/1002), the latter however citing al-ʔaxfaš al-ʔawsaṭ (d. 215/830) (see Blanc 1979, 171; Versteegh 1995, 96 f.; Larcher 2018).

tion we should ask is whether the language of the Quran had a full inflectional system or not, a question which should be treated separately from the question of whether the system is proper to a vernacular or poetic register. Here we cannot turn to later sources, but we must base ourself on the earliest linguistic source that we have for the Quran: the QCT.

In an earlier article, my colleague Phillip W. Stokes and I have argued that, while the language of the Quran had not completely lost case inflection, the system had been significantly reduced (van Putten and Stokes 2018). We argue that word-final *-an* had shifted to *-ā* and that all other forms of final short vowels and nunation (i.e. *-a, -i, -u, -un* and *-in*) had been lost without a trace, not just in pause but also in connected speech. Only with nouns in construct, case appears to have been (perhaps optionally) retained. The arguments we present in favour of this view, rely on a careful study of the orthographic behaviour and internal rhyme patterns of the QCT. It seems worthwhile to summarize the main points here again, before we move on with the discussion.

1. **Pausal spelling cannot account for the lack of marking of *ʔiʕrāb* and especially *tanwīn*.**
   The 1sg. endings *-nī* 'me' and *-ī* 'my' are shortened in pausal environments, and this is reflected in the orthography of the Quran only in pause. Had 'pausal spelling' been a general principle, we would expect this shortening to be reflected in the consonantal text consistently. To this we may now also add the appearance of a final *-h* in pausal forms of the imperative and apocopate, which likewise only shows up in the QCT if such a word actually stands in a pausal position (see Appendix A.4.14). It therefore does not seem to be true that the orthography of the Quran always spells words as they are pronounced in pause. This therefore fails to explain the absence of signs for *ʔiʕrāb* and especially *tanwīn* in the spelling in non-pausal position.
   While the feminine noun being usually spelled with *hāʔ* in construct position is often invoked as evidence for the 'pausal spelling principle', it is nothing of the sort. The feminine noun in construct is unusual, and certainly orthographic, but its behaviour is unlike any other noun in construct, which are not spelled in their pausal form at all. For example, the construct form of *banūna* is simply spelled بنوا in construct not in its pausal form بنون and ابى لهب spells the construct form as ابى the way it is pronounced in construct as well, and not in its pausal form اب. Authors who continue the myth that Arabic spelling is based on the pronunciation in pause are unjustly generalizing from the exceptional behaviour of the feminine ending to the orthography of the whole Quran.[2]

2 The explanation through a principle of pausal spelling is not a recent one, it is how the

2. **The distribution of the spelling of *tāʔ maftūḥah* and *tāʔ marbūṭah* for the feminine ending points to a dialectal distribution: -*at* in construct and -*ah* everywhere else.**
   The feminine ending is occasionally written with ـت rather than ـه, this invariably occurs when the noun stands in construct. In this position it is fairly common, occurring 22% of the time. Outside of construct it is invariably spelled with ـه. Had the feminine ending been pronounced -*at* in all non-pausal environments, we would be at a loss to explain why it is not spelled ـت similarly often in non-construct, non-pausal position. What we find, however is that the feminine ending, in the 1800+ times that the feminine ending is not in construct, not once is it spelled with ـت. If we reasonably take the 22% of construct feminine nouns as the baseline for accidental phonetic spelling instead of pausal spelling, we would similarly expect non-construct feminines outside of pause to occur spelled with ـت about 22% of the time, i.e. about 400 times. The actual score, however, is zero. This strongly suggests that outside of construct the feminine ending was never pronounced -*at*, not in pause nor in context. Thus, this distribution suggests that the feminine ending was always pronounced -*ah* except in construct where it was pronounced -*at*. So this distribution points to a morphology of the noun identical to that of modern Arabic dialects with -*at* in construct and -*ah* everywhere else.[3]
3. **Internal rhyme suggests that "pausal" pronunciations were used in non-pausal positions[4]**
   Examples include: ***xayran la-hum*** rhyming with ***ʔarḥāma-kum*** (Q47:21–22), suggesting /xayrā la-hum/; and the rhyming epithet pairs in formu-

---

medieval Arab grammarians explained the unusual mismatch between the Arabic orthography and its classical pronunciation. For example, Ibn al-Sarrāǧ (d. 316 AH) in his *Kitāb al-Xaṭṭ* lays out the principle explicitly: *wa-l-ʔaṣlu ʔayḍan fī kulli kalimatin ʔan tuktaba ʕalā l-lafẓi bi-hā mubtadaʔatan wa-mawqūfan ʕalay-hā* "And the principle is also that for each word that it be written with the pronunciation of it at the beginning of an utterance, and if it was paused upon." (Ibn al-Sarrāǧ *Kitāb al-Xaṭṭ*, 67). We of course cannot blindly rely on a 4th c. AH source to tell us how the orthographic rules of the 1st c. AH worked. The explanation is just as much a *post hoc* justification as it is for a modern scholar to hold this view.

3 In fact this exact distribution is seen as evidence for a modern dialectal type feminine ending in Middle Arabic texts (e.g. Blau 1967, §24.1; 2002, 34; Blau and Hopkins 1987, §47a). If this argument is deemed convincing for Middle Arabic, it should also be accepted for Quranic Arabic.

4 For several examples of internal rhymes that seem to operate on "pausal" forms, see also Larcher (2014). In a recent article Larcher (2021) explores one more possible case of internal rhymes using pausal forms and, seemingly independently, explicitly adopts the same conclusions as Van Putten & Stokes (2018).

lae such as *ʔinna ḷḷāha samīʕun ʕalīm* (Q49:1) and *wa-kāna ḷḷāhu ʕalīman ḥakīmā* (Q48:4) suggesting /samīʕ ʕalīm/ and /ʕalīmā ḥakīmā/.

4. **Several words reflect the regular outcome of the loss of the final short vowels and *n*, in places where they are not morphologically *ʔiʕrāb* and *tanwīn*.**

 For example, the apocopate **yakun* spelled as يك (Q8:53) and the energic forms **la-nasfaʕa-n* and **la-yakūnan* being spelled لنسفعا (Q96:15) and ليكونا (Q12:32) respectively.

On the basis of these arguments, it seems likely to me that the Quran, far from having a fully classical *ʔiʕrāb/tanwīn* system as is generally believed, had a much reduced one. However, we cannot admit a full reworking of the text towards a Classical Arabic system by later grammarians/philologists from something more-or-less identical to the modern dialectal Arabic system as Vollers would have had it. This would have required a reworking of the QCT, we now have access to early manuscripts that closely follow the standard text that can be securely dated before the period of the development of Arabic grammatical theory, as its canonization almost certainly happened during the reign of ʕuṯmān b. ʕaffān.[5]

The absence of any transmission of reading traditions that lacked *ʔiʕrāb* seems to have been the main objection of Nöldeke against Vollers' *ʔiʕrāb*-less ur-Quran. A spirited defense of Vollers' hypothesis was put forward in three articles by Kahle (1947, 78–84; 1948, 163–182; 1949) who, aiming to counter Nöldeke's claim, proffers over a hundred prophetic, and non-prophetic narrations admonishing people not to read the Quran without *ʔiʕrāb*. Many of these narrations must be outright fabrications, unless we accept that a full-fledged grammatical terminology was part of the common parlance of the prophet and his companions. Nevertheless, they show an important point: there were in fact people reading the Quran without *ʔiʕrāb*, and this was happening early enough that an authority as early as al-Farrāʔ (d. 207/822) felt the need to relate such narrations to discourage it. This made short work of Nöldeke's unusually weak criticism of Vollers. However, this does not seem to have swayed later authors who continue to cite Nöldeke's review. Rabin (1955) agrees with Nöldeke and is right to point out that, just because there were people who read the Quran without *ʔiʕrāb*—something clearly considered to be disturbing to those who relate these narrations—this does not mean that there was an *ʔiʕrāb*-less ur-Quran. Conversely, however, the opposite is of course also true: that reading

5 Considering the limited accessibility to early Quranic manuscripts, or the lack of sound philological arguments for an early canonization of the text in the 19th century, it would be unfair to criticize Vollers anachronistically for not taking this into account.

the Quran without (or with reduced) *ʔiʕrāb* was considered bad by third century AH authorities, a time after the activity of most of the canonical reciters had come to prominence can hardly be used as an argument that it was *always* considered wrong. These narrations reveal something important: Later readers and grammarians thought that any form of language could not be considered *al-ʕarabiyyah* unless it was supplied with *ʔiʕrāb*, which being the *maṣdar* of the C-stem of the root √*ʕrb* literally means "to make Arabic". Therefore, there is no *al-ʕarabiyyah* without *ʔiʕrāb*. It is not surprising that so few of the traditions seem to acknowledge a once existing form of Quranic Arabic that did not have *ʔiʕrāb* even if it did exist; By the time the narrations were fabricated, and certainly when the reading traditions are canonized with Ibn Muǧāhid in the fourth Islamic century, the superiority of the *ʕarabiyyah* that had *ʔiʕrāb/tanwīn* was well-established and completely unassailable.

Rabin (1955) criticizes Kahle's argumentation, but misses his point. He is, of course right, that the exhortations to *not* read the Quran without *ʔiʕrāb*, and that *laḥn* is to be avoided does not prove that the language of the Quran was without case. I do not believe that Kahle was arguing for this. What Kahle aimed to show is that the very paradigm of reading the Quran, in this period *necessitated* the used of *ʔiʕrāb*, any manner of reading without it, or not even following the strict model presented by the readers-*cum*-(proto-)grammarians, would by definition not be considered proper by the people who ended up deciding what the norms of reading the Quran would be. With the narrations brought by al-Farrāʔ, we are one generation removed from the canonical reader and grammarian al-Kisāʔī, as well as Sībawayhi. In fact, Rabin and Kahle seem to agree to a large extent, Rabin (1955, 27) says: "If, however, the language of the Koran made concessions to the literary *koinē*, the *ʿArabiyya*, then it must needs (sic) have accepted also the case-endings, that feature which was felt to be so essential that it was called by the same word as the use of the language itself, *iʿrāb*."

Despite what Rabin seems to think, he and Kahle are not in disagreement on this point. The disagreement stems from the fact that Rabin, and with him many others, take for granted that the language of the Quran made these concessions to the *ʕarabiyyah* already at the time of composition during the lifetime of the prophet. Rabin takes this for granted, believing that al-Farrāʔ, who could not possibly conceive of the language of the Quran being anything but a language with the *ʔiʕrāb* and *tanwīn* intact, is in fact correct in his inability to conceive of this. That assumption, however, is never substantiated in any way. The evidence of the QCT, as I see it, rather speaks against it.

Looking for evidence in the reading traditions for traces of the original language of the Quran in terms of the case system is therefore something that is not possible as that was not the goal of the readers. What we can recover, however, is evidence that the readers of the Quran were not trying to syllable-for-syllable transmit the pronunciation as they received it from their teacher, but instead, much like we saw in the previous chapter and chapter 3, sought to beautify the language, and chose forms that they rationalized to be the correct pronunciation—even if that led to pseudocorrect readings. The choice of *ʔiʕrāb* by the readers was part of their job, a rational endeavour and one where different readers could and did have different intuitions and came to different solutions.

A clear place where disagreements on *ʔiʕrāb* frequently occur between the readers is on names of places and tribes, which may either occur as triptotes or as diptotes in the classical language. Sībawayh (III, 246–256) tells us that a name of a people may either be triptotic if it refers either to the eponymous father of a tribe or a *ḥayy* 'clan', while when it is diptotic, it refers to a *qabīlah* 'tribe'. As Van Putten (forthcoming) shows, the distinction between *ḥayy* and *qabīlah* does not seem to be based on any genealogical basis: both the primordial confederacy of *maʕadd* and the famous tribe of *qurayš*, a tribe that belongs to *maʕadd* are designated as *ḥayy* whereas *tamīm* is a *qabīlah*. The difference between *ḥayy* and *qabīlah* comes down to formal characteristics. In the case of a *qabīlah* the tribe as a whole is treated as dipotic while the eponymous father is triptotic, and it can be denoted as 'sons of [eponymous father]', this constitutes a *qabīlah*, e.g. *Tamīmu* 'the tribe Tamīm'. *Tamīmun* 'the eponymous father of the tribe, Tamīm', *banū tamīmin* 'sons of Tamīm, the father = the tribe Tamīm'. Such constructions cannot be formed with *Qurayš*, at least according to Sībawayh, and this prescription seems to be adhered to quite faithfully even today.[6]

For names of peoples or countries that occur in the Quran, however, the practical context to make this distinction was lacking, and as a result the readers quite plainly disagree with one another. *sabaʔ* 'Shebah' occurs twice, both in a genitive position (Q27:22; Q34:15). Ibn Kaṯīr (in the transmission of al-Bazzī, for Qunbul see §7.1.1) and ʔabū ʕamr treat this name as a diptote, i.e. *sabaʔa*, whereas the other readers take it to be a triptote, *sabaʔin*. Indeed, if we look at how this distinction is explained, e.g. by Ibn Xālawayh (*Ḥuǧǧah*, 270) he says: "whoever treats it triptotic considers it to be the name of a mountain or the name of the father of the tribe; whoever does not conjugate it, makes it to be the name of a land or a woman, so it becomes heavy from the definiteness and

6 A google search for "بنو تميم" yields 193.000 results, while a search for "بنو قريش" yields only 3.840.

femininity." In his book on what should be treated triptotic and what should be treated diptotic, al-Zaǧǧāǧ (*Mā Yanṣarif*, 59) presents a different opinion: "ʔabū ʕamr treats *sabaʔ* as a diptote, so he considers it to be the name of a tribe (*qabīlah*)."

What should be clear from these treatments is that it is not actually *known* by anyone what the proper treatment of this noun should be, and rather than giving a consistent answer of what *sabaʔ* refers to—which of course should be a land, the Sabaean kingdom—we get multiple solutions by the readers, seemingly not based on any real knowledge of what the conjugation should be, but rather through a rationalization from however the word should be conjugated.

This rationalization becomes even more obvious when it causes some conflict with the QCT, namely with the name of the people of Thamud. This has been discussed once before by Van Putten (forthcoming) but I will summarize the discussion here. When we look at the QCT, we find that *ṯamūd* functions as a triptote. Whenever it stands in the nominative and genitive it is spelled ثمود whereas when it occurs in the accusative it is spelled ثمودا (Q11:68; Q25:38; Q29:38; Q53:51), there is one exception to this in Q17:59 اتينا ثمود الناقه مبصره "and we gave Thamud the she-camel as an evident (sign)". For the latter exception there are a variety of explanations.

Despite the clear behaviour of the QCT of this word as triptotic, the canonical readers display a rather mixed treatment. The readers invariably treat the nominative as a diptote, reading *ṯamūdu* not *ṯamūdun*. The genitive is likewise treated as a diptote, reading *ṯamūda* rather than *ṯamūdin*. There is a single exception to this, which we will return to shortly. As for the accusative, most readers follow the *rasm* suddenly switching categories for this noun, reading it as *ṯamūdan*, but Ḥafṣ ʕan ʕāṣim, Ḥamzah and Yaʕqūb ignore the *rasm* and read *ṯamūda* instead. Šuʕbah ʕan ʕāṣim only follows them in the diptotic reading in Q53:51 (Ibn al-Ǧazarī, § 3298–3299). It is clear from these examples that there is somewhat of a consensus between the readers that in principle *ṯamūd* should be diptotic, but there is a difference of opinion as to whether one is free to ignore the *rasm* when it is unambiguous in its triptosy.

Later discussions dutifully follow the distinction as presented by Sībawayh, and cast this discussion into terms of *ḥayy* versus *qabīlah*, e.g. Ibn Xālawayh (*ḥujjah*, 188): "whoever treats it as triptotic, there are two opinions (as to why): one of them is: that he considers it to be the name of a *ḥayy* or a chieftain (of a tribe), and the other is that they consider it to be a *faʕūlan* noun from the root *ṯmd*, and this is a small amount of water. The one who treats it as a diptote considers it to be the name of a *qabīlah*."

This discussion of the much earlier al-Farrāʔ however, is very interesting and quite different, and provides an explanation as to why his teacher al-Kisāʔī reads the triptotic genitive *ṯamūdin* in Q11:68 only while he reads *ṯamūda* elsewhere (al-Farrāʔ *Maʕānī*, II, 20):

> The reciters disagreed on *ṯamūd*: among them there were those who treated it as triptotic in each case.[7] As for those who treat it diptotic in this case, Muḥammad ← al-Farrāʔ ← Qays ← ʔabū ʔisḥāq ← ʕabd al-Raḥmān b. al-ʔaswad b. Yazīd al-Naxaʕī ← his father reports that he would never treat *ṯamūd* as a triptote in the whole Quran, and Ḥamzah read it thus. There are among them those who treat *ṯamūd* triptotically in the accusative **because it is written with an *ʔalif* in the whole Quran**, except in one place *ʔātaynā ṯamūda n-nāqata mubṣirah* (Q17:59), and this is what al-Kisāʔī adopted, he treated it triptotically in the accusative, and diptotically in the genitive and nominative, except in one case, in HIS speech *ʔa-lā ʔinna ṯamūdan kafarū rabba-hum ʔa-lā buʕdan **li-ṯamūdin*** (Q11:68)". So, they asked him about this and he said: "it is read with the genitive of triptosy; **it is ugly to have a word occur twice in two places (within the same verse) and then have them disagree [on triptosy/dipotsy], so I treated it [*ṯamūdin*] as a triptote because of it being close to it [*ṯamūdan*]**. (emphasis my own)

This extraordinary discussion reveals a view of the transmission of the readings strikingly different from how modern Islamic orthodoxy views the readings.[8] Al-Farrāʔ explains the existence of a reading being explicitly based on its spelling, rather than the writing being seen as accommodating a preexistent oral tradition. Second, he brings a report from his teacher who gives an explicitly aesthetic argument for his choice to read ثمود (Q11:68) as *ṯamūdin* rather than *ṯamūda*.

While this account of course does not prove that the Quran was once composed without *ʔiʕrāb*—for that we have to rely on the philological arguments presented at the start of this section—what it does show is how readers themselves thought about their role in applying *ʔiʕrāb* in recitation. Their role was not to faithfully verbatim the *ʔiʕrāb* as had been taught to them, but rather to

7 N.B. not a single one of the canonical readers reads it thus. It is reported for prominent non-canonical readers such as al-ʔaʕmaš and Yaḥyā (Ibn Xālawayh *muxtaṣar*, 50). It is also attested in vocalized Quranic manuscripts, but seemingly only ever marked as a secondary reading: Arabe 334(d), 58r, l. 2.; Arabe 347(b), 81r, l. 4.; Cod. Guelf. 12. 11. Aug. fol., 5r, l. 4; Arabe 340(d), 64v, l. 8; Arabe 351, 147r, l. 4; Arabe 341(b), 180r, l. 1; Ms.orient.Quart.1208 (VI), 6r, l. 6; Arabe 359(c), 79r, l. 5; Arabe 325(k), 133r, l. 5; Arabe 335, 3r, l. 6; Arabe 354(c), 31r, l. 5; Arabe 350(b), 233v, l. 3; Arabe 333(d), 74r, l. 15; Arabe 350a, 135r, l. 2.

8 The relevance of this passage was already remarked upon by Nöldeke et al. (2013, 543).

argue and rationalize why a word should have the *ʔiʕrāb* that they would give it. In such cases even purely aesthetic arguments such as the one cited, was apparently enough to deviate from the way their teacher taught it (Ḥamzah, al-Kisāʔī's direct teacher reads *ṯamūda* and *li-ṯamūda* in the relevant verse). As such the application of *ʔiʕrāb* by these readers can tell us nothing at all about the use of *ʔiʕrāb* of the original language of the QCT. However, given that the choice of *ʔiʕrāb* was a rational endeavour explicitly based on both the *rasm* and aesthetic preference rather than prophetic example, it becomes quite easy to envision that the presence of this very system was not original to the text, but was rather imposed on it sometime after the standardization of the QCT by ʕuṯmān.

In some cases, we can see that to the readers certain words were no longer transparently analysable, and as a result the application of case end up being pseudocorrect. For example, the question word *ʔayyāna* 'when?' (Q7:187; Q16:21; Q27:65; Q51:12; Q75:6; Q79:42) is universally read as such by the canonical readers. This word is generally analysed as a CaC̄āC pattern of a root √ʔy/wn whence also *ʔān* 'time', which subsequently receives a final *-a* as other question words such as *ʔayna* or perhaps denotations of time such as *yawma* 'on the day' and *ḥīna* 'at the time'. However, this question word is clearly a univerbation of *ʔayya ʔānin* 'at which time?', where the *hamzah* of *ʔān* was lost. This indeed appears to have been recognized by al-Farrāʔ who is quoted in the *Lisān al-ʕarab* (183a) as saying:

> the base [*ʔaṣl*] of *ʔayyāna* is *ʔayya ʔawānin*, so they drop the vowel [*faxaffafū*] of the *yāʔ* of *ʔayy* and removed the *hamzah* of *ʔawān*, and then and then the vowelless *yāʔ* and the *wāw* after it meet, so the *wāw* was assimilated to the *yāʔ*, and he told this on the authority of al-Kisāʔī.

While it is probably better to derive the second part of *ʔayyān* from *ʔān* rather than *ʔawān*,[9] this etymology is, of course, otherwise the correct one. What is interesting in the line of reasoning, however, is that at no point the final short vowel is discussed. The explanation that is given would predict the form *ʔayyānin* rather than the now recited *ʔayyāna*. Other grammarians, perhaps for this reason, preferred different explanations for this word, but the fact

9 Al-Farrāʔ considered the origin (*ʔaṣl*) of *ʔān* to also be *ʔawān* (*lisān al-ʕarab*, 193b). The awkward choice to argue from the form *ʔawān* to explain this form is typical of Arabic linguistic thought, which does not like to take surface forms as input for a certain output, and instead argues from the development of a kind of platonic ideal of the word (*ʔaṣl*) and how that word leads to different surface forms.

remains that this is evidently the most straightforward etymology. However, it only works if we assume that the case vowels were only applied later, and that the form that yielded *ʔayyāna* was in fact /ayy ān/, or perhaps /ayya ān/ without the final case vowel, which was subsequently later applied to the word /ayyān/ when it was no longer analysed as a compound phrase, yielding the form *ʔayyāna* rather than the expected ****ʔayyānin*.

7.1 Lack of Final Short Vowels in the Reading Traditions

From the examples above, it should be clear that the placement of final short vowels and *tanwīn* in the recitation of the Quran tells us very little about what the situation was like in the original language of composition. Choosing *ʔiʕrāb* was the duty of the reciter which could and did lead to disagreements among the readers. The fact that readers all agree that the Quran is to be read with *ʔiʕrāb* is part of the ideology that gave rise to the science of recitation in the first place. Yet, from time-to-time we encounter isolated cases of words that are unexpectedly read without final short vowels.

Considering how strongly reading without final short vowels was disfavored by the grammarians early on, the very fact that such forms are transmitted at all should probably be understood as a genuine attempt of transmitting earlier forms otherwise lost to the tradition, as it is difficult to imagine how readers would have chosen to *innovate* transmissions without case vowels on purpose.

Of course, the existence of such forms cannot prove that the original language of the Quran lacked these final short vowels any more than their presence can—the only way to establish that is by going back to the QCT—but the existence of such transmissions does suggest that in the earliest times of the transmission of the Quran, there were transmissions going around that had forms without final short vowels. These transmissions have not come down as complete readings, but like many other cases are simply retained as singular lexical exceptions.

7.1.1 *Sabaʔ*

While most readers either treat the name of the South Arabian kingdom of *sabaʔ* as a triptote or a diptote, there is also a transmission of Ibn Kaṯīr through the canonical transmitter Qunbul (a teacher of Ibn Muǧāhid) who simply read it without any *ʔiʕrāb*, i.e. *sabaʔ* rather than *sabaʔa* or *sabaʔin* in Q27:22 and Q34:15 (Ibn al-Ǧazarī, § 3803). Ibn Muǧāhid (480) considered this *ʔiʕrāb*less reading a mistake (*wa-huwa wahm*), affirming that the transmission of al-Bazzī is the correct one, but despite that he also brings a single strand transmission independent of Qunbul that likewise transmits this *ʔiʕrāb*less form (Al-Ḥasan b. Muḥammad b. ʕubayd aḷḷāh b. ʔabī yazīd ← Šibl ← Ibn Kaṯīr). It is interesting to note that Al-Dānī seems disturbed enough by this, even in his *al-Taysīr*—a book that normally does not spend much time explaining certain forms—that he feels it is necessary to qualify why Qunbul would read it as such, saying that it is "with the intention (for it to be) the pausal form" (*ʕalā niyyati l-waqf*) (Al-Dānī *taysīr*, 27).

This caseless transmission presents a problem for scholars who wish to explain this form, as the grammatical framework that the grammarians have set up do not normally allow for the absence of any inflection in the middle of a verse, and as such only *post hoc* explanations are adduced. For example, Ibn Xālawayh (*Ḥuǧǧah*, 270) says: "whoever quiesces the *hamzah* would say: This noun is feminine, and that is heavier than masculine; it is definite, and that is heavier than indefinite; it is *hamzat*ed and that is heavier than not having a *hamzah*, as these features come together in the noun that we have mentioned, the heaviness is lessened by quiescence of the final short vowel."

7.1.2 *As-sayyiʔ*

The noun *as-sayyiʔ* السيا[10] occurs in its definite form twice in the same verse (Q35:43). Ḥamzah reads the first occurrence without *ʔiʕrāb*, i.e. *as-sayyiʔ*, while the second one is read as *as-sayyiʔu* (Ibn al-Ǧazarī, § 3991). It should be noted here that one cannot argue that this is a pausal pronunciation, as Ḥamzah drops the *hamzah* in pause, i.e. *as-sayyī*, a distinction specifically commented on with regard to this verse by al-Dānī (*taysīr*, 182 f.)

Ibn Xālawayh (*Ḥujjah*, 297) cannot use the same argumentation why this form is caseless as he did for *sabaʔ*, as this noun is not feminine. Instead, he suggests that it was "lightened" because of the meeting of two *kasrah*s in a row. He likens this to ʔabū ʕamr's reading of *bāriʔi-kum* as *bāriʔ-kum* (Q2:54; see § 7.2.5). This explanation is, of course, *ad hoc* as Ḥamzah does not read *bāriʔi-kum* without the case vowel, nor *min šāṭiʔi l-wād* (Q28:30) which is more comparable in terms of phonetic context.

7.1.3 *Maḥyā-y*

Nāfiʕ and ʔabū Gaʕfar are unique in reading محياى (Q6:162) as *maḥyā-y* (Qālūn; ʔabū Ǧaʕfar) *maḥyā̆-y* (Warš) rather than *maḥyā-ya* (Ibn al-Ǧazarī, § 2513). This is irregular within these readings. Other cases of nouns ending in *ʔalif maq-*

10 The spelling سيا rather than the CE سيى is the standard spelling in early manuscripts (van Putten 2018, 115).

ṣūrah followed by the 1sg. ending simply have *-ya*, e.g. هداى (Q2:38) is *hudā-ya* (Qālūn; ʔabū Ǧaʕfar) or *hudā̆-ya* (Warš).

7.1.4 *Yā-bunay*

There is disagreement among the readers on how to read يبنى 'o my son' in its six attestations (Q11:42; Q12:5; Q31:13, 16, 17; Q37:102) (Ibn al-Ǧazarī, § 3291). Ḥafṣ ʕan ʕāṣim read it as *yā-bunay-ya* whenever it occurred. Šuʕbah ʕan ʕāṣim follows him in Q13:13 and Q31:17 only. In all other cases he read *yā-bunayy-i* with the more typical shortened vocative 1sg. ending *-i* as also found in يابت *yā-ʔabat-i* 'o my father', يرب *yā-rabb-i* 'o my lord', يقوم *yā-qawm-i* 'o my people'. All other readers follow the reading *yā-bunayy-i* instead.

For Ibn Kaṯīr, there is an exception, he specifically reads Q31:13 as *yā-bunay*, without final *-i*, nor with gemination of the final consonant. It might be that it simply means 'O son!' rather than 'O my son', but even in that case one would have expected *yā-bunayyu* rather than no case vowel at all. This is therefore clearly an uninflected form in Ibn Kaṯīr's reading. This *ʔiʕrāb*less form occurs again in Q31:17, which is read as *yā-bunay* by Qunbul whereas Ibn Kaṯīr's other canonical transmitter, Al-Bazzī reads it as *yā-bunay-ya*, while he usually read *yā-bunayy-i* elsewhere.

7.1.5 *Yartaʕ/nartaʕ*

An interesting case of the loss of final short vowels is يرتع (Q12:12). This is read by most readers as a jussive *yartaʕ* or *nartaʕ*, and is taken to be from a root √*rtʕ* which in this G-stem supposedly means 'to graze' and figuratively 'to revel, indulge freely (in)'. However, several readers read it as the jussive Gt-stem of *raʕā* 'to pasture', i.e. *nartaʕi* (Ibn Kaṯīr) or *yartaʕi* (Abū Ǧaʕfar and Nāfiʕ).[11]

irtaʕā 'to graze; pasture' and *rataʕa* 'to graze; to revel' are obviously related and the latter must be considered a reanalysis of the former. This, however, is only possible from a stage of the language where final short vowels were lost. In Quranic Arabic, final long *ī* is lost completely in pause, and such shortened forms are occasionally also used outside of pause (van Putten and Stokes 2018, 156 ff.). The imperfective of *irtaʕā* would thus be *yartaʕī* or *yartaʕ* and in pause exclusively *yartaʕ#*. The jussive form would always be *yartaʕ*. These shortened forms without final short vowels in the prefix conjugation look identical to the prefix conjugation of a verb derived from a root √*rtʕ*. The root √*rtʕ* must be

11 Ibn Muǧāhid does not mention this disagreement among the readers at all. Al-Dānī (*taysīr*, 128) reports it. He says that most readers read *nartaʕ*; That ʕāṣim, Al-Kisāʔī and Ḥamzah and Nāfiʕ read *yartaʕ* and that the Ibn Kaṯīr and Nāfiʕ read it with a final *i*, i.e. *nartaʕi* and *yartaʕi* respectively. Abū Ǧaʕfar also reads it with the final *i* (Ibn al-Ǧazarī, 293).

the result of a reanalysis of the prefix conjugation *yartaʕ*, which allowed for a reanalysis that is only readily possible in a variety of Arabic that has lost final short vowels.[12] We must therefore see the root √*rtʕ* as an artifact of grammatical thought of the Arab grammarians who were confronted with the reading *yartaʕ* lacking final short vowels—a form which would be incorrect in the Arabic which retained final short vowels—unless it was the jussive of a non-existent root √*rtʕ*. From there a new verb with this root √*rtʕ* was coined. This reanalysis is unlikely to have happened in a variety that had full *ʔiʕrāb* present, as the jussive *yartaʕi* is not homophonous to ***yartaʕ*.

7.1.6 *Tatran, tatrā, tatrē*

An example where the readers show disagreement on whether a noun should have *tanwīn* or not can be found in تترا 'one after another, in succession' (Q23:44) which is read by Ibn Kaṯīr, ʔabū ʕamr and ʔabū Ǧaʕfar as *tatran*, whereas the rest reads it as *tatrā* or *tatrē*, depending on whether they apply *ʔimālah* to the *-ā* feminine suffix (Ibn al-Ǧazarī, § 3690). Traditionally this word is interpreted as either a CaCC derivation of *watira* 'to string' or a CaCCā derivation of the same (Ibn Xālawayh *Ḥuǧǧah*, 257). The initial *t* is explained as an alternation of *w* and *t* in the way that we see it in *turāṯ* 'inheritance' from *wariṯa* 'to inherit', but such an explanation in either case is not particularly attractive. This *w/t*-alternation is otherwise only found in in tuCāC and tuCaCah (e.g. *tuxamah* 'indigestion') derivations from I-*w* verbs (Fischer 2002, § 240.3). Whatever the actual derivation of this noun, it is clear that because of the obscurity of this *hapax legomenon* and its derivation, readers could not agree whether the word was to have *tanwīn* or not, and hence we are confronted with both options.[13]

7.1.7 *Tuḍār*

تضار (Q2:233) is variously read by the canonical seven as *tuḍārru* (Ibn Kaṯīr, ʔabū ʕamr, Yaʕqūb, Ibn ʕāmir) or *tuḍārra* (Nāfiʕ, Ḥafṣ ʕan ʕāṣim, Ḥamzah, al-Kisāʔī, Xalaf). However, Abū Ǧaʕfar reads it in a completely *iʕrāb*-less form *tuḍār*. He also read يضار (Q2:282) without *ʔiʕrāb*.[14] (Ibn al-Ǧazarī, § 2774).

---

12 The root √*rtʕ* also lacks Semitic cognates, unlike, *raʕā* which is easily reconstructible for Proto-Semitic as **raʕaya* (cf. Aram. *rʕā* 'to grave; pasture'; Hebr. *råʕå*; Gz. *raʕaya*; ASA *rʕy*; Akk. *reʔû*).

13 See also Nöldeke et al. (2013, 417, n. 184) who are equally skeptical about the derivation.

14 Moreover, both with degemination of the final consonant, a feature reported for Middle Arabic (Blau 2002, § 10).

7.1.8 *The 3sg.m. Suffix -h*

A striking category of words that lack expected final (long!) vowels in the Quranic reading traditions are the final weak verbs that occur in the apocopate or imperative followed by the third person masculine clitic pronoun *-hū/-hī*. Verbs of this type occur sixteen times in the Quran, and every single one of them is reported among at least one of the canonical readers without the expected final vowel, and occasionally with a short form *-hi/hu* rather than *-hī/hū*. There is a good amount of disagreement among different works on the Qirāʔāt, for simplicity's sake, the following table is based on Ibn al-Ǧazarī (§ 1213–1219).

	IK/K/X	Wš	IA	Qā	Y	AJ	AA	Ḥ/Š	Ḥṣ
Q3:75 يوده	-hī	-hī	-hī, -hi, -h	-hi	-hi	-h (-hi)	-h	-h	-hī
Q3:75 يوده	-hī	-hī	-hī, -hi, -h	-hi	-hi	-h (-hi)	-h	-h	-hī
Q3:145 نوته	-hī	hī	-hī, -hi, -h	-hi	-hi	-h (-hi)	-h	-h	-hī
Q3:145 نوته	-hī	hī	-hī, -hi, -h	-hi	-hi	-h (-hi)	-h	-h	-hī
Q4:115 نوله	-hī	-hī	-hī, -hi, -h	-hi	-hi	-h (-hi)	-h	-h	-hī
Q4:115 نصله	-hī	-hī	-hī, -hi, -h	-hi	-hi	-h (-hi)	-h	-h	-hī
Q42:20 نوته	-hī	-hī	-hī, -hi, -h	-hi	-hi	-h (-hi)	-h	-h	-hī
Q27:28 فالقه	-hī	-hī	-hī, -hi, -h	-hi	-hi	-h (-hi)	-h	-h	-h
Q24:52 يتقه	-hī	-hī	-hī, -hi, -h	-hi	-hi	-h, -hi, -hī	-h	-h, -hī	-q-hi
Q20:75 ياته	-hī	-hī	-hī	-hi (-hī)	-hi	-hī	-h, -hī	-hī	-hī
Q7:111 ارجه	-ʔhū/-hī	-hī	-ʔhū/i	-hi	-ʔhu	-hi, -hī	-ʔ-hu	-h	-h
Q26:36 ارجه	-ʔhū/-hī	-hī	-ʔhū/i	-hi	-ʔhu	-hi, -hī	-ʔ-hū	-h	-h
Q39:7 يرضه	-hū	-hu	-hū, -hu, -h	-hu	-hu	-h (-hū)	-h, -hu, -hū	-h, -hu	-hu
Q90:7 يره	-hū	-hū	-hū	-hū	-hu, -hū	-hu, hū	-hū	-hū	-hū
Q99:7 يره	-hū	-hū	-hū, -h	-hū	-hu, -hū	-h, -hu, -hū	-hū	-hū	-hū
Q99:8 يره	-hū	-hū	-hū, -h	-hū	-hu, -hū	-h, -hu, -hū	-hū	-hū	-hū

It is possible to make several generalizations on the basis of this table. First, al-Kisāʔī, Xalaf and Ibn Kaṯīr do not show any unusual behaviour in these verbs, and simply follow their general rules of the pronouns. Warš ʕan Nāfiʕ follows them almost completely, only making an exception at *yarḍa-hu*.

Yaʕqūb consistently treats these apocopates/imperatives that have a final *-i* as if they ended in final *-ī*, and therefore vowel length disharmony is triggered. This behaviour is reminiscent of another part of his reading that we have discussed earlier (§ 3.6.3): Yaʕqūb does not harmonize the third person plural suffix *-hum* to *-him* if *ay* or *ī* precede. Rawḥ ʕan Yaʕqūb likewise treats apocopates as if they ended in final *-ī* and does not apply vowel harmony either. This parallel is unlikely to be a coincidence.

Qālūn ʕan Nāfiʕ, like Yaʕqūb consistently has a short pronominal form after apocopates that end in *-hi*. Unlike Yaʕqūb, Qālūn has no other examples where he seems to treat apocopate *-i* as if it were *ī*. For Qālūn with apocopates that end in *-a* length disharmony does not get triggered either, although there are transmissions for Yaʕqūb that lack it too, and thus we see *yara-hū* (Q90:7; Q99:7, 8). But for *yarḍa-hu* (Q39:7), like Warš he has a short vowel.

Taking the imperfect as the basis of the vowel length disharmony rule is indeed how it is explained in *Ḥuǧǧah* literature, Ibn Xālawayh (*Ḥuǧǧah*, 111) for example says: "those who pronounce the vowel (of *-hV*) short take the base (*ʔaṣl*) of it to be *yuʔaddī-hi*, and then the *yāʔ* disappears because of it being an apocopate, and the shortened vowel remains because of what its base (*ʔaṣl*) was."

This type of reading however, can hardly be understood as the outcome of natural language. The rule of vowel disharmony not being affected by the shortening of the *ī* is imaginable if the vowel-length disharmony of the pronominal suffix predates the shortening of the vowel in the apocopate. The phonological process would then have been phonologized due to this development. However, the order of development is reversed: apocopate forms of the verb go at least as far back as Proto-West-Semitic, evidence of them being present, for example, in Hebrew (*yiḇnī* 'he builds' *way-yiḇɛn* 'and he built' < *yabniyu, *yabni), whereas it seems clear that the vowel length disharmony is a (Classical) Arabic internal development. The use of the short form of the pronoun, therefore should be considered an explicit grammarian rationalization from the view that apocopates are shortened forms of the imperfective, rather than a natural outcome of the language.

The vowelless forms as found in the readings of Šuʕbah, Ḥamzah, ʔabū ʕamr and ʔabū Ǧaʕfar rather appear as overzealous application of the grammatical rules of apocopation. All of them more-or-less consistently have no vowel on the pronoun at all on the apocopates that end in in *-i*.

What this seems to stem from is that all of these readers start with a surface imperfective form, e.g. *yattaqī-hi*, and subsequently apply the rule to make an apocopate form to both parts of the word, shortening final *-ī* and dropping final *-i*. Indeed al-Farrāʔ (*Maʕānī*, I, 224) was aware that some readers seem to view it as such, although he considers it a mistake:

> Al-ʔaʕmaš and ʕāṣim used to drop the vowel of the *hāʔ* in *yuʔaddi-h, yuwalli-h mā tawallī, ʔarǧi-h wa-ʔaxā-hu, xayran yara-h,*[15] *šarran yara-h*. And there are two ways of viewing this for them [*wa-fīhi la-humā maḏhabān*]: One of these is that the people considered it to be the apocopate of the *hāʔ*, in fact [what is apocopated] is in front of the *hāʔ*. So, this—if it is the case that they supposed that—is a mistake.

The second option that al-Farrāʔ presents, however, is not particularly convincing as an explanation of these forms. He gives cases where Arabs may pronounce the pronoun as *-h*, but none of the cases he cites account for the environment in which we see this behaviour:

> As for the other option, either there are among the Arabs those who apocopate the *hāʔ* when there is a short vowel before it. So, they say: *ḍarabtu-h ḍarban šadīdā*, or one removes from the *hāʔ* the *rafʕ* of its base as is the case with *raʔaytum* and *ʔantum*. Do you not see that the *mīm* is quiesced while its base is *rafʕ* [In al-Farrāʔ's framework, the base of these words is *raʔaytumū* and *ʔantumū*]?

Al-Farrāʔ is clearly bothered by the first explanation, as it evidently stems from ignorance of the grammatical model the grammarians—him included—rely upon, but it is also evidently less *ad hoc* than his other option, which does not explain at all why these shortened formed only occur specifically with the imperative and apocopate of III-*y/w* verbs.

It might be possible that the origin of this overzealous application of this rule may have to do with transmissions that originally lacked final short vowels. In the nascent period of grammatical theory—readers like al-ʔaʕmaš (d. 148) and ʕāṣim (d. 127) predate Sībawayh by one to two generations—it seems possible that in other contexts the application of the apocopation rules was less

15 This reading has not come down to us through transmissions of the canonical readers. Al-Farrāʔ usually appears to report ʕāṣim's reading from Šuʕbah.

ambiguous than with the final weak verbs, and therefore these were classicized properly, whereas the final weak verbs went under the radar and their quiescent forms were retained.

There are some irregularities among the readers with fully vowelless forms, but Ibn Muǧāhid (211 f.) reports a zero vowel for every form for Ḥamzah → al-Kisāʔī → al-Farrāʔ and ʕāṣim → Šuʕbah → Yaḥyā b. ʔādam. The latter is also reported by al-Farrāʔ in his *Maʕānī* and is likely to have been the original transmission, considering how close al-Farrāʔ is to the source. There do not seem to be transmissions on ʔabū ʕamr's authority with short vowels however. Al-Dānī (*Ǧāmiʕ*, 457), however, does bring reports of the expected form *yara-h* for al-Dūrī ← ʔabū ʕamr.

An obvious explanation for the exceptional status of the forms *yara-hū* is that two of the three cases stand in a rhyme position. It is likely that the original transmission simply transmitted these forms in their pausal for *yara-h*—the natural pronunciation in this position—and only on further inquiry by later transmitters, were non-pausal forms invented, this time not following the overzealous apocopation rule of the early readers, but rather one that simply followed the Classical Arabic rules, which would generate *yara-hū*, the one other case of *yara-hū* subsequently followed suit.

A truly baffling transmission is the reading of Ḥafṣ ʕan ʕāṣim of يتقه 'fears him' (Q24:52). While the other readers have *yattaqi-h(i/ī)*, as one would expect, Ḥafṣ drops the short vowel of the jussive altogether, while retaining a short harmonized form of the pronoun. There does not seem to be an obvious way to account for such a form from Classical Arabic grammar. The most obvious explanation is that it comes from an underlying form *yattaq-h* where the final *i* is epenthetic to avoid a word-final two consonant cluster—something avoided in Classical Arabic. This is the explanation given by Ibn Xālawayh (*Ḥuǧǧah*, 263), the reason why the apocopate would have lost the final *i*-vowel in this position, however, can only be explained by deriving it from a variety where at least in some positions the apocopate of final weak verbs lost the final *-i*, presumably a dialect which (at least) lost the final short vowel *-i*,[16] which was then analogically spread to non-final position. Indeed, Ibn Xālawayh seems to attest the existence of such a form, citing a line of poetry that has the form *yattaq*.

All the specific complexities and disagreements of these forms aside, it is clear that there was great disagreement on how to treat these cases, something that is difficult to imagine if the Quran had been transmitted in its predictable

16 Blau (1977, 15 f.) seems to suggest that the Meccan dialect would have been such an old Arabic dialect.

classical form. Both the forms with long vowels *-hū/ī* and *-hu/i* can be understood as later grammarian intervention, especially the latter being dependent on specific grammatical analysis that cannot be thought to have existed before the rise of Arabic grammatical theory. The *-h* forms, however, are clearly the *lectio difficilior* here. While it can certainly be envisioned that these too were generated by nascent grammatical theory with an overapplication of apocopation rules, it also seems possible that simply original transmissions without final short vowels shine through here instead.

7.1.9 *The Mysterious Letters*

A special case of words being unexpectedly pronounced without any form of *ʔiʕrāb* in the reading traditions are the mysterious letters at the beginning of Sūrahs. The names of the letters in Classical Arabic are simply inflected, just like any other noun in the language, and in principle there is no reason why الم would not be read as *ʔalifun lāmun mīmun*, but instead all of the letters are universally read without their inflectional endings. This could perhaps be understood as pausal pronunciations of these letters, and this is how ʔabū Ǧaʕfar treats them, who introduces a pause after every single mysterious letter (Ibn al-Ǧazarī, §1592). The rest of the readers, however simply treat these words as if they are nouns that lack all inflection, and pronounce them in context. As such, these letters may even undergo assimilation with each other, and the following words, e.g. Q26:1, Q28:1 طسم is pronounced with assimilation of the *n* of *sīn* to the *m* of the following word by most readers (see Ibn al-Ǧazarī, §1907–1917 for a full discussion).

The form of the mysterious letters is fairly easy to understand from a situation that started out as lacking inflectional endings, which were classicized. As these mysterious letters have no obvious syntactical function, it is difficult to classicize these into an inflectional paradigm. The inverse, however, is more difficult to understand. There is no reason why the mysterious letters would be uninflected, if the base language of the Quran was inflected.

7.2 Was ʔabū ʕamr's Reading an ʔiʕrāb-less Reading?

The most recent work on the potential absence of case in a reading tradition of the Quran, and by extension the possible caselessness of an Ur-Quran was put forward by Jonathan Owens (2006, 119–136), who argues that the reading of ʔabū ʕamr originally represented a reading tradition that did not inflect for case, and was only later classicized to have case. This is essentially a continuation and further elaboration of Vollers' (1906) original theory concerning this topic, bringing to bear modern linguistic insights in understanding ʔabū ʕamr's phenomenon on 'Major Assimilation' (*al-ʔidġām al-kabīr*), i.e. assimilation of consonants across word boundaries, even when there is an intervening short vowel. If Owens' argument is correct, it would mean that it is not just the QCT (as argued by van Putten and Stokes 2018), but even one of its canonical readings that originally lacked the case system of Classical Arabic. However, the arguments put forward by Owens are not quite convincing, as we will see in the following sections. The major assimilation of ʔabū ʕamr is not as alien to the model of the grammarians as Owens makes it out to be, and I will show that ʔabū ʕamr's reading can only be understood if we assume the underlying presence of some kind of case system as part of his system.

7.2.1 *Al-ʔidġām al-kabīr*

All reading traditions of the Quran have some amount of assimilation across word boundaries, but this usually only happens with *tanwīn* or consonants that are not followed by a vowel. ʔabū ʕamr's reading is unique in that it frequently occurs across word boundaries when there is an intervening short vowel, yielding forms such as: *qāla rabbu-kum* → *qārrabbukum* (Owens 2006, 127).

Such assimilations take place when either the final consonant of the first word and the first consonant of the second word are identical, or close in terms of place of articulation. Owens represents this Major Assimilation through two rules, where C_a is an 'assimilatable' consonant:

1. $C_{1a}\check{v}\ \#C_{2a} \rightarrow C_{1a}\ \#C_{2a}$
2. $C_{1a}\ \#C_{2a} \rightarrow C_{2a}C_{2a}$

He considers these rules "linguistically odd", as rule 2 cannot precede rule 1, but rule 1 *only* applies when 2 also applies (Owens 2006, 130).[17] As such, rule 1 seems to anticipate rule number 2 before it has taken place. The dependency of rule 2 on rule 1 prompts Owens to suggest that rule 1 was not originally operative, and that the base form simply lacked the case vowels that are elided through this rule. Later classicization would then have included these case vowels into the reading, wherever assimilation did not prevent this from happening.

---

17 While the kind of 'permeability' of final vowels for assimilation is certainly rare, the Awadhi language (and Eastern-Hindi language, spoken in India and Nepal) provides a strikingly close parallel to ʔabū ʕamr's major assimilation. Awadhi as three short high vowels /i/, /u/ and /e/, which are devoiced in word-final position. When these vowels stand between two consonants with the same place of articulation they are syncopated. Depending on the consonants that come to stand next to each other, this may subsequently lead to further assimilations, e.g. bɦɑːgi gʌwɑː → bɦɑːggʌwɑː 'ran away', bɦɑːtu dɑːri̥ → bɦɑːddɑːri̥ 'rice and pulse', cʌli diɦɑː → cʌldiɦɑː 'started' (Saksena 1937, 94). I thank Hamza Khwaja for providing me with this reference.

I have trouble seeing why the rules as formulated by Owens are "linguistically odd". Major assimilation of this type occurs frequently in the Quran and its readings—albeit irregularly, and contrary to Owens' (2006, 130) claim, it is covered quite extensively by Sībawayh. Returning back to the assimilation rules 1 and 2, Owens says: "For Sibawayh, then type (8a) [rule 1, MvP] applies within words, and between words only when the two consonants are identical; (8b) [rule 2, MvP] applies across word boundaries, with an input in which two consonants abut one another." (Owens 2006, 131). For the example of the assimilation happening within a word, Owens cites *yaqtatil* → *yaqittil*. However, his claim that such assimilations are only described by Sībawayh when they involve identical consonants, is incorrect. In fact, on the very page that Owens cites for the assimilation *yaqtatil* → *yaqittil* (Sībawayh in the Derenbourg edition, vol. II, 459) there are three examples of this assimilation where the assimilation happens within a word where the two consonants are not identical. Sībawayh cites here *irtadafa* → *raddafa*, al-Ḥasan al-Baṣrī's reading *ixtaṭafa* → *ʔillā man xaṭṭafa l-xatfah* (Q37:10);[18] and a reading of the people of Mecca *murtadifīna* → *muruddifīna* (Q8:9).[19] This is far from the only time that Sībawayh discusses this kind of development happening within word-boundaries. Other examples he cites are: *yatasammaʕūna* → *lā yassamaʕūna* (Sībawayh IV, 463),[20] *ṯalāṯatu darāhima/ʔaflusin* → *ṯalāttu* (Sībawayh IV, 464), *yataṣāliḥā* → *yaṣṣāliḥā* (Sībawayh IV, 467),[21] *yaxtaṣimūna* → *yaxaṣṣimūna* (Q36:49), *yataṭawwaʕūna* → *yaṭṭawwaʕūna*, *yataḏakkarūna* → *yaḏḏakkarūna* (Q2:121 and others), *yataṭayyarū* → *yaṭṭayyarū bi-mūsā* (Q7:131), *taṭawwaʕa* → *iṭṭawwaʕa*, *taḏakkara* → *iḏḏakkara*, *tadāraʔtum* → *fa-ddāraʔtum fīhā* (Q2:72), *tazayyanat* → *wa-zzayyanat* (Q10:24), *tazayyunan* → *izzayyunan*, *taddāruʔan* → *iddāruʔan*, *taṭayyarnā* → *iṭṭayarnā bika* (Q27:47), also the acceptability of *yahtadūna* → *yahiddūna* is implied, though not explicitly mentioned[22] (Sībawayh IV, 474–475).

Admittedly, Sībawayh cites very few examples of major assimilation of dissimilar consonats across word boundaries, although I have found one example.

---

18 Recorded by Ibn Xālawayh (*muxtaṣar*, 127) as *xiṭṭifa* for al-Ḥasan, Qatādah and ʕīsā.

19 The Meccan Ibn Kaṯīr simply reads *murdifīna* (Ibn al-Ǧazarī, § 3169).

20 He is citing Q37:8 لا يسمعون here, which is read by Ḥafṣ ʕan ʕāṣim, Ḥamzah, al-Kisāʔī and Xalaf as an assimilated tD-stem, where the rest reads it as *yasmaʕūna* (Ibn al-Ǧazarī § 4030). His comments that "unassimilated is proper Arabic" should perhaps be seen as a subtle jab at the Kufans.

21 Sībawayh cites Q4:128 يصلحا here, which is read by most readers as *yaṣṣāliḥā*, only the four Kufans read *yuṣliḥā* (Ibn al-Ǧazarī § 2961).

22 But compare the Quranic reading Q10:35 *yahiddī, yahaddī, yahăddī, yahddī, yihiddī* (besides *yahdī*) (Ibn al-Ǧazarī § 3256).

Sībawayh (IV, 450) cites the assimilation of ʕ to *h*, in which case both consonants are shifted to *ḥ*. Here he cites both word-internal and word-external examples *maʕa-hum* 'with them' → *maḥḥum* and *maʕa hāʔulāʔi* 'with these' → *maḥḥāʔulāʔi* a feature specifically attributed to the Banū Tamīm. On the same page he also cites a line of poetry which underwent *masḥi-hī* 'his anointment'→ *masḥḥī* (→ *masḥī*?).

The absence of extensive assimilation of this type across word-boundaries, however, does not help Owens' argument. Owens' main objection to the possibility that such an assimilation took place against word boundaries is that it does not take place word-internally, the above examples should make abundantly clear that they do. Where across word-boundaries we may doubt whether the underlying form had an intervening vowel, we cannot make this case for the word-internal cases. So, whether this assimilation across vowel is "linguistically odd" or not, it is evident that it is happening, even in word-internal position, and therefore it is difficult to invoke this intuition as an argument against the presence of intervening short vowels.

Nöldeke was therefore right to dismiss Vollers' use of major assimilation as evidence for the complete absence of *ʔiʕrāb*, and Owens has not made a compelling case against it. Moreover, the presence of clear cases of word-internal major assimilation in the QCT (there are many more examples besides those that Sībawayh cites, see also Appendix A.3.5) prove that we are not dealing with Sībawayh's grammatical invention, but with actually attested linguistic forms.

While major assimilation in ʔabū ʕamr's reading cannot serve as evidence for the absence of case vowels, it certainly does not prove that they existed either. However, there are several other features of ʔabū ʕamr's reading that clearly require us to presuppose the presence of case vowels, which we will look at in more detail in the following sections.

7.2.2 *I-umlaut*

Many other aspects of ʔabū ʕamr's reading are dependent upon the presence of case vowels, as admitted by Owens himself (Owens 2006, 132). One of these is the *ʔimālah* of any stem-final *ār* (see § 3.6.2).[23] Whenever stem-final *ār* is followed by *i* (but not *ī*),[24] e.g. *an-nāri* > *an-nēri* (Q2:39); *kaffārin* > *kaffērin*

23 Note that this means that stem internal *āri* sequences do not undergo *ʔimālah*, so *bāridun* (Q38:42) is not read with *ʔimālah*. It explicitly applies only if the *r* is the third root consonant (see also § 3.6.2).

24 There is one verse specific exception, on which thransmitters of ʔabū ʕamr disagreed: *al-ǧāri* (Q4:36, both occurrences) (Ibn al-Ǧazarī, § 2050).

(Q2:276). This *i*-umlaut operates even if *al-ʔidġām al-kabīr* causes the triggering *kasrah* to be dropped hence *ʕalā l-kuffāri ruḥamāʔu* > *ʕalalkuffērruḥamāʔu* (Q48:29) (Ibn al-Ǧazarī, § 1192). The underlying phonological representation therefore needs the presence of the case vowel, despite its absence in the surface form.

7.2.3 *Rawm and ʔišmām*

Owens (2006, 132 ff.) suggests that the use of *ʔišmām* and *rawm* in ʔabū ʕamr's reading point to more examples of reduced case distinction. However, they actually show the opposite. Owens' position seems to stem from a misunderstanding of his sources. The first misunderstanding seems to be what these two terms mean and the second is where they occur. Owens labels *rawm* as 'labialization' and *ʔišmām* as 'fronting and rounding'. This is incorrect.[25] It is helpful to cite ʔabū ʕamr al-Dānī's description of the two concepts here, which I find particularly clear (al-Dānī *taysīr*, 58 f.).[26]

> As for the meaning of *rawm*: it is when you weaken the sound of the vowel until it has gone almost completely, so that you will hear it as a concealed sound. A blind person can perceive it with his sense of hearing.
>
> As for the meaning of *ʔišmām*: you bunch up your lips after the, originally, vowelless (final) letter. A blind person cannot perceive that information, because it is seen with the eye and nothing else.

In other words: *rawm* denotes ultra-short vowels while *ʔišmām* is labialization, and indeed this is how it is taught today. It is true that ʔabū ʕamr has the option to use *rawm* and *ʔišmām*, but it is incorrect that these neutralize short high vowels. Again, it pays to look at the descriptions of the Qirāʔāt works, al-Dānī continues:

---

25 Confusion on this topic is understandable, the terminology has been used in different ways by different grammarians. Ibn al-Ǧazarī for example reports that the Kufan grammarians used the two terms in the opposite manner from the general discussion (III, 1863), and that the use of the term *rawm* had a slightly different meaning amongst the grammarians than among the readers (Ibn al-Ǧazarī, III, 1878; § 2295). Needless to say, when discussing the terminology in the context of ʔabū ʕamr's reading, we should be sticking to the way that the reciters use it. As far as can be gleaned from Sībawayh's (IV, 168 ff.) description, it seems to mostly agree with what the readers say (except for him also *fatḥah* can undergo *rawm*). While neither *rawm* and *ʔišmām* is explicitly defined, it is pointed out that *ʔišmām* only applies with *ḍammah*.

26 But other descriptions leave no doubt that they are in fact the same, there is no difference of opinion between Ibn al-Ǧazarī (§ 2277, § 2278) and al-Dānī here.

> So as for the *rawm*, it is applied by the readers with the *rafʕ*, *ḍammah*, *ǧarr* or *kasrah*, and they do not employ it for the *naṣb* or *fatḥ* because of their lightness.
>
> As for *ʔišmām*, it only occurs for the *rafʕ* and *ḍammah*, and nothing else.

In other words when *rawm* is applied, it is to *u* and *i* and there is, in fact, no neutralization: *u* is articulated as *ŭ* and *i* as *ĭ*. As for *ʔišmām* it is sensibly only used for the nominative and imperfect. When a reciter decides to recite with *rawm* or *ʔišmām*, they are applied whenever the context allows, while, when the context does not, the recitation resorts back to full assimilation. So rather than neutralizing distinctions it in fact creates *more* distinctions not present if a reciter of ʔabū ʕamr's reading opts for no *ʔišmām* or *rawm* and simply adhered to *ʔidġām* only. It should also be added that, when ʔabū ʕamr opts for *rawm*, the consonants are not actually assimilated. Keeping this in mind, Owens' (2006, 133) example *qaala rabb-u-kum* → ***qaar*^{w} *rabbukum* does not occur at all. Even when opting to include *ʔišmām* or *rawm* in recitation this would always be pronounced with assimilation and no labialization: *qārrabbukum*. The table below summarizes the outcomes of these three processes in his recitation.

	Input		*ʔidġām*	With *ʔišmām*	With *rawm*
$C_a aC_a$	*qāla rabbu-kum*	→	*qārrabbukum*[27]	*qārrabbukum*	*qārrabbukum*
$C_a iC_a$	*al-ʕumuri li-kaylā*	→	*alʕumullikaylā*	*alʕumullikaylā*	*alʕumurĭ likaylā*
$C_a uC_a$	*yaškuru li-nafsi-hī*	→	*yaškullinafsihī*	*yaškul*^{w}*linafsihī*	*yaškurŭ linafsihī*

Owens' confusion about the terminology here is understandable, as Ibn Muǧāhid (156) uses the verb *ʔašamma* in a non-technical way in some places of his discussion. For example, on the discussion of the words *yuʕallimu-hum* (Q2:129) and *yalʕanu-hum* (Q2:159) he says that, in a transmission of ʕalī al-Hāšimī, ʔabū ʕamr "used to give taste (*yušimmu*) to the *mīm* of *yuʕallimu-hum* and the *nūn* of *yalʕanu-hum*—both before the *hāʔ*—of *ḍamm* without full pronunciation (*ʔišbāʕ*) and it is like that for *ʕan ʔasliḥati-kum wa-ʔamtiʕati-kum* (Q4:102), he gives a little bit of the taste to the *tāʔ* for both of them of the *ǧarr*". The fact that Ibn Muǧāhid makes a distinction here between giving the taste

27 Technically speaking the vowel *ā* may be pronounced overlong, i.e. *qāārrabbukum*, as long vowels before long consonants are regularly lengthened.

of the vowel *u* and *i* suggests first of all that we are not dealing with *ʔišmām* in the technical sense (which cannot apply to *u*), but also that these vowels were distinct (i.e. it is *rawm*) and it is not merged into a single epenthetic vowel *ə* as Owens suggests.

7.2.4 *Tanwīn Blocks Assimilation*

Whenever a noun has *tanwīn*, *al-ʔidġām al-kabīr* cannot operate. This is explicitly stipulated for ʔabū ʕamr's assimilation rules by ibn Muǧāhid (117). Whenever *tanwīn* is present, case vowels are also present. It seems possible to argue that a caseless version of ʔabū ʕamr's reading had *tanwīn* but no distinction between case vowels before it. In that case, ʔabū ʕamr's reading would be similar to modern dialects with 'dialectal tanwīn' (Stokes 2020). There is however nothing to indicate that this is the case, and the *i*-umlaut *ʔimālah* still cause by the genitive case in the indefinite rather argues against this.

7.2.5 *A Non-literalist Reading of ʔabū ʕamr's Traditions*

Owens admits the problems with his theory brought up by the *i*-umlaut and *tanwīn*. But, he argues for a "non-literalist" reading of ʔabū ʕamr's tradition: "Against a literalist reading, I would argue that the status of many grammatical elements in the *Qiraaʔaat* tradition still awaits comparative treatment, and that in some instances reconstructed forms may be necessary, which are not attested directly in any single variant" (Owens 2006, 132). While the complete transmission of ʔabū ʕamr indeed only first appears in the fourth century AH,[28] several centuries after ʔabū ʕamr's lifetime (d. 154 AH), the transmissions of his reading among different authorities are independent enough that we can be reasonably confident that the features, along with those that require the presence of case vowels can be confidently attributed to him. Nevertheless, I believe that Owens does observe something important in his discussion of ʔabū ʕamr's recitation, and that his "non-literalist reading" of the tradition is warranted. Througout ʔabū ʕamr's reading along with traces in Ibn Kaṯīr's reading we see a fairly frequent cases of syncope (or ultrashort realization) of the *ʔiʕrāb* vowels *i* and *u* in phonetically very similar environments. While for neither reader this syncope is regular, the conditioning in which it occurs is consistent, and seems to reflect at least a memory of a variety of Arabic that had a case system quite distinct from that of Classical Arabic. Thus, Ibn Muǧāhid (155 f.)

28 Ibn Muǧāhid's description is in fact extremely short and of little help to a person who would want to recite ʔabū ʕamr's reading with assimilation. His student Ibn Xālawayh has a more detailed description, which does not differ significantly from later descriptions (Ibn Xālawayh *Badīʕ*, 307–317).

mentions several cases where word-final *u* and *i* are either pronounced ultrashort (*ŭ* or *ĭ*) or syncopated altogether whenever heavy pronomonial suffixes follow,[29] e.g. *bāriʔ(ĭ)-kum* (Q2:54), *yaʔmur(ŭ)-kum* (Q2:67), *yuʕallim(ŭ)-hum, yalʕan(ŭ)-hum, ʕan ʔasliḥatĭ-kum wa-ʔamtiʕatĭ-kum* (Q2:102), and *yağmaʕ(ŭ)-kum* (Q64:9).[30] Among his canonical transmissions there are many more cases of shortening like this, and even complete loss of *ʔiʕrāb* is reported. This is broadly transmitted for the words *bāriʔ(ĭ)-kum, yaʔmur(ŭ)-kum, yaʔmur(ŭ)-hum, yanṣur(ŭ)-kum* and *yanšir(ŭ)-kum* whenever they occur (al-Dānī *taysīr*, 73), but Ibn al-Ğazarī (Ibn al-Ğazarī, § 2655) brings marginal transmissions of many more cases, some even transmitting that every verb that ends in -*ru-h/kum* loses or makes ultrashort the mood ending of the verb. Traces of a similar process can also be found in the canonical transmissions of ʔabū ʕamr's Meccan teacher Ibn Kaṯīr who read *ʔar-nā* (Q2:128; Q4:153; Q41:29) and *ʔar-nī* (Q2:260; Q7:143), for the C-stem imperative of of *raʔā*, and ʔabū ʕamr follows him in this as well, though some transmit an ultrashort vowel *ʔarĭ-nā/nī* instead (Ibn al-Ğazarī, § 2728). It is worth pointing out that Ibn Muḥayṣin, one of ʔabū ʕamr's other Meccan teachers and one of the 4 pseudo-canonical readers after the 10, seems to have had a much more regular application of this syncope than either ʔabū ʕamr or Ibn Kaṯīr (Sabṭ al-Xayyāṭ *al-Mubhiğ*, II, 370).[31]

While this system is not regular, it seems clear that the traces that are present here are related to a phenomenon that is reported as a dialectal tendency of Tamīm and ʔasad, which happens, according to al-Farrāʔ (*Luġāt*, 30) "because of the continuous succession of vowels" (*tawālī al-ḥarakāt*) citing forms such as *yaʔmur-kum, yaḥzun-hum, ʔa-nuzlim-kumū-hā, ʔaḥad-hum, ʔaḥad-humā, li-ʔaḥad-himā*. He explicitly points out that "the people of the Hijaz pronounce this clearly and do not weaken it, and this is the more preferable of the two options to me (*wa-huwa ʔaḥabbu l-wağhayni ʔilayya*)." Considering that this only affects the high vowels *u* and *i*, among Najdi tribes, it seems that this should be considered to be part of the broader syncopating tendencies of *u* and *i* among these tribes (as discussed in § 2.2.4 and § 3.3.2). In this pattern, it seems worthwhile to also mention the existence of a different type of syncope before heavy suffixes in ʔabū ʕamr's reading, that is the syncope of the vowel

---

29 The opinion that ʔabū ʕamr pronounced these vowels ultrashort rather than syncopating them altogether seems to be an ancient one. Even Sībawayh (IV, 202) already explicitly mentions the reading of ʔabū ʕamr *bāriʔĭkum* with an ultrashort vowel.

30 N.B. explicitly without neutralization of these short vowels.

31 Ibn al-Ğazarī (IV, 2165) cites Ibn Muḥayṣin as reading *yuʕallim-hum, naḥšur-hum* and *ʔaḥad-humā* (Ibn al-Ğazarī, IV, 2165). I have been unable to find reports of the reading *ʔaḥad-humā* for Ibn Muḥayṣin.

before the case vowel of *subul* and *rusul* (and in a non-canonical transmission *nuzul*) before heavy suffixes, e.g. *ruslunā, rusluhum, ruslukum, nuzluhum* etc. (Ibn al-Ǧazarī, §2678; Ibn Muǧāhid, 623).

While it seems that the transmission of ʔabū ʕamr's reading tradition is stable enough that we can be reasonably confident that he indeed had the rather irregular and incomplete system of syncopation that is reported for him, but in a non-literalist interpretation of the reported fact, we can certainly see how ʔabū ʕamr and his Meccan teachers Ibn Kaṯīr and Ibn Muḥayṣin clearly retain the memory of a regular system of syncopation, similar to the one that al-Farrāʔ describes. This would not lead us to conclude that their readings (or their ancestral predecessors) were entirely caseless, but they do point to a more reduced case system, where in some environments *u* and *i* dropped out completely, neutralizing the case contrast between the nominative and the genitive. It is worth noting here as well that when it comes to ʔabū ʕamr's *ʔidġām kabīr* a distinction in treatment between *u* and *i* as against *a* can be observed as well. When assimilating dissimilar consonants, more phonotactic environments allow assimilation when *u* or *i* intervene than when *a* intervenes. For example, a superheavy syllable due to the assimilation of *dāl* may only happen if the vowel in between is *u* or *i*, e.g. *min baʕdi ẓulmīhī* → *min baʕẓẓulmihī* (Q5:39) and *yurīdu ẓulman* → *yurīẓẓulman* (Q3:108) but no assimilation in *baʕda ẓulmihī* (Ibn al-Ǧazarī, §1169).

That the dropping of the case vowels *u* and *i* was considered ideologically problematic already very early on is quite clear. We have already mentioned al-Farrāʔ's opinion that forms without syncope are better, and a central part of disagreement within ʔabū ʕamr's transmissions are the many conflicting opinions as to whether he read the words under discussion above ultrashort or with no vowel at all. This controversy about ʔabū ʕamr's reading was clearly already set in motion the generation after his lifetime (he dies 154 AH), as Sībawayh (d. ca. 180 AH) already explicitly takes the stance that ʔabū ʕamr did not drop the vowel in *bāriʔĭ-kum*, but instead pronounced it ultrashort (Sībawayh, IV, 202).

In conclusion, we can say that there are aspects of ʔabū ʕamr's reading that irregularly, but frequently point to this dialectal tendency to syncopate the final short vowels *u* and *i* in when they are suffixed by heavy pronominal clitics. This, along with reports of grammarians like al-Farrāʔ, certainly shows that in the second century AH the strict Classical Arabic (never syncopating) case system did not have the universal prestige that it holds today. Moreover, it seems to suggest that speakers of dialects of Tamīm and ʔasad indeed did not have a system that fully conformed to the standard Classical system. However, the evidence does not allow for a reconstruction a recitation of the Quran attributed to ʔabū ʕamr, or his teachers that lacked the final short vowels and *tanwīn* altogether.

It also clearly points to a different case system than the one Van Putten & Stokes (2018) have reconstructed for Quranic Arabic on the basis of the QCT.

7.2.6 *Ḥamzah's ʔidġām kabīr*

While ʔabū ʕamr's major assimilation is clearly part of a regular, but quite likely artificial, system of reading, making it difficult to see these as traces of a Quran without final short vowels, this major assimilation also occurs in Ḥamzah's reading. In his reading, however, it is not the result of a regularly recurring system, but just forms a set of lexical exceptions, which cannot be understood from the regular linguitic systems of Ḥamzah's reading (Ibn al-Ǧazarī, § 1194–1195):

bayyata ṭāʔifah → *bayyaṭṭāʔifah* (Q4:81)

wa-ṣ-ṣāffāti ṣaffā → *wa-ṣ-ṣāffāṣṣaffā* (Q37:1)
fa-z-zāǧirāti zaǧrā → *fa-z-zāǧirāzzaǧrā* (Q37:2)
fa-t-tāliyāti ḏikrā → *fat-tāliyāḏḏikrā* (Q37:3)

wa-ḏ-ḏāriyāti ḏarwā → *wa-ḏ-ḏāriyāḏḏarwā* (Q51:1)
Fa-l-mulqiyāti ḏikrā → *fa-l-mulqiyāḏḏikrā* (Q77:5; only Xallād ʕan Ḥamzah)
fa-l-muġīrāti ṣubḥā → *fa-l-muġīrāṣṣubḥā* (Q100:3; only Xallād ʕan Ḥamzah)

Seemingly equally eligible phrases are not included. For example, *fa-s-sābiḥāti sabḥā, fa-s-sābiqāti sabqā* (Q79:3–4) never assimilate.

Especially because it does not seem to be part of a larger system it becomes tempting to see these as genuine transmissions of forms without case vowels. But here too, as with ʔabū ʕamr's reading, this may be a memory not of a caseless recitation of the Quran, but rather one with a more pervasive assimilation across word-boundaries.

7.3 A Phonetic Rule That Requires Absence of Full *ʔiʕrāb*

Throughout the Quranic reading traditions, once occasionally finds forms that, in principle follow the classical *ʔiʕrāb* system, but whose distribution cannot be understood within such a system. An example of this is the inflection of *mayyit* 'dead' in the reading of Ḥafṣ ʕan ʕāṣim, Ḥamzah, al-Kisāʔī, and Xalaf. These readers have the short form of the stem *mayt-* whenever is occurs as an indefinite masculine accusative or in any form of the feminine. The distribution as formulated for the four Kufans exactly matches the distribution as described by al-Farrāʔ (*Luġāt*, 47) and has been tabulated below:

	Indefinite	**Definite**	**Feminine**
nom.	*mayyitun*	–	*al-maytatu*
gen.	*mayyitin*	*al-mayyiti*	–
acc.	*maytan*	*al-mayyita*	*al-maytata, maytatan*

ʔabū Ǧaʕfar always has the uncontracted form, whereas Yaʕqūb and Nāfiʕ mostly follow the pattern of the four Kufans mentioned above but Nafiʕ has an uncontracted form at Q36:33 *al-mayyitatu*, Q6:122, Q49:12 *mayyitan* and Q7:57, Q35:9 *mayyitin*. Yaʕqūb has Q6:122 *mayyitan* uncontracted and Ruways ʕan Yaʕqūb also reports Q49:12 *mayyitan*. The remaining readers always have the shortened form (Ibn al-Ǧazarī § 2745).

It is difficult to make sense of the Kufan distribution if we assume that full *ʔiʕrāb* was present. Why, for example, would the following short *a* in *al-maytata* cause shortening of the stem, whereas in *al-mayyita* it does not? However, if we take the forms that Van Putten & Stokes (2018) reconstruct as the case system of Quranic Arabic as the basis, i.e. a system identical to the Classical Arabic "pausal" pronunciation, the distribution becomes readily transparent: the vowel *i* simply syncopates whenever it stands in an open syllable, an exceedingly common phonological development in the modern Arabic dialects as well. Only the indefinite accusative *-ā* and the feminine ending *-ah* would have this environment.

	Indefinite	**Definite**	**Feminine**
nom.	*mayyit*	–	*al-maytah*
gen.	*mayyit*	*al-mayyit*	–
acc.	*maytā*	*al-mayyit*	*al-maytah, maytah*

The only way I see how this distribution can be explained as being present in the Quranic recitations with its Classical Arabic case endings is by assuming that these forms stemmed from a variety of Arabic that had a case system just like the one Van Putten & Stokes reconstruct for Quranic Arabic. The fact that grammarians report this—to them morphological—conditioning with the Classical Arabic case endings, is a clear example of Grammarians "classicizing" their dialectal data. The *ʔiʕrāb* was felt as such a central part of proper Arabic, that all linguistic data gets filtered through that lens, regardless of whether this is appropriate or not.[32]

Traces of similar cases of syncope, seemingly triggered by an originally reduced case system may also be found in the distribution of some of the CuCuC nouns. For example, for *nuḏur* 'warnings' is universally unsyncopated among all Quranic readers when it is in the definite form, or in the non-accusative indefinite. But Ḥafṣ ʕan ʕāṣim, ʔabū ʕamr, Ḥamzah, al-Kisāʔī and Xalaf all syncopate this word in the indefinite accusative *nuḏran*, while the rest reads *nuḏuran*. It is probably no coincidence that the readers that read in this manner are the same ones that have the *mayyit~maytā* alternation (Ibn al-Ǧazarī, § 3694).[33] A similar distribution is attested for *nukur* 'denial' which is read without syncopation in the non-accusative form by all readers but Ibn Kaṯīr. The indefinite accusative however, is read as the syncopated *nukran* by a once again familiar list of readers: Ḥafṣ ʕan ʕāṣim, Ḥamzah, al-Kisāʔī, Xalaf and ʔabū ʕamr. In this case also Hišām ʕan Ibn ʕāmir has the syncopated form (Ibn al-Ǧazarī, § 2685).[34]

7.4 Conclusion

We have argued that two main features that distinguish the Quranic reading traditions from the language as it is reflected in the QCT are the introduction of

32 This is a trend we will continue to see throughout the history of linguistic writings within the Arabic tradition. For example the famous Himyaritic sentence رأيك بخلم كولدك ابنا من طيب "I saw in the dream that I gave birth to a son of Gold", where 'son' is conjugated as *ibnan*, with the Classical Arabic indefinite accusative, must probably be seen as classicization of a form of the language which was clearly rather far removed from Hijazi and Classical Arabic (Rabin 1951, 48). Rabin likewise quotes a few lines of apparent Himyaritic poetry, where he quite rightly comments that "there is obviously some admixture of Classical Arabic": *yā bna Zubayrin ṭāla mā ʕaṣayka; wa-ṭāla ma ʕannaykanā ʔilayka; la-taḥzananna bi-llaḏī ʔatayka; la-nadṛiban bi sayfina qafayka* "Son of Zubair, long hast thou been disloyal, long hast thou troubled us to come to thee. Thou wilt be grieved for what thou hast committed (or: what is coming to thee). Yea, with our sword we shall cut off thy neck."

33 With the exception that ʔabū ʕamr is included in this distribution.

34 Ibn Kaṯīr also has the syncopated form, but he also syncopates the genitive form *nukrin* (Ibn al-Ǧazarī, § 2688).

the *hamzah* and the use of the full Classical Arabic system of final short vowels and nunation. If my thesis is correct in this regard, this must mean that these features were consciously introduced into the Quran, and that Quranic Arabic has been "linguistically reworked" by the early Arab philologists. In the case of such reworking, one would probably expect to see traces of this process. It should be clear from the previous and current chapter that these occur in copious amounts.

There are many examples in the reading traditions where the *hamzah* was artificially inserted in places that never etymologically had them, and likewise there are many more examples of words that inexplicably lack the *hamzah*, where for all intents and purposes we would predict that the regular rules of the treatment of *hamzah* in these readings would have required them. From this behaviour we should conclude that the early Arabic philologists did not always have access to accurate information on the place where the *hamzah* should appear, and would make their own (sometimes incorrect) rationalizing judgments. This is explicitly admitted by the tradition. We have fairly credible early reports of some of the canonical readers specifically commenting on their rationalization process in applying the *hamzah*.

Demonstration of a change in the case system is more complex. The *ʔiʕrāb* and *tanwīn* system being the quintessential feature of Classical Arabic, and therefore the one feature that binds together all of the reading traditions, it is of course impossible to recover from these traditions a reading that lacked this feature altogether. Nevertheless, close examination of the readings does reveal that here too, we see that the application of *ʔiʕrāb* and *tanwīn* was not a matter of accurate transmission from a prototypical source, but rather a rational endeavour. We have a direct citation from the student of al-Kisāʔī of him citing explicitly aesthetic arguments why he chose to conjugate *ṯamūd* in a certain way. Also, a form like *ʔayyāna*, which quite rightly, is analysed as coming from *ʔayya ʔānin*, can only be understood as a hyperclassicism of an input that lacked case vowels altogether. The fact that some words among the readers such as *mayyit/maytah/maytā* seem to undergo syncope conditioned by a case system different from the Classical Arabic system—but rather the one that can be reconstructed for Quranic Arabic, is a clear indication that the case system has been imposed onto the Quranic language.

Furthermore, there are a good number of cases where final short vowels, and in one case *tanwīn*, are inexplicably missing. This even seems to be a regular phenomenon for apocopate/imperative III-*y/w* verbs followed by a pronominal suffix for some readers. Considering the ideological commitment to *ʔiʕrāb* and *tanwīn*, showcased by the many injunctions not to recite the Quran without it (see Kahle 1947, 49–84; 1948; 1949), it is difficult to see how such unclassical forms would have entered the language, if they do not point to some genuine attempt to retain the proper recitation of such words.

While Vollers was, as Owens (2006, 77, n. 42) put it, "essentially shouted down [...] by his German colleagues" for his views on the language of the Quran, it is especially his arguments for this reworking which I believe have not been given the adequate evaluation that they deserved. Vollers' arguments for a wholesale transition from an Ur-Quran without case to the fully Classical case inflection were indeed rather weak,[35] but one thing he does conclusively show is that the readers of the Quran clearly reworked the readings according to grammatical and philological principles. As Vollers did not rely on very direct sources on the reading traditions,[36] he missed many cases of such artificiality in the readings that I have shown in chapter 3, 6 and the current chapter, but nevertheless on many occasions noticed clear cases of pseudocorrection among both canonical and non-canonical readers (such as the canonical reading of *saʔqay-hā* for *sāqay-hā*).

Nöldeke (1910, 1f.) criticized Vollers for not realizing that many of the readings cited as evidence for philological reworking of the Quran are canonical.[37] But these readings being accepted as canonical does not alleviate the problem that Vollers highlights. Nöldeke admits that the recitation of the Quran was linguistically reworked, but believes that under the layers of artifice a true language always shines through (Nöldeke 1910, 2). But how can we be so certain that it is the "true language" that shines through? What philological evidence based on primary source material of the Quran has been adduced? Nöldeke, nor any of Vollers' other critics ever adequately address this crucial point. Why would this one central feature—one so laden with ideological commitment as the *ʔiʕrāb* system—be the one system that the readings accurately reflect while so many other features carry "artificial decorations"?

35 Although these arguments have only been seldomly adequately addressed by his critics. See Van Putten & Stokes (2018, 145f.) for a discussion.

36 He primarily relied on reports found in the *ʔanwār al-Tanzīl wa-ʔasrār al-Taʔwīl* by the very late scholar Nāṣir al-Dīn al-Bayḍāwī (d. 685 AH) for his information on the Qirāʔāt.

37 This was a misrepresentation of Vollers' understanding of the situation, e.g. Vollers (1906, 25) explicitly speaks of "al Kisâ'i († um 180), einer der kanonischen Qorânleser", clearly showing awareness of this distinction. While it is an unfair criticism of Vollers, it would in fact have been a perfectly reasonable criticism of several scholars who would later give his work short shrift, such as Wehr (1952) and Zwettler (1978). Both authors seem to be almost entirely unaware of the existence of any linguistic differences of the Quranic reading traditions and what effect this may have for our understanding of what the *ʕarabiyyah* is.

As it is clear that all the canonical Quranic readings (and as far as we can see, also the non-canonical ones) have been linguistically reworked, we must be careful to generalize from these sources to make any pronouncements about the original language of the Quranic composition. Of course, that is not to say that the reading traditions are devoid of interest to the researcher who wishes to reconstruct the language of the QCT, and indeed its original composition. The linguistic variation found in the reading tradition is a massive font of linguistic data that allows us to gain insight into the kinds of linguistic variation that existed in the literary language of the early Islamic period. The transmissions of this data frequently predate the activity of our earliest grammarian authors, and record wider linguistic variation. These allow the researcher to quickly generate a number of different hypothetical pronunciations, which may then be checked against the QCT. An example where the reading traditions clearly retain the original linguistic situation as reflected in the QCT can be found with the preservation of a word-final *ā/ē* contrast as preserved in the readings of al-Kisāʔī, Ḥamzah, Xalaf and Warš ʕan Nāfiʕ, which rhyme and orthography of the QCT clearly show are an accurate reflection of the system as found in Quranic Arabic.

If it is the case that all of the Quranic readings, canonical or otherwise, have been linguistically reworked, how can we be certain that any part of these readings is in any way a reflection of the actual language as intended by the QCT, or indeed of its original composition? This question simply cannot be answered, as it traditionally has been, through the sole examination of the Arabic literary tradition. I hope that this work has shown that the tradition is too late, too artificial, too contradictory and too ideologically invested in the ideal of the *ʕarabiyyah* to function as the sole reliable source on the language of the Quran. For this reason, we must turn to the actual primary source material that is by far the closest to the time of composition of the text: the Quranic Consonantal Text itself.

CHAPTER 8

From Hijazi beginnings to Classical Arabic

وَلَسْنَا مُتَعَبَّدِينَ بِأَقْوَالِ نُحَاةِ ٱلْبَصْرَةِ

ABŪ ḤAYYĀN, *Baḥr al-Muḥīṭ*

The previous chapters have been concerned with four general topics. The first of these asked the question what the *ʕarabiyyah* was according to the earliest grammarians—demonstrating that these early grammarians had a much less prescriptive view of the language than what we later come to define as Classical Arabic. This is cause for us to rethink what it means for the language of the Quran to be the *ʕarabiyyah*, and forces us to ask a more precise question: what was the language of the Quran really like, which of the myriad competing features of the *ʕarabiyyah* were the ones that were proper to the language of the Quran, if any?

Turning to the Quranic reading traditions, we find that far from giving a uniform answer as to the linguistic features of Quranic Arabic are, they frequently employ many different forms reported by the grammarians. This shows that in this period the concept of what the *ʕarabiyyah* was and was not, was still very much under debate. Moreover, it was shown that the linguistic system that the Quranic reading traditions reflect do not seem to form consistent linguistic systems that agree very well with the Arabic dialects as described by the grammarians. Moreover, they frequently go beyond what falls under the purview of the grammarians, incorporating linguistic features that must be thought of as artificial. Because of the great amount of disagreement between the readings, as well as their artificial nature, the Quranic readings cannot be seen as giving a clear and undeniable insight into what the language of the Quran truly was at the time of its composition.

Subsequently, I proposed that we do away with the mixed signals that come in through the Quranic reading traditions, and instead focus on the linguistic features that can be deduced from the one part of the Quranic corpus that clearly stems from the early Islamic period, namely the Quranic Consonantal text of the Uthmanic Archetype. Once we look at the features that can be

 | DOI:10.1163/9789004506251_009

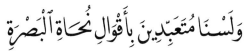

deduced from this earliest stratum of the Quran, a surprisingly consistent picture emerges: Nearly all isoglosses that can be deduced from the QCT, align with Hijazi Arabic.

The fact that such a consistent picture emerges from the study of the QCT is not at all obvious from the perspective of the tradition. The Arabic philological tradition was not troubled by features in the Quran being mixed and matched from a variety of different dialects, and there was no focus on arguing that whatever occurred in the Quran had to be Hijazi Arabic. The fact that, despite this, such a clear picture presents itself suggests both that we should take the QCT as a linguistic source seriously, as well as conclude that the language of the Quran has been reworked and 'Classicized' over time, to yield the much more Classical looking forms of Arabic in which the text is recited today. In the previous chapters, I have demonstrated that there is in fact quite a lot of evidence in the way the readings behave as well as in the literary sources that this is indeed what happened: the readers were actively aiming to make the language of the Quran more in line with what they considered to be the proper *ʕarabiyyah*. This can be clearly seen from the fact that readers were concerned with questions of pseudocorrect application of the *hamzah*—a feature said to be absent in the language of the Hijaz. But also, perhaps more controversial, I suggest we can see traces of the Classical Arabic case system having been imposed onto the original language as reflected in the QCT, which had lost most of its word final short vowels and *tanwīn*.

The title of this book is "Quranic Arabic: from its Hijazi Beginnings to its Classical Arabic readings." Having arrived at the end of this work, it seems worthwhile to provide here a chronological reconstruction of the development of the language of the Quran up until the language of the reading traditions as we see it today, and finally, place the emergence of a standard Classical Arabic within this framework.

8.1 The Prophet's Career

We do not have a perfect direct source of the composition of the Quran as it was recited by the prophet Muhammad during his career. Nevertheless, considering that the Quran is a rhyming text, and the QCT normally agrees with the phonetics that seem to be reflected in the rhyme, it seems fairly safe to say that the language of the QCT was close to the language Muhammad would have used during his career as a prophet in the early seventh century. The language of composition would not have been Classical Arabic, but instead the local vernacular of Mecca and/or Medinah: Hijazi Arabic—*luġat ʔahl al-Ḥiǧāz*.

Although the Quranic verses that affirm that the Quran itself and its language are *ʕarabiyy* have sometimes been interpreted as the Quran affirming that it is composed in Classical Arabic—or at least a high language distinct from the vernacular, I believe that Al-Jallad's (2020b) analysis of the *ʕarabiyy* verses is much more probable. He suggests that these verses are specifically meant to affirm that the Quran was revealed in the local vernacular in contrast to the scriptures of, for example, the Jews and Christians which would have been *ʔaʕǧamiyy* 'foreign, unintelligible' which is especially clear in Q16:103, where this conflict between *ʕarabiyy* and *ʔaʕǧamiyy* is highlighted: ولقد نعلم انهم يقولون انما يعلمه بشر لسان الذى يلحدون اليه اعجمي وهذا لسان عربى مبين /wa-laqad naʕlam annahum yaqūlūn innamā yuʕallimu-h bašar; lisānu lladī yulḥidūn ilayh aʕǧamī wa-hāḏā lisān ʕarabī mubīn/ "We have certainly learned that they say that it is just a human that is teaching him; but the language which they refer to is foreign, while this is the clear Arabic tongue."

The dichotomy between Classical Arabic and the "vernacular" should not be seen in such stark terms as it often is within the field. Just because the Quran is composed in the local vernacular does not mean it cannot have retained many of the highly archaic features that we associate today with Classical Arabic, rather than the modern vernaculars. The idea that the "vernacular" nature of the language needs to imply the loss of these archaic features—leading to an rapprochement to the modern vernaculars—is unwarranted, but a view that appears frequently in the literature (e.g. Blau 1977; Zwettler 1978). Whatever vernacular was spoken in the Hijaz in the early seventh century would, of course, quite likely be much more archaic in many regards than those spoken more than a millennium later. Vollers' (1906) theory posited that the Hijazi vernacular was very close to the widespread modern vernaculars such as the Egypto-Levantine dialect bundle, having lost case distinctions in all environments. The evidence does not support such a conclusion.

8.2 The Uthmanic Recension (ca. 30 AH/650 CE)

While the details of the when and by whom of the canonization of the Uthmanic text type have been debated for some time, a new focus on the use of primary source material in the form of early Islamic manuscripts has made it quite clear that this canonization was most likely undertaken during the reign of the third caliph ʕuṯmān b. ʕaffān, who had four copies made that were distributed to Kufa, Basra, Syria (likely Homs, see Sidky 2021, 171–174) and Medina. The orthography of this archetype has been extraordinarily well-preserved and quite clearly reflects the Hijazi dialect—something universally acknowledged, even by scholars who did not conclude from this that the language it intended to represent was also Hijazi.

The clear agreement between the orthography and the Quranic rhyme shows that the language of the Uthmanic recension was certainly not very far removed from the language of the original composition. Likewise, the orthographical and linguistic features as found in the Uthmanic recension show clear and obvious connections to the administrative language of the early Arabic papyri.

The various reports that the Quran was revealed in the language of the Qurayš and that ʕuṯmān explicitly ordered the Quran to be written in the language of the Qurayš should, in light of the discoveries presented in this work, be reevaluated. Kahle brings one such a report, quoted by al-Farrāʔ:[1]

> ʿUmar b. al-Khaṭṭāb heard a man reading *ʿattā ḥina* (sic) in the meaning of *ḥattā ḥīna*. He said: ʻWho taught you to recite thus?' He said: "Abdallāh b. Masʿūd.' So, he wrote to ʻAbdallāh b. Masʿūd: ʻThe Koran came down in the language of the Ḳuraish and it came not down in the language of the Hudhail. So, do you teach men to recite it in the language of the Ḳuraish and not in language of the Hudhail.'

Zwettler, and with him Rabin do not accept that the Quran was composed in the language of the Qurayš, and instead believe the Quran was composed in the ʻpoetic koiné'. Zwettler reads part of the section that Kahle translates from al-Farrāʔ, as evidence for this. Al-Farrāʔ argues that the Qurayš dialect was superior to all others, and interestingly cites a couple of reasons, pointing out it lacks the *ʕanʕanah* of the Tamīm (pronouncing *ʕayn* as *ʔalif*), nor the *Kaskasah*

---

1 While the attribution of this discussion to al-Farrāʔ is certainly how it appears in the manuscript CBL MS. Arab. 705, a work on Quranic verse counts falsely attributed to al-Farrāʔ, one has to wonder about the accuracy of this attribution. Larcher (2005, 802f.) speculates that the text is an extract from al-Farrāʔ's *Luġāt al-Qurʔān*, but since Larcher's writing, that text has now become available to us. If it was ever part of that text, it has not come down in the recension we have access to today. There are some reasons to doubt the attribution of the citation to al-Farrāʔ: it does not seem to be quoted in any other known works even though al-Farrāʔ gets cited so frequently in a large variety of medieval works, that a large portion of *Luġāt al-Qurʔān* and *al-Maʕānī* could be reconstructed from citations alone (and for *Luġāt al-Qurʔān*, Rabin at times indeed does, see the discussion on hollow root *ʔimālah* in § 5.9). It would be quite surprising for an account as interesting for linguistic ideologies as this one to not be cited at all in works perhaps more relevant to linguistic questions than a book on verse counts. I will proceed on the assumption that the quote indeed comes from al-Farrāʔ, though the identity of the author of the quote does not significantly impact our conclusions here.

of Rabīʕah (pronouncing the pausal 2sg.f. ending *-ki* as *-kis*[2]) nor the *kasr* of the Qays in *tiʕlamūna, tiʕlam* (Barth-Ginsberg alternation) and *biʕir, šiʕir* (for *baʕir* and *šaʕir*, see § 2.2.3).

It is an anachronism to think that these features, absent in the modern standard of Classical Arabic, where absent in the poetic koiné/*ʕarabiyyah*, as they are described in detail by Sībawayh and other early grammarians. It would, moreover, be a mistake to take this discussion of al-Farrāʔ to equate the most eloquent form of the *ʕarabiyyah*—the one that later becomes to standard Classical Arabic—with the dialect of the Qurayš. In fact, when we examine al-Farrāʔ's writing in a broader perspective including his *Luġāt al-Qurʔān* and *Maʕānī al-Qurʔān*, he clearly has no issue assigning linguistic features to the Qurayš that he almost certainly did not employ himself in Quranic recitation. For example, he reports that the Qurayš did not apply vowel harmony to of the third person pronouns *-hū, -humā, -hum* and *-hunna* (al-Farrāʔ *Luġāt*, 10 f.), that they did not have the front rounded vowel for passive hollow verbs *qüla* (al-Farrāʔ *Luġāt*, 14), but rather *qīla* and that they read *mustahziʔūna* without *hamzah* as *mustahzūna* (al-Farrāʔ *Luġāt*, 15). His teacher, al-Kisāʔī, recites the Quran with the non-Qurašī option in all three of those cases. The other Kufan reciters have the Qurašī option for *qīla*, but for the other options are non-Qurašī. Al-Farrāʔ is a transmitter of al-Kisāʔī's reading and clearly sees no problem in terms of eloquence of reading in such a manner, as he does not explicitly denounce any of these manners of readings, not in his *Luġāt al-Qurʔān*, nor in his *Maʕānī al-Qurʔān*.

Clearly, to al-Farrāʔ, there was no inherent contradiction between the statement that the Quran was revealed in the dialect of the Qurayš, and the Quran being recited in something that was self-evidently to al-Farrāʔ not the language of the Qurayš.[3] This does not prove that the language of the Quran was Classical Arabic/poetic koiné, as Zwettler would have it. It proves that the original language of recitation was not relevant to how the Quran was recited. This makes it significantly more plausible that the traces of Classicization of the language of the Quran that we see were considered acceptable to this late second century AH authority.

---

2 This is sometimes understood as referring to a palatalization of pausal *-k* to *-tˢ*. I find the evidence for this not particularly compelling, and will stick to the literal reading here.

3 On the apparent contradiction between Qurayš being the most eloquent of languages, and at the same time the most eloquent language, the *ʕarabiyyah*, being nothing like the language of the Qurayš see the excellent discussion by Larcher on this text by al-Farrāʔ in relation to a similar text by Ibn Fāris (Larcher 2005).

Clearly, not all grammarians were equally satisfied with this dialectal identification of the Quran's language. In the interpretation of the *sabʕat ʔaḥruf* ḥadīṯ, ʔabū ʕubayd al-Qāsim b. Sallām (d. 224 AH/838 CE) reports that the much debated *ʔaḥruf* refer to seven different dialects of Arabic, Ibn al-Ǧazarī (§ 65) quotes ʔabū ʕubayd as claiming these seven dialects were: Qurayš, Huḏayl,[4] Taym al-Rabāb, al-ʔazd, Rabīʕah, Hawazān and Saʕd b. Bakr, but no such specific reference is given in ʔabū ʕubayd's *Faḍāʔil al-Qurʔān*, where he does mention that the Quran was revealed in seven dialects (attributing this claim to the companion Ibn ʕabbās), without specifying which seven those were (ʔabū ʕubayd *Faḍāʔil al-Qurʔān*, 340).

Regardless of the historicity of al-Farrāʔ's report, we can conclude that whatever language the Quran was composed in, the Quranic reading traditions are not only linguistically clearly not a guide to what that language of the Quran was (as I have argued in chapter 3), but also that these early influential authorities seem to agree with that conclusion.

While the above report, cited by al-Farrāʔ without *ʔisnād*, may very well be late, there is another well-attested bundle of reports about the process of the Uthmanic recension, which seems to have been extraordinarily early, Motzki (2001) through his detailed *isnad*-cum-*matn* analysis shows that the common link of this report is Ibn Šihāb al-Zuhrī (d. 124 AH/741–742 CE). This report usually includes the mention that ʕuṯmān's recension of the Quran should be written in the dialect of the Qurayš because it was revealed in their language, and that part of the report independently goes back to our common link Ibn Šihāb.[5]

Thus, through ʔibrāhīm b. Saʕd and Šuʕayb[6] both on the authority of al-Zuhrī we get a virtually identical report:

> *ʔanna ʕuṯmāna daʕā*[7] *Zayda bna Ṯābitin wa-ʕabda llāhi bna Zubayr wa-Saʕīda bna l-ʕāṣi*[8] *wa-ʕabda r-raḥmāni bna l-Ḥāriṯi bni Hišāmin fa-nasaxū-hā fī l-maṣāḥif. Wa-qāla ʕuṯmānu li-l-rahṭi l-qurašiyyīna ṯ-ṯalāṯah: ʔiḏā xta-*

4 Note that this is in direct conflict with the report of ʕumar cited by al-Farrāʔ.

5 The version reported by al-Ṭabarī lacks this section (Comerro 2012, 37). The partial common link of al-Ṭabarī's version is Yūnus, transmitting from the common link Ibn Šihāb al-Zuhrī (Motzki 2001, 25).

6 The partial common link of Šuʕayb's version forms a partial common link one generation later, at ʔabū l-Yamān (Motzki 2001, 25).

7 Šuʕayb opens with *qāla fa-ʔamara ʕuṯmān* "Uthman said and ordered" instead.

8 Šuʕayb reverses the two preceding figures in the order they are mentioned.

> *laftum ʔantum wa-Zaydu bnu Ṯābitin fī šayʔin mina l-qurʔān,*[9] *fa-ktubū-hu bi-lisāni Qurayš, fa-ʔinnamā nazala bi-lisāni-him.*[10] *fa-faʕalū ḏālik.*[11]
>
> ʕuṯmān called Zayd b. Ṯābit, ʕabd aḷḷāh b. Zubayr, Saʕīd b. Al-ʕāṣ and ʕabd al-Raḥmān b. al-Ḥāriṯ b. Hišām—they copied the manuscripts of the Qurʔān. ʕuṯmān said to the Qurashis (everyone but Zayd): If you disagree with Zayd b. Ṯabit on anything in the Quran, write it down in the dialect of the Quraysh, because the Quran was revealed in their language. And so, they did that
>
> *Saḥīḥ al-Buxārī*: *al-Manāqib* 61, *Bāb Nazala al-Qurʔān bi-Lisān* Qurayš, #3506; *Faḍāʔil al-Qurʔān* 66, *Bāb nazala al-Qurʔān bi-Lisān Qurayš wa-l-ʕarab*, #4984

Schwally (Nöldeke et al. 2013, 260) dismissed the historicity of this part of the report as an outright forgery, saying: "generally, any tradition connecting the ʿUthmānic text in any way with dialectal questions must be rejected, since the Koran is not written in a local dialect at all but rather has a language identical to that of the pre-Islamic poems." While this has been the *communis opinio* before him and after him, I hope that the current work has shown that the identity of the Quranic language with poetry has so far only been asserted and has not been demonstrated, and that the QCT indeed quite clearly reflects Hijazi Arabic. Considering the earliness of the report and how well it aligns with the facts of the early Quranic manuscripts, we can carefully conclude that this report may very well retain a historical memory of the original language of composition of the Quran.

8.3 The Era of the Readers (ca. 40 AH–250 AH)

While the original language of the Quran, as shown by the QCT and affirmed by the tradition appears to have been Hijazi Arabic (or specifically Qurashi), at some point linguistic norms—at least in the recitation of the Quran—shift drastically, giving rise to the classicized reading traditions that we know among the canonical, and non-canonical readers alike.

---

9 Šuʕayb has *fī ʕarabiyyatin min ʕarabiyyati l-qurʔān* "on the Arabic from among the Arabic of the Qurʔān" instead.

10 Šuʕayb has *fa-ʔinna l-qurʔāna ʔunzila bi-lisāni-him* "for the Quran" instead.

11 Šuʕayb lacks *ḏālika*.

Al-Jallad (2020b, 69 f.) draws a tentative initial history of this development. He suggests that Old Hijazi, the language of the QCT, was the literary and prestige dialect of the Medinan state, and continued to be so as it transitioned into the early Umayyad empire. He suggests that in the Umayyad period another literary form of Arabic gains prestige, namely the language of the Qaṣīdah, with its strict metered and rhymed system. While the exact linguistic features of these odes are obscured by the inexorable forces of revision towards the later literary standard,[12] one feature is undeniable: the system of final short vowels and *tanwīn* forms an integral part of its structure confirmed by the rhyme and metre.

It seems possible that this new literary standard that enters into the sociolinguistic arena, vying for prestige should be identified as the dialect of the Maʕadd. Al-Jallad follows Peter Webb's highly thought-provoking observation that the main label of group identity in the pre-Islamic qaṣīdahs is *Maʕadd* (Webb 2017, 70 ff.), who these Maʕadd were and how their qaṣīdahs gained prestige in the Umayyad period is a question that we hope Al-Jallad will address in the future research project he mentions in his book (Al-Jallad 2020b, 69).

However we interpret this relation to Maʕadd exactly, one thing is abundantly clear and I follow Al-Jallad completely in his conclusion: "the Qaṣīdah belong to a different literary culture than that of the Ḥigāz, as its form is not found in the Quran. And even though the Quran refers to poets, there [is] nothing to suggest that these poets were producing poems belonging to the same style as the pre-Islamic Qaṣīdah." In a footnote he adds: "the very fact that the Quran had to tell its audience that the speaker was not a "poet" suggests a structural similarity between the text and what the audience would have considered poetry. If the Classical Qaṣīdah was the prototype, no such warning would have been necessary."

When exactly this literary variety starts to play a central role in influencing Arabic literary prose is frustratingly difficult to answer, due to the dearth of primary source material that dates from the period and is likewise vocalized, but when it comes to the period that this "qaṣīdah register" starts playing a role in Quranic recitation puts us on firmer ground. The transmission of many Quranic readers is rather strong, and there can be little doubt that the form in which they have been transmitted to us is very close to how they actually recited the Quran.

The earliest reader by far would certainly be Ibn ʕāmir, who is said to have lived from 8 to 118 AH, but his transmission is problematic for a variety of rea-

12 Something already clearly noticed and impeccably formulated by (Nöldeke 1910, 3).

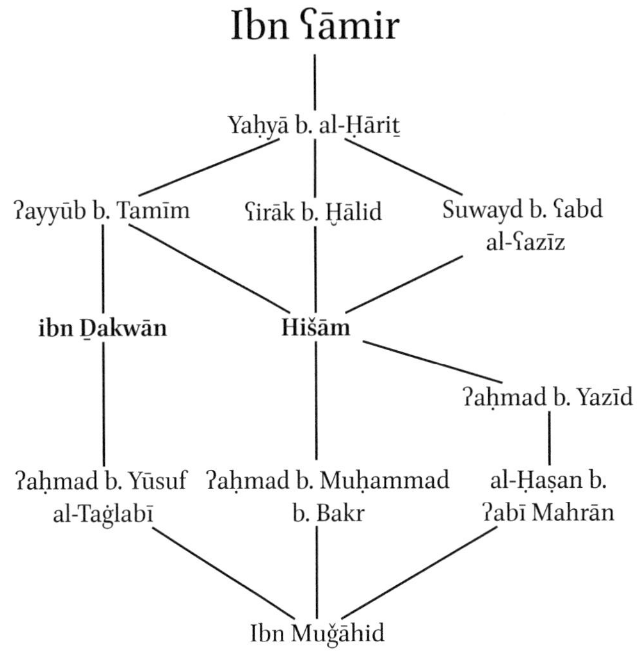

FIGURE 3 *ʔisnād* of Ibn ʕāmir as reported by Ibn Muǧāhid (85–87)

sons. First, his astounding age of 110 years should raise some eyebrows, but even granting that, his transmission has only come down to us through one transmitter, Yaḥyā b. al-Ḥāriṯ (d. 145 AH) and the two canonical transmitters (Hišām, 153 AH–245 AH and Ibn Ḏakwān, 173 AH–242 AH) are removed two more generations from Yaḥyā sharing, partially, the same teachers. So, this reading may have taken its Classical shape as late as the mid second century AH.

al-Ḥasan al-Baṣrī (110 AH) and Ibn Muḥayṣin al-Makkī (d. 123 AH) along with the canonical reader Ibn Kaṯīr (d. 122 AH) (see al-Ḏahabī 46, 69, 89) make up the next group of earliest readers, and their readings can be more securely attributed to their lifetimes. Therefore, somewhere in their lifetimes this register formerly proper to the pre-Islamic Qaṣīdah had gained enough prestige to come to be accepted as part of the prestigious Quranic recitation.

The bulk of the canonical and well-attested non-canonical readers alike, have their death dates all throughout the middle of the second until the middle of the third century.[13] It seems reasonable to conclude that recitation with *ʔiʕrāb* and *tanwīn* (and seemingly at least some amount of the application of

13 ʕāṣim (d. 127), ʕāṣim al-Ǧaḥdarī (d. 128), ʔabū Ǧaʕfar (d. 130), al-ʔaʕmaš (d. 148), ʔabū ʕamr

the *hamzah*) rose to dominance in this period. At its earliest, at the start of the Umayyad period, but probably became firmly established some decades after the beginning of the Umayyad period (perhaps around 80 AH).

This seems to be independently confirmed by the primary source material in the form of early Quranic manuscripts. The earliest manuscripts, those that can be dated to the seventh century, lack any form of vocalization signs and purely reflect the standard Uthmanic text, a consonantal skeleton (e.g. CPP, BL, Arabe 330g, Birmingham, Cadbury Research Library, Islamic Arabic 1572b). By the 8th century a system of red dots developed to write the vowel signs. Of course, the absence of vowel signs does not necessarily suggest that in this period the Quran was still recited in a purely Hijazi manner, but it stands to reason to consider the development of the vowel signs to suit a need, and this need would have quite naturally been to aid recitation in the linguistic style of the now popular Qaṣīdahs.

The fact that vocalization in manuscripts is primarily focused not on marking the word internal vowels—that part was clearly considered quite uncontroversial—but to primarily mark (1) word final short vowels and *tanwīn* and (2) The place of the *hamzah*, is a strong indication that it was specifically these two features that were salient and of prime importance to be conveyed in this period of developing reading traditions.

For an illustration of this system I have transcribed below a single page of R 119, f. 23a (for the photo see Déroche (2014), fig. 17). Every section in **bold** is expressed in the vocalization. Of the 112 cases of vocalization, only 23 are used to mark word-internal vowels, the remaining 89 express stem-final short vowels, *ʔiʕrāb/tanwīn*, or *hamzah*.

1. wa-lā liyahdiya-hum **ṭarīqan. ʔillā** ṭarīqa ǧahannama xālidīna fīhā **ʔabad-**
2. **-an** wa-kāna ḏālika ʕalā **l̠lāhi yasīran. Yā-ʔayyuhā** n-nāsu qad **ǧēʔa-**
3. **kumu** r-rasūlu bi-l-ḥaqqi min rabbi-**kum fa-ʔāminū xayran lakum wa-ʔin**
4. **yakfurū fa-ʔinna** lillāhi mā fī s-samāwāti **wa-l-ʔarḍi wa-kāna**
5. **l̠lāhu ʕalīman ḥakīman. Yā-ʔahla** l-kitābi lā **taġlū** fī **dīnikum wa-**
6. **lā taqūlū** ʕalā **l̠lāhi ʔillā** l-**ḥaqqa. ʔinnamā** l-**masīḥu ʕīsā bnu**
7. **maryama rasūlu l̠lāhi wa-kalimatuhū ʔalqā-hā ʔilā maryama wa-rūḥun**
8. **minhu fa-ʔāminū bi-llāhi wa-rusulihī wa-lā taqūlū ṯalāṯatun-i ntahū**
9. **xayran lakumū ʔinnamā l̠lāhu ʔilāhun wāḥidun subḥānahū ʔan yakūna lahū wa-**
10. **-ladun lahū** mā fī s-samāwāti wa-mā fī **l-ʔarḍi wa-kafā bi-**

(d. 148), Ḥamzah (d. 156), Nāfiʕ (d. 169), Sallām (d. 171), al-Kisāʔī (d. 189), Yaʕqūb (d. 205), ʔabū ʕubayd al-Qāsim b. Sallām (d. 224), Xalaf (d. 229), ʔabū Ḥātim al-Siǧistānī (d. 255).

11. -llāhi wakīlan. Lan yastankifu l-masīḥu ʔan yakūna ʕabdan li-llāhi wa-
12. lā l-malāʔikatu l-mufarrabūna wa-man yastankif ʕan ʕibādatihī

Of course, it is frequently very difficult to be establish whether the red dotting is in fact contemporary with the writing of the text, and we only become more certain of this when we reach manuscripts of the classical Kufic B.II and D styles, which generally date to around the middle to end of the third century AH (Déroche 1992, 36f.), where the vocalization appears in virtually all manuscripts in these styles, clearly indicating that they were considered an integral part of the manuscript's creation.

Addition of vocalization is certainly unlikely to post-date the third century, as by the early fourth century Ibn Muǧāhid canonizes the seven canonical readers, after which these rapidly become the dominant readings reflected in manuscripts. Before this canonization, however, more often than not the readings represented in these manuscripts are clearly non-canonical, and unlikely to have been added to such manuscripts in, say, the fourth century AH or later.

Several manuscripts show nascent forms of the vocalization system, expressing *hamzah* in ways that are somewhat different from later manuscripts. Most prominent is Kairouan, Musée des arts islamiques R 38, a manuscript which from its ornamentation and script style should clearly be considered part of the imperial Umayyad Qurans, which uses not red dots but red dashes, and seem to predate the innovation of doubling the vowel sign to mark *tanwīn*, as it uses only a single dot where one expects two to be written. It stands to reason to consider this a very early example of this system, and may very well be contemporaneous to this manuscript, which likewise follows a non-canonical reading.

BnF Arabe 334a, studied by Cellard (2015) and edited by Van Putten (2019a) is a more developed system of vocalization, already using doubling of the vowel sign to use nunation, but employing not red dots but somewhat thicker red dashes than R 38. Also, its system of marking the *hamzah* seems to be somewhat different than that in other vocalized manuscripts. The vocalization, as shown by Van Putten (2019a), follows a non-canonical but perhaps Hijazi reading style, with as a prominent feature the absence of any form of vowel harmony on the third person pronominal suffixes. While lack of harmony in the pronouns becomes extraordinarily popular in the B.II manuscripts, those consistently harmonize *bihī* only (van Putten and Sidky forthcoming), this manuscript also leaves that unharmonized as *bihū*. These features likewise give it the impression of being rather more archaic than the regular vocalization style.

While the details differ on how the *hamzah*, *ʔiʕrāb* and *tanwīn* is expressed in these manuscripts, they likewise agree that the system is only rarely employed to express word-internal short vowels. I believe that we can place the rise of the vocalized manuscript, and especially the one with a focus on the final short vowels and *hamzah*, in the Umayyad period, continuing into the Abbasid period, contemporaneous with the rise of activity of Quranic readers.

It is of course also quite significant that the eponymous readers to which all these readings are attributed come from this crucial era in the early 8th to 9th century. It would have been extraordinarily attractive to attribute the readings not to historically rather insignificant figures like the eponymous readers, but rather to companions of the prophet or the prophet himself, but this does not happen. This is because it is precisely these readers that constructed these classicized readings in this era.

A final, but much more scanty piece of evidence for the shift from a classicization of the Quran may perhaps be found in the grammatical terminology as it is used by the early exegetical works as studied by Versteegh (1993). A striking difference between the very earliest transmitted *tafsīr* of Muǧāhid b. Ǧabr (d. 104/722) compared to some of the slightly later exegetes such as Muḥammad b. al-Sāʔib al-Kalbī (d. 146/763), Muqātil b. Sulaymān (d. 150/767) and Sufyān al-Ṯawrī (d. 161/778) is exactly the complete absence of the former of any terminology for *ʔiʕrāb* and *tanwīn*, and even in Sufyān al-Ṯawrī's commentary such terminology is almost entirely absent, he only uses the verb *nawwana* "to apply nunation" once (Versteegh 1993, 113). This is quite different from Muḥammad al-Kalbī who shows a concern for variant readings and in discussing them displays a full set of terms for final short vowels (Versteegh 1993, 125 ff.). It is difficult not to notice that Muḥammad al-Kalbī's is exactly the generation of many of the great Quranic reciters such as ʔabū ʕamr (d. 154/770) and ʕāṣim (d. 127/745) and Nāfiʕ (d. 169/785), while Muǧāhid clearly precedes them, and thus perhaps also the widespread classicization of the language of the Quran.

This era marked an explosion of different linguistic forms, and a negotiation of what the linguistic features of the *ʕarabiyyah* were going to be. This much is already clear from the disagreement on the linguistic details between the canonical readers (as we saw in chapter 3), but also other non-canonical readers show an even broader amount of linguistic variation than is allowed within the canonical ten. Also, within the vocalized Quranic manuscripts, a wealth of different forms and unusual recombinations of features are found.[14] What the *ʕarabiyyah* was, was not yet straightforward, and this period must be seen as

14 For an in-depth study of just one part of the variation of linguistic systems, namely the pronouns, both in the transmitted tradition and the manuscripts see Van Putten & Sidky (forthcoming).

a negotiation towards a new standard, truly only one central feature remains constant throughout this experimentation and that is that the final short vowels and *tanwīn*, the one feature that is perpetuated by every line of the new central literary form: the *qaṣīdah*.

8.4 Crystallization of Classical Arabic (ca. 250–350 AH)

There is a reason why we speak of Classical Arabic in a much more restricted sense than the *ʕarabiyyah* that the early grammarians sought to describe. Indeed, at some point, the negotiation of what the *ʕarabiyyah* starts to crystallize and a fairly uniform system emerges which is more or less identical to grammar books such as Fischer, Wright and Thackston. When exactly this complete crystallization takes place, is as of yet, not entirely clear. Research into the linguistic norms of non-Quranic literary manuscripts of the third and fourth centuries is still a desideratum. But I will provide some initial observations.

The papyrus copy of *al-Ǧāmiʕ* by Ibn Wahb (d. 197 AH), copied in 275 AH/889 CE and published by David-Weill (1939) is remarkable for being strikingly unclassical in its language. Despite being unvocalized, it has many features that would not be considered part of the Classical Arabic language that we know today. Middle Arabists such as Blau (1999, Appendix I) have often taken this work to be a reflection of 'Middle Arabic', a form of Arabic that mixes Classical Arabic and colloquial features. However, if Blau is right to suppose that the unusual linguistic features present in this manuscript are rather reflective of the peculiarities of Ibn Wahb's Arabic rather than of its copyist, we are dealing with a manuscript stemming right from the period that the parameters of the literary language were still being negotiated. Regardless of whether some of the unusual features of Ibn Wahb's text as the result of interference of the author's colloquial Arabic, seeing his deviations from Classical Arabic as deviations from an established standard is anachronistic. For example, it is highly problematic to declare forms like اربعة[عشر] *ʔarbaʕ(a)taʕšar* as a non-Classical form (Blau 1999, 124), while ʔabū Ǧaʕfar (d. 130 AH) who recites Q74:30 تسعة عشر as *tisʕataʕšar* (Ibn al-Ǧazarī, § 3205) which would make it *ʕarabiyyah* by definition. Clearly, the jury was still out on whether such a form was to become part of Classical Arabic.

The copy of ʔabū ʕubayd al-Qāsim b. Sallām's (d. 224 AH) *Ġarīb al-Ḥadīṯ*, copied in 252 AH, and with that the oldest known dated paper manuscript in Arabic, held at the Leiden University Library under the shelf mark Or. 298 is another data point worthy of examination. This manuscript is vocalized with the modern vowel signs that are clearly contemporary with the main text, and this gives us an insight into some of the linguistic features. Many of the features that we associate with standard Classical Arabic are present, even though the orthography is exceptionally archaic, thus *ʔuxrā-hā* and *ʔūlā-hā* are spelled with typically Quranic orthographic practice of using *yāʔ* for the *ʔalif maqṣūrah* even before a pronominal clitic: اخريها and اوليها (Leiden University Library, Or. 298,[15] 2r, l. 13). But despite this spelling, which has sometimes been interpreted as indicating *ʔimālah*, the spelling with *fatḥah* before this *ʔalif maqṣūrah* suggests that it already employed the standard Classical Arabic -*ā*. Likewise, the plural pronouns are short, and they undergo vowel harmony, and the appearance of *hamzah* appears to be quite conservative.

But a question is, to what extent these features that are present in the manuscript are indicative of a crystallization of the Classical norms. We are lucky enough to have a transmission of ʔabū ʕubayd's own reading of the Quran, and for each of these features he indeed follows the Classical norm. Yet there are indications that not all users of the literary Arabic language in the early third century would stick perfectly to this Classical Arabic norm. For example, in his Quranic recitation, ʔabū Ḥātim al-Siǧistānī (d. 255 AH) still has the non-standard Classical Arabic lack of vowel harmony after -*ay* for the plural pronoun, i.e. *ʕalayhum* but *fīhim, bihim* (van Putten and Sidky forthcoming). Whether ʔabū Ḥātim would have employed such pronominal behaviour outside of his reading tradition and in his Classical Arabic prose, is sadly something that cannot be confirmed, as we lack any autographs, or in fact any copies at all of his works, but I see little reason assume a difference between recitation and Classical Arabic prose *a priori*.

What is definitely clear is that about a century later, in Ibn Xālawayh's *Kitāb al-Badīʕ*, of which we have a copy from his death year (380 AH, CBL Ar 3051), all the features part of the standard Classical Arabic have been firmly established.[16] This is independently confirmed by the literary tradition, the contemporary author Ibn Mihrān (d. 381 AH) in his description of the pronominal system of the Quranic readers, strikingly different from most other sources in the genre, only mentions deviations from the Classical norm, leaving it implicit that anyone whom he does not mention explicitly, simply has the Classical Arabic harmonizing short suffixes (see van Putten and Sidky forthcoming).

15 For more information on this manuscript see Witkam (2007, 1:149–152).

16 Although occasional surprising variants show up, still from a normative perspective, for example the plural proximal deictic *hāʔulāʔi* is spelled هولا implying *hawlāʔi* (5r., l. 3), a variant recognized to exist by Al-Farrāʔ (*lughāt*, 22), but not generally considered part of the normative classical register.

It seems then that quite soon after (if not already during) the period I labelled 'the Era of the Readers' the typical features that we now associate with standard Classical Arabic became firmly established. Some of the typical features that became fixed, which at the time of the early readers and grammarians were clearly still up for debate are:

- Harmonization of *-hū* and *-hum* (and vowel length disharmony of *-hū/-hu, -hī/-hi*), a feature generally associated with the Najdi dialects.
- Short plural pronouns, rather than the long forms *-humū, ʾantumū* etc.
- Conservative syllable structure, typical for the Hijazi dialects (*rusul* and *kalimah*, not *rusl* and *kalmah, kilmah*).
- Conservative retention of the *hamzah*, typical of Najdi dialects.
- Generalization of the *a*-vowel in prefix conjugation typical of the Hijaz, rather than the Najdi forms like *tiʕlamu*.
- Absence of *i*-umlaut *ʔimālah*, a feature associated with Najd.
- Complete loss of the fourth phonemic vowel *ē* for III-*y* nouns and verbs, considered to be a Najdi feature by the grammarians, but clearly also part of Quranic Arabic originally.

This rather chaotic combination of features of standard Classical Arabic should make it quite clear that the rather popular notion that Classical Arabic is primarily influenced by the Najdi dialects is not really borne out by the evidence. While the vowel harmony of the pronouns and the conservative use of the *hamzah* are indeed striking features associated with Najd, many other features typical of Najd like the far-reaching syncope of *i* and *u* in open syllables, the front vowel prefixes in the verb and *ʔimālah* are entirely absent.

Moreover, much of the morphology that is reflected by the actual consonantal skeleton, such as the shape of the deictic pronouns is almost invariably in agreement with the Hijazi forms, while the Najdi *ḏāka* occurs occasionally in Classical Arabic prose, *ḏālika* far outnumbers it, and *tīka/ḏīka, hāḏī* and (*hā-*)*ʔulā* instead of *tilka, hāḏihī* and *hāʔulāʔi* are almost entirely unheard of. Contrary to popular belief, I would therefore also say that it is in fact Hijazi Arabic that is the main contributor to the phonology and morphology of Classical Arabic rather than Najdi Arabic. This is, no doubt, due to the massive influence the Quran had on the emerging literary tradition of Arabic. That this influence has not been realized sooner, primarily seems to rest on the fact that whenever the Quran agreed with standard Classical Arabic it has been considered to be normal and unremarkable and in line with the conclusion that the Quran was composed in standard Classical Arabic.

Despite a crystallization of most of the main Classical Arabic norms being complete around the 4th century AH, it remains possible to encounter non-textbook features occur in perfectly Classical Arabic prose until surprisingly late. While certainly outside the scope of the current book, let me highlight a few salient cases that I have noticed.

Syncopation of *huwa* and *hiya* after *wa-*, *fa-*, *la-* to *wa-hwa*, *fa-hya* (§ 2.2.4.3) sticks around in Classical Arabic prose until surprisingly late. For example, *al-Maǧmūʕ al-Rašīdiyyah* (BnF Arabe 2324) dated to 710 AH regularly has this syncope throughout its text (see 3r, l. 12; 10r, l. 10; 22r, l. 3; 34v, l. 16; 40v, l. 6; 50v, l. 6, etc.), it also attested the Hijazi form of 'to see' *rāʔa-hū* (§ 5.11) rather than the textbook form *raʔā-hu* (5v, l. 8). Even later, in a copy of *Risālat ibn ʔabī Zayd* from 1059 AH we find evidence of *an-nubūʔah* 'prophecy' instead of the textbook *an-nubuwwah* (BnF Arabe 1058, 5v, l. 8), a form often considered to be a "hyperclassicism" (§ 6.5.1.1). Also, the dropping of *hamzah* in places where the textbook norms do not prescribe it is attested surprisingly late, e.g. *mašiyyatuka* for *mašīʔatuka* in a copy of al-Ǧazūlī's *Dalāʔil al-Xayrāt* from 1170 AH (BnF Arabe 6859, 36r, l. 10).

8.5 Conclusion

I hope that this work has shown that there is still much to be discovered about the Quranic Arabic language, and that both Quranic Arabic, the reading traditions of the Quran and the emergence of the standard Classical Arabic deserve to be studied in their own right. I hope to have shown that the way we think about the language of the Quran needs to be approached from a (historical) linguistic point of view, and should be reframed not from a position where we anachronistically impose later standards onto the text, but starting from its primary source material: the Quranic Consonantal Text.

Undoubtedly much more is to be discovered. There are two main topics I wish to highlight here. First is the corpus of early Islamic papyri and inscriptions. These share many linguistic similarities with the language of the Quran, and should likewise be seen as products of their time. Deviations from the standard should not anachronistically be assumed to be deviations from the not yet established Classical Arabic standard, but instead should be compared against other documents of their time, including the QCT. Only this way we can deduce what the contemporary linguistic norms were.

Another question is the linguistic position of pre-Islamic and early Islamic poetry. The equation of the poetry with standard Classical Arabic and the language of the Quran all too often means that interesting linguistic variation that occurs in the poetry gets glossed over. These corpora deserve careful linguistic study in their own right. While certainly the poetry is much more linguistically mixed than other sources of early Arabic, it strikes me as likely that different poets from different regions are likely to use certain features more than others. The amount of times we must assume the loss of *hamzah* due to meter in the poetry of Ibn ʔabī Rabīʕah, as shown by Schwarz (1901), for example, is quite striking and should probably be seen in the context of him being a Hijazi poet. Any comments of this kind have mostly been impressionistic and incidental and a systematic linguistic study of the material is direly needed.

APPENDIX A

Notes on Orthography, Phonology and Morphology of the Quranic Consonantal Text

A.1 Introduction

This appendix serves as a more detailed discussion for some of the topics of the language of the Quranic Consonantal Text that have come up throughout this book. As previous works on the language and orthography of the Quran have mostly relied on the Cairo Edition, which is not always an accurate reflection of the Uthmanic Text, this appendix aims to add some more detailed discussion to questions of orthography, phonology and morphology of Quranic Arabic. Throughout the book there are several references to this appendix, but I have also included topics of note here which do not receive direct discussion in the book. It is hoped that this appendix can function as a short but useful guide to some of the main features of Quranic Arabic on its own. In some cases, discussions here rely on observations and generalizations of the orthography found in early Quranic manuscripts. Whenever I do so, I refer to Appendix B, which is a list of relevant tables that compares the orthography of certain words across early Quranic manuscripts.

A.2 Orthography

The Quranic orthography was studied in great detail by Werner Diem (1976; 1979; 1980; 1982) in a series of highly insightful and in-depth articles which trace the rise and development of Quranic orthographic practice from its Nabataean Aramaic origins. Diem exclusively relied on the orthography as found in the Cairo Edition, which has occasionally caused him to draw the wrong conclusions about the principles of Quranic orthography as they must have been present in the UT. Quite often, we find that early Quranic manuscripts consistently agree with each other on certain topics of orthographic practice, where the Cairo Edition differs from this practice. In this section I will discuss the main orthographic practices of Quranic Arabic, which will necessarily overlap on occasion with the observations made by Diem.

A.2.1 *The Spelling of* ā

In Pre-Islamic Arabic written in the Nabataean script, and transitional Nabataeao-Arabic there was no way to write word-internal *ā* (unlike *ī*, and *ū*). With the loss of the glottal stop in Quranic Arabic, the *ʔalif* gave rise to a new word-internal *mater lectionis* for /ā/ (Diem 1979, § 60–68; van Putten 2018).[1] In the QCT, the use of *ʔalif* for writing /ā/ is still largely optional, and it is one of the main points of disagreement between different Quranic manuscripts (van Putten 2019c, 281–286). Despite this unstable status of the spelling, several generalizations can be made about its spelling.

In the QCT defective spellings of *ā* are very common, but highly uncommon in words of the shape CāC and CāC̄ (Diem 1979, § 67). The exception to this being the spelling of the verb 'to say' /qāl/ which in early Islamic documents is almost without exception spelled defectively قل, an archaic spelling retained in this one high frequency word, the same is true for, for example its plural form قلوا.[2] In the CE the special status of the verb *qāla* has almost completely disappeared, and is generally spelled *plene* as other verbs of this type. However, قل recited as *qāla* occurs in Q21:112, Q23:112,114 and Q43:24.[3]

The defective spelling of the feminine plural ending /-āt/ is standard in the Uthmanic orthography. In the CE only بنات 'daughters' is regularly spelled *plene*. Besides these there are three specific exceptions: Q41:12 سموات 'heavens' (versus 189 times that it is spelled سموت), Q41:16 ايام نحسات 'unfortunate days' and Q42:22 روضات الجنات 'the flowering meadows of the gardens'. These unique exceptions of these verses do not seem to be a feature of the UT. For الجنات /ǧannāt/ 'gardens', the *plene* spelling is regular in early manuscripts, just like بنات /banāt/ 'daughters', and not just used in the position Q42:22. It appears that if the stem + the feminine plural ending would only be three letters long if the feminine

1 This same feature is well-attested in early Islamic Arabic, and generally recognized to be part of Pre-Classical orthography (Blau 1967, § 9.1; 2002, 35, § 26; Hopkins 1984, § 10).

2 A lack of awareness of the special status of *qāla* has led to some confusion in epigraphic research. The extremely common formula اللهم اغفر [...] لمن قل/قال امين 'O God, forgive [...] whoever says Amen', is misread by Grohmann (1962, 148–149; Z 256, Z 257) as اللهم اغفر [...] لمن فا امين 'O God, grant pardon [...] to everyone who returns, Amen'. cf. the same formula with قال (al-Kilābī 2009, nos. 78, 215) and with قل (al-Kilābī 2009, nos. 49, 90). A similar misunderstanding is found in the edition of the 31 AH gravestone inscription from Aswan, where line 4–5 استغفر له اذا قرا هذا الكتب وقل امين should be understood as "and ask (Allah) pardon for him (the deceased) when he reads this writing and says Amen", and not how it is translated "(passer by) When reading this inscription ask pardon for him (the deceased) and say Amen!" (El-Hawary 1930, 322).

3 In all of these cases, the choice of spelling these defectively seems to be an attempt to accommodate the other canonical readings, which in these places disagree on the reading of this word. Some of them thus read it as *qul* (Ibn al-Ǧazarī, § 3640, § 3705, § 3706, § 4154).

plural ending was spelled defectively, the ending is spelled *plene* (van Putten 2019c, 284). As for سموت, نحسات and روضات, these are normally spelled defectively in these positions, following the regular rule of defective spelling of *-āt* in early manuscripts (see B.1).[4]

In the QCT, *ā* two syllables removed from the stress, such as in plural G-stem active participles and duals *CāCiCū/īn, CāCiCāt* and *CāCiCān/ayn* (as well as العلمين /al-ʕālamīn/) are consistently spelled defectively. Diem (1979, § 67.2; 1980, § 105) notices this rule too, but observes that in the CE, hollow verbs break this patterns and are consistently spelled *plene* (as are the singulars), e.g. Q7:4 قايلون 'sleeping at noon'. This is however an idiosyncracy of the CE. In early Quranic manuscripts these words simply follow the same rule as other plurals of this pattern and are spelled defectively (van Putten 2018, 108 f.).

The vocative prefix /yā-/ is consistently spelled defectively throughout the Quran, and this is without exception, e.g. يموسى 'O Mūsā' (Q2:55 and *passim*), يمريم 'O Maryam' (Q3:37 and *passim*), etc.[5]

Whenever the 1pl. suffix *-nā* is followed by any other clitic, it is consistently spelled defectively, e.g. رزقنهم 'we provided them' (Q2:3), ارسلنك 'we have sent you' (Q2:119).

A.2.2 *Questions of Double* yāʔ, wāw *and* ʔalif

Diem (1979, § 37–43) discusses the avoidance of double *matres yāʔ* and *wāw* in detail, and argues that the sequences of *yī* and *wū* are typically written with only a single *yāʔ* and *wāw* respectively, whereas other phonetic sequences may still have these two consonants in a row. However, the facts as they appear in the CE are not very representative of the UT, and as a result the analysis does not hold up.

For the ى, Diem cites cases such as CE ولى /waliyy-ī/ 'my friend' (Q7:196; Q12:101); CE يحى /yuḥyī/ 'he revives' (Q2:73) and CE يستحى /yastaḥyī/ 'he is ashamed' (Q2:26). However, in early Quranic manuscripts all of these are consistently spelled with two *yāʔ*s, and therefore the UT had two *yāʔs* (see B.2).[6]

---

4 The common defective spelling of the feminine plural ending also occurs in early Islamic inscriptions, but is misunderstood by Grohmann (1962, Z 48), who interprets صلوت الله as a singular 'the blessing of God' rather than 'the blessings of God', cf. صلوات الله (al-Rāšid 2009, 242). Likewise, Grohmann translates رحمت الله وبركته عليك 'the Mercy and blessing of God may be upon you' taking بركته as a singular (Grohmann 1962, Z 150, Z 171), but this formula certainly has the plural /barakāt-uh/, cf. رحمت الله وبركاته عليكم (Grohmann 1962, Z 225).

5 This practice is also attested in early Islamic Papyri (Hopkins 1984, § 10d), in the Ibn Wahb literary papyrus (Blau 1999, 124). Several clear cases are found in early Islamic inscriptions as well, e.g. يرحمن (al-Kilābī 2009, no. 35), يرب 'O my lord' (Grohmann 1962, nos. 165, 232).

6 The origin of this innovation in the Cairo Edition appears to come from Al-Dānī's *al-Muqniʕ*

	UT	CE
Q7:196, Q12:101	وليي	ولى
e.g. Q2:73	يحيي	يحى
e.g. Q2:26	يستحيي	يستحى
Q2:258	احيي	احى
Q15:23, Q50:43	نحيي	نحى

With these forms shown to be innovations of the CE, the amount of examples where a single ى is used to write a sequence /yī/ becomes very small, whereas there are several more examples where a double ى is used even in de CE, e.g. يحييكم /yuḥyī-kum/ 'he revives you' (Q2:28; Q8:24; Q22:66; Q30:40; Q45:26); يحيين /yuḥyī-n/ 'he revives me' (Q26:81); يحييها /yuḥyī-hā/ 'he will give them life' (Q36:79); حييتم /ḥuyyītum/ 'you are greeted' (Q4:86); افعيينا /ʔa-fa-ʕayīnā/ 'where we then tired?' (Q50:15) and عليين /ʕilliyyīn/ 'Elyon' (Q83:18).

Diem (1979, § 41) considers the outcome of *baʔīs* (Q7:165) spelled بيس to be a reflection of /bayīs/, but it seems doubtful that this is the correct analysis. First, it is not clear that **baʔīs* is the word which بيس is supposed to represent, as in the canonical reading traditions it is variously recited as *bīsin, biʔsin, bayʔasin* and *baʔīsin* (Ibn al-Ǧazarī, § 3150).[7] **biʔsin* would of course yield /bīs/, for which بيس is the only acceptable spelling, and **bayʔasin* would presumably yield /bayas/ or /bayyas/, again بيس being the only acceptable spelling. But even if Diem is right to assume that **baʔīs* is the origin of what بيس represents, it is quite probable that the outcome of **baʔīs* after the loss of **ʔ* was not *bayīs* but rather *bayyis* aligning with the outcome of the CaCīC adjectival pattern of hollow roots such as *mayyit* 'dead' (cf. Blau 1967, § 11.4.1.1) for which, once again, بيس would be the expected spelling. For these reasons this word is not a very good example of avoidance of two *yāʔ*s in the sequence *yī*.[8]

The examples that are left, then all have in common that they either have they correspond to the Classical Arabic sequence *iyyī/īʔī* or *āʔī*. The examples are given below.

---

who mentions that the Qurans of Medina and Iraq spell these words with only one *yāʔ*, a practice copied by the Cairo Edition (Al-Dānī *al-Muqniʕ*, 56).

7 Among the non-canonical readings there are moreover reports of *bayʔisin, bīsin, baysin* and *biʔīs* (Ibn Xālawayh *muxtaṣar*, 47).

8 One might also consider the reading /bāyis/ < *bāʔisin, which would be in line with the orthography بايس attested in BnF Arabe 6140a, although this could also be analysed as a case of historical hamzah spelling see A.2.7.

The reading traditions	QCT	
an-nabiyyīna, an-nabīʔīna (Q2:61 & *passim*)[9]	النبين	'the prophets'
al-ḥawāriyyīna (Q5:111; Q61:14)	الحوارين	'the apostles'
al-ʔummiyyīna (Q3:20, 75; Q62:2)	الامين	'the gentiles'
rabbāniyyīna (Q3:79)	ربنين	'worshippers of the lord'
ʔābāʔ-ī, ʔābāʔ-iya (Q12:38)[10]	اباى	'my fathers'
warāʔ-ī, warāʔ-iya, warā-ya (Q19:5)[11]	وراى	'behind me'
šurakāʔ-ī, šurakāʔ-iya (Q41:47)	شركاى	'my associates'
duʕāʔ-ī, duʕāʔ-iya (Q71:6)	دعاى	'my prayer'
ʔisrāāʔīl (Q2:40 & *passim*)	اسريل	'Israel'
ǧibrīl, ǧabrīl, ǧabraʔil, ǧabraʔīl (Q2:97, 98)[12]	جبريل	'Gabriel'
mīkāl, mīkāʔil, mīkāāʔil, mīkāāʔīl (Q2:98)[13]	ميكيل	'Michael'

As the apparent absence of double *matres* is phonetically conditioned, it seems like they should be considered the result of a genuine phonetic development, rather than an orthographic convention. In the case of the nouns that have a Classical Arabic sequence *iyyīna* or *īʔīna* it is likely that we are dealing with a contraction to /-īn/. Diem (1979, § 39) deems this unlikely, as he argues that an oblique plural الامين /al-ummīn/ should have had a nominative **الامون /al-ummūn/. To my mind, it seems perfectly possible to have an asymmetrical paradigm nom. /al-ummiyyūn/ obl. /al-ummīn/ without necessarily undergoing analogical leveling in one direction or the other. This is, in fact, a possibility in the *ʕarabiyyah*, e.g. أعجمين *ʔaʕjamīna* 'the non-Arabs' (Fischer 2002, § 116, note 2).[14]

As for the nouns that in Classical Arabic end in *āʔ* followed by the 1sg. possessive marker, it seems likely that the sequence *āʔ-ī* or *āʔ-iya* simply collapsed

9 Ibn al-Ǧazarī (§ 1531).

10 Ibn al-Ǧazarī (§ 2493).

11 Ibn al-Ǧazarī (§ 2519). *Warā-ya* is attributed to Ibn Kaṯīr in a non-canonical transmission (Ibn Muǧahid, 407).

12 Ibn al-Ǧazarī (§ 2714).

13 Ibn al-Ǧazarī (§ 2715).

14 The only exception to this contraction is عليون /ʕilliyyūn/, عليين /ʕilliyyīn/ 'Elyon'. As this is likely a loanword from Hebrew *ʿɛlyon* 'upper part of something; epithet of God' (Jeffery 2007, 215–216), it should not surprise us that this contraction does not take place, as it may have been borrowed at a time postdating the contraction.

to /ā-y/ after the loss of the *hamzah* and final short vowels. A trace of this development seems to have been retained in transmission of Ibn Kaṯīr's reading as *warā-ya*.

This leaves us with اسريل 'Israel', جبريل 'Gabriel' and ميكيل 'Michael'. At first sight one might want to read these as /ʔisrāyil/, /ǧibrāyil/ and /mīkāyil/. However, because اسريل stands in a /UR/ rhyme eight times (Q7:105, 134; Q26:17, 22, 59, 197; Q32:23; Q43:59), such a reading would break the rhyme. The reading that would be consistent with both the rhyme and the spelling is, in fact, /ʔisrīl/, paralleling the development that we see in the majority reading of جبريل as /ǧibrīl/. By extension it seems probable that ميكيل is to be understood as /mīkīl/.[15]

While double *yāʔ* avoidance when spelling *yī* does not appear to have been an orthographic principle, this seems to be different for double *wāw* avoidance when spelling *wū* (cf. Diem 1979, § 40). In post-consonantal position, the sequence /wū/ is indeed written with a single *wāw*. This is exemplified by forms of the verb *lawā* 'to distort; to turn around': يلون /yalwūn/ 'they distort' (Q3:78), تلون /talwūn/ 'you will [not] turn around' (Q3:153) and تلوا /talwū/ 'you distort' (Q4:135).[16] We can likewise see this avoidance of two *wāw*s in word-initial position we find وري /wūrī/ 'was concealed' (Q7:20). It seems likely that we can also count فاوا /fāwū/ 'so retreat!' (Q18:16) and الغاون /al-ġāwūn/ 'the deviators' (Q26:224). The pronunciation of داود, دواد 'David' is difficult to determine, so it is not entirely certain whether that should be interpreted as an example of double *wāw* avoidance (see A.2.8).

Diem takes ancient sequence **aʔū*(*na*) of III-*ʔ* stems in the plural as having developed to /awū(n)/. It seems likely however that III-ʔ and III-w/y stems have merged completely and these should rather be read as /aw(n)/. From spellings such as يستهزون /yastahzūn/ < **yastahziʔūna* it is clear that at least the **iʔū* sequence has merged completely with III-*w/y* stems. Indeed, in the reading traditions we see this with some of these verbs, with etymological *-aʔūna* forms, e.g. ʔabū Ǧaʕfar's *yaṭawna* 'they step' < **yaṭaʔūna* and *murǧawna* 'postponed' probably < **murǧaʔūna* (see § 6.5.5).

Diem likewise analyses the adjectives روف 'compassionate' and يوس 'despairing' as evidence of *aʔū* > *awū* being represented by a single *wāw*. Once again one has to wonder whether this is a correct identification. For روف, Diem

15 I thank Ahmad Al-Jallad for suggesting this analysis to me.

16 تلوا 'you distort' (Q4:135) is also read as *talū* by Ḥamzah and Ibn ʕāmir (Ibn al-Ǧazarī § 2962), so may not represent an example of this. The interpretation of the reading *talū* seems somewhat controversial. Al-Farrāʔ (*Maʕānī* I, 291) derives it from a root *lʔy*, which he claims has the same meaning as *tatawallaw* 'they follow in succession'. Ibn Xālawayh (*Ḥuǧǧah*, 127) see it as a G-stem of the root *wly*.

implicitly assumes that the Ḥafṣ reading *raʔūf* is the origin of the word represented, and thus reconstruct /rawūf/, however, all other Kufan readers read *raʔuf* (Ibn al-Ǧazarī, § 2731), which would presumably yield /rawuf/ or perhaps /rawf/ after the loss of the *hamzah*, where spelling with a single *wāw* would be expected. يوس is universally recited as *yaʔūs*, but *yaʔus* is reported in Arabic lexicography (*Lisān* 4945c), thus likewise opening up the possibility of the reading /yawus/. If his assumption that these come from CaCūC adjectival patterns holds up, however, these may indeed be good examples of *wū* being spelled with a single wāw, assuming that **aʔū* did not yield /awwu/ rather than /awū/ in this position.

To this he adds several other probable examples of this orthographic practice like *al-mawʔūdah* الموده /al-mawūdah/ 'the buried alive girl' (Q81:8) and يوده /yawūdu-h/ 'it tires him' (Q2:255). After the loss of *hamzah* روس 'heads' probably became /rūs/ (Q2:279) as the plural of /rās/ in analogy to /sāq/ pl. /sūq/ (incidentally also read as *suʔūq*, see § 6.4.10), but /ruwūs/ cannot be excluded.

Like double *wāw*, the sequence of double *ʔalif* is avoided. This is clearest in the case of nouns that end in *ʔalif mamdūdah*, followed by an indefinite accusative. Rhyme confirms that such sequences where indeed pronounced with two syllables, e.g. انشا /inšāʔā/ 'a creation' (Q56:35), yet they are spelled with only one *ʔalif*.

This same avoidance is found with the question particle ا /ʔa-/. When it combines with words that start with /ʔa-, ʔi-, ʔu-/, it is generally spelled with just a single *ʔalif*, e.g. انتم /ʔa-ʔantum/ (or /āntum/?) 'are you?' (Q2:140), انك /ʔa-(y)innaka/ 'are you?' (Q37:52), انزل /a-(w)unzila/ 'has it been revealed?' (Q38:8). Occasionally however, such sequences are spelled phonetically rather than morpho-phonemically, in which case a glide is written in the place of the word-initial vowel that followers the question particle, e.g. اينكم /a-yinna-kum/ 'do you?' (Q6:19), اونبيكم /ʔa-wunabbī-kum/ 'shall I inform you?' (Q3:15). Both spellings may even occur in a single verse, e.g. ايذا متنا وكنا ترابا وعظما انا لمبعوثون /a-yiḏā mutnā wa-kunnā turābā wa-ʕiẓāmā a-(y)innā (*or* innā)[17] la-mabʕūṯūn/ 'When we die and become dust and bones, will we be resurrected' (Q56:47, cf. also the identical phrase in Q23:82 and Q37:16, where /a-(y)iḏā/ is spelled اذا).

A.2.3 *ʔalif al-Wiqāyah*

A place where the orthography of the QCT diverges rather sharply from Classical Arabic orthography is in its use of the so-called *ʔalif al-wiqāyah*. In Classical

17 There is significant disagreement among the readers whether to read these words with a question particle in front of both, for a discussed see Ibn al-Ǧazarī (§ 1413).

Arabic, an *ʔalif* is written after word-final *wāw* only when this *wāw* denotes the verbal plural ending (Wright 1896, § 7a). In the QCT, its use is much more widespread, and regularly appears after any word-final /ū/ or /aw/, regardless of whether it is the plural verb or not (Nöldeke et al. 2013, 418 f.). This highly morphological spelling of Classical Arabic is thus an innovation. Examples of the broader use of the *ʔalif al-wiqāyah* are, e.g. كفروا /kafarū/ 'they disbelieved' (*passim*), مشوا /mašaw/ 'they walked' (Q2:20), يدعوا /yadʕū/ 'he calls' (Q2:221);[18] ملقوا ربهم /mulāqū rabbi-hum/ 'meeting of their lord' (Q2:46); ناكسوا روسهم /nākisū rūsi-hum/ 'the hanging of their heads' (Q32:12). The relative pronoun /ḏū/ which in the CE follows the Classical Spelling ذو, is consistently spelled ذوا in early Quranic manuscripts (Déroche 2009, 65).

There is only one case in the QCT where *ʔalif al-wiqāyah* is not used for word-final /-ū/, where we would expect it to be spelled, namely يعفو /yaʕfū/ 'that he forgive' (Q4:99) (see B.3). An exception to the general rule that whenever word-final /-aw/ occurs it should be written with *ʔalif al-wiqāyah*, are cases where a /w/ immediately precedes. Thus we find اوو /ʔāwaw/ 'they gave shelter' (Q8:72, 74) and لوو /lawwaw, lawaw/[19] 'they turn aside' (Q63:5). This orthographic practice is lost in the CE, but is consistent in early Quranic manuscripts (see B.4). There are two other words that end in /-aw/ words which in the CE are written without *ʔalif al-wiqāyah*, one of them certainly had the *ʔalif al-wiqāyah* in the UT, namely, سعوا /saʕaw/ 'they strove' (Q34:5) and another whose data is a bit more ambiguous, as several very ancient manuscripts have the *ʔalif al-wiqāyah* while (mostly) later ones lack it, namely: عتو(ا) /ʕataw/ 'and they became insolent' (Q25:21), see B.4.

Nöldeke et al. (2013, 418 f.) object to the possibility that the *ʔalif al-wiqāyah* is intended to represent the phonetic value /ū/ and /aw/, and instead suggest that "every final و is followed by an ا" and "exceptions to the rule can be easily explained". However, one of the main exceptions is not addressed at all: All nouns that end in a consonantal /w/, either when preceded by a consonant, or when part of word-final /uww/ are consistently spelled without *ʔalif al-wiqāyah*. Examples of word-final *-Cw* are: العفو /al-ʕafw/ 'the surplus; the forgiveness' (Q2:219; Q7:199), باللغو /bi-l-laġw/ (Q2:225; Q5:89; Q25:72), اللغو /al-laġw/ (Q23:3; Q28:55), لغو /laġw/ (Q52:23) 'idle talk', لهو /lahw/ (Q6:32; Q29:64; Q31:6; Q47:36; Q57:20), اللهو /al-lahw/ (Q62:11) 'amusement', البدو /al-badw/ 'the desert'

18 Thus, Quranic orthography is unable to make the distinction between the homophonous *yadʕū* 'he calls' and *yadʕū* 'they call (subjunctive/jussive)' which in Classical orthography is expressed as يدعو versus يدعوا.

19 Ibn al-Ǧazarī (§ 4397) reports both variants *lawaw* (Nāfiʕ and Rawḥ) and *lawwaw* (the rest).

(12:100). Words that end in word-final *-uww* are: عدو /ʕaduww/ 'enemy' (Q2:36, and *passim*), العدو /al-ʕaduww/ 'the enemy' (Q63:4), بالغدو /bi-l-ġuduww/ 'in the mornings' (Q7:205; Q13:15; Q24:36), لعفو /la-ʕafuww/ 'surely oft-pardoning' (Q22:60; Q58:2), عتو /ʕutuww/ 'arrogance' (Q67:21). The rule as formulated by Nöldeke et al. does not account for this, whereas the phonetic definition (which they object to): *wāw+ʔalif al-wiqāyah* denotes /ū/ or /aw/, does.

Diem (1979, § 47) tries retain the orthographic rule formulated by Nöldeke et al. while taking these forms into account. The orthographic rule he formulates, however, is sufficiently complex that it would take a linguist to be able to spell correctly. He suggests that the *ʔalif al-wiqāyah* is only used of the *ʔalif* could not be mistaken for the indefinite accusative. This does a reasonable job at explaining *laġwun* لغو (Q52:23) versus *laġwan* لغوا (Q56:25), although even this requires a rather complex process of the scribe of needing to work through counterfactual readings, in order to ensure the *ʔalif* does not get written accidentally. But it becomes especially difficult to square with the fact that the definite form does not take the *ʔalif al-wiqāyah* either, e.g. *al-laġwi* اللغو (Q23:3), a context where writing the *ʔalif al-wiqāyah* could never lead to a confusion with the indefinite accusative.

Moreover, Diem's rule is based on the mistaken assumption that *luʔluʔ* 'pearl' distinguishes the indefinite accusative *luʔluʔan* لولوا from the other cases لولو for *luʔluʔun* and *luʔluʔin*. This, however, is an idiosyncrasy of the CE. In the UT, this word always received the *ʔalif al-wiqāyah* also in the nominative and genitive form (see B.6).

Since indeed the use of *ʔalif al-wiqāyah* in these words is most readily explained phonetically, it being used whenever it is vocalic /ū/ or diphthongal /aw/, whereas when it is consonantal it is spelled without, it seems to me that contrary to the popular belief, the *ʔalif al-wiqāyah* does represent a phonetic value, rather than it being a purely orthographic practice (and certainly not a 'word-divider').

The reason why /ū/ and /aw/ are treated the same may be up for debate. First, it is of course possible that Quranic Arabic had lost final /aw/ of the verbs. In many modern dialects, e.g. Damascene Arabic, the final weak ending *-aw* has been lost completely and merged with *-ū*, e.g. *katabu* 'they wrote' and *banu* 'they built' not ***bano* (Cowell 1964, 55, 61). It is possible that these merged in Quranic Arabic although a more conservative reconstruction seems prudent.

Another point of comparison here is the treatment of diphthongs in the Old Arabic as reflected in the Safaitic inscriptional corpus. Safaitic orthography never writes vowels with *matres lectionis*. Thus, /ū/ is never expressed with ⟨w⟩. Perhaps surprisingly, the diphthong /aw/ is treated the same, and is likewise never expressed in writing whereas consonantal /w/ is expressed with

⟨w⟩. Thus, to the speakers of the Safaitic Old Arabic dialect, the diphthong /aw/ was treated as a true diphthong, that is more similar to a long vowel than a vowel+consonant sequence (Al-Jallad 2015, 37 f.).

The treatment of /aw/ and /ay/ as being distinct from other consonantal uses, and more akin to the long vowels, is also something we see in their treatment in the Arabic grammatical tradition. Thus, the *ḥurūf al-līn* are the use of *ʔalif*, *yāʔ* and *wāw* when a vowel precedes, in words like: *nār* 'fire'—envisioned as /naAr/, *dār* /daAr/ 'house', *fīl* /fiyl/ 'elephant', *qīla* /qiyla/ 'it is said', *ḥūla* /ḥuwla/ 'it was changed' *ġūl* /ġuwl/ 'ogre', *bayt* 'house' and *ṯawb* 'garment' (*Lisān*, 4117c).[20]

In light of this it seems quite likely, and phonologically plausible that the *ʔalif al-wiqāyah* was used as a tool to write word-final 'vocalic' uses of *wāw*, i.e. /ū/ and /aw/ as opposed to consonantal uses of *wāw*.

Another argument that Nöldeke et al. bring up to not take this as a phonological spelling, but rather a 'place *wāw* after every *wāw*' rule is that it is placed after verbs in the subjunctive, such as تعفوا ,يعفوا (Q2:237), لتتلوا (Q13:30), لن ندعوا (Q18:14), ان اتلوا (Q27:92) ليربوا (Q30:39), ليبلوا (Q47:4) نبلوا (Q47:31), which according to them must be verbs ending in *-uwa* not *-ū*. This presupposes that the Quranic reading traditions are an accurate representation of the language of the QCT, and final short vowels were not lost in such verbs. Neither of these assumptions are justified. The fact that these verbs are treated exactly the same as verbs that end in *-ū* in Classical Arabic rather speaks in favour of the loss of the final short vowels, something that I have also argued on different grounds in Chapter 7 and Van Putten & Stokes (2018).

An exceptionally difficult issue is the treatment of the *ʔalif al-wiqāyah* in roots that originally contained *hamzah*. While some of these behave exactly as expected, it is especially the historical sequences **-aʔu* and **āʔu* that paint a rather complex picture. Nöldeke et al. (2013, 419) object to seeing the *ʔalif al-wiqāyah* as a phonetic marking for /ū/ and /aw/ as against consonantal /w/, because many words of the type have final *hamzah*. This, again, presupposes that the Quranic reading traditions are an accurate reflection of the language of the QCT, which certainly in the case of the *hamzah* cannot be accepted. It is quite clear that Quranic Arabic had lost *hamzah* completely (see § 5.2) which

20 Ibn al-Ǧazarī (§ 948, § 950, § 1234, § 1343) makes an explicit distinction between *ḥurūf al-madd* (*ū, ī, ā*) and *ḥarfay al-līn* (*aw, ay*). This does not appear to be a distinction systematically made by the early grammarians like Sībawayh, which seems to use the terms indiscriminately, and often uses the compound term *hurūf al-madd wa-l-līn*. Even if it were an ancient distinction, the two terms are still clearly distinguished from uses of *wāw* and *yāʔ* were a consonant, rather than a vowel, precedes.

has given rise to many forms of artifical and pseudocorrect *hamzah* use all throughout the reading traditions (see Chapter 6 and § 3.6.1). In the following sections we will discuss the different contexts where *ʔalif al-wiqāyah* appears where the words etymologically contained a *hamzah*.

A.2.3.1 ʔalif al-wiqāyah for Stem Final *uʔ

When it comes to stem final **uʔ*, regardless of what vowel would historically follow, the word is always spelled with *ʔalif al-wiqāyah*. Thus امروا /imrū/ 'man' (Q4:176), لولوا /lūlū/ 'pearl' (Q52:24), اللولوا 'the pearl' (Q55:22; Q56:23). In the Cairo Edition some these forms of 'pearl' are spelled without *ʔalif al-wiqāyah*, but this not original to the UT, see B.6.

In the case of the indefinite لولوا 'pearl', the spelling is thus ambiguous whether it represents nominative/genitive /lūlū/ or accusative /lūluwā/. This ambiguity has indeed lead to disagreement in the Quranic reading traditions where the word may be read both as a genitive *luʔluʔin, lūluʔin* and as an accusative *luʔluʔan, lūluʔan* (Q22:23; Q35:33, see Ibn al-Ǧazarī, § 3652).

A.2.3.2 Treatment of Stem-Final *ūʔ

In nouns, etymological sequences of stem-final **ūʔ* behave exactly the same as stem-final /uww/, and thus are spelled without *ʔalif al-wiqāyah*: قرو /quruww/ (< *qurūʔ-*) 'menstruations' (Q2:228) سو /suww/ (< **sūʔ-*) 'the wickedness of …' (Q2:49, and *passim*), بالسو 'wickedness' (Q2:169, and *passim*), السو 'wickedness' (Q4:17, and *passim*). Of course, in the indefinite accusatives, these receive a final *ʔalif* as the mark of the indefinite accusative, e.g. سوا /suwwā/ 'wickedness' (Q4:110)

In the verbal system, however, we find these spelled with *ʔalif al-wiqāyah* in the two instances that it occurs. What is recited in the reading tradition as *la-tanūʔu* is spelled لتنوا 'would be a burden' (Q28:76) and what is recited as *tabūʔa* is spelled تبوا 'that you bear' (Q5:29). This is likely the result of analogical leveling due to a partial paradigmatic levelling of the II-*w*, III-*ʔ* imperfect paradigm with the III-*w* paradigm:

	Proto-Arabic		**Hamzaless Arabic**	
	III-w	II-w, III-ʔ	III-w	II-w, III-ʔ
3sg.m.	**yaʕlū*	**yabūʔu*	*yaʕlū*	**yabuww >> yabū*
3pl.m.	**yaʕlū(na)*	**yabuʔū(na)*	*yaʕlū(n)*	*yabū(n)*
3pl.f.	**yaʕlūna*	**yabuʔna*	*yaʕlūn*	*yaʕlūn*

The merger of II-*w*, III-*ʔ* verbs with III-*w* verbs towards ending in /-ū(n)/ may perhaps be visible in ليسوا /li-yasū/ (Q17:7) which is variously read as *li-yasūʔū* 'so that they will sadden', *li-yasūʔa* 'so that he will sadden' and *li-nasūʔa* 'so that we will sadden' (Ibn al-Ǧazarī, § 3447). If the majority reading *yasūʔū* was indeed the grammatical form intended, then it seems that the Quranic Arabic pronunciation of this was /li-yasū/.

A.2.3.3 Treatment of Word-Final *āʔū

Unlike Classical Arabic spelling, II-*w/y*, III-*ʔ* verbs in the in the perfect 3pl.m. form are spelled without an *ʔalif al-wiqāyah*, e.g. وباو /bāw/ 'they returned' (Q2:61); فاو /fāw/ 'they returned' (Q2:226),[21] جاو /ǧāw/ 'they came' (Q3:184) and also راو /rāw/ 'they saw'[22] (Q2:166; Q7:149; Q10:54; Q12:35; Q19:75; Q28:64; Q34:33; Q37:14; Q40:84, 85; Q42:44; Q62:11; Q72:24). The last of these is spelled راوا in the Cairo Edition, but this is not original to the UT, see B.7. As word-final /ū/ is otherwise always spelled with *ʔalif al-wiqāyah*, this suggests that word-final **āʔū* shifted to /āw/, rather than ***āwū* as Diem (1979, § 65) suggests.

Of exceptional status is اسوا 'they did evil' (Q30:10; Q53:31) which is universally recited as *ʔasāʔū* and thus we would rather expect the spelling **اساو. But indeed, in early Quranic manuscripts, the spelling is as it is found in the Cairo edition (see B.16). This spelling thus seems to suggest a pronunciation /ʔasaw/ rather than /ʔasāw/. As this is the only C-stem perfect in the 3pl.m. of stems of this type, it is difficult to be sure about this analysis.

A.2.3.4 Word-Final *aʔū

Plural hamzated verbs that historically end in **aʔ-ū* are likewise spelled with the *ʔalif al-wiqāyah* and are presumably pronounced /-aw/: تبروا /tabarraw/ 'they disown' (2:167), فادروا /fa-draw/ 'so avert!' (3:168), اقروا /iqraw/ 'recite!' (Q69:19), فاقروا /fa-qraw/ 'so recite!' (Q73:20).

One verb lacks the final *ʔalif al-wiqāyah*: تبوو /tabawwaw/ 'they settled' (Q59:9), thus showing similar behaviour as the verbs without an original **ʔ* that have /w/ before a final /-aw/, like اووا /ʔāwaw/ 'they gave shelter' (Q8:72, 74) and لووا /lawwaw, lawaw/ 'they turn aside' (Q63:5) discussed above.

---

21 It is worth appreciating how the QCT aptly distinguishes this word from فاوا /fāwū/ < **fa-ʔwū* 'so retreat!' (Q18:16), which would have been homographic had the Classical Arabic rule of the *ʔalif al-wiqāyah* been adhered to.

22 The Quranic Arabic perfect of 'to see' was /rāʔ/, not /raʔā/, see § 5.11 for a discussion.

A.2.3.5 Word-Final *aʔu(n)

As for **aʔu* sequences, verbs are overwhelmingly spelled with *wāw* and *ʔalif al-wiqāyah*, with a couple of exceptions where it is simply spelled with *ʔalif*, e.g. يبدوا /yabdaw/ 'he begins' (Q10:4, 34 (2×); Q27:64; Q30:11, 27), تفتوا /taftaw/ 'you will not cease' (Q12:85), يتفيوا /yatafayyaw/ 'it inclines' (Q16:48), اتوكوا 'I lean' /atawakkaw/ (Q20:18), لا تظموا /lā taẓmaw/ 'you will not be thirsty' (Q20:119) يدروا /yadraw/ 'he knows' (Q24:8), ما يعبوا /mā yaʕbaw/ 'will not concern himself' (Q25:77), ينشوا /yunaššaw/ 'is brought up' (Q43:18), ينبوا /yunabbaw/ 'will be informed' (Q75:13). There are three exceptions to this general rule, namely يستهزا /yustahzā/ 'it is being ridiculed' (Q4:140), يتبوا /yatabawwā/ 'he settles' (Q12:56), نتبوا /natabawwā/ 'we settle' (Q39:74).

For nouns, the *ʔalif* spelling is more common, although the spelling with *ʔalif al-wiqāyah* occurs as well. Thus for **al-malaʔu* 'the chieftains' we see: الملا /al-malā/ (Q7:60 66, 75, 88, 90, 109, 127; Q11:27; Q12:43; Q23:33; Q28:38; Q38:6) and الملوا /al-malaw/ (Q23:24; Q27:29, 32, 38). The other noun, from **nabaʔu* 'the news of', on the other hand, occurs more often in the *wāw* + *ʔalif al-wiqāyah* spelling: نبوا /nabaw/ (Q14:9; Q38:21; Q64:5) but نبا /nabā/ (Q9:70). The indefinite form **nabaʔun* 'news' is likewise spelled نبوا (Q38:67) (see B.8, B.9).

The presence of these spelling with final *wāw* and *ʔalif al-wiqāyah* seems to have an important implication for the relative chronology of final short vowels and the *hamzah*, as it requires that *hamzah* was lost before the final short vowels were lost. The forms that are simply spelled with *ʔalif* are perhaps analogical levelling of the default form, as verbs that end in *-ā* do not usually show a distinction between the imperfective and aorist/apocopate, and likewise nouns that end in *-ā* do not usually show a distinction between the nominative versus the accusative after the loss of final short vowels.[23]

A.2.3.6 Word-Final *āʔu

An especially vexing case of the issue of the *ʔalif al-wiqāyah* in words that etymologically end in *ʔalif mamdūdah* followed by the nominative or imperfect **-u*. First of all, it should be said that unlike the reflexes of **aʔu*—where the distribution is almost 50/50—the vast majority of the words in this group are simply spelled with the final *ʔalif*. However, there are 18 cases in the CE where a spelling with *wāw* + *ʔalif al-wiqāyah* shows up. However, a closer look at the data in early Quranic manuscripts shows that not all of these can be successfully reconstructed with that spelling in the UT. B.10, B.11, B.12, B.13, and B.14 tabulate

23 The genitive seems to show similar free variation, but there is only evidence for it in construct e.g. نباى المرسلين (Q6:34) but من نبا موسى (Q28:3).

the attestations of the relevant words as they appear in early manuscripts. Here I will give a summary of the conclusions we can draw from this examination. Below, I have also included a few cases where an unusual spelling occurs where the CE has *ʔalif*.

	Qirāʔāt	CE	UT
Q5:18	*ʔabnāʔu*	ابنوا الله	ابنا الله
Q6:5	*ʔambāʔu*	انبوا ما	انبوا ما
Q26:6	*ʔambāʔu*	انبوا ما	انبا ما (probably)
Q6:94	*šurakāʔu*	شركوا	شركا
Q42:21	*šurakāʔu*	شركوا	شركوا
Q30:13	*šufaʕāʔu*	شفعوا	شفعا
Q14:21	*aḍ-ḍuʕafāʔu*	الضعفوا	الضعفوا
Q40:47	*aḍ-ḍuʕafāʔu*	الضعفوا	الضعفوا
Q35:28	*al-ʕulamāʔu*	العلموا	العلموا
Q26:197	*ʕulamāʔu*	علموا بنى اسريل	علما بنى اسريل
Q60:4	*buraʔāʔu*	بروا	بروا
Q11:87	*našāʔu*	نشوا	نشوا or نشاو
Q37:106	*al-balāʔu*	البلوا	البلا
Q44:33	*balāʔun*	بلوا	بلا
Q40:50	*duʕāʔu*	دعوا الكفرين	دعا الكفرين
Q5:29	*ǧazāʔu*	جزوا الظلمين	جزاو الظلمين
Q5:33	*ǧazāʔu*	جزوا الذين	جزاو الذين
Q20:76	*ǧazāʔu*	جزا من	جزاو من
Q39:34	*ǧazāʔu*	جزا المحسنين	جزاو المحسنين
Q42:40	*ǧazāʔu*	جزوا سييه	جزاو سييه
Q59:17	*ǧazāʔu*	جزوا الظلمين	جزا الظلمين

Of the 19 words spelled with the *ʔalif al-wiqāyah*, only six appear to have been spelled as such in the UT, with one (نشوا Q11:87) being somewhat unclear. In five cases *ǧazāʔu* is not spelled as جزوا or جزا but as جزاو instead, whereas the spelling جزوا is entirely absent. The normal spelling of *ʔalif mamdūdah* nouns with simple *ʔalif* remains the majority spelling however (10 cases).

All cases of the او spelling are nouns in construct (a place where final short vowels appear to have been retained), and thus جزاو may very well represent /ǧazāwu/, with optional weakening of stem final *hamzah*, whereas جزا in identical context would represent /ǧazāʔu/. With a clitic following, this noun is variously spelled with and without the final glide in the UT (A.4.11). This spelling would then align with the proposed theory here that *wāw* not followed by *ʔalif al-wiqāyah* represent consonantal /w/. The only fly in the ointment is انبوا (Q6:5) which is likewise stands in construct but has the *ʔalif al-wiqāyah*. A possible solution is to not read this as a *ʔaCCāC* plural, but rather as a *ʔaCCuC* plural, i.e. **ʔanbuʔu* > *ʔanbū*, which would explain this spelling. Admittedly, however, this solution is rather *ad hoc*.

The remaining words with the *ʔalif al-wiqāyah* spelling are all diptotic CuCaCāʔu plurals that *do not* stand in construct. Among these nouns, spellings of this type are fairly common with, five times appearing with the *wāw+ʔalif al-wiqāyah* in the nominative, and 19 cases where it is spelled with *ʔalif*. Rabin (1951, 110, §w) speculates (following Vollers) that these forms represent /aḍḍuʕafō/ with a final vowel /ō/, and he seems to think that there is no special relationship between this spelling and the nominative. The fact that we never see such spellings in non-nominative contexts (which are by no means uncommon) however make this rather unattractive to assume that the original case vowel plays no role here.

However, it is similarly unlikely to take these spelling as representing /āwu/, or even /āʔu/ (as suggested by Diem 1981, §184a; and Nöldeke et al. 2013, 422). In contexts much less ambiguous than the very specific context of *CuCaCāʔu*-plurals, it seems to be clear that with such a sequence the spelling او would be expected, at least usually (see the reflexes of **āʔū*, and **ǧazāʔu* above). I would tentatively suggest that for reasons currently not entirely clear, the outcome of diptotic *CuCaCāʔu indeed is /CuCaCō/, creating a diptotic case distinction not dissimilar to the sound masculine plural with /CuCaCō/ in the nominative and /CuCaCāʔ/ (or /CuCaCā/?) in the oblique. Quranic Arabic then represents a stage where such nominatives have mostly, but not entirely, been analogically levelled.

The difference in behavior of the diptotic plurals may very well be because of their lack of nunation. Thus **-āʔu, *āʔa* became /-ō, -ā/, because there was no nunation to guard this contraction, whereas **-āʔun, *āʔin, *āʔan* were exempt from this contraction and became /-āʔ, -āʔ, -āʔā/. This may also explain why **ʔawliyāʔu-* when followed by pronominal clitics appears to behave as ending in *ʔalif maqṣūrah* /ʔawliyā-hum/ rather than *ʔalif mamdūdah* **/ʔawliyāwu-hum/ (see A.4.11). Without further data this hypothesis will have to remain speculative.

A.2.3.7 ربا ,الربوا

A final word whose spelling appears to contain an *ʔalif al-wiqāyah* is الربوا 'usury' (Q2:275 (3×), 276, 278; Q3:130; Q4:161), which in the indefinite appears spelled as ربا (Q30:39) (see B.15). This alternation between وا and ا spelling may at first glance seem similar the treatment of the *CuCaCāʔu plurals discussed above. However, unlike the nouns above, this spelling is not unique to the nominative, but is found in all cases but the nominative, e.g. الذين ياكلون الربوا "those who devour usury (acc.)" (Q2:275), مثل الربوا "like usury (gen.)" (Q2:275).

It is quite unclear what the etymological background of this word is and how to interpret it. In the Quranic reading traditions it is either read as *ar-ribā* or *ar-ribē* (Ibn al-Ǧazarī, § 1974), but on the basis of the spelling with *wāw*, it has been argued that it should be /ar-ribō/ (Rabin 1951, 105; Nöldeke et al. 2013, 418). As Rabin points out, this is an opinion, already endorsed by al-Zamaxšarī (*Kaššāf*, I, 319). However, there are no other stems with /ō/ as a word-final vowel, regardless of case—and there is no obvious etymological origin for this vowel to appear in this context. As shown by Van Putten (2017a), **awV-* yields /ā/ in Quranic Arabic, not /ō/, and thus we would expect *ar-ribawa to have yielded **الربا /ar-ribā/, or perhaps even الربى /ar-ribē/.[24] Due to the unusual position of this word, Rabin (1951, 109, §u) seems justified in assuming that the word is likely a borrowing of some kind, but the exact linguistic origin remains unclear.

A.2.3.8 Summary

The table below summarizes the distribution of the different spelling of *ʔalif al-wiqāyah* and *wāw* (as well as the spellings او and simply ا). Excluded from this table are several highly frequent particles which are never spelled with *ʔalif al-wiqāyah*. These are هو, او and لو. In the cases where the distribution is not absolute, I have shaded the cell with the dominant spelling.

	**ū, *uwa*	**uʔv(n)*	**aw*	**aʔū*	**aʔu(n)*	**āʔu(n)*	**āʔū*	**uwwv(n)*	**ūʔv(n)*	*Cwv(n)
وا	3461	3(+2?)	218	6	22	6(+1?)	2		2	
او						5(+1?)	20			
و	1		3 (*-waw)(+1?)	1 (*-waʔū)				31	47	16
ا					16	221				

24 Some Arab Grammarians appear to have argued that unlike *CaCaw- stems, like عصا "stick", originally *CiCaw- and *CuCaw- stems shifted their final root consonant to *y*, something that also happened in Quranic Arabic الضحى /aḍ-ḍuḥē/ 'the forenoon' (Q93:1) and العلى /al-ʕulē/ 'highest (plural)' (Q20:4). For a brief discussion see Ibn al-Ǧazarī (§ 1974).

It should be clear that the two spellings وا and و(ا) are in quite strict complementary distribution, clearly suggesting a phonetic origin for these spellings. The only environment where such spellings appear to be in competition is in the *-āʔu(n) sequence. However, as we saw above even here the two spellings appear to be mostly in complementary distribution, where او is reserved for triptotic nominative nouns in construct, and وا is reserved for diptotic nouns in the nominative definite and indefinite form. It therefore seems quite reasonable to suggest that indeed وا is used to write /-ū/ and /-aw/, whereas و marks word-final consonantal /w/.

A.2.4 *Spelling of* la- *'Indeed' as* لا

In the Quran the asseverative *la-* is frequently spelled لا before 1sg. form of the verb.[25] It is attested once in the CE in لااذبحنه /la-ʔaḏbaḥanna-h/ 'I will surely slaughter him' (Q27:21), but attested in quite a few more places in Early Quranic Manuscripts, for example فلااقطعن /fa-la-ʔuqaṭṭiʕann/ 'So surely I will cut off' (Q20:71 in SM1a); لاكيدن /la-ʔakīdann/ 'surely I will plan' (Q21:57 in W, T[26]); لاملن /la-ʔamlānna/ 'I will surely fill' (Q32:13 in W,[27] T;[28] Q38:85 in BL); ولاغوينهم /wa-la-ʔuġwiyanna-hum/ 'and surely I will mislead them' (Q15:39 in Arabe 334c); ولامرنهم /wa-la-ʔāmuranna-hum/ 'I will surely command them' (Q4:119 in W, Arabe 330b); ولاادخلنكم 'I will certainly admit you' (Q5:12 in Arabe 324c);[29] لااقتلنك /la-ʔaqtulanna-k/ 'I will surely kill you' (Q5:27 in W,[30] CPP, BL[31]); لااتينهم /la-ʔatiyanna-hum/ 'I will surely come to them' (Q7:17 in S, SM1a, K); لااصلبنكم /la-ʔuṣallibanna-kum/ 'I will surely crucify you' (Q7:124 in CPP,[32]); لاازيدنكم /la-ʔazīdanna-kum/ 'I will surely increase you' (Q14:7 K[33]); لااعذبنه /la-ʔuʕaḏḏibanna-hū/ 'I will surely punish him' (Q27:21 in W, T).

Besides these extra places in the Quran where we attest such spellings, there are also some disagreements among the reading traditions about whether certain phrases should be read with *lā* or asseverative *la-* that seem to stem from this spelling practice. For example, Qunbul ʕan Ibn Kaṯīr reads Q10:16 لو شا الله

25 Blau (1967, § 8.2) gives several clear examples of this same orthographic feature in early Christian Arabic, e.g. لااقرن 'I shall admit', لااعدلن 'I shall return', لاابيعنك للبربر 'I swear I shall sell you to the Berbers', لااصنعها 'I shall do it', etc.

26 The extra *ʔalif* has been removed.

27 The extra *ʔalif* has been removed.

28 The extra *ʔalif* has been added by a later hand.

29 The extra *ʔalif* has been removed.

30 The extra *ʔalif* has been added by a later hand.

31 The extra *ʔalif* has been added by a later hand.

32 The extra *ʔalif* has faded, and was perhaps removed on purpose.

33 The extra *ʔalif* has been removed.

ما تلوته ولاادريكم به *law šāʔa llāhu mā talawtu-hū ʕalaykumū wa-la-ʔadrā-kumū bi-hī* "and if Allah had willed it he would have not have recited it to you, and he would have made it known to you" rather than reading ولاادريكم به as *wa-lā ʔadrā-kum bi-hī* "nor would he have made it known to you" (Ibn al-Ǧazarī, § 3247).[34] Qunbul ʕan Ibn Kaṯīr also reads لااقسم بيوم القيمه (Q75:1) as *la-ʔuqsimu bi-yawmi l-qiyāmah* 'I definitely swear by the day of resurrection', while the rest reads *lā ʔuqsimu bi-yawmi l-qiyāmah* 'No! I swear by the day of resurrection' (Ibn al-Ǧazarī, § 3247).[35]

Sidky (2021, 181) points out that it was already noticed early on that this surprising early orthography could yield significant ambiguities as both the asseverative and negative indicative would end up being spelled exactly the same, which al-Farrāʔ criticitices as being "of the terrible spelling practices of those of old" (*wa-huwa min sūʔi hiǧāʔi l-ʔawwalīna*) (Al-Farrāʔ *Maʕānī*, I, 295 f.).

The spelling as لا is not just restricted to cases of the asseverative particle before a 1sg. verb, but can occur before any word that starts with a *hamzah*; Al-Dānī (*Muqniʕ*, 36) reports the spelling لااوضعوا 'they were active' (Q9:47), which is indeed attested in early manuscripts (GK; BL; Rampur Raza). And likewise, for the asseverative particle combined with the preposition الى we find the spelling لاالى (Q3:158: S, W,[36] Q47, GK,[37] CPP; Q37:68: W, Arabe 333d), as pointed out by Diem (1979, § 26). A close examination of early manuscripts will likely uncover even more cases.

A.2.5 *The Prepositions* ʕalā, ḥattā *and* ladā *Are Often Spelled* حتا، علا، لدا

It is common in early copies of the Kufic C style to write the prepositions *ʕalā* and *ḥattā* as علا and حتا rather than the now standard على and حتى (Cellard 2015, 208–213), manuscripts of this type appear to always be of Medinan regionality (Cellard 2015, 168–186; see also van Putten 2019a, see especially 356, note 122). This alternate spelling is also found once in the CE for *ladā*: لدى (Q40:18) and لدا (Q12:25). These three words are exactly the words with *ʔalif maqṣūrah* that reading traditions that have III-*w ʔimālah* (see § 3.3.3.3) normally read as /ā/, despite their spelling (Ibn al-Ǧazarī, § 1973),[38] and *ḥattā* is explicitly mentioned

34 Surprisingly, this reading is not mentioned by Ibn Muǧāhid (121), despite Qunbul being his direct teacher.

35 Most works mention explicitly that Q75:2 ولا اقسم بالنفس اللوامه is read as *wa-lā ʔuqsimu bi-n-nafsi l-lawāmah* 'And nay! I swear by the reproaching soul' even by Qunbul, although here too a reading *wa-la-ʔuqsimu* seems more natural.

36 The *ʔalif* has been removed.

37 The *ʔalif* has been removed.

38 Also, the preposition الى is read as /ʔilā/ rather /ʔilē/, but this word is not commonly spelled الا (but see the corrected spelling of الا to الى in Q46:5 in CA1).

as being an exception by Sībawayh (IV, 135). It seems to be the case that these words in Quranic Arabic were probably pronounced /ḥattā/, /ʕalā/ and /ladā/, despite their spelling. The spelling with ى for these words should probably be considered historical spellings, rather than reflecting the pronunciation of Quranic Arabic (van Putten 2017a, 62).[39]

The most likely explanation for this exceptional spelling of /ā/ with ى can probably be explained through their respective etymologies. It seems likely that in the history of Quranic Arabic these prepositions were **ʔilay*, **ʕalay*, **laday*, and **ḥattay*.[40] When these would be combined with a noun starting with the definite article, it would create a **aya* triphthong which would then contract to **ē* and get subsequently shortened to *a* in a closed syllable, e.g. **ʕalay al-rağuli* > **ʕalē l-rağuli* > *ʕala l-rağul*. From this realization *ʕala* before definite articles, one could easily get a preposition *ʕalā* through backformation.

A.2.6 *Words Starting with /l/ Preceded by the Definite Article.*

The definite article when it precedes a word that starts with ل, is sometimes written with only a single *lām*. This is regular for اليل 'night', and was probably original for الولوا 'the pearls', which is written with only a single *lām* in two rather early manuscripts (see B.6). All forms of the relative pronoun in the Quran are spelled with a single *lām*, rather than the Classical Arabic practice which only maintains this spelling for the singular and masculine plural forms, whereas all other forms write it with two *lāms* (see A.4.5).

The vast majority of the words whose stem starts with *lām* however, are written with two *lāms*, most notably, of course, ٱللَّٰه /aḷḷāh/. The fact that even before the *lām* the definite article is usually spelled morphologically rather than phonetically (unlike Nabataean Arabic) was one of the reasons for Van Putten (2019b, 15) to suggest that the definite article was probably assimilated in Quranic Arabic, as it is in Classical Arabic, and that at the very least it cannot tell us that it was unassimilated as it is in the Damascus Psalm fragment.

A.2.7 *Historical* Hamzah *Spelling with* ای

Šayʔ 'thing', in early Quranic manuscripts, is written both شى and شاى, apparently haphazardly but with a clear preference to spelling it with *ʔalif*. In the

39 Such spellings also occur in the early papyri (Hopkins 1984, § 10d, only mentioning حتا) and Christian Arabic (Blau 1967, § 10.1). Considering the special position of these prepositions in the reading traditions and the grammarians, the spelling of these prepositions cannot be used as evidence that the vowel /ē/ and /ā/ have merged (*pace* Hopkins 1984, § 12c; Blau 2002, § 16).

40 On the etymology of *ḥattā*, see Al-Jallad (2017b).

Cairo edition لشاى is attested in Q18:23. There is no special significance to this position in early manuscripts, where the spelling may occur elsewhere, and some manuscripts spell it لشى in Q18:23 as well (e.g. SM1a).[41] I side with Diem (1980, §127–128) that this is likely a historical spelling. There are many cases where an original *ʔ next to a *y or in a position where it would become a *y* is spelled with the orthographic اى. Other cases of this found in the Cairo edition are:

الملايه/ملايهم /al-malayi-h(um)/ 'his/their chiefs' (Q7:103; Q10:75, 83; Q11:97; Q23:46; Q28:32; Q43:46)
جاى /ǧīy/ 'it was brought' (Q39:69; Q89:23)
من نباى المرسلين /min nabay(i) al-mursalīn/ 'of the tidings of the messengers' (Q6:34)
افاين /a-fa-(y)in/ 'but if not …' (Q3:144; Q21:34)
مايه، ماتين /miyah, miyatayn/ 'one/two hundred' (Q2:259 (2×), 261; Q8:65 (2×), 66 (2×); Q18:25; Q24:2; Q37:147).
السواى /as-sūwē/ 'the evil' (Q30:10)
يايس، تايسوا /yayas, tayasū/ 'he despairs/(do not) despair' (Q12:87 (2×); Q13:31).[42]

In early Quranic manuscripts, the verb شا 'to want' and جا 'to come' in the suffix conjugation also occasionally employs this spelling:

شايت 'you want' (SM1a, Q18:77; T, Q24:62) شايتم 'you (pl.) want' (Arabe 331, Q2:223; DAM 01–21.3, Q7:161). جايت 'you came' (T, Q19:27)

Several other examples have been identified by Puin (2011, 164).

سايل /sīl/ 'it was asked' (Q2:108, in S, DAM 01–28.1)
ساى /sīy/ 'he was distressed' (Q11:77, in S)

---

41 The spelling شاى is also well-attested in the early Islamic Papyri (Hopkins 1984, §15d).

42 Diem (1980, §127) explores the possibility that this might in fact represent /yāyas/, the outcome of the metathesized root *ʔayisa* 'to despair' as attested in several modern dialects, as well as in the Classical Arabic lexicons. He suggests this is not likely, as the perfect form does not point to this metathesis. I tentatively follow this conclusion, although it could be that *yʔ* > *ʔy* was a regular metathesis, which eventually gave rise to the perfect stem being analogically remodeled towards *ʔayisa*. This other reading with metathesis is possible, and is in fact attested among the reading traditions, al-Bazzī ʕan Ibn Kaṯīr reads *istāyasū* (Q12:80), *tāyasū*, *yāyasu* (Q12:87), *istāyasa* (Q12:110), *yāyas* (Q13:31), (Ibn al-Ǧazarī §1528). The metathesized perfect form of this verb is attested in the early Islamic papyri (Hopkins 1984, §56).

رايي /rūyā-y/ 'my vision' (Q12:100 in CPP; W; SM1a; Q12:43 in W, SM1a, GK)
بايس /bayyis/ 'wretched' (Q7:165 in A6140a[43])

An apparent application of this same spelling practice is found in the spelling of classical *as-sayyiʔah*. While this is spelled السييه in the CE, occasionally in early manuscripts we find السايه, with the etymological *ʔalif* seemingly before the wrong consonant in terms of the seat of the *hamzah*.

Q7:95 السايه /as-sayyiyah/ (CPP; BL)

A similar process is found on word-boundaries. Whenever a word is preceded by *bi-* or *li-* and the consonant *after* the *ʔalif* is a *yāʔ*, a second *yāʔ* is written. In the CE this only occurs three times بايم /bi-(y)āyyām/ 'in the days of …' (Q14:5), بايد /bi-(y)ayd/ 'with strength' (Q51:47), بايكم /bi-(y)ayyi-kum/ 'which of you' (Q68:6). But this practice is much more widespread in early Quranic manuscripts than it is in the CE. The spelling is especially common in the phrase بايت 'with the signs/verses of …' which is subjected to a rigorous study by Déroche (2014, 47). Also, the singular بايه 'with the sign/verse of …' is usually spelled in this manner. There are, at least, occasionally cases where the same spelling is employed after the prefix *li-* (van Putten 2018, 111).

bi-ʔayyi is invariably spelled as بايي in early manuscripts, as can be easily seen in the oft-repeated فبايي in Q55 (see Arabe 331, W, SM1a, Top etc.). In other places in the Quran, we likewise find the same spelling regularly: فبايي (Q7:185; Q45:6; Q53:55; Q77:50), بايي (Q31:34; Q81:9) and لايي (Q77:12).

Van Putten (2018, 109f.) suggested that these spellings are hybrid spellings that represent both the original etymological *ʔalif*, but use the *yāʔ* to point out that these forms were now pronounced as /bi-yāyāt/, /bi-yayyi/ etc. Some evidence for this reading is furthermore found in the Quranic reading traditions. Al-ʔaṣbahānī ʕan Warš ʕan Nāfiʕ is said to have pronounced every instance of *fa-bi-ʔayyi* as [fabiyayyi], and there is some disagreement within his transmission whether *bi-ʔayyi-kum* (Q68:6) and *bi-ʔayyi* (Q31:34) are read this way (Ibn al-Ǧazarī, § 1492–1493). There is however no mention of Q81:9, nor *li-ʔayyi* Q77:12, and nothing on *bi-ʔāyāt*, *bi-ʔaydin* or *bi-ʔayyām*.

While Van Putten (2018) does not comment on this, it is very striking that whenever such a spelling takes place across word boundaries, it invariably

43 It is possible that the original reading of this word was rather /bāyis/, something both بايس and the more generally attested بيس also supports as a reading. There does not seem to be a significantly difference in meaning between *bāʔis* and *baʔīs*.

involves a word that starts with ا and has ى later in the word. This is unlikely to be a coincidence. Perhaps the loss of word-initial *ʔ did not undergo the same developments as word-internal *ʔ (something suggested by other parts of its orthographic behaviour as well) and a secondary sound-law takes place where *ʔ > y /i_ǎy. The rather specific context in which the sound law takes place, however, is *ad hoc* and another solution may be thought of, but it seems that any explanation must account for the fact that this spelling practice seems to be conditioned by a *y* later in the word.[44]

A.2.8 *The Spelling of* dāwūd *as* دواد *and* ruʔūs *as* رواس

A rather puzzling spelling practice which may be related to the marking of historical *hamzah* when it stands next to *ū* can be found in the name *dāwūd*. In the CE this name is spelled داود, but in early manuscripts it is frequently spelled دواد (Marx and Jocham 2015, 29ff.). It seems possible that this reversed order of the *ʔalif* and *wāw* represents an alternative pronunciation of the name: /duwād/ or /duʔād/,[45] similar to the appearance of the spelling ابرهم and ابرهيم for *ʔibrāhām* and *ʔibrāhīm* (van Putten 2020b). Unlike the spellings of ابرهم, ابرهيم no clear pattern arises of the two spellings being used in fixed places across manuscripts. In general, manuscripts either have the دواد or داود spelling (see B.17).

Such an explanation is less obvious for the representation of *ruʔūs* however. It likewise occurs spelled as رواسهم in two manuscripts (Q14:43, Is. 1615 I, CA1). Here we can hardly argue that the pronunciation was *ruwās* or *ruʔās*. It seems then that, for whatever reason the وا sequence may reflect a historical sequence *ʔū, with the etymological position of the *ʔ transposed, perhaps because it was no longer pronounced, much like what we saw with the historical spelling اى for words that involved *yāʔ*, where the *ʔalif* also often does not stand in the right place, e.g. جاى < *ǧīʔa. If this is also the case for دواد, the spelling may still represent /dāwūd/, which would then have come from an earlier *dāʔūd.[46] Note however, other manuscripts occasionally attest an etymological *hamzah* spelling for words with similar syllable structure, where the *ʔalif* does stand in

44 This spelling convention on word-boundaries is not reported on for non-Quranic early Islamic Arabic, but it is at least found on the Dome of the Rock inscription which spells as بايات (dotted as such!) (Kessler 1970, 6).

45 Cf. the Muʕtazilī ʔaḥmad b. ʔabī Duʔād (d. 240 AH), see EI^2: s.v. Aḥmad b. Abī Du'ād. Of course, we may also entertain the idea that this is a later spelling pronunciation and in fact Ibn ʔabī Dāʔūd was intended.

46 Which in turn could, in fact, come from *dāwūd* again, due to the presence of a shift of *wu* and *wū* to *ʔu*/*ʔū* well-attested in Classical Arabic, and also found in the QCT once (see A.3.11).

the etymologically correct position, e.g. براوسكم (Q5:6, ms.or.fol. 4313), likewise *yaʔūsan* is spelled with a historical spelling ياوسا (Q17:83, Or. 2165) (see B.18).

A.2.9 *Plene Spelling of Short* u

Occasionally, the Quran attests examples where what was likely short *u* is spelled with a و. This is well attested in forms of the plural demonstrative element **ʔul-* such as اوليك /ulāyik/ 'those', اولا /ulāʔ/ 'those'; اولوا /ulū/ 'those of (masculine, nominative)'; اولى /ulī/ 'those of (masculine, genitive/accusative)'; اولات /ulāt/ 'those of (feminine)'. For words of this type, this spelling practice continues to be the regular spelling all throughout the written history of Arabic.[47] As it is unusual to find short vowels being spelled with a long vowel sign in the QCT, as this is not at all the norm, one might consider the possibility that these forms in Quranic Arabic originally had long vowels, as per their spelling. This option appears to be supported by Rabin (1951, 153), who however does not comment on it explicitly and also says that Classical Arabic has *ʔūlāʔi*, which to my knowledge only occurs with a short vowel (Fischer 2002, § 7, n. 7). However, the short vowel is in better agreement with the cognates of this plural morpheme in other Semitic languages, which all universally point to a short vowel. The spelling of short *u* with و is attested once in a context other than the plural pronoun base *ʔul-*, namely, ساوريكم /sa-urī-kum/ 'I will show you' (Q7:145; Q21:37).

A.2.10 *Defective Spelling of Word-Final Long Vowels before* ʔalif al-waṣl

While long vowels before *ʔalif al-waṣl* are generally spelled plene, it appears that these long vowels were shortened, at least, before the *ʔalif al-waṣl* of the definite article, and this shortening is on occasion expressed in the orthography, as pointed out by Nöldeke et al. (2013, 409).

The vocative *ʔayyuhā* is usually spelled ايها in the QCT, but a spelling ايه occasionally occurs. In all cases this happens in front of a noun with the definite article, ايه المومنون 'O believers' (Q24:31), يايه الساحر 'O sorcerer!' (Q43:49) and ايه الثقلان 'O two dependents' (Q55:31).[48] To my knowledge no other cases of defective final *ā*.

For defective *ū* we find: يدع الانسان 'man supplicates' (Q17:11), ويمح الله 'and God eliminates' (Q42:24), يدع الداع 'the caller calls' (Q54:6), سندع الزبانيه 'we will call the angels of Hell' (Q96:18), صلح المومنين 'the righteous ones of the believers' (Q66:4).

---

47 Puin (2011, 150) identified several early Quranic manuscripts where words of this type are occasionally spelled without the و, e.g. فاليك /fa-ulāyik/, الى /ulī/.

48 Cf. early Christian Arabic with the same practice (Blau 1967, § 9.2).

Most common, however, is the shortening of *ī* before *ʔalif al-waṣl*: سوف يوت الله 'God will bring' (Q4:146), نتج المومنين 'we save the believers' (Q10:103), بالواد المقدس 'in the sacred valley' (Q20:12; Q79:16), لهاد الذين 'verily a guide of those who' (Q22:54), واد النمل 'the valley of ants' (Q27:18), اتين الله 'God has given me' (Q27:36),[49] شطى الواد الايمن 'the rightmost side of the valley' (Q28:30), بهد العمى 'guide of the blind' (Q30:53),[50] يردن الرحمن 'The beneficent intends for me' (Q36:23), صال الجحيم 'the burning one in hell' (Q37:163), يعباد الذين 'O my slaves who …' (Q39:10), الجوار المنشيت 'the elevated ships' (Q55:24),[51] الجوار الكنس 'running, disappearing' (Q81:16).

A special case is يقص الحق (Q6:57) which is variously read as *yaqḍi l-ḥaqq* and *yaquṣṣu l-ḥaqq* (Ibn al-Ǧazarī, § 3029). Only in the former option are we dealing with the shortening of *ī* before *ʔalif al-waṣl*. However, I agree with Sadeghi (2013) that the second reading is probably original.

A.3 Phonology

A.3.1 *Consonants*

The consonantal system as can be reconstructed for Quranic Arabic based on the QCT has been illustrated in Van Putten (2019b). The table below reproduces the reconstructed phonological system, when the sign used in the transcription does not correspond to the IPA realization, the IPA realization is written behind it. In some cases, I have simplified technically ambiguous realizations of sounds to the most likely realization based on modern *taǧwīd* realizations. For a more detailed discussion of other likely realizations, I refer the reader to Van Putten (2019b).

The ⁼ sign, which usually marks 'unaspirated' is here to be understood as the glottis standing in prephonation state, i.e. a somewhat closed glottis which stops strong turbulent airflow (which leads to aspiration in stops and "voicelessness" in fricatives). For the stops this auditorily presents itself as unaspirated stops, and for the ṣ which is likewise *maǧhūr*, as a fricative without turbulent airflow (van Putten 2019b, 7–12).

---

49 See Van Putten (forthcoming) for a discussion on the spelling of this word and other cases of *ʔalif maqṣūrah* followed by the clitic *-ni/nī*.

50 Read by Ḥamzah as *tahdi l-ʕumya* (Ibn al-Ǧazarī: § 3896).

51 المنشات in the CE, but this is an idiosyncrasy of this edition. See A.4.10 for a discussion on the spelling of this adjective.

	Labial	Dental	Lateral	Palatal/Dorsal	Pharyngeal	Glottal
Stop	*b*	*t* [tʰ], *d*, *ṭ* [tˤ⁼]		*k* [kʰ], *ǧ* [ɟ], *q* [q⁼]		(*ʔ*)
Fricative	*f*	*ṯ* [θ], *ḏ* [ð], *ẓ* [ðˤ]	ḍ [ɮˤ]	*x* [χ], *ġ* [ʁ]	*ḥ* [ħ], *ʕ*	
Sibilant		*s*, *z*, *ṣ* [sˤ⁼]		*š* [ʃ]		
Nasal	*m*	*n*				
Approximant		*r*	*l*	*y* [j], *w*		

A.3.2 *The Loss of the Hamzah*

As has long been recognized, the orthography of the Quran seems to reflect a dialect that has lost the *hamzah* in most environments. In an earlier article, I have shown that rhyme confirms that this is not purely an orthographic idiosyncrasy, but is an accurate reflection of how the Quran was pronounced (van Putten 2018).[52] The table below illustrates the main phonological developments caused by the loss of *hamzah*, along with examples.

Development	Example
***Cʔv > Cv**	**yasʔalu* > يسل /yasal/ (Q70:10)
	**al-ʔafʔidati* > الافده /al-afidah/ (Q104:7)
	**ǧuzʔun* > جز /ǧuz/ (Q15:44)
***vʔC > v̄C**	**yaʔkulu* > يا كل /yākul/ (Q10:24)
	**yuʔminu* > يومن /yūmin/ (Q2:232)
	**aḏ-ḏiʔbu* > الذيب /aḏ-ḏīb/ (Q12:13)
***Uʔ > i/uWW**	**barīʔun* > بري /bariyy/ or /barī/[53] (Q6:19)
	**sūʔun* > سو /suww/ (Q3:174)
Final *āʔ remains unchanged	**as-samāʔi* > السما /as-samāʔ/ (Q14:24)
	**ʔinšāʔan* > انشا /inšāʔā/ (Q56:35)
***aʔa > ā**	**saʔala* > سال /sāl/ (Q70:1)
***aʔi/u > aWi/u?**	**baʔisa* > بيس /bayis/ (Q11:99)
	**naqraʔu-hū* > نقروه /naqrawu-h/ (Q17:93)
***i/uʔă > i/uWā**	**muʔaḏḏinun* > موذن /muwaḏḏin/ (Q7:44)
	**fiʔatun* > فيه /fiyah/ (Q3:13)

52 On the topic of the *hamzah* spelling see also Diem (1976; 1980, § 116–128).

53 See A.3.9.

(*cont.*)

Development	Example
*i/uʔU > U	**mustahziʔūn* > مستهزون /mustahzūn/ (Q2:14) **al-mustahziʔīna* > المستهزين /al-mustahzīn/ (Q15:95) **ruʔūsakum* > روسكم /rūsakum/ (Q2:196)
*aʔU > aW	**yaṭaʔūna* > يطون /yaṭawn/ (Q9:120) **baʔīsin* > بيس /bays/[54] (Q7:165)
*āʔi/u > āWi/u	*sāʔilun > سايل /sāyil/ (Q70:1) *duʕāʔu-kum > دعاوكم (Q25:77)

A.3.3 *Vowels*

As for the vowel system of Quranic Arabic, it shares with Classical Arabic the short vowel system *a, i, u* and likewise shares the long vowels *ā, ī* and *ū*. However, the Classical Arabic *ā* corresponds to *ā, ē* and *ō*. The table below represents the phonemic system of Quranic Arabic that can be reconstructed from the QCT.

	Front		Central		Back/Rounded	
High	*i*	*ī*			*u*	*ū*
Mid		*ē*				*ō*
Low			*a*	*ā*		

Besides the Classical Arabic long vowels /ā/, /ī/ and /ū/, Quranic Arabic had a fourth phonemic vowel which was written with a *yāʔ* and likely pronounced as /ē/, e.g. هدى /hadē/ 'he guided' (*passim*). It is clear from the rhyme that this was a separate sound from final /ā/ written with *ʔalif*, § 5.8, as they do not cross-rhyme. This fourth vowel /ē/ should not be seen as a variant of *ā*, which its Arabic name *ʔalif maqṣūrah bi-ṣūrat al-yāʔ* 'the shortened *ʔalif* with the shape of the *yāʔ*' might suggest, nor should its pronunciation *ʔimālat al-ʔalif*

54 This is the reading of Ibn Šihāb al-Zuhrī (Ibn Xālawayh *muxtaṣar*, 47). Some other possible interpretations of this rasm, e.g. /bayyis/ seems possible too. For a discussion see A.2.2.

naḥw al-yāʔ 'The leaning of *ā* in the direction of *ī*' be understood as a historical process, which was not the concern of the Arab grammarians. Instead, these are purely descriptive terms. Van Putten (2017a) has shown that not only is the *ʔalif maqṣūrah bi-ṣūrat al-yāʔ* in the Quran pronounced differently, it also has a different historical background from the *ʔalif maqṣūrah bi-ṣūrat al-ʔalif* and is fully phonemic so that it cannot be understood as an allophone. The table below gives an overview of some of the instances of Quranic Arabic /ē/ and the etymological origins from which it develops. It likewise shows that the outcome of the original triphthongs containing **y* is orthographically distinct from those that contain **w* and original **ā*.[55]

QCT	Quranic Arabic	Proto-Arabic	Classical Arabic	Gloss
هدى	/hadē/	**hadaya*	هَدَى	'he guided'
هدى	/hudē/	**hudayun*	هُدًى	'guidance'
ذكرى	/ḏikrē/	**ḏikrayu*	ذِكْرَى	'a reminder'
هديه	/hadē-h/	**hadaya-hu*	هَدَاهُ	'he led him'
تقيه	/tuqēh/	**tuqayata*	تُقَاةً	'a precaution'
دعا	/daʕā/	**daʕawa*	دَعَا	'he invoked'
دعاه	/daʕā-h/	**daʕawa-hu*	دَعَاهُ	'he called him'

Verbs with final /ē/ in early Quranic manuscripts, dissimilate to /ā/, written as ـا or defectively when the pronominal suffix *-nī/-ni* follows (ـنى or ـن). This same development happens when the 1sg. suffix *-ya* (ـى) follows a noun that ends in /ē/. Van Putten (forthcoming) has argued that, since this spelling difference is phonetically conditioned, we are likely dealing with a regular dissimilation of *ē* to *ā* in the vicinity of *ī* or *y*. This difference in spelling has mostly been lost in the CE, where these verbs and nouns are treated exactly the same before the

55 The Cairo Editions contain a few exceptions to this orthographic practice. For example, *iǧtabā-hu* (Q16:121) is spelled اجتبه; Early Quranic manuscripts, however consistently spell this اجتبيه (e.g. B, W, BL, SM). The same is true for the same word in Q68:50 (e.g. W, SM). Likewise, *ʕuqbā-hā* (Q91:15) spelled عقبها in the Cairo Edition, is simply found as عقبيها in early manuscripts (e.g. SM, G) (see B.27). However, while مضى /maḍē/ 'departed' (Q43:8) has the expected spelling in the CE, early Quranic manuscripts surprisingly seem to converge on the spelling مضا (see B.28).

1sg. suffixes as before any of the other pronominal suffixes. For a full overview see Van Putten (forthcoming) but, one finds for example Q7:143: ترانى (W; SM1a; GK; BL; CPP; 330g; DAM29 ترنى) where the CE has تريني.

A small group of nouns in Quranic Arabic are written with a final ـوه. These are صلوه 'prayer' (*passim*), زكوه 'alms' (*passim*), حيوه 'life' (*passim*), منوه 'Manāt' (Q53:20), بالغدوه 'in the morning' (Q6:52; Q18:28); النجوه 'the salvation' (Q40:41) and كمشكوه 'like a niche' (Q24:35). While these words are often explained as representing an orthographic innovative way of writing word-internal /ā/, based on Aramaic spellings of some of these words, Al-Jallad (2017c) shows that this explanation is not very convincing. It is clear that all the words of Arabic origin in this list originally had a sequence **awat* which monophthongized to /-ōh/ (see also § 5.3).

Another word that may have had the phoneme /ō/ is الربوا /ar-ribō/ 'usury' (Q2:275 (3×), 276, 278; Q3:130; Q4:161). The spelling with *wāw ʔalif* while in Classical Arabic ending up as *ā*, similar to the /ō/ of /ṣalōh/ becoming *ṣalāh, ṣalāt* may suggest that this word was /ar-ribō/. The etymology of this word is rather unclear (Rabin 1951, 109, § v), and current accounts of the phoneme /ō/ do not predict native words to have /ō/ in word-final position (Al-Jallad 2017c; van Putten 2017a). There is also no forthcoming explanation why the indefinite form of this noun apparently shifts this /ō/ to /ā/, as it is spelled ربا (Q30:39). Some nouns that etymologically end in a stem **-āʔ* may have shifted to **-āʔu* to /ō/ in the nominative, as is discussed in more detail in A.4.11.

A.3.4 *Loss of Final Short Vowels and* tanwīn

From the internal rhyme found in the Quran, it seems clear that what are considered the pausal pronunciations of final short vowels and *tanwīn* are in fact also the pronunciation in verse internal position as well (van Putten and Stokes 2018). Hence the developments that have taken place are the following, **u*, **i*, **a*, **un* and **in* are lost word-finally, whereas **an* has shifted to *ā*. Case and mood vowels appear to have been retained in construct, however. This reconstruction seems to be further confirmed by the Quranic orthography which indeed lacks any sign of regular *tanwīn* that we would have otherwise expected.

While throughout most of the corpus the generalization of this reduced case/mood system is borne out, there are a couple of Sūrahs that appear to tell a different story, at least in pausal position. In several final short **-a* appears to have been lengthened. In some cases, this appears in the QCT, and is further confirmed by the rhyme, e.g.: الظنونا /aẓ-ẓunūnā/ 'the assumptions' (Q33:10), الرسولا /ar-rasūlā/ 'the messenger' (Q33:66) and السبيلا /as-sabīlā/ 'the way' (Q33:67). To this we may add as well the diptotic plural with an apparent diptotic accusative ending: قواريرا /qawārīrā/ 'crystal clear' (Q76:15, 16)[56] and سلسلا /salāsilā/ 'chains' (Q76:4).

In other cases, the spelling is not changed, but the rhyme that such words appear in make it clear that they are to be read with final /-ā/, thus every other case of the accusative of *as-sabīl* in rhyme is spelled السبيل but certainly rhymed /as-sabīlā/ (Q4:44, Q25:17, Q33:4). Likewise, two subjunctives seem to rhyme with final /-ā/ ان ازيد /an azīdā/ 'that I should add' (Q74:15) and لن يحور /lan yaḥūrā/ 'he will not return' (Q84:14). Note that these are isolated exceptions, and both the definite accusative and the subjunctive occurs hundreds of times in rhyme where they are *not* pronounced as /-ā/. How to understand the exceptional status of these rhymes (which mostly concentrate and Q33 and Q76) requires further research.[57]

A.3.5 *Assimilation Across Vowels*

A major feature of Quranic Arabic that distinguishes it quite clearly from later Classical norms is its assimilation of identical and coronal consonants across vowels, while some of these ambiguous cases lead to disagreement between the Quranic readers, there is not a single reading that shows no signs of this assimilation at all.

For assimilation across vowels where the consonants are identical, it mostly concers with the first-person clitics *-nī* and *-nā*. The table below illustrates the examples. In some of these cases there is a disagreement between the regional codices, where one of the codices has an unassimilated form where the other does, in such cases I have given the abbreviated code (S = Syria, M = Medina, B = Basra, K = Kufa, C = Mecca) of the regional codex that has the minority variant. The unmarked version is then the variant that occurs in all other codices (see Sidky 2021; Cook 2004).

56 The form in Q76:16 does not occur in rhyme, but is the first word of the verse, directly following the previous word spelled like this. This being said, the later Basran codices seem to change this spelling to the expected قوارير. For a discussion on the reports on this spelling and its attestations in early manuscripts see Sidky (2021).

57 For a further discussion on these rhymes see also Van Putten & Stokes (2018, 161–163).

QCT	Pronunciation	Quranic recitation
اتحجونى (Q6:80)	/ʔa-tuḥāǧǧūn-nī/	*ʔa-tuḥāǧǧūn-nī, ʔa-tuḥāǧǧū-nī*[58]
تامرونى (Q39:64)	/tāmurūn-nī/	*taʔmurūn-nī/-niya, tāmurūn-nī, taʔmurū-niya, tāmurū-niya*[59]
تامروننى (Q39:64, S)	/tāmurūna-nī/	*taʔmurūna-nī*
تامنا (Q12:11)	/tāman-nā/	*taʔmanʷ-nā, tāmanʷ-nā, tāman-nā*[60]
مكنى (Q18:95)	/makkan-nī/	*makkan-nī*[61]
مكننى (Q18:95, C)	/makkana-nī/	*makkana-nī*
فنعما (Q2:271)	/fa-naʕim-mā/	*fa-naʕim-mā, fa-niʕim-mā, fa-niʕm-mā, fa-niʕĭm-mā*[62]
نعما (Q4:58)	/naʕim-mā/	*naʕim-mā, niʕim-mā, niʕm-mā, niʕĭm-mā*
انى (Q2:30 & *passim*)	/ʔin-nī/	*ʔin-nī*
انى (Q2:47 & *passim*)	/ʔan-nī/	*ʔan-nī*
انا (Q2:14 & *passim*)	/ʔin-nā/	*ʔin-nā*
انا (Q4:66 & *passim*)	/ʔan-nā/	*ʔan-nā*
لياتينى (Q27:21)	/la-yātiyan-nī/	*la-yaʔtiyan-nī, la-yātiyan-nī*[63]
لياتيننى (Q27:21, C)	/la-yātiyanna-nī/	*la-yaʔtiyanna-nī*
ترينى (Q23:93)	/turiyan-nī/	*turiyan-nī*

One might be tempted to understand such assimilation taking place as evidence that in Quranic Arabic the intervening short vowels of these stems had been lost, even before clitics. Interpreted in this way, these would not be examples of assimilation across short vowels. For early Christian Arabic, which shows similar cases, e.g. اخزنى /ʔaxzan-nī/ 'he grieved me', امكنى /ʔamkan-nī/ 'it was possible for me', يدينى /yadīn-nī/ 'you judge me'. Blau (1967, §35.4; §41.4) indeed interprets these as evidence for that.

It is worth making several more observations here however: even when the previous consonant is completely unvocalized in the reading traditions, identical consonants following each other may be written twice, thus the jussive يدركم (Q4:78) recited as *yudrik-kum* '(death) will overtake you' is written with

58 Ibn al-Ǧazarī (§3037).
59 Ibn al-Ǧazarī (§4091).
60 Ibn al-Ǧazarī (§1209).
61 Ibn al-Ǧazarī (§1208).
62 Ibn al-Ǧazarī (§2806).
63 Ibn al-Ǧazarī (§3801).

two *kāf*s, يوجهه (Q16:76) recited as *yuwağğih-hu* and يكرههن (Q24:33) recited as *yukrih-hunna* are written with two *hāʔ*s. But assimilation written out may also happen as found in the jussive تفتنى (Q9:49) recited as *taftin-nī*. As such, the fact that e.g. يدعوننى (Q12:33) 'they call me' is written with two *nūn*s does not necessarily prove the pronunciation /yadʕūna-nī/, it could just as well stand for /yadʕūn-nī/ with morphophonological spelling. However, in light of the fact that nouns followed by pronominal clitics appear to have kept their final short vowels (A.3.4), it seems reasonable to assume that this is the case for verbs too. The examples given above are therefore not evidence for the lack of final short vowels, but rather examples of assimilation across vowels, a phenomenon of which there are many more examples in Quranic Arabic where we cannot propose the absence of an intervening vowel as we will see below.

Assimilation of identical consonants across a vowel also rarely occurs in the jussives of geminated verbs like *yamdud*. These forms are far outnumbered by cases where the metathesis did not take place, but it is worth mentioning all the cases here. If the same word also occurs elsewhere unassimilated, I have included them in this table as well. When regional variants play a role letter codes are given once again.

QCT	Pronunciation	Quranic recitation
يرتدد (Q2:217)	/yartadid/	*yartadid*
يرتدد (Q5:54, SM)	/yartadid/	*yartadid*[64]
يرتد (Q5:54)	/yartadd/	*yartadda*
يرتد (Q27:40)	/yartadd/	*yartadda*
يشاقق (Q4:115)	/yušāqiq/	*yušāqiq(i)*
يشاق (Q59:4)	/yušāqq/	*yušāqq(i)*
يضار (Q2:282)	/yuḍārr/	*yuḍārra, yuḍār*[65]
تضار (Q2:233)	/tuḍārr/	*tuḍārra, tuḍārru, tuḍār*[66]

Another place where the QCT irregularly has assimilation across short vowels is in the tD- and tL-stems, where the *ta*- prefix may be optionally assimilated to the following coronal consonant. This may happen both in the suffix con-

64 Ibn al-Ǧazarī (§ 2989).
65 Ibn al-Ǧazarī (§ 2774).
66 Ibn al-Ǧazarī (§ 2774).

jugation and in the prefix conjugation, although in the latter it is much more common. The seven cases of this assimilation in the prefix conjugation are the following.

QCT	Pronunciation	Reading Traditions
فادرتم (Q2:72)	/fa-ddārātum/	*fa-ddāraʔtum(ū), fa-ddārātum(ū)*
فاطهروا (Q5:6)	/fa-ṭṭahharū/	*fa-ṭṭahharū*
اداركوا (Q7:38)	/iddārakū/	*iddārakū*
اثاقلتم (Q9:38)	/iṯṯāqaltum/	*iṯṯāqaltum(ū)*
وازينت (Q10:24)	/wa-zzayyanat/	*wa-zzayyanat*
اطيرنا (Q27:47)	/iṭṭayyarnā/	*iṭṭayyarnā*
ادرك (Q27:66)	/iddārak/	*iddāraka*

For the prefix conjugation there are many more examples, but are cause for some disagreement between the readers. When a *ya-* prefix precedes an assimilated tD/tL-stem, all readers are in agreement that the prefix assimilates, but when it stands before a *ta-* prefix, some rather see it as the haplological avoidance of the sequence *ta-ta-* > *ta-*, similar to ولا تفرقو /wa-lā tafarraqū/ 'do not become disunited' (Q3:103) but ولا تتفرقوا /wa-lā tatafarraqū/ 'id.' (Q42:13). As both haplology avoidance and assimilation occur in the QCT, it is not possible to be certain in those cases whether we are dealing with assimilation or haplology. The table below gives several illustrative examples of the problem using the common verb *taḏakkara* as the basis for examples.

QCT	Pronunciation	Reading Traditions
يذكر (Q2:269)	/yaḏḏakkar/	*yaḏḏakkaru*
يتذكر (Q13:19)	/yataḏakkar/	*yataḏakkaru*
تتذكرون (Q6:80)	/tataḏakkarūn/	*tataḏakkarūna*
تذكرون (Q6:152)	/taḏḏakkarūna/, /taḏakkarūna/	*taḏakkarūna, taḏḏakkarūna*

There is no way to decide what the intended pronunciation was of a second person, or third person feminine prefix conjugation verb when the next consonant can be assimilated, and the Quranic readings do not seem to retain a historical memory of it, and rather have complex generalized rules. For example, the Kufans always read *ta-* followed by an assimilatable consonant assuming haplology (thus *taḏakkarūna*), whereas the other readers always assume assimilation (thus *taḏḏakkarūna*) (Ibn al-Ǧazarī § 3084).

Other coronal consonants may occur assimilated as well, are unattested in the prefix conjugation:

QCT	Pronunciation	Reading Traditions
يشقق (Q2:74)	/yaššaqqaq/	*yaššaqqaqu*
يطوف (Q2:158)	/yaṭṭawwaf/	*yaṭṭawwafa*
يصدقوا (Q4:92)	/yaṣṣaddaqū/	*yaṣṣaddaqū*
يضرعون (Q7:94)	/yaḍḍarraʕūn/	*yaḍḍarraʕūna*
يدبروا (Q23:68)	/yaddabbarū/	*yaddabbarū*
يسمعون (Q37:8)	/yassammaʕūn/	*yassammaʕūna*
يزكى (Q80:3)	/yazzakkē/	*yazzakkā, yazzakkē, yazzakkā̈*

As was the case with the assimilation of identical consonants across vowels, this type of assimilation is also cause for some disagreement between the regional codices, for Q7:3 the Syrian codex has تتذكرون recited by Ibn ʕāmir as *yataḏakkarūna* whereas the non-Syrian codices have تذكرون variously recited as *taḏakkarūna* or *taḏḏakkarūna*. In light of the non-Syrian reading, the more natural reading of Q7:3 in the Syrian codex is probably *tataḏakkarūna*, a reading that is indeed reported for Ibn ʕāmir (as a non-canonical transmission) and for ʔabū al-Dardāʔ (Ibn Xālawayh *muxtaṣar*, 42; Ibn Muǧāhid, 278). ʔabū al-Dardāʔ was one of the companions of the prophet who indeed died in Damascus, and was one of Ibn ʕāmir's teachers (Ibn al-Ǧazarī, § 627), it is therefore no surprise that he would have the expected Syrian variant.

The assimilation across vowels of *ta-* to a following coronal may even happen if the *ta-* is preceded by a consonant. This seems to occur in the Ct-stem *istaṭāʕa* 'to be able', but may, depending on the interpretation, also occur with the Gt-stems *ihtadā* and *ixtaṣama*, for a discussion on the interpretation of the Gt cases see § 5.10. The table below illustrates some examples.

QCT	Pronunciation	Reading Traditions
استطاعوا (Q18:97)	/istaṭāʕū/	*istaṭāʕū*
اسطاعوا (Q18:97)	/isṭṭāʕū/	*isṭāʕū, isṭṭāʕū*[67]
لم تستطع (Q18:78)	/lam tastaṭiʕ/	*lam tastaṭiʕ*
لم تسطع (Q18:82)[68]	/lam tasṭṭiʕ/	*lam tasṭiʕ*
يهتدى (Q10:108)	/yahtadī/	*yahtadī*
يهدى (Q10:35)	/yahddī/ (or /yahdī/?)	*yahiddī, yahaddī, yahăddī, yahddī, yahdī*[69]
تعتدوا (Q2:190)	/taʕtadū/	*taʕtadū*
تعدوا (Q4:154)	/taʕddū/ (or /taʕdū/?)	*taʕddū, taʕaddū, taʕăddū, taʕdū*[70]
يختصمون (Q26:96)	/yaxtaṣimūn/	*yaxtaṣimūna*
يخصمون (Q36:49)	/yaxṣṣimūn/ or /yaxṣimūn/	*yaxiṣṣimūna, yaxaṣṣimūna, yaxăṣṣimūna, yaxṣṣimūna, yaxṣimūna*[71]

These examples should make it clear that syncope of short vowels between two identical consonants, and assimilation of *t* to coronals across a vowel happens quite frequently all throughout the QCT. It seems to have always been optional, and for almost every single example of such a phenomenon there are examples where the assimilation did not take place as well. Its distribution does not present an obvious explanation for this variation. The fact that both لم تستطع and لم تسطع occur only several verses apart, and استطاعوا and اسطاعوا even occur in the same verse, give us little reason to suggest that this is due to multiple authors or scribes for different parts of the Quran. It seems that we must conclude that such assimilations across vowels were a free variant option in the language of the Quran, which infrequently occurred regardless of environment.

The freedom between different assimilated and unassimilated forms is in fact so close, that almost perfectly parallel verses may occur both with assimilated and unassimilated forms, for example:

---

67 Ibn al-Ǧazarī (§ 3540).

68 The Manuscript Ma VI 165 has تستطع for both Q18:78 and Q18:82.

69 Ibn al-Ǧazarī (§ 3256).

70 Ibn al-Ǧazarī (§ 2969).

71 Ibn al-Ǧazarī (§ 4010).

> Q6:42 *wa-laqad* ***ʔarsalnā*** *ʔilā ʔumamin min qabli-ka fa-****ʔaxaḏnā****-hum* ***bi-l-baʔsāʔi wa-ḍ-ḍarrāʔi laʕallahum*** **yataḍarraʕūna**
>
> We have sent already unto peoples that were before thee, and we visited them with tribulation and adversity, so that perhaps they might grow humble.
>
> Q7:94 *wa-mā* ***ʔarsalnā*** *fī qaryatin min nabiyyin ʔillā* ***ʔaxaḏnā*** *ʔahla-hā* ***bi-l-baʔsāʔi wa-ḍ-ḍarrāʔi laʕallahum*** **yaḍḍarraʕūna**
>
> And we sent no prophet unto any town except to visit its people with tribulation and adversity, so that perhaps they might grow humble.

Another case of this process is attested in the non-canonical readings, and is well-attested in vocalized Quranic manuscripts for the verb يخصفان (Q7:22; Q20:121) 'they covered (themselves)', which is read by the canonical readers as *yaxṣifāni* but is attested vocalized as *yaxaṣṣifāni, yaxiṣṣifāni* in kufic manuscripts (e.g. Q7:22 in Arabe 334j; Q20:121 in Arab 325j, 347a), which is clearly an assimilated form of the Gt-stem *yaxtaṣifāni*. These forms are attested in the Šāḏḏ literature too, e.g. Ibn Xālawayh (*muxtaṣar*, 42, 90).

A.3.6 *Pausal Shortening of* -ī

Quranic Arabic has two realizations of word-final *-ī*, it can either be written with a ى or with no *mater* at all. This concerns any type of word-final *yāʔ*: (1) Final *-ī* of definite III-*y* nouns, e.g. الواد 'the valley' (Q89:9); (2) 1sg. Object pronoun *-nī*, e.g. فاتقون 'fear me' (Q2:41); (3) 1sg. possessive pronoun *-ī*, e.g. دين 'my religion' (Q109:6); (4) The *-ī* of imperfect verbs (only once): يسر 'it passes' (Q89:4).

Van Putten & Stokes (2018, 156–158) showed that these shortened forms are overwhelmingly favoured in pausal positions. While long forms rarely occur in pause, and shortened forms only occasionally occur outside of pause. Thus, pause seems to be quite clearly the origin for the shortening. The fact that these forms stand in rhyme where the vowel is entirely unpronounced, suggests that the *-ī* was not shortened, but dropped altogether, which would mean the pausal form of the 1sg. possessive marker was zero-marked.

A.3.7 *sayyiʔāt *as* سيات *Reflecting* /sayyāt/

Original **sayyiʔāt-* 'evil deeds' in the CE is regularly spelled as سيات, السيات seemingly with an *ʔalif* in the position of the **ʔ*.[72] In early manuscripts this

72 This spelling also appears to be common in early Christian Arabic (Blau 1967, §11.4.1.2B).

spelling is not always regular. It is outside the scope of the current work to examine this spelling in every single manuscript. Instead, below I have listed the spellings for every single occurrence of the word in the CPP. It becomes clear that the spelling سييت, more in line with the normal orthographic practices of the QCT, occurs besides سيات.

> سياتنا (Q3:193), السيات (Q10:27)
> سييتهم (Q3:195; Q25:70), السييت (Q4:18; Q7:153, 168; Q42:25; Q45:21, 33), سييتكم (Q4:31; Q5:12; Q8:29), سييته (Q65:5)

As with most other CayyiC adjectives, *sayyiʔ* has a contracted by-form *sayʔ* in Classical Arabic (*Lane*, 1491a, see also al-Farrāʔ *Luġāt*, 30), cf. *ḍayyiq-*, *ḍayq-* 'narrow' (*Lane*, 1868b), *mayyit-*, *mayt-* 'dead' (*Lane*, 2800b) and *layyin-*, *layn-* 'soft' (*Lisān*, 4117b). It seems then that the spelling سيات should be considered the outcome of this contracted form, i.e. /sayyāt/ or /sayāt/, whereas the spelling سييت represents the uncontracted form /sayyiyāt/. The *ʔalif* then is not a sign for the *hamzah*, but rather the result of the regular rule for the plene spelling of the plural feminine ending which occurs if the word would otherwise consist of only three letters (see Appendix A.2.1).

Whether the QCT indeed originally showed free variation between the contracted or uncontracted form, or whether the CE is correct in only showing the contracted form is a question that cannot be addressed in the current work.

A.3.8 *A Case of* N*-Assimilation?*

While by no means regular, there are two examples in the QCT where the sequence of two *nūn*s is simplified to just a single *nūn*, namely: Q21:88 نجى 'we save', Q12:110 فنجى 'so we save' (cf. Q10:103 ننج 'we save') which are read as *nuǧǧī*/*nunǧī* and *fa-nuǧǧiya*/*fa-nunǧī* respectively.[73] If this is not simply a writing error that has been propagated from the archetype, this should probably be understood as an isolated case of an assimilated *n* to the following *ǧ*.

A.3.9 *The Genitilic Adjective Ending*

In most modern dialects, the gentilic adjective ending (*Nisbah*) is *-ī* for the masculine and *-iyya(h)* for the feminine. While the masculine form has become a fairly common place transcription of the Classical Arabic gentilic adjec-

---

73 Ibn al-Ǧazarī (§ 3354; § 3633), who considered Q21:88 a hapological reduction of *nunaǧǧī*. Ibn Muǧāhid (430), surprisingly considers it to be the passive perfect *nuǧǧiya* with dropped final *-a*. This is grammatically quite problematic considering the following noun *al-muʔminīna* is in the accusative.

tive, normatively it is to be pronounced as *-iyy* even in pausal pronunciation. The Quranic rhyme suggests that the simplification of *-iyy* to *-ī* took place in Quranic Arabic as well, whereas the indefinite accusative remained *-iyyā*.

> Q20:85, 87 السامرى /as-sāmirī/ 'The Samaritan' rhymes with Q20:86 موعدى /mawʕid-ī/ 'promise to me', Q20:88 فنسى /fa-nasī/ 'so he has forgotten' and Q20:95 يسمرى /yā-sāmirī/ 'O Samaritan!' rhymes with Q20:94 قولى /qawl-ī/ 'my word' and Q20:95 نفسى /nafs-ī/ 'my soul'.
>
> Q19:16 مكانا شرقيا /makānā šarqiyyā/ 'an eastern location' rhymes with Q19:17 بشرا سشيا /bašarā sawiyyā/ 'an able-bodied man'.

The feminine gentilic adjective ending would presumably have been /-iyyah/, but it is unattested in rhyme position.

A.3.10 *ʔalif al-waṣl*

In Classical Arabic, there is a significant group of words that start with an initial vowel, which is elided when another vowel precedes it.[74] These can be found in five main environments.

1. The definite article: (*a*)*l-bašar*
2. A small group of nouns such as (*i*)*sm* 'name', (*i*)*bn* 'son', (*i*)*mruʔ* 'man', (*i*)*mraʔah* 'woman'.
3. Imperative verbs, (*i*)*fʕal*, (*u*)*ktub*
4. Gt-, N- and Ct-stem verbs: (*i*)*ftaʕala*, (*i*)*nfaʕala*, (*i*)*stafʕala*
5. Assimilated tD- and tL-verbs: (*i*)*ḏḏakara*, (*i*)*ṯṯāqala*

From the QCT, it is not at all clear that such an elision takes place in Quranic Arabic, as the prothetic vowel is spelled morphophonologically, so even when a particle precedes that would cause the *ʔalif al-waṣl* to be elided, is still written. From the orthography it is therefore equally possible that the *ʔalif* was actually pronounced in such cases.

From the Damascus Psalm fragment, we learn that it need not be the case that all contexts of the *ʔalif al-waṣl* are equal in this regard. There the *ʔalif al-waṣl* of the definite article is elided in much the same way as in Classical Arabic e.g. οελναρ /wa-l-nār/ 'and the fire' (v. 21), βιλλαυ /bi-ḷḷāh/ (v. 22), φιλ·β[...] /fi l-b[ariyyah]/ 'in the wilderness' (v. 52), φιλ·βαχερ /fi l-bašar/ 'among men' (v. 60), λιλ·σεβ· /li-l-sab(y)/ 'into captivity'. However, the Gt- and N-stems seem to have a true *hamzat al-qaṭʕ*, e.g. οα·αβ·τε·λεῦ /wa-ʔabtalaw/ 'they tempted' (v. 56) and φα·ανκα·λε·β(ο)υ· /fa-ʔanqalabū/ 'and they turned their backs' (v. 57) (for the analysis of the Damascus Psalm Fragment see Al-Jallad 2020b, 79 ff.). As already

---

74 In poetry, the ʔalif al-waṣl may sometimes be treated as a true *hamzah* (Nöldeke 1896, 7).

pointed out by Al-Jallad (2020b, 51, 60), it is therefore not a given that the QCT orthography represented a linguistic situation identical to Classical Arabic rather than the situation identical to that of the Damascus Psalm Fragment. In this section we will examine each of the five environments, and considered the evidence for the elision of the *ʔalif al-waṣl* in each of them.

In the QCT, it is regular to drop the *ʔalif al-waṣl* of the definite article when *la-* or *li-* precedes, e.g. الحمد لله /al-ḥamd li-llāh/ 'praise be to God' (Q1:2), هدى للمتقين /hudē li-l-muttaqīn/ 'a guidance to the god fearing' (Q2:2), وانه للحق من ربك /wa-inna-h la-l-ḥaqq min rabbi-k/ 'for this is indeed the truth from your lord' (Q2:149). In early manuscripts this behaviour is quite frequent, although never regular, when *bi-* precedes the definite article. This is especially common in the phrase بالحق /bi-l-ḥaqq/ 'with the truth' (Cellard 2018, 8), although not exclusively, e.g. بلمعروف /bi-l-maʕrūf/ 'what is fair' (Cellard 2018, ٤٧-٤٨, l. 5), بلامس /bi-l-ams/ 'yesterday' (Cellard 2018, ٧٧-٧٨, l. 6). Very rarely the preposition *ka-* has the same effect, e.g. كلمهل /ka-l-muhl/ 'like molten brass' (Cellard 2018, ١٩٩-٢٠٠, l. 10). If *wa-* or *fa-* or *fī* precede, the *ʔalif al-waṣl* is always written.

The only possible example that may be cited of an example where the *ʔalif al-waṣl* of the definite article is perhaps left unwritten is the phrase ولدار الاخره (Q12:109; Q16:30). This is recited as a construct phrase as *wa-la-dāru l-(ʔ)āxirati*, however وللدار الاخره (Q6:32), recited as *wa-la-d-dāru l-(ʔ)āxiratu*,[75] suggests that this might not be a construct phrase with the asseverative particle *la-* in front of it, but rather the single *lām* represents the definite article, i.e. /wa-d-dār al-āxirah/ (Nöldeke et al. 2013, 397, fn. 56).

Despite the frequent morphophonological spelling then, it seems clear that indeed the vowel of the definite article was elided if a particle preceded. This is further confirmed by the fact that, occasionally, word-final long vowels are spelled defectively when they immediately precede a definite article, e.g. سوف يوت الله المومنين اجرا عظيما /sawf yūti (< yūtī) llāh al-mūminīn ağrā ʕaẓīmā/ 'Allah will bring the believers a great reward' (Q4:146), صلح المومنين /ṣāliḥu (< ṣāliḥū) l-mūminīn/ 'the righteous among the believers' (Q66:4) and ايه اللذين امنوا /ayyuha (< ayyuhā) l-mūminūn/ 'O believers!' (Q24:31) (see A.2.10).

There is very little direct evidence that the *ʔalif al-waṣl* on words such as *imraʔah* and *imruʔ* was elided. However, the *basmalah* formula is written بسم الله /bi-smi llāh/ and never باسم الله. This is a strong indication of the elision of this *ʔalif al-waṣl*. Outside of the *basmalah*, *bi-smi* occurs occasionally with the morphophonological spelling as well, though this is cause for some disagree-

75 Except by the Syrian canonical reader Ibn ʕāmir who reads it *wa-la-dāru l-ʔāxirati*, because the Syrian Muṣḥaf spells this ولدار الاخره rather than وللدار الاخره (Ibn al-Ğazarī § 3017; Cook 2004, 92, (S4)).

ment among early Quranic manuscripts, e.g. باسم ربك /bi-smi rabbi-ka/ (Q56:74) (see B.19). The CE attests يبنوم /ya-bna-wumm/ (Q20:94) 'O son of my mother!', which would be a good example of the elided *ʔalif al-waṣl* before ابن, however this word is consistently spelled يابنوم in early Quranic manuscripts (see B.20).

While several I-*ʔ* verbs have irregular biradical imperatives such as *kul* 'eat!' and *xuḏ* 'take!', most verbs are treated as regular triradical verbs, with the loss of the *hamzah* in Quranic Arabic, however, these develop a special allomorphy, where the unprefixed imperative have an initial long vowel /ī/ whereas when they are prefixed by *wa-* or *fa-* these merged into /wā-/ and /fā-/. This behaviour can only be understood if we assume that such imperatives in an early stage of the language indeed had a non-phonemic initial *i-* in absolute initial position, **(i)ʔti* > /īt/ but **fa-ʔti* > /fāt/.

	wa-	fa-	
ايت /īt/ (Q10:15)		فات /fāt/ (Q2:258)	'come/bring!'
ايتوا /ītū/ (Q20:64)	واتوا /wātū/ (Q2:189)	فاتوا /fātū/ (Q2:23)	'come (pl.)!'
		فاتيا /fātiyā/ (Q26:16)	'come (du.)!'
ايذن /īḏan/ (Q9:49)			'permit!'
		فاذنوا /fāḏanū/ (Q2:279)	'be informed (pl.)!'
	وامر /wāmur/ (Q7:145)		'order!'
		فاوا /fāwū/ (Q18:16)	'retreat (pl.)!'

While this behaviour clearly proves that such verbs had an *ʔalif al-waṣl* historically, it is not entirely clear that this is the case synchronically. Verbs of this type do not have the same morphological behaviour as in Classical Arabic. For example: قل الذين لا يرجون لقانا ايت بقران غير هذا او بدله can really only be understood as /qāl allaḏīn lā yarǧūn **liqāʔa-nā īt** bi-qurān ġayr hāḏā baddil-(u)h/ "Those who do not expect to meet us say: 'bring a recital other than this or change it'". Had the Classical pronunciation /liqāʔa-na ʔti/ or with loss of *hamzah* /liqāʔanāti/[76] been intended, we would not expect ايت to have been spelled with the *yāʔ*. This behaviour clearly cannot be attributed to pausal spelling, as had that been the case, we would expect the form with *wa-* or *fa-* in front of it to also be written with the *yāʔ*, i.e. **فايت 'come/bring!'.[77]

76 As is the recitation of Warš ʕan Nāfiʕ, ʔabū Ǧaʕfar and optionally for ʔabū ʕamr.

77 This is thus one of the many examples where the alleged "pausal spelling principle" is violated in Quranic orthography. See Van Putten & Stokes (2018, 152–158) for a more detailed discussion.

Synchronically, it therefore seems that verbs of this type had a *ʔalif al-qaṭʕ* when there was not a direct proclitic in front of it. It seems possible that واغفر 'and forgive!' (Q2:285), وانظر 'and see!' (Q2:259), واعلم 'and know!' (Q2:26) are read as /wa-ġfir/, /wa-nẓur/ and /wa-ʕlam/ respectively, which would assume some amount of morphophonological spelling (something that is clear for the definite article as well) but alternatively /wa-iġfir/, /wa-unẓur/ and /wa-aʕlam/ cannot be excluded. The fact that, unlike the definite article, we never find phonetic spellings without the prothetic *ʔalif* may be interpreted as an indication that these indeed had *ʔalif al-qaṭʕ*.

When *li-* and *la-* precede the definite article, they always trigger an elided spelling of the *ʔalif al-waṣl*. This is not the case when *la-* precedes the *ʔalif al-waṣl* of derived verbs of the N-, Gt- or Ct-stem, which may suggest that, similar to the Damascus psalm fragment, these derived verbs indeed had a prefix *ʔa-* rather than *ʔalif al-waṣl*, e.g. لاختلفتم /la-ʔaxtalaftum/ 'you would have differed' (Q8:42), لانفضوا /la-ʔanqaḍḍū/ 'they would have dispersed' (Q3:159), لاستكثرت /la-ʔastakṯart/ 'I would have multiplied' (Q7:188).

There is one case against the presence of an *ʔalif al-qaṭʕ* in the Gt-stem. لتخذت 'you would have taken' (Q18:77) is recited as *la-ttaxaḏtā, la-ttaxatta* by most readers, despite the absence of the *ʔalif al-waṣl* in the QCT. The reading of Ibn Kaṯīr, ʔabū ʕamr and Yaʕqūb is *la-taxiḏta, la-taxitta*, which would not imply the elision of the *ʔalif al-waṣl* (Ibn al-Ǧazarī, § 3525). However, it is quite clear that this is the inferior reading. *Ittaxaḏa* is an irregular Gt-stem. Instead of the expected ***iʔtaxaḏa*, Quranic Arabic treats it as a derivation of a I-*w* verb. The G-stem *taxiḏa* is transparently an analogical backformation from *ittaxaḏa*. As the G-stem of *ittaxaḏa* is just the original *ʔaxaḏa* everywhere else in the Quran, e.g. اخذتهم /ʔaxaḏtu-hum/ (Q22:44), it is difficult to accept the sudden use of *taxiḏa* in this place only. Thus, the more natural reading of لتخذت is indeed /la-ttaxaḏt/, which suggests that the *ʔalif al-waṣl* was unpronounced, in line with Classical Arabic, and different from the Arabic of the Damascus psalm fragment. There is however a question whether the spelling لتخذت is in fact archetypical to the UT. While a good number of manuscripts indeed exhibit this spelling, several quite ancient manuscripts point to the expected spelling لاتخذت, such as Saray Medina 1a (corrected to لتخذت by a later hand) (see B.21). If the spelling with the elided *ʔalif al-waṣl* is not original to the UT, then it once again becomes quite likely that the initial cluster was preceded by an *ʔalif al-qaṭʕ* instead.

Finally, the tD- and tL-stems as with the derive N-, Gt-and Ct-stems always write the *ʔalif al-waṣl* with an *ʔalif*, regardless of whether it is preceded by a proclitic or not. However, the only proclitics that occur before it are *wa-* (وازينت /wa-(v)zzayyanat/ 'and is embellished', Q10:24) and *fa-* (فادرتم /fa-(v)ddārātum/

'so they disputed', Q2:72). These same proclitics also do not cause the elision of the *ʔalif al-waṣl* of the definite article in the orthography, which in proncuniation it was almost certainly unpronounced. As such, it is not readily possible to determine whether stems like these retained their epenthetic initial syllable if a clitic precedes.

A.3.11 *An Isolated Case of Word-Initial* *wu > ʔu

The Arab grammarians record the possibility of shifting word-initial **wu* and **wū* to *ʔu* and *ʔū*, e.g. *wulida* > *ʔulida*, and in *wuǧūh* > *ʔuǧūh* (Sībawayh IV, 331). This rule has made its way, not entirely regularly, into the textbook Classical Arabic as well (Fischer 2002, § 36b). While most of the time, this shift does not occur in the QCT, e.g. ولد (Q19:15) /wulid/ 'he was born' and وجوه (Q3:106) /wuǧūh/ 'faces', there is a single occurrence of this development, namely, اقتت /ʔuqqitat/ 'the time has come' (Q77:11)[78] transparently from the root √wqt.[79]

A.4 Morphology

A.4.1 *Independent Pronouns*

Almost the complete paradigm of the independent pronouns is attested in the QCT, only the second person feminine plural is unattested.

		Singular		Dual		Plural
3m	هو	/hū/, /huww/?	هما	/humā/	هم	/hum/
3f	هى	/hī/, /hiyy/?			هن	/hunn/
2m	انت	/ant/	انتما	/antumā/	انتم	/antum/
2f	انت	/ant/			–	
1	انا	/anā/			نحن	/naḥn/

78 ʔabū ʕamr reads *wuqqitat* and ʔabū Ǧaʕfar reads this *wuqitat*, ignoring the dropping of the hamzah suggested by the *rasm* (Ibn al-Ǧazarī § 4494).

79 This phenomenon is also attested occasionally in early Christian Arabic. Blau (1967, § 83) reports اجد 'was found', الد 'was born', اقفت 'she was placed' and اعظت 'you have been instructed'.

From the fact that the masculine plurals are spelled هم and انتم rather than هموا and انتموا make it obvious that Quranic Arabic did not employ the long forms of the plural pronouns, unlike some of the Hijazi reading traditions (§ 3.6.5).

The reconstruction of the phonetics of the third person singular pronouns requires some discussion. In the *ʕarabiyyah* these pronouns are consistently *huwa* and *hiya*, unless they stand in an environment where they may syncopate to *wa-hwa* and *fa-hya* (§ 2.2.4.3). From a Semitic perspective, the *ʕarabiyyah* forms are surprising, the Hebrew forms *hū* הוא and *hī* היא are best understood as reflexes of Proto-West-Semitic **hūʔa* and **hīʔa* (Suchard 2019, 211). Both the loss of length and the loss of the **ʔ* in the *ʕarabiyyah* are irregular. Many modern dialects of Arabic have forms such as *huwwa* and *huwwe* (besides *hū*, *hī*) (Fischer and Jastrow 1980, 80) which do not appear to be reflexes of **huwa* and **hiya* but rather of **hūʔa-h* and **hīʔa-h*, i.e. the Proto-West-Semitic pronouns followed by the *-h* pronominal extension also found in the Hebrew second person masculine pronoun *ʔattå* < **ʔanta-h*, and in the third person pronouns as well in the dead sea scrolls הואה, היאה (Suchard 2019, 210). For a discussion on these stem extensions see Al-Jallad (2014b).

The expected reflex of Classical Arabic **huwa* in Quranic Arabic, after the loss of final short vowels, would be ***hū*. As we saw in A.2.3, word-final *-ū* is usually written with an *ʔalif al-wiqāyah*, and therefore the expected spelling of our hypothetical ***hū* would be هوا. Instead, we regularly find هو, which would be the expected spelling for the reflex of **hūʔa* > *huww*. On this basis we might want to posit the third person pronouns as **hūʔa* > /huww/ and **hīʔa* > /hiyy/ for Quranic Arabic. However, the fact that the pausal form هيه (Q101:10) rhymes as /hiyah/, seems to suggest that Quranic Arabic indeed goes back to a form closer to the one we find in Classical Arabic instead, which would make a reading as /hū/ and /hī/ more attractive, in which case the spelling of هو is irregular.[80]

A.4.2 *Clitic Pronouns*

The pronominal system of the Quranic reading traditions shows a large amount of variation, most of which is not continued in Classical Arabic (van Putten and Sidky forthcoming). As final short vowels are lost in Quranic Arabic, some of this variation present in the reading tradition was presumably not expressed at all. It is unclear to what extent there was vowel harmony between the case vowel and the following pronominal suffix in the masculine plural clitics, but

80 Al-Farrāʔ (*Luġāt*, 29) reports that Banū ʔasad uses *hū* and *hī* for *huwa* and *hiya*, and he cites poetry using the *hī* form. Such monosyllabic forms of the independent pronouns occur on occasion in poetry.

reports of grammarians suggest that it was typical of the Hijaz to not have vowel harmony. This leads me to tentatively suggest that Quranic Arabic lacked vowel harmony as well, although there is no independent way to confirm this.

Lengthened forms of the singular pronouns *-hū* and *-hī* were certainly absent, as we would expect those to have been written as ـهو and ـهى. The same is true for the lengthened pronominal forms *-humū, -himī, himū* and *-kumū* which would be expected to be written ـهموا, ـهمى and ـكموا. The long form of the second person plural pronoun only occurs four times before other clitic pronouns (Q8:44; Q11:28; Q15:22; Q47:37). The table below illustrates the probable reconstruction of the pronominal suffix paradigm.

	Singular	Dual	Plural
3m	ـه /-h/		ـهم /-hum/
		ـهما /-humā/	
3f	ـها /-hā/		ـهن /-hunn/
2m			ـكم, /-kum/,
	ـك /-k/	ـكما /-kumā/	ـكمو /-kumū-/ (before pronouns)
2f			ـكن /-kunn/
1 (verbal)	ـنى, /-nī/,		
	ـن /-n/		ـنا /-nā/
1 (nominal)	ـى, /-ī/, /v̄-y/, /ē/,		
	∅ -∅		

Special mention needs to be made of the 1sg. pronoun which has several different allomorphs. Due to pausal shortening of final **-ī* both the verbal /-nī/ and nominal /-ī/ also occur as /-n/ and /-∅/ respectively (see A.3.6). After long vowels, the 1sg. nominal suffix is /-y/. Finally, there likely was a special vocative 1sg. marker that shows up in expressions of woe, e.g. ياسفى /yā-ʔasaf-ē/ 'O my sorrow!' (Q12:84), يحسرتى /yā-ḥasrat-ē/ 'O my regret!' (Q39:56), and يويلتى /yā-waylat-ē/ 'Woe is me!' (Q5:31; Q11:72; Q25:28). While technically the spelling with ى could be read as *-ī* as well,[81] the normal 1sg. ending, this is unlikely to be the intended reading here. Vocatives throughout the Quran consistently have the short pausal 1sg. ending, e.g. يقوم /yā-qawm-∅/ 'O my people!', يابت /yā-abat-

81 Indeed, some non-canonical readers would read it as such, see Ibn Xālawayh (*muxtaṣar*, 32).

∅/ 'O my father!', يرب /yā-rabb-∅/ 'O my lord!'.[82] Had the vocatives of woe had the normal 1sg. ending, we would have expected it to have been shortened as well. Moreover, in the canonical Quranic reading traditions this vocative 1sg. is indeed consistently read as *-ē/-ǟ/-ā*, as expected (Ibn al-Ǧazarī, § 1973, § 2041–2042).

The first singular possessive clitic *-ī* occurs a few times in pausal position (all in Q69) with a final *h*, clearly confirmed by the rhyme to represent a reading /-iyah/: كتبيه /kitāb-iyah/ 'my book' (Q69:19, 25); حسابيه /ḥisāb-iyah/ 'my reckoning' (Q69:20; Q69:26); ماليه /māl-iyah/ 'my property' (Q69:28) سلطنيه /sulṭān-iyah/ 'my authority' (Q69:29). Elsewhere in the Quran the pausal 1sg. /-∅/ is used in verse final position.

A.4.3 *Verbal Endings*

The suffix conjugation of the perfective verb appears to have been identical to the pausal pronunciations of Classical Arabic. The 1p suffix /-nā/ is always spelled defectively in the QCT when it is followed by a pronominal clitic. This is presumably defective spelling, and does not indicate an actual shortening of the suffix to /-na/ in that context.

	Singular		Dual		Plural	
3m	∅	-∅	ـا	/-ā/	ـوا	/-ū/, /-aw/
					ـو	/-w/
3f	ـت	/-at/	ـتا	/-atā/	ـن	/-n/
2m	ـت	/-t/	ـتما	/tumā/	ـتم	/-tum/
					ـتمو	/-tumū-/ (before clitic pronouns)
2f	ـت	/-t/			ـتن	/-tinn/
1	ـت	/-t/			ـنا،	/-nā/
					ـنـ	

The third person masculine plural ending ـوا /-aw/ would be the form that occurs in verbs that end in *ʔalif maqṣūrah*. This is indistinguishable from /-ū/ in the orthography of the QCT, but it seems reasonable to assume that Quranic

82 This, incidentally, seems to suggest that in the original prosody of Quranic recitation, such epenthetic vocatives had a minor pause following them, explaining the pausal form.

Arabic retained this distinction. The third person masculine plural ending ـو /-w/, never followed by an *ʔalif al-wiqāyah* occurs on hollow roots with *hamzah* as final root consonant such as جاو /ǧāw/ 'they came' (e.g. Q3:184) and also راو /rāw/ 'they saw' (e.g. Q7:149).[83]

The prefix conjugation has two different sets of ending, depending on whether it represent the imperfective, or the subjunctive/jussive. Invariably the imperfective form is longer, and those forms are given in between brackets when necessary. The vowel of the prefix appears to have occurred in two forms either with an *a* (used for the G-, tD-, tL-, Gt-, N- and Ct-stems) and *u* (used for the D-, L- and C-stems). In Quranic Arabic there was no alternation in the prefix vowel between *a* and *i* as reported for some eastern dialects (see § 4.7).

		Singular		Dual		Plural
3m	يـ	/ya-/, /yu-/	يـ...ـا(ن)	/ya-, /yu/.../-ā(n)/	يـ...ـوا/ـون	/ya-/, /yu-/.../-ū(n), -aw(n)/
3f	تـ	/ta-/, /tu-/	تـ...ـا(ن)	/ta-/, /tu-/.../-ā(n)/	يـ...ـن	/ya-/, /yu-/.../-n/
2m	تـ	/ta-/, /tu-/	تـ...ـا(ن)	/ta-/, /tu-/.../-ā(n)/	تـ...ـوا/ـون	/ta-/, /tu-/.../-ū(n), -aw(n)/
2f	تـ	/ta-/, /tu-/.../ī(n), -ay(n)/	تـ...ـا(ن)	/ta-/, /tu-/.../-ā(n)/	تـ...ـن	/ta-/, /tu-/.../-n/
1	ا	/a-/, /u-/			نـ	/na-/, /nu-/

A.4.4 *Demonstrative Pronouns*

The near deixis demonstrative pronouns of Quranic Arabic have much less variation than is reported for Classical Arabic. It is seemingly a Hijazi innovation to always prefix the deictic pronouns with *hā-* (see § 4.5), save for certain specific archaic constructions, where traces of the ancient forms without *ḏā* are retained (see below).

Near deixis	Singular	Dual	Plural
masculine	هذا /hāḏā/	هذن /hāḏān/	هولا /hāwulāʔ/ or /hawlāʔ/
feminine	هذه /hāḏih/	هاتين /hātayn/[84]	

83 See A.2.3 for the discussion of the use of the *ʔalif al-wiqāyah* and § 5.11 on the Quranic Arabic use of /rāʔ/ and /nāʔ/ instead of Classical *raʔā* and *naʔā*.

84 The plene spelling of this pronoun seems to be the common spelling in early Quranic manuscripts (see B.29).

In Classical Arabic, the dual of the near deixis inflects for case, as a dual noun would, i.e. nom. *hāḏāni* gen./acc. *hāḏayni*. There is no evidence that this is the case in Quranic Arabic. The masculine dual occurs twice, once at Q22:19 هذان خصمان /hāḏān xaṣmān/ 'these are two enemies', with nominative function, and the other is the famous verse Q20:63 ان هذن لاسحرن /in(n) hāḏāni la-sāḥirān/ 'indeed, these are two magicians', where it functions as an accusative, where Classical Arabic would require *hāḏāyni*. However, as this is the only attestation of the near deixis dual pronoun in an accusative position, there is no reason to believe that this dual inflected for case.

The feminine dual is only attested in the gen./acc. and has the expected form هاتين. This could either mean that at an earlier stage of Quranic Arabic, it did inflect for case and the masculine and feminine generalized different case forms, or that Q20:63 really is an error.

The far deixis in Quranic Arabic is marked by the deictic pronominal base, followed by a typically Hijazi element -*l*(*i*)- in the singular followed by the second person pronoun suffix, which can agree with the addressee.

Far Deixis	Singular	Dual	Plural
masculine	ذلك /ḏāli-k/ (2sg.)	ذنك /ḏāni-k/ (2sg)	اوليك /ulāyi-k/ (2sg.)
	ذلكما /ḏāli-kumā/ (2du.)	—	—
	ذلكم /ḏāli-kum/ (2pl.m.)	—	اوليكم /ulāyi-kum/ (2pl.m.)
	ذلكن /ḏāli-kunn/ (2pl.f.)	—	—
feminine	تلك /til-k/ (2sg.)	—	
	تلكما /til-kumā/ (2du.)	—	
	تلكم /til-kum/ (2pl.m.)	—	
	—	—	

While ذلك and تلك can clearly be used in environments where the addressee is plural, the other forms seem to always be explicitly used in addressee agreement. Fischer (2002, § 275.2) suggests that the addressee agreement in pre-classical Arabic no longer holds. This may be true for the poetry where these forms occur, but the system is evidently productive in the Quran.[85]

The locative deictics follow the same pattern as the pronominal deictics, where the near deixis always has the prefix *hā*- and the far deixis always

85 Al-Mubarrad (III, 275) discusses the full system of addressee agreement.

has the *-li-* stem extension. There is no evidence for addressee agreement for the locative deictic.

	Near deixis	Far deixis
Locative	ههنا /hāhunā/	هنالك /hunāli-k/

The Arab grammarians report forms of the short demonstrative without prefix *hā-* as a possible forms, this use of ذا /ḏā/ has fallen out of use in Quranic Arabic. In the QCT it is only attested after the interrogatives من /man/ 'who' and ما /mā/ 'what'. The long interrogative /man ḏā/ is only used in the cleft construction من ذا الذى /man ḏā allaḏī/ 'who is it that …?' (Q2:245, 255; Q3:160; Q33:17; Q57:11). ما ذا /mā ḏā/ (*passim*)[86] shows no obvious difference in meaning or syntax from /mā/.[87] The long deictic can also be combined with من /man/: امن هذا الذى /ʔam-man hāḏā allaḏī/ 'or who is it that …?' (Q67:20, 21).

Classical Arabic has a construction of independent pronouns followed by the deictic elements with a presentative function. In such cases, the deictic lacks the *hā-* prefix but it may stand in front of the independent pronoun e.g. *hā-ʔana ḏā* 'here I am!', *ʔanta ḏā* 'here you are', *hā-naḥnu ʔulāʔi* 'here we are!' (Fischer 2002, § 279). Quranic Arabic attests this construction twice, both times with plural pronouns: هانتم اولا تحبنهم /hā-antum ulāʔ tuḥibbūna-hum/ 'Here you are loving them' (Q3:119) هم اولا على اثرى /hum ulāʔ ʕalā aṯar-ī/ 'Here they are on my track' (Q20:84).

Such constructions may also have the *hā-* prefix on the demonstrative after the pronoun, and the *hā* prefix may also occur on both: انتم هولا تقتلون انفسكم /antum hāwulāʔ taqtulūn anfusa-kum/ 'Here you are killing one another' (Q2:85); هانتم هولا حججتم فيما لكم به علم /hā-antum hāwulāʔ ḥāǧaǧtum fī-mā la-kum bi-h ʕilm/ 'Here you are, having argued about that of which you have knowledge' (Q3:66), see also Q4:109 and Q47:38.

86 This word is normally interpreted as a single word *māḏā* and written as such in typewritten Arabic. There is no way to distinguish ما ذا from ماذا in handwritten Arabic, as a space between unconnected letters is of the same size in between words as within it. In light of من ذا above, it seems best to interpret the form as /mā ḏā/ in Quranic Arabic. The ambiguity whether these phrases should be seen as one word or not seems to also underlie the reports that the Muṣḥafs of Ibn Masʕūd would write *man ḏā* as a single word منذا (Al-Farrāʔ *Maʕānī*, III, 132).

87 Sībawayh (II, 416–419) specifically discusses constructions of this type.

A.4.5 *Relative Pronouns*

The relative pronouns, unlike the Classical Arabic spelling, is spelled with a single *lām* in Quranic Arabic in all its forms.[88]

	Singular	Dual	Plural
masculine	الذى /allaḏī/	nom. الذان /allaḏān/ obl. الذين /allaḏayn/	الذين /allaḏīn/
feminine	التى /allatī/	—	التى /allātī/ الى، الاى /allāy/

While Classical Arabic allows for two forms of the feminine plural relative pronoun, the form besides *allātī* is normally *allawātī*. Such a form does not occur in the Quran. Instead, a pronoun spelled variously in early manuscripts as الاى or الى, presumably /allāy/, is used, with no discernable difference in function.[89] Where the other pronominal forms are quite clearly the definite article *al-* + a particle *la* followed by a demonstrative element, the origin of the /-āy/ of /allāy/ is not entirely clear.

A.4.6 *The Relative Possessive Demonstrative*

The relative possessive demonstrative which created constructions like "those of X" inflect for case and gender. For the plural two competing stems occur, the /ulū~ī/ and /ḏawī/.

	Singular	Dual	Plural
masculine	ذوا، ذى، ذا /ḏū, ḏī, ḏā/	ذوا، ذوى /ḏawā, ḏaway/	اولى ،[90]اولوا/اولا /ulū, ulī/ ذوي /ḏawī/ (gen.) Q2:177
feminine	ذات /ḏāt/	ذواتا، ذواتى /ḏawātā, ḏawātay/	اولت /ulāt/

88 This is a spelling practice it shares with early Christian Arabic (Blau 1967, § 26.3.2).

89 It is tempting to see in الى the ubiquitous relative pronouns *illi* of the modern dialects, but the spelling الاى seems to preclude such an interpretation. It is, moreover, unclear how a pronoun as rare as the feminine plural relative pronoun would be likely to spread to all positions and become the dominant relative pronoun.

90 When *ulū* stands before a CC cluster, early Quranic manuscripts frequently write the

A.4.7 *Short Compound Interrogatives with mā*

Prepositional compounds with *mā* occur several times in the Quran in short forms, where the interrogative is only written as a single *mīm*. All of these occur besides the long form. Whether the lack of an *ʔalif* should be understood as them ending in a short /ma/, or ending in /m/ cannot be deduced from the QCT, and is dependent on the relative chronology of these shortened forms in Quranic Arabic. It is worth noting that these shortened forms predominantly occur when the combination of preposition + *mā* is interrogative in function, only Q86:5 appears to have a relative function with the short مم.

لم /li-m(a)/ (Q3:183; Q4:77; Q5:18; Q7:164; Q9:43; Q19:42; Q20:125; Q27:46; Q41:21; Q61:2, 5; Q66:1)	لما /li-mā/ (e.g. Q2:41)
فيم /fī-m(a)/ (Q4:97; Q79:43)	في ما /fī mā/ (e.g. Q2:240)
بم /bi-m(a)/ (Q15:54; Q27:35)	بما /bi-mā/ (e.g. Q2:4)
مم /mim-m(a)/ (Q86:5)	من ما /min mā/ (e.g. Q30:28), مما /mim-mā/ (Q2:23)
عم /ʕam-m(a)/ (Q78:1)	عن ما /ʕan mā/ (e.g. Q7:166), عما /ʕan-mā/ (e.g. Q2:74)

كم 'how much?', which in Classical Arabic is invariably read as *kam*, may also be considered the result of this historical shortening of *-mā* in compound interrogatives, with lexical specialization. Historically, it seems to derive from **ka-mah* literally 'like what?', as can be seen in Semitic comparanda such as Hebrew *kammå* 'how much?' (with irregular gemination also found in *låmmå* 'why?') and Aramaic *kəmā, kammā* 'how much?' (Brockelmann 1908, 326). The fact that the form ends up as *kam* in the Classical language and not as *kama* might be an indication that the shortened pronoun was indeed pronounced /-m/ in Quranic Arabic, rather than /-ma/.

The semantic development of *ka-mā* 'like what?' → *ka-ma* 'how much?' also finds a parallel in another interrogative with the same meaning, namely *ka-ʔayyin*, likewise 'like' + 'what?', as attested in the Quran in the phrase كاين من 'how much of!' (Q3:146; Q12:105; Q22:45, 48; Q29:60; Q47:13; Q65:8), with fossilized nunation written out (see van Putten and Stokes 2018, 170). In Classical Arabic *ka-ʔayyin* can even have the interrogative function of *kam* 'how much?' (*Lane*, 134a) rather than only serving as an expression wonder.

demonstrative as اولا. The reasons for this are not entirely clear. For a rather speculative account on this phenomenon see Puin (2011, 154). See also Sidky (2021) for a discussion of this phenomenon, but also lacking a solution. A dedicated study of this orthographic phenomenon is warranted.

A.4.8 *Noun Inflection*

Van Putten & Stokes (2018) have argued that Quranic Arabic had a reduced case system where only triptotic nouns distinguished the indefinite accusative with /-ā/ but otherwise lost inflect, except in construct. Case was retained in the Dual and Sound masculine plural. The paradigms of nouns can be reconstructed as follows:

	Indefinite	Definite	Construct
nom.	كتب /kitāb/ (Q2:89)	الكتب /al-kitāb/ (Q2:2)	كتب /kitābu/ (Q11:17)
gen.	كتب /kitāb/ (Q20:52)	الكتب /al-kitāb/ (Q2:85)	كتب /kitābi/ (Q5:44)
acc.	كتبا /kitābā/ (Q3:145)	الكتب /al-kitāb/ (Q2:44)	كتب /kitāba/ (Q4:24)

Triptotes

	Indefinite	Definite	Construct
nom.	رجلان /rağulān/ (Q5:23)	الولدان /al-wālidān/ (Q4:7)	رسولا /rasūlā/ (Q20:47)
gen.	شهرين /šahrayn/ (Q4:92)	الولدين /al-wālidayn/ (Q4:135)	ابنى /ibnay/ (Q5:27)
acc.	رجلين /rağulayn/ (Q16:76)	الذكرين /ad-dakarayn/ (Q6:143)	ابويكم /abaway-kum/ (Q7:27)

Dual

	Indefinite	Definite	Construct
nom.	بنون /banūn/ (Q26:88)	البنون /al-banūn/ (Q18:46)	بنوا /banū/ (10:90)
obl.	بنين /banīn/ (Q17:6)	البنين /al-banīn/ (Q37:153)	بني /banī/ (Q17:4)

Sound masculine plural

	Indefinite	Definite	Construct
nom.	مغنم /maġānim/ (Q4:94)	القوٰعد /al-qawāʕid/ (Q24:60)	مفتح /mafātiḥu/ (Q6:59)[91]
gen.	مغنم /maġānim/ (Q48:15)	القوٰعد /al-qawāʕid/ (Q2:127)	مسكن /masākini/ (Q14:45)
acc.	مغنم /maġānim/ (Q48:19)	القوٰعد /al-qawāʕid/ (Q16:26)	مسجد /masāǧida/ (Q2:114)

Diptotes

	Indefinite	Definite	Construct
nom.	رحمه /raḥmah/ (Q2:157)	الرحمه /ar-raḥmah/ (Q57:13)	رحمت /raḥmatu/ (Q11:73)
gen.	رحمه /raḥmah/ (Q2:159)	الرحمه /ar-raḥmah/ (Q17:24)	رحمه /raḥmati/ (Q15:56)
			رحمت /raḥmati/ (Q19:2)
acc.	رحمه /raḥmah/ (Q3:8)	الرحمه /ar-raḥmah/ (Q6:12)	رحمه /raḥmata/ (Q39:9)
			رحمت /raḥmata/ (Q2:218)

Feminine singular

	Indefinite	Definite	Construct
nom.	بينت /bayyinät/ (Q3:97)	البينت /al-bayyinät/ (Q2:209)	جنات /ǧannātu/ (Q13:23)
obl.	بينت /bayyinät/ (Q2:99)	البينت /al-bayyinät/ (Q2:87)	جنات /ǧannāti/ (Q5:65)

Sound Feminine plural

A.4.9 *III-w and III-y Nouns with Preceding a Vowel.*

Nouns that end in stem-final **-ay-* and **-aw-*, unlike Classical Arabic, appear to be distinct in Quranic Arabic, where the former collapsed to /ē/ and the latter to /ā/ (§ 5.8). The tables below give paradigm for both types of nouns.

91 The use of the plural pattern CaCāCiC for 'keys' is somewhat surprising. Strict Classical Arabic grammar would require the plural of *miftāḥ* to be *mafātīḥ*. The use of this pattern for stems with a long vowel in the last syllable seems to be more common in early Islamic Arabic papyri (Hopkins 1984, § 87b). Generalization of CaCāCiC over CaCāCīC is also a

	Indefinite	Definite	Construct
nom.	هدى /hudē/ (Q2:2)	الهدى /al-hudē/ (Q2:120)	هديهم /hudē-hum/ (Q2:272)
gen.	هدى /hudē/ (Q2:5)	الهدى /al-hudē/ (Q17:94)	هديهم /hudē-hum/ (Q16:37)
acc.	هدى /hudē/ (Q17:2)	الهدى /al-hudē/ (Q20:47)	هدى الله /hudē llāhi/ (Q6:71)

Words that end in /ā/ are rarer, and thus a full paradigm cannot be recovered.

	Indefinite	Definite	Construct
nom.			عصاك /ʕaṣā-k/ (Q7:117)
gen.		الصفا /aṣ-ṣafā/ (Q2:158)	بعصاك /bi-ʕaṣā-k/ (Q26:63)
acc.			عصاه /ʕaṣā-h/(Q7:107)

A.4.10 *III-w/y and III-ʔ Nouns*

Final weak nouns whose stem ends in historical **-iy-* such **wādiy-* 'valley, river' have some amount of variation due to the appearance of shortened forms of the stem-final *-ī*. The defective spelling of the definite form is especially common in pause, and seems to be the result of a process of pausal shortening of final *ī* that we find throughout the Quran (see A.3.6). The short spellings in construct are presumably simply context spellings of the shortening of the long vowel before the CC cluster of the following definite article.

	Indefinite	Definite	Construct
nom.	قاض /qāḍ/ (Q20:72)	الزانى /az-zānī/ (Q24:2)	اتى /ʔātī/ (Q19:93)
		المهتد /al-muhtad#/ (Q17:97)	لهاد /la-hādi/ (Q22:54)

typical isogloss of the modern Maghrebi Arabic dialects (Fischer and Jastrow 1980, 91). The Lisan al-ʕarab (*Lisān*, 3337c) explains this unusual plural as corresponding to a singular **miftaḥ* rather than *miftāḥ*, but the only evidence cited for it is the present Quranic verse, which seems to confirm it exceptional status. Note that Ibn Xālawayh (*muxtaṣar*, 35) cites a non-canonical reading for this verse with the singular, which would be equally acceptable to the *rasm*.

(*cont.*)

	Indefinite	Definite	Construct
gen.	بواد /bi-wād/ (Q14:37)	الداع /ad-dāʕ/(Q2:186)	بهدى /bi-hādī/ (Q27:81)[92] بهد /bi-hādi/ (Q30:53)
acc.	واديا /wādiyā/ (Q9:121)	الداعى /ad-dāʕī/ (Q20:108)	عليها /ʕāliya-hā/ (Q11:82)

As in Classical Arabic, final weak plurals that are in origin diptotic have a slightly different form in the indefinite accusative form, lacking the final /-ā/. Here again we find shortened forms in the definite forms (besides long forms) although they do not occur in obvious pausal positions.

	Indefinite	Definite	Construct
nom.	غواش /ġawāš/ (Q7:41)	الجوار /al-ǧawār/ (Q55:24)	
gen.	ليال /layāl/ (Q69:7)	المثانى /al-maṯānī/ (Q15:87) كالجواب /ka-l-ǧawāb/ (Q34:13)	موليكم /mawālī-kum/ (Q33:5)
acc.	مولى /mawālī/ (Q4:33)	المولى /al-mawālī/ (Q19:5)	

Nouns which end in an original stem-final *-iʔ- are barely attested, but when they appear, they seem to behave identically to final weak nouns, although pausal forms with shortening are unattested.

	Indefinite	Definite	Construct
nom.		البارى /al-bārī/ (Q59:24)	
gen.			باريكم /bārī-kum/(Q2:54)
acc.	خاسيا /xāsiyā/ (Q67:4)		شانيك /šāniy(a)-k/(Q108:3)

One other noun that has a *hamzah*-final stem is المنشيت (Q55:24). This word is spelled in the CE as المنشات, but this is clearly not original to the UT, as all

92 Q27:81 and Q30:53 are read by *hamzah* as *tahdi l-ʕumya* (Ibn al-Ǧazarī: § 3825).

early manuscripts retain the spelling المنشيت (see B.22). This word is read by the majority of the readers as a passive participle of *ʔanšaʔa*, i.e. *munšaʔāt* '(sails) raised', whereas Ḥamzah reads it as an active participle *munšiʔāt* 'raising (its sails)' (Ibn al-Ǧazarī, § 4316). The *rasm* is only consistent with Ḥamzah's reading, pointing to /munšiyāt/. If the majority reading is indeed intended, it means that the adjective *munšaʔ* has merged completely with III-*y* adjectives, and must be understood as coming from a paradigm m.sg. */munšē/ m.pl */munšawn/; f.sg. */munšēh/ f.pl. /munšayāt/.

The noun which in Classical Arabic would be *sayyiʔ* is consistently spelled السيا in early Quranic manuscripts (van Putten 2018, 115). This is similar to verbs ending in the same sequence: هيا *hayyiʔ* (Q18:10) and يهيا *yuhayyiʔ* (Q18:16). The reasons for this are unknown. It is tempting to see this as a historical *hamzah* spelling.

A.4.11 *Nouns in *-āʔ in Construct*

In the discussion of the *ʔalif al-wiqāyah* above, we already saw that nouns ending in *-āʔ* in the construct nominative sometimes are spelled not with final *ʔalif*, as is the normal spelling, but rather with *ʔalif*+*wāw* (most notably with *ǧazāʔ-* spelled as جزاو) and one time as wāw+ʔalif, ابنوا (see B.11 and B.14). Also, the genitive is occasionally expressed with a glide *yāʔ* in construct. This seems to be reconstructible for the following words in the UT: تلقى 'the accord of' (Q10:15), اناى 'the hours of' (Q20:130) and perhaps als ايتاى 'the giving of' (Q16:90) (see B.23).

When nouns of this type are followed by a pronominal clitic, they always reflect the case vowel with *wāw* in the nominative and *yāʔ* in the genitive in the CE. But this is a quirk of the CE, and examination of early Quranic manuscripts reveals that both spellings with and without the glides are attested (van Putten and Stokes 2018, 172–176). While previously, Van Putten & Stokes (2018, 159, 160f.) have interpreted this as evidence that case vowels in construct could optionally be lost, I now believe that a more natural interpretation of this data is to see this as related to the special status of this word-final *hamzah* after /ā/.

From Quranic rhyme it is clear that the *hamzah* was retained in this position, thus الدعا (Q3:38) clearly rhymes with other words that end in /āG/, which suggests a pronunciation /ad-duʕāʔ/. Moreover, انشا (Q56:35) stands in an /āGā/ rhyme, thus suggesting that the indefinite accusative was pronounced with final /āʔ-ā/, i.e. /inšāʔā/.

Presumably those forms that lack the glides are cases where the stem-final *hamzah* (spelled with the *ʔalif*) was retained. While those that show a glide have optional elision of the *hamzah* in this non-word-final position. The paradigm of nouns of this type must therefore be something along these lines as shown in the table below.

	Indefinite	Definite	Construct	Construct+Pron
Nom.	فجزا (Q5:95) /fa-ǧazāʔ/	السما (Q25:25) /as-samāʔ/	جزاو (Q5:29) /ǧazāwu/ جزا (Q2:85) /ǧazāʔu/	جزاوهم (Q17:98) /ǧazāwu-hum/ فجزاه (Q4:93) /fa-ǧazāʔu-h/
Acc.	جزا (Q5:38) /ǧazāʔā/	الجزا (Q53:41) /al-ǧazāʔ/	دعا (Q24:63) /duʕāʔa/, /duʕā(.a)/	دعا كم (Q35:14) /duʕāʔa-kum/ /duʕā(.a)-kum/
Gen.	دعا (Q41:51) /duʕāʔ/	الدعا (Q3:38) /ad-duʕāʔ/	اناى (Q20:13) /ʔānāyi/ دعا (Q41:49) /duʕāʔi/	دعايهم (Q46:5) /duʕāyi-hum/ بدعاك (Q19:4) /bi-duʕāʔi-ka/

The noun *ʔawliyāʔ* 'allies; protectors' is of exceptional status. While it is a noun that historically end in *-āʔ*, when the noun stands in construct the glide for the case vowel never appears, not when it stands in construct with a noun, nor when a pronominal suffix follows. This idiosyncrasy is not retained in the CE, but can be reconstructed for the UT, see B.24 (see also Nöldeke et al. 2013, 422). It thus seems that this noun has merged with nouns that end in *-yā* such as الدنيا /ad-dunyā/ 'world' (*passim*), الحوايا /al-ḥawāyā/ 'intestines' (Q6:146) and خطيكم /xaṭāyā-kum/ 'your sins' (Q2:58).

	Indefinite	Definite	Construct	Construct+Pron
Nom.	اوليا (Q46:32) /awliyā/		اوليا (Q5:51) /awliyā/	اوليهم (Q2:257) /awliyā-hum/
Acc.	اوليا (Q3:28) /awliyā/		اوليا (Q4:76) /awliyā/	اوليه (Q3:175) /awliyā-h/
Gen.	اوليا (Q11:20) /awliyā/			اوليهم (Q6:121) /awliyā-hum/

This shift of category seems to be unique to this noun, ادعييهم /ʔadʕiyāyi-hum/ 'adopted sons' (Q33:37) is consistently spelled with the glide for the genitive in early manuscripts (see B.25).

A.4.12 *Confusion between Subjunctive and Apocopate*

There is one example in the QCT where we find confusion between the subjunctive and the apocopate. The following verse uses an apocopate stem, in a clearly subjunctive context:

رب لولا اخرتنى الى اجل قريب فاصدق واكن من الصلحين (Q63:10)

/rabb-∅, lawlā axxarta-nī ilā ajal qarīb fa-aṣṣaddaq **wa-akun** min aṣ-ṣāli-ḥīn/

My lord, if only you would delay me for a brief term so I would give charity and be among the righteous[93]

A.4.13 *Partial Merger of III-ʔ Verbs and III-y/w Verbs*

In Classical Arabic grammar III-*w/y* verbs and III-*ʔ* are kept clearly distinct. This is, as far as we can tell from the defective spelling, not the case in Quranic Arabic, where we see a certain amount of merger of the two stem types. This merger is certainly less complete than it is in the modern dialects, but nevertheless we can deduce mergers from the QCT that did not take place in Classical Arabic.

G-stems of III-*ʔ* verbs are still clearly distinct from III-*y* and III-*w* verbs, e.g. قرات /qarāt/ 'you recited' (Q16:98) vs. نجوت /nağawt/ 'you fled' (Q28:25) and قضيت /qaḍayt/ 'you decided' (Q4:65), and even in derived stems there are clear examples where they are distinct, e.g. نبات /nabbāt/, or /nabbaʔat/ 'she informed' (Q66:3), نباتكما /nabbātu-kumā/ 'I informed you' (Q12:37); اخطاتم /axṭātum/ 'you have sinned' (Q33:5); امتلات /imtalāt/ 'you filled' (Q50:30).

In the imperfect stem and nominal derivations, however, these verbs merge to a large extent throughout the whole paradigm. With the loss of the *ʔ*, word-final *iʔ* yielded -*ī*, merging in most places with word-final -*ī* of final weak roots. This can be clearly seen in some of the derived stems of final glottal stop roots that in the imperfect plural forms as well as the participial plural forms have merged with the III-*y/w* verbs.

يستهزى /yastahzī/ (Q2:15) < **yastahziʔu*
مستهزون /mustahzūn/ (Q2:14) < **mustahziʔūna*

---

93 It is interesting to note here that, while most reading traditions simply follow the *rasm* and read this word as an apocopate *ʔakun*, ʔabū ʕamr ignores the *rasm* and reads it as the Classically normative *ʔakūna* (Ibn al-Ğazarī, § 4401).

يستهزون /yastahzūn/ (Q6:5, etc.) < **yastahziʔūna*
تستهزون /tastahzūn/ (Q9:65) < **tastahziʔūna*
والصبون /wa-ṣ-ṣābūn/ (Q5:69) < **aṣ-ṣābiʔūna*
والصبين /wa-ṣ-ṣābīn/ (Q2:62; Q22:17) < **aṣ-ṣābiʔīna*
اتنبون /ʔa-tunabbūn/ (Q10:18) < *tunabbiʔūna*
فالون /fa-mālūn/ (Q37:66; Q56:53) < **fa-māliʔūna*
يطفوا /yuṭfū/ (Q9:32; Q61:8) < **yuṭfiʔū*
ليواطوا /li-yuwāṭū/ (Q9:37) < **yuwāṭiʔū*
الخطون /al-xāṭūn/ (Q69:37) < **al-xāṭiʔūna*
(لـ)خطين /(la-)xāṭīn/ (Q12:29, 91, 97; Q28:8) < **xāṭiʔīna*
متكين /muttakīn/ (Q18:31, etc.) < **muttakiʔīna*
خاسين /xāsīn/ (Q2:65; Q7:166) < **xāsiʔīna*

This merger has led to some amount of disagreement whether certain verbs are III-*y* or III-*ʔ* among the canonical readers, see § 6.5.5 for a discussion.

Words ending in **aʔūna* are technically ambiguous in terms of their interpretation, due to the tendency to not write double *wāw* sequences for representing /wū/ (see A.2.2). It however stands to reason that these would have merged to /-awn/, e.g.

يطون /yaṭawn/ (Q9:120) < *yaṭaʔūna
يقرون /yaqrawn/ (Q10:94; Q17:71) < *yaqraʔūna
يدرون /yadrawn/ (Q13:22; Q28:54) < *yadraʔūna
مبرون /mubarraʔūn/ (Q24:26) < *mubarraʔūna
مرجون /murǧawn/ (Q9:106) < *murǧaʔūna

In the *ʕarabiyyah*, the apocopate and imperative would be places where III-*ʔ* and III-*w/y* verbs would remain distinct, even if one were to pronounce them with the loss of *hamzah*. The imperative of صلى *ṣallā* 'to bless' would be صل *ṣalli* 'bless!', whereas the imperative of نبأ *nabbaʔa* 'to inform' would be نبئ *nabbiʔ* which with dropping of the *hamzah* should yield *nabbī*.

In the QCT we see that a merger between the two stem types is under way, no doubt due to their complete merger in the imperfective and subjunctive stems. The table below illustrates the examples of apocopates and imperatives of historically III-*ʔ* verbs and how they appear in the QCT.

QCT		Classical Arabic
ارجه (Q7:111; Q26:36)	/arǧi-h/	أَرْجِئْهُ
نبنا (Q12:36)[94]	/nabbi-nā/	نَبِّئْنَا
نبى (Q15:49)	/nabbī/	نَبِّئْ
نبيهم (Q15:51; Q54:28)	/nabbī-hum/	نَبِّئْهُمْ
انبيهم (Q2:33)[95]	/anbī-hum/	أَنْبِئْهُمْ

One final verb could perhaps be added here, namely نسها (Q2:106), which is either read *nunsi-hā*, an apocopate of *ʔansā* 'to cause to be forgotten' or *nansaʔ-hā* from *nasaʔa* 'to cause to be delayed' (Ibn al-Ǧazarī, § 2720). If the latter reading is correct, this would be yet another hamzated apocopate that appears to function as a final weak verb. But **aʔ* usually does not show this merger, e.g. لم ينبا /lam yunabbā/ 'he was not informed' (Q53:36), اقرا /iqrā/ 'recite!' (Q17:14; Q96:1, 3). Semantically, *nunsi-hā* seems like a better fit in this verse: ما ننسخ من ايه او ننسها نات بخير منها او مثلها "whatever we abrogate from a verse or cause it to be forgotten we bring one better or equal to it.", and thus I think it is better taken as the regular outcome of a final weak verb.

Finally, the verb *hayyaʔa* 'to make ready' is consistently spelled with a final *ʔalif* in early Quranic manuscripts: *hayyiʔ* هيا (Q18:10); *yuhayyiʔ* يهيا (Q18:16). This spelling should be reconstructed for the Uthmanic archetype, but its interpretation is not very clear, for a suggestion and other words with such spellings, see Van Putten (2018, 115).

A.4.14 *Pausal Imperatives/Apocopates of* III-*y/w Verbs Iqtadih, yatasannah*

III-*w/y* apocopates and imperatives throughout the Quran are consistently without any reflex of the final radical, thus we see, e.g. يرم /yarmi/ 'throws' (Q4:112), يدع /yadʕ(u)/ 'invokes' (Q23:117), يلق /yalq(a)/ 'meets' (Q25:68); ايت /īt(i)/ 'come!' (Q10:15), ادع /udʕ(u)/ 'invoke!' (Q2:68).

94 This word is spelled نبينا in the CE, but in early Quranic manuscript نبنا is regular. See B.26 for an overview.

95 Most manuscripts have the *rasm* انبيهم but DAM 01–32.1 has انبهم. This latter *rasm* is not

However, the only two times that an imperative and apocopate occur in pause, these stems are suffixed with a final *hāʔ*: فبهديهم اقتده /fa-bi-hudē-hum iqtadih#/ "so follow after their guidance." (Q6:90),[96] which is followed by the قلے pausal sign in the CE, which indicates an optional pause, with a preference towards pausing.[97] The other case is found in قل بل لبثت مايه عام فانظر الى طعامك وشرابك لم يتسنه /qāl bal labiṯt miyah ʕām fa-nẓur ilā ṭaʕāmi-k wa-šarābi-k lam yatsannah#/ "He said: Nay, you have remained for a hundred years, look at your food and your drink; it did not age." (Q2:259), which is followed by the صلے pausal sign in the CE, which indicates an optional pause, with a preference towards continuing.[98] Based on these two examples it seems that in Quranic Arabic imperatives and apocopates received /h/ in pause.

It is worth noting that the fact that this *hāʔ* only shows up in pausal position, is yet another piece of evidence that 'pausal spelling' is not a governing principle in Quranic orthography. Had that been the case, all apocopates and imperatives should have received a final *h*, not just the one that stand in a pausal position.

A.4.15 *Partial Merger of the I-ʔ and I-w Verbs in Derived Stems*

Due to the loss of the *hamzah* (see § 5.2) D- and L-stems of verbs with a *ʔ* as their initial consonant merge with D- and L-stems of verbs with *w* as their initial consonant, e.g. **yuʔaxxiru-hum* > يوخرهم /yuwaxxiru-hum/ 'he gives respite to them' (Q14:42); **yuʔāxiḏu* > يواخذ /yuwāxiḏ/ 'he would punish' (Q35:45). Such verbs usually remain distinct in the perfect where you get forms like **ʔaxxara* > اخر /ʔaxxar/ 'left behind' (Q75:13). The partial merger of these verb types is no doubt the origin of the pseudocorrect use of *hamzah* in *muʔṣadah* for *mūṣadah* (§ 6.4.2).

A more pervasive merged with I-*w* is found in the Gt-stem of the verb *ʔaxaḏa*, which is treated as a I-*w* in the QCT. This idiosyncrasy also finds its way into Classical Arabic, e.g. اتخذ /ittaxaḏ/ 'he took' (e.g. Q18:4). Other Gt stems of

---

common, but it is consistent with the reading of al-Ḥasan al-Baṣrī *ʔanbi-himī* (Ibn Xālawayh *muxtaṣar*, 4).

96 Ibn ʕāmir treats this final *hāʔ* as a pronoun, reading it *iqtadi-hi* or *iqtadi-hī* (Ibn al-Ǧazarī, § 2375). This reading is grammatically rather awkward. It is difficult to take it as a resumptive pronoun of the preceding object (*bi-hudā-hum*) since that object is marked with *bi-*, thus we would expect *iqtadi bi-hī* rather than *iqtadi-hī*. Ibn Muǧāhid (262) shared this sentiment and explicitly calls it a mistake (*wa-hāḏā ġalaṭun*) because this is a pausal *hāʔ*, not a pronoun.

97 See also Saǧāwindī (*ʕilal al-Wuqūf*, 333).

98 See also Saǧāwindī (*ʕilal al-Wuqūf*, 482).

I-ʔ verbs continue to behave distinctly from I-*w* verbs, e.g. لا ياتل /lā yātal/ 'may they not swear' < **yaʔtali* (Q24:22).

A.4.16 */yak/ besides /yakun/*

The verb كان /kān/ 'to be', has an anomalous form in the apocopate. Besides the regular stem form يكن which is identical to that of Classical Arabic, quite often we find the form يك. Van Putten & Stokes (2018, 168–170) argue that this is best understood as the regular outcome of this verb in Quranic Arabic. As word-final nunation and case vowels were lost, the word final **-un* of **yakun* would also regularly be lost, yielding /yak/. The long form is then an analogically restored version of the apocopate.

A.4.17 **raʔaya 'to See' and *naʔaya 'to Be Distant' as* را *and* نا

The regular spelling of the verbs *raʔā* 'to see' and *naʔā* 'to be distant', both historically final weak verbs with a medial *hamzah*, is را and نا respectively in the QCT. Their orthographic behaviour suggests that they have merged with hollow roots with a final *hamzah*, e.g. جا /ǧāʔ/, جات /ǧāt/ جاو /ǧāw/ 'to come', at least in the 3rd person masculine singular and plural forms, hence we find spellings را /rāʔ/ راو /rāw/. The spelling را occurs twenty times in the Quran, and only *Sūrat al-Naǧm* attests the form راى (Q53:11, 18), which at least in the first verse seems to be the use of a dialectal form /raʔē/ to accommodate the rhyme. The exact interpretation of the unusual behaviour in this Sūrah, however, should not distract us from the fact that the regular Quranic form is را, which is not likely to have been a spelling for /raʔē/.

How exactly را and نا took on the shapes that they have is not entirely obvious. One might imagine that at an earlier stage of Quranic Arabic, the **y* and **ʔ* were regularly metathesized, **raʔaya* > **rayaʔa* which then regularly yielded /rāʔ/. Alternatively, one might imagine that the intervocalic *hamzah* had dropped yielding **raʔaya* > *rāya* which then, similar to **samāy* 'sky' shifted its word final *y* to *ʔ*, likewise yielding /rāʔ/.

In the former development one would expect the verb to have completely merged with verbs of the type جا /ǧāʔ/, in which case one would predict the first and second person forms to be like جيت /ǧīt/. But this does not seem to be the case. The Cairo edition attests both ارءيت 'did you see?' (e.g. Q18:63) and رايت 'you saw' (e.g. Q47:20).[99] In Early Quranic manuscripts it is not at all uncommon to only see the spelling ريت, but رايت spellings do occur. Considering these

99 There is a certain conditioned distribution between these two spellings in the Cairo edition, but this appears to be absent in early Quranic documents (see van Putten 2018, 107 f.).

spellings, it seems that the suffixed forms were probably /rāy-t/ 'you saw', etc. In which case the second scenario which requires *hamzah* to be lost before the **āy* > *āʔ* shift, becomes more probable. This specific behaviour with partial merger, *rāʔa* but *raʔaytu* (or *rāytu*), is exactly what is reported by al-Farrāʔ as being a typical Hijazi isogloss (§ 5.11).

APPENDIX B

Orthographic Comparison

This study tries to uncover the linguistic features of Quranic Arabic by focusing on the earliest layer of the written text, Quranic Consonantal Text. This is the standard philological approach to studying languages of antiquity, but doing this to the Quran is not without its problems. As of writing, there is no critical edition of the Quranic text, and the field generally relies on the standard text established by the Cairo Edition. This edition is by no means a poor edition, as its orthography is explicitly archaizing. It has attempted to reconstructed the original Uthmanic *rasm* as much as possible by relying on medieval *rasm* works such as al-Dānī's *muqniʕ*. As a result, much of how the orthography is presented in this edition is a fairly accurate representation of what 5th century AH sources reported about manuscripts that predated them by yet another couple of centuries.

Comparison with Quranic manuscripts shows that these descriptions indeed are fairly reliable guides to the orthography as it appears in the earliest manuscripts. However, they are not always accurate, and throughout this work I have sometimes had to draw upon the orthographic practices as they appear in early manuscripts rather than how they appear in the CE. When I do so, I refer to entries in this Appendix, which presents tables of certain important lexical items and it examines how they appear in early manuscripts. These comparative tables will function as "critical editions" not of the full Quranic text, but of the individual specific words that are being examined.

From the following tables it will quickly become clear that, most of the time the manuscript records show a remarkably consistent picture, all sharing the same spelling with only the occasional exception. Not infrequently, the Cairo Edition is the odd one out. When such a consistent picture emerges, there can be little doubt that what we find in these manuscripts can be confidently reconstructed for the archetype, despite the Cairo Edition showing something different.

Throughout this appendix, I have consistently drawn on several manuscripts to see if the relevant words occur in these. The abbreviations that I use in the tables are given here. On occasion it has been relevant to cite other manuscripts, in which case I will discuss them individually below the relevant table. Unless stated otherwise I have accessed these manuscripts in digitized form, using the Corpus Coranicum (http://www.corpuscoranicum.de) and Gallica (http://gallica.bnf.fr) websites.

The selection of the manuscripts consulted is based to a large extent on availability. All of these manuscripts contain a significant portion of the Quranic text, and a good number of them are considerably early. Several of the ones consulted (especially GK, S, M-Ali, and S-Ali) are probably to be dated somewhat later than the other manuscripts consulted here. These, however, are rather complete examples, and therefore frequently allow us to establish what the orthography continued to look like in later manuscripts (more often than not, there is hardly a difference between earlier and later manuscripts in this regard).

1615I **Dublin, Chester Beatty Library, Is 1615 I + Doha, Museum of Islamic Art Ms. 68.2007, Ms. 69.2007, Ms. 70.2007, Ms. 699.2007 + Houston, Vahid Kooris Private Collection**
47 folios; ^{14}C: 591–643 CE, σ2 (95.4%); "330g style"
I have only been able to access the folios of the CBL.

330g **Paris, Bibliothèque nationale de France, Arabe 330g + Dublin, Chester Beatty Library, Is 1615 II + St. Petersburg, National Library, Marcel 16 + Manama, Bayt al-Qurʔān, Ms. 1611-MKH235 + auctioned folios: Rennes Enchères 2011, Lot 151**
43 folios; first century; "330g style"
I have only been able to access the folios of the BnF and CBL.

331 **Paris, Bibliothèque nationale de France, Arabe 331 + Leiden, Leiden University Library, Or. 14.545 b + c**
58 folios; first century, ^{14}C: 652–763 CE, σ2 (95.4%); Kufi B Ia (Déroche 1983, 67, no. 14).

BL **London, British Library, Or. 2165 + Paris, Bibliothèque nationale de France, Arabe 328e + Kuwait, Dār al-ʔāṯār al-ʔislāmiyyah, LNS 19 CA^{ab} (bifolio)**
128 folios; second half of the first century (Dutton 2004, 66); Hijazi II (Déroche 1983, 62, no. 7).
Reading of LNS folio is based on the transcription on the Corpus Coranicum website. Or. 2165 has been accessed from the British Library website and the Parisian section on Gallica.

CA1 **Codex Amrensis 1**
75 folios; ca. first half second century(?) (Cellard 2018, 15); Late Hijazi (Cellard 2018, 7)/Hijazi I (Déroche 1983, 59, no. 1).
Edited and published by Cellard (2018).

CPP **Codex Parisino-Petropolitanus**
98 folios; c. third quarter of the first/seventh century (Déroche 2009, 177); Hijazi I (Déroche 1983, 59 f., nos. 2 & 3).

Edited and published by Déroche (2009). For the Parisian folios I have checked these myself through the digitizations available on the Corpus Coranicum and Gallica websites. For the other folios, I have relied on Déroche's transcriptions.

D29 **Sanaa, Dār al-Maxṭūṭāt, DAM 01–29.1**
35 folios; ca. 1st century. Various styles: Hijazi I, Kufi B.Ia.
I have had private access to these folios, as I am currently preparing an edition of this manuscript together with Michael Marx.

GK **Kairo, al-Maktaba al-Markaziyya li-l-Maxṭūṭāt al-ʔislāmiyyah: Großer Korankodex**
1087 folios; not before 700; Kufi B.Ib or B.II.

M-Ali **The Mashhad codex attributed to ʕaliyy b. ʔabī Ṭālib**
341 folios; ca. 2nd/3rd century; Kufi B.II.
Edited and published by Altıkulaç et al. (2017)

Q **Cairo, Dār al-Kutub MS 247 (Qaf 47) + Berlin, Staatsbibliothek, Ms. Or. Fol. 4313**
36 folios; first century, ^{14}C: 606–652, $\sigma 2$ (95.4%) (Marx and Jocham 2015); "330g style"

S **Berlin, Staatsbibliothek: Samarkand Codex (Facsimile)**
353 folios; ca. 750–850. Kufi D I.

S-Ali **al-Muṣḥaf al-Sharīf attributed to ʿAlī b. Abī Ṭālib (the copy of Sana'a)**
275 folios; ca. 2nd/3rd century. Kufi C.III.[1]
Edited and published by Altıkulaç (2011).

SM1a **Gotthelf-Bergsträßer Archive: Saray Medina 1a**
308 folios; late first/early second century; various styles: Hijazi, B.Ia, O.I.

SM1b **Gotthelf-Bergsträßer Archive: Saray Medina 1b**
134 folios; 2nd/3rd century; C.III.

SU = Codex Ṣanʿāʾ I, upper text **Sanaa Dār al-Maxṭūṭāt, DAM 01–27.1 + Ḥamdūn** (2004) + **auctioned folios: Christie's 2008; Bonhams 2000; Sotheby's 1992 and Sotheby's 1993.**
80 folios; 578–669 CE 2σ (95.4%)/606–649, $\sigma 2$ (95.4%) (Coranica); Hijazi I.
The upper text of the Sanaa palimpsest must of course post-date the lower text, but can still be considered an early Quranic manuscript from the first or early second century on the basis of its orthography.

1 For an approximate dating of the C.III style see Cellard (2015, 212).

T **Tübingen, Universitätsbibliothek, Ma VI 165**
77 folios; ^{14}C: 649–675, σ2 (95.4 %); Kufi B.Ia.

Top **Istanbul, Topkapı Sarayı Müzesi: H.S. 44.31**
408 folios. Late first/seventh, early second/eight century; Kufi C.I
Edited and published by Altıkulaç (2007).

W **Berlin, Staatsbibliothek: Wetzstein II 1913 (Ahlwardt 305) + BnF Arabe 6087.**
216 folios.; Second half first century/early second century, ^{14}C: 662–765, σ2 (95.4 %); Kufi B/Ia (Déroche 1983, 67, no. 160).

In some cases, some changes have been made in manuscripts to the relevant word that is being considered. The following symbols are used in the following:

(...) letter added later.
{...} letter removed.
[...] absent in the text.
ش < س word س was changed to word ش.

B.1 Samāwāt, naḥ(i)sāt, rawḍāt

	CE	Qirāʔāt	BL	CPP	SM1a	CA1	W	1615I	S	GK	S-Ali	Top	M-Ali
Q41:12	سموات	*samāwātin*	سموت		سموت	سموت	سموت	سموت	سماوت	سماوت	سموت	سموت	سموت
Q41:16	نحسات	*naḥisātin, naḥsātin*	نحست		نحست	نحست	نحست	نحست	نحست	نحست	نحست	نحست	نحست
Q42:22	روضات	*rawḍāti*	روضـ[ـت]	روضت	روضت		روضات	روضت	روضت	روضت	روضت	روضت	روضات

B.2 Yī with Two yāʔs

As *yuḥyī* and *yastayī* are rather commonly attested, to save space I have not included every single instance of them in this table. Nevertheless, as you will see in the following table, the spelling with two *yāʔ*s in early manuscripts is clearly regular, and quick examinations have shown that this is no different for the attestations that have not been included here.

	CE	Qirāʔāt	BL	CPP	SM1a	CA1	SU	D29	W	331	T	1615I	330g	SM1b	S	GK	S-Ali	Top	M-Ali
Q7:196	ولى	*waliyyiya*	ولي	ولي	ولي		ولي		ولي	ولي			ولي			ولي		ولي	ولي
Q12:101	ولى	*waliyyī*	ولي	ولي	ولي	ولي			ولي							ولي	ولي	ولي	ولي
Q2:258	احى	*ʔuḥyī*					احي		احي	احي					احي	احي	احي	احي	احي

(*cont.*)

	CE	Qirāʔāt	BL	CPP	SM1a	CA1	SU	D29	W	331	T	1615I	330g	SM1b	S	GK	S-Ali	Top	M-Ali
Q15:23	نحى	*nuḥyī*	نحيي	نحيي	نحيي	نحيي			نحيي	نحيي					نحيي	نحيي	نحيي	نحيي	نحيي
Q50:43	نحى	*nuḥyī*			نحيي	نحى		نحيي	نحيي	نحيي						نحيي	نحيي	نحيي	نحيي
Q7:158	يحى	*yuḥyī*	يحيي	يحيي	يحيي		يحيي		يحيي							يحيي	يحيي	يحيي	يحيي
Q9:116	يحى	*yuḥyī*		يحيي	يحيي	يحيي			يحيي				يحيي			يحيي	يحيي	يحيي	يحيي
Q28:4	يستحى	*yastaḥyī*		يستحيي	يستحيي						يستحيي			يستحيي		يستحيي	يستحيي	يستحيي	يستحيي
Q33:53	فيستحى	*yastaḥyī*	فيستحيي		فيستحيي			فيستحيي	فيستحيي		فيستحيي	فيستحيي				فيستحيي	فيستحيي	فيستحيي	فيستحيي
Q33:53	يستحى	*yastaḥyī*	يستحيي		يستحيي			يستحيي	يستحيي		يستحيي	يستحيي				يستحيي	يستحيي	يستحيي	يستحيي
Q7:127	نستحى	*nastaḥyī*	نستحيي	نستحيي	نستحيي		نستحيي		نستحيي				نستحيي			نستحيي	نستحيي	نستحيي	ستحيي

B.3 ʔalif al-wiqāyah on yaʕfū/yaʕfuwa

	CE	Qirāʔah	BL	CPP	SM1a	SU	W	331	Is1615I	330g	Q47	S	GK	S-Ali	Top	M-Ali
Q2:237	يعفوا	*yaʕfuwa*					يعفوا	يعفوا					يعفوا	يعفوا	يعفوا	يعفوا
Q4:99	يعفو	*yaʕfuwa*		يعفوا		يعفوا	يعفو(ا)			يعفو	يعفو	يعفو	يعفو	يعفو	يعفو	يعفوا

(*cont.*)

	CE	Qirāʔah	BL	CPP	SM1a	SU	W	331	Is1615I	330g	Q47	S	GK	S-Ali	Top	M-Ali
Q5:15	يعفوا	*yaʕfū*	يعفوا	يعفوا							يعفوا		[يعفوا]ا	يعفوا	يعفوا	يعفوا
Q24:22	ليعفوا	*l-yaʕfuwa*	ليعفوا		ليعفوا		ليعفو						ليعفوا	ليعفوا	ليعفوا	ليعفوا
Q42:25	يعفوا	*yaʕfū*	يعفوا	يعفوا	يعفوا	يعفوا	يعفوا		يعفوا			يعفوا	يعفوا	يعفوا	يعفوا	يعفوا
Q42:30	يعفوا	*yaʕfū*	يعفوا	يعفوا	يعفوا		يعفوا		يعفوا			يعفوا	يعفوا	يعفوا	يعفوا	يعفوا

B.4 Lack of ʔalif al-wiqāyah on Words Ending in -waw

	CE	Qirāʔāt	BL	CPP	SM1a	CA1	SU	W	331	330g	GK	S-Ali	Top	M-Ali
Q8:72	اووا	*ʔāwaw*	اوو	اوو	اوو	اوو	اوو	اوو	اوو		اوو	اوو	اوو	اوو
Q8:74	اووا	*ʔāwaw*	اوو	اوو	اوو	اوو	اوو	اوو	اوو	اوو	اوو	اوو	اوو	اوو
Q63:5	لووا	*lawwaw, lawaw*		لوو	لوو			لووا	لوو		لووا		لوو	لووا
Q59:9	تبوو	*tabawwaʔū*			تبوو	تبوو		تبووا	تبوو		تبووا	تبوو	تبوو	تبووا

B.5 Spelling of saʕaw and ʕataw

	CE	Qirāʔāt	BL	CPP	SM1a	SU	D29	W	331	T	1615I	330g	SM1b	S	GK	S-Ali	Top	M-Ali
Q22:51	سعوا	*saʕaw*	سعوا		سعوا		سعوا	سعوا[a]		سعوا			سعوا		سعوا	سعوا	سعوا	سعوا
Q34:5	سعو	*saʕaw*	سعوا		سعوا		سعوا	سعوا		سعوا	لسعو[b]				سعو	سعوا	سعوا	سعوا
Q7:77	عتوا	*ʕataw*	عتوا	عتوا	عتوا	عتوا		عتوا						عتو	عتوا	عتوا	عتوا	عتوا
Q7:166	عتوا	*ʕataw*	عتوا	عتوا	عتوا	عتوا		عتوا	عتوا			عتوا			عتوا	عتوا	عتوا	عتوا
Q25:21	عتو	*ʕataw*	عتوا	عتوا	عتوا	عتو		عتو		عتو{ا}					عتو	عتو	عتو	عتو
Q51:44	فعتوا	*faʕataw*						فعتوا	فعتوا						فعتوا	فعتوا	فعتوا	فعتوا

a Perhaps the final *ʔalif* is a later addition.
b (sic!)

B.6 Luʔluʔ

All forms of /lūlū/ 'pearl' should probably be reconstructed with an *ʔalif al-wiqāyah* for the UT, although the CE reports lacks these in some cases.

	CE	Qirāʔah	BL	CPP	SM1a	SU	W	331	T	1615I	SM1b	GK	S-Ali	Top	M-Ali
Q22:23	لولوا	*luʔluʔan, luʔluʔin, lūluʔan, lūluʔin*	لولوا		لولوا		لولوا		لولوا	لولوا	لولو(ا)	لولوا	لولوا	لولوا	لولوا
Q35:33	لولوا	*luʔluʔan, luʔluʔin, lūluʔan, lūluʔin*		لولوا	لولوا		لولوا		لولوا			لولوا	لولوا	لولوا	لولو
Q52:24	لولو	*luʔluʔun, lūluʔun*			لولو{ا}		لولوا	لولو{ا}				لولوا	لولوا	لولوا	لولوا
Q55:22	اللولو	*al-luʔluʔu, al-lūluʔu*			اللولو	الولو	اللولوا	الولو{ا}				اللولوا	اللولوا	اللولوا	اللولو
Q56:23	اللولو	*al-luʔluʔi, al-lūluʔi*			اللولوا	الولو{ا}	اللولوا	الولوا				اللولوا	اللولوا	اللولوا	اللولو
Q76:19	لولوا	*luʔluʔan, luʔluʔin, lūluʔan, lūluʔin*			لولوا							لولوا		لولوا	لولوا

B.7 Raʔaw

	CE	Qirāʔah	BL	CPP	SM1a	SU	D29	W	311	T	1615I	330g	SM1b	S	GK	S-Ali	Top	M-ali
Q2:166	راوا	*raʔawu*					راو	راو	راو					راو	راو		راو	راو
Q7:149	راوا	*raʔaw*	راو	راو	راو	راو	راوا	راو				راو			راو	راو	راو	راو
Q10:54	راوا	*raʔawu*	راو	راو	راو	راو		راو					راو		راو	راو	راو	راو
Q12:35	راوا	*raʔawu*	راو		راو{ا}	راو		راو					راو			راو	راو	راو
Q19:75	راوا	*raʔaw*	راو		راو			راو		راو				راو	راو{ا}	راو	راو	راو
Q28:64	راوا	*raʔawu*	راو		راو{ا}	راو				راو	راو		راو		راو	راو	راو	راو

(*cont.*)

	CE	Qirāʔah	BL	CPP	SM1a	SU	D29	W	311	T	1615I	330g	SM1b	S	GK	S-Ali	Top	M-ali
Q34:33	راوا	*raʔawu*	راو		راو					راو	راو{ا}				راو	راو	راو	راو
Q37:14	راوا	*raʔaw*	راو		راو			راو			راو			راو	راو	راو	راو	راو
Q40:84	راوا	*raʔaw*	راو		راو			راو			راو				راو	راو	راو	راو
Q40:85	راوا	*raʔaw*	راو		راو			راو			راو				راو	راو	راو	راو
Q42:44	راوا	*raʔawu*	راو	راو	راو	راو		راو			راو			راو	راو	راو	راو	راو
Q62:11	راوا	*raʔaw*		راو	راو			راو							راو		راو	راو
Q72:24	راوا	*raʔaw*			راو		راو	راو							راو		راو	راو

B.8 Al-malaʔu

	CE	Qirāʔāt	BL	CPP	SM1a	CA1	SU	W	T	1615I	Q47	SM1b	S	GK	S-Ali	Top	M-Ali
Q7:60	الملا	*al-malaʔu*	الملا	الملا	الملا		الملا	الملا					الملا	الملا	الملا	الملا	الملا
Q7:66	الملا	*al-malaʔu*	الملا	الملا	الملا		الملا	الملا					الملا	الملا	الملا	الملا	الملا
Q7:75	الملا	*al-malaʔu*	الملا	الملا	الملا		الملا	الملا					الملا	الملا	الملا	الملا	الملا
Q7:88	الملا	*al-malaʔu*	الملا	الملا	الملا		الملا	الملا					الملا	الملا	الملا	الملا	الملا

(*cont.*)

	CE	Qirāʔāt	BL	CPP	SM1a	CA1	SU	W	T	1615I	Q47	SM1b	S	GK	S-Ali	Top	M-Ali
Q7:90	الملا	*al-malaʔu*	الملا	الملا	الملا		الملا	الملا					الملا	الملا	الملا	الملا	الملا
Q7:109	الملا	*al-malaʔu*	الملا	الملا	الملا		الملا	الملا						الملا	الملا	الملا	الملا
Q7:127	الملا	*al-malaʔu*	الملا	الملا	الملا		الملا	الملا						الملا		الملا	الملا
Q11:27	الملا	*al-malaʔu*	الملا	الملا	الملا < الملوا	الملا		الملا			الملا	الملا		الملا	الملا	الملا	الملوا
Q12:43	الملا	*al-malaʔu*	الملا		الملا		الملا	الملا						الملا	الملا	الملا	الملا
Q23:24	الملوا	*al-malaʔu*	الملوا	الملوا	الملوا			الملوا	الملوا			الملا		الملوا	الملوا	الملوا	الملا
Q23:33	الملا	*al-malaʔu*	الملا	الملا	الملا			الملا						الملا	الملا	الملا	الملا
Q27:29	الملوا	*al-malaʔu*	الملوا	الملوا	الملوا			الملوا	الملوا			الملوا	الملوا	الملوا	الملوا	الملوا	الملوا
Q27:32	الملوا	*al-malaʔu*	الملوا	الملوا	الملوا			الملوا	الملوا < الملا			الملوا	الملوا	الملوا	الملوا	الملوا	الملوا
Q27:38	الملوا	*al-malaʔu*	الملوا	الملوا	الملوا[a] <?			الملوا	الملوا			الملوا		الملوا	الملوا	الملوا	الملوا
Q28:38	الملا	*al-malaʔu*	الملا	الملا	الملا < الملوا				الملا	الملا		الملا		الملا	الملا	الملا	الملا
Q38:6	الملا	*al-malaʔu*	الملا		الملا			الملا		الملا			الملا	الملا	الملا	الملا	الملا

a This appears to be an autocorrection.

B.9 Nabaʔu(n)

	CE	Qirāʔāt	BL	CPP	SM1a	CA1	SU	W	1615I	330g	S	GK	S-Ali	Top	M-Ali
Q9:70	نبا	*nabaʔu*	نبا	نبا	نبا	نبا	نبا	نبا		نبا		نبا	نبا	نبا	نبوا
Q14:9	نبوا	*nabaʔu*	نبوا	نبوا	نبو(ا)			نبو(ا)				نبو	نبوا	نبوا	نبوا
Q38:21	نبوا	*nabaʔu*	نبوا		نبوا			نبوا	نبا		نبوا	نبوا	نبوا	نبوا	نبوا
Q38:67	نبوا	*nabaʔun*	نبوا	نبوا	نبوا			نبوا	نبوا			نبوا		نبوا	نبوا
Q64:5	نبوا	*nabaʔu*			نبوا			نبوا				نبوا		نبوا	نبوا

B.10 Balāʔ

	CE	Qirāʔāt	BL	CPP	SM1a	SU	D29	W	1615I	330g	S	GK	S-Ali	Top	M-Ali
Q2:49	بلا	*balāʔun*						بلا			بلا	بلا		بلا	بلا
Q7:141	بلا	*balāʔun*	بلا	بلا	بلا	بلا	بلا	بلا		بلا		بلا	بلا	بلا	بلا
Q14:6	بلا	*balāʔun*	بلا	بلا	بلا			بلا				بلا	بلا	بلا	بلا
Q37:106	البلوا	*al-balāʔu*	البلا		البلا	الـ]ـبلا		البلا	البلا > البلوا			البلا	البلا	البلوا	البلوا
Q44:33	بلوا	*balāʔun*		بلا	بلا			بلا	بلوا			بلا	بلا	بلا	بلو

B.11 ʔanbāʔ, ʔabnāʔ, duʕāʔ

	CE	Qirāʔāt	BL	CPP	SM1a	SU	W	331	T	1615I	S	GK	S-Ali	Top	M-Ali
Q6:5	انبوا	*ʔambāʔu*	انبوا				انبوا				انبوا	انبوا	انبوا	انبوا	انبوا
Q26:6	انبوا	*ʔambāʔu*	انبا		انبا > انبوا		انبوا > انبا	انبوا	انبوا			انبا	انبا	انبا	انبوا
Q28:66	الانبا	*al-ʔambāʔu*	الانبا		الانبا	الانبا			الانبا	الانبا		الانبا	الانبا	الانبا	الانبا
Q5:18	ابنوا	*ʔabnāʔu*	ابنوا	ابنا > ابنوا			ابنا > ابنوا					ابنا	ابنا	ابنا	ابنا
Q13:14	دعا	*duʕāʔu*	دعا	دعا	دعا		دعا					دعا	[د]عا	دعا	دعا
Q40:50	دعوا	*duʕāʔu*			دعا		دعا			دعا		دعوا	دعا	دعا	دعا

B.12 Fuʕalāʔ plurals

	CE	Qirāʔāt	BL	CPP	SM1a	CA1	SU	D29	W	331	T	1615I	SM1b	S	GK	S-Ali	Top	M-Ali
Q26:224	الشعرا	*aš-šuʕarāʔu*	الشعرا		الشعرا				الشعرا		الشعرا		الشعرا			الشعرا	الشعرا	الشعرا
Q4:12	شركا	*šurakāʔu*		شركا			شركا		شركا					شركا	شركا	شركا	شركا	شركا
Q6:94	شركوا	*šurakāʔu*	شركوا	شركا	شركوا > سركا			شركا	شركا > شركوا					شركا	شركا		شركوا	شركوا
Q6:139	شركا	*šurakāʔu*		شركا	شركا				شركا					شركا	شركا		شركا	شركا

(*cont.*)

	CE	Qirāʔāt	BL	CPP	SM1a	CA1	SU	D29	W	331	T	1615I	SM1b	S	GK	S-Ali	Top	M-Ali
Q39:29	شركا	*šurakāʔu*	شركا		شركا				شركا			شركا			شركا		شركا	شركا
Q42:21	شركوا	*šurakāʔu*	شركوا	شركا	شركوا > سركا				شركا			شركوا			شركوا	شركوا	شركوا	شركوا
Q68:41	شركا	*šurakāʔu*			شركا									شركا	شركا		شركا	شركا
Q2:266	ضعفا	*ḍuʕafāʔu*							ضعفا					ضعفا	ضعفا	ضعفا	ضعفا	ضعفا
Q14:21	الضعفوا	*aḍ-ḍuʕāfāʔu*	الضعفوا	الضعفوا	الضعفوا	الصعفا			الضعفوا	الضعفوا					الضعفوا	الضعفوا	الضعفوا	الضعفوا
Q40:47	الضعفوا	*aḍ-ḍuʕāfāʔu*			الضعفوا > الضعفا				الضعفوا			الضعفا			الضعفوا	الضعفوا	الضعفوا	الضعفوا
Q35:28	العلموا	*al-ʕulamāʔu*	العلموا	العلموا	العلموا				العلموا		العلما	العلما			العلموا	العلموا	العلما	العلموا
Q26:197	علموا	*ʕulamāʔu*	علما		علموا				علما		علموا		علموا	علما	علما	علموا	علما	علموا
Q30:13	شفعوا	*šufaʕāʔu*	شفعا		شفعا						شفعا	شفعا	شفعوا		شفعوا	شفعوا	شفعوا	شفعا
Q60:4	بروا	*buraʔāʔu*			بروا	بروا			بروا						بروا		بروا	بروا

B.13 Našāʔu

	CE	Qirāʔāt	BL	CA1	SM1a	SU	W	SM1b	S	GK	S-Ali	Top	M-Ali
Q11:87	نشوا	*našāʔu*	نشوا	تشوا[a]	نشاو	نساو	نشو(ا)	نشـ{ـا}و	نشوا	نشوا	نشوا	نشاو	نشوا

a *tašāʔu* is a non-canonical reading attribute to ʕalī b. ʔabī Ṭālib and al-Ḍaḥḥāk (Ibn Xālawayh *muxtaṣar*:61).

B.14 Ǧazāʔu

	CE	Qirāʔāt	BL	CPP	SM1a	CA1	SU	D29	W	331	T	1615I	330g	Q47	SM1b	S	GK	S-Ali	Top	M-Ali
Q2:85	جزا	*ǧazāʔu*							جزا							جزا	جزا		جزا	جزاو
Q2:191	جزا	*ǧazāʔu*							جزا									جزا	جزا	جزاو
Q5:29	جزوا	*ǧazāʔu*		جزاو				جزاو	جزاو					جزاو			جزاو	جزاو	جزاو	جزاو
Q5:33	جزوا	*ǧazāʔu*		جزاو			جزاو	جزا(و)	جزا(و)					جزاو			جزاو	جزاو	جزاو	جزاو
Q5:85	جزا	*ǧazāʔu*					جزا		جزا					جزا			جزا	جزا	جزا	جزاو
Q9:26	جزا	*ǧazāʔu*	جزا	جزا	جزا	جزا	جزا		جزا	جزا			جزا					جزا	جزا	جزاو
Q10:27	جزا	*ǧazāʔu*	جزا	جزا	جزا	جزا	جزا		جزا				جزا		جزا		جزا	جزا	جزا	جزاو
Q12:25	جزا	*ǧazāʔu*	جزا		جزا		جزا		جزا						جزا		جزا	جزا	جزا	جزاو

(*cont.*)

	CE	Qirāʔāt	BL	CPP	SM1a	CA1	SU	D29	W	331	T	1615I	330g	Q47	SM1b	S	GK	S-Ali	Top	M-Ali
Q20:76	جزا	*ǧazāʔu*	جزاو		جزا(و)		جزاو	جزا	جزاو		جزاو					جزاو	جزاو	جزاو	جزاو	جزاو
Q34:37	جزا	*ǧazāʔu*	جزا		جزا						جزا	جزا					جزا	جزا	جزا	جزا
Q39:34	جزا	*ǧazāʔu*	جزاو		جزو > جزا				جزاو								جزاو		جزا	جزاو
Q41:28	جزا	*ǧazāʔu*	جزا		جزا	جزا			جزا			جزا				جزا	جزا	جزا		جزاو
Q42:40	جزوا	*ǧazāʔu*	جزاو	جزاو	جزاو				جزاو			جزاو > جزوا				جزاو	جز(ا)و	جزاو	جزا	جزاو
Q55:60	جزا	*ǧazāʔu*			جزا		جزا		جزا	جزا							جزا	جزا	جزا	جزاو
Q59:17	جزوا	*ǧazāʔu*			جزا				جزا	جزا							جزا	جزا	جزاو	جزاو

B.15 Ribā

	CE	Qirāʔāt	BL	CPP	SM1a	SU	W	T	1615I	330g	Q47	S	GK	S-Ali	Top	M-Ali
Q2:275	الربوا	*ar-ribā, ar-ribē*					الربوا				الربوا		الربوا	الربوا	الربوا	الربوا
Q2:275	الربوا	*ar-ribā, ar-ribē*					الربوا						الربوا		الربوا	الربوا
Q2:275	الربوا	*ar-ribā, ar-ribē*					الربوا				الربوا		الربوا		الربوا	الربوا

(*cont.*)

	CE	Qirāʔāt	BL	CPP	SM1a	SU	W	T	1615I	330g	Q47	S	GK	S-Ali	Top	M-Ali
Q2:276	الربوا	*ar-ribā, ar-ribē*		الربوا			الربوا						الربوا	الربوا	الربوا	الربوا
Q2:278	الربوا	*ar-ribā, ar-ribē*		الربوا			الربوا				الربوا		الربوا	الربوا	الربوا	الربوا
Q3:130	الربوا	*ar-ribā, ar-ribē*		الربوا		الربوا	الربوا				الربوا	الربوا	الربوا	الربوا	الربوا	
Q4:161	الربوا	*ar-ribā, ar-ribē*		الربوا		الربوا	الربوا			الربوا			الربوا	الربوا	الربوا	الربوا
Q30:39	ربا	*riban*	ربا		ربا	ربوا		ربا	ربا			ربا	ربا	ربا	ربا	ربا

B.16 ʔasāʔū

	CE	Qirāʔāt	BL	SM1a	1615I	W	331	T	SM1b	GK	S-Ali	Top	M-Ali
Q30:10	اسوا	*ʔasāʔū*	اسوا	اسوا	اس{ـا}ـوا			اسوا	اسوا	اسوا	اسوا	اسوا	اسوا
Q53:31	اسوا	*ʔasāʔū*		اسوا		اسوا	اسوا			اسوا	اسوا	اسوا	اسوا

B.17 Dāwūd

	CE	Qirāʔāt	BL	CPP	SM1a	SU	W	331	T	1615I	330g	Q47	SU	D29	S	GK	S-Ali	Top	M-Ali
Q2:251	داود	*dāwūdu*				داود	دواد < داود	داود								داود	داود	داود	داود
Q4:163	داود	*dāwūda*		دواد		داود	دواد < داود				داود					داود	داود	داود	داود
Q5:78	داود	*dāwūda*				داود	دواد < داود					دواد				داود	داود	داود	داود
Q6:84	داود	*dāwūda*		داود	داود		دواد < داود							داود	داود	داود	داود	داود	داود
Q17:55	داود	*dāwūda*	داود		دواد < داود		داود		دواد < داود				داود			دود	داود	داود	داود
Q21:78	داود	*dāwūda*	دواد < داود		دود < داود		دواد < داود		دواد < داود							داود	داود	داود	داود
Q21:79	داود	*dāwūda*			دود < داود		دواد < داود		دواد < داود				داود			داود	داود	داود	داود
Q27:15	داود	*dāwūda*	داود	داود	داود		دواد < داود		دواد				داود		داود	داود	داود	داود	داود
Q27:16	داود	*dāwūda*	داود	داود	داود		دواد < داود		دواد						داود	داود	داود	داود	داود
Q34:10	داود	*dāwūda*	داود		داود				دواد	دواد < داود						داود	داود	داود	داود
Q34:13	داود	*dāwūda*	داود		داود				دواد < داود	دواد < داود						داود	داود	داود	داود
Q38:17	داود	*dāwūda*	داود		داود		دواد < داود			دواد					داود	داود	داود	داود	داود
Q38:22	داود	*dāwūda*	داود		داود		دواد < داود			دواد					داود	داود		داود	داود

(*cont.*)

	CE	Qirāʔāt	BL	CPP	SM1a	SU	W	331	T	1615I	330g	Q47	SU	D29	S	GK	S-Ali	Top	M-Ali
Q38:24	داود	*dāwūdu*	داود		داود		دواد > داود			دواد					داود	داود	داود	داود	داود
Q38:26	يداود	*yā-dāwūdu*	يداود		يدود > يداود		يدواد > يداود			يدواد					يداود	يداود	يداود	يداود	يداود
Q38:30	لداود	*li-dāwūda*	لداود		لداود		لدواد > لداود			لدواد						لداود		لداود	لداود

B.18 Ruʔūs

	CE	Qirāʔāt	BL	CPP	SM1a	SU	D29	W	331	T	1615I	Q47	GK	S-Ali	Top	M-Ali
Q2:196	روسكم	*ruʔūsakum*						روسكم					روسكم	روسكم	روسكم	روسكم
Q2:279	روس	*ruʔūsu*		روس		روس		روس				روس	روس	روس	روس	روس
Q5:6	بروسكم	*biruʔūsikum*		بروسكم				بروسكم				براوسكم	بروسكم	بروسكم		بروسكم
Q14:43	روسهم	*ruʔūsihim*	روسهم	روسهم	روسهم		روسهم	روسهم	روسهم		رواسهم		روسهم		روسهم	روسهم
Q17:51	روسهم	*ruʔūsahum*	روسهم		روسهم	روسهم		روسهم		روسهم			رووسهم	روسهم	روسهم	روسهم
Q21:65	روسهم	*ruʔūsihim*	روسهم		روسهم	روسهم		روسهم		روسهم			روسهم	روسهم	روسهم	روسهم

(*cont.*)

	CE	Qirāʔāt	BL	CPP	SM1a	SU	D29	W	331	T	1615I	Q47	GK	S-Ali	Top	M-Ali
Q22:19	روسهم	*ruʔūsihim(u/i)*	روسهم		روسهم			روسهم		روسهم			روسهم	روسهم	روسهم	روسهم
Q32:12	روسهم	*ruʔūsihim*	روسهم		روسهم			روسهم		روسهم			روسهم	روسهم	روسهم	روسهم
Q37:65	روس	*ruʔūsu*	روس		روس			روس			روس		روس	روس	روس	روس
Q48:27	روسكم	*ruʔūsakum*			روسكم			روسكم	روسكم				روسكم	روسكم	روسكم	روسكم
Q63:5	روسهم	*ruʔūsahum*		روسهم	روسهم			روسهم	روسهم				روسهم		روسهم	روسهم

B.19 Bi-smi

	CE	Qirāʔāt	BL	CPP	SM1a	CA1	SU	W	331	T	330g	Q47	SM1b	S	GK	S-Ali	Top	M-Ali
Q11:41	بسم	*bismi*	بسم		بسم	بسم	بسم	بسم				بسم	بسم		بسم	بسم	بسم	بسم > باسم
Q27:30	بسم	*bismi*	بسم	بسم	بسم			بسم		بسم				بسم	بسم		بسم	بسم
Q56:74	باسم	*bismi*		باسم	بسم			باسم	باسم						باسم	باسم	باسم	باسم
Q56:96	باسم	*bismi*		باسم	بسم			باسم	باسم						باسم	باسم	باسم	باسم
Q69:52	باسم	*bismi*		باسم	باسم			باسم							باسم		باسم	باسم
Q96:1	باسم	*bismi*			بسم						باسم				باسم		باسم	باسم

B.20 Ibn ʔumma/I, ya-bana ʔumma/i

	CE	Qirāʔāt	BL	CPP	SM1a	SU	D29	T	W	330g	GK	S-Ali	Top	M-Ali
Q7:150	ابن ام	*ibna ʔumma/i*	ابن ام	ابن ام	ابن ام	ابن ام	ابنوم		ابن ام > ابنوم	ابنوم	ابن ام	ابن ام	ابن ام	ابن ام
Q20:94	يبنوم	*yabnaʔumma/i*	يابنوم		يابنوم	يابنوم	يابنوم	يابنوم	يابنوم		يابنوم	يابنوم	يابنوم	يابنوم

B.21 La-ttaxaḏta

	CE	Qirāʔāt	BL	SM1a	W	T	SM1b	GK	S-Ali	Top	M-Ali
Q18:77	لتخذت	*la-ttaxaḏta, la-ttaxaṯṯa, la-taxiḏta, la-taxiṯṯa*	لتخذت	لتخذت > لاتخذت	لاتخذت > لتخذت	لتخذت	لاتخذت > لتخذت	لتخذت	لتخذت	لتخذت	لتخذت

Paris, Bibliothèque Nationale de France, Arabe 334k has لاتخذت.

B.22 Al-munša/iʔāt

	CE	Qirāʔāt	SU	SM1a	GK	W	331	M-Ali	Top	S-Ali
Q55:24	المنشات	*al-munšaʔāt, al-munšiʔāt*	المنشيت	المنشيت	المنشيت	المنشيت	المنشيت	المنشيت	المنشيت	المنشيت

B.23 Genitive Construct Nouns in Ending in -āʔi

	CE	Qirāʔāt	BL	CPP	SM1a	SU	D29	W	331	T	1615I	330g	SM1b	S	GK	S-Ali	Top	M-Ali
Q10:15	تلقاى	*tilqāʔi*	تلقى	تلقى	تلقا			تلقى				تلقى	تلقاى		تلقى	تلقى	تلقاى	تلقاى
Q16:90	ايتاى	*ʔītāʔi*	ايتى		ايتا	ايتى > ايتا[a]	ايتا	ايتا					ايتا	ايتى	ايتى		ايتا	ايتاى
Q24:37	ايتا	*ʔītāʔi*	ايتا	ايتا	ايتا					ايتا					ايتا		ايتا	ايتا
Q20:130	اناى	*ʔānāʔi*	اناى		انا		اناى	اناى		انا(ى)				اناى	اناى	اناى	اناى	اناى
Q6:31	بلقا	*bi-liqāʔi*		بلقا				بلقا							بلقا	بلقا	بلقا	بلقا
Q6:154	بلقا	*bi-liqāʔi*		بلقا	بلقا	بلقا		بلقا						بلقا	بلقا	بلقا	بلقا	بلقا
Q7:147	لقا	*liqāʔi*	لقا	لقا	لقا	بلقا	لقا	لقا				لقا			لقا	لقا	لقا	لقا
Q10:45	بلقا	*bi-liqāʔi*	بلقى	بلقا	بلقا	بلقاى		بلقا					بلقا		بلقى	بلقا	بلقاى	بلقا

a This looks like an autocorrection.

(*cont.*)

	CE	Qirāʔāt	BL	CPP	SM1a	SU	D29	W	331	T	1615I	330g	SM1b	S	GK	S-Ali	Top	M-Ali
Q13:2	بلقا	*bi-liqāʔi*	بلقا	بلقا	بلقا			بلقا							بلقا	بلقا	بلقا	بلقا
Q23:33	بلقا	*bi-liqāʔi*	بلقا	بلقا	بلقا			بلقا		بلقا					بلقا	بلقا	بلقا	بلقا
Q30:8	بلقای	*bi-liqāʔi*	بلقا		بلقا					بلقا			بلقا		بلقی	بلقای	بلقای	بلقا
Q30:16	لقی	*liqāʔi*	لقا		لقا					لقا	لقا		لقای		لقی	لقا	لقای	بلقا
Q32:10	بلقا	*bi-liqāʔi*	بلقا		بلقا			بلقا		بلقا			بلقا		بلقا	بلقا	بلقا	بلقا
Q41:54	لقا	*liqāʔi*	لقا	لقا	لقا	لقا		لقا			لقا				لقا	لقا	لقا	لقا
Q11:71	ورا	*warāʔi*			ورا	ورا		ورا						ورا	ورا	ورا	ورا	ورا
Q33:53	ورا	*warāʔi*	ورا		ورا		ورا	ورا		ورا	ورا				ورا	ورا	ورا	ورا
Q42:51	ورای	*warāʔi*	ورای	ور(ا)ی	ورا			ورا			ورا			ورای	ورای	ورا	ورا	ورای
Q49:4	ورا	*warāʔi*			ورا		ورا	ورا	ورا						ورا	ورا	ورا	ورا
Q59:14	ورا	*warāʔi*			ورا			ورا	ورا						ورا	ورا	ورا	ورا

B.24 ʔawliyāʔ in Construct

	CE	Qirāʔāt	BL	CPP	SU	W	331	T	1615I	330g	Q47	S	GK	SM1a	CA1	SU	D29	S-Ali	Top	M-Ali
Q2:257	اولياوهم	*ʔawliyāʔu-hum(ū)*			اولياهم	اوليهم	اوليهم					اولياهم	اوليهم					اوليهم	اوليهم	اولياهم
Q6:121	اوليايهم	*ʔawliyāʔi-him(ū)*		اوليهم		اوليهم						اوليايهم	اوليهم	اوليهم				اولياهم	اولياهم	اوليايهم
Q6:128	اولياوهم	*ʔawliyāʔu-hum(ū)*		اوليهم		اوليهم						اولياوهم	اوليهم	اوليهم					اوليهم	الياهم
Q8:34	اولياوه	*ʔawliyāʔu-hū*	اوليه		اولياه	? > اولييه	اولياه			اوليه	اوليه		اوليه	اوليه	اوليه		اولياه	اولياه	اولياه	اولياه
Q33:6	اوليايكم	*ʔawliyāʔi-kum(ū)*	اوليكم			اوليكم		اوليكم	اولييكم				اوليكم	اوليكم		اوليا كم		اوليكم	اوليكم	اوليكم
Q41:31	اولياوكم	*ʔawliyāʔu-kum(ū)*	اوليكم			اوليكم			اوليكم			اوليكم	اوليكم	اوليكم		اوليكم		اوليكم	اوليكم	اوليكم

B.25 ʔadʕiyāʔihim

	CE	Qirāʔāt	BL	SM1a	SU	W	T	1615I	GK	S-Ali	Top	M-Ali
Q33:37	ادعيايهم	*ʔadʕiyāʔi-him(ū)*	ادعييهم	ادعييهم	ادعيهن > ادعييهم	ادعييهم	ادعييهم	ادعييهم	ادعييهم	ادعييهم	ادعييهم	ادعييهم

B.26 Arjih, nabbiʔnā, nabbiʔ, nabbiʔhum, ʔanbiʔhum

	CE	Qirāʔāt	BL	CPP	SM1a	SU	CA1	W	331	T	S	GK	S-Ali	Top	M-Ali
Q7:111	ارجه	*ʔarǧih, ʔarǧihi, ʔarǧihī, ʔarǧiʔhū, ʔarǧiʔhu, ʔarǧiʔhi*	ارجه	ارجه	ارجه	ارجه		ارجه				ارجه	ارجه	ارجه	ارجه
Q26:36	ارجه	*ʔarǧih, ʔarǧihi, ʔarǧihī, ʔarǧiʔhū, ʔarǧiʔhu, ʔarǧiʔhi*	ارجه	ارجه	ارجه			ارجه		ارجه		ارجه	ارجه	ارجه	ارجه
Q12:36	نبينا	*nabbiʔnā*	نبنا		نبنا	نبنا		نبنا				نبنا	نبنا	نبنا	نبنا
Q15:49	نبى	*nabbiʔ*	نبى	نبى	نبى		نب > نبى[a]	نبى	نبى		نبى	نبى	نبى	نبى	نبى
Q15:51	نبيهم	*nabbiʔhum*	نبيهم	نبيهم	نبيهم		نبيهم	نبيهم	نبيهم		نبيهم	نبيهم	نبيهم	نبيهم	نبيهم
Q54:28	نبيهم	*nabbiʔhum*			نبيهم			نبيهم				نبيهم	نبيهم	نبيهم	نبيهم
Q2:33	انبيهم	*ʔanbiʔhum*						انبيهم			انبيهم	انبيهم		انبيهم	انبيهم

a This appears to be an autocorrection.
Sanaa, Dār al-Maxṭūṭāt 01-32.1 has انبهم for Q2:33 (accessed through Corpus Coranicum).

B.27 Fa-ğtabā-hu, ʕuqbā-hā

	CE	Qirāʔāt	W	SM1a	330g	GK	M-Ali	Top
Q68:50	فاجتبه	*fa-ğtabā-hu, fa-ğtabā-hū, fa-ğtabē-hu*	فاجتبيه	فاجتبيه		فاجتبيه	فاجتبيه	فاجتبيه
Q91:15	عقبها	*ʕuqbā-hā, ʕuqbē-hā*		عقبيها	عقبيها	عقبيها	عقبيها	عقبيها

B.28 Maḍā

	CE	Qirāʔāt	BL	CPP	SM1a	CA1	W	1615I	S	GK	S-Ali	M-Ali	Top
Q43:8	مضى	*maḍā, maḍē*	مضا	مضا	مضى	مضا	مضا	مضا	مضا	مضا	مضا	مضا	مضا

B.29 Hātayni

	CE	Qirāʔāt	BL	CPP	SM1a	T	1615I	SM1b	GK	S-Ali	Top	M-Ali
Q28:27	هتين	*hātayni*	هاتين	هاتين	هاتين	هاتين	هاتين	هاتين	هاتين	هاتين	هاتين	هاتين

Bibliography

Abbott, Nabia. 1939. *The Rise of the North Arabic Script and Its Ḳur'ānic Development: With a Full Description of the Ḳur'ān Manuscripts in the Oriental Institute*. Chicago, IL: University of Chicago Press.

Abu-Haidar, Farida. 1991. *Christian Arabic of Baghdad*. Wiesbaden: Harrassowitz.

'Abū Ḥayyān, Muḥammad. 2010. *Al-Baḥr al-Muḥīṭ fī al-Tafsīr*. Edited by Ṣidqī Muḥammad Ǧamīl. 11 vols. Beirut: Dār al-Fikr.

'Abū 'Ubayd, al-Qāsim b. Sallām. 1995. *Faḍā'il al-Qur'ān*. Edited by Marwān al-'Aṭiyyah, Muḥsin Ḫarābah, and Wafā' Taqiyy al-Dīn. Damascus & Beirut: Dār Ibn Kaṯīr.

al-'Aḫfaš al-'Awsaṭ, 'Abū Ḥasan Sa'īd b. Mas'adah. 1990. *Ma'ānī al-Qur'ān*. Edited by Hudā Maḥmūd Qarrā'ah. Cairo: Maktabat al-Ḫāniǧī.

al-Ḫalīl b. 'Aḥmad. 2003. *Kitāb al-'Ayn Murattaban 'alā Ḥurūf al-Mu'ǧam*. Edited by 'Abd al-Ḥamīd al-Hindāwī. Beirut: Dār al-Kutub al-'Ilmiyyah.

Al-Jallad, Ahmad. 2014a. "*Aṣ-Ṣādu llatī ka-s-Sīn*—Evidence for an Africated *Ṣād* in Sibawayh?" *Folia Orientalia* 51: 51–57.

Al-Jallad, Ahmad. 2014b. "Final Short Vowels in Ge'ez, Hebrew *'atta*, and the Anceps Paradox." *Journal of Semitic Studies* 59 (1): 315–327.

Al-Jallad, Ahmad. 2015. *An Outline of the Grammar of the Safaitic Inscriptions*. Leiden & Boston: Brill.

Al-Jallad, Ahmad. 2017a. "Graeco-Arabica I: The Southern Levant." In *Arabic in Context*, edited by Ahmad Al-Jallad, 99–186. Leiden & Boston: Brill.

Al-Jallad, Ahmad. 2017b. "The Etymology of *Ḥattā*." In *To the Madbar and Back Again. Studies in the Languages, Archaeology, and Cultures of Arabia Dedicated to Michael C.A. Macdonald*, edited by Laïla Nehmé and Ahmad Al-Jallad, 338–345. Leiden & Boston: Brill.

Al-Jallad, Ahmad. 2017c. "Was It *Sūrat Al-Baqárah*? Evidence for Antepenultimate Stress in the Quranic Consonantal Text and Its Relevance for صلوه Type Nouns." *Zeitschrift der Deutschen Morgenländischen Gesellschaft* 167 (1): 81–90.

Al-Jallad, Ahmad. 2017d. "The Arabic of the Islamic Conquests: Notes on Phonology and Morphology Based on the Greek Transcriptions from the First Islamic Century." *Bulletin of the School of Oriental and African Studies* 80 (3): 419–439.

Al-Jallad, Ahmad. 2018a. "The Earliest Stages of Arabic and Its Linguistic Classification." In *The Routledge Handbook of Arabic Linguistics*, edited by Elabbas Benmamoun and Reem Bassiouney, 315–331. London & New York: Routledge.

Al-Jallad, Ahmad. 2018b. "What Is Ancient North Arabian?" In *Re-Engaging Comparative Semitic and Arabic Studies*, edited by Daniel Birnstiel and Na'ama Pat-El. Wiesbaden: Harrassowitz.

Al-Jallad, Ahmad. 2020a. "Notes on the Language of the Hismaic Inscriptions and a Re-

Reading of Line 4 of the Madaba Hismaic Inscription." *Journal of the Royal Asiatic Society* 30 (3): 561–569.

Al-Jallad, Ahmad. 2020b. *The Damascus Psalm Fragment: Middle Arabic and the Legacy of Old Ḥigāzī*. Chicago, IL: Oriental Institute.

Al-Jallad, Ahmad. forthcoming. "One Wāw to Rule Them All: The Origins and Fate of Wawation in Arabic and Its Orthography." In *Scripts and Scripture*, edited by Fred Donner and Rebecca Hasselbach. Chicago, IL: Oriental Institute.

Al-Jallad, Ahmad, Zeyad Al-Salameen, Yunus Shdeifat, and Rafe Harahsheh. 2020. "Gaius the Roman and the Kawnites: Inscriptional Evidence for Roman Auxiliary Units Raised from the Nomads of the Ḥarrah." In *Landscapes of Survival: The Archaeology and Epigraphy of Jordan's North-Eastern Desert and Beyond*, edited by M.M.G. Akkermans, 355–389. Leiden: Sidestone Press.

Al-Jallad, Ahmad, and Karolina Jaworska. 2019. *A Dictionary of the Safaitic Inscriptions*. Leiden & Boston: Brill.

Al-Jallad, Ahmad, and Ali al-Manaser. 2015. "New Epigraphica from Jordan I: A Pre-Islamic Arabic Inscription in Greek Letters and a Greek Inscription from North-Eastern Jordan." *Arabian Epigraphic Notes* 1: 51–70.

Al-Jallad, Ahmad, and Marijn van Putten. 2017. "The Case for Proto-Semitic and Proto-Arabic Case: A Reply to Jonathan Owens." *Romano-Arabica* 17: 87–117.

Altıkulaç, Tayyar. 2011. *Al-Muṣḥaf al-Sharīf: Attributed to ʿAlī b. Abī Ṭālib, the Copy of Sana'a*. Istanbul: Research Centre for Islamic History, Art and Culture.

Altıkulaç, Tayyar, Ḥamīd Riżā Mustafīd, and Morteza Tavakoli. 2017. *Muṣḥaf-i Šarīf. Mansūb ba-Imām ʿAlī b. Abī Ṭālib*. Tehran: Markaz Ṭabʿ wa-Našr Qurʾān Karīm.

As-Said, Lahib. 1975. *Recited Koran: A History of the First Recorded Version*. Princeton, N.J.: Darwin Pr.

Azami, Muhammad Mustafa al-. 2003. *The History of The Qur'anic Text: From Revelation to Compilation: A Comparative Study with the Old and New Testaments*. First Edition. Leicester: UK Islamic Academy.

Bearman, P., Th. Bianquis, C.E. Bosworth, E. van Donzel, and W.P. Heinrichs, eds. 1960. *Encyclopaedia of Islam*. Second edition, Online version. Leiden & Boston: Brill.

Beck, Edmund. 1945. "Der ʿUṯmānische Kodex in der Koranlesung des zweiten Jahrhunderts." *Orientalia* N.S. 14: 355–373.

Beck, Edmund. 1946. "ʿArabiyya, Sunna und ʿĀmma in der Koranlesung des zweiten Jahrhunderts." *Orientalia* N.S. 15: 180–224.

Behnstedt, Peter. 1987. *Die Dialekte der Gegend von Ṣaʿdah (Nord-Jemen)*. Wiesbaden: Harrassowitz.

Blachère, Régis. 1947. *Introduction au Coran*. Paris: G.P. Maisonneuve.

Blanc, Haim. 1964. *Communal Dialects in Baghdad*. Cambridge: Harvard University Press.

Blanc, Haim. 1979. "Diachronic and Synchronic Ordering in Medieval Arab Grammatical Theory." In *Studia Orientalia Memoriae D.H. Baneth Dedicata*, edited by Joshua Blau, Shlomo Pines, Meir Jacob Kister, and Shaul Shaked, 155–180. Jerusalem: The Magnes Press.

Blau, Joshua. 1967. *A Grammar of Christian Arabic. Based Mainly on the South-Palestinian Texts from the First Millennium*. 3 vols. Louvain: Secrétariat du CorpusCO.

Blau, Joshua. 1970. *On Pseudo-Corrections in Some Semitic Languages*. Jerusalem: The Israel Academy of Sciences and Humanities.

Blau, Joshua. 1977. "The Beginnings of the Arabic Diglossia: A Study of the Origins of Neoarabic." *Afroasiatic Linguistics* 4 (4): 175–202.

Blau, Joshua. 1999. *The Emergence and Linguistic Background of Judaeo-Arabic: A Study of the Origins of Middle Arabic*. 3rd revised edition. Jerusalem: Ben-Zvi institute for the Study of Jewish Communities in the East.

Blau, Joshua. 2002. *A Handbook of Early Middle Arabic*. Jerusalem: The Max Schloessinger Memorial Foundation.

Blau, Joshua, and Simon Hopkins. 1987. "Judeo-Arabic Papyri—Collected, Edited, Translated and Analysed." *Jerusalem Studies in Arabic and Islam* 9: 87–160.

Bloch, Ariel A. 1967. "The Vowels of the Imperfect Preformatives in the Old Dialects of Arabic." *Zeitschrift der Deutschen Morgenländischen Gesellschaft* 117 (1): 22–29.

Brockelmann, Carl. 1908. *Grundriss der vergleichenden Grammatik der semitischen Sprachen. I. Band: Laut- und Formenlehre*. Berlin: Verlag von Reuther & Reichard.

Bursi, Adam. 2018. "Connecting the Dots: Diacritics, Scribal Culture, and the Qurʾān in the First/Seventh Century." *Journal of the International Qurʾanic Studies Association* 3: 111–157.

Cantineau, Jean. 1978. *Le Nabatéen. II. Choix de Textes, Lexique*. Osnabrück: Otto Zeller.

Carter, Michael G. 2004. *Sibawayhi*. Oxford: Oxford University Press.

Cellard, Éléonore. 2015. "La Vocalisation des manuscrits coraniques dans les premiers siècles de l'Islam." In *Les Origines du Coran, le Coran des origines, actes de colloque*, edited by François Déroche, Christian Robin, and Michel Zink, 161–186. Paris: Académie des Inscriptions et Belles-Lettres.

Cellard, Éléonore. 2018. *Codex Amrensis 1*. Leiden & Boston: Brill.

Cellard, Éléonore. 2021. "The Ṣanʿāʾ Palimpsest: Materializing the Codices." *Journal of Near Eastern Studies* 80 (1): 1–30.

Comerro, Viviane. 2012. *Les Traditions sur la constitution du muṣḥaf de ʿUthmān*. Beirut: Ergon Verlag.

Cook, Michael. 2004. "The Stemma of the Regional Codices of the Koran." *Graeco-Arabica* 9–10: 89–104.

Cowell, Mark W. 1964. *A Reference Grammar of Syrian Arabic*. Washington, D.C.: Georgetown University Press.

Ḏahabī, Šams al-Dīn al-. 1995. *Maʿrifat al-Qurrāʾ al-Kibār ʿalā al-Ṭabaqāt wa-l-ʾAʿṣār*. Edited by Tayyar Altıkulaç. Istanbul: ISAM.

Dānī, 'Abū 'Amr al-. 1978. *Al-Muqniʿ fī Rasm Maṣāḥif al-'Amṣār ma'a Kitāb al-Naqṭ*. Edited by Muḥammad Al-Ṣādiq Qamḥāwī. Cairo: Maktabat al-Kulliyāt al-'Azhar.

Dānī, 'Abū 'Amr al-. 1984. *Al-Taysīr fī al-Qirā'āt al-Sabʿ*. Edited by Otto Pretzl. Beirut: Dār al-Kitāb al-'Arabī.

Dānī, 'Abū 'Amr al-. 1994. *Al-Bayān fī 'Add 'Āy al-Qur'ān*. Edited by Ġānim Qaddūrī al-Ḥamad. Kuwayt: Markaz al-Maḫṭūṭāt wa-l-Turāṯ.

Dānī, 'Abū 'Amr al-. 2005. *Ǧāmiʿ al-Bayān fī al-Qirā'āt al-Sabʿ al-Mašhūrah*. Edited by Muḥammad Ṣaddūq al-Ǧazā'irī. Beirut: Dār al-Kutub al-'Ilmiyyah.

David-Weill, J. 1939. *Le Djâmiʿ d'Ibn Wahb. I. Texte et Planches*. Cairo: Imprimerie de l'institut français.

Déroche, François. 1983. *Les Manuscrits du coran. Aux origines de la calligraphie coranique*. Paris: Bibliothèque nationale.

Déroche, François. 1992. *The Abbasid Tradition. Qur'ans of the 8th to the 10th Centuries AD*. Oxford: Oxford University Press.

Déroche, François. 2009. *La Transmission écrite du Coran dans les débuts de l'islam: Le Codex Parisino-Petropolitanus*. Leiden & Boston: Brill.

Déroche, François. 2014. *Qur'ans of the Umayyads: A First Overview*. Leiden & Boston: Brill.

Diem, Werner. 1973. "Die nabatäischen Inschriften und die Frage der Kasusflexion im Altarabischen." *Zeitschrift der Deutschen Morgenländischen Gesellschaft* 123 (2): 227–237.

Diem, Werner. 1976. "Some Glimpses at the Rise and Early Development of the Arabic Orthography." *Orientalia* N.S. 45: 251–261.

Diem, Werner. 1979. "Untersuchungen zur frühen Geschichte der arabischen Orthographie I. Die Schreibung der Vokale." *Orientalia* N.S. 48: 207–257.

Diem, Werner. 1980. "Untersuchungen zur frühen Geschichte der arabischen Orthographie II. Die Schreibung der Konsonanten." *Orientalia* N.S. 49: 67–106.

Diem, Werner. 1981. "Untersuchungen zur frühen Geschichte der arabischen Orthographie III. Endungen und Endschreibungen." *Orientalia* N.S. 50: 332–383.

Diem, Werner. 1982. "Die Entwicklung der Derivationsmorpheme der t-Stämme im Semitischen." *Zeitschrift der Deutschen Morgenländischen Gesellschaft* 132 (1): 29–84.

Durie, Mark. 2018. *The Qur'an and Its Biblical Reflexes. Investigation into the Genesis of a Religion*. Lanham, Boulder, New York & London: Lexington Books.

Dutton, Yasin. 2001. "An Early Muṣḥaf According to the Reading of Ibn 'Āmir." *Journal of Qur'anic Studies* 3 (1): 71–89.

Dutton, Yasin. 2004. "Some Notes on the British Library's 'Oldest Qur'an Manuscript' (Or. 2165)." *Journal of Qur'anic Studies* 6 (1): 43–71.

El-Hawary, Hassan Mohammed. 1930. "The Most Ancient Islamic Monument Known, Dated A.H. 31 (A.D. 652), from the Time of the Third Calif 'Uthman." *The Journal of the Royal Asiatic Society of Great Britain and Ireland* 2: 321–333.

Fārisī, ʾAbū ʿAlī al-. 1971. *Al-Ḥuǧǧah fī ʿIlal al-Qirāʾāt al-Sabʿ*. Edited by ʿĀdil ʾAḥmad ʿAbd al-Mawǧūd and ʿAlī Muḥammad Muʿawwaḍ. Beirut: Dār al-Kutub al-ʿIlmiyyah.

Farrāʾ, ʾAbū Zakariyyā Yaḥyā al-. 1983. *Maʿānī al-Qurʾān*. Edited by Muḥammad ʿAlī al-Naǧǧār and ʾAḥmad Yūsuf al-Naǧātī. Beirut: ʿĀlam al-Kutub.

Farrāʾ, ʾAbū Zakariyyā Yaḥyā al-. 2014. *Kitāb fīh Luġāt al-Qurʾān*. Edited by Ǧābir b. ʿAbd Aḷḷāh al-Sarīʿ. Unpublished, freely downloadable.

Ferguson, Charles A. 1959. "The Arabic Koine." *Language* 35 (4): 616–630.

Fiema, Zbigniew T., Ahmad Al-Jallad, Michael C.A. Macdonald, and Nehmé, Laïla. 2015. "Provincia Arabia: Nabaea, the Emergence of Arabic as a Written Languages, and Graeco-Arabica." In *Arabs and Empires before Islam*, edited by Greg Fisher, 11–89. Oxford: Oxford University Press.

Fischer, Wolfdietrich. 2002. *A Grammar of Classical Arabic, Third Revised Edition*. Translated by Jonathan Rogers. New Haven & London: Yale University Press.

Fischer, Wolfdietrich, and Otto Jastrow. 1980. *Handbuch der arabischen Dialekte*. Wiesbaden: Harrassowitz.

Fleisch, Henri. 1947. *Introduction à l'étude des langues sémitiques*. Paris: A. Maisonneuve.

Foreman, Alex. forthcoming. "Some Jahili Knowns and Unknowns: Naturally, A Preliminary."

Fox, Joshua. 2013. *Semitic Noun Patterns*. Leiden & Boston: Brill.

Fück, Johann. 1950. *Arabiya. Untersuchungen zur arabischen Sprach- und Stilgeschichte*. Berlin: Akademie-Verlag.

Ǧabbūrī, Yaḥyā al-. 1968. *Dīwān al-ʿAbbās b. Mirdās al-Sulamī*. Baghdad: Dār al-Ǧumhūriyyah.

Ǧazarī, ʾAbū al-Ḫayr ibn al-. 2006. *Ġāyat al-Nihāyah fī Ṭabaqāt al-Qurrāʾ*. Edited by Gotthelf Bergsträsser. 2 vols. Beirut: Dār al-Kutub al-ʿIlmiyyah.

Ǧazarī, ʾAbū al-Ḫayr ibn al-. 2018. *Našr al-Qirāʾāt al-ʿAšr*. Edited by ʾAyman Rušdī Suwayd. 5 vols. Beirut & Istanbul: Dār al-Ġawṯānī.

Geyer, R. 1909. "Review of Vollers' *Volksprache und Schriftsprache im alten Arabien*." *Göttingische Gelehrte Anzeigen* 171: 10–56.

Ǧinnī, ʾAbū al-Fatḥ ʿUṯmān ibn. 1903. *Kitāb al-Muġtaṣab*. Edited by Edgar Pröbster. Leipzig: August Pries.

Grohmann, Adolf. 1962. *Arabic Inscriptions*. Leuven: Publications Universitaires.

Ḫālawayh, ʾAbū ʿAbd Aḷḷāh ibn. 1979. *Al-Ḥuǧǧah fī al-Qirāʾāt al-Sabʿ*. Edited by ʿAbd al-ʿĀl Sālim Makram. Beirut: Dār al-Šurūq.

Ḫālawayh, ʾAbū ʿAbd Aḷḷāh ibn. 1992. *ʾIʿrāb al-Qirāʾāt al-Sabʿ wa-ʿIlaluhā*. Edited by ʿAbd al-Raḥmān b. Sulaymān al-ʿUṯaymīn. Cairo: Maktabat al-Ḫāniǧī.

Ḫālawayh, ʾAbū ʿAbd Aḷḷāh ibn. 2007. *Al-Badīʿ*. Edited by Ǧāyid Zīdān Muḫallaf. Baghdad: Markaz al-Buḥūṯ wa-l-Dirāsāt al-ʾIslāmiyyah.

Ḫālawayh, ʾAbū ʿAbd Aḷḷāh ibn. 2009. *Muḫtaṣar fī Šawāḏḏ al-Qurʾān min Kitāb al-Badīʿ*. Edited by Gotthelf Bergsträsser. Berlin: Klaus Schwarz.

Ḥamdūn, R.Ġ. 2004. "Al-Maḫṭūṭāt al-Qur'āniyyah fī Ṣan'ā' Munḏu al-Qarn al-'Awwal al-Hiǧrī wa-Ḥifẓ al-Qur'ān al-Karīm bi-l-Ṣuṭūr." MA Thesis, Sanaa: Al-Yemenia University.

Hilali, Asma. 2017. *The Sanaa Palimpsest: The Transmission of the Qur'an in the First Centuries AH*. Oxford, New York: Oxford University Press.

Hock, Hans Henrich. 1991. *Principles of Historical Linguistics*. Second Revised and Updated Edition. Berlin & New York: Mouton de Gruyter.

Holes, Clive. 2010. *Colloquial Arabic of the Gulf. The Complete Course for Beginners*. London & New York: Routledge.

Hopkins, Simon. 1984. *Studies in the Grammar of Early Arabic. Based upon Papyri Datable to before 300 A.H./912 A.D.* Oxford: Oxford University Press.

Hopkins, Simon. 2020. "*Alif Maqṣūra*, Final *Imāla*, and Pre-Classical Arabic." In *Semitic, Biblical and Jewish Studies in Honor of Richard C. Steiner*, edited by Aaron J. Koller, Mordechai Z. Cohen, and Adina Moshavi, 72–86*. Jerusalem: Michal Schard Yeshiva University Press.

Houtsma, M.Th., T.W. Arnold, R. Basset, and R. Hartmann, eds. 1913. *Encyclopaedia of Islam, First Edition*. Leiden & Boston: Brill.

Huehnergard, John. 2012. *An Introduction to Ugaritic*. Peabody, MA: Hendrickson Publishers.

Huehnergard, John. 2017. "Arabic in Its Semitic Context." In *Arabic in Context. Celebrating 400 Years of Arabic at Leiden University*, edited by Ahmad Al-Jallad. Leiden & Boston: Brill.

Ingham, Bruce. 1994. *Najdi Arabic: Central Arabian*. Amsterdam: John Benjamins.

Jeffery, Arthur. 2007. *The Foreign Vocabulary of the Qur'ān*. Leiden & Boston: Brill.

Kahle, Paul E. 1947. *The Cairo Geniza*. London: Oxford University Press.

Kahle, Paul E. 1948. "The Qur'ān and the 'Arabiya." In *I. Goldziher Memorial Volume*, edited by József Somogyi and D.S. Loewinger, 163–182. Budapest: [s.n.].

Kahle, Paul E. 1949. "The Arabic Readers of the Koran." *Journal of Near Eastern Studies* 8 (2): 65–71.

Kessler, Christel. 1970. "'Abd Al-Malik's Inscription in the Dome of the Rock: A Reconsideration." *Journal of the Royal Asiatic Society* 102 (1): 2–14.

Khan, Geoffrey. 2013. *A Short Introduction to the Tiberian Masoretic Bible and Its Reading Tradition*. Second edition. Piscataway: Gorgias Press.

Kilābī, Ḥayāt al-. 2009. *Al-Nuqūš al-'Islāmiyyah 'alā Ṭarīq al-Ḥaǧǧ al-Šāmī bi-Šimāl Ġarb al-Mamlakah al-'Arabiyyah al-Su'ūdiyyah (Min al-Qarn al-'Awwal 'ilā al-Qarn al-Ḫāmis al-Hiǧrī)*. Riyadh: Maktabat al-Malik Fahd al-Waṭaniyyah.

Kossmann, Maarten, and Benjamin Suchard D. 2018. "A Reconstruction of the System of Verb Aspects in Proto-Berbero-Semitic." *Bulletin of the School of Oriental and African Studies* 81 (1): 41–56.

Labov, William. 1994. *Principles of Linguistic Change, Vol. 1: Internal Factors*. Oxford: Blackwell Publishers.

Laher, Suheil. forthcoming. "Phonological Flux: The Qurrā' and the Ḥijāzī-Tamīmī Cleavage."

Lane, E.W. 1863. *An Arabic-English Lexicon*. London: Williams and Norgate.

Larcher, Pierre. 2005. "D'Ibn Fāris à al-Farrā' ou un retour aux sources sur la Luġa al-Fuṣḥā." *Asiatische Studien/Etudes Asiatiques* 59 (3): 797–814.

Larcher, Pierre. 2014. "Le Coran: Le dit et l'écrit." In *Oralité et écriture dans la Bible et le Coran. Actes du colloque international, IREMAM-MMSH, 3–4 Juin 2010, Aix-En-Provence (France)*, edited by Philippe Cassuto and Pierre Larcher, 53–67. Aix-en-Provence: Presses Universitaires de Provence.

Larcher, Pierre. 2018. "Une Relecture critique du chapitre XVII du 'Īḍāḥ d'al-Zaǧǧāǧī." In *Case and Mood Endings in Semitic Languages—Myth or Reality?*, edited by Manuel Sartori, Lutz Edzard, and Philippe Cassuto, 45–67. Wiesbaden: Harrassowitz.

Larcher, Pierre. 2021. "Une «rime cachée» dans Cor 23, 12–14? Histoire du texte et histoire de la langue." *Arabica* 68 (1): 36–50.

Levin, Aryeh. 1992. "The Authenticity of Sībawayhi's Description of the *'Imāla*." *Jerusalem Studies in Arabic and Islam* 15: 74–93.

Macdonald, Michael C.A. 2000. "Reflections on the Linguistic Map of Pre-Islamic Arabia." *Arabian Archaeology and Epigraphy* 11: 28–79.

Manẓūr, Muḥammad b. Mukarram ibn. n.d. *Lisān Al-ʿArab*. Cairo: Dār al-Maʿārif.

Marx, Michael Josef, and Tobias J. Jocham. 2015. "Zu den Datierungen von Koranhandschriften durch die ^{14}C-Methode." *Frankfurter Zeitschrift für Islamische Theologie*, 9–43.

Melchert, Christopher. 2008. "The Relation of the Ten Readings to One Another." *Journal of Qur'anic Studies* 10 (2): 73–87.

Mihrān, 'Aḥmad ibn. 1986. *Al-Mabsūṭ fī al-Qirā'āt al-ʿAšr*. Edited by Subayʿ Ḥākimī. Damascus: Mağmaʿ al-Luġah al-ʿArabiyyah.

Mihrān, 'Aḥmad ibn. 1990. *Al-Ġāyah fī Qirā'āt al-ʿAšr*. Edited by Muḥammad Ġayyāṯ al-Ǧanbāz. 2nd ed. Riyadh: Dār al-Šawwāf li-l-Našr wa-l-Tawzīʿ.

Miles, George C. 1948. "Early Islamic Inscriptions Near Ṭā'if in the Ḥijāz." *Journal of Near Eastern Studies* 7 (4): 236–242.

Motzki, Harald. 2001. "The Collection of the Qur'ān. A Reconsideration of Western Views in Light of Recent Methodological Developments." *Der Islam* 78: 1–34.

Mubarrad, 'Abū ʿAbbās Muḥammad b. Yazīd al-. 1994. *Kitāb Al-Muqtaḍab*. Edited by ʿAbd al-Ḫāliq ʿUḍaymah. 5 vols. Cairo.

Muğāhid, 'Abū Bakr ibn. 1972. *Kitāb al-Sabʿah fī al-Qirā'āt*. Edited by Šawqī Ḍayf. Third Edition. Cairo: Dār al-Maʿārif.

Müller, W.W. 1982. "Das Altarabische der Inschriften aus vorislamischer Zeit." In *Grundriß der arabischen Philologie. Band 1: Sprachwissenschaft*, edited by Wolfdietrich Fischer, 32–33. Wiesbaden: Reichert.

Nasser, Shady Hekmat. 2013a. "The Two-Rāwī Canon before and after Ad-Dānī (d. 444/

1052–1053): The Role of Abū ṭ-Ṭayyib Ibn Ghalbūn (d. 389/998) and the Qayrawān/Andalus School in Creating the Two-Rāwī Canon." *Oriens* 41: 41–75.

Nasser, Shady Hekmat. 2013b. *The Transmission of the Variant Readings of the Qurʾān: The Problem of Tawātur and the Emergence of Shawādhdh*. Leiden & Boston: Brill.

Nasser, Shady Hekmat. 2020. *The Second Canonization of the Qurʾān (324/936): Ibn Mujāhid and the Founding of the Seven Readings. The Second Canonization of the Qurʾān (324/936)*. Leiden & Boston: Brill.

Nehmé, Laïla. 2018. *The Darb Al-Bakrah. A Caravan Route in North-West Arabia Discovered by Ali I. al-Ghabban. Catalogue of the Inscriptions*. Riyadh: Saudi Commission for Tourism and National Heritage.

Nöldeke, Theodor. 1896. *Zur Grammatik des classischen Arabisch*. Wien: Gerold.

Nöldeke, Theodor. 1904. *Beiträge zur semitischen Sprachwissenschaft*. Strassburg: Karl J. Trübner.

Nöldeke, Theodor. 1910. *Neue Beiträge zur semitischen Sprachwissenschaft*. Strassburg: Karl J. Trübner.

Nöldeke, Theodor, Friedrich Schwally, Gotthelf Bergsträßer, and Otto Pretzl. 2013. *The History of the Qurʾān*. Leiden & Boston: Brill.

Owens, Jonathan. 2006. *A Linguistic History of Arabic*. New York: Oxford University Press.

Prochazka, Theodore. 1988. *Saudi Arabian Dialects*. London & New York: Routledge.

Puin, Gerd-R. 2011. "Vowel Letters and Ortho-Epic Writing in the Qurʾān." In *New Perspectives on the Qurʾān. The Qurʾān in Its Historical Context 2.*, edited by Gabriel Said Reynolds, 147–190. London & New York: Routledge.

Putten, Marijn van. 2017a. "The Development of the Triphthongs in Quranic and Classical Arabic." *Arabian Epigraphic Notes* 3: 47–74.

Putten, Marijn van. 2017b. "The Archaic Feminine Ending *-at* in Shammari Arabic." *Journal of Semitic Studies* 62 (2): 357–369.

Putten, Marijn van. 2017c. "The Feminine Ending *-at* as a Diptote in the Qurʾānic Consonantal Text and Its Implications for Proto-Arabic and Proto-Semitic." *Arabica* 64 (5–6): 695–705.

Putten, Marijn van. 2018. "Hamzah in the Quranic Consonantal Text." *Orientalia* N.S. 87 (1): 93–120.

Putten, Marijn van. 2019a. "Arabe 334a. A Vocalized Kufic Quran in a Non-Canonical Hijazi Reading." *Journal of Islamic Manuscripts* 10 (3): 327–375.

Putten, Marijn van. 2019b. "Inferring the Phonetics of Quranic Arabic from the Quranic Consonantal Text." *International Journal of Arabic Linguistics* 5 (1): 1–19.

Putten, Marijn van. 2019c. "'The Grace of God' as Evidence for a Written Uthmanic Archetype: The Importance of Shared Orthographic Idiosyncrasies." *Bulletin of the School of Oriental and African Studies* 82 (2): 271–288.

Putten, Marijn van. 2020a. "Classical and Modern Standard Arabic." In *Arabic and*

Contact-Induced Change, edited by Christopher Lucas and Stefano Manfredi, 57–82. Berlin: Language Science Press.

Putten, Marijn van. 2020b. "Hišām's ʾIbrāhām: Evidence for a Canonical Quranic Reading Based on the Rasm." *Journal of the Royal Asiatic Society* 30 (2): 231–250.

Putten, Marijn van. 2020c. "The History of the Maltese Short Vowels." In *Maltese Linguistics on the Danube*, edited by Slavomír Čéplö and Jaroslav Drobný, 59–90. Berlin & Boston: De Gruyter Mouton.

Putten, Marijn van. forthcoming. "Dissimilation of *ē* to *ā* in the Quranic Consonantal Text." *Journal of the International Qurʾanic Studies Association*.

Putten, Marijn van. forthcoming. "Ṯamūd: Reading Traditions; The Arabic Grammatical Tradition; And the Quranic Consontantal Text." In *Language Change in Epic Greek and Other Oral Traditions*, edited by Lucien van Beek. Leiden & Boston: Brill.

Putten, Marijn van, and Hythem Sidky. forthcoming. "Pronominal Variation in Arabic Among the Grammarians, Quranic Reading Traditions and Manuscripts," in *Formal models in the History of Arabic Grammatical and Linguistic Tradition*, edited by Raoul Villano special issue of *Language & History* 65:1.

Putten, Marijn van, and Phillip W. Stokes. 2018. "Case in the Qurʾānic Consonantal Text." *Wiener Zeitschrift für die Kunde des Morgenlandes* 108: 143–179.

Rabin, Chaim. 1955. "The Beginnings of Classical Arabic." *Studia Islamica* 4: 19–37.

Rabin, Chaim. 1951. *Ancient West-Arabian*. London: Taylor's Foreign Press.

Rāšid, Saʿd b. ʿAbd al-ʿAzīz al-. 2009. *Al-Ṣuwaydirah (al-Ṭarf Qadīman). ʾĀṯāruhā, Wa-Nuqūšuhā al-ʾIslāmiyyah*. Riyadh: Layan Cultural Foundation.

Ratcliffe, Robert R. 1998. *The "Broken" Plural Problem in Arabic and Comparative Semitic. Allomorphy and Analogy in Non-Concatenative Morphology*. Amsterdam & Philadelphia: John Benjamins.

Revell, E.J. 1975. "The Diacritical Dots and the Development of the Arabic Alphabet." *Journal of Semitic Studies* 20 (2): 178–190.

Ritt-Benmimoun, Veronika. 2014. *Grammatik des arabischen Beduinendialekts der Region Douz (Südtunesien)*. Wiesbaden: Harrassowitz.

Rosenthal, Franz. 1961. *A Grammar of Biblical Aramaic*. Wiesbaden: Harrassowitz.

Sabṭ al-Ḫayyāṭ. 1984. "Al-Mubhiǧ fī al-Qirāʾāt al-Ṯamān wa-Qirāʾat al-ʾAʿmaš, wa-bn Muḥayṣin wa-Ḫtiyār Ḫalaf wa-l-Yazīdī." Edited by ʿAbd al-ʿAzīz b. Nāṣir al-Sabr. PhD Thesis, Riyadh: Al-Imam Mohammad Ibn Saud Islamic University.

Sadeghi, Behnam. 2013. "Criteria for Emending the Text of the Qur'ān." In *Law and Tradition in Classical Islamic Thought: Studies in Honor of Professor Hossein Modarressi*, edited by Michael Cook, Najam Haider, Intisar Rabb, and Asma Sayeed, 21–41. Palgrave Series in Islamic Theology, Law, and History. New York: Palgrave Macmillan US.

Sadeghi, Behnam, and Uwe Bergmann. 2010. "The Codex of a Companion of the Prophet and the Qurʾān of the Prophet." *Arabica* 57: 343–436.

Sadeghi, Behnam, and Mohsen Goudarzi. 2011. "Ṣanʿāʾ 1 and the Origins of the Qurʾān." *Der Islam* 87 (1–2): 1–129.

Saksena, Baburam. 1937. *Evolution of Awadhi*. Delhi, Patna, Varanasi: Motilal Banarsidass.

Sara, Solomon I. 2007. *Sibawayh On ʔimālah (Inclination)*. Edinburgh: Edinburgh University Press.

Sarrāǧ, ʾAbū Bakr Muḥammad ibn al-. 1971. *Kitāb al-Ḫaṭṭ*. Edited by Khawla Saleh Houssein Al-Jubouri. Beirut: Dār al-Kutub al-ʿIlmiyyah.

Sarrāǧ, ʾAbū Bakr Muḥammad ibn al-. 2009. *Al-ʾUṣūl fī al-Naḥw*. Edited by Muḥammad ʿUṯmān. 2 vols. Cairo: Maktabat al-Ṯaqāfah al-Dīniyyah.

Schwarz, Paul. 1901. *Der Diwan des ʿUmar ibn Abí Rebīʿa*. Leipzig.

Shahpasand, Elaheh, and Ala Vahidnia. 2018. "Taʾsīr Aaqīda-yi ʿMuḏakkar Angāri-yi Qurʾānʾ bar Qirāʾāt-i." *Muṭāliʿāt-i Qurʾān wa-Ḥadīṯ* 11 (2): 111–134.

Sībawayh, ʾAbū Bišr ʿUṯmān. 1881. *Le Livre de Sîbawayh. Traité de grammaire arabe par Sîboûya, dit Sîbawayhi*. Edited by Hartwig Derenbourg. Paris: Imprimerie Nationale de France.

Sībawayh, ʾAbū Bišr ʿUṯmān. 1988. *Kitāb Sībawayh*. Edited by ʿAbd al-Salām Muḥammad Hārūn. Cairo: Maktabat al-Ḫāniǧī.

Sidky, Hythem. 2020. "On the Regionality of the Quranic Codices." *Journal of the International Qurʾanic Studies Association* 5: 133–210.

Sidky, Hythem. forthcoming. "Consonantal Dotting and the Oral Quran."

Sinai, Nicolai. 2014a. "When Did the Consonantal Skeleton of the Quran Reach Closure? Part I." *Bulletin of the School of Oriental and African Studies* 77 (2): 273–292.

Sinai, Nicolai. 2014b. "When Did the Consonantal Skeleton of the Quran Reach Closure? Part II." *Bulletin of the School of Oriental and African Studies* 77 (3): 509–521.

Sinai, Nicolai. 2020. "Beyond the Cairo Edition: On the Study of Early Quranic Codices." *Journal of the American Oriental Society* 140 (1): 189–204.

Spitaler, Anton. 1935. *Die Verszählung des Koran nach islamischer Überlieferung*. München: Verlag der Bayerischen Akademie der Wissenschaften.

Stokes, Phillip W. 2020. "A Reanalysis of the Origin and Diachronic Development of ʿDialectal Tanwīnʾ in Arabic." *Journal of the American Oriental Society* 140 (3): 639–666.

Suchard, Benjamin D. 2019. *The Development of the Biblical Hebrew Vowels: Including a Concise Historical Morphology*. Leiden & Boston: Brill.

Suchard, Benjamin D. 2016. "The Hebrew Verbal Paradigm of Hollow Roots: A Triconsonantal Account." *Zeitschrift der Deutschen Morgenländischen Gesellschaft* 166 (2): 317–332.

Suchard, Benjamin D. 2018. "The Vocalic Phonemes of Tiberian Hebrew." *Hebrew Studies* 59 (1): 193–207.

Suchard, Benjamin D., and Jorik (F.J.) Groen. 2021. "(Northwest) Semitic Sg. *CVCC-, Pl.

*CVCaC-ū-: Broken Plural or Regular Reflex?" *Bulletin of the School of Oriental and African Studies* 84 (1): 1–17.

Suyūṭī, Ǧalāl al-Dīn al-. 1998. *Hamʿ al-Hawāmiʿ fī Šarḥ Ǧamʿ al-Ǧawāmiʿ*. Edited by ʾAḥmad Šams al-Dīn. Beirut: Dār al-Kutub al-ʿIlmiyyah.

Testen, David. 2005. "Literary Arabic and Early Hijazi Contrasts in the Marking of Definiteness." In *Perspectives on Arabic Linguistics XI: Papers from the Eleventh Annual Symposium on Arabic Linguistics*, edited by Niloofar Haeri, Mushira Eid, and Elabbas Benmamoun, 207–225. Amsterdam & Philadelphia: John Benjamins.

Thackston, Wheeler M. 1994. *An Introduction to Koranic and Classical Arabic*. Bethesda, Md: IBEX Publishers.

Tov, Emanuel. 1992. *Textual Criticism of the Hebrew Bible*. Minneapolis: Assen [etc.]: Fortress Press; Van Gorcum.

Versteegh, Kees. 1984. *Pidginization and Creolization. The Case of Arabic*. Amsterdam & Philadelphia: John Benjamins.

Versteegh, Kees. 1993. *Arabic Grammar and Qurʾānic Exegesis in Early Islam*. Leiden & Boston: Brill.

Versteegh, Kees. 1995. *The Explanation of Linguistic Causes. Az-Zağǧāǧī's Theory of Grammar. Introduction, Translation, Commentary*. Amsterdam & Philadelphia: John Benjamins.

Versteegh, Kees. 2014. *Arabic Language*. Edinburgh: Edinburgh University Press.

Vollers, Karl. 1906. *Volkssprache und Schriftsprache im alten Arabien*. Strassburg: Karl J. Trübner.

Wansbrough, John. 1977. *Quranic Studies; Sources and Methods of Scriptural Interpretation*. Amherst, NY: Prometheus Books.

Watson, Janet C.E., and Barry Heselwood. 2016. "Phonation and Glottal States in Modern South Arabian and San'ani Arabic." In *Perspective on Arabic Linguistics XXVIII: Papers from the Annual Symposium on Arabic Linguistics, Gainesville Flordia, 2014*, edited by Youssef A. Haddad and Eric Potsdam, 3–36. Amsterdam: John Benjamins.

Watt, William Montgomery, and Richard Bell. 1991. *Introduction to the Qur'an*. Edinburgh: Edinburgh University Press.

Webb, Peter. 2017. *Imagining the Arabs: Arab Identity and the Rise of Islam*. Edinburgh: Edinburgh University Press.

Wehr, Hans. 1952. "Review of Fück ʿArabīya." *Zeitschrift der Deutschen Morgenländischen Gesellschaft* 102: 179–186.

Wehr, Hans. 1979. *A Dictionary of Modern Written Arabic: (Arabic-Engl.)*. Edited by J. Milton Cowan. 4th ed. Wiesbaden: Harrassowitz.

Wellhausen, Julius. 1897. *Reste arabischen Heidenthums*. 2nd ed. Berlin: Georg Reimer.

Wensinck, A.J. 1927. *A Handbook of Early Muhammadan Tradition. Alphabetically Arranged*. Leiden: Brill.

Witkam, Jan Just. 2007. *Inventory of the Oriental Manuscripts of the Library of the University of Leiden. Vol. 1*. Leiden: Ter Lugt Press.

Wright, William. 1896. *A Grammar of the Arabic Language: Translated from the German of Caspari and Edited with Numerous Additions and Corrections. 2 vols*. Cambridge: Cambridge University Press.

Yaʿīš, Muwaffaq al-Dīn ibn. 2001. *Šarḥ al-Mufaṣṣal li-l-Zamaḫšarī*. Edited by ʾĪmīl Badīʿ Yaʿqūb. Beirut: Dār al-Kutub al-ʿIlmiyyah.

Zağǧāğ, ʾAbū ʾIsḥāq al-. 1971. *Mā Yanṣarif wa-mā lā Yanṣarif*. Edited by Hudā Maḥmūd Qarrāʿah. Cairo: s.n.

Zamaḫšarī, ʾAbū Qāsim Maḥmūd al-. 1879. *Al-Mufaṣṣal fī al-Naḥw*. Edited by Jens Peter Broch. Christiania: Libraria P.T. Mallingii.

Zamaḫšarī, ʾAbū Qāsim Maḥmūd al-. 1966. *Al-Kaššāf ʿan Ḥaqāʾiq al-Tanzīl wa-ʿUyūn al-ʾAqāwīl*. Cairo.

Zwettler, Michael. 1978. *The Oral Tradition of Classical Arabic Poetry: Its Character and Implications*. Columbus: Ohio State University Press.

Index of Tribes, Groups and Regions

Al-ʔazd 144, 220
Al-Hāriṯ b. Kaʕb 116
Al-Rabāb 78, 177, 220
ʔanṣār 138
ʔasad 22, 28, 31–32, 37–38, 58, 62–63, 66–67, 70–71, 71n31, 77–81, 102–104, 108–111, 116, 124, 135, 139, 141, 177, 207–208, 274n

Bakr b. Wāʔil 22, 32, 63–64, 78, 103, 123, 144
Basra 9, 25, 41, 45, 50–51, 54–55, 59, 70, 77, 79, 85n40, 108, 163–164, 172, 180, 217, 261, 261n56

Damascus 50–51, 54, 93, 180, 241, 265
Dubayr 31, 37, 66
Ḍabbah 140

Faqʕas 31, 66, 124

Ġaṭafān 122, 141

Hawāzin 138
Hijaz 1, 6, 13–14, 17, 22–23, 25, 28, 30–31, 33, 36–38, 40, 57–71, 71n32, 72–73, 77–81, 85, 88, 98, 100–125, 125n, 126–127, 133–150, 153, 155, 168, 171–173, 182–183, 207, 211n32, 216–218, 221–222, 224, 220–230, 275, 277–278
Homs 54, 217
Huḏayl 65, 102n, 138, 144, 148, 218, 220

Kalb 80, 124, 140
Kinānah 22, 37, 122, 138
Kufa 9, 41, 45, 50–51, 54, 54n10, 55–56, 59, 66n24, 74–77, 79, 86–87, 93–95, 104, 108, 133, 137, 168, 170, 180, 202n20, 204n25, 210, 217, 219, 239, 261, 265

Maʕadd 150, 188, 222
Mecca 2, 15, 21, 50–51, 70, 77, 116, 129, 131n15, 138n23, 142, 146, 168, 180, 199n, 202, 202n19, 207–208, 216, 261
Medina 2, 9, 50–51, 54, 54n10, 55, 63, 76–77, 108, 108n, 129, 131n15, 138, 146, 155, 161n8, 171–172, 180–181, 216–217, 222, 236n6, 250, 261

Najd 25–28, 31–32, 34, 34n12, 35–36, 36n15, 38, 40, 42, 46, 58–59, 63–66, 68–70, 73, 78–81, 102, 104, 108, 110–111, 118, 125–127, 129, 133–136, 140–141, 143–145, 207, 229

Petra 146n

Saʕd b. Bakr 22, 103, 103n3, 138, 220

Tamīm 22, 25–26, 28, 31–33, 37–38, 58, 60–65, 67, 69–70, 71n31, 72, 78–81, 102–103, 105, 107–111, 115–116, 123–124, 135–137, 139–142, 144, 148, 188, 203, 207–208, 218
Ṯaqīf 144
Ṭayyiʔ 102, 118

Qayn 124, 140
Qays 22, 25, 28, 31–32, 38, 58, 63–64, 66–67, 69–70, 72, 78–81, 102–103, 108–111, 124, 134–137, 139–141, 144, 219
Quḍāʕah 71n31, 140
Qurayš 22, 37, 42, 57, 66, 77, 81, 103, 121–125, 138–141, 144–145, 147–149, 173, 188, 218–221

Rabīʕah 22, 32–33, 37–38, 64, 81, 102–103, 111, 139, 219–220

Syria 9, 54, 54n10, 55, 108, 108n, 138n21, 179, 182–183, 217, 261, 265, 270n

ʕuḏrah 124, 140
ʕuqayl 31, 66

Index of Subjects

ʔalif al-tafxīm XVII, 24, 30, 30n6, 123
Akkadian 88n, 166n16, 195n12
Ancient South Arabian 88n, 195n12
Arabic
Hismaic 45, 101, 114, 118, 122, 135
Pre-Islamic 18, 28, 36, 36n15, 43, 100–102, 104–106, 112–114, 118, 120, 135, 143–145, 151, 159, 161n7, 167, 182–183, 221, 230, 241–242
Nabataean 101, 105, 114, 118, 120, 122, 135, 144, 146n, 151, 159, 182–183, 233–234, 251
modern dialectal 112, 113, 125, 132n, 140n28, 146, 151, 161n7, 179, 210, 217, 241, 252n42, 268, 274, 280n87, 284n, 288
Graeco- 44, 106, 134, 144
Middle 43, 159, 185n3, 195n14, 227
Old *see* Pre-Islamic
Proto- 36, 89, 106, 106n, 112, 113, 115, 124, 124n3, 125n, 140n26, 142, 151–152, 161, 161n7, 179n, 182–183, 243, 259
Safaitic 26, 28, 44, 101–102, 104n6, 105, 113–114, 118, 120, 122–123, 124n3, 135, 143, 143n31, 146, 151, 159, 161n7, 167, 183, 241–242
ʕanʕanah 218
ʕarabiyyah 1, 3–7, 12–13, 15–19, 25, 29, 32–33, 35–42, 42n, 43–47, 55–56, 79, 90, 96, 98, 100, 112, 114, 121, 142, 145, 147, 151, 157, 163–164, 166n18, 168, 172, 173n, 176, 187, 213–216, 219, 219n3, 226–227, 237, 274, 289
Aramaic 36, 36n15, 101, 123–124, 141, 157, 161n7, 162n10, 166, 166n16, 167, 172–173, 176, 195n12, 233, 260, 281

Barth-Ginsberg 36–38, 46, 80, 106–107, 118, 219

Cairo Edition (CE) 9, 10, 12, 47, 123, 233–235, 235n6, 236, 236n6, 240–241, 243–244, 246, 249, 250, 252–253, 256n50, 259, 259n, 260, 267–268, 285, 287, 290n94, 291–292, 292n, 294, 301

Dadanitic 101, 114

Ethiopic, Classical 26, 28, 84, 88n, 101, 112, 176, 195n12

Gəʕəz *see* Ethiopic, Classical
Greek 106, 124, 164

Hebrew 6n5, 28–29, 36, 69n30, 91, 113, 132, 157, 164, 166, 166n16, 167, 172–173, 176, 178–179, 179n31, 195n12, 197, 237n, 274, 281
Hismaic *see* Arabic, Hismaic

ʔidġām kabīr 201, 204–206, 208–209
ʔiʕrāb 4–5, 151–154, 182, 184, 186–188, 190–195, 200, 203, 206–207, 209–212, 223, 225–226
ʔimālah 20, 23–29, 39, 43, 44n, 67–70, 75–76, 83–86, 90, 95, 104, 133n, 135–136, 145, 195, 203, 203n23, 206, 218n, 228–229, 250
ʔišmām 31, 31n8, 66–67, 74, 74n34, 204, 204n25, 205, 206

Kaskasah 218
Koiné, poetic 1–3, 13, 15–16, 19, 52, 100, 103, 117, 146, 148, 183, 187, 218–219, 221

Latin 124–125

Mā Ḥiǧāziyyah 108–109, 118
Mandaic 167, 167n20

Persian 166n17
Pre-Islamic poetry 2–4, 15–17, 100, 150, 151, 221–223, 230

Quranic Consonantal Text (QCT) 8–11, 13–14, 39, 98, 100–112, 114–117, 119–125, 133, 135–147, 149–153, 155, 158, 172, 174, 176, 179, 183–184, 186–187, 189, 191, 201, 203, 208, 211, 214–216, 221–222, 230, 233–235, 237, 239–240, 244n21, 254n46, 255–256, 258–260, 262–266, 268–270, 272–273, 276, 279, 281, 288, 291–292, 294

Rasm 10, 53–55, 108n, 138–139, 147, 153, 174, 176, 180, 189, 191, 258n, 273n76, 284n, 286, 288n, 290n95, 294
rawm 204, 204n25, 205–206
Rhyme 8, 99, 119, 126–131, 133, 143, 151, 153–155, 164, 165n13, 168, 176, 181, 216, 218, 258, 269
Regional variants 9, 108n, 250, 261, 263, 265

Safaitic *see* Arabic, Safaitic
Semitic 26, 36, 88n, 101, 113, 131–132, 157, 159, 166–167, 179, 179n, 180, 195n12, 255, 274, 281
  North-West 106n9
  West- 112, 166–167, 197, 274
Syncope 32–35, 46, 59–65, 130, 132, 145, 206–208, 211–212, 229–230, 266
Syriac 132, 179

Taltalah *see* Barth-Ginsberg
Tawātur 52n
Tanwīn 44–45, 150–154, 160, 182, 184, 186, 192, 195, 201, 206, 208, 212, 216, 222–223, 224–227, 260

Ugaritic 107n10, 166–167
Uthmanic Text (UT) 8, 10, 53–54, 99, 215, 217–218, 220–221, 233–235, 241, 243–247, 272, 285–287, 294, 301
Vowel harmony 20, 22, 31–33, 34n12, 36, 43, 46, 58, 63, 71n31, 77, 85, 85n39, 86–87, 93n47, 95, 197, 219, 225, 228–229, 274–275

Index of Modern Authors

Abbott, Nabia 11n11
Abu-Haidar, Farida 69n29
Al-Jallad, Ahmad 18, 28, 30, 36, 36n15, 44–45, 100–102, 105–106, 107n10, 109, 113–114, 117, 122–123, 124n3–4, 134n–135, 144, 150–152, 159, 167, 179, 182–183, 217, 222, 238n15, 242, 251n40, 260, 269–270, 274
As-Said, Lahib 76, 95
Altıkulaç, Tayyar 296–297
Azami, Mughammad Mustafa al- 77

Beck, Edmund 82
Behnstedt, Peter 125n, 143n31, 161n7
Bell, Richard 50
Bergsträßer, Gotthelf 52
Blachère, Régis 57n, 100n
Blanc, Haim 24n, 43, 183n
Blau, Joshua 42–44, 119, 142, 151, 153, 159, 167, 181–183, 185n3, 195n14, 199n, 217, 227, 234n1, 235n5, 236, 249n25, 251n39, 255n48, 262, 267n72, 273n79, 280n88
Bloch, Ariel 36, 38
Brockelmann, Carl 161n7, 281
Bursi, Adam 10

Cantineau, Jean 101, 135
Carter, Michael 16–17, 56n, 57n
Cellard, Éléonore 225, 250, 270, 295, 296n
Comerro, Viviane 220n5
Cook, Michael 9, 54, 99, 261, 270n
Cowell, Mark W. 241

David-Weil, J. 227
Déroche, François 224–225, 240, 253, 295–297
Diem, Werner 8n6, 112, 119–121, 141, 151, 233–238, 241, 244, 247, 250, 252, 252n42, 257n52
Dutton, Yasin 9, 295
Durie, Mark 146n

El-Hawary, Hassan Mohammed 234n2

Ferguson, Charles A. 151
Fiema, Zbigniew T. 105
Fischer, Wolfdietrich 3–4, 17, 19–20, 22, 25, 31, 33–35, 37–39, 45, 64n20, 65, 91, 102, 115n, 172, 174, 174n25, 177n29, 195, 227, 237, 255, 273–274, 278–279, 284n
Fleisch, Henri 2, 15, 100n
Flügel, Gustav 6, 9, 147
Foreman, Alex 2n
Fox, Joshua 78, 132
Fück, Johann 152, 161n8

Ǧabbūrī, Yaḥyā al- 173n
Geyer, R. 1
Groen, Jorik 63
Grohmann, Adolf 234n2, 235n4, 235n5

Ḥamdūn, R.Ġ. 296
Heselwood, Barry 91
Hock, Hans Henrich 57, 75, 83
Holes, Clive 112
Hopkins, Simon 11n12, 42–44, 185n3, 234n1, 235n5, 251n39, 252n41–42, 283n
Huehnergard, John 38, 107n10

Ingham, Bruce 36, 36n4

Jastrow, Otto 91, 274, 284n
Jaworska, Karolina 123, 135, 159, 167
Jeffery, Arthur 162n10, 173, 176, 237n14
Jocham, Tobias J. 254, 296

Kahle, Paul E. 9, 147–148, 186–187, 212, 218
Kessler, Christel 254n44
Khan, Geoffrey 9
Kilābī, Ḥayāt al- 234n2, 235n5

Labov, William 75
Laher, Suheil 86
Larcher, Pierre 45n, 164n, 183n, 185n4, 218n, 219n3
Levin, Aryeh 23, 23n, 27, 69n29, 104n6

Macdonald, Michael C.A. 101
Manaser, Ali al- 36, 36n15, 44–45, 106, 182

Marx, Michael Josef 254, 296
Melchert, Christopher 95
Miles, George C. 134
Motzki, Harald 220, 220n5–6
Müller, W.W. 101

Nasser, Shady Hekmat 50, 50n, 52n, 53, 74n, 94n
Nehmé, Laïla 106
Nöldeke, Theodor 1, 6, 8n6, 47n, 50, 52, 65n21, 97–98, 119, 133, 142, 186, 190n8, 195n13, 203, 213, 221–222, 240–242, 247, 248, 255, 269n, 270, 287

Owens, Jonathan 133n, 183, 186, 200–206, 213

Prochazka, Theodore 112
Puin, Gerd-R. 252, 255n47, 281n
Putten, Marijn van 1, 8, 8n6, 24, 26, 30, 36, 41, 54, 54n7, 58, 72, 77, 85n39, 85n40, 88, 91, 99, 100, 114, 119–123, 133, 140n26, 141–144, 150–155, 161n7, 165n13, 172, 176, 177n28, 183–184, 185n4, 188–189, 193n10, 194, 201, 209–211, 213n35, 225, 226n, 228, 234–235, 242, 248, 250–251, 253–254, 256, 256n49, 257, 259–260, 261n57, 267, 271n77, 274, 281–282, 286, 290, 292, 292n

Rabin, Chaim 2, 3, 7, 8n6, 15, 16, 18–19, 30, 31, 39–42, 52, 55, 56, 59, 66n24, 67n24, 82n, 93n, 100, 100n, 101–102, 103n4, 105, 105n, 106n, 107–108, 108n, 109, 114–121, 123–124, 132–134, 133n, 136, 138, 142–143, 148, 172, 186–187, 211n32, 218, 218n, 247–248, 255
Rāšid, Saʿd b. ʿAbd al-ʿAzīz, al- 235n4
Ratcliffe, Robert R. 132
Revell, E.J. 11n11, 11n13
Ritt-Benmimoun, Veronika 112
Rosenthal, Franz 101

Sadeghi, Behnam 9n8, 54n7, 256
Saksena, Baburam 201n
Sara, Solomon 24–26, 83
Shahpasand, Elaheh 53n
Schwally, Friedrich 2, 221
Schwarz, Paul 231
Sidky, Hythem 9–10, 41, 54, 54n9, 58, 77, 85n39–40, 88, 89n, 95, 138n21, 138n23, 150, 162n11, 217, 225, 226n, 228, 250, 261, 261n56, 274, 281n
Sinai, Nicolai 1, 9n, 99, 151
Spitaler, Anton 93, 129, 131n15, 143n30
Stokes, Phillip W. 100, 142, 150–152, 154, 184, 185n4, 194, 201, 206, 209–211, 213n35, 242, 260, 261n57, 267, 271n77, 281–282, 286, 292
Suchard, Benjamin D. 28–29, 36n14, 63, 69n30, 72, 91, 113, 274

Testen, David 123
Thackston, Wheeler M. 15, 19, 52, 227
Tov, Emanuel 9

Vahidnia, Ala 53n
Versteegh, Kees 3, 15, 17, 45n, 82, 119, 151, 183, 1893n, 226
Vollers, Karl 1, 2, 6–8, 146–147, 150–152, 154, 158n4, 161n8, 166n17, 172, 186, 186n, 200, 203, 213, 213n37, 217, 247

Wansbrough, John 8n7
Watt, William Montgomery 50
Watson, Janet C.E. 91
Webb, Peter 16, 222
Wehr, Hans 115n, 213n37
Wellhausen, Julius 167
Witkam, Jan Just 228n15
Wright, William 4, 17, 19, 25, 39, 102, 227, 240

Zwettler, Michael 3, 5n, 6, 6n4, 11n11, 15, 119, 148, 172, 182, 213n37, 217–219

Index of Medieval Muslim Figures and Authors

ʕabbās b. Faḍl *ʕan* ʔabū ʕamr 60
ʔabū al-Dardāʔ 265
ʔabū al-Hāriṯ *ʕan* al-Kisāʔī *see* al-Layṯ ʕan al-Kisāʔī
ʔabū al-Xaṭṭāb 64
ʔabū ʕamr 6n3, 51, 54n10, 58–59, 61–62, 62n17, 63–64, 66, 68, 70, 74, 78, 83, 87–88, 90–91, 91n45, 95, 116, 130, 133, 139n, 156, 158, 160, 168–169, 177, 178, 180, 188–189, 193, 195, 197, 199–201, 201n, 203, 203n24, 204, 204n25, 205–206, 206n, 207, 207n29, 208–209, 211, 211n33, 223n, 226, 271n76, 272, 273n78, 288n
ʔabū Ǧaʕfar 6n3, 7, 51, 54, 54n10, 55, 58–59, 59n, 60–63, 66–67, 74, 76–79, 83, 88, 95, 108n, 117, 130–131, 138, 138n22, 156–157, 167n19, 168–169, 173, 177–178, 180, 193–194, 194n, 195, 197, 200, 210, 223n, 227, 238, 271n76, 273n78
ʔabū Ḥātim al-Siǧistānī 224n, 228
ʔabū Ḥayyān 162, 163n12, 165, 168
ʔabū Hišām *ʕan* Sulaym *ʕan* Ḥamzah 74
ʔabū ʔisḥāq 75n
ʔabū ʕubayd al-Qāsim b. Sallām 50n, 220, 224n, 227–228
ʔaḥmad b. Qālūn 88
ʕāʔišah 105n8, 117
Al-ʕabbās b. Mirdās 173n
Al-ʔaʕmaš 41, 81, 122n, 148, 163, 164, 190n7, 198, 223n
Al-ʔaʕraǧ 163, 164
Al-ʔaṣbahānī's *ṭarīq* of Warš *ʕan* Nāfiʕ 52, 87n, 157, 176, 253
Al-ʔaxfaš 20, 21, 27, 169, 183n
Al-ʔazraq's *ṭarīq* of Warš *ʕan* Nāfiʕ 52, 68, 90n, 156, 157, 173, 177
Al-Bazzī *ʕan* Ibn Kaṯīr 51, 63–64, 158, 165, 181, 188, 192, 194, 252n42
Al-Ḏahabī- 155n, 169, 170n22, 223
Al-Ḍaḥḥāk 308
Al-Dānī 21, 48n3, 50, 52, 53, 61n17, 74, 75n, 83, 85, 89, 92, 94, 108, 143n30, 162, 169, 181, 193, 194n, 199, 204, 207, 235n6, 236n6, 250, 294
Al-Dūrī *ʕan* al-Kisāʔī 51, 70, 83, 84n37
Al-Dūrī *ʕan* ʔabū ʕamr 51
Al-Fārisī 165n14
Al-Farrāʔ 3, 16, 20–23, 25–28, 28n4, 29–37, 37n16, 38, 38n20, 39–41, 42n, 43, 45, 56–57, 57n, 59–60, 62–64, 66, 66n23, 67–71, 71n31, 72–74, 77, 78, 80, 81, 88, 93, 94, 97, 101–102, 102n, 103–104, 106–111, 115–116, 121–122, 122n, 123–124, 133, 133n, 134–139, 140n27, 141–142, 142n, 143–144, 147–148, 148n34, 163, 163n, 165n13, 168, 177–178, 186–187, 189–191, 191n, 198, 198n, 199, 207–208, 210, 218, 218n, 219–220, 220n4, 228n16, 238n16, 250, 268, 274n, 279n86, 293
Al-Ḥasan al-Baṣrī 202, 202n18, 223, 291n95
ʕalī b. ʔabī Ṭālib 308
Al-Kisāʔī 7, 22, 28n4, 37, 37n16, 41, 51, 53n, 54, 56, 59, 59n, 61, 64, 66, 66n23–24, 67n24, 68, 73–79, 85–87, 90, 92, 93, 95, 95n, 104, 128, 130, 133, 133n, 137, 154, 156, 160, 164, 169, 170, 170n22, 176–178, 187, 189–191, 194n, 195, 197, 199, 202n20, 209, 211–212, 213n37, 214, 219, 224n
Al-Mubarrad 20–21, 25, 27, 30n6, 38n20, 278n
Al-Mufaḍḍal *ʕan* ʕāṣim 88, 109n14
Al-Musayyabī *ʕan* Nafiʕ 88
Al-Šāṭibī 50
Al-Sulamī 75n
Al-Sūsī *ʕan* ʔabū ʕamr 51, 89
Al-Suyūṭī 93n
Al-Ṭabarī 50n, 53, 220n5
Al-Zaǧǧāǧ 163, 189
Al-Zaǧǧāǧī 183n
Al-Zamaxšarī 39, 43, 104, 158, 174n27, 183, 248
Al-Layṯ *ʕan* al-Kisāʔī 51, 85
ʕāṣim 5, 29, 47, 53–54, 58, 61, 75, 77–79, 81, 87–88, 93–94, 116, 122n, 130, 148, 156, 158, 164, 167, 194n, 195, 198, 198n, 199, 223n, 226
ʕāṣim al-Ǧaḥdarī 47n, 223n

Ḥafṣ *ʕan* ʕāṣim 5, 7, 47, 47n2, 48–49, 51, 54n10, 61, 63, 66, 68, 72, 74, 78, 79, 86–

Ḥafṣ ʕan ʕāṣim (*cont.*) 88, 93, 93n, 94–95, 116, 130, 147, 158, 164, 177, 189, 194–195, 199, 202n20, 209, 211, 239
Ḥamzah 6n3, 28n4, 29, 39, 41, 51, 53, 53n, 54–55, 58, 61, 63–67, 67n25, 68, 70, 74–79, 86–87, 87n, 89–90, 93, 95–96, 117, 124, 124n5, 128, 130, 133, 133n, 137, 154, 157–158, 160, 164, 169–170, 177, 189–191, 193, 194n, 195, 197, 199, 202n20, 209, 211, 214, 224n, 238n16, 256n50, 286
Hišām ʕan ibn ʕāmir 51, 54n8, 61n15, 61n16, 66, 68, 69, 157, 211, 223

Ibn ʕabbās 124
Ibn ʔabī Rabīʕah 231
Ibn al-Sarrāǧ 30n6, 185n2
Ibn ʕāmir 51, 54n8, 55, 58, 61, 64, 66, 69–70, 78–79, 87, 108n, 116, 130, 138n21, 163, 164, 180, 195, 222, 238n16, 265, 270n, 291n96
Ibn al-Bawwāb 12
Ibn Ḏakwān ʕan ibn ʕāmir 51, 61n15, 61n16, 67, 69, 70, 83, 131, 138, 156, 169, 173, 178, 223
Ibn Fāris 219n3
Ibn Fulayḥ ʕan Ibn Kaṯīr 158
Ibn Ǧinnī 116, 183n
Ibn al-Ǧazarī 51–54, 54n10, 55, 58–60, 61n17, 62–64, 66–67, 67n25, 67n26, 68–74, 75n, 78–79, 83, 84n37, 85–87, 87n, 88–90, 90n, 91n45, 94, 108n, 116–117, 124n5, 128, 128n8, 130–131, 136, 137n, 138, 138n21, 138n22, 138n23, 138n24, 139n, 155n, 156–160, 164–165, 167–169, 171, 173, 175–181, 189, 192–194, 194n, 195, 196, 200, 202n19–22, 203n24, 204, 204n25, 207, 207n31, 208–211, 211n34, 220, 227, 234n3, 236, 237n9–13, 238n16, 239, 239n, 240n19, 242n, 243–244, 248, 248n, 250, 252n42, 253, 256, 262n58–63, 263n64–66, 265, 266n67, 266n69–71, 268n, 270n, 272, 273n76, 276, 285n, 286, 288n, 290, 291n96
Ibn Ġalbūn, ʔabū al-Ṭayyib 50, 94
Ibn Ǧammāz ʕan ʔabū Ǧaʕfar 51
Ibn Ǧammāz ʕan Nāfiʕ 88, 171
Ibn Kaṯīr 7, 21, 51, 54–55, 58, 61, 66, 70, 77, 79, 86–89, 95, 116, 130–131, 138, 156, 158–159, 165, 168, 174–176, 188, 192–194, 194n, 195, 197, 202n19, 206–208, 211, 211n34, 223, 237n, 238, 272
Ibn Masʕūd 53, 53n, 148, 218, 279n86
Ibn Mihrān 67n26, 92, 228
Ibn Muǧāhid 50, 50n, 51, 60, 62, 62n17, 68n27, 73, 74n, 88, 89, 93–94, 95n, 96, 109n14, 124n5, 133, 148n34, 155, 158, 161–162, 162n9, 165, 165n14, 171, 171n, 174, 181, 187, 192, 195n, 199, 205–206, 206n28, 208, 225, 237n11, 250n34, 265, 268n, 291n96
Ibn Muḥayṣin 77, 207, 207n31, 208, 223
Ibn Šihāb al-Zuhrī 105n8, 220, 220n5, 258n
Ibn Wahb 227
Ibn Wardān ʕan ʔabū Ǧaʕfar 51
Ibn Xālawayh 60, 72n33, 109n14, 160, 166, 173, 178, 188–190, 193, 195, 197, 199, 202n18, 206n28, 228, 236n7, 238n16, 258n, 265, 267, 275n, 284n, 291n95, 308
Ibn Yaʕīš 136
ʔidrīs ʕan Xalaf 51
ʔiṣḥāq ʕan Xalaf 51
ʔismāʕīl b. Ǧaʕfar ʕan Nāfiʕ 88

Kuṯayyir ʕazzah 29

Muhammad (prophet) 47, 76, 105n8, 187, 191, 216, 226
Muslim b. Ǧundab 155

Nāfiʕ 5, 6, 48, 51, 54–55, 58, 61, 63–64, 66–67, 76–79, 83, 87–89, 95, 96, 108n, 130, 163–164, 167, 171, 171n, 172–173, 176, 180, 193–194, 194n, 195, 210, 224n, 226
Nuṣayr ʕan al-Kisāʔī 92

Qālūn ʕan Nāfiʕ 51, 55, 58–59, 68n27, 88–89, 155–156, 160, 178, 193–194, 197
Qunbul ʕan Ibn Kaṯīr 51, 158, 165, 188, 192–194, 249–250, 250n34
Qutaybah ʕan al-Kisāʔī 92

Rawḥ ʕan Yaʕqūb 51, 63, 78, 85, 197
Ruways ʕan Yaʕqūb 51, 66, 85–86, 210

Ṣabt al-Xayyāṭ 207
Saǧawindī 291n97, 291n98
Sallām ʔabū al-Munḏir 85n39, 224n

Sībawayh 3, 5–6, 16–17, 20–30, 30n6, 31, 31n8–9, 32–38, 38n18, 39–41, 43, 45, 56, 56n, 57n, 58–59, 64–71, 73, 83–85, 88, 97, 101–102, 105, 105n7, 106–109, 115, 117, 121, 123, 124n2, 124n3, 125–126, 133–136, 142–143, 143n30, 162, 165n13, 168, 171n, 172, 174–176, 177n29, 187–189, 198, 202–203, 204n25, 207n29, 208, 219, 242n, 251, 273, 279n87
Šibl *ʕan* Ibn Katīr 193
Šuʕbah *ʕan* ʕāṣim 51, 61, 63, 66, 68, 72, 78, 87–88, 93–95, 95n, 131, 148n34, 158, 160, 178, 180, 189, 194, 197, 198n, 199

ʔubayy 53
ʕumar b. al-Xaṭṭāb 148, 218, 220n4
ʕuṯmān b. ʕaffān 9, 10, 54, 99, 150, 163, 186, 191, 217–218, 220–221

Warš *ʕan* Nāfiʕ 5–6, 48, 49–52, 58, 68, 68n27, 70, 74, 83, 87–90, 94, 133, 154, 156–157, 160, 169, 171, 173, 176–178, 193–194, 197, 214, 271n76

Xalīl b. ʔaḥmad 6n4, 172
Xalaf 51, 54, 61, 63–64, 66–68, 74–76, 78–79, 86–87, 95, 130, 133, 154, 156, 164, 169–170, 176, 178, 195, 197, 202n20, 209, 211, 214, 224n
Xalaf *ʕan* Ḥamzah 51, 74, 75
Xallād *ʕan* Ḥamzah 51, 67n26, 170, 209
Xāriǧah *ʕan* Nāfiʕ 162, 163

Yaḥyā b. ʔādam *ʕan* Šuʕbah *ʕan* ʕāṣim 74, 199
Yaḥyā b. al-Ḥāriṯ *ʕan* ibn ʕāmir 223
Yaḥyā b. Waṯṯāb 72n33, 75n, 190n7
Yaʕqūb 51, 55, 58, 61, 64, 66, 70, 71n32, 74, 78, 79, 85, 85n39, 88, 130, 131, 156, 189, 195, 197, 210, 224n, 272

Zayd b. ʕalī 163, 164
Zayd b. Ṯābit 220, 221

Index of Quranic verses

Q1:2 270
Q2:1 58
Q2:2 270, 282, 284
Q2:3 92, 235
Q2:4 92, 281
Q2:5 284
Q2:6 87, 92
Q2:8 108
Q2:10 67
Q2:11 124
Q2:14 122, 156, 258, 262, 288
Q2:19 139
Q2:20 240
Q2:23 271, 281
Q2:24 116
Q2:26 123, 235, 236, 272
Q2:28 236
Q2:30 262
Q2:31 122
Q2:33 290, 318
Q2:35 111
Q2:36 241
Q2:38 194
Q2:39 203
Q2:40 237
Q2:41 267, 281
Q2:44 282
Q2:46 240
Q2:47 262
Q2:49 243, 305
Q2:54 193, 207, 285
Q2:55 139, 235
Q2:60 139
Q2:61 237, 244
Q2:62 167, 289
Q2:65 156, 289
Q2:67 207
Q2:68 290
Q2:72 202, 264, 273
Q2:73 235, 236
Q2:74 265, 281
Q2:76 27
Q2:81 122
Q2:85 73, 279, 282, 287, 308
Q2:87 283
Q2:89 282
Q2:97 237
Q2:98 237
Q2:99 283
Q2:102 207
Q2:106 290
Q2:108 252
Q2:111 179
Q2:114 283
Q2:119 235
Q2:120 284
Q2:121 202
Q2:124 153
Q2:128 207
Q2:129 205
Q2:138 69
Q2:140 239
Q2:143 113, 133
Q2:144 111
Q2:149 270
Q2:150 177
Q2:157 283
Q2:158 265, 284
Q2:159 205, 283
Q2:164 84
Q2:166 244, 302
Q2:167 244
Q2:168 63
Q2:169 243
Q2:177 280
Q2:190 266
Q2:186 180, 285
Q2:189 271
Q2:191 308
Q2:196 258, 312
Q2:208 78
Q2:209 283
Q2:211 122
Q2:217 108, 263
Q2:218 283
Q2:219 240
Q2:221 240
Q2:223 252
Q2:225 240
Q2:226 244
Q2:228 243
Q2:231 136

Q2:232	257	Q3:153	238
Q2:233	84, 108, 195, 263	Q3:154	104
Q2:237	242, 299	Q3:157	72, 87
Q2:240	281	Q3:158	72, 87, 250
Q2:245	279	Q3:159	272
Q2:251	311	Q3:160	279
Q2:255	239	Q3:168	244
Q2:257	287, 317	Q3:174	257
Q2:258	123, 236, 271, 298	Q3:175	287
Q2:259	252, 272, 291	Q3:176	84n37
Q2:260	207	Q3:183	281
Q2:264	177	Q3:184	244, 277
Q2:266	307	Q3:193	268
Q2:269	264	Q3:195	268
Q2:271	138, 262	Q4:7	282
Q2:272	284	Q4:8	152
Q2:275	247, 248, 260, 309	Q4:9	70, 96
Q2:276	204, 310	Q4:12	306
Q2:278	247, 260, 310	Q4:16	70
Q2:279	239, 271, 312	Q4:17	243
Q2:282	59n, 107, 108, 141, 195, 263	Q4:18	268
		Q4:24	282
Q2:285	272	Q4:31	268
Q3:8	283	Q4:33	285
Q3:13	48, 257	Q4:36	203n24
Q3:15	239	Q4:38	177
Q3:20	237	Q4:44	261
Q3:28	287	Q4:58	138, 262
Q3:37	235	Q4:65	288
Q3:38	133, 286, 287	Q4:66	262
Q3:44	136	Q4:76	287
Q3:66	279	Q4:77	281
Q3:73	133	Q4:78	262
Q3:75	72, 72n, 87, 106, 196, 237	Q4:81	209
		Q4:86	236
Q3:76	111	Q4:91	107
Q3:78	238	Q4:92	265, 282
Q3:79	237	Q4:93	287
Q3:91	176	Q4:94	12, 54, 283
Q3:97	283	Q4:97	281
Q3:103	264	Q4:99	240, 299
Q3:106	273	Q4:102	60, 205
Q3:108	208	Q4:104	107
Q3:114	84n37	Q4:109	279
Q3:119	279	Q4:110	243
Q3:130	247, 260, 310	Q4:112	290
Q3:144	252	Q4:115	108, 196, 263
Q3:145	196, 282	Q4:119	249
Q3:146	281	Q4:128	202n21

Q4:135 238, 238n16, 282
Q4:140 245
Q4:146 256, 270
Q4:153 207
Q4:154 136, 137, 266
Q4:161 247, 260, 310
Q4:162 117n
Q4:163 311
Q4:165 177
Q4:176 243
Q5:4 69
Q5:6 137, 255, 264, 312
Q5:12 249, 268
Q5:16 72
Q5:18 246, 281, 306
Q5:23 282
Q5:24 104
Q5:26 107
Q5:27 249
Q5:29 243, 246, 287, 308
Q5:31 84, 275
Q5:33 84, 246, 308
Q5:38 287
Q5:39 208
Q5:41 84n37
Q5:44 282
Q5:51 287
Q5:52 84n37
Q5:54 55, 108, 108n, 263
Q5:62 84n37
Q5:65 283
Q5:68 107
Q5:69 117n, 167, 289
Q5:85 308
Q5:89 240
Q5:95 287
Q5:96 72n, 73
Q5:111 84, 237
Q5:112 84
Q5:117 73
Q6:5 246, 247, 289, 306
Q6:12 283
Q6:19 239, 257
Q6:31 315
Q6:32 240, 270
Q6:34 245n, 252
Q6:42 267
Q6:46 87n
Q6:52 260
Q6:57 54, 256
Q6:59 283
Q6:71 284
Q6:76 138
Q6:77 138
Q6:78 138
Q6:80 137, 262, 264
Q6:84 311
Q6:90 291
Q6:94 113, 246, 306
Q6:99 140
Q6:121 287, 317
Q6:122 84, 210
Q6:128 317
Q6:139 306
Q6:143 282
Q6:150 107
Q6:152 264
Q6:154 315
Q6:162 193
Q7:3 265
Q7:4 235
Q7:10 161
Q7:12 84
Q7:17 249
Q7:18 140
Q7:20 238
Q7:22 267
Q7:27 282
Q7:38 264
Q7:41 285
Q7:44 257
Q7:57 210
Q7:60 245, 303
Q7:66 245, 303
Q7:76 245, 303
Q7:77 301
Q7:88 245, 303
Q7:90 245, 304
Q7:93 107
Q7:94 265, 267
Q7:95 253
Q7:97 6n3
Q7:99 107
Q7:103 252
Q7:105 238
Q7:107 284
Q7:109 245, 304
Q7:111 88, 180, 290, 318

Q7:117	284
Q7:123	107
Q7:124	249
Q7:127	245, 299, 304
Q7:131	202
Q7:134	238
Q7:137	84
Q7:141	55, 305
Q7:143	207, 260
Q7:145	255, 271
Q7:147	315
Q7:149	244, 277, 302
Q7:150	314
Q7:153	268
Q7:158	268, 299
Q7:161	252
Q7:164	281
Q7:165	236, 253, 258
Q7:166	156, 281, 289, 301
Q7:176	21
Q7:185	253
Q7:187	191
Q7:188	272
Q7:196	235, 236, 298
Q7:199	240
Q7:205	241
Q8:24	236
Q8:29	268
Q8:34	317
Q8:42	140, 272
Q8:44	275
Q8:47	177
Q8:53	186
Q8:61	78
Q8:65	252
Q8:66	79, 252
Q8:67	73
Q8:70	73
Q8:72	240, 244, 300
Q8:74	244, 300
Q9:3	140, 153
Q9:8	107
Q9:26	308
Q9:30	167
Q9:32	107, 156, 289
Q9:37	173, 180, 289
Q9:38	264
Q9:40	140
Q9:43	281
Q9:47	250
Q9:49	92, 263, 271
Q9:65	289
Q9:70	178, 305
Q9:102	180
Q9:106	180, 289
Q9:109	76
Q9:112	69
Q9:116	299
Q9:120	180, 258, 289
Q9:121	285
Q10:4	245
Q10:15	271, 286, 290, 315
Q10:16	249
Q10:18	156, 289
Q10:22	54n10, 111
Q10:24	202, 257, 264, 272
Q10:27	268, 308
Q10:30	54
Q10:34	245
Q10:35	136, 202n22, 266
Q10:45	315
Q10:54	244, 302
Q10:75	252
Q10:83	252
Q10:90	282
Q10:94	180, 289
Q10:103	256, 268
Q10:108	136, 266
Q11:20	287
Q11:27	177, 245, 304
Q11:28	275
Q11:41	68, 86, 313
Q11:42	194
Q11:68	189, 190
Q11:70	111
Q11:72	275
Q11:73	283
Q11:77	252
Q11:82	285
Q11:87	246, 308
Q11:97	252
Q11:99	257
Q12:5	194
Q12:11	106, 138, 262
Q12:12	194
Q12:13	170n22, 257
Q12:17	170
Q12:25	250, 308

Q12:29	156, 289
Q12:31	109
Q12:32	156, 186
Q12:33	263
Q12:35	244, 302
Q12:36	290, 318
Q12:37	288
Q12:38	237
Q12:43	245, 304
Q12:56	245
Q12:58	111
Q12:64	107
Q12:80	107, 252n42
Q12:82	176
Q12:84	275
Q12:85	245
Q12:87	252, 252n42
Q12:91	156, 289
Q12:97	156, 289
Q12:100	241, 253
Q12:101	235, 236, 298
Q12:105	281
Q12:109	270
Q12:110	252n42
Q13:13	139
Q13:14	306
Q13:15	241
Q13:19	264
Q13:22	289
Q13:23	283
Q13:30	242
Q13:31	252, 252n52
Q14:5	253
Q14:6	305
Q14:7	249
Q14:9	245, 305
Q14:18	111
Q14:21	246, 307
Q14:37	285
Q14:42	291
Q14:43	254, 312
Q14:45	283
Q15:20	161
Q15:22	275
Q15:23	236, 299
Q15:39	249
Q15:44	257
Q15:49	290, 318
Q15:51	290, 318
Q15:53	106
Q15:54	281
Q15:56	283
Q15:85	69
Q15:87	285
Q15:95	156, 258
Q16:21	191
Q16:26	283
Q16:27	181
Q16:30	270
Q16:37	284
Q16:43	176
Q16:48	245
Q16:76	263, 282
Q16:83	111
Q16:90	286, 315
Q16:91	140, 159
Q16:98	288
Q16:103	217
Q16:121	259n
Q17:2	284
Q17:4	115, 282
Q17:6	282
Q17:7	244
Q17:11	255
Q17:14	290
Q17:23	47
Q17:24	283
Q17:35	67
Q17:43	115
Q17:51	312
Q17:55	311
Q17:59	189, 190
Q17:64	63
Q17:71	180, 289
Q17:72	68
Q17:83	138, 255
Q17:93	115, 257
Q17:94	284
Q17:97	284
Q17:98	287
Q17:106	21
Q18	129
Q18:1–64	127
Q18:4	129, 291
Q18:5	128
Q18:8	130
Q18:10	286, 290
Q18:14	242

Q18:16 238, 244n21, 271, 286, 290
Q18:18 130, 140, 158
Q18:19 63, 148
Q18:22 85
Q18:23 252
Q18:25 129, 252
Q18:28 130, 260
Q18:31 156, 289
Q18:32 129
Q18:37 128
Q18:39 129
Q18:44 130
Q18:45 128
Q18:46 282
Q18:51 128
Q18:52 181
Q18:54 143
Q18:55 130
Q18:56 130
Q18:60 130
Q18:63 87, 292
Q18:65–83 127
Q18:74 76, 131
Q18:77 252, 272, 314
Q18:78 266
Q18:82 266
Q18:87 131
Q18:88 131
Q18:95 138, 262
Q18:97 266
Q18:102 131
Q18:103 131n15
Q18:104 131
Q18:106 130
Q18:107 131
Q19 115
Q19:2 283
Q19:3 164
Q19:4 287
Q19:5 237, 285
Q19:8 115
Q19:9 119, 121
Q19:15 273
Q19:16 269
Q19:17 269
Q19:23 72, 140
Q19:27 252
Q19:30 121
Q19:31 73
Q19:41 121
Q19:42 121, 281
Q19:49 121
Q19:51 121
Q19:53 121
Q19:54 121
Q19:55 115
Q19:56 121
Q19:60 121
Q19:66 72
Q19:67 121
Q19:68 115
Q19:69 115
Q19:72 115
Q19:74 121, 122, 178
Q19:75 244, 302
Q19:76–98 127
Q19:77 129
Q19:88 129
Q19:91 129
Q19:92 129
Q19:93 284
Q20 90
Q20:4 248n
Q20:10 87n
Q20:12 256
Q20:13 287
Q20:15 69
Q20:18 245
Q20:24 141
Q20:43 141
Q20:52 282
Q20:63 70, 109, 116, 278
Q20:64 271
Q20:66 115
Q20:71 107, 249
Q20:72 284
Q20:75 196
Q20:76 246, 309
Q20:84 279
Q20:85 269
Q20:86 269
Q20:87 269
Q20:88 269
Q20:94 269, 271, 314
Q20:95 269
Q20:97–115 127
Q20:97 142

Q20:108 285
Q20:119 245
Q20:121 267
Q20:125 281
Q20:130 286, 315
Q21:15 67
Q21:24 179
Q21:34 72, 252
Q21:37 255
Q21:42 122
Q21:53 69
Q21:57 249
Q21:65 312
Q21:73 69
Q21:79 311
Q21:81 111
Q21:84 69
Q21:88 268, 268n
Q21:90 84n37
Q21:106 69
Q21:112 234
Q22:7 69
Q22:11 113
Q22:17 117n, 167, 289
Q22:19 70, 84, 116, 278, 313
Q22:23 243, 302
Q22:27 139
Q22:44 272
Q22:45 281
Q22:48 281
Q22:51 301
Q22:54 256, 284
Q22:60 241
Q22:66 236
Q23:3 240, 241
Q23:24 245, 304
Q23:33 245, 304, 316
Q23:35 72
Q23:44 195
Q23:46 252
Q23:47 69
Q23:56 84n37
Q23:61 84n37
Q23:68 265
Q23:82 72, 239
Q23:93 262
Q23:112 234
Q23:114 234
Q23:117 290
Q24:2 143, 252, 284
Q24:8 245
Q24:21 27
Q24:22 292, 300
Q24:26 289
Q24:31 60, 255, 270
Q24:33 70, 263
Q24:35 71, 160, 260
Q24:36 241
Q24:37 315
Q24:43 133
Q24:52 88, 196, 199
Q24:60 283
Q24:62 252
Q24:63 287
Q25:5 141
Q25:17 261
Q25:21 115, 240, 301
Q25:25 287
Q25:28 275
Q25:38 189
Q25:53 111
Q25:68 290
Q25:69 86
Q25:70 268
Q25:72 240
Q25:77 245, 258
Q26:1 200
Q26:6 246, 306
Q26:16 271
Q26:17 238
Q26:22 238
Q26:36 88, 180, 290, 318
Q26:44 115
Q26:49 107
Q26:59 238
Q26:63 284
Q26:81 236
Q26:88 282
Q26:94 92
Q26:96 266
Q26:146 104
Q26:197 238, 246, 307
Q26:224 306
Q27:6 140
Q27:14 115
Q27:15 311
Q27:16 311
Q27:18 256

Q27:21	249, 262
Q27:22	188, 192
Q27:28	88, 196
Q27:29	245, 304
Q27:30	313
Q27:32	245, 304
Q27:35	281
Q27:36	256
Q27:38	245, 304
Q27:39	70
Q27:40	70, 263
Q27:44	165
Q27:46	281
Q27:47	202, 264
Q27:64	179, 245
Q27:65	191
Q27:66	264
Q27:81	285, 285n
Q27:92	242
Q28:1	200
Q28:3	245n
Q28:4	299
Q28:8	289
Q28:25	288
Q28:27	70, 116, 319
Q28:29	70, 87n
Q28:30	193, 256
Q28:32	70, 252
Q28:34	122, 176
Q28:38	245, 304
Q28:54	289
Q28:55	240
Q28:61	59n
Q28:62	181
Q28:64	244, 302
Q28:66	306
Q28:71	158
Q28:74	181
Q28:75	179
Q28:76	243
Q28:81	22
Q28:83	115
Q29:3	111
Q29:38	189
Q29:60	281
Q29:64	240
Q30:10	244, 252, 310
Q30:11	245
Q30:13	246, 307
Q30:27	245
Q30:28	281
Q30:39	242, 248, 260, 310
Q30:40	236
Q30:53	256, 285, 285n
Q30:54	79
Q31:6	240
Q31:13	194
Q31:16	194
Q31:17	194
Q31:34	253
Q32:12	240, 313
Q32:13	249
Q32:23	238
Q33	261
Q33:4	261
Q33:5	285, 288
Q33:6	317
Q33:10	67, 69, 260
Q33:11	70
Q33:14	140
Q33:17	279
Q33:18	107
Q33:27	180
Q33:37	287, 317
Q33:51	180
Q33:53	144, 299, 316
Q33:66	260
Q33:67	261
Q33:68	53
Q34:5	240, 301
Q34:10	311
Q34:13	285, 311
Q34:14	122
Q34:15	188, 192
Q34:33	244, 303
Q34:37	309
Q34:52	122
Q35:9	210
Q35:11	62n17
Q35:14	287
Q35:28	152, 153, 307
Q35:33	243, 302
Q35:43	193
Q35:45	291
Q36:23	256
Q36:31	177n28
Q36:32	117
Q36:33	210

Q36:35	54n10
Q36:39	69
Q36:47	92
Q36:49	136, 137, 202, 266
Q36:51	140
Q36:56	156
Q36:67	115
Q36:73	69
Q36:79	236
Q37:1–3	112
Q37:1	209
Q37:2	209
Q37:3	209
Q37:8	202n20, 265
Q37:10	202
Q37:14	244, 303
Q37:16	72, 239
Q37:52	239
Q37:53	72, 115
Q37:65	313
Q37:66	156, 289
Q37:68	250
Q37:102	194
Q37:106	246, 305
Q37:142	170
Q37:147	252
Q37:153	282
Q37:163	256
Q38:6	245, 304
Q38:8	239
Q38:14	62n18
Q38:17	311
Q38:21	245, 305
Q38:22	311
Q38:24	312
Q38:26	312
Q38:30	312
Q38:33	165
Q38:42	203n23
Q38:63	67
Q38:67	245, 305
Q38:76	84
Q38:85	249
Q39:7	88, 196
Q39:9	283
Q39:10	256
Q39:29	307
Q39:34	246, 309
Q39:56	275
Q39:60	92
Q39:64	138, 262
Q39:69	252
Q39:74	245
Q40:16	93
Q40:18	250
Q40:26	54n10
Q40:34	67
Q40:41	260
Q40:47	307
Q40:50	246, 306
Q40:59	69
Q40:84	244, 303
Q40:85	244, 303
Q41:12	234, 298
Q41:16	234, 298
Q41:21	281
Q41:28	309
Q41:29	70, 207
Q41:31	317
Q41:44	87
Q41:47	181, 237
Q41:49	287
Q41:51	138, 287
Q42:13	264
Q42:20	196
Q42:21	107, 246, 307
Q42:22	234, 298
Q42:24	255
Q42:25	268, 300
Q42:30	300
Q42:32	85
Q42:40	246, 309
Q42:44	244, 303
Q42:51	316
Q43:8	259n, 319
Q43:18	245
Q43:24	234
Q43:35	117
Q43:46	252
Q43:49	255
Q43:59	238
Q43:71	54n10
Q43:81	69
Q44:33	246, 305
Q44:47	58
Q45:6	253
Q45:21	268
Q45:26	236

Q45:33	268
Q46:5	250n38, 287
Q46:15	70
Q46:32	287
Q47:13	281
Q47:20	292
Q47:21–22	185
Q47:31	242
Q47:35	78
Q47:36	240
Q47:37	275
Q47:38	279
Q48:4	186
Q48:10	87
Q48:15	283
Q48:19	283
Q48:25	180
Q48:27	313
Q48:29	165, 204
Q49:1	186
Q49:4	63, 316
Q49:6	54
Q49:12	210
Q50:3	72
Q50:15	236
Q50:30	288
Q50:43	236, 299
Q51:1–4	127
Q51:1	209
Q51:3	131
Q51:7–9	127
Q51:12	191
Q51:44	301
Q51:47	253
Q52:23	240, 241
Q52:24	243, 302
Q52:42	115
Q53	90
Q53:11	292
Q53:17	141
Q53:18	292
Q53:20	260
Q53:22	159
Q53:26	107
Q53:31	244, 310
Q53:36	290
Q53:41	287
Q53:50	160
Q53:51	189
Q53:53	178
Q53:55	253
Q54	127
Q54:1	127
Q54:2	127
Q54:5	131
Q54:6	131, 255
Q54:7	128
Q54:10	128
Q54:13	130
Q54:15	128
Q54:16	131
Q54:17	128
Q54:20	128
Q54:21	131n14
Q54:22	128
Q54:23	131n14
Q54:24	130
Q54:26	128
Q54:28	290, 318
Q54:30	131n4
Q54:31	128
Q54:37	131n14
Q54:39	131n14
Q54:40	128
Q54:41	131n13
Q54:42	128
Q54:43	130
Q54:44	128
Q54:47	130n11
Q54:51	128
Q54:52	130n12
Q54:55	128
Q55	253
Q55:15	84
Q55:19	111
Q55:22	243, 302
Q55:24	85, 256, 285, 315
Q55:29	119, 121
Q55:31	255
Q55:35	84
Q55:60	309
Q56:23	243, 302
Q56:25	241
Q56:35	239, 286
Q56:47	72, 239
Q56:53	156, 289
Q56:65	142
Q56:72	156

Q56:74	271, 313
Q56:86	115
Q56:96	313
Q57:11	279
Q57:13	283
Q57:20	240
Q57:23	107
Q57:29	177
Q58:2	109, 241
Q59:4	108, 263
Q59:9	244, 300
Q59:14	316
Q59:17	246, 309
Q59:24	285
Q60:4	246, 307
Q61:2	281
Q61:5	281
Q61:7	70
Q61:8	289
Q61:14	84, 237
Q62:2	237
Q62:11	240, 244, 303
Q63:4	241
Q63:5	244, 300, 313
Q63:10	288
Q64:5	245, 305
Q64:9	207
Q65	127
Q65:4	131
Q65:5	268
Q65:7	131
Q65:8	131, 281
Q66:1	281
Q66:3	288
Q66:4	255, 270
Q66:5	69
Q67:4	180, 285
Q67:20	279
Q67:21	115, 241, 279
Q68:6	253
Q68:19	6n3
Q68:41	307
Q68:42	165
Q68:45	141n
Q68:50	259n, 319
Q69	276
Q69:7	285
Q69:9	121, 178
Q69:11	141
Q69:19	244, 276
Q69:20	276
Q69:25	276
Q69:26	276
Q69:28	276
Q69:29	276
Q69:30	21
Q69:35	104
Q69:37	156, 289
Q69:47	109
Q69:52	313
Q70:1	180, 257–258
Q70:10	257
Q71:6	237
Q72	127
Q72:3	129
Q72:5	128
Q72:8	130
Q72:24	244, 303
Q73:6	180
Q73:14	115
Q73:20	244
Q74:15	261
Q74:30	227
Q74:37	113
Q75:2	250n35
Q75:6	191
Q75:13	245, 291
Q75:29	165
Q76	261
Q76:4	261
Q76:15	261
Q76:16	261, 261n56
Q76:19	302
Q77:1–6	127
Q77:2	111
Q77:5	209
Q77:6	131
Q77:11	273
Q77:12	253
Q77:32–33	127
Q77:50	253
Q78:1	281
Q79:1–5	127
Q79:3–4	209
Q79:16	256
Q79:17	141
Q79:37	141
Q79:42	191

Q79:43 281
Q80:3 265
Q80:25–31 127
Q81:8 239
Q81:9 253
Q81:11 141
Q81:16 85, 256
Q83:3 67, 110
Q83:18 236
Q84:14 261
Q84:18 116
Q86:4 116
Q86:5 281
Q86:11–14 127
Q88:5 69
Q89:1–5 127
Q89:4 143, 267
Q89:9 143, 267
Q89:23 252
Q90:7 87, 196
Q90:20 158
Q91 90
Q91:15 259n, 319
Q93:1 248n
Q95:1 178
Q96:1 290, 313
Q96:3 290
Q96:15 186
Q96:18 255
Q97 127
Q98:6 173
Q98:7 173
Q99:5 111
Q99:7 196
Q99:8 196
Q100:1–5 127
Q100:3 209
Q101:10 274
Q103 127
Q104:7 257
Q104:8 158
Q107:5 93
Q107:6 93
Q108:3 285
Q109:1 70
Q109:3 69
Q109:4 69
Q109:5 69
Q109:6 267

Printed in the United States
by Baker & Taylor Publisher Services